INSECTS
OF THE
WORLD

INSECTS OF THE WORLD

W. Linsenmaier (signature)

Drawings, Photographs, and Text

by

Walter Linsenmaier

Translated from the German by

Leigh E. Chadwick

McGraw-Hill Book Company

New York St. Louis San Francisco
Toronto London Sydney Johannesburg Singapore New Delhi

Frontispiece:
Mimic and beetle.
As a means of defense the goliath
beetle has a sharp-edged groove
between the dorsal thoracic plate
and the wing covers.

NOTE TO THE READER
Each illustration in the book has a double number, such as 42/1; the first number indicates the page on which the illustration appears. [24/3] is a text reference to a color illustration. (→ 104/6) is a reference in a caption of a black-and-white illustration to the same illustration in color.

A McGraw-Hill Co-Production
Design and production:
Emil M. Bührer, Franz Coray and Robert Tobler
Copyright © 1972 by Walter Linsenmaier
All rights reserved
No part of this publication may be reproduced,
stored in a retrieval system, or transmitted
in any form or by any means, electronic,
mechanical, photocopying, recording, or
otherwise, without the prior written permission
of the publisher.
Library of Congress Catalog Card Number: 78–178047
07–037953–X
German language edition published by
Droemersche Verlagsanstalt Th. Knaur Nachf.,
München/Zürich
Printed in Switzerland by
C. J. Bucher AG, Lucerne

Foreword

Walter Linsenmaier's *Insects of the World* is an outstanding accomplishment—unique in the entomological literature.

So numerous are the different kinds of insects and so varied are the ways in which they cope with the problems of living that it is today a great feat to produce a survey of the group in its totality.

Fortunately for those who have wanted to know about insects, in the past many people have compiled their own observations and those of others. But these works share a common shortcoming, for practically without exception they have been written by zoologists. Thus, their works are characterized by a more or less uniform outlook.

This is where the uniqueness of Walter Linsenmaier's approach lies, for fundamentally he is not a professionally trained zoologist, even though through his own deep interest and efforts he has earned full right to such a scientific label. First and foremost he is an artist—a painter. When he views an insect, his eye leaps to its shape, coloring, and motions; thoughts about its physiology, its behavior, and its place in the overall scheme do present themselves, but later.

As an artist Linsenmaier has made penetrating studies of how the insect's artistic attributes come about, and he explains these devices for us; for himself he has taken on the even more difficult task of mastering the techniques for depicting such phenomena. He has examined and drawn many of the most outstanding exotic species in their natural habitats, and this book contains some of the most magnificent illustrations in the whole of biological art.

So fresh and vivid is this treatment of entomology that I am impelled to urge this work not only upon all present and prospective entomologists but also upon all others who wish to learn about the vital part played by insects in our world.

Leigh E. Chadwick
Sargentville, Maine

CONTENTS

Insects and Their Ways

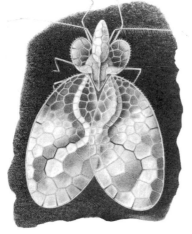

9/1
The tiny lace bugs are among the most fascinating creatures in the world of insects. (→ 132/13)

9/2
Insects have many methods of protection and defense. These moths startle their enemies with a terrifying "mask."

PAGE 8

8/1
The most ancient insect fossils come from the Coal Age, the Carboniferous Period, 320 million years ago. But these insects must already have had millions of years of evolution behind them. The majority of their genera, which lived in the now-fossilized coal-producing forests, are long since extinct; yet a few have persisted even up to now, like the cockroaches (Blattaria) and the dragonflies (Odonata), though the species are no longer so gigantic as they were then. For example, the wingspan of the giant dragonfly Meganeura monyi, discovered in coal at Commentry in France, was more than a yard!

Insects are so fantastic they often seem like creatures from another world. Almost every imaginable shape—beautiful, bizarre, grotesque, ugly, or commonplace—can be found among the insects. Much of the ornamentation, architecture, and technical creations of our own world existed in the insect world long ago. The instruments and techniques developed by insects in the course of their evolution are so highly refined and so numerous that we still cannot completely understand them, let alone duplicate them in laboratory or factory. Nevertheless, even in their most unrestrained developments, the insects remain true to definite basic patterns. In doing so, they exhibit a harmony that man often fails to achieve in his own creations.

Ancient Insects

Insects apparently came into being more than 350 million years ago, during the Paleozoic Era. About this time the larger green plants also began to populate the land. No traces of these earliest insects exist, but we think they must have developed from certain many-legged marine animals.

The first insects to leave a permanent record of themselves, in the form of fossils found in rocks, were more highly evolved forms from the Pennsylvanian Period of the Paleozoic Era, some 300 million years ago. Almost all these species have since vanished. They either died out or were gradually reshaped into different forms. But a few, such as the cockroaches and the primitive, wingless insects of the subclass Apterygota, have preserved their ancient shapes to the present.

Among the fantastic creatures of the Pennsylvanian woods were huge dragonfly-like insects *(Meganeura)* whose wings spanned 30 inches. Little is known about the life of these phenomenal insects that flew among the tree ferns, seal trees, and scale trees.

The flies and beetles appeared much later, in the Triassic Period of the earth's middle age, the Mesozoic Era. The butterflies and the nerve-winged insects followed in the Jurassic Period, about 170 million years ago. With the full burgeoning of flowering plants during the Cretaceous Period of the Mesozoic, and, later, during the Cenozoic, the world of insects was able to develop fully.

From time to time during the Cenozoic, small insects were caught fast and sealed in the resinous gum that dripped from the trees of the coniferous forests. Locked in beautiful, transparent amber coffins, these delicate creatures have been preserved to this day. They are quite like living insects; some are even identical with them.

INSECTS TODAY

In number of species, insects far surpass all other kinds of living things; and the total number of individual insects is beyond estimation. To date there are taxonomic descriptions of about a million species, and the complete tally is estimated to be in the neighborhood of three million. Without insects, many plants and animals would cease to exist, and the world would be a different place to live.

Insects have the phenomenal ability to preempt every available space, to take possession of almost every square yard of our planet except the oceans, and to thrive and multiply in these places. In their billions and trillions, these often fragile beings survive the thousandfold dangers of an inimical environment. Their reproductive capacity is fabulous: a single female may produce hundreds, even thousands, of tiny eggs. And the change in form, or metamorphosis, that insects undergo in their development from egg to adult opens still more opportunities for them to occupy all types of living space. For in places where the mature insect might not be able to exist, its larva can do so. Furthermore, many insects have resting stages capable of surviving seasonal extremes of weather.

The insect world has developed specialists that can take advantage of widely different environments. But this very specialization, though of great value to insects as a whole, carries drastic limitations for the individual species. A slight change in climate or the disappearance of a single plant species can cause the extinction of one or more species of insects.

Although most insects are capable of almost unlimited multiplication, this is not the only means of guaranteeing an adequate number of survivors. Even species that produce few eggs manage to complete their life cycles year after year. Important to the survival of many of these insects is their ability to defend themselves, if only by means of concealment. But often we cannot detect any defensive ability whatsoever. We then talk of natural balance, where neither dangers nor enemies are numerous enough to wipe out a species.

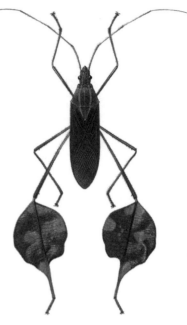

10/1
This leaf-footed bug makes a most conspicuous display of its hind legs, which are adorned with banners. (→ 129/6)

CAPTIONS FOR PAGES 13 TO 19

13/1
Termite in amber, encaged in this gum for some 40 million years.
13/2
African ground beetle and kingfisher, both well armed for self-defense.

PAGES 14 AND 15

Insects in the woods of North America (enlarged). In order to insert an egg into a horntail wasp larva feeding deep in the wood, the ichneumon wasp in the middle has put out from between the two halves of its sheath her threadlike ovipositor, which is carried between the legs.
On page 14 the "caterpillar hunter," a most useful forest ground beetle, is laying hold of a saddleback caterpillar that is protected by poisonous spines; above it is a dying caterpillar, studded with the cocoons of a small parasitic wasp species, and below is a potter wasp building a clay jar as a home for her offspring. On page 15 at the right a singing tree cricket is vibrating its fore wings, that serve as resonators.

PAGES 16 AND 17

Artists in dissimulation, as seen in the woods of Rio de Janeiro. All sorts of plant parts are imitated, and with many insects disturbance causes the emergence of contrasting colors from the dark disguise, giving effects like flashes of lightning. The diagram for identifying the insects is on page 12.

PAGES 18 AND 19

Warning colors and mimicry in the woods at Rio de Janeiro. Insects attempt, frequently successfully, to scare off enemies by means of double spots that give the effect of eyes and by means of bright, varicolored costumes. Many of these colorful insects are toxic or for other reasons inedible, and other unprotected kinds survive because they have similar warning garb. The assemblage of Lepidoptera of almost identical appearance forms a "mimicry ring," containing poisonous and nonpoisonous species from distinct families. Along with them, as further examples of mimicry, are some wasps with their understudies, as well as a poisonous black-banded beetle with two of its imitators. The diagram of the illustration for identifying the insects is on page 12.

INSECT BIOTYPES

The insect population of a region is determined by the environment, especially by the plants that are found there. The tropics, where there are no winter interruptions and where optimal climatic conditions prevail, are particularly heavily inhabited by insects. Nevertheless, except for a few common kinds, intensive search uncovered only a small number. In order to find all the insects shown in the illustrations, special methods of collection were needed; the most effective was light trapping at night. Innumerable species were turned up only in this way.

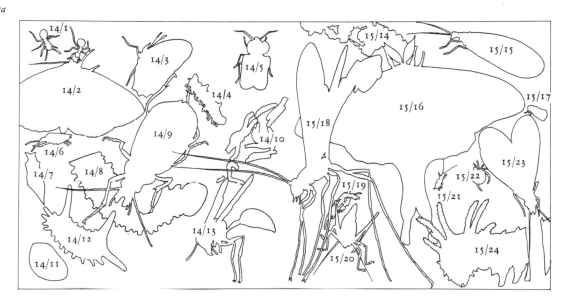

FOR IDENTIFICATION OF THE INSECTS ON PAGES 14 AND 15:

INSECTS OF THE NORTH AMERICAN BUSH

14/1
Carpenter ants (enlarged 1.5×).
14/2
Underwing moth (enlarged 1.5×).
14/3
Satyrid butterfly (enlarged 1.5×).
14/4
Sphinx moth caterpillar, infested by braconid wasps; the parasitic larvae made their way out of the host's dying body, and then pupated in the cocoons (0.6 natural size).
14/5
Lace bug (enlarged 10×).
14/6
Stink bug (enlarged 1.5×).
14/7
Pupa of a swallowtail butterfly (enlarged 1.5×).
14/8
The caterpillar of a giant silkworm moth, spinning its cocoon (enlarged 3×).
14/9
Tiger beetle attacking a slug

caterpillar (enlarged 3×).
14/10
Tent caterpillars on their communal silken nest (0.6 natural size).
14/11
Gall made by a gall wasp (enlarged 3×).
14/12
Saddleback caterpillar, with its toxic spines (enlarged 3×).
14/13
Potter wasp, building a clay pot as a home for her progeny (enlarged 4×).
15/14
Scale insects (enlarged 2×).
15/15
Green lacewing (enlarged 4×).
15/16
Male luna moth (enlarged 2×).
15/17
Planthopper (enlarged 1.5×).
15/18
Ichneumon wasp sinking her egg into a wood wasp larva that is feeding deep in the wood.

The long, boring ovipositor is carried between the coxae; and from it the two halves of the sheath curl upward elastically, while their tips remain in contact with the wood. Soon they will slide off and the empty ovipositor sheath will protrude rearward (enlarged 3.5×).
15/19
Scale insects (0.6 natural size).
15/20
Katydid (natural size).
15/21
Long-horned beetle (enlarged 1.3×).
15/22
Spider (not an insect).
15/23
Male tree cricket, chirping (enlarged 5×).
15/24
Hickory horned devil, the harmless caterpillar of the royal walnut moth *Citheronia regalis* (enlarged 2×).

INSECT LIFE IN THE SOUTH AMERICAN FOREST, RIO DE JANEIRO

16/1–17/31 CONCEALING GARB

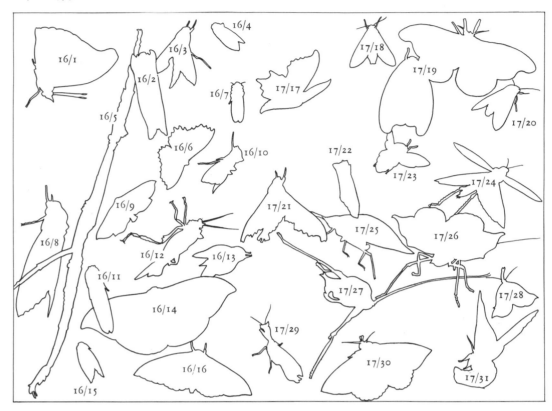

18/1–19/34 WARNING COLORS, EYESPOTS, AND MIMICRY

16/1   Brush-footed butterfly (nat. size).
16/2   Prominent moth (enl. 2×).
16/3   Sphinx moth (natural size).
16/4   Carpenterworm moth (nat. size).
16/5   Walkingstick (natural size).
16/6   Geometrid moth (enl. 2×).
16/7   Leafhopper (enlarged 2×).
16/8   Sphinx moth (natural size);
(its caterpillar 18/8).
16/9   Pyralid moth (enlarged 2×).
16/10   Noctuid moth (enlarged 1.5×).
16/11   Prominent moth (enlarged 2×).
16/12   Katydid (enlarged 1.5×).
16/13   Royal moth (slightly reduced).
16/14   Giant silkworm moth (nat. size).
16/15   Prominent moth (0.5 nat. size).
16/16   Royal moth ♀ (natural size).
17/17   Moth (enlarged 1.5×).
17/18   Arctiid moth (enlarged 1.5×).
17/19   Giant silkworm moth ♂
(enlarged 2×).
17/20   Arctiid moth (enlarged 1.5×).
17/21   Sphinx moth (enlarged 1.5×).
17/22   Prominent moth (natural size).
17/23   Golden bee (natural size).
17/24   Grasshopper (0.5 natural size).
17/25–27 Katydids (natural size).
17/28   Noctuid moth (enlarged 1.5×).
17/29   Praying mantid (natural size).
17/30   Noctuid moth (natural size).
17/31   Giant silkworm moth (nat. size).

18/1   Lantern fly, a fulgorid
planthopper (natural size).
18/2–3 White butterflies. (2) ♀; (3) ♂
(0.6 natural size).
18/4–6 Leafhoppers (enlarged 4×).
18/7   Syntomid moth (enl. 1.3×).
18/8   Larva of a sphinx moth
(natural size).
18/9   Geometrid moth (enl. 2×).
18/10   Syntomid moth (enl. 2×).
18/11   Noctuid moth (enl. 1.5×).
18/12   Click beetle (enlarged 2×).
18/13   Arctiid moth (enlarged 2×).
19/14   Morpho butterfly (slightly enl.).
19/15   Waxen-tailed planthopper
(natural size).
19/16   Milkweed butterfly (nat. size).
19/17–18 Heliconian butterflies.
(17) *Heliconius narcaea;*
(18) *H. silvana robigus* (0.6 nat. size).
19/19–21 Ithomiid butterflies.
(19) *Melinaea ethra;*
(20) *Ceratinia vallonia daeta;*
(21) *Mechanitis nessaea lysimnia*
(0.6 natural size).
19/22   Brush-footed butterfly
(0.6 natural size).
19/23   Treehopper (enlarged 2×).
19/24   Mydas fly (natural size).
19/25   Spider wasp (natural size).
19/26   Red-mouthed wasp (enl. 1.6×).
19/27   Syntomid moth (enl. 1.6×).
19/28   Aristolochia swallowtail
butterfly (0.5 natural size).
19/29   Spider wasp (enlarged 1.3×).
19/30   Assassin bug (enlarged 1.3×).
19/31   Syntomid moth (enl. 1.75×).
19/32   Net-winged beetle (enl. 1.75×).
19/33   Long-horned beetle
(enlarged 1.75×).
19/34   Ant bug (enlarged 2×).

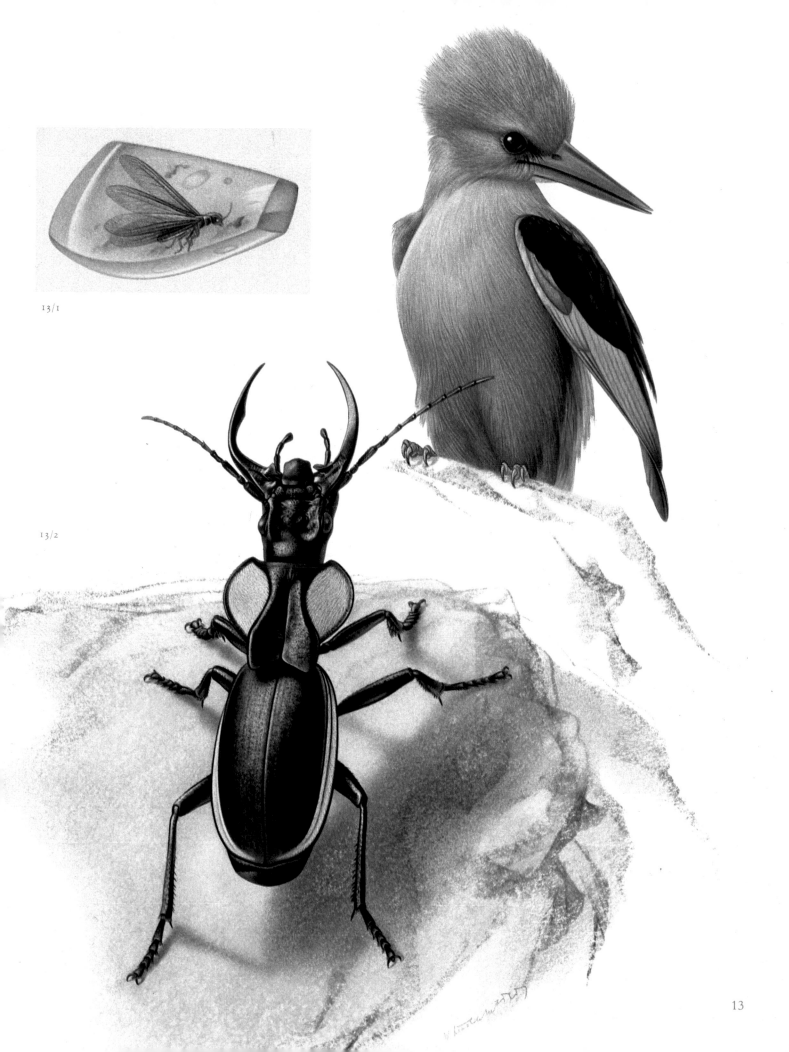

13/1

13/2

13

W Linsenmaier

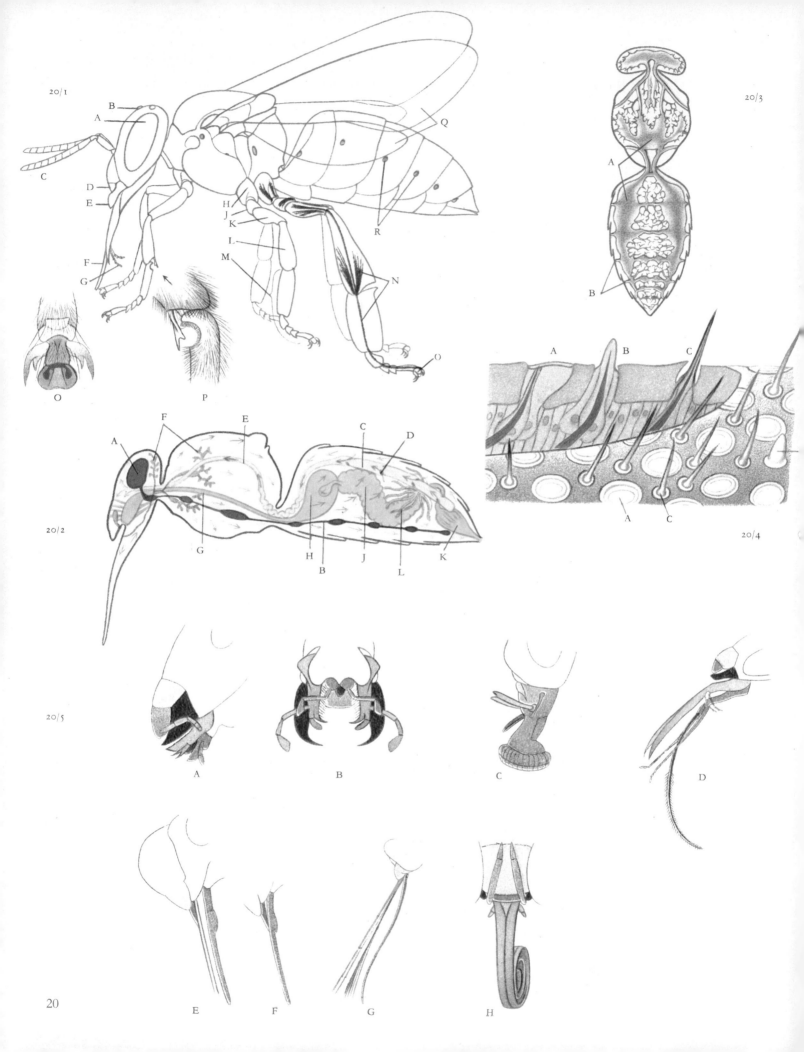

20/1

20/2

20/3

20/4

20/5

20

The Insect Body

The lofty success of insects in the battle for survival hinges partly on the way in which the insect body is organized. This body organization is characteristic of the *Arthropoda*, the phylum (main division) of animals whose principal members, besides the insects, are the crustaceans and the arachnids, including spiders, scorpions, mites, and others. Instead of having a body supported by means of an internal skeleton, these animals have muscles and other inner organs suspended from an outer covering. This surface layer often is stiffened into a hard, chitin-containing shell that remains flexible thanks to its subdivision into many separate small plates joined together by thin membranes. This arrangement, however, evidently places strict limitations on the body size attainable, for with each increase in growth an animal must shed its shell and replace it with a larger one.

INTERNAL ANATOMY

Some vital organs of the insect body seem strangely displaced in comparison with the corresponding organs of the human body. For instance, though the central nervous system of an insect begins in the head with a brain, the nerve cord extending from the brain runs along the lower part of the insect body instead of along the back.

The circulatory system is no more than a simple pipe, part of which serves as a heart. Contractions of the heart pump blood from the pipe directly into the body cavity, where the blood bathes the internal organs. The blood distributes only nutrients, not nutrients and oxygen as does our blood. Insect blood is nearly always greenish; it lacks hemoglobin.

Breathing does not take place through a nose or mouth in the head, but through numerous holes along the abdomen and through a few on the thorax. The holes are called spiracles, or stigmata, and are the openings of a tubular respiratory system that branches throughout the body. In connection with it, there are several air sacs. No doubt the compression and expansion of these sacs, as a result of changes in the shape of the body and its organs as well as changes in internal fluid pressure, cause them to act as pumps that promote the exchange of air and that regulate its flow through the system.

In contrast to the organs of circulation and respiration, the organs of digestion and reproduction have a fairly normal appearance.

This brief outline is not intended to give the impression that the insect body is a simple structure. On the contrary, one could write a book on the anatomy of a wasp.

EXTERNAL DETAILS

Not only does the internal anatomy of insects seem strange to us, but certain external features do, too. For example, the organ of hearing sometimes resides in the upper part of the leg, the organs of smell and taste may be on the feet and lower legs as well as on the antennae, and the eyes may seemingly rest on the neck.

Among the arthropods, the crustaceans have ten legs, and adult arachnids eight; but insects, at least the mature ones, have six legs. Like other arthropods, insects are characterized by the division of the body into rings or segments. They are distinguished from other arthropods by the possession of three definite body regions—the head, thorax, and abdomen—which are set off sharply from one another, at least in the fully developed insect.

The ancestor of the insects may be imagined as a multisegmented wormlike creature, with a pair of legs on each segment. It probably looked something like a millipede. In the course of millions of years, according to theory, the several pairs of legs nearest the front end were modified to form the mouthparts (and possibly the antennae); meanwhile, the first four to six body segments were fused together into the head, and the next three consolidated into the composite thorax. Some eleven segments became the abdomen, and the abdominal appendages became vestigial and disappeared.

The wings could not have been derived from modified legs, as were the wings of birds. Insect wings are outgrowths of the body wall. They were already present in many of the earliest known insects.

The lack of dependence on an internal skeleton has made possible a multiplicity of wing forms and techniques of flying that would be altogether unimaginable among other flying creatures, whose method of flying was based on the foreleg. Not infrequently, at all events, the wings, even in winged insects, have become more or less degenerate, even to the point of total absence; or they have been partially sclerotized, as for instance in the beetles, where the membrane of the fore wings has changed into chitinous wing covers, which reduces flight ability. This is also so for the "true bugs" (Heteroptera) although here the wingtips have remained membranous. Actually the powers of flight do not depend on the wings alone but primarily also on the wing musculature, which in good fliers occupies the greatest part of the thorax.

The various wing areas, cells, principal veins, their branches, and cross veins are designated in the technical literature by definite generally accepted names, letters, and numbers. Venation—the course and arrangement of veins in the wing—is often the principal (frequently, as with the *Neuroptera,* the only) criterion for distinguishing between

orders, families, genera, and species of insects. The more ancient insect forms have a more abundant venation, quite similar on all wings, whereas reduced venation is a later specialization. Additionally, greater separation of the bases of fore and hind wings is characteristic of more primitive insect status.

The insect leg is conspicuous by its slenderness and noteworthy for its rigidity, but it does not differ in its subdivisions from the accustomed pattern of arthropod legs. Thus we find, in series, a coxa, a trochanter, a femur, a tibia, and a tarsus. The tarsus is divided into several subsegments, and most authorities distinguish further the terminal leg segment as the pretarsus. Despite its subdivisions, the leg as a whole is an internally musculated tubular structure.

Although the leg pattern is common to all insects, the legs have manifold forms, each of which fits a particular way of life. For instance, legs may be used for jumping, swimming, clinging, seizing prey, digging, or spinning. And we often find on the legs, in addition to certain sensory organs, highly refined mechanisms for cleaning the body, gathering food, injecting fluids, or applying suction. The tarsus almost always ends in two claws (rarely only one) and often has an adhesive lobe (pulvillus) that lies beneath these. This lobe, variously shaped and frequently divided, serves primarily for clinging to smooth surfaces. When it is absent, the lower tarsal surface may bear adhesive pads. [20/1]

The feelers, or antennae, of insects are amazing instruments. They may be nearly covered by tens of thousands of sensory hairs and pits. Using its antennae to smell and probe at the same time, an insect is able to detect fantastically dilute odors and to evaluate the plastic shapes of its surroundings, its fellows, and other living creatures. In this way, an insect finds the proper plants for feeding or for depositing eggs, a parasitic female tracks down its animal host, and an insect of one sex seeks out the opposite sex. Some female insects possess scent glands, consisting of hairs, hair bundles, or scales that become active at mating time. The antennae of males of the same species often are made more sensitive by being expanded into numerous side branches, like the feather of a bird, which provide room for a larger number of sense cells. The males of certain moths appear to respond from a distance of as much as seven miles to the odor released from a female upwind, but it is still not certain what fraction of the behavior is the result of odor perception and what

22/1
The highly differentiated wing forms of threadwinged Neuroptera (Kemopteridae). (→ 188/1)

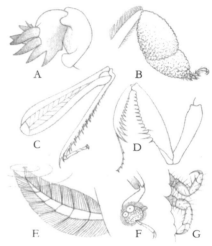

22/2A–G
Insect legs are not always merely for walking, but often have very special functions: (A) digging legs (mole cricket); (B) legs for harvesting (bee); (C) jumping legs (grasshopper); (D) prehensile legs (praying mantis); (E) swimming legs (diving beetle); (F) adhesive soles (diving beetle); and (G) clasping legs (head louse).

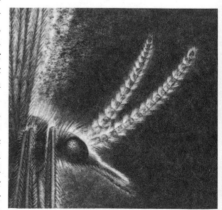

22/3
The antennae, with their almost infinite number of different forms, are the most versatile of insect sense organs. A moth fly. (→ 279/5)

fraction the result of a tendency to fly upwind. In some species the male has a scent that attracts the female. [245/1]

Eyes and Vision

The insect's compound eyes are globes that often shimmer with magnificent hues. Frequently, we can see without magnification the marvelous honeycomblike structure of their curving outer surface, which is revealed as a complex of intersecting arcs of tiny six-sided figures. Each of these hexagons is the upper transparent cuticle of an individual organ of sight, a long, slender cylinder that narrows as it goes inward.

Immediately beneath the cuticular cornea of each organ is a lens, a long crystalline cone at the lower end of which lies a rod-shaped bundle of from seven to fourteen (most often eight) retinal cells. The base of each cell gives off an optic nerve fiber. Thus a bee with 4,000 facets to the eye sees through the medium of 8,000 eyes, 64,000 retinal cells, and a like number of optic nerve fibers. And some insects have as many as 30,000 facets in each of their compound eyes! Many compound eyes are hemispherical, oval, or elongated; some are shaped like half-moons, like kidneys, or are otherwise variously indented.

Insects have yet other eyes. These are the little frontal eyes, or so-called dorsal ocelli, that lie between the compound eyes. Usually, there are three of these simple eyes. Though somewhat different in structure from a human eye, an ocellus is nevertheless often composed of identical parts: a curving cornea, a lens, an iris, a vitreous body, a retina, and a darkly pigmented wall at the rear. Ocelli seem to be very sensitive to light and are much enlarged in nocturnal insects. Yet they cannot perceive images, and their function is not clearly understood. Many insect larvae and nymphs possess only these simple eyes, in numbers that vary from group to group. [29; 314]

Optics of the Compound Eye

The optics of the compound eye differ from the optics of all other eyes. Every facet, isolated from its neighbors by a layer of dark pigment, functions independently. Each facet gathers only the light that falls directly upon it—that is, the light coming from that sector of the surroundings that lies within its own visual angle—and concentrates this light on the retinal cells. In the retina as a whole, these segments or spots of light are combined into a mosaic picture (which is not reversed, as the image is in our own eyes). This mosaic picture consists of as many single elements as there are bundles of retinal cells, and there are as many bundles as there are facets. The more of these bundles there are, the finer and more concentrated are the individual points that make up the picture, and the clearer and sharper is the total image.

With such an analysis we can indeed get some idea of the nature of an image in this kind of an optical system, but we have no knowledge of the way in which the image is interpreted by the insect brain.

Thanks to innumerable experiments, we have learned that most insects, with the exception of many butterflies and certain flies, are red-blind. But although they cannot see red, many of these insects regularly visit red flowers. The reason they do so is because most red flowers have a tinge of yellow or violet, which the insects can perceive; or else the red flowers reflect not only red but also ultraviolet light that, though invisible to us, is perceived by certain insects. The flowers look red to us, but they look yellow, violet, or ultraviolet to the insects, and are distinguished on this basis. The qualities of color that bees see seem to be limited to four: ultraviolet, blue, yellow, and bluegreen. Bees see bluegreen in place of our white; so white flowers appear bluegreen to bees.

Polarized Light

Amazingly, insects see another kind of light invisible to us. This is polarized light, which is produced when sunlight passes through the earth's atmosphere. Because insects can see polarized light, the vault of the sky is not of nearly uniform brightness for them as it is for us, but is dismembered into sectors that differ in color or intensity. The position of this pattern shifts relative to the animal with any change in his line of vision or direction of flight. The insect therefore has a sensitive optical compass that is functional as long as a small piece of blue sky is within sight.

Many insects are able to orient accurately even under a solid cloud cover or at night. For want of further understanding such behavior has sometimes been attributed to the perception, as yet little studied, of magnetic or electric forces. For the most part, however, orientation in space is mediated, as in ourselves, by conspicuous objects, such as well-lighted rocks and silhouettes of the horizon or of trees. Above all, insects orient themselves by the position of the sun. Thus, if one throws a shadow on a column of ants and then presents them with a mirrored

23/1
The eyes of whirligig beetles, that live mostly on top of the water, enable them to see above and below the surface at the same time.

23/2
The duplex "turbaned eyes" of mayflies are among the most highly evolved known.

23/3
Scale insect males have rather primitive visual organs, namely only simple eyes (ocelli) but no compound eyes. (→ 112/2)

reflection of the sun, they turn and go off in the wrong direction.

Many of the more primitive insects lack well-developed compound eyes. The eye facets of springtails *(Collembola)*, for example, are not closed complexes, as they are in more advanced insects, but consist of a few single eyes gathered into loosely knit groups. In certain insects that spend their lives in the dark, as in soil or in caves, organs of vision are altogether lacking.

INSECT INSTRUMENTS

The variations of the insect mouth and mouthparts are nearly limitless. Here we find an assemblage of instruments such as only a surgeon, an artisan, or a burglar might wish for—from a harmless sucking proboscis, through implements for boring, sawing, pinching, and cutting, to such devilish contraptions as poison syringes or stilettos that snap out to pierce the prey. [20/5]

Also highly refined are various mechanisms for egg-laying and stinging found in the female abdomen. There one may see exquisite hypodermic needles of improbable length, slenderness, and elasticity that bore deep into the hardest wood. In fact, insects can cope with nearly all materials, even metals.

Insects wield their tools with complete mastery even though they have never received any instruction in the use of these tools. Insect workers include born bricklayers, coopers, weavers, tailors, spinners, miners, sappers, and patternmakers; they make silk, paper, mortar, paste, wax, honey, and sugar; and they cultivate fungi and cause plant galls.

COMMUNICATION

Insects converse with their own kind by means of signs and sounds, songs and dances. Many of the tones they produce are so high that we don't hear them. The ability to hear ultrasounds not only enables insects to communicate with one another, but occasionally has other survival value. For example, bats hunt moths on the wing with the aid of a kind of radar. A bat emits ultrasounds and hears the echoes as they bounce back from the moths' bodies. But since a moth can intercept the ultrasounds, it frequently is able at the last minute to make evasive maneuvers and escape the pursuing bat.

INSTINCT

The guidepost of insect behavior is the inborn intelligence called instinct. Rarely can an insect escape the compulsion of instinct, even when instinct leads to catastrophe.

Instinct causes a female solitary bee to dig a chamber in the ground; to collect pollen and shape it into a ball that stands in the chamber on three short legs, and to deposit eggs on the pollen ball, which serves as food for the young after they hatch. The three legs keep the ball from coming into close contact with the damp earth and hence from getting moldy. But never does such a bee live long enough to learn that mold could grow on a pollen ball; thus she is warding off harm of a kind that is wholly unknown to her.

A caterpillar instinctively spins a cocoon around itself before it turns into a pupa, the resting stage from which the adult emerges. The cocoon is so hard that the emerging butterfly would find it a prison if there were not a built-in escape hatch. At the upper end of the cocoon the caterpillar builds an exit in the form of a circular lock made of bristles. The bristles meet at the center of the lock, their tips facing outward and pressed together as though under tension from a spring. The bristles make the cocoon hard to enter. But they part easily when pressure is exerted by the butterfly within. [274/6; 310/1]

REPRODUCTION

Insect reproduction generally is dependent on mating, but also occurs frequently by means of unfertilized females, a phenomenon known as parthenogenesis. In the latter case, only females or only males—rarely both sexes—develop from the unfertilized eggs. In social insects—bees and ants, for example—the fertilized eggs yield female offspring, and the unfertilized ones males. When parthenogenesis is of constant occurrence, females are produced more or less exclusively. Males are either unknown or extremely rare. This is the case with walkingstick insects, some sawflies, gall wasps, parasitic wasps, and certain moths of the family Psychidae.

In numerous species of insects, only males appear when a female has remained unfertilized. Her plight may well have resulted from a dearth of males, a state of affairs that is alleviated by the production of purely masculine progeny. When a generation including males is occasionally interpolated in a whole series of female generations, as occurs in plant-lice, we speak of heterogony. Another type of heterogony occurs when bisexual and purely female generations alternate, as happens in many gall wasps. When generations alternate in these fashions, differences in form and in biology arise.

From Egg to Adult

25/1-2

The defenseless tentacle prominent moth (2) is forced to depend on concealment, but its well-armed caterpillar (1) has a very striking appearance. (→ 62/5-6)

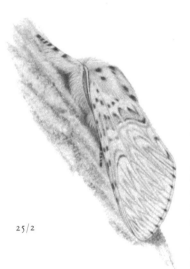

25/2

An ugly, plodding caterpillar becomes a beautiful, flitting butterfly, and a soft white grub changes into a beetle clad in armor. A dingy underwater creature sheds its skin and is suddenly a dragonfly. Changes like these mark the development of an insect from egg to adult and are known as its metamorphosis. This is probably the most astounding phenomenon in the insect empire.

Metamorphosis as a way of life makes possible a very small beginning. Hundreds or thousands of tiny eggs can be produced in the insect body and then deposited in all kinds of places, even inside dead or living plant or animal tissue. The plasticity and adaptiveness of the wormlike early stages of many insects permit the use of each and every source of food. So, chewing and sucking go on everywhere, for is it not the exclusive function of these larvae—these maggots, grubs, and caterpillars—to grow into adults?

One might think so. And yet certain facts prompt second thoughts. Many insects live for several years as larvae, but perhaps for only a few days or even a few hours as mature beings; and these may do practically nothing except mate and lay eggs, some not even taking a meal. And is it not odd that so many of the merely preliminary stages display a gamut of form, a phantasy of color, and an ingenuity of self-defense far surpassing those of the mature insect? For example, gaudily colored caterpillars of terrifyingly fantastic form, equipped with poisonous spines or with acid-dispensing syringes, may turn into dull-colored moths lacking all means of self-protection.

On the stage in this scene from life, the caterpillar apparently has become the leading actor. Elsewhere, the eggs may play a prominent role, as veritable works of art. And occasionally the pupae, those pauses in insect life whose usual chore is to remain unseen, may even have an excessively striking appearance. [30; 62/5, 6; 254–255; 274]

Complete Metamorphosis

Metamorphosis occurs in many animals, especially in aquatic ones. But a pupal stage appears only among insects. Insects that go through a pupal stage are said to have complete metamorphosis.

The first stage in the development of insects is the egg. Most insects lay eggs, but some give birth to living young that have developed from eggs inside the mother's body. The larvae of some insects are full-grown at birth and immediately turn into pupae. Certain flies that live among termites give birth to fully mature offspring, the entire course of metamorphosis having taken place within the mother's body.

Larval Stage

In hatching from the egg, many larvae open the eggshell with special teeth or hooks on the mouth, forehead, or thorax. These teeth or hooks may serve no other function. The freshly hatched larvae often have a different form than they have during the middle or later stages of their development, a difference that frequently may be accounted for by a radical alteration in the way of life. And here we again stand in amazement before that tireless urge that without an apparent goal lets the most immature, so-to-speak the most anonymous forms hatch with the richest of colors and in the most bizarre of shapes. A creature adorned in so unlikely a manner feeds and grows, climbs from its skin when the latter gets too tight, and then can be recognized no more. Today decked with thorns, pegs, and hairs; tomorrow, bare and smooth. Now black, then red, and later green; spotted at first, and afterwards patterned with rings or stripes.

The number of molts of an insect varies from four to eight for most insects, but may go as high as twenty or more for some insects. These molts are triggered by the periodic activity of certain hormones. First, the outer chitinous layer of the insect's skin is loosened, together with the internal coat of the respiratory tubes and of certain parts of the digestive tract, which have a similar

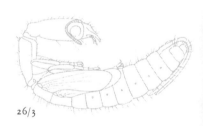

26/1–2
The first, highly motile stage and the second, sessile stage (1) of a strepsipterous larva (twisted-winged parasite) ; and the larva of a tortoise beetle that has disguised itself with "antlers" made from a sausage-shaped lump of dung (2).

constitution. Meanwhile, the epidermis (hypodermis) constructs a new superficial layer. During this event the old skin is pressed farther and farther backward by the integrated muscular contraction and expansion of the body segments. Finally, it breaks in the region of the neck and is stripped away toward the rear.

Many larvae and nymphs devour the empty skin (exuviae), just as the eggshell often is consumed by the hatching immature insect. Shortly after every molt, the young insects swallow air (or water, in the case of aquatic species). In this way they may achieve sudden, astonishing increases in size.

A molt involves much risk for an insect. Consider the caterpillar. Defenseless, unable to move, and for the most part anchored fast in its silken carpet, the caterpillar may sit still for days before the actual molting process begins; the process itself may last only for minutes and frequently occurs at night. Usually it is successful, but not always. A slight injury can cause deformation and death.

Larval life may be completed in hours or days, but usually lasts for weeks or months, and sometimes for years. For the most part it is interrupted by periods of rest (diapause) that are correlated with climatic changes. The rest periods may carry the insect through the winter or, more rarely, through a hot, dry summer. At such times a few species of beetles turn temporarily into so-called "false pupae." After molting they assume a mummy-like simplified form in which legs and mouthparts are reduced in size; they either remain entirely within the cast skin of the previous instar (stage between molts) or else lie with only the abdomen so enclosed. Some insects undergo states of diapause that are not correlated with climate and that are of no known value to the insect.

Pupal Stage

Before the final larval molt, insect larvae make great and often marvelous preparations: they build, glue things together, spin shelters and fabrics of every imaginable kind, dig chambers or hollow them out, weave hammocks, and make themselves fast with belts or cushions. For at the last molt there comes to light that wholly different being—the pupa.

During its first few minutes or hours of existence, the pupa is still soft and perhaps even without its form-to-be, but it soon assumes its intended shape. This may be the stiff, active or inactive, mummylike pupa of a moth or butterfly, in which indications of the head, antennae, legs, and wings of the future insect are visible and in which future form and color are foreshadowed in thousands of ways. Or the pupal form may be coarctate, like that of a muscoid fly; the last larval skin is changed into a rigid case containing the true pupa. Or it may be the soft, pale, and almost ghostly pupa of a beetle, bee, or wasp, with its rudimentary appendages sculptured in bas-relief; or the strangely elfin, very active, floating pupa of a gnat. [33/2; 138/30; 279/3D, 5A; 364/3D]

Within the pupa, particularly during its first minutes, hours, or days of life, sweeping events take place. Many internal organs melt away and turn to liquid. From the sausage-like mass of the pupa, the rudiments of legs and wings begin to grow. An entire head takes shape from what was nothing but a deep, open throat. Dramatic happenings of this sort are the commonplace events of insect life, as any ordinary maggot will show us.

After this radical developmental event, a brief resting stage usually occurs, preceding the adult stage. The interruption ordinarily lasts longer in insects that have but one generation a year, and may even occupy several years. This offers the insect a chance of simply bypassing an unfavorable climatic period. But little use is made of the possibility. The great majority of adult insects come forth automatically exactly at the time set for the species, whether the climatic conditions are favorable or not. The slight alterations in schedule that sometimes occur usually are a matter only of a week or a few weeks, as they are with the blossoming time of various plants, on which the insects, of course, depend.

There exists in all insects a hidden clock that orders their whole life cycle and takes note of the dry, the wet, or the cold seasons. This clock, controlled by hormones, can be slowed or speeded up in the laboratory by changing the insect's living conditions. For instance, the insect's resting period may frequently (but not always) be shortened greatly by exposing the insect prematurely to artificial cold. But tampering with its clock may also kill the insect. If, for example, we remove an insect of the temperate zone entirely from exposure to the customary cold of winter, it will cease development and will die. Such techniques are now employed to destroy harmful insects.

Insects usually pass the winter as eggs or in some subsequent immature form, although

26/3

26/4
→ 138/30

26/5
→ 274/5

26

27/1
When we are confronted with the spotless beauty of newborn insects, we imagine we are breathing in the freshness of morning dew. (→ 30/4)

there are many that overwinter as adults. When an insect is in the stage of development in which it normally spends the winter, it often withstands freezing temperatures by producing glycerin-like substances that prevent the body fluids from solidifying. [139]

THE ADULT

When the adult insect is ready to emerge from the pupa, a further process of completion sets in; this is concerned especially with the strengthening and the pigmentation of the insect. The development of pigmentation is a striking sight. The eyes darken first, and then the whole body. From hour to hour the pattern becomes clearer; finally the colors shine forth.

And then comes the signal—who knows from where to break free. For weeks, months, or even for years, there lay a "thing." True enough, it was gripped in the process of formation, and its blood pulsed; yet it was completely quiescent and unable to move, a casting within the rigid mold of the pupal skin. Then, one day or night, between one second and the next, there is a sudden twitch, a bursting of the pupal rind at some predestined spot, and legs begin to grope about outside.

Many flies, beetles, and wasps only need to push, bite, or dissolve their way out of the nest, out of the ground, or out of wood, and then to wait quietly for the hardening of their armor and wings. But the breakout does not always happen so easily and quickly. The moths and butterflies, for instance, frequently struggle intermittently, between compulsory rest periods, to draw the wings and the proboscis from their sheaths, before the body is released by the pupal shell. Often clinging to the pupal case or running feverishly about in search of a suitable spot to seize onto, often only gradually working themselves out of the depths of the ground or dissolving their way out of the tightly spun cocoon with the help of their saliva, they begin to prepare for a specially significant event: the expansion of the wings. This usually starts immediately after emergence and converts rudimentary wings into the powerful, magnificent airfoils with which we are familiar.

The butterfly or moth prepares for the expansion by taking a position that lets the wings hang freely downward. Every insect wing is originally a narrow outpocketing of the integument. It consists of a double

26/3–5
Pupal forms: Motile form (free pupa) of the snakefly (3), the coarctate pupa of a long-horned beetle (4) (→ 138/30), and the mummylike pupa of a moth (5) (→ 274/5). (The freely projecting proboscis betrays the long trunked sphinx moth.)

membrane between whose surfaces run air tubes, the so-called wing veins. The pumping of air through the air tubes and of blood between the membranes gradually extends and expands the wing. After half an hour or so the wings attain full size. The blood is then withdrawn, and the double membrane becomes glued together, forming a single, slowly hardening structure. The air tubes remain filled with air, and blood continues to circulate in narrow channels along the air tubes and here and there elsewhere. Usually, a butterfly is ready for flight in two to four hours.

Not every butterfly survives this dangerous phase of wing expansion, for at that time enemies cannot be evaded. Besides, many a butterfly is crippled irreparably by some small misfortune, as when the spreading of the wings, once started, is interrupted for too long a time. [30/1]

From a freshly emerged insect there emanates an enchanting aura. The glass-clear wing membranes sparkle with a delicate and attenuated gloss; the colors of a butterfly are touched with the sheen of satin, and the arched wing covers of a beetle might be of molten silk. What an unforgettable instant, when a butterfly first spreads its wings! During their development, they are held folded together over the back, but now they open wide like a bedewed blossom, to the accompaniment of a delicate aroma; at the same time a scarcely perceptible tremor runs along the dainty wing margins and through the soft down and stiffer hairs, out to the very tips of the antennae. Next, the whole body begins to pulsate, in quivering waves that more and more strongly grip the wings, until these begin to beat with ever-growing force. The entire organism is agitated beyond control and hurls itself violently into the air. Once we have witnessed that event, we have had a truly moving experience. [246]

INCOMPLETE METAMORPHOSIS

A great many insects gradually develop into adults, without going through a pupal stage. This is incomplete metamorphosis, and the young insects are known as nymphs. In the primitive wingless insects, such as the bristletails and springtails, the young look almost exactly like the adults, except in size. Other insects, including dragonflies, mayflies, cockroaches, and true bugs more or less resemble their parents, but lack reproductive organs and wings. These develop slowly, getting larger after each molt, but attain their final dimensions in a large spurt during the last molt. Or sometimes wing rudiments become outwardly visible only at the molt to the last nymphal stage. Aquatic nymphs, which do not resemble the adults, though they are not profoundly different, are often called naiads.

Insects with long legs molt in a hanging position. For some, such as the walkingstick insect, this bit of acrobatics becomes the height of grotesquerie, a living enactment of "wire sculpture." [31/3]

The early stages of some insects have an astonishing power of regeneration: such lost structures as whole legs may be replaced in the course of ensuing molts. In contrast, a minor wound occurring even in the earliest instars of insects with complete metamorphosis causes damage that is impressed in one way or another on the imago, provided the insect ever does reach maturity.

In insects with incomplete metamorphosis, coloration generally changes less abruptly during successive stages than in those with complete metamorphosis. After the final molt, attainment of the definitive color pattern may take longer than usual, perhaps requiring days or weeks after the insect has matured. In some species of grasshoppers, the final coloration may vary in accordance with the background against which they are living. [31/2]

In considering the final appearance of insects, we come to the most striking visible manifestation of the insect world: their shaping by means of color, outline, and sculpture.

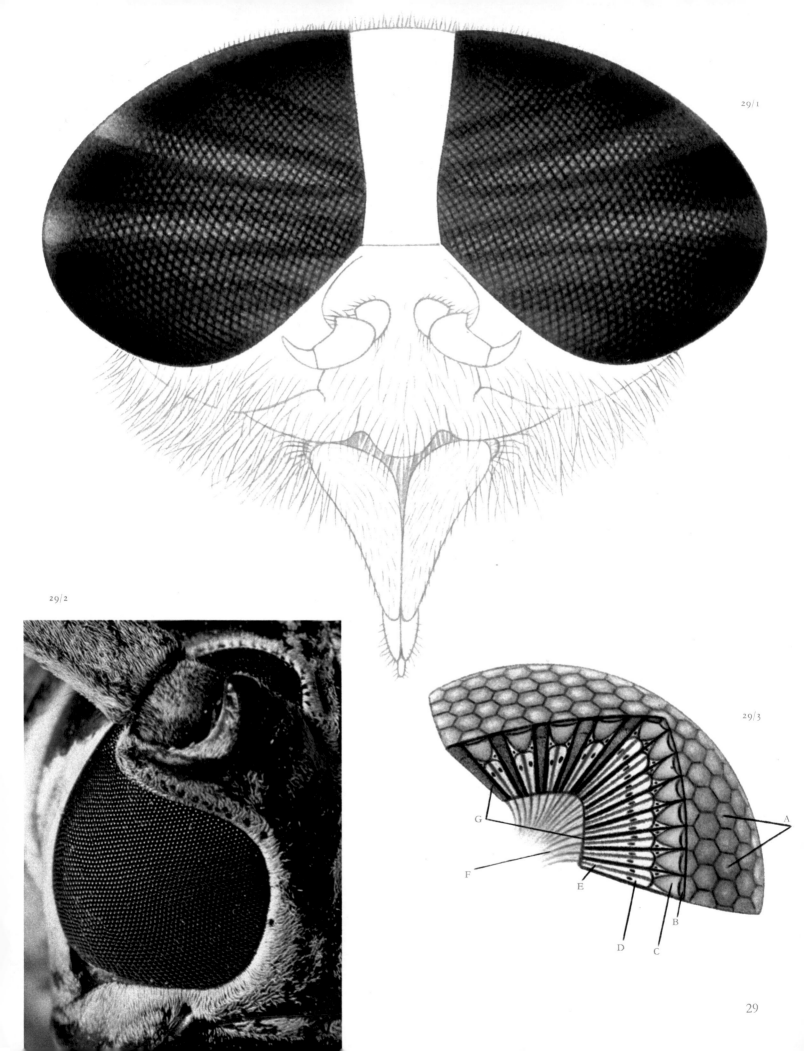

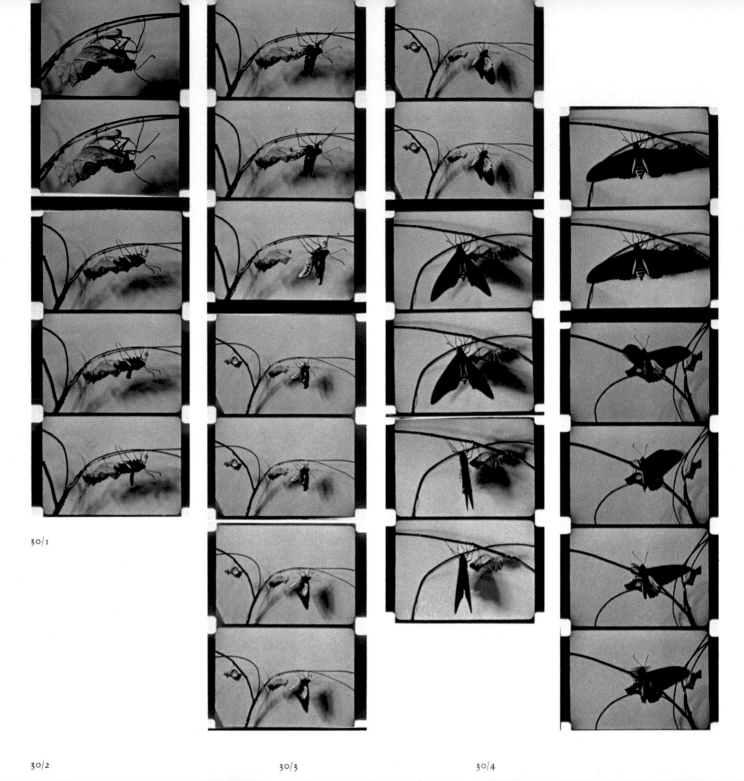

30/1

30/2　　　　　　　　　　　　　30/3　　　　　　　　　　　　　30/4

30

31/1

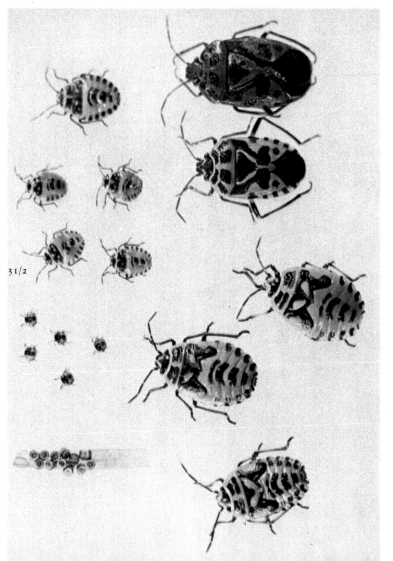

31/2

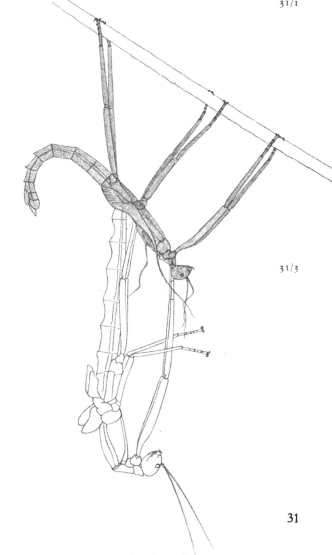

31/3

31

32/1

32/2

32/3

32/4

32/5

32/6

32/7

32

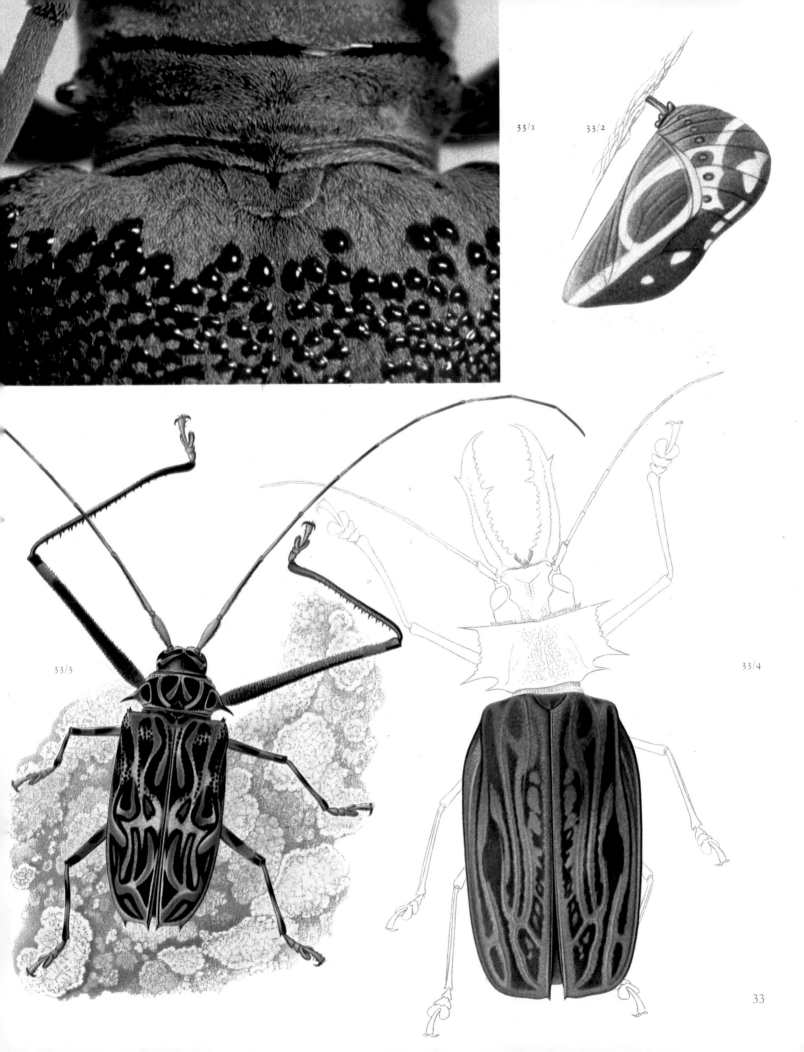

33/1   33/2

33/3   33/4

33

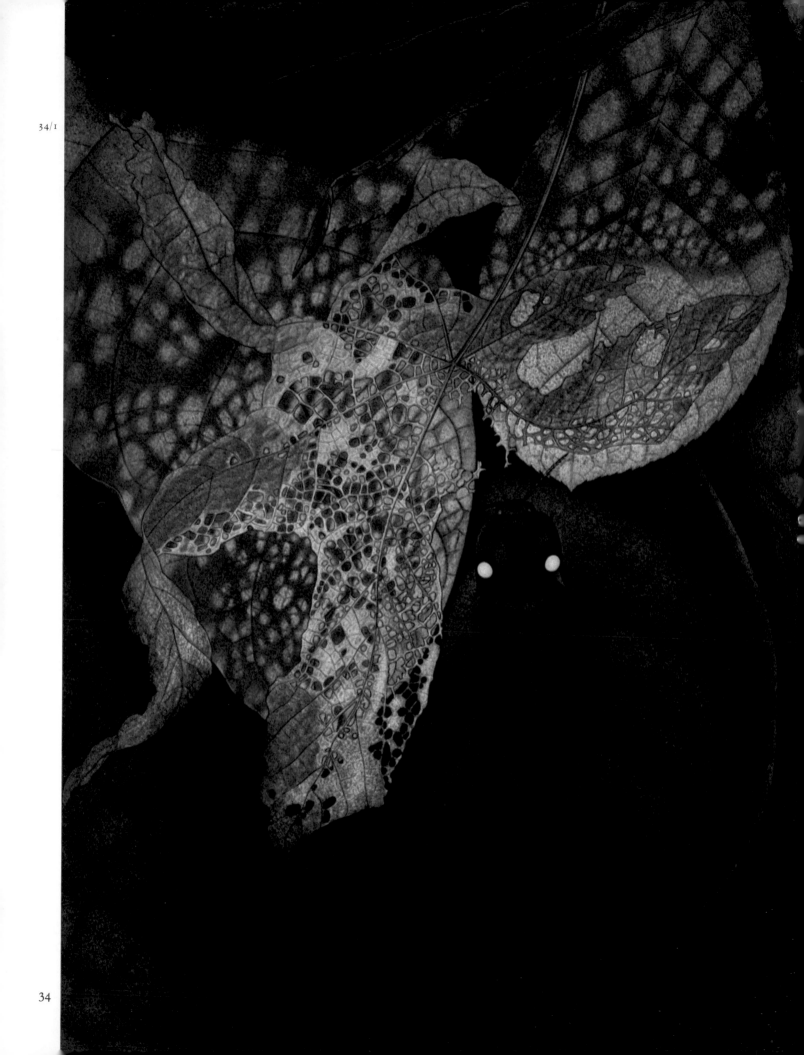

35/1

35/2

35/3

35/4

35/5

35

36/1

36/2 – 3

36/4 – 5

36/6

36/7

36/8 – 10

36/11 – 13

Living Works of Art

PAGE 36

36/1
Examples of a very variable species from the family of tiger moths. Photograph.

36/2–5
The fundamentally varicolored hind wings of the underwing moths have in a few species a tendency to evolve toward melanism, especially in the inner, basal portion. With the blue underwing (4), this area is naturally black, but it can be brightened up again experimentally, through the action of high concentrations of oxygen during a particular, labile stage of the pupa; the adults so obtained display what is probably the more primitive coloration (5).

36/6–7
With many insects, different generations also differ; above, the dry season form and, below, the rainy season form of an African butterfly.

36/8–13
Geographic races of an apollo butterfly (genus Parnassius), a group with a special propensity for forming races, inasmuch as the mountain areas available for flying are often small and isolated. Photograph.

In color, outline, and sculpture, insects represent perhaps the most phenomenal artistry on earth. The forms out of which this art is created include all the components of life, used simultaneously. We can imagine the effects of climatic, physical, chemical, and biological influences. But the really decisive force is life itself.

The "canvas" on which much of this art is displayed is the insect integument. This external skeleton, or shell, is not merely a rigid casting, but has a complex structure consisting mostly of superimposed, interwoven layers. The integument, which includes the wing surfaces, may be more or less colorless and transparent, milky, or opalescent white; but the greater part of the mature insect's surface is brown, ranging from yellowish-brown through reddish-brown to nearly black.

Many insects, particularly numerous beetles, occur only in the uncolored condition, but in other insects the colorless areas are scattered like islands among regions that are brightly pigmented or covered with colorful hairs or scales. The unadorned surface may be employed, then, even in its raw state, as an ornamental element. This can be very impressive when the integument is molded into such marvelous sculptural details as protruding tubercles or deep recesses. Especially in butterflies, the transparent wing membrane gains a similar artistic significance when parts of it are left opaque.

The colors themselves may be deposited in or on the integument, or close beneath it in the epidermis, or even further down, in the inner organs. Often, too, the hairs and particularly the scales bear colors. In addition, the surface may have a powdery, readily removed overcoating that is yellow, bright blue, or white. [33/1; 107/8; 245]

PIGMENT COLORS

Much of an insect's coloration results from the presence of pigments, particularly black, brown, red, and yellow, with their intermediates, and to some extent white, green, blue, and violet. Pigments come from the blood or arise from metabolic reactions as uric acid derivatives. They are various complex chemical compounds from which particular shades are produced in the epidermal cells by means of such processes as atmospheric oxidation. We distinguish two main groups of pigments: (1) blood pigments (melanins), ranging from yellowish-brown to black; and (2) fat pigments (lipochromes), including yellows and reds.

Variation in coloring is achieved not only by differences in chemical composition, but also through unequal concentration of the pigment granules. For example, yellow pigment in high concentration produces an orange shade, but is bright yellow when dilute. In addition, an inexhaustible wealth of combinations occurs when different colors and pigments are laid down one above the other. In conjunction with these effects, the epidermis and lower layers of the integument serve as reflectors, as do the white and yellow portions of the deeper-lying fat body. Other factors, too, may play a part, such as the green plant chlorophylls that caterpillars and grasshoppers take up with their food. Most pigments are not very light-fast, and many get bleached by the sun even in the living insect.

STRUCTURAL COLORS

The most striking colors are not produced by pigments at all, even though pigments deposited among or beneath them contribute to the overall effect. These are the silvers, golds, silky and metallic greens, blues, violets, and purples, and the colors that shimmer and shine, glittering and iridescent, like opals or mother-of-pearl. They are not chemicals but structural colors—colors resulting from interference and refraction of light, as in a rainbow.

The refraction of the rays of light takes place in complex surface layers or inclusions within the integument. The inclusions consist of microscopic rods or lamellae (leaf-like plates) arranged in single, double, or multiple layers; these layers may also contain air bubbles, as do almost all the metallic scales of the butterfly wing. Less frequently, interference colors are produced by an excreted layer that has hardened in relief into appropriately sculptured shapes, as in tiger beetles and ground beetles.

All structural colors change in accordance with the angle at which light falls on them. As the angle becomes smaller, they get cloudier, duller, darker, and finally disappear altogether. A silken gleam is produced by close horizontal stratification of thin, thread-like rods; a satiny effect is given by tiny, closely appressed vertical hairs or by scales standing on edge. [31/1; 32/1; 314–15]

LIVING LIGHTS

Insects that produce light at night or at dusk are particularly fascinating. Among these, the lightning bugs are the most familiar. Light-producing organs occur on various parts of the insect body and are found not only in adults, but in pupae, larvae, and eggs. In fact, even unfertilized eggs within the female body can give off light, which comes from their innermost substance, the yolk. Some insects shine without benefit of special light-producing organs, merely by means of the cells of the fat body, a kind of tissue distributed here and there throughout the insect's body. For that matter, the more highly developed light-producing organs of other insects have been derived from the fat body.

The luminous substance, which seems to consist of chemically altered proteins, is peculiar to the insect body. It is not of bacterial origin, as is the luminous material of many organisms in the sea. The light organs lie close beneath transparent patches of skin and are plateshaped or lenslike complexes. They have an upper layer of light-producing cells and an inferior layer of cells that reflect light upward and outward. The whole organ is penetrated by nerves and air tubes; the latter branch profusely among the light-producing cells and thus make possible a rich supply of oxygen and the high rate of oxidation essential for the production of light. The light itself may be whitish, yellow, red, or even blue, but it is usually greenish.

In some lightning bugs, luminescence is important in the mutual attraction of the sexes. In some other insects the lights, which look like two eyes and shine forth most brightly when their possessor is disturbed,

are assumed to be a means of scaring enemies away. We know that the lights of certain cave-dwelling gnat larvae entice food in the form of small insects into the webs of the larvae. However, no particular function has as yet been discerned for most instances of light production in insects.

Finally, the reddish glint in the eyes of moths flying to an electric light should be mentioned. This light, however, is not produced by the moth, but is reflected by the moth's eye—specifically, by a tight network of tiny air tubes, acting as a mirror, that lies behind the eye's visual cells. The reflected light does not last long, for when the eye is strongly stimulated the incoming rays are soon screened from the reflecting tracheal layer by dark pigment granules. [34; 136/6, 7; 146; 190]

FUNCTIONS OF COLORS

Body colors generally are regarded as protection against excessively intense radiation of light and heat. Their function therefore is not solely concerned with appearance. Yet they may serve to bring the sexes together, and no doubt their principal significance is as a means of protection and deception in the struggle for existence. In countless instances, however, no uses can be found for the satin and silk, the silver and gold, the cuffs, collars, skirts, trains, and all the thousand other varieties of insect adornment. [109]

PICTORIAL DESIGN

We have spoken of substance and color, but there is yet more; we are forced to ascend still further beyond the limits of what we can comprehend. For we have not yet taken note of the way in which these elements are applied—of their simultaneous, mutually interdependent action, which creates the unparalleled blend of artistry that marks the insect's body. Often this artistry is achieved with spots and lines that spread over the most varied parts of the body and merge into a unified composition, just as if a wing were not one thing, an abdomen or a head something else.

These and other structures are developing quite separately as early as the larval stage. And yet the pupal organism frequently acquires a colored spot here and one or more lines there, many of which combine and form the reasonably complete sketch that is outlined coarsely on the pupal exterior. And then, when the final color pattern of the mature insect is being laid down inside, there

38/1
The difference between the sexes may take odd forms. To this elegant, brilliantly metallic female of the Chalcidids there belongs an ugly, louse-shaped male.

38/2
Longitudinal striping and transverse striping arise in fundamentally different ways. During the growth of mussels and snails, if dark pigment is deposited at the shell margin uninterruptedly and always at the same distinctly separated points, then longitudinal stripes result; contrariwise, if the deposition of pigment

develop on the various parts of the body surface those definitive and quite different designs that unite to yield the marvelous predestined patterns of the adult.

How should one attempt in phylogenetic terms to comprehend the origin of such total images as being merely the sum of details, each diagrammed on a wholly different part of the body? In any event, all present conceptions of the origin of species, by natural selection of those individuals best equipped to survive the struggle for existence, do not suffice to explain the many-sided riddles brought forward by coloration and design. [32/2; 186/42; 211/1; 249; 252/6; 255/3]

The basic elements in the coloration of insects are dark spots, stripes, and bands. Usually, the close relationship of these elements to the courses of nerves, tracheae, or wing veins is understandable, for the creative forces must first find expression upon or near the pathways of pulsating life.

The most primitive designs are made of more or less similar spots, perhaps arranged in series. Or they are made of rather cloudy, undulant darkenings that tend to thicken along certain lines of the body, such as the dorsal and lateral lines, and that thus are able to form figures peculiar to the several species. Next there come sharper, more definite, better outlined lengthwise stripes and transverse bands, of which the former seem to have an earlier origin. In any case, many transverse bands can be derived from a fusion of spots that originally occurred independently, on both sides, and that were left close together by the dissolution of still earlier longitudinal stripes. This is an evolutionary course that points toward the possible source of networks or screen patterns. Almost everywhere one sees a tendency for the pigments to be distributed both lengthwise and transversely at the same time, but the transverse distribution is much more frequent and the formation of longitudinal stripes less so.

It is a deeply moving riddle, this operation of the forces and tendencies of the body. They concentrate this here and that there, on one occasion produce color at a certain spot, push some things apart, combine others, cause substances to flow along parallel lines or to intersect. Never is this done at random, but always in conformity to the laws of the genus and the species.

How uncannily limited and controlled such dynamic energy is! Its basic formulas are by no means so numerous as one might suppose: the wealth of outcome that confuses us resides rather in their thousandfold variants.

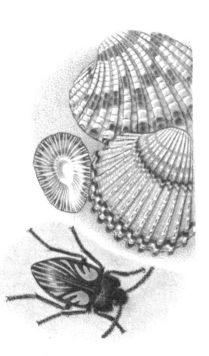

is interrupted in time but not spatially, transverse stripes are produced. Irregularities in these processes cause spotting, and jagged or meshed patterns. With insects too the designs depend heavily on internal, rhythmic processes, but in their case on those of circulation and metabolism. (→ 32/4)

APPEARANCE AND SEX

The males and females of many kinds of insects are so similar that we can scarcely distinguish them. By far the majority, however, have slight or more evident differences in size, shape, and pattern. In some species the differences are so great that the affinity of the sexes is completely unrecognizable, as when the male has wings but the female is wingless.

Frequently, the males, which generally emerge from the pupa somewhat earlier than the females, have more magnificent coloring and more fantastic shapes, but the female pattern sometimes is the richer one. Presumably, at one time in the distant past, both sexes were alike. In many instances it seems that the male, in agreement with his more lively temperament, subsequently has undergone a more violent development of form and color, whereas the female, in adaptation to her calmer way of life and greater need of protection, has kept closer to the original shape and coloration.

Utterly fantastic, among insects whose sexes are so different, are the gynandromorphs, those rare individuals that have characteristics of both sexes. In the bilateral gynandromorph, one half with its corresponding pair of wings is male, and the other is female; the separation runs along the midline of the body, though the antennae may be oppositely exchanged. In contrast, the left fore wing and the right hind wing of a crossed gynandromorph are male, their opposites female. And in the incomplete gynandromorph the color pattern of both sexes is strewn irregularly over the wings of one individual. [35/2, 3; 179/2; 213/12; 220/11]

FREAKS

Only exceptionally do freaks occur among insects, as when two or three legs arise where one should have been, or when antennae occur in duplicate or terminate in leg segments with claws. At times larval nutrition may play an important part in the later development of the imago. For instance, when larval food is scarce, not only may unusually small beetles be produced, but these may emerge with defective or rudimentary skeletal structures. [35/1, 4, 5]

VARYING GENERATIONS

In many insects that produce two generations a year, the two populations differ slightly or more markedly. This phenomenon, known as seasonal dimorphism, appears most impressively in certain butterflies both in temperate and tropical zones. The tropical butterflies have forms characteristic of the dry and rainy seasons, and the temperate butterflies have forms characteristic of spring and summer. The successive generations of the same species are so unlike that they have at times been described as completely different species. The summer and dry season forms are generally smaller and have different, brighter colors, but a less conspicuous pattern. One generation, usually the spring or wet season form, is typical of the species. [36/6, 7; 220/5, 6]

INDIVIDUAL VARIATION

No two individuals of a species are ever alike in all particulars. There is always variation among individuals. The extent of the variation is slight for many species, but for others the extremes are so far apart that they sometimes have been described as two or more species. The nature of individual variants is such that they might all be offspring of a single pair.

ABNORMAL COLORING

Occasional individuals are abnormal: they have suffered a disturbance in development or some other pathological damage. For instance, the interruption of the ordinary course of coloration by heat or cold, dampness, or deficiency of light may cause a reddish pigmentation to replace the normal dark or black. This condition, called rufinism, may even become the rule for insects at high altitude, in caves, or under other extreme conditions. Again, external influences may cause the body pigments of an insect to whiten in various regions of the body and the wings. This effect is called albinism. Albinism also may occur in some insects as an inherited abnormality.

Abnormal coloring may also be non-pathological. An example of this is flavinism, the shift from a normally reddish color toward yellow. Another is the change toward a darker form that crops up in insects again and again. This change shows itself in two ways. The dark pigments may come to predominate more and more, covering the entire surface like a veil and yet letting the underlying pattern shine through. This is melanism. Or else the black parts of the original pattern may expand to the point where they fuse, leading frequently to a complete blackening, known as nigrism. Flavinism, melanism, and

nigrism, though often influenced by cold and dampness, are inherited abnormalities of insects. They are caused by mutations, those abrupt changes that originate not as the result of external influences but because of sudden alterations in the genetic material. By their very nature, mutations are of the utmost significance in investigations of the origins of species. [36/1; 215/2; 243/17]

GEOGRAPHIC VARIATION

With a few exceptions, most of the widely distributed insect species have developed more or less clearly distinct local forms called geographic races, or subspecies. These races have arisen often quite abruptly through mutation. They are shaped by the totality of the climatic, geologic, and faunistic relationships peculiar to their range, and mingle with each other at most along the boundaries of the areas they occupy. Because there is some interbreeding here, the races seldom become completely distinct from one another. But such interbreeding at the margins cannot occur in races that occupy widely separated islands, except in the few species with extraordinary powers of flight; consequently these inhabitants of islands have gone far in their special, peculiar modifications and may even have become so different that they have attained the status of distinct species. Even on the mainland one finds sharply isolated localities, each with its own strikingly modified insect races. These localities include desert oases, mountains, isolated bodies of water, and distinctive soil formations with their special types of vegetation. [36/8–13; 49/1–12]

Not surprisingly, in places of this sort a majority of the species, although they are from different families of insects, have certain features in common. Most desert insects display the light color of the sand. Nordic and alpine species share the distinction of a long, thick, protective covering of hairs. And the males of certain butterflies and moths of both Australia and the Sahara Desert possess enormously enlarged antennae, with a consequent enlargement of olfactory end organs, that help them locate their females over extraordinary distances.

Somewhat less understandable is the fact that in certain countries numerous species of insects have experienced a striking coarsening of their sculptured pattern. And then there is the problem that never does every one of the species develop the adaptation common to the majority. But the matter becomes completely mysterious when we see that, even in a relatively small locality, various

40/1
Melanism in a butterfly. There are variations of many kinds, namely, individual ones (aberrations, mutations); geographic races or local forms, as well as ecological ones—that is, those resulting from differences in life styles (some are designated as subspecies); differences between the sexes (sexual dimorphism); differences between generations in a single year (seasonal dimorphism); pathological alterations (monstrosities). Photograph. (→ 243/17)

41/1
An assemblage of Brazilian butterflies of different families in similar garb. Here toxic and nontoxic species fly together, cannot be distinguished, and hence are protected in common from enemies. (→ 19)

41/2–3
To this same "mimicry ring" there belongs also the female of a white (pierid) butterfly (2). However, the male (3) is wearing the white dress typical of his family, and therefore remains unprotected. (→ 18–19)

41/3

rather distantly related insects have acquired a distinctive, brightly colored pattern, almost like a uniform.

In the Philippines, for example, a whole assemblage of beetle species is decorated with a network of scales that glisten with all the colors of the rainbow; and certain golden wasps, whose close relatives normally are uniformly greenish or bluish, have fiery red heads such as are seen nowhere else in the world. The tropics of South and Central America are famous for their uniformly-clad associations of butterfly species, each pattern typical of a single locale and yet differing from country to country, or even from one forest to another. In considering these matters we have hit upon a specially touchy problem—that of mimicry. [49/13–33]

MIMICRY AND CAMOUFLAGE

The doctrine of mimicry was founded in 1861, in Darwin's time, by the English naturalist H. W. Bates. In a single place in the primeval forest of Brazil he saw numerous brightly colored butterflies that, although of different families, were so similar in color, pattern, and behavior that they could not be distinguished in flight. Bates correctly assumed that one of the species in such a group, thanks to a disagreeable smell or taste, or to poisonous body fluids, was more or less shunned by birds. The several other, edible species, then, would have the advantage of being let alone because they looked like the undesirable species.

A variation in mimicry was recognized shortly thereafter by a German scientist, Fritz Müller. He also saw great groups of similar-appearing butterflies. But in each of these groups two or more species were distasteful to birds. By their resemblance to one another, these distasteful species apparently increased their protection. In total individuals, the distasteful species outnumbered the intrinsically unprotected species in the company.

Later, as many as 19 species of similarly colored butterflies from different families and genera were counted in a mimicry ring. In some species of this nature only the females bear the common uniform. The males are less in need of such protection from the viewpoint of the species and also less likely to be flying in companies of this sort. They wear quite different garb, of a type characteristic of their genus and species.

Butterfly mimicry occurs everywhere in the tropics. In Africa, *Papilio dardanus,* a species that ranges from the deep south as far north as Ethiopia, gives a dramatic performance of mimicry. The males occur throughout the range in the normal, long-tailed costume of the papilios. But the females have a different coloration and wing shape in each locality. In several places, the females are deceptively like other, inedible butterfly species. Some 24 distinct geographical races of the females have been identified. In rare instances, difficult to explain, sexually dissimilar patterns do not depend on geographical separation of races, but are found among the offspring of a single pair.

Many kinds of insects besides butterflies are protected by their stench or by poisons, as well as by sharp spines and various other defense measures. And many are the defenseless and unprotected insects that owe their lives to a similarity to these defensively equipped species. One must be careful, however, in designating examples of mimicry. Insects often show a remarkable resemblance to others with which they have no contact. This resemblance sometimes is incorrectly called mimicry. But true mimicry can occur only between different species that live together in the same place at the same time. How it happens that two widely separated species of insects come to resemble one another is unknown.

It is not hard to see how harmless insects might profit by a resemblance to wasps or bees. Although hunted by certain birds, wasps and bees are generally avoided because of their defensive stings. So we are not so greatly surprised that some flies and beetles, thanks to their coloring, or that certain butterflies with especially narrow, usually extended, transparent wings, display such a general similarity. But we find it strange that certain of the true bugs or even grasshoppers have taken on the appearance of insects so foreign to their nature as ordinary wasps or parasitic wasps.

Our amazement grows, moreover, when we discover that mimicry is not confined to general similarities, but goes to remarkable lengths in duplicating the outward appearance of definite individual species. Thus the similarity of a certain butterfly to a species of wasp is refined to the point where the illusion of the wasp's red mouth is given by the butterfly's palpi (mouthpart processes) and forecoxae (foreleg segments nearest the body). Another species from the same family of butterflies, in imitation of the ovipositor of a parasitic wasp, has developed a long caudal extension that is completely alien to butterfly anatomy.

Also unusual is the wasp-waist developed by certain beetles. Such models of deceit walk and move just like the insects they resemble. For instance, certain beetles and true bugs disregard their own heritage and hold their wings as the wasps do; and, in further imitation, they wave their legs and antennae, and arch their customarily straight abdomen upwards in the middle, bending the tip downward.

Among beetles, the net-winged beetles (Lycidae) are particularly unpopular as food for birds because of their toxic or at least unpleasant blood. Many net-winged beetles are resembled by beetles of other families, particularly the long-horned beetles. Some of the latter mimic certain yellowish-brown net-winged beetles. Both have black stripes running across the broad elytra (fore wings) that, oddly enough, are flattened like the wings of moths. This mimicry circle has been joined by an entirely different order, namely moths of the family Syntomidae. Most species of this family of moths have an entirely different appearance. [19; 50/1, 2; 224/18]

Moths whose legs and motions and caterpillars whose shapes are like those of bristly spiders are less widely known, but are extraordinarily striking. It is interesting to see how a moth of the family Noctuidae moves its monstrous legs, and perhaps sidles a little, as a spider does. Moths of the family Limacodidae also mimic spiders; at times during their day-long sleep they hold up their thick hairy legs in spectral stiffness. In addition, one might mention the rather rare similarity to ants displayed by certain true bugs and grasshoppers, particularly in their immature stages. There are, in addition, a few small spiders that look like ants. [19/34: 50/3; 56/4]

NATURAL SELECTION

The existence of mimicry can be explained by the theory of natural selection, which holds that the fittest are selected by nature to survive. For example, the enemies of insects, mainly the birds, prefer certain species of insects as food. The species of insects that are the least desirable as food have the best chance of surviving and reproducing their own kind. The characteristics that enabled these species of insects to survive are passed on to succeeding generations and tend to become perpetuated. But before natural selection can begin, there must be something to be selected—in this example, the least desirable insects.

A clear example of such natural selection has occurred recently in centers of heavy industry in Britain, where the light-colored individuals of the peppered moth gradually have been replaced by dark variants, which elsewhere are present in only a small minority. In industrial areas the dark forms have a better chance of surviving long enough to reproduce, because their enemies can find them much less easily than their light-colored relatives on the soot-covered treetrunks. This kind of selection could begin, however, only because of the presence of mutants that were dark and therefore adjusted to the changed state of affairs.

As another example, flying insects are at a disadvantage on certain islands at sea, because these islands are exposed constantly to stormy winds that tend to carry the flyers out to sea. Some of these islands now provide homes only for flightless insects, whose wings are reduced to rudiments or may even be lacking altogether. But the wind could only select the flightless individuals because these cripples occurred there occasionally, as they do everywhere else.

One can suppose that selection is able to refine an adaptation. But it can scarcely be responsible for the most complete adaptations; for often these far exceed the degree of adaptation needed for preservation of the species. Thus certain insects look like perfect leaves, whereas other insects even resemble leaves with such characteristic blemishes as moldy spots or raggedly chewed margins. But one can hardly assume that the second group is any less likely to be found and eaten by birds than the first group. Incomplete mimics may endure equally as well as complete mimics; and it may be that mimicry, as well as protective patterns and warning coloration, is responsible for the survival of only a small percentage of individuals. Even

42/1
Mimicry of wasps. The looks of well-armed wasps are feigned by butterflies and moths, but also by flies, true bugs (Hemiptera), beetles, and grasshoppers. In one moth (on the right), for instance, the illusion of a wasp's red mouth is given by red palps and forecoxae. (→ 19/26–27)

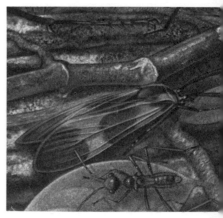

42/2–3
A fly simulates the dreaded Pepsis spider wasp. (→ 19/24, 25)

43/1
Insects that have cryptic garb imitate those parts of their habitat where they spend the greater portion of their life. Their capabilities range from depicting a simple clod to feigning a complete resemblance to a flower. (→ 54/6)

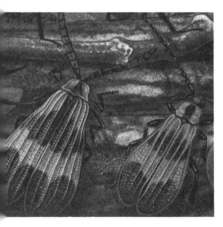

43/2–5
Mimicry of beetles and ants. In the center a toxic soft-bodied beetle, at the right a harmless long-horned beetle, and at the left a moth. Below, a leaf bug that looks like an ant. (→ 19/31–34)

so, it may serve as a decisive safeguard for the preservation of the species.

PROTECTIVE COLORATION AND FORM

The commonest colors among insects are gray, yellow, and brown, in all their shades, and green; these are the colors of the ground and of plants, and thus aid in the concealment of insects. Countless insects have the simplest garb and shape, remain more or less hidden when at rest without any special expenditure on their part, and survive very well. And yet, inconspicuousness alone evidently will not suffice for all insects, for we see a wide range of protective costumes and an intriguing play between costume and posture.

Some insects flatten themselves against the background, often aided by fringes of hairs along the lateral lines of the body or by other extensions that prevent them from casting a sharp shadow. Certain moths turn from a head-upward position on a tree trunk through an angle of 90 degrees, until their spread wings point one upward and one downward. As a result, the pattern of the moth merges precisely with the sculpturing of the bark.

Many green caterpillars have a light-colored back and a gradually-darkening ventral surface; they hang upside-down on leaves and twigs, with their darker surface turned upward. Such a caterpillar is hardly more prominent than the flat leaves surrounding it, because its own shadow darkens its light-colored back, while light from above illuminates its underside. Any impression of depth that the body might give is thus eliminated. The same use of this antagonistic shading is seen in certain caterpillars that cling vertically to hanging leaves; the body is light-colored in front and grows darker and darker toward the rear.

When these insects do not take their intended stance relative to the source of light, they are more conspicuous than they would be with plain coloring. Do they ordinarily adopt a certain position because it suits their coloring, or are they so colored because this is the way they sit? One could imagine light and warmth from above affecting the epidermal cells in such a way that they would deposit more or darker pigment. Yet these problems are never so simple as they seem.

In nymphal dragonflies, and in some grasshoppers that may be peppered with all colors of the soil, experiments have determined that a color-forming stimulus—that is, an imprinting of the environmental coloration—is mediated by the eyes. In other words, the optic nerves release factors that initiate the expression of a color pattern adapted to the background. This finds fulfillment at the ensuing molt. But only a few of these grasshoppers "voluntarily" accommodate their color to that of the surroundings. Most of them appear to seek out a background suited to their individual coloration, or, in localities with a uniformly-colored soil, all individuals have an appropriate ground-color from birth.

Many young insects, especially young bugs and beetles, disguise themselves in a peculiar fashion by bestrewing themselves with sand, soil, or even with their own excrement. They may be studded with hooks or bristles that help to hold these materials. [16–17; 51; 255/8]

A much-varied means of optical deception practiced by butterflies and other insects is the apparent dissolution of the form of the body (somatolysis) by means of strikingly sharp, visually disruptive designs. These may arrest the hunter's attention and thereby leave the true contours of the insect unrecognized. As is usual with all protective dress in insects, such effects are closely associated with the resting positions, where there can be a cooperative image that extends over both the body and the wings. [51]

Other performances aimed at invisibility go still further. False twigs, thorns, bits of wood, lichens, leaves, seed pods, and bird droppings are formed. We are peering into the curious, buffoonish world of mimesis. The ordinary shape and venation of many insect wings give them a leaflike appearance. But this is not enough. Extravagant refinements far beyond any necessity are added. The venation of the simulated leaf, for example, frequently runs directly counter to the insect's own vein-pattern. In addition, the "leaf" may appear to have translucent holes and, as already mentioned, spots of mold, as well as irregular edges that look as though insects had gnawed on them. Even the leafstalk is sometimes included, either appearing to be hanging unattached in the air or to be connected to a twig.

Many insects not only have the form and color of twigs, bark, and lichens, but they carry the deception further. They frequently rest in a posture, characteristic of each species, that seems quite impossible. The forepart, abdomen, or some other body region may extend stiffly from a support, or almost the whole body may stick out. Often the body contours are distorted by undulating or stiffly erect tufts of hair.

A person may be acquainted with hundreds and thousands of species of moths, having seen them predominantly with symmetrically extended wings, as is usual in technical illustra-

44/1
The larva of the assassin bug makes its own disguise out of little bits of dirt or dust. (→ 53/1)

tions or in museum collections. But if he spends a few nights in the virgin tropical forest and observes the moths at rest, he begins to perceive how little he knows, after all. What was long familiar is not to be discerned, for a variety of figures are generated by the specifically different positions taken by fundamentally similar moths. These together with the moths' picturesque designs, which are given complete expression only through the posture peculiar to each species, make an impression far different from the stereotyped arrangement of a museum drawer. [16–17; 50/7; 52–56; 255/6]

Many insects, such as certain butterflies, dragonflies, bees, and wasps, assemble in sleeping companies. Pressed tightly together, they often cling to twigs or straws by means of their legs or mandibles. At times they give the impression of a spray or bed of flowers. This is exemplified beautifully by little moth-like homopterous insects of the family Flatidae, whole groups of which join in sucking the juices of plant stems.

The nymphs of certain praying mantids resemble the flowers on which they sit. The resemblance results not only from their shapes and colors, but above all from their postures. Indeed, many mature mantids closely resemble either green leaves or dry leaves, an imitation whose effectiveness is enhanced by the peculiar to-and-fro movement of the insect, as though it were a leaf swaying in the wind. Particularly unusual are those few species whose prothorax bears varicolored ventral developments that simulate a flower; when these are exposed, they attract other insects, which fly straight into a waiting pair of prehensile claws. Bright colors on the thorax and forecoxae are normally kept hidden by many mantids, only to be displayed abruptly—flashing into view and seeming to strike an enemy with terror—when the mantid attacks. These phenomena lead us to consider the complex of bright and varied colors that have irritant, startling, or warning effects. [56/1; 324]

FLASH COLORS

Concealing (cryptic) garb combined with brightly colored adornment that is hidden when the insect is at rest appears most often among the butterflies, grasshoppers, walking-stick insects, true bugs, and members of the Homoptera. The signals that shine forth so unexpectedly when the animals are disturbed are known as flash colors. Occasionally they occur on the abdomen, but almost always they are on the hind wings. They are found,

as a rule, on insects that lack weapons of defense. In species that take flight hastily they usually have the form of a red, yellow, blue, or more rarely a white patch whose contrasting effect is heightened by black stripes or spots.

These contrasting colors may well cause enemies to become excited, at least initially. The pursued thus gains time for a mad, short flight, then dives into a new resting place and makes the conspicuous colors vanish suddenly by covering the bright spots on the wings or body with the nondescript fore wings. This is observed most frequently in grasshoppers, whose contrasting coloration appears on the hind wing and on the inner surface of the hind femur. But probably this coloration in grasshoppers functions primarily as an optical means for mutual attraction of the sexes. [17; 56/3; 57/1–3; 106/1–8]

EYESPOTS

Slower-moving or poorer-flying insects, or those that cannot take to the air fast enough when they are at rest because they first must raise their body temperature by means of respiratory or other vibrations, frequently display strikingly peculiar designs instead of simple contrasting colors. With the aid of twitching movements they create strangely nightmarish sights that are to us suggestive of evil. For example, hanging from a tree branch is an unimpressive-looking "leaf" that perhaps does not quite fool a smart bird. The bird gives it a tentative peck, and the "leaf" at once drops to the ground. There, it dances a while in a regular, clumsy rhythm, looking like a mask dominated by two now visible goggle-eyes, each of which is supplied with a pane of "glass" that flashes in the incident light. But soon it stops in a stiffly erect position. The bird hesitates, withdraws a little, moving about indecisively nearby, and then returns—to nothing. During its dance the moth was making itself ready to fly; and now a "leaf" again is hanging, but in a quite different place, where none was before.

The greatest abundance of such "startling eyes" is presented by the family of the giant silkworm moths *(Saturniidae)*. Many of them do not drop at once when disturbed, but are content to spread their wings suddenly and perhaps let them play in a slow rhythm of rising and falling. The central element of the saturniid pattern is an eyespot on each of the four wings. Usually it is effaced or at least reduced on the undersides.

In many species the spots on the upper surfaces of the fore wings have disappeared,

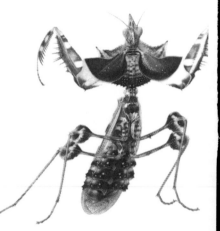

44/2
While certain insect species merely come together in groups for sleeping, many others live in assemblages all the time and may look like a cluster of flowers on a plant, such as these plant-hoppers. (→ 56/2).

44/3
An African praying mantis, the notorious "devil's flower"; its outstretched forelegs make it look like a flower, and it is alleged to attract insects by this means. (→ 101/4)

44/4
Warning colors on the hind wings of an owlet moth. (→ 17/30)

45/1

Eyelike designs on insect body or wings, used as a means of frightening off enemies, occur in infinite variety; their modifications range from the simple doubled spot to artistic masterpieces. (→ 58/1)

45/2–3

On a praying mantis (above) (→ 60/1) they appear as a spiral, and on the huge Australian carpenterworm moth (below) the "eye" is actually raised in relief, as though it had been hammered out of the wing surface. (→ 249)

and those on the hind wings are more prominent. A minority of these species has eyespots on the undersides of the fore wings, too, so that eyespots can be seen simultaneously from above or below. These species settle less frequently than others on flat surfaces that would block the underside spots from view. When there are four equally developed "eyes" on the upper wing surfaces, these are visible when the moth is at rest. The insect's active participation in the surprise effect has been eliminated.

An unusual eyespot design is displayed in the South American forests by huge butterflies of the genus *Caligo* that fly briefly at dusk. Like other, related butterflies, they sit at rest in the shrubbery near the ground, with their wings clapped together over the back, excellently disguised by their wavy brown-and-light-gray coloring. But, strange to say, the disguise is broken by a huge eye on the hind wing facing the view. Where otherwise there would be practically nothing to be seen, this single eye goggles out of the darkness of the underbrush, lighting up rather devilishly whenever an errant sunbeam strikes it. Drawings of such butterflies frequently show them with extended wings, in which position they give a genuinely owl-like two-eyed effect. But in life the insects always rest with closed wings and always fly with rapid wing movements, so that the two eyespots are never visible simultaneously.

A magnificent single-eyed design is also found in certain praying mantids. It attains a special intensity of coloration through the superposition of the mantid's semitransparent wing covers, each of which bears the same design. But when the mantid assumes its defensive posture, with wings spread, suddenly two "eyes" instead of one appear. In many insects, especially beetles, the effect of eyes is produced by two spots set side by side somewhere on the body and more or less contrasting with it, or often even raised in relief. [18; 57/5; 58–60; 63; 244–245; 255/3]

MOVEMENT AND DESIGN

How great is the alarming power of eyespots and other spectacular designs? Only experiments can provide the answer, and many of these will be difficult to carry out convincingly. Yet it is surely obvious that effectiveness is intended wherever the insect, by means of body movements, participates actively in the display of these designs. This happens in the majority of cases. For instance, a sphinx moth caterpillar pulls in its head,

puffs out its thorax like a balloon, and exposes on the swollen surface the eyespots that lie on the two sides. Or it lifts the front part of its body and writhes around its own axis as a means of displaying the startling designs on the lower surface of its thorax.

To be sure, the general basis of such movements lies in reactions typical of certain families of these caterpillars. Even those species that lack special alarm designs raise the forepart and pull in the head. And yet a last item of behavior is missing, such as the inflation of the body or the twisting motion, which makes sense only in combination with the appropriate patterns.

The behavior of adult sphinx moths also illustrates an evolving series of defensive movements coordinated with coloration. Before beginning preparations for flying, almost all of these moths react to disturbances with rhythmically repeated elevations of the body. The middle of the abdomen arches upward and displays, from the midst of its muted gray or brown protective garb, the strikingly contrasting color pattern of the back.

Other species, especially those that have bright display colors on the hind wings, simultaneously raise the wings as they raise the body. When the eyed sphinx moths (*Smerinthus*) follow this pattern, their blue-ringed eyespots, twitching in the rhythm of the body movements, are set off against the brightly shining red background of the exposed part of the hind wing.

Another peak performance is given by the death's-head moth (*Acherontia*), which takes its name from markings resembling a human skull on the forepart of its back. This satiny-dark, massive shadow of the night rears up in a startling, demoniac dance. The effect is produced not only by the death mask, but also by the uncanny impression given by the straddling, suggestively shaped forelegs, and a continual musical accompaniment, which sounds something like creaking leather. Over the middle of the abdomen, which is raised again and again, runs a blue band; and the ochre-yellow sides, like the hind wings which now come into view, are waspishly striped in black. A truly fantastic, unique phenomenon of the insect world! [61; 248/5]

However, the movements and dances that insects use to defend themselves, that harmonize so astoundingly with shape and design, cannot be evoked at will. Rather, they quickly grow weaker with repeated annoyance, and instead the insect reacts by running away. Only after a rather long rest period can the dances be reactivated in their full intensity, like a storage battery that has been recharged.

Of particular interest too are those effects, seen in numerous different insects at rest, that seemingly are intended to divert the enemy from the victim's front end. In these insects the posterior portion is much more noticeable because of its form and color and may even be strikingly emphasized as a false head by means of antenna-like appendages. After an attack, a bird, misled by such devices, might find in its beak no more than a small shred of the wings, or some other insignificant part of the body. [57/3; 187/9]

WARNING COLORS

Many brightly colored insects, particularly larvae, show themselves openly and are conspicuous from afar. These insects do advertise their presence with warning colors, for they enjoy the protection of distasteful, even toxic, body fluids. There are many examples. Caterpillars that feed on poisonous herbs may carry the toxic effect through their development even to the mature form. The blister beetles *(Meloidae)* contain cantharidin, a toxin dangerous to man and beast. Many caterpillars are clothed with urticating (stinging) hairs or with thorns, some of which are filled with acid. Certain larval moths *(Dirphia)* imitate this kind of caterpillar not only in the coloration and specific hair pattern of the abdomen, but also in the contortions the body goes through.

Let us not leave unmentioned the protective sting of female wasps and the piercing beak of the assassin bugs and other predatory bugs. Nor should we neglect the chemical armament of various brightly colored insects. Toxic blood or acids are squirted out through the skin, from leg joints, wing covers, and body openings, or sprayed forth or spit out, or even exuded in a sweatlike foam. Odorous glandular reservoirs are everted, in the form of threads, horns, or swellings, from excrescences on the sides, thorax, or neck; and from hidden glands unpleasant smells and stenches come into play. Notable practitioners of chemical warfare are the bombardier beetles, which expel from the anus a cloud of gas that explodes with a modest pop.

Thanks to unpleasant experiences many an enemy learns sooner or later to let such brightly colored creatures alone. On this fact rests the effectiveness of all warning colors—and of mimicry, too. And it is for this reason that mimicry supposedly does not occur in nocturnal insects, for at night no colors can be seen. However, it is strange that most of the moths of the family Arctiidae, which are endowed with distasteful body fluids and particularly bright warning colors, are active mainly at night. By day they conceal themselves so well that only rarely are many specimens discovered. Nevertheless, many other harmless larval moths, of the most disparate families, are clad in part as though they had copied the arctiids precisely. [62/1–4; 152/1; 248/5]

Obviously, the many-sided richness of insect life cannot be forced into a single mold and leaves no rule unbroken. Even insects without particular coloration defend themselves well enough, whether it is through speed or stealthy nocturnal activity, whether it is by dropping suddenly into the grass or assuming a condition of "feigned death." Some insects stretch the abdomen forward over the back as though they were scorpions. Others bite and pinch with tonged mandibles or other mechanisms, or scratch an enemy's hide with thorns on their legs; in fact, these rigid prongs, sticking out in all directions, make it almost impossible for such insects to be eaten.

But by far the majority of insects are harmless and absolutely defenseless. And even the small minority that uses mimicry, defiant color, and other weapons is vulnerable to certain enemies. Protective shape and coloration are wasted on parasitic wasps and other parasites that locate their victim with their sense of smell, and on bats, which hunt by echolocation. Nor does camouflage prevent bacterial and other diseases from taking their toll.

Among the larger enemies of insects is man himself. When insects threaten harm to him, man battles them with ever new poisons, of which one after the other loses its efficacy. For a few of the poisoned insects always survive, thanks to peculiarities of their constitutions, and these insects father new races that inherit the peculiarities and are able to withstand the poisonous chemicals, too. So man begins to fight with biological means; he cultures the enemies of the insects and lets parasites and disease loose on them. And because of the troubles that a few insect species bring him, he all too easily forgets the absolute dependence of all higher organisms on the existence of insects and, equally important, the role of insects as a significant and inexhaustible source of scientific and aesthetic knowledge.

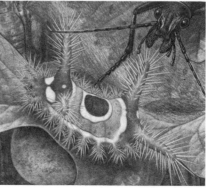

46/1
Many grasshoppers are studded with spines and are thus well protected. (→ 54/5)

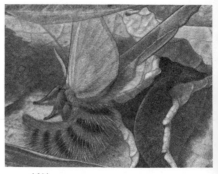

46/2–3   2
*Certain caterpillars, like this American saddleback (2), are dotted with poisonous spines or stinging hairs. (→ 14/12)
This is an advantage also to those few moths that actually are harmless but that, with their abdomen, are able to simulate such a nettlelike larva (3).
(→ 17/31)*   3

46/4
A bombardier beetle shooting off an explosive mixture of gases. (→ 62/1)

Insects around the World

Despite the threats to their existence, insects thrive. They have taken possession of almost the whole world, having left vacant only the most extreme localities. They are found amid snow and ice, on the skin of penguins, in burning deserts, in the raging winds and rushing streams of the mountains, in the dark silence of caves, and inside plants and animals.

Distribution

The earth can be divided into regions according to the type of animal and plant life. In zoogeography we distinguish the following: *Holarctic* (arctic and north temperate zones), including the Nearctic and the Palearctic; *Ethiopian* (African and Madagascan); *Oriental* (Indian); *Australian; Neotropical* (South American); and *Antarctic.* Over these geographical areas are spread the ecological regions: forest (arboreal), plains and deserts (eremian), tundra (tundral), and snow and ice (nival).

These ecological regions make the greater impressions on the insects that live in them. Thus desert species throughout the world have definite characteristics in common, as also do forest species. But the geographic regions, too, in some degree display their own peculiar forms. From the study of the relationships between these forms, significant conclusions may be drawn about the history of the earth and its organisms, particularly with reference to connections and relationships that existed eons ago between parts of the world that are separated by oceans today.

In the Holarctic there is much in common between the Nearctic (North America) and Palearctic (Europe and Northern Asia) regions; certain species actually have a circumpolar distribution. There also is a similarity between the organisms of the African and Oriental regions, in particular between the Madagascan and Indian. And the distantly separated Neotropical and Australian faunas have many common insect associations, whereas Africa and South America show less similarity. Of course, the boundaries between neighboring regions—as, for example, Africa–India or India–China (Palearctic)—are not everywhere sharply drawn; marked interchanges occur, and many a tropical element presses far northward into the temperate zone. The faunas of North and South America are interspersed quite fully: many forms occur both in the northern part and much farther south, below the tropical belt.

The Oriental and Australian regions are extraordinarily interfingered, partly because the latter includes New Guinea, the Moluccas, Celebes, and other similar islands, whereas the Philippines, Java, and Borneo, more closely related to the Asiatic mainland, have a great affinity with the Orient. Here is a world of island forms, of the cleavage of races, and of complex paleontological problems. Opposed to it there stands Africa, a closed continent, a land where individual species have enormously wide distributions.

Most insect families occur in all the regions of the world, but when we subdivide families into genera we find that many genera are peculiar to and characteristic of the area they inhabit. For example, in the Holarctic the bumblebees (genus *Bombus*) have a circumpolar distribution, but only vestiges of this extend into the tropics. Especially characteristic of the Palearctic region are the ground beetles *(Carabus)* and the alpine apollo butterflies *(Parnassius),* a few of which still exist in North America. Likewise limited to the northern hemisphere are the moths of the genus *Catocala* (underwings); these large moths with their brilliantly colored hind wings constitute the noble peak of their family (Noctuidae).

Africa may justly be called the land of ants and termites, but its most striking and unique insects probably are the flower beetles (Cetoniinae), particularly the goliath beetles *(Goliathus),* which may reach a length of 4 inches or more. The Madagascan region, too, has its peculiarities, with relationships simultaneously to India and Africa. And yet fewer of its insects are out-of-the-way than one might expect from the extremely odd flora and fauna.

The Oriental-Australian regions scintillate with the largest of all butterflies, the bird-wing butterflies *(Ornithoptera),* which are related to the swallowtails *(Papilio).* Here,

47/1
A short-horned grasshopper, not yet too severely threatened, going into hiding as a precautionary measure before jumping away; if danger does not come nearer, but merely changes place slowly, the insect will continue to creep behind the stalk at exactly the same rate.

For identification of the insects
on page 51

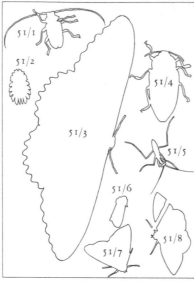

CAPTIONS
FOR PAGES 49 TO 63

49/1–12
Geographic forms of a ground beetle.
Distinctive differences are less a matter
of colors than of sculptural refinements.
Photograph.

49/13–29
Many diurnal insects of the plains and
deserts, such as bees, digger wasps,
wasps, and certain flies, are light in
color, in adaptation to the extreme
conditions of illumination; often only
their shadow is to be seen as they flit
rapidly along near the ground. This
increase in lightness is achieved
by breaking down the black pigments
or by making them reddish, or else
by thickening and extending the light
components of the body hair. Frequently
the eyes of these insects are an intense
green, light blue, or light red (slightly
enlarged). Photograph.

49/30–33
Four quite different but similarly
colored redheaded cuckoo wasps that
occur like this only in the Philippines;
a striking example of so-called "regional
convergence" (enlarged 3×).
Photograph.

PAGE 50
50/1
Mimicry of wasps. Many syntomid
moths not only look like wasps, but also
move like them (enlarged 4×).

50/2
Mimicry of bees. Many clearwing
moths, aided by the extraordinary coat
of hairs on their legs, simulate bees
(enlarged 4×).

50/3
Mimicry of spiders. An owlet moth
that simulates a spider (enlarged 2×).

50/4–6
Mimicry of butterflies. In front the
monarch, protected by its toxic body
fluids, and especially famous
as a migratory butterfly, followed by its
"mimic" (5), a representative of the
nonpoisonous group of admiral butterflies, the normal garb of which is shown
by the third species below (6).

50/7
Mimesis. A member of the family
of carpenterworm moths displays
a costume that dissolves the body
contours.

PAGE 51
51/1–8
Cryptic coloration in a forest in Rio
de Janeiro. On the left, a stink bug
and a beetle; in the center, an owlet
moth that has the longest wingspan

of all Lepidoptera (natural size).
Below, and to the right, are a beetle,
a small praying mantis, and three moths.
See above for their identification.

PAGES 52 AND 53
Passive and active concealment.
The clucking moth from the tent
caterpillar family (52/5, enlarged)
drops when disturbed and lies motionless
on its side, and the assassin bug larva
(53/1, enlarged) makes its own disguise
with bits of dirt or dust. The lower
wing surface of the leaf butterfly
Kallima (52/4, enlarged) varies to an
exceptional degree in coloration and
in the extent to which the "fungal
spots" are developed, whereas the many-
colored upper surface varies but little.

PAGES 54 AND 55
Insects that imitate leaves (leaf
mimesis). Particularly renowned is the
wandering leaf (54/4) from the
walkingstick family; the grasshoppers
shown below (54/5, 54/6); and a praying
mantis (55/1). Holes gnawed into the
leaf are simulated on the wing membrane
by a lack of scales or an absence
of pigmentation, and dew drops by scales
that glitter like silver; many moths fold
their wings to resemble leaves. The ribs
of leaves may at times be represented
by the wing venation, but also by a pattern
of lines that run diametrically opposite
(as is the case in the leaf butterfly,
54/1). (Natural size.)

PAGES 56 AND 57
56/1
Flower mimesis. A praying mantis,
concealed like a hunter in a blind,
waiting for insects to fly in
(enlarged 3×).

56/2
A group of flatid planthoppers living
together and simulating a cluster of
flowers. Various other insects come
together similarly only for sleeping
purposes.

51/1 Long-horned beetle, Dry-
octenes scrupulosus (Cerambycidae)
51/2 Stink bug, Phloea
longirostris (Pentatomidae)
51/3 Owlet moth, Thysania
agrippina (Noctuidae)
51/4 Metallic wood-boring
beetle, Euchroma gigantea
(Buprestidae)
51/5 Mantid (Mantidae)
51/6 Prominent moth, Notoplusia
(Notodontidae)
51/7–8 Noctuid moths (Noctuidae)
(7) Parallelia expediens
(8) Blosyris Pandrosa

56/3, 57/1–3
Raising the fore wings lets the warning
colors—placed on hind wings or abdomen,
or on both—appear with the utmost
abruptness. Red, yellow, or blue hind
wings occur in many band-winged
grasshoppers (57/1), and in owlet
moths of the underwing genus Catocala
(56/3), while a red back is displayed
by many true bugs and moths, in certain
species of which the rear end takes
on the appearance of a head (57/3).

56/4–12
Resting Brazilian microlepidoptera
and moths of larger size, part of them
imitating beetles, part spiders. At the
top, in the middle, is an adult of the
bagworm moth family that on being
disturbed jerks its rear end upward
into an arch, like a scorpion. At the
upper right is a flatid planthopper,
below it a micromoth, and at the bottom
the forepart of a leaf-footed bug.
(enlarged 3×).

57/4–5
The gigantic South American Caligo
butterflies have "goggle-eyes" on the
lower surface of the hind wings. In the
species on the left, the "eyes" can be
seen faintly through the wings.
Photograph.

PAGES 58 AND 59
58/1–5
In the American genus Automeris of
giant silkworm moths, warning eyelike
designs within the cryptic costume are
presented in an especially resourceful
series of modifications.

59/1
One episode in the defensive dance of an
African giant silkworm moth, which goes
hopping around with its wingtips
striking the ground again and again,
until at last it stops sharply erect with
wings outspread (somewhat reduced).

PAGE 60
60/1
An African praying mantis and a
cuckoo (natural size). The eyespot

design of these insects is constructed from
a spiral.

PAGE 61
61/1
Death's-head sphinx moth keeping
a dormouse at bay.

61/2–6
Dorsal designs of various related species
(natural size).

PAGE 62
62/1
A bombardier beetle in action
(enlarged 5×).

62/2–4
A butterfly and moths with warning
colors. At the top one of the
Heliconiidae, which are famous for
their mimicry groups (enlarged 1.5×).

62/5–6
An inconspicuous adult tentacle
prominent moth, and its very conspicuous
caterpillar (enlarged 1.5×).

62/7
The noctuid moth's sense of hearing
(tympanal organ) is located on both
sides of the back part of the thorax,
and enables moths to perceive the ultra-
sound vibrations emitted by bats on the
hunt (much enlarged).

PAGE 63
63/1
A giant silkworm moth and a bat
(somewhat enlarged).

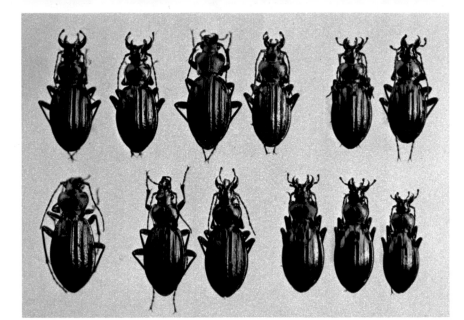

49/1-6

49/7-12

49/13 49/14 49/15 49/19 49/20 49/21

49/16 49/17 49/18 49/22 49/23 49/24

49/25 49/26 49/27 49/28 49/29

49/30-33

49

50/2

50/6

50/3

50/7

50

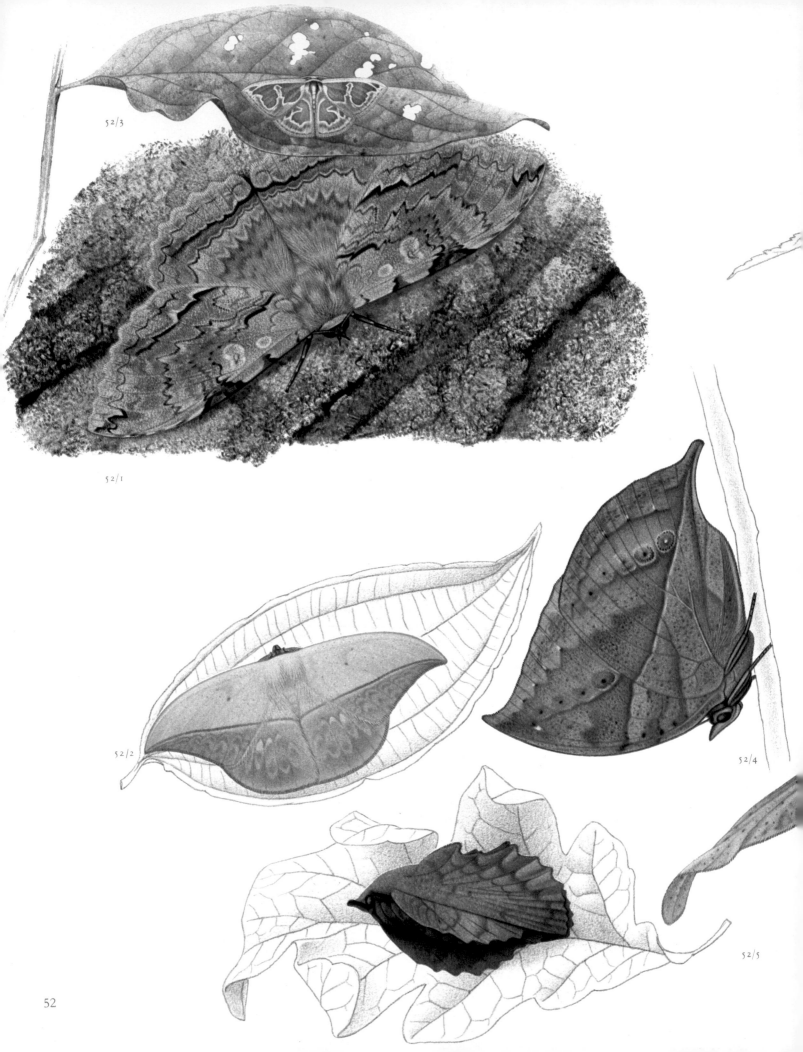

52/3

52/1

52/2

52/4

52/5

52

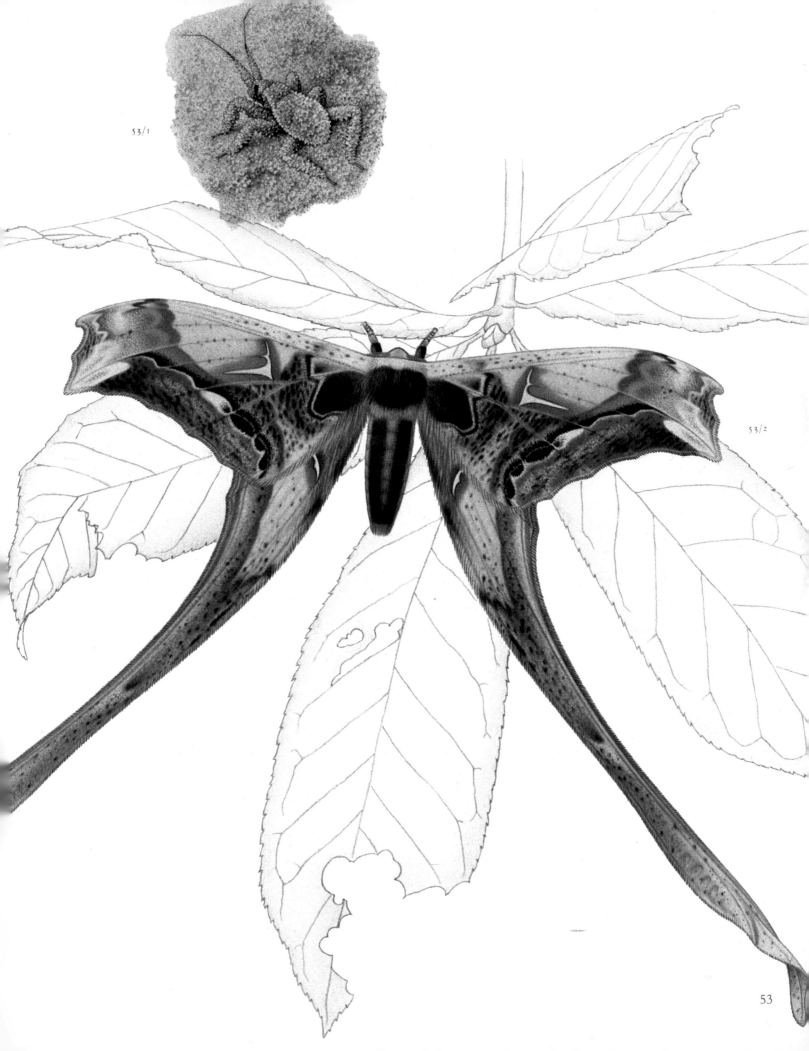

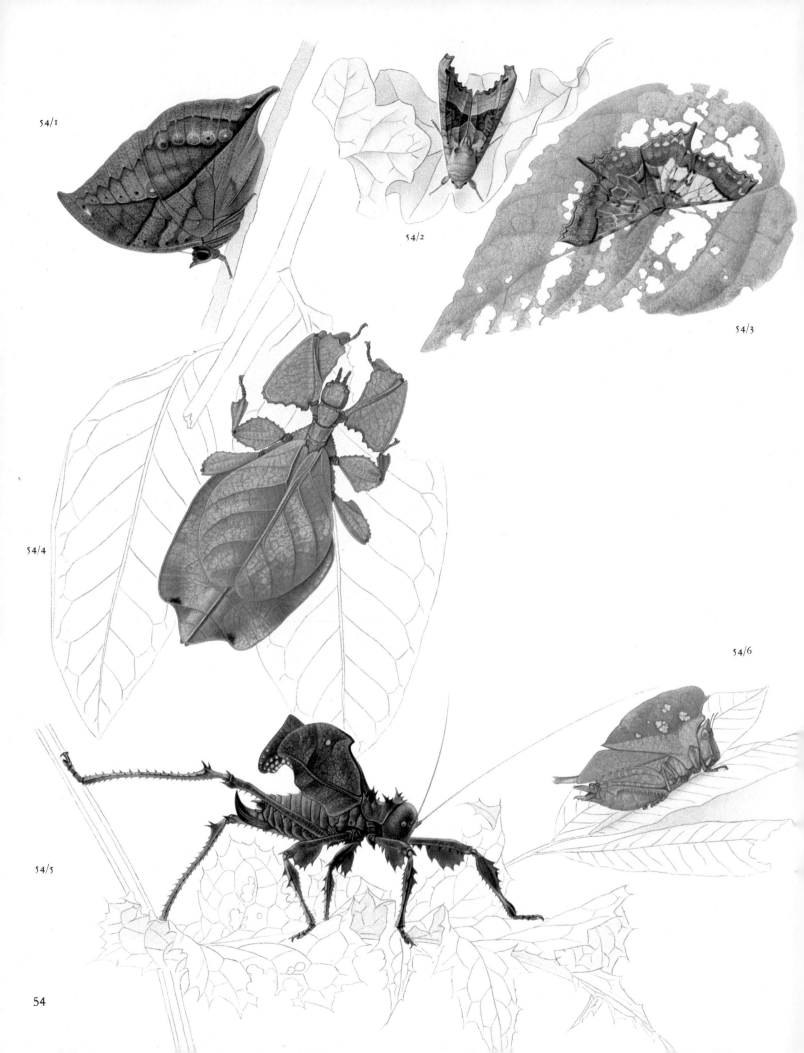

54/1

54/2

54/3

54/4

54/6

54/5

54

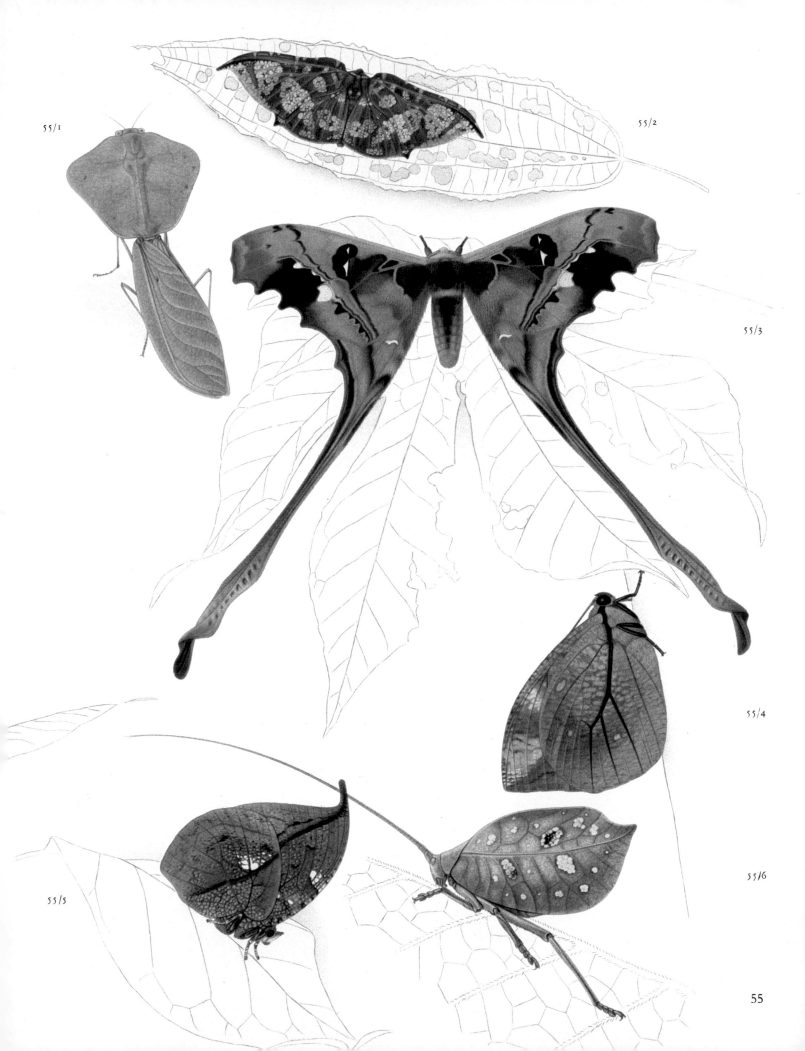

55/1

55/2

55/3

55/4

55/5

55/6

55

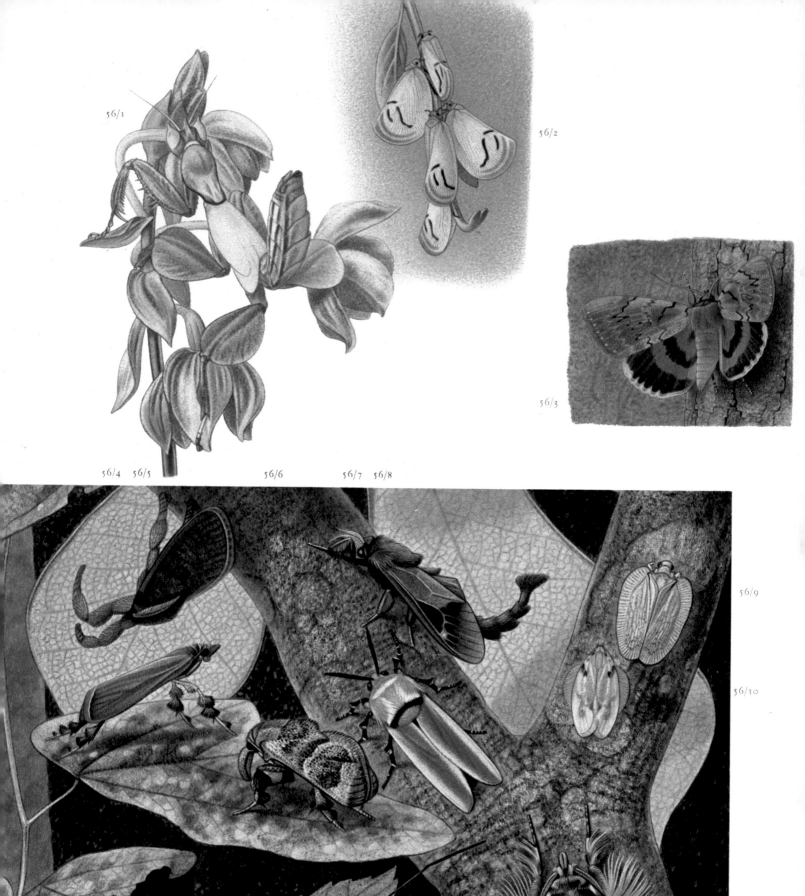

56/1

56/2

56/3

56/4 56/5

56/6

56/7 56/8

56/9

56/10

56/11

56/12

57/1

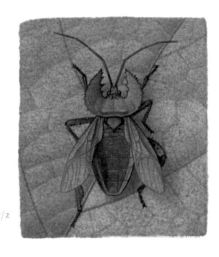

57/2

57/3

57/4

57/5

58/1

58/2

58/3

58/4

58/5

58

59/1

61/1

61/2-7

61

62/1

62/7

62/2

62/4

62/3

62/5

62/6

62

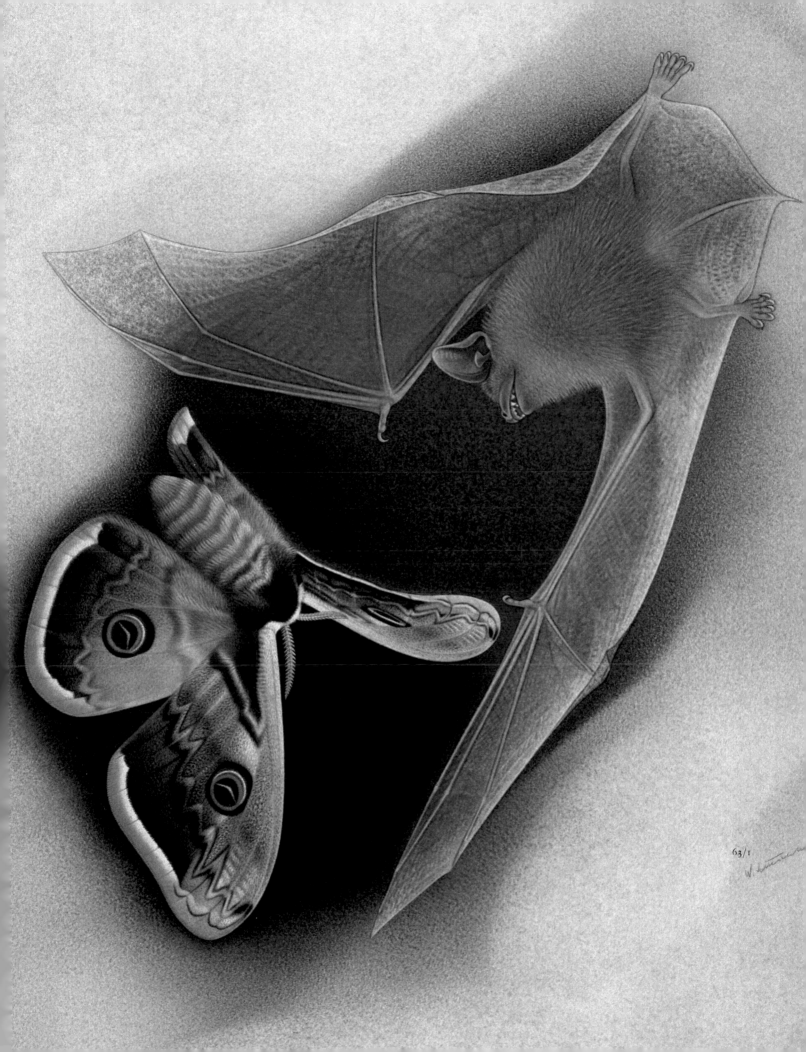

64/1
*The giant silkworm moth Graellsia
isabella, which inhabits only
a few localities in Spain and
southern France, is perhaps the
most striking relic species of the
Ice Age (male at left, female at
right). Photograph.*

64/2
*White butterflies (pierids) on
migration.*

64/3
*The thistle butterfly (or painted
lady), Vanessa (Pyrameis)
cardui, its races and its
migrations. In spite of the
enormous area of distribution
(yellow on the map), it has
evolved only two geographic races
as a consequence of its widespread
migrations: namely cardui
japonica in East Asia and
Japan (dark yellow), with a very
similar form in Java, and cardui
kershawi in Australia and
New Zealand (orange).
The migrations of the type form
of the species, cardui cardui,
are toward the north in spring
or summer, but southward
in autumn, may flood over
a country for weeks on end,
and may extend for more than
1,250 miles. But thistle butterflies
also migrate as individuals or in
small groups, and have repeatedly
been seen flying over the Atlantic
(red dots).*

too, live the largest moths in the world, the Atlas silk moths (*Attacus*), from the family of the saturniids. Other inhabitants include the biggest of all walkingstick insects (phasmids), as well as gigantic snout beetles (*Protocerius* and *Cryptotrachelus*) and the rare phantom ground beetle (*Mormolyce*).

The peak of creative production, however, probably is reached in South and Central America, in the Neotropical region. This is the area of the harshest coloration, as evidenced by the harlequin garb of butterflies, caterpillars, and beetles, and of the most striking mimicry, as shown by the unique butterfly genus *Heliconius* and its hundreds of imitators. It is also the home of all imaginable sorts of butterflies with glassy-transparent wings, and the abode of the *Morpho* butterflies, those blue spirits of the virgin forest and the most gorgeous phenomena of the insect world.

Here live the mighty hercules beetles and elephant beetles (Dynastinae), as well as the largest beetle in the world, the huge, long-horned *Titanus giganteus*, which reaches 8 to 9 inches in length. Other residents include the snout beetle *Entimus*, glittering incomparably, as though bejeweled; the firefly *Pyrophorus*; the powerful wasps of the genus *Pepsis*, which hunt the large, hairy bird spiders; and the dreaded leafcutting ant *Atta*. But these few extravagant examples should not let us forget that most living insects are inconspicuous in size, color, and form. [42/1]

Zoogeographical studies are among the most fascinating that nature has to offer. Here we can touch only briefly upon their possible import. For instance, we find northern species living at high altitudes quite far south, although they are altogether absent at lower altitudes in intervening areas. An islandlike distribution of this kind has come about because cold-climate insects, able to range widely during the Ice Age, could survive only where climate remained cold after the glaciers retreated. Species once widely distributed but now limited to narrowly bounded regions are known as relics. A particularly impressive example within the Palearctic fauna is the moth *Graellsia isabella*, which persists as a relic of the Ice Age only in a few places in Spain and southern France. [64/1]

MIGRATION

The innate urge of many insects to migrate plays an important part in the history of insect distribution. Truly penetrating studies of this tendency have been begun only recently. Migration occurs among the most different insects; the migratory movement of individuals is probably the general rule and is significant for the spread of species.

Rather rare, in contrast, are the migrations of whole swarms of insects over what often are enormous distances. Thanks to tests in which individual butterflies in such companies were labeled, we know a little about the duration, distance covered, and route followed in such pilgrimages. But what it is that impels millions of insects of certain species to depart simultaneously on a long journey is still poorly understood. Sometimes, but not always, it is because an excessive increase in insect numbers has brought on a food shortage. This happens in the case of the armyworm moth (*Pseudaletia unipuncta*) of North America, whose hordes of larvae roll onward, devouring all vegetation in their way.

Of a different nature are the wanderings of the larvae of the mourning gnat, *Neosciara*, formerly feared as harbingers of war or famine. These larvae stick themselves together with a slimy excretion in snakelike columns as much as 13 feet long and glide over the forest floor in search of a site for pupation. It is evident that many insect larvae are seized with a great unrest shortly before they pupate and may wander hurriedly about at random for hours or days until, for no good reason, they find the peace essential to their preparation for transformation. But what drives those gnat maggots to associate in countless numbers and to stick themselves together in the form of a "snake"? This is a complete riddle.

Another riddle is: what determines the direction of a migration? Is it polarized light, as in the orientation of a bee, for instance? Is it the stars by night? Is it magnetic or electrical influences? Scientists have determined that migrating locusts are borne in a given direction by the prevailing wind. Also, certain moths that fly northward over the Alps, despite unfavorable weather, apparently are carried aloft by thermal air currents. Many other insects may be similarly transported. Yet one sees butterflies holding a course undismayed, even directly against the wind. What is more, they do not change course when they encounter obstacles like trees, cliffs, and buildings, but instead fly right over them.

Groups of migrating insects usually move in loose formations, some of which may be 100 yards to a few miles in width. For hours or days one may see an individual flying past every few seconds or minutes. Frequently

these insects proceed in single file, though they cannot see one another; it is as if they were following a string stretched invisibly through the air. In a day they may travel 15 to 25 miles; under favorable conditions, perhaps more. Sphinx moths (Sphingidae) fly 30 miles per hour or faster, yet their daily or nightly period on the wing is shorter than that of the slower day fliers.

The temperature has a great effect on flight: it must be neither too low nor too high. A temperature of about 30° C (54° F) is necessary to release the urge for flight or migration. Before flying, an insect normally raises its internal temperature by muscular vibration to about 40° C (72° F). But if the internal temperature rises too far, because of too much heat from the sun or because of high air temperature combined with excessive humidity, flight ceases; a butterfly goes into rigor and dies if the body temperature reaches as much as 45° C (81° F).

What triggers the migratory urge? In addition to a numerical increase and a lack of food, a sort of "mass suggestion" is suspected; thus insects quite unrelated to a migrating group join the procession, as when dragonflies participate in a butterfly migration. Unfavorable environmental conditions and meteorological factors also have been pointed to. It seems certain that the urge to migrate is a tendency fixed by inheritance. Always it is the same relatively few species that migrate in groups over long distances.

An outstanding long-distance migrator is *Danaus plexippus,* the monarch butterfly of North America. The monarchs are strong fliers and excel in gliding ability. In autumn they travel southward from Canada and northern United States to Florida, Mexico, and California, their chief wintering places. Here they congregate in great crowds on certain kinds of trees, notably pines. In the spring, they begin their flight north, laying their eggs along the way and then dying. New generations replace the old, and with the coming of fall the butterflies again undertake a journey of perhaps 2,000 or more miles. [50/4; 64/2, 3]

Sometimes, migration results in the destruction of the migrators. For example, certain sphinx moths fly from Africa to northern Europe, singly in some years and in groups in others, frequently passing high above the Alps. In the far Northland, these moths either die sterile in the autumn or else lay eggs that develop into pupae that generally are unable to withstand the cold winter.

For obvious reasons we are best informed about the migrations of the dreaded migratory locusts. Again and again they wreak devastating damage on all continents and, by eating every green thing within sight, they may endanger or even eradicate countless other species of insects. Over and over, from certain areas in their homeland, swarms of 100,000 to 10 billion locusts pour out, hissing, rustling, crackling, and darkening the skies. They inundate hundreds and thousands of acres, leaving no green thing standing where they rattle to earth.

Each swarm is a single company (population) whose members have grown up together, but is divided into groups that often crisscross during flight. Observations from airplanes have shown that the locusts do not strive toward a fixed goal, but let themselves be wafted at random by the wind. They make use of head and tail winds in taking off and landing. Usually, however, locusts begin a migration even before they became adults. As unwinged nymphs, they start to march, and the mass pattering of their feet is clearly audible.

In many countries the problem with migratory locusts is one of a single species, but more often several are involved. An odd fact is that each such species occurs in the form of two different races—the so-called phases— which are distinct both biologically and morphologically. Specifically, there is a sedentary or solitary phase, choosy about its food and colored inconspicuously green, gray, or reddish; and a migratory phase, which devours any and all plants, is marked with more contrasting colors, and usually has longer wings.

Either phase can be formed from the other, without the necessity of intervening generations. But only the earlier stages of one phase can be transformed into the other, as has been shown experimentally when individuals of a group in one phase are transferred to a group in the other phase. Under such conditions, insects of the solitary phase may yield the migratory phase, or vice versa. One may therefore imagine that the transformation of the shifted individual is caused by some psychological suggestion emanating from its new companions; yet the finer reasons for this astounding phenomenon of the phases, and hence for the origin of the migratory swarms, are not yet fully explained. Problems of this kind are rendered especially complex by the great differences between the life cycles of the various locust species, whose enormous reproductive potential again and again conjures up new calamities.

66/1
Map to show the distribution and migrations of the monarch butterfly, Danaus plexippus.

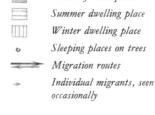

	Areas of development
	Summer dwelling place
	Winter dwelling place
	Sleeping places on trees
	Migration routes
	Individual migrants, seen occasionally

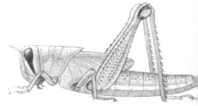

66/2
Young stages of a species of migratory locust. At the left, the solitary, sessile phase; on the right, the swarm-forming, migratory phase (somewhat enlarged). (→ 106/9)

CLASSIFICATION OF INSECTS

In classifying insects, entomologists divide them into groups of basically different structure. These groups form the main divisions of insects, the so-called orders. Since variation is the soul of life, these orders are to some extent "disorders," because they contain nonidentical groups. Hence we have to divide each order into families. Even within the families, one can distinguish different groups, which we call genera (singular, genus). In the genera are assembled the final natural entities, the species.

But even this "ultimate" category knows no peace. On the contrary, nature's urge toward the creation of new forms surges ahead within the species. Sizes, forms, designs, colors, and sculpturing vary. In order to achieve some clarity in our classifications, we are compelled to split the species into subspecies, or races. (Let us merely whisper that we also require other subclassifications and superclassifications, such as superclasses and subclasses, superorders and suborders, superfamilies and subfamilies, subgenera, cohorts, sections, divisions, tribes, and who knows what all else.) So at last we construct a systematics by which we can classify every insect.

SCIENTIFIC NAMES

Each species receives a Latin name of at least two parts—a name recognized throughout the world. The first part designates the genus to which the insect belongs, the second part is the species. This is the system of binary nomenclature, introduced in 1735 by the Swedish doctor and botanist Carolus Linnaeus. Since the double label is placed under the emblem of a definite family, which occupies a place in one of the 31 orders, we are able not only to assign each insect properly, but also to indicate where any newly discovered one belongs. And we can do this even though these names may run into the millions.

Countless species have been redescribed and named anew twice, thrice, or ten times, because one discoverer often does not know too much about his past and present colleagues! But there actually are far more than a million species of insects, a quantity that should register particularly on our consciousness if we compare it with the approximately 67,000 vertebrate species of the globe.

INSECT ORDERS: LIST OF 31 ORDERS

The class Insecta is divided into some 25 to 35 orders, depending upon the entomologist's point of view. Authorities differ on the number of orders because in a few cases one order may be subdivided into two or more, or two or more orders can be combined into one.

As is customary, the orders are listed in the sequence in which they are thought to have first appeared on the earth. There is, however, wide disagreement over this sequence. Moreover, the arrangement should not be taken to suggest that there was a single line of descent, with each order descending from the previous one. Most authorities, in fact, recognize at least three evolutionarily distinct lines.

The first four orders may be grouped as the subclass Apterygota, the primitive wingless insects. These small insects are wingless in all stages and are believed always to have been so. They are distributed throughout the world, but encompass few species. After hatching from the egg, they develop with no apparent changes in body form, or only slight changes. The insect molts an indefinite number of times during its development and even after it reaches sexual maturity.

The rest of the orders, which include the vast majority of insects, form the subclass Pterygota. Almost all the members of this group are flying insects. A few have degenerate wings or lack wings altogether. But these wingless species are descended from winged ancestors, a fact that distinguishes them from the wingless insects of the subclass Apterygota.

In the accompanying list, the orders of the subclass Pterygota are numbered from 5 through 31. Insects of orders 5 through 22 develop gradually through several nymphal stages, but only after the final molt do they become sexually mature and gain the ability to fly. Orders 23 through 31 undergo a different metamorphosis. After hatching from the egg, the insect goes through several larval stages and then forms a pupa, the resting stage from which the sexually mature, winged insect emerges at the final molt.

CLASS INSECTA

SUBCLASS APTERYGOTA
WINGLESS INSECTS

1. ORDER THYSANURA
BRISTLETAILS

2. ORDER DIPLURA
CAMPODEIDS AND JAPYGIDS

3. ORDER PROTURA   TELSONTAILS

4. ORDER COLLEMBOLA
SPRINGTAILS

SUBCLASS PTERYGOTA
WINGED INSECTS

5. ORDER EPHEMEROPTERA
MAYFLIES

6. ORDER ODONATA
DRAGONFLIES AND DAMSELFLIES

7. ORDER BLATTARIA
COCKROACHES

8. ORDER MANTODEA   MANTIDS

9. ORDER ISOPTERA   TERMITES

10. ORDER ZORAPTERA
ZORAPTERANS

11. ORDER PLECOPTERA
STONEFLIES

12. ORDER NOTOPTERA
(GRYLLOBLATTODEA)
GRYLLOBLATTIDS

13. ORDER PHASMIDA
(PHASMATODEA)
WALKINGSTICKS AND LEAF INSECTS

14. ORDER SALTATORIA
(ORTHOPTERA)
GRASSHOPPERS AND CRICKETS

In the chapters that follow, the insects are presented in groups that in some cases represent orders and in other cases represent families. Furthermore, the groups have been arranged so that all social insects are covered in one section and all aquatic insects in another.

15. ORDER EMBIODEA
(EMBIOPTERA)
EMBIIDS, OR WEBSPINNERS

16. ORDER DERMAPTERA   EARWIGS

17. ORDER PSOCOPTERA
BOOKLICE, BARKLICE, AND DUSTLICE

18. ORDER MALLOPHAGA
CHEWING LICE

19. ORDER ANOPLURA
SUCKING LICE

20. ORDER THYSANOPTERA   THRIPS

21. ORDER HOMOPTERA
CICADAS, LEAFHOPPERS, WHITEFLIES, APHIDS, SCALE INSECTS, AND OTHERS

22. ORDER HETEROPTERA
(HEMIPTERA)   TRUE BUGS

23. ORDER COLEOPTERA   BEETLES

24. ORDER NEUROPTERA
NERVE-WINGED INSECTS

25. ORDER MECOPTERA
SCORPIONFLIES

26. ORDER TRICHOPTERA
CADDISFLIES

27. ORDER LEPIDOPTERA
BUTTERFLIES AND MOTHS

28. ORDER DIPTERA   FLIES, MOSQUITOES, AND GNATS

29. ORDER APHANIPTERA
(SIPHONAPTERA)   FLEAS

30. ORDER STREPSIPTERA
TWISTED-WINGED PARASITES

31. ORDER HYMENOPTERA
WASPS, BEES, ANTS, ICHNEUMONS, CHALCIDS, AND SAWFLIES

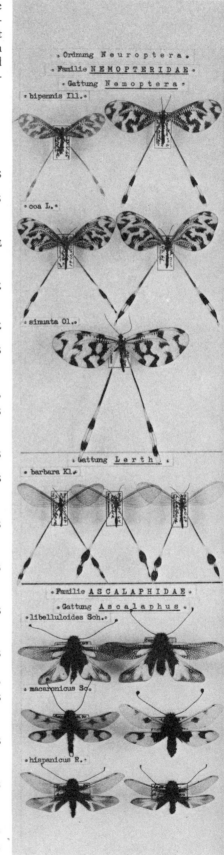

WINGLESS INSECTS
SUBCLASS APTERYGOTA

Insects of the subclass Apterygota are small and primitive in structure. They are distributed throughout the world, but encompass few species. They are, so to speak, living fossils. They lack wings, and their metamorphosis is scarcely detectable; during growth and even after maturity there are many molts in the course of which no morphological changes, or only slight ones, become apparent. At the same time, these insects possess a strong power of regeneration. If they lose legs, antennae, palpi, or other appendages, these are little by little rebuilt completely. Members of the Apterygota are unique among insects in that their abdominal segments have processes and exsertile vesicles that are thought to be vestigial legs; however, these have little significance in locomotion. The insects are grouped in four orders, descriptions of which follow.

BRISTLETAILS   ORDER THYSANURA

These small, agile insects have long, thin bodies usually covered with gleaming scales of various colors. The insects, few of which exceed half an inch in length, are most active at night or in the dark. They have chewing mouthparts, long threadlike antennae, and three similar caudal bristles at the hind end of the body. The abdomen bears rudimentary legs, in the form of small protuberances (styli), and frequently also has vesicles (subcoxal sacs) that can be extruded by means of blood pressure. It appears that moisture is taken up through them.

In most of the 350 species, males are far less common than females, and apparently new individuals are produced frequently from unfertilized eggs by the process of parthenogenesis. Usually sexual maturity is attained within a year, perhaps in as few as eight months, in cold climates—for instance, in the Alps, where species of the family Machilidae have been found at altitudes of two miles. But maturation can take as long as three to four years. The relatively large eggs are scattered singly and often are disguised by tiny bits of plants or soil that stick to them.

Members of the Thysanura have a nearly worldwide distribution. They are grouped in two families. The spindleshaped bristletails (family Machilidae) have relatively large compound eyes and three dorsal ocelli (simple eyes). On the abdomen they have subcoxal sacs and styli, the latter on the legs as well. These warmth-loving but moisture-needing insects are often handsomely decorated, but

readily lose their coat of scales on contact. They live in stony places under leaves, bark, or rocks, and feed on algae and lichen. One also sees them day after day on cliffs and treetrunks, where their erratic leaps betray their presence.

At rest, they are rendered invisible by their coloration and their habit of snuggling into cracks with the antennae laid back and the caudal bristles lined up with them. The bristles are spread apart when the insects move, as are the antennae, which feel out the terrain in advance of every forward motion. The long maxillary palpi—appendages of the secondary jaws that extend forward beneath the mouth—also are used as feelers during forward progress, and at times function as supports. Bristletails can jump, though not toward any particular goal. Some genera, notably *Petrobius,* live only on rocky seacoasts.

In contrast with the bristletails of the family Machilidae, members of the family Lepismatidae have flattened bodies. Their compound eyes, absent in some species, are small and far apart. They have only a few small lateral ocelli, or even no lateral eyes at all; and dorsal ocelli are lacking, as are the styli of the legs. Subcoxal sacs on the abdomen also are absent in most species. Distributed in about 220 species throughout the world, these insects live beneath leaves, bark, or stones; occasionally they are found in the nests of swallows. But they prefer to live in caves (a life for which a few forms, some of them blind, are specialized) and in the houses of man.

The extraordinarily light-shy, rapidly running silverfish (*Lepisma saccharina*), which

The scientific collection. Some samples showing groups belonging to two families (spoonwings and owlflies) of the order Neuroptera (nerve-winged insects). Each specimen in the collection bears a label indicating name, date, place of capture, name of the collector, and, in case the insect was scientifically examined and identified, name of the scientist. Insect collections decay easily and remain intact only under professional care.

inhabits houses, is frowned upon because it gnaws on books, paper, leather goods, and even foodstuffs. A rarer member of the family, the firebrat *(Thermobia domestica)*, prefers the warmer and even the hottest parts of our dwellings. Certain other lepismatids (for instance, *Atelura*) thrive in the constant warmth and moisture of the nests of ants or termites, where they live in the thousands. These lodgers are tolerated more or less voluntarily by their hosts, even though, some observers claim, they subsist by stealing food. [97/2, 3]

CAMPODEIDS AND JAPYGIDS ORDER DIPLURA

These are delicate, wingless insects with thin bodies. The largest of the 400 species is 2 inches long, but most are a quarter inch or less in length. Their chewing mouthparts are enclosed within the head capsule; they have vestiges of legs (styli and subcoxal sacs) on the abdomen. Usually whitish and without eyes, they live in darkness under moss or rocks, or in the ground. A few kinds occur in ants' nests or are specialized cavern-dwellers. These insects are found throughout the world. They eat materials of plant and animal origin. They dig little hollows in the soil and attach a bunch of some 10 to 22 eggs to a downward-projecting stalk.

Only two families are known, namely the Campodeidae, with two caudal bristles, and the rarer Japygidae (more often confined to warmer countries), with a single bristle at the rear. Insects of these families grasp living prey and bring it at once to the mouth, or else drag it about for a while. The japygid females, like earwigs, wrap themselves protectingly around their eggs and even around the young that have hatched, an astonishing phenomenon in so primitive an insect. A fairly common U.S. species of campodeid is *Campodea staphylinus*.

TELSONTAILS ORDER PROTURA

Telsontails are extremely small, slender, wingless insects. Soft and colorless, they lack antennae and eyes; they have piercing-sucking mouthparts. The front pair of legs is extended as organs of touch, and only the second and third pairs are used for walking. The first two or three abdominal segments have rudimentary legs (styli and subcoxal sacs). Unique in the insect world is the increase from eight abdominal segments in the newly hatched proturan to twelve in the mature individual;

at each molt a new segment is added just in front of the rear end. The twelfth segment, absent in other insects, is known as the telson and gives these insects their name. To ward off enemies, the telsontail curves its abdomen forward over the head and discharges a sticky excretion from a gland at the abdomen's hind tip.

The way of life of the telsontails is little known; it appears that they impale springtails *(Collembola)* on their sickle-shaped claws and suck out the prisoners' juices. The telsontails live in the ground and under moss or bark. Two families with about 50 species are known, namely Eosentomidae and Acerentomidae. They were first discovered in 1907, and have since been found in all parts of the world. [98/8]

SPRINGTAILS ORDER COLLEMBOLA

Springtails are minute, wingless insects. Their soft bodies are covered with hairs or scales. The first abdominal segment of the body bears on its underside a tube from which two sacs can be protruded. These sacs secrete a sticky substance that enables the springtail to adhere to smooth surfaces.

Most species can jump by means of a forked leaping organ extending downward from just in front of the rear end ("spring tail"). When not in use, the organ is bent forward under the body and is caught by a special hook; in jumping it is set free suddenly against the surface on which the insect is resting and, like a metal spring, hurls the insect forward at random some 15 body lengths. This type of movement occurs only during flight from an enemy; normally a springtail moves about by walking on the tips of the claws. In most species the tibia and tarsus of the leg are fused into one segment, the tibio-tarsus, to which the claws are attached.

A springtail's compound eyes consist of a few single facets grouped loosely together, and its dorsal ocellus (simple eye) is a primitive organ, lying beneath the integument and visible outwardly only as a small dark spot. Many springtails lack specialized visual organs and are quite blind, but most are nevertheless very sensitive to light. The body color protects them from light. Many species have typical dark spotted designs that change shape perceptibly under the influence of light and moisture. Darkness causes them to become lighter; light and moisture make them grow darker and even completely black.

In some species the pigment granules in the individual body cells disperse in darkness,

70/1
The fantastic mating games of the bristletails. Small silverfishes, the male on the left (enlarged 2×). Of special interest among the silverfish and bristletails is the mating process, which is to some degree artificial, with indirect fertilization. In an out-of-the-way place, the male silverfish spins a definite arrangement of threads and puts a drop of semen beneath it. Then the female walks under the longer of the threads, halts as soon as her back touches it, and palpating the ground with her abdomen, picks up the semen. All this takes place while both partners are executing a series of ritual movements. Among the bristletails the male himself holds taut the thread, which is fastened to the ground and bears a few drops of semen; he wraps himself about the female and shoves her in the proper direction. This action too is preceded by a dance. (→ 97/2)

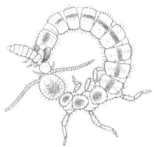

71/1-2
Diplurans devouring a springtail/ and guarding a clutch of eggs suspended by a stalk in a cavity in the earth (greatly enlarged).

concentrating at the cell margins and thus producing a dark network. But under the influence of light, they gather in the center of the cells, producing quite different, spotted patterns. Frequently young springtails are whitish and grow darker at each molt as they increase in age. The well-known ability of certain species to give off light apparently depends on their eating luminous parts of molds; these then shine out through the gut and tissues with a white or bluish light.

The mouthparts of the springtails are enveloped by the head capsule, and are either of the chewing or piercing-sucking type. Their food is derived primarily from plants and often is in a decaying state, but animal matter of all sorts also is consumed. Many springtails live on and in fungi, others in flowers, and many beneath bark; but the majority live in the ground, often at depths of several feet where—for instance, in cemeteries—they are

of much importance in the conversion of dead organic materials. This is particularly so because in number of individuals the springtails rank among the most numerous. Certain species live on the water; the tips of their forked leaping organ are expanded like leaves, and their ventral tube allows them to cling to the water's surface layer.

Springtails deposit their eggs in large batches, and the young develop to maturity in two to three weeks. There are nine families and some 2,000 species of springtails distributed throughout the world, for the most part in the temperate and arctic zones. In extreme climates, as in arctic areas, they may be the only insects capable of surviving. The snow-flea *(Isotoma saltans)* is a striking biological phenomenon. Billions of snowfleas sometimes cover the snow and ice of high mountain peaks; these insects exist on pollen and other wind-borne organic material. [98/1–6]

WINGED INSECTS
SUBCLASS PTERYGOTA

COCKROACHES Order Blattaria

The cockroaches are a primeval group of insects. Richly represented as early in time as the Carboniferous Period, they have persisted to the present in a direct evolutionary line and with only minor modifications. We are not fond of cockroaches, at least not of those few species that share our dwellings and foodstuffs. But the cockroach is not easy to catch. It can run very fast thanks to its especially strong coxae, the leg segments that join with the body. And the insect's flattened, oval build allows it to take refuge in narrow crevices, within which it even can move backward, feeling its way with a posterior pair of appendages (cerci) that might almost be dubbed "abdominal antennae."

71/3
A cockroach of the forest floor.
(→ 99/4)

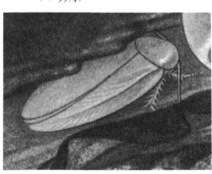

Cockroaches range from a fraction of an inch to several inches in length. The cockroach head, with its slanting forehead and chewing mouthparts, lies beneath the prothorax. The two compound eyes are relatively large, and in most species there are two dorsal ocelli also. The long antennae are very motile and flexible, and the four richly veined wings are laid flat one pair above the other on the body, the hind wing folded beneath the more or less hardened fore wing. In many species, and particularly in the females, the wings are degenerate or entirely absent. With the possible exception of some of the large tropical species, which may be as much as 4 to 5 inches long and which fly readily to light, the cock-

roaches are poor fliers, more given to fluttering; they use their wings for the most part as parachutes and extend them, after a jump, before they land.

These insects spread from place to place on foot; occasionally they go on short migrations. Certain species have been transported by man over the whole earth, particularly on ships, where cockroach infestations may be a source of great annoyance. The principal followers after civilization are the American cockroach *(Periplaneta americana)*, the Indian or Australian cockroach *(Periplaneta australasiae)*, the Oriental cockroach *(Blatta orientalis)*, and the German cockroach *(Blattella germanica)*.

Cockroaches are fond of warmth. The 3,500 species live mainly in the tropics; but some species occur in every part of the world except the arctic and antarctic regions. Most of them avoid the light, living in concealment under leaves, bark, and stones; some are lodgers in the nests of ants, wasps, or termites. And a few species even are found in water, where the wingless females and nymphs swim and dive extremely well.

Cockroaches are omnivorous, but vegetable matter probably predominates in their diet; some cannibalism has been seen among them. In libraries they have caused much damage, by chewing on books for the sake of the paste in the bindings. They locate their food by means of sensory mouthparts (palpi). Certain species eat wood, which they digest with the help of specific unicellular organisms (Protozoa) living in their gut, a type of symbiosis that occurs regularly in many other insects.

Cockroaches always are cleaning themselves industriously; they seize the antennae with the forelegs, draw them to the mouth, and lick them clean; they polish the wings by stroking them with the spiny hindlegs. However, they lack special cleaning devices, such as are displayed by many other insects.

The color of the majority of cockroaches is brown (in any of its shades); the rest are pale green or brightly striped or spotted with black, yellow, and even red. Frequently the back of the prothorax bears a handsome decorative design, and occasionally there are metallic colors. Some few species are shaped like woodlice (isopod crustaceans) and can roll up like them when danger threatens. Protection is also provided by stink glands on the abdomen of most species. The most dangerous enemies of the cockroach are little parasitic wasps (Evaniidae), sometimes known as "famine wasps" because of their disproportionately small abdomen; the larvae of these wasps develop in and feed on the cockroach eggs.

Many cockroaches perform an odd courtship before mating. The male taps the female with his antennae and suddenly turns around. The female then licks at a glandular secretion on the male's back, while he bends his antennae rearward and lets them play over hers.

The eggs, numbering from five to fifty, are placed together in a bundle, the shape of which varies from species to species. Inside the bundle the eggs lie in a series of chambers arranged in two rows. In most species the female carries the egg cocoon (ootheca) around on the end of the abdomen for some time, then simply drops it or tucks it into a carefully prepared hollow. But certain species carry the egg capsule until the young begin to hatch. In a few tropical species the eggs develop to completion in a brood pouch inside the female body. In such instances only a rudimentary egg cocoon is formed, or maybe none at all. The young of these cockroaches are born alive, and some species even shelter their young beneath the wings for some time afterwards. Thus we see here an uninterrupted series of stages leading to care of the young.

The newborn are white (as the older cockroaches are immediately after each molt), but become colored after a few hours. In accordance with their incomplete metamorphosis, their shape and motions are like those of the parents, except they have no wings. Maturity is reached after about six molts, usually in some three to six months or longer. After the final molt the wings are expanded by blood pressure to their full length, and the full-grown cockroach lives for some six months or more. On occasion the species *Periplaneta americana* has been kept in the laboratory for over three years. [98/9–21]

MANTIDS ORDER MANTODEA

Over there sits a creature that looks something like a grasshopper. Odd how it twists its head, keeping its eyes ever fastened on us. Now it tries to get away and creeps almost sinuously through the grass. But when threatened it halts; raises its head high; spreads its forelegs, revealing astonishing designs; and fans its rattling wings in and out.

The name of this amazing creature is the mantid, mantis, or soothsayer. It is also called praying mantis because it holds the forelegs out in front like a pair of supplicating hands. But appearances could not be more deceiving, for these are instruments that deal in death.

The praying mantis is a sight to see. The attentive motionlessness, relieved by a plantlike swaying to and fro, the fierce rapacious temperament, the uncanny visage that despite its masklike rigidity moves so freely on the slender outstretched neck, and the tremulous shimmer that plays over the globular eyes— these make the mantids among the most fascinating spectacles of the animal world. Since ancient times all manner of human superstition has been associated with them.

Mantids are moderately close relatives of the cockroaches, a relationship that manifests itself in various similarities, including the two small posterior outgrowths (the cerci) of the abdomen, the form and position

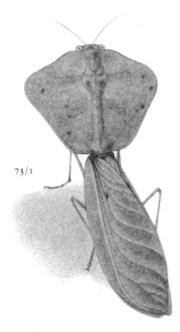

73/1

73/1–2
Many praying mantids simulate leaves. (→ 55/1 ; 17/29)

73/2

of the coxae (parts of legs nearest the body), and the wings. But there are also striking differences. The mantid's trunk and prothorax are very slender, and out in front of them there sits, free and extraordinarily movable, the triangular head with the antennae, which usually are very thin.

Mantids hunt with their particularly large, strongly vaulted compound eyes, which may even protrude like towers, but whose color is scarcely noticeable. The facets near the center of the eye's curved surface are more highly developed; in particular they have longer lenses and thus afford better acuity. This explains why the mantids so frequently turn the head about, for they try to fixate every moving thing with this central zone of their eyes. Another characteristic peculiarity is a certain shifting of the eye pigment when darkness approaches in the evening. As a result the eyes take on a darker, purplish hue. This occurs only in active individuals, not in those at rest—a phenomenon connected with better utilization of the dwindling light. On the frons (forehead), between the compound eyes, there are three well-developed ocelli, or simple eyes.

All mantids have predatory forelegs, quite distinct from the rest of the legs. Each foreleg is a pair of hinged prehensile shears equipped with rows of spines as sharp as needles, from which there is no escape for the victim. Forelegs are not used in locomotion except in rare instances, such as in climbing; in their stead the middle pair of legs is turned forward somewhat more than usual, providing broader support for the body. In the act of taking prey, the wide-open shears of the forelegs lash out like lightning, clamp the booty between them, and pull it back to the razor-sharp mouthparts, where it is cut to pieces and eaten.

In other respects the mantids have an extraordinary variety of forms. Besides the normal spindle shape, there are flat mantids, often having leaflike outgrowths even on the legs. These disguises render the insects invisible both to their enemies and to their prey. Some mantids imitate lichens and bark; others look like green or brown leaves, some even flowers, assisted at times by a very bizarre posture; also there are some very long, thin, rod-shaped species.

Because of such differences, it is particularly hard to classify the mantid family properly with reference to their more fundamental relationships with one another, a task that has not yet been accomplished satisfactorily. We know about 1,700 species, mostly green, brown, or gray, but certain ones have beautiful bright coloring; in Australia there are mantids of about 1 to 6 inches in length that exhibit metallic colors. These tropical and subtropical insects depend on warmth, are active by day, and usually lead a solitary existence.

Occasionally mantids are transported from one country to another by man, particularly in egg capsules fastened to plants. As a result, one finds in the vicinity of New York today not only the European *Mantis religiosa,* which has both a green and a brown form, but also two Asiatic species, *Tenodera angustipennis* and *Tenodera sinensis.* Mantids are not great fliers; flight is limited pretty much to males and unfertilized females. Also, no migrations have been seen, so that the natural distribution of mantids apparently is a slow process.

Gluttonous creatures that they are, mantids devour all sorts of insects, not excepting their own kin. Huge praying mantids occasionally even snatch at lizards or small birds. Grasshoppers are a preferred food, and tiny immature mantids feed principally on plant-lice. The females frequently indulge in the custom of eating the male immediately after mating, as some spiders also are known to do. This cannibalistic act often begins during the very process of mating, and in some species it even happens that the male can start to mate only after his head and neck have been bitten off. A headless mantid is able to mate only because the nerve centers concerned lie in the abdomen and function independently of the actual brain.

Like the cockroaches, the mantids lay their eggs in packets made of a hardened foamy secretion. The capsules differ greatly in shape from one species to another; the eggs are arranged in rows of compartments. The egg cocoon always is fastened to something—a stone, a twig, bark, grass, or leaves; and its production takes about four or five hours.

From the tip of the female abdomen there issues simultaneously with the eggs a secretion, beaten into a foam with special implements and then shaped appropriately by spiral movements of the abdomen. While this process is going on, the insect moves forward slowly, successively adding an egg to each newly formed chamber. One egg cocoon may contain 50 to 400 eggs; and regularly a female produces several capsules, as also is the case with cockroaches.

In the temperate zone the eggs pass the winter in the cocoon, where they are well protected so long as they are not parasitized by tiny wasps (Chalcididae). Within the cocoon the young hatch in spring. They are incompletely developed, ugly beings that molt for the first time either just as they break out through the wall of the capsule or immediately afterward. Thereupon they leave their common shelter as proper mantids, though still lacking wings—a swarm of little, agile, bizarre creatures.

During the summer the young grow up; the number of molts required may vary somewhat, depending on temperature and sex. *Mantis religiosa,* for instance, undergoes five to six molts; other species, seven to ten. Not until the last nymphal stage do short wing stubs appear, and the actual wings unfold and extend to their full size after the molt to maturity. In the temperate zone the entire course of development takes three to five months, and the adults live a few months thereafter. Their most important enemies are birds. In general, mantids are seldom seen. Few fossils of them have been found. [51/5; 56/1; 60; 100–101]

ZORAPTERANS Order Zoraptera

The zorapterans are minute insects, measuring at most about a tenth of an inch long. Slender and pale-colored, they have chewing mouthparts and are related to the termites. Their thoracic segments are separate from one another, instead of two or all three being fused, as is usually the case with other insects. Some species lack both eyes and wings; others have two compound eyes and three widely separated dorsal ocelli, as well as four long wings with reduced venation. Certain species, however, like termites, lose the wings soon after reaching maturity. Metamorphosis is incomplete.

The zorapterans live together under moss or bark, in piles of old sawdust, or in the ground. These insects were first discovered in 1913, and as yet only a single family, Zorotypidae, and one genus, *Zorotypus,* with less than 20 species, has been found in North and South America, Java, and Ceylon.

The zorapterans, mantids, termites (treated in "Social Insects"), and cockroaches can be classified as the superorder Blattoidea, while the next five orders (orders 11 to 15) constitute the superorder Orthopteroidea. All of them have incomplete metamorphosis.

GRYLLOBLATTIDS

Order Notoptera

There are only six known species of these mountain insects, considered by some entomologists as a family (Grylloblattidae) of the order Orthoptera and by others as a separate order (Grylloblattodea or Notoptera). Wingless and primitive, they measure 0.8 to 1.2 inches in length and are pale brown or pale yellow. At the rear of the slender body are two moderately long filaments (cerci). These insects live above treeline under moss and stones, retaining full activity at temperatures only slightly above freezing. The species *Grylloblatta campodeiformis* was the first of these insects to be discovered, in 1914, in the Canadian mountains; others were found later in the United States, Russia, and Japan. They seem to represent a primitive grasshopperlike insect of the type that may have been the ancestor of the grasshoppers and crickets (Orthoptera). [102/1]

WALKINGSTICKS AND LEAF INSECTS

Order Phasmida (Phasmatodea)

The walkingsticks and leaf insects are noted for their near-perfect imitations of plants. Some that resemble twigs are drawn out to improbable lengths, measuring as much as 13 inches; others are flattened and expanded like a leaf. They are nocturnal insects that move slowly and clumsily as they feed on green leaves of trees and bushes. During the day they hang motionless from plants, with forelegs stretched out stiffly in front of the head, occasionally letting themselves drop under the influence of sunlight or if disturbed by shaking.

There are approximately 2,000 phasmid species, which live mostly in warm countries and owe their existence largely to their penchant for catalepsy (trancelike state), for even the most deceptive "twig" or perfect "leaf" loses its disguise when it walks. And with few exceptions these insects move too slowly to escape most pursuers. Nevertheless, they are not entirely defenseless. In the phasmid's thorax are two protective glands from which a milky, sharp-smelling, and corrosive liquid is squirted out for some distance; this liquid occasionally makes it impossible for a person to remain under trees inhabited by phasmids. Also, many species are so thoroughly studded with strong, sharp spines that the prospect of eating them is hardly an attractive one to any animal.

A typical phasmid has two small compound eyes and three dorsal ocelli (simple eyes), as well as thin, fairly short antennae. The head is generally elongate oval in shape

74/1
*Zorotypus brasiliensis
(greatly enlarged).*

74/2
The huge walkingsticks include the longest of all insects. (→ 16/5)

and may be clothed with spines or hairs. In the big species a rounder form makes the head look somewhat like a bald skull, an appearance accented by a bare, flabby, segmented body of primeval appearance. Characteristic of the phasmids is the very short anterior section of the trunk (prothorax), which is not fused with the rest of the thorax but is joined flexibly to it.

Some phasmids, especially females, lack wings. All the species living in the United States are wingless except *Aplopus mayeri,* of Florida. The largest U.S. species, *Megaphasma denticus,* may be up to 6 inches long.

A number of phasmids have only one well-developed pair of wings, almost always the back pair; the front pair is greatly shortened or rudimentary. The hind wings then have a hardened anterior marginal zone, beneath which the remaining membranous portion, with many lengthwise folds, lies close against the abdomen. It is a great surprise when a thin walkingstick suddenly extends great, broad buzzing wings, generally brightly colored. No doubt this serves as a means of scaring enemies off, for even winged phasmids do not fly much and use their wings as parachutes only in case of need.

75/1
The few species of "wandering leaves" are among the most perfect examples of leaf mimesis. (→ 54/4)

These insects do not leap, either; their legs are better adjusted to climbing and walking. The insect moves its legs slowly and when at rest stretches them out and places them, almost invisibly, against the body (except when they have deceptive leaflike shapes). Phasmids suspend themselves with a minimum of attachment; frequently only the front legs are used for this purpose, with perhaps one middle or hind leg as a diagonal prop. The suspended walkingstick is twiglike in its stiffness and rigidity; occasionally it rocks to and fro as though swayed gently by the wind. Some species press close against a branch, and others let almost the entire body stick out stiffly from a branch into the air. Certain South American species that live near mountain streams cling to rocks over which the water washes.

The walkingsticks are predominantly gray, brown, or green, but many species have bright colors on the hind wings and on the inner surface of the femur (third leg segment from the body) of each front leg. Most species can change their color under the influence of light, temperature, and humidity, from brown to green or vice versa. The change may occur slowly, as when one skin pigment gradually dominates the others, or it may take place rapidly, as when the pigments shift position under the influence of light. Phasmids are dark-colored at night and light by day. Coldness and dampness cause darkening, and warmth and dryness cause paling; this results in an automatic adaptation to the environment, for in warm, dry localities phasmids take on the paler coloration of the surroundings.

Walkingstick insects are used in zoological laboratories as experimental animals for tests concerned with hypnosis (catalepsy), color change, the regeneration of lost parts, and parthenogenesis. Parthenogenetic reproduction, in which a new individual develops from an unfertilized egg, is frequent among walkingsticks, and for many species males are altogether unknown; even in the unusually familiar walkingsticks of Europe (genera *Bacillus* and *Dixippus*) a male hardly ever is obtained, despite much culturing in laboratories. In certain other species, some two to seven males occur for every 2,000 to 3,000 females.

The tough-skinned, brown eggs of walkingsticks resemble seeds or little covered vessels. The female scatters them at random, up to about 10 a day, or 90 to 200 in all. Then she dies. The smaller and scarcer males live much longer and may even survive two generations of females.

The eggs hatch at night; the young insects raise themselves up in the eggs, back first, pulling all their legs out only at the last. They are surprisingly large and look much like adults. During their development, which lasts three to six months, the young insects molt six times and have a great capacity for regenerating lost body parts. The adult female may live another three to six months.

Enemies of walkingsticks are lizards, birds, spiders, parasitic wasps, and parasitic flies, the last two of which develop within the phasmid body. Although dense populations of walkingsticks are uncommon, some species appear in great numbers. These may damage plants by defoliating them. For instance, *Diapheromera femorata* in North America strips the leaves from oaks and roses, and *Podacanthus wilkinsoni* in Australia defoliates eucalyptus trees. [31/3]

The most beautiful phasmids probably are the green "wandering leaves" of the genus *Phyllium* from southern and southeast Asia. These insects live on certain trees, particularly the cacao. The females, which cannot fly, are marvelous leaf imitations, especially because of their hardened fore wings, beneath which the hind wings lie as tiny flaps that are fused with the back. The rare males, on the other hand, have well-developed hind wings and only little, stumpy front wings.

It is a rare and queer experience to see a "leaf" walking, as it sets one leg slowly after the other and rocks the abdomen from side to side. These wandering-leaf insects can climb up the smooth surfaces of leaves or even glass; and for days at a time they hang with their leaf-shaped front legs stretched out among the leaves. A lizard doesn't notice them, even when its head is right beside them; and, ironically, their disguise is so good that leaf-eating insects, including their own kind, mistakenly bite at them.

Despite the effectiveness of their disguise, these insects are uncommon. The reason is that they reproduce slowly. A female lives some three months and lays an egg or two every day, for a total of about 100 eggs. The eggs, which look like seeds, take five or more months to hatch. The young initially are red-brown and wingless. With the abdomen tilted ludicrously upward, they climb a bush or tree until they reach the tender terminal leaves, which also are mostly reddish. After a week or two the nymphs become yellow-green, but still have many irregular brown patches, as also do many mature specimens, especially those that feed on the cocoa plant. Some remain brown all over like a wilted leaf, while others have unpigmented, transparent blotches that if anything increase the deceptive similarity to leaves. The nymphs take several months or more to mature. Parthenogenetic reproduction is frequent with these phasmids, as with walkingsticks, but apparently cannot be continued indefinitely, for it has been observed that females from as early as the second generation remain infertile. [102/2, 3; 103]

GRASSHOPPERS AND CRICKETS

ORDER SALTATORIA (ORTHOPTERA)

With tones as pure as a bell, the field crickets chirp outside their holes on the grassy slopes; their clear, high notes fill the valley day and night. Summer would not be summer without the vibrant symphony of the crickets and grasshoppers, this ringing whir that hangs in the air and buzzes in our ears. From the nether world, as though from afar, the mole cricket announces his presence, like a purring miniature motor. Within our dwellings the hearth crickets are heard at night. With ringing chirps the tree crickets call through the branches, much more loudly than one would believe possible for these ghostly pale, delicate little creatures. And

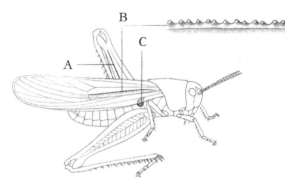

from all directions, seemingly from everywhere and nowhere—now here, now growing silent over yonder and then starting up again—there comes the rhythmic song of untold long-horned and other grasshoppers.

The 10,000-plus species of grasshoppers and crickets are grouped in several families belonging to the order Orthoptera. They range from a few tenths of an inch to 4 inches in length. Long-horned grasshoppers and crickets have long antennae, whereas other grasshoppers, sometimes called short-horned grasshoppers, have short antennae.

MUSIC MAKING

Every species has its own distinctive "song," which often identifies the singer more clearly than does its appearance. Crickets and certain long-horned grasshoppers produce the purest tones; those of the European field cricket (*Liogryllus campestris*) have a musical pitch of four octaves above middle C, some 4,200 vibrations per second, with the wings rubbing together seven times in this interval. Many studies have been made of the sounds produced by American crickets such as *Acheta* and *Nemobrus*.

With few exceptions, only the males can sing. Coldblooded creatures that they are, they respond to the warmth of their surroundings by bursting into song. As the temperature rises, their life processes speed up, and their song becomes more rapid and intense. From the tempo of successive chirps of certain tree crickets (*Oecanthus*) we can determine the air temperature precisely. In the case of the snowy tree cricket (*Oecanthus fultoni*), for example, we simply count the number of chirps in 15 seconds, add 39, and the total is the temperature in degrees Fahrenheit.

The musical instruments (organs of stridulation) are simple in construction and use. A scraper, often comblike, with a row of pegs or transverse ridges, is rubbed across a file (or stridulatory vein), which may be either smooth or knobby.

Grasshoppers (family Acrididae) have a scraper on the inside of the middle segment

(femur) of each hind leg and rub the scrapers lengthwise over stridulatory veins on the wing covers (fore wings). This sets the wing membranes in vibration, and the membranes amplify the sound. Even amplified, the song of the grasshopper is not loud; and it is more of a scraping sound than music. In certain wingless species a file may be formed along the side of the abdomen.

Long-horned grasshoppers and katydids (Tettigoniidae) and crickets (Gryllidae) have their file and scraper on the wing covers, which are rubbed together in rapid succession to produce the chirps; the scraper is formed by a sharp-edged bowed-out region of the wing margin. In long-horned grasshoppers one wing (usually the left one) bears the file, and the other wing the scraper. In crickets both file and scraper are present on each wing. Most crickets employ them unilaterally; for example, the scraper of the right wing is drawn across the file on the left wing. But the mole cricket *(Gryllotalpa)* alternates them; the female of this species is exceptional, furthermore, in possessing a musical instrument, although she uses it little or not at all.

The purity of tone and the often powerful intensity of the songs of crickets and long-horned grasshoppers depend on specially constructed resonant areas ("drumheads") on the front wings, the same wings that have the stridulatory organs. These transparent roundish or oval drums are stretched between definite wing veins. In certain species, the entire wing, more or less, constitutes a resonating system; in others the abdomen is inflated to act as an additional resonator.

When music is made the wing covers are elevated; crickets lift them high and often hold them almost vertically. Since the outer margins of the wings are bowed downward, a space that amplifies the sound is formed beneath them. Certain tropical long-horned grasshoppers have wings so shaped as to produce an even larger cavity. [15/23; 014/3, 5]

Musicians must have ears if they are to hear the tunes they make, and these insects have a hearing organ manifested outwardly as a rounded eardrum. Crickets and long-horned grasshoppers bear their eardrums one beneath the "knee" of each foreleg; other grasshoppers have an eardrum on either side of the front part of the abdomen. But all the silent species lack such organs.

COURTSHIP SONGS AND SIGNALS

The songs of grasshoppers and crickets are not merely an expression of well-being,
but are used by males in attracting and courting females as well as in rivalry among themselves. Mute insects must use means other than music; certain long-horned grasshoppers, for example, entice their females with odors issued from glandular vesicles. Different sounds serve for each phase of courtship. There are courting songs, mating calls, and cries of rivalry; there are ticks produced by snapping the hind tibiae, mandibular noises ("gnashing the teeth"), and drumming on the ground with the hind legs or the abdomen. In addition, sounds are produced voluntarily by the beating of the wings either in flight or not in flight. In some species these wingbeats make a surprisingly loud rattling or buzzing. The sounds result from the special structure and position of veins on the forepart of the hind wings. Altogether there is an astonishingly rich repertory of sounds, whose stimulatory foundation and tactics of application we have just begun to seek in tedious, zoopsychological investigations.

Often we may hear the rival songs of two male long-horned grasshoppers. They alternate in sending forth their tunes, each singing during the pauses of the other. In this way they attract yet other males and set up a vehement concert that serves to attract the females. But if there is no female nearby, all this rival song soon changes over into the customary "national hymn" of the species.

When a male encounters a potential mate, he shifts to his wooing song, a gentler-sounding melody hardly audible to us; with what seems like rising emotion, the singing becomes ever more rapid until the moment when it is broken off abruptly, often in the middle of a phrase. A single tick, or perhaps a few, thereupon indicate the initial steps of mating. The rest of the crickets meanwhile continue their musical rivalry.

Especially astonishing are the customs of those short-horned grasshoppers in whose behavior both optical and acoustical signals play a part. Their "national colors" on the hind legs and on the wings are as resplendent as heraldic emblems. By whipping the femora up and down or by beating the wings—now noisily, now silently, depending on how demonstrative their mood—these creatures entice one another or drive each other away. Each species has its own language.

Observing the behavior of these grasshoppers is time-consuming but rewarding. Perhaps we see one male grasshopper making a bow before his mate. Or another beckons in a ludicrous manner with its upstretched

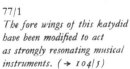
77/1
The fore wings of this katydid have been modified to act as strongly resonating musical instruments. (→ 104/5)

hind legs. A female gives her partner an invitation by flapping her wings energetically. Another shakes her hind legs and drums with her feet because at the moment she wants nothing to do with a male who has come too close. And this male lashes out backward with its long, spiny hind legs, like a kicking horse, because it wants to get rid of an onlooking rival, who actually may be sitting in front or at the side. Another grasshopper whirs above a single spot, waiting for some female to give a sign of her presence. And yet another male flirts with his "beloved" by flying about her in tight curves. Finally we may assume, perhaps, that the red lights displayed by small luminescent grasshoppers in the virgin forest of South America serve to attract females.

Every species has its methods and its ritual. Only recently have we become more fully acquainted with them, as in the case of *Oedipoda coerulescens*. Though this species has brightly marked hind wings, at rest it is one of the best-disguised insects. Each individual seeks out in a bare or sparsely covered terrain those places that most closely match its own body color. So effective is the disguise that a male searching for a mate cannot find one, not even when he comes almost close enough to touch her. A sense of smell evidently does not function here, and the eyes seem to see only what is moving. The females stay quite still most of the time, which is of decisive importance for their disguise. But now and then one of them takes off suddenly in a quick, short flight of only a few yards, alerting the males with her brilliant wing pennons and rattling flight.

The males chirp in excitement and fly in pursuit, attempting to land as near the female as possible. This apparently is not easy, for she flies fast and without advance notice dives sharply downward into hiding. The pursuing males then bounce to a landing, turning a cartwheel and gazing back in the direction from which she came; she has vanished, as though swallowed up by the earth. Enemies that might have noticed the conspicuous flight are also misled. Now the males explore, turning about in all directions, climbing up on rocks and other points of vantage, and waiting for a sign from the female. Invisible to them, she sits as still as a piece of wood. When she beckons with slow, silent motions of her colorful hind femora, the nearest male hastens to her. But if a male discovers and approaches a female without her invitation, she rejects him with an upraised femur. [57/1; 106/1-8]

The leg-mummery of the grasshoppers can vary almost without end. Different modes of expression are communicated by the angle through which the femora are moved or at which they are placed, by whether both move at once and in the same direction, by whether they alternate and perhaps work antagonistically, by whether they are held out from the body or else brush along the wings and thus produce sound, by whether they move at longer or shorter intervals, and by whether they are raised with the tibiae flexed, moderately open, or even fully outstretched. Much observation has confirmed that such nuances constitute definite rules of behavior, fixed for each species. But despite this great wealth of theatrical communication and sound language, grasshoppers seem nowhere to have developed relationships that might induce us to include them among the social insects.

MIGRATING LOCUSTS

Among grasshoppers, association without higher forms of social life is frequent, and the dreaded classic example is the migratory locust. The latter is a biological concept, not a taxonomic one. Any grasshoppers that join in group migrations are called migratory locusts. Individuals of one and the same species may be migratory locusts or non-migrating grasshoppers.

The individual species of migratory locusts, when in their normal solitary phase, are distributed over broad areas. In certain invariably identical, relatively small localities, excessive overpopulation occurs periodically and leads to development of the swarming phase. This often happens after a series of years in which climatic conditions have been favorable. In addition to ample supplies of food, such swarming grounds must have, within a limited area, a definite range of temperature and humidity. These requirements are met between humid mountain ranges and dry plains, and on the shores of rivers, lakes, and seas when these are bordered by arid regions.

Floodplains are particularly appropriate as swarming grounds. Here, great hordes of grasshopper nymphs, attracted by the ubiquitous moisture, become concentrated into ever-narrowing areas when water begins to dry up and food gets scarce. The crowding causes the nymphs to disturb one another, and this continual mutual disturbance rises to a level of irritation that leads to the production of the swarming phase. The nymphs develop a spotted, much darker coloration

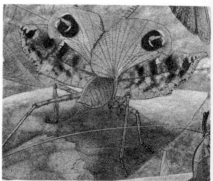

78/1
A very few tropical katydids possess eyespots, which may be of use for scaring enemies off and in the mating ritual. In favor of this last hypothesis is the fact, extremely rare in insects, that these wonderful designs, like windowpanes, shine out conspicuously only with transmitted light, i.e., when viewed from below against the light sky, and that they are dull and turbid under other circumstances.
(→ 17/26)

and hence absorb more warmth. Their body temperature is 5° to 8° C (9° to 14° F) higher than that of individuals of the solitary phase; this again heightens their sensitivity to stimulation and increases their activity.

In conjunction with a distinct tendency for imitation, the whole company finally begins to advance on foot on a broad front, as though under the influence of a mass psychosis, carrying with it every individual in the region and covering some 300 to 350 yards a day. Rivers are crossed by swimming; cliffs and chasms scarcely constitute obstacles, although good-sized forests do. In the course of the march, the nymphs gradually grow into mature locusts and begin to take to the air.

Although locusts prefer to ride the winds, swarms have been seen in flat calms over the open sea, hundreds of miles from shore; of course, they perished, as do those that happen to fly into the desert. If living conditions are unfavorable in the place to which the locusts have migrated, the progeny of the locusts may die off entirely or may diminish in numbers from generation to generation. When the numbers required for the swarm-forming mass psychosis are no longer attained, only the solitary nonmigrating phase of the locust develops. In spite of such obstacles, during the years 1926 to 1931 migratory locusts crossed and recrossed all of North Africa in the course of ten generations.

The most important migratory species in North America is the Rocky Mountain locust (*Melanoplus spretus*). Insects alleged to be of this species caused enormous damage as recently as the beginning of this century. From breeding grounds on the warm, dry plateaus of the Rocky Mountains these locusts thrust to the south, southeast, and east, perhaps as far as Texas, and then returned as a new generation.

Another serious pest is *Locusta migratoria,* commonly called the migratory locust. It is distributed in several races throughout most of the world except North and South America. These breed in Africa along the Niger river, on the Sudanese coast of the Red Sea, and along the northern border of the Sahara; in Arabia, Iran, and Pakistan; in China along the Hwang-Ho river; and from Central Asia to the Black Sea at river mouths, beside lakes, and along seacoasts. Swarms of these locusts have penetrated repeatedly as far north as Germany.

In North Africa, the Moroccan locust (*Dociostaurus maroccanus*) is particularly injurious. It is smaller than the others (about ¾ to 1⅔ inches long) and makes shorter migrations. In the south of Africa the chief mischief makers are the red locust *(Nomadacris septemfasciata)* and the brown locust *(Locustana pardalina)*. These ravage cornfields in particular. In Australia the most feared locusts are *Chortoicetes terminifera* and, especially in the north, *Gastrimargus musicus.* By clearing forests that act as natural barriers to these locusts, man has contributed to their mass outbreaks.

In South America locust swarms appear almost exclusively in cultivated areas, where their natural enemies and other hazards are scarce. Hordes of *Schistocerca paranensis,* a species that usually begins to swarm only after reaching maturity, originate mainly in the agricultural regions of Argentina. Setting their course by climatic conditions, they fly first southwesterly, then turn and move northward along the Andes. The swarms overwinter in northwestern Argentina, often heaped into piles a yard high during the cold nights, and fly back southward in the spring. Near Buenos Aires they split up, one part heading westward, another going northward along the Andes again, and the rest falling out over Uruguay. [106/9]

The weight of a big swarm has been estimated at 15,000 tons, and its daily food consumption as equivalent to that of 1.5 million people. For days at a time, even for a week, locusts may darken the sky in a given region, coming to earth when the temperature drops in the evening and covering everything with a crawling layer. Where they settle almost nothing remains, not even the bark of trees less than two years old. And the eggs they leave behind are the seeds of new invasions.

After a locust invasion, many animals starve to death or die from eating the poisonous plants spurned by the locusts. Famine and destitution descend on the people. We cannot always cope with these calamities of nature. We are forced to spray poisons, but in doing so we kill the very creatures that eat the locusts. In North Africa, for example, large numbers of locust-eating storks have been killed in this way.

Except for a few sluggish species, locusts are active insects, and they like warmth. They begin to migrate only on a day when the temperature reaches about 25° C (77° F); once begun, migration continues at night if the temperature is above 27° C (81° F). If the temperature rises to more than 40° C (104° F), say at noontime, the migration is interrupted.

The locust, like many other insects, regulates its body warmth by changing its position relative to the sun. For warmth it chooses a well-protected resting-place that strongly reflects the sun's rays; for coolness it selects a spot swept by the wind. During certain stages of its development a locust can stand temperatures from 40° C to 46° C (104° F to 115° F); it dies of heat only when the temperature reaches 47° C to 50° C (117° F to 122° F). The locust is much more sensitive to cold. It dies at 0.5° C to 1° C (about 33° F to 34° F).

All grasshoppers and crickets are heavy eaters, and most eat almost any vegetable food, which they masticate with their strong chewing mouthparts. The geologically ancient grasshoppers, which already were in existence about 300 million years ago in the Carboniferous Period, were predatory insects. Even now the more primitive groups (for example, tettigoniids, sagines, decticines, stenopelmatids) are carnivorous, at least when they are mature; their forelegs, equipped with strong, inward-facing spines, function for seizing prey. They prefer to eat other grasshoppers, but also welcome flies, caterpillars, snails, and worms. Certain species, such as the mole cricket, live on a mixed diet of vegetable and animal food.

In almost all grasshoppers and crickets, the last pair of legs is developed into powerful organs used for leaping. In the mole cricket, however, it is the forelegs that are different; they are digging organs that resemble the front feet of a mole.

Grasshopper wings are modified in many ways. Some species have only hind wings, and certain others have none at all. In species having two pairs of wings, the slenderer, harder fore wings function in flight mainly as supporting surfaces; the membranous back wings act as both supporting surfaces and propellers.

The flight ability of grasshoppers and crickets is in general feeble; it is more highly developed in only a few groups, especially in the migratory locusts, which fly with about 20 wingbeats per second and at about 10 to 12 miles per hour. These fliers steer conspicuously badly.

Grasshoppers often put the wings to use in their flying leaps. Before they jump one often may observe a peculiar seesawing motion of the whole body, during which time the feet have not budged; these are the so-called movements of "getting set," and they appear also as rituals in the relations of the sexes.

The grasshopper normally moves about by creeping and uses its hind legs surprisingly little. It usually hops only when fleeing an enemy; after a few leaps many species crawl into the vegetation and cannot be flushed out again. It is interesting to watch grasshoppers climbing about. They change frequently from one blade of grass or twig to another by first pulling the distant support close with one hind leg, which is often extended sideways to a remarkable degree. In climbing, these insects use only the tarsi of the legs, and not the tibiae as well, as most other insects do.

In contrast with ordinary grasshoppers, most of which live on the ground, the long-horned grasshoppers do more climbing. Their feet have specially adherent soles formed from a layer of fine tubes standing on end; these are dampened over and over by being drawn through the mouth, and they stick firmly to a support.

CLEANING HABITS

Crickets and grasshoppers clean themselves industriously. Ordinary grasshoppers dust off their short, stiff antennae with their front legs; long-horned grasshoppers and crickets pull their long, flexible, threadlike antennae to the mouth and lick them clean. The legs of grasshoppers and crickets are freed of dirt, in part by licking them with the mouth, in part by rubbing them together, and in part by scraping them against the underlying support. The body is attended to with the legs and feet. A particularly farcical sight is a grasshopper washing its face, which it moistens with saliva and wipes against the ground, twisting the head from side to side as it walks along. Equally ludicrous to the observer is the way a grasshopper, when presented with a ball of dung, kicks it backward with surprising accuracy to a distant goal.

The relatively large, not very movable head of crickets and grasshoppers almost always is set nearly vertically on the freely moving anterior thoracic segment (prothorax). The two compound eyes are puite big, and three dorsal ocelli nearly always are present. The antennae originate on the "forehead," and in crickets and long-horned grasshoppers frequently are of enormous length.

REPRODUCTION AND DEVELOPMENT

The female long-horned grasshopper has at the hind end of her abdomen a long ovipositor, shaped like a sword in most species, that she uses to insert her eggs into

80/1
In flying grasshoppers and katydids fore and hind wings are not moved to the same extent nor precisely at the same time.
(→ 17/24)

81/1
Mimesis of leaves and lichens in katydids. (→ 16/12)

81/2
With repeated stings a blue mud-dauber wasp has paralyzed a cricket and is dragging it into the underground nest. (→ 312/9)

the ground or into the stems or leaves of plants. Most crickets have lance-shaped ovipositors through which eggs are passed into the soil or into twigs.

Female short-horned grasshoppers, although their ovipositors are mere stubs, use them to drill into the ground. The abdomen of the female stretches out like a telescope to an unbelievable length, enabling her to make a deep hole. In the hole, often lined with secretion, she lays sausage-shaped eggs, row on row, in a gradually hardening mass of foam. Smaller species may lay from 2 to 10 eggs, larger species from 40 to 50, some as many as 100. The mouth of the hole is stoppered with a plug made of the same foamy secretion and then is covered over with earth. The entire act of egg-laying lasts some two to four hours, and one female makes several such chambers, up to 11; she may produce 400 to 500 eggs. [104/4; 106/9]

Certain grasshoppers insert the eggs in the soft pith of stems or twigs, or else in rotten wood. The mole crickets *(Gryllotalpa),* which feed on roots, insects, and worms in the burrows they dig, make an enlarged subterranean chamber in which their females lay their eggs. A female mole cricket watches over her 200 to 300 eggs for nearly three weeks until they hatch, and then for another four weeks supervises the young, meanwhile not eating any food. [104/1]

The young grasshopper or cricket opens the eggshell with the help of a hard ridge on its head or by pressure from a cervical vesicle (neck sac) inflated with blood. Still enclosed in a membrane, the young insect is shaped rather like a worm. Immediately after hatching, it molts into a nymph that is quite similar to the parents. Wings first appear as short stubs that grow larger in the course of the four to seven nymphal stages (there are five stages on the average, but as many as ten in crickets). Not until after the last molt are the wings extended to their full size; the process takes some 20 minutes.

When ready to molt, a grasshopper suspends itself by the feet, inflates itself by swallowing air, and bursts the old skin down the back. All increase in length takes place only at molts; on each occasion the body becomes longer by about a quarter. As a rule successive molts occur when the body weight has doubled. Similarly, the mature insect attains reproductive capability only after it has doubled its weight; the attainment of sexual maturity can usually be recognized by changes in coloration.

The duration of development in grasshoppers and crickets is dependent on temperature; larger species take some 40 to 70 days to reach maturity. In the temperate zone these insects usually live for two to three months thereafter and die in autumn. Their eggs generally last through the winter and hatch the following spring. The eggs of a few species, however, hatch in the fall, and these species overwinter as nymphs. The only species whose sequence of generations is wholly independent of the seasons is *Gryllus domesticus,* the cricket that lives in our houses. A seasonal interruption in generations occurs even in the tropics, because of the dry season there. Nevertheless, three to four generations are possible during favorable years in the tropics.

The nymphs have considerable capacity gradually to replace lost antennae and legs other than the jumping legs; the latter get broken off easily and often, yet are seldom or never regenerated. Parthenogenesis, or virgin reproduction, occurs rather rarely in grasshopper species, and in most of these species it is the exception; yet apparently it is the rule in some species, such as the European *Saga,* males of which never have been seen.

FORM AND COLOR

Grasshoppers and crickets have a wealth of different body forms that serve above all else for disguise. Like many walkingstick and leaf insects, they are deceptively similar to green or dry leaves, twigs, or bark. Species that live in the grass frequently are long and thin, and are marked with contrasting, lengthwise lines that obscure the contours of the body; often they have a long, pointed head, and even the antennae, held close together, imitate the tip of a blade of grass. Species that inhabit the bare ground have earthy colors and often have short, heavy bodies, frequently with a grainy surface.

Crickets and grasshoppers are relatively poor in surface sculpturing. Nevertheless one often sees comblike or warty outgrowths or spines; the latter may be so strong and numerous that they protect against enemy attacks. Also, certain desert crickets have peculiar, gigantic rags of skin on the front of the head.

The coloration of grasshoppers ranges chiefly from green to brown or gray, but also includes brilliant yellow, red in all shades, blue, and black; metallic colors are rare. Varicolored alarm costumes, conspicuous from afar, are worn by a few species, principally the sluggish ones that when threatened let blood seep out of the thorax or even squirt it from the coxae of the legs. This fluid is presumed to taste unpleasant to birds. Some other grasshoppers perspire a toxic foam. Usually, however, the defensive capabilities of grasshoppers go no further than spitting out harmless digestive juices, biting, or scratching with the sharp-spined tibiae of the hind legs. Some larger tropical species can kick backward and sideways so powerfully that they can tear a bloody gash in a person's hand. [15/20; 16/12; 17/24–27; 54/5, 6; 55/6; 57/1; 104–106]

ENEMIES

Danger surrounds the grasshopper or the cricket. Its chief enemies are birds, from little songbirds to birds of prey. One enemy, the stork, can eat as much as 4 pounds of grasshoppers a day. Many birds follow locust migrations and may nest in the areas that locusts invade. Countless mammals, reptiles, and spiders also destroy grasshoppers and crickets. To these enemies must be added predatory insects such as the digger wasps (*Sphex*), robber flies (asilids), praying mantids, and the many predatory species of their own kind. In some countries, human beings eat grasshoppers; when roasted, they are said to taste something like nuts.

Grasshopper eggs are eaten by certain beetle larvae of the families Meloidae (*Zonabris, Epicauta*) and Cleridae (*Trichodes*) and by larvae of many flies, such as bombyliids, muscids, sarcophagids, anthomyiids, chloropids; and they are parasitized by tiny wasps (scelionids). Also, many adult flies (tachinids, sarcophagids) fasten their eggs to grasshopper adults and nymphs, no matter whether these are resting, jumping, or flying. The hatching fly maggots bore into the host's body and batten on fat, muscle, and entrails.

Another enemy is the female of the red mite *Eutrombidium*. The female mites force their way into the subterranean egg chambers of grasshoppers, suck the eggs dry, achieve sexual maturity while so doing, and thereby attract males. Later, each female lays 300 to 700 eggs in a little hollow slightly below the surface of the ground. After hatching, the young attach themselves to grasshoppers in all stages of development, later let themselves fall again to earth in a full-grown but not yet sexually ripe condition (nymphal stage). These mites may destroy a third to almost half of the grasshopper eggs.

Finally, diseases also decimate these insects; whole swarms may perish of bacterial and fungal infections.

DISTRIBUTION

Grasshoppers and crickets are found throughout the world, except in polar regions; they are most numerous in warm countries. Most species, because they demand special environmental conditions, have small, often island-like areas of distribution. Many grasshoppers are glacial relics: they are native both to the cool northland and to mountain ranges much farther south.

Some crickets and grasshoppers live in caverns, and most of these are distinguished by extremely long antennae and legs, by little or no pigmentation (a few are brightly colored), and by degenerate eyes. Other specialists include little grasshoppers that build houses by rolling up leaves and fastening them with a solidifying secretion. Some tree crickets, only about a tenth of an inch long, live as unwelcome guests of ants. Finally, a few grasshopper species, usually in their nymphal stage, are mimics that resemble wasps, parasitic wasps, or ants.

EMBIIDS, OR WEBSPINNERS
ORDER EMBIODEA (OR EMBIOPTERA)

The webspinners are mostly about 0.2 inch long and seldom as much as 0.8 inch. Only a few more than 100 species are known, most of them tropical; less than 10 species extend into the southern United States. The webspinners are slender and usually dark brown, with a large head and a long, narrow thorax. Although the majority are wingless, the males of many species have four wings. Because these wings have few supporting veins, they lack rigidity and produce a weak, fluttery flight. The insects have chewing mouthparts and eat vegetable food.

The webspinners, also called embiids, have an ability unique in the world of insects: they can spin silken threads with their feet. The threads are formed from a secretion that comes out of a few tubular bristles and hardens immediately on contact with the air. With these threads, the insects build pipes or tunnels in which they can move forward or backward equally well. These webbed passageways occur under stones, leaves, bark, and other objects, where large assemblages of embiids often live. Even the nymphs take part in the construction of the webs, which serve for protection against predacious insects, for regulating humidity, and for a place where the eggs are laid.

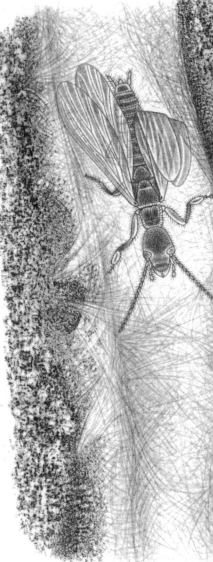

82/1
A pair of webspinners, the male above, in their silken tunnel (greatly enlarged).

82/2
Unique in being multiply creased in both the longitudinal and transverse directions, the earwig wing often can be spread only with the help of the legs (enlarged).

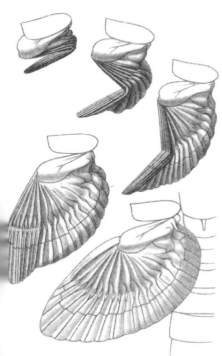

EARWIGS ORDER DERMAPTERA

The typical earwig is a long, thin insect with a pair of pincers at the end of its body. In several languages its common name incorporates the word for ear. One or more reasons may account for this. First, the extended wing of certain species of earwigs looks like an ear. Second, the earwig's pincers resemble instruments once used to pierce women's ears for the insertion of earrings. Third, there was once a widespread notion that earwigs crept into the ears of sleeping persons. This notion is true only in the sense that earwigs are active at night, like to crawl into crevices, and therefore may by chance get into an ear now and then.

The 1,000 species of earwigs have flattened longish bodies ranging from a few tenths of an inch to about 2 inches in length. The mostly brown body has a leathery look or a weak metallic luster.

The weapons of earwigs include stink glands on the abdomen and two hooklike appendages (cerci) at the end of the abdomen. The hooks vary greatly in shape and length, even within a single species, and are bigger and stronger in the males. When an earwig defends itself, it bends the abdomen, scorpion-like, so far forward over the back that the points of the hooks lie above the earwig's head. Certain species run around all the time with the abdomen curled up in this way. From such a stance, thrusts are made in a forward direction, often with a sidewise tearing motion, and can badly wound even spiders much stronger than the embattled earwig.

Of course, earwigs also are able to pinch with these tongs, even though this usually is hardly perceptible to a person. Furthermore, the earwigs may seize prey with the hooks and bring it to the mouth. In addition, these instruments have been known to help in opening and closing the insect's relatively large, fan-shaped hind wings; these are folded together in an extraordinarily artful and complicated manner so that they lie beneath the smaller, scale-like wing covers (elytra).

Many earwigs either are poor fliers or lack wings and cannot fly at all. With their equal-sized legs and their exceptionally motile body, however, these insects are very rapid runners. When fleeing along a surface above the ground, they let themselves drop swiftly and scurry to safety. The flat body usually is pressed close against the ground or into a narrow crevice.

Earwigs lead a thoroughly nocturnal existence, and spend the day in humid hiding places such as beneath rocks or bark, under or among leaves, or in flowers, seed clusters, or fruits. Usually they gather in groups, occasionally as many as several hundred beneath a single stone.

In earwigs the sense of touch plays a dominant role. The antennae continually feel out the surroundings and remain in contact with the ground or other support even when the insect is at rest. The head, which moves freely, has two flattish yet well-developed compound eyes and no dorsal ocelli (simple eyes). Like the head, the anterior part of the thorax (prothorax) is articulated freely to the body.

Earwigs have chewing mouthparts and are extraordinarily greedy. Their food consists of the tender parts of plants, of fruit, and of decaying vegetable and animal matter. Frequently these insects do damage in truck gardens or orchards, but also are useful in pollination and in destroying plantlice and fruit caterpillars. Most species eat all kinds of smaller insects, not excepting their own kin. The enemies of earwigs are insectivorous mammals, birds, lizards, insects, spiders, and centipedes.

Because they like warmth, earwigs are distributed mainly in the tropics and subtropics; yet, with the exception of the arctic and antarctic, they occur everywhere, even at snowline in the mountains, which is well above 6,000 feet altitude in the Alps. They are common in Europe, but scarce in America. Certain species live on the seashore, at times swimming in the water. A southeastern Asia species, *Arixenia esau,* lives on the throat of the naked bat *(Chiromeles torquatus)* and rears its young there. Species of *Hemimerus* dwell in the coat of African rats *(Cricetomys).* In accordance with their peculiar way of life, both *Arixenia* and *Hemimerus* produce living young rather than eggs and are strongly modified in structure, having simple paired antenna-like appendages (cerci) instead of hooks and having poorly developed eyes. [107/6, 7]

FAMILY LIFE

Earwigs are especially interesting to us because of their "family life," which apparently is based on their innate sociability. Beginning at mating time, earwigs display customs that seem rare among insects. In the temperate zone, pairing of males and females begins in crevices occupied by the whole community. Mating may occur at various times throughout the year, but often takes place in fall. With the onset of cold weather each female tries to withdraw from her male for the winter rest and uses her mouth to dig a hole in the ground. But she seldom gets rid of the male; in the spring, after the pair has overwintered together, they remain paired until the female lays her eggs, which takes two to four days. Then the female drives her partner out of the "house" and closes the entrance with dirt. With the mother instinct now awakened, the female grows aggressive and will attack anything in defense of her nest.

In the chamber the female piles the long, shiny eggs carefully in a round heap and stretches her head and forelegs over them. There usually are 40 to 55 eggs, but may be as few as 20 or as many as 80. She licks the eggs over and over again. Without such treatment they soon dry and decay. If the chamber proves too damp or too dry for the brood, or if there is any disturbance, she makes a new hole and carries the eggs one by one in her mouth into the hole. During the time it takes the eggs to hatch, usually two to eight weeks, depending on the temperature, the female earwig eats no food. The young hatch and molt at the same time. Each nymph, by means of an "egg tooth" on its head, bursts the eggshell.

A different egg-hatching pattern is displayed by *Prolabia arachidis,* the earwig that lives in greenhouses in Europe. The female lays her eggs one after the other just before they are ready to hatch; as each egg is laid, she sets the young nymph free by biting away the chorion (outer shell of the egg).

Except for their color, the newly hatched nymphs look much like their parents. In winged species, the nymphs are also distinguished by the absence of wings, which do not appear until the last nymphal stage.

At first the nymphs stay together under their mother's supervision; she washes the young by licking them and fetches back any that have run off. After the second molt, they begin to forage for food by themselves at night, always returning to the nest. Eventually, the whole company reassembles in the nest after a customary nocturnal search for food; the old female, having become steadily weaker, finally dies and is eaten by the nymphs. Details of the rearing procedure differ in other species. Nymphal development usually includes four or five molts and lasts five to six months; the mature insects live together another six to eight months.

The entire sequence of brood care is an automatic series of instinctive acts. If one takes the eggs away from a female and gives them back two to four days later, her instinct to care for the brood has disappeared and she unhesitatingly eats them. But if they are returned sooner, there ensues a gripping contest between her natural urges. She takes an egg in her mouth and remains motionless a long time. Suddenly she begins to lick the egg, perhaps letting it fall and taking another. Or she may begin to eat it. Usually, however, she continues to care for the brood even though her maternal instinct seems weakened, as shown by the fact that she no longer defends her brood so vehemently.

The strength of the normal defensive tendency of female earwigs is shown when several females, instead of digging individual holes, lay their eggs in a single hole that is already available. The strongest female does not rest until she has raked all the eggs together for herself alone and has driven the others away. [107/6, 7]

BOOKLICE, BARKLICE, AND DUSTLICE ORDER PSOCOPTERA

The more than 1,100 species of these delicate insects are distributed throughout the world. Most are only about a tenth of an inch in length, a few reaching a half inch. They have a somewhat louselike, compressed appearance and are usually seen only when we look for them. A few domestic species, sometimes called dustlice, attract our attention when they get into foodstuffs or damage carpeting, upholstery, or even wood. One of the commonest of these is the booklouse, *Liposcelis divinatorius.* But the great majority of these insects live in the open.

Many of these insects, known as barklice, gather together in colonies on the bark of trees as well as on all kinds of plants, where they feed on algae, fungi, and lichens. Their social tendency may go so far that a whole assemblage moves like a flock of sheep—the individual members moving simultaneously, with identical motions and in the same direction—to graze on a mat of mold or on a rust fungus. Such a company may be composed of several species.

Frequently barklice protect themselves with a common covering of spun silk, produced by their oral spinning glands. Even the young assist in the construction of this web. The silken net protects colonies that cling to the underside of a leaf from falling, but its greatest significance probably is as a

84/1
Mating activity in one species of barklice; above, the fore wing of another species (greatly enl.).

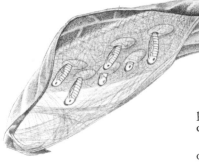

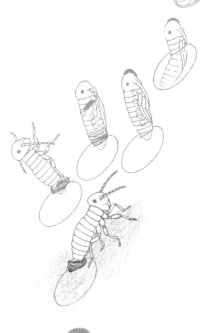

85/1
Barklouse embryos, whose mother has spun a safety net beneath them, hatching from the egg.

The hatching stages and a detail of the head to show the saw that the embryo uses as an eggburster (greatly enlarged).

85/2

A book scorpion with a captured dustlouse (greatly enlarged).

protection against too much moisture or dryness.

In the temperate zone the insects of this order live mainly on the edges of woods, where it is not too sunny, or in forests, particularly on conifers. A few species live in ants' nests, some in the combs of bees and wasps, and others in birds' nests. All are sluggish, fleeing from danger by leaping backward, but rarely taking to the air. Nevertheless, occasionally swarms are seen letting themselves be borne along by the wind, apparently in satisfaction of a nascent urge to migrate.

The rounded wings of these insects, laid rooflike over the abdomen, are distinctly handsome, because of the pattern of their venation and often because of their dark-colored design. Beneath the fore wings lie the much smaller hind wings, and in flight both are fastened together by an ingenious mechanism so that they form a single supporting surface. Frequently, however, wings are reduced in size, especially in females, and in a single species there may be both long- and short-winged individuals, the latter of which are apt to frequent the lower vegetation. Some species are wingless.

The inability of wingless and short-winged species to fly is accompanied by a reduction of the eyes. Normally there are two rather large, strongly vaulted compound eyes and three dorsal ocelli (simple eyes); but when the eyes are reduced, the dorsal ocelli usually are absent altogether, and the compound eyes may have regressed to the point where each is represented by a single facet (prosommatidium).

These insects have long antennae and highly specialized mouthparts used for chewing or rasping. They eat both vegetable and animal materials, and some engage in cannibalism. Usually their coloration is inconspicuous: greenish, yellowish, or from brown to nearly black; tropical species may have bright-colored, gleaming, metallic scales.

In the congress of the sexes, a variety of behavior is displayed. In courtship, for example, a male may dance about a female with his wings half-opened and with his face constantly turned toward her, buzzing from time to time, and butting her again and again with his head. Or, certain female dustlice may attract males by pounding whatever surface they are sitting on five or six times a second with a buttonlike or T-shaped callosity on the lower side of the rear end, the act perhaps lasting for as much as an hour

with only brief pauses. If the surface can vibrate, as when it happens to be of paper, the sound is audible to a person and resembles the ticking of a watch. Because superstition associated this ticking with death, and because the ticking was attributed, perhaps mistakenly, to the booklouse (*Liposcelis divinatorius*), this insect became known as the "deathwatch." (The name is shared by the anobiid beetle *Xestobium,* which makes a similar noise by banging its head against the walls of its burrow inside wood.) It is suspected that females of some other species can make music, for they have on their coxae what appears to be an instrument for sound production (organ of stridulation) in the form of rows of teeth and a resonant membrane.

The females glue their oval eggs to the substrate, both singly and in masses, often either covering them with a cement of secreted substance plus bits of dirt or of plants, or wrapping them in a web of silk. The embryos hatch with the help of a cephalic eggburster, a hard, often saw-toothed ridge that cuts or saws through the eggshell. A fantastic sight it is, when whole ranks of these creatures rise as though on command from the glistening white web that covers the eggs. With rear ends still held fast within, they tarry awhile like mummies, protruding stiffly upward, before they swallow air, burst their embryonic membranes, and with muscular contractions that travel backward in waves strip the membranes back completely into piles at the rear.

After a period of delay, during which the legs harden until they are able to grasp the supporting surface, the newborn insects run off and begin to eat. They differ little from the mature insects. Their wing rudiments first appear in the second instar, between the first and second molts. Usually there are six molts. Dorsal ocelli come out only after the last one, at which time the wings turn into transparent membranes. The entire course of development from egg to imago (mature adult) generally requires 25 to 27 days.

In the temperate zone there are from one to three generations a year depending on the species. As a rule, these insects pass the winter as eggs, but certain genera overwinter as nymphs, to whose covering of hairs bits of dirt and plants are stuck, forming a protective layer.

The most prominent enemies of the order Psocoptera are certain other insects, such as digger wasps (sphecids), ants, capsids, and assassin bugs (reduviids). A capsid sticks its proboscis through the covering web into an egg and sucks it dry. Psocopterans also are parasitized by tiny parasitic wasps (mymarids). In our houses, dustlice are exterminated by the book scorpions.

CHEWING LICE

ORDER MALLOPHAGA

Chewing lice are small, flattened insects related to booklice, barklice, and dustlice. They are whitish, yellowish, reddish, brown, or black, and are sometimes adorned with spotted designs or fine sculpturing. They are from about 0.02 inch to 0.4 inch long and have chewing mouthparts. Their eyes are either greatly reduced or completely lacking and none have wings.

The chewing lice live on the bodies of birds and mammals, from the hummingbird to the elephant, and eat feathers, hair, scales, and fatty matter from the sebaceous glands of the skin; occasionally a few species take blood from wounds or from the bases of young feathers. The individual genera and species are specialized to live on particular hosts; the more than 2,675 species described to date are spread over the entire world and are found on mammals and birds even in the polar zones. The majority occur on birds, in particular on birds of prey; the dependence of these insect species on certain kinds of animals is so complete that they cannot exist on other kinds. The presence of particular chewing lice on what appeared to be wholly unlike kinds of birds has repeatedly indicated that the bird hosts were, in reality, closely related. And today, when identical chewing lice occur on closely related yet different birds, we can conclude that in the course of evolution these insects have been modified almost not at all, or at least much less than their hosts.

Chewing lice dwell on different parts of their hosts—on mammals, especially on the neck, the nape, the bases of the horns, and the tail; and on birds, mainly beneath the wings and on the neck and head, particularly around the eyes. If two or more species occur on one host, they occupy distinct, separated regions. With free-living animals they seldom reach the status of a harassing infestation, but occasionally do so with domesticated species, particularly, of course, with neglected ones. The so-called "chicken louse" *(Menopon pallidum)*, which infests domestic fowl throughout the world, constantly demands control. Another worldwide pest is the cattle-biting louse *(Bovicola bovis)*.

Many species are of interest in studies of the physiology of nutrition because their digestion is carried out with the help of fungi or bacteria living within their bodies. These *symbionts,* as members of such an association are called, have amazing methods of getting into the eggs in the maternal body and thus being transmitted to the next generation.

The eggs, the maximum number of which may be about 100 per female, are glued to hairs or feathers on the insect's host. The eggs are marvelous works of art, with an unusual decoration of thin outgrowths that resemble delicate plant sprouts. The eggs have a steeple-like cap that is pushed off by the hatching young. The young look much like their elders and molt about three times in the course of growth. The entire period of development lasts three to four weeks. There seem to be scarcely any interruptions in the life cycle of Mallophaga, inasmuch as temperature and humidity relationships are kept constant by the body of the host. When the latter dies and grows cold, these lodgers soon perish, too. Only an especially lucky chance would permit them to shift to a new host, as they often do among living animals.

Enemies that have been seen are the lizards found in Mediterranean sea-gull colonies and among cormorants in the guano islands off Peru; these reptiles subsist on Mallophaga from the birds.

SUCKING LICE ORDER ANOPLURA

This ugly group of insects is in ill repute as a carrier of disease. Man and other mammals are the hosts and victims of these tiny bloodsuckers that measure a mere 0.08 inch to 0.2 inch long. All of the 250 known species live exclusively on warm blood and will starve to death without it in half a day to two or three days at most. Their wingless bodies are whitish, yellowish, or brownish in color. Their eyes are small, but in some species protrude considerably; other species lack eyes altogether. The feet have a single huge claw that can be flexed sideways; between it and an opposing thumblike projection, a hair of the host is clamped as in a vise. Lice cling so doggedly to hairs that they scarcely can be torn away.

Lice have an equally firm hold on life. Once attached to its host, a louse continues sucking even after one has cut the body away. The louse body itself can withstand a load of about 2 pounds. Besides these

86/1
A chicken louse (Mallophaga).

86/2
A pigeon louse (Mallophaga).

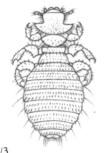

86/3
A guinea-pig louse (Mallophaga).

87/1
In hatching, the chicken louse embryo lifts the bulb-shaped cover from the egg. The bristly rings around the egg, each consisting of bristles of a different shape, hinder it from falling from the host's plumage (greatly enlarged).

things, lice can survive for one to two days under water by closing off their respiratory openings (stigmata) with a special apparatus that differs from genus to genus. Lice that are parasitic on seals take along with them under water, as a reserve for breathing, a layer of air held between their modified scales or hairs.

Specific kinds of lice usually live on specific kinds of mammals. The presence of the same genera of lice on both man and ape is evidence of the family relationship of the two. The size of lice does not depend on the size of the animal they live on; those peculiar to the elephant, for example, are no larger than those of other species.

Lice may wander from one host to another, guided by radiant heat and odor, when the hosts come within 2 inches to a foot of each other. They are transferred between humans on clothes and other objects. But the wind and even flies can provide transportation. Between animals, the so-called louseflies serve this purpose; these flies are so named not because they serve as transports, but because they themselves have a louselike shape and way of living.

Lice attempt to climb at once onto any object that comes near. As a result, they have a good chance of getting back on the host if they have fallen off—for instance, in the animal's nest. Lice are most active at a temperature of 30° C to 35° C (86° F to 95° F), but even at 20° C (68° F) they run at the rate of about 10 inches per minute.

Two louse species live on man: the crab louse *(Phthirus pubis)* and two races of the species *Pediculus humanus*. The crab louse lives particularly in the pubic hair of the body, the head louse *(Pediculus humanus capitis)* in the hair of the head, and the body louse *(Pediculus humanus corporis)* on the rest of the body and in the eyebrows and beard. The body lice lay up to 300 eggs in about 40 days, preferably on clothing. The young, shaped like the parents, hatch in 6 to 15 days, depending on the temperature, and begin to suck blood at once if they are in a position to do so. They molt three times and mature in about two weeks. Thus the whole duration of development from egg to maturity takes approximately a month, and the adults may live about three weeks thereafter. On persons destitute from war or other causes, lice may increase to enormous numbers; as many as 16,000 have been found on an individual. Among some primitive tribes the presence of lice is suffered for religious or other cultural reasons.

The louse's proboscis, when at rest, is retracted into the head. When used for biting, it is extended and bored deep into the skin, while the louse, often clinging to a hair, stands on its lowered head. A secretion injected into the wound causes inflammation around the puncture. Yet, barring an extremely heavy louse infestation, this inflammation would be relatively harmless, were there not frequently dangerous microbes in the gut of these insects.

Particularly as a consequence of squashing and grinding up the lice by scratching, a person may inoculate himself with these disease agents. They are the primary cause of typhus fever, of relapsing fever, and of trench fever, which often enough are fatal. The great casualties of Napoleon's armies in Russia in 1812 are attributable to a great extent to an epidemic of typhus fever. And without our modern agents of chemical control the number of victims during World War II might well have been millions higher. Even today the possibility of new outbreaks of such epidemics of louse-borne fever persists in many places in the world. In addition, the bacilli of bubonic plague and of typhoid fever occur in the digestive tract of lice, which also are able to transmit skin diseases.

Unpleasant though they are, lice make useful objects of study and provide insight into stirring miracles of nature. Especially interesting is the relationship between lice and the bacteria that live in them as symbionts. The lice provide the bacteria with a place to live, and the bacteria, in turn, are thought to assist the louse in its digestion. There are different bacteria in almost every species of louse. When eggs form in the female louse, bacterial symbionts living in her body move into the eggs; after an egg has been laid, the symbionts migrate into the body of the developing embryo.

Fascinating also are the arrangements and methods employed by lice with their eggs and embryos. The hard, pressure-resistant egg (popularly called a "nit") is attached with a water-insoluble blob of cement to a hair in such a way that the embryo within lies with its underside turned toward the support. In the eggs of most species, the eggcap has canals and air chambers for circulating air. The hatching embryo, using the egg tooth on its head, first cuts an opening in this cap and then swallows large amounts of air as well as the fluid egg contents, a part of which it excretes rearward. In this way the embryo, simultaneously increasing rapidly in volume, is forced upward against the eggcap, lifting

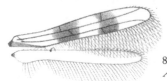

88/1

A pair of thysanopteran (thrips) wings (greatly enlarged).

it off; thereupon the young louse strips off the embryonic membranes and climbs out.

The Anoplura are classified by some authorities as a suborder of the Mallophaga (chewing lice). At all events the highly specialized elephant louse, *Haematomyzus elephantis* (Haematomyzidae), occupies a special transitional position. [107/1–5]

THRIPS   ORDER THYSANOPTERA

The sultry prelude to a summer thunderstorm exerts an almost paralyzing depression on man, but makes insects livelier. If we happen to walk near cultivated grain fields on such a day, we may be forced to beat a sudden and rapid retreat by tiny winged pests. Rising from the fields in heavy swarms, these insects descend on us, crawling over our face and into our eyes and ears. Although the insects do not bite, our skin reddens and itches almost unbearably.

These "thunderstorm flies" are known as thrips. In some places they are called "bladder-footed insects," for their feet, instead of ending with claws and a pulvillus, terminate in retractable bladderlike vessels that permit the insects to cling to smooth surfaces. It is these vessels that cause the torturing irritation of our skin.

Thrips are slender, flattened, dark-colored insects, usually from 0.02 to 0.1 inch in length and rarely 0.16 to 0.2 inch long, though some exceptional tropical species measure as much as 0.4 inch. Thrips are plant feeders. They have peculiar, specialized, piercing-sucking mouthparts, so shaped that the lower part of the face has a strikingly unequal, asymmetrical construction, a most uncommon feature among insects.

All over the world thrips are dreaded as pests of all sorts of cultivated plants, such as flowers, vegetables, fruit, grains, cotton, flax, and tobacco. Some are adapted to one or a few plant species, but others attack almost everything. An especially versatile harmful species, *Thrips tabaci,* attacks cabbage, tobacco, onions, and many other plants.

One genus may cement great masses of eggs to bark or a similar surface, whereas another inserts eggs into plant tissues by means of a piercing ovipositor. A female is able to produce as many as 200 eggs, and if only half of them develop, the first-generation offspring will number 100, the second, 10,000; and three to four generations a year are possible! The increase in population, then, is enormous and extremely rapid, and with many species is accomplished by parthenogenesis—reproduction without males.

Not all of the 3,170 species of thrips distributed over the world, however, are harmful to man; a great many live only in wild flowers and other uncultivated plants, and others suck on fungi, sponges, lichens, and algae that grow on bark or beneath fallen leaves. Moreover certain thrips are predatory and suck out the juices of other thrips and plantlice. Some species engender plant galls.

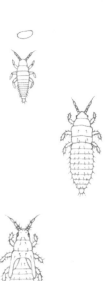

Thrips have wings that are as peculiar as they are characteristic. They are long, narrow, membranous flaps with only a few veins and with long fringes of hairs on the margins; the fringes probably are important in enlarging the effective wing surface. The name Thysanoptera means "fringe-winged," yet many species have either no wings or greatly reduced ones. Frequently there are long- and short-winged individuals in one and the same species. Wingless specimens lack dorsal ocelli, or simple eyes, but the two compound eyes always are well-developed. These are very active insects, some of which are able to jump by snapping the abdomen upward, as do, for example, earwigs and certain short-winged beetles (staphylinids).

The nymphs are similar to the full-grown insects, but often have a livelier coloration (in certain species they even are red). Also, they lack wings, which sets them apart from the adults of winged species. They become more or less mature as early as the second instar, the stage following the first molt. Subsequent instars are most peculiar. The third is a prepupa with a moving body and legs; the females of some species mate with the males during this stage. After the ensuing molt there appears a similarly constructed, likewise motile pupa, which in the winged species has the rudiments of wings; following this, some species have a second pupal stage.

Both prepupae and pupae live in hiding places or in the ground, often withdrawn into a cocoon they have spun, without feeding further. In the temperate zone certain species (often only the females) overwinter as mature adults, others as nymphs or as pupae. Frequently the young stages of thrips are called larvae rather than nymphs; their metamorphosis in some respects is intermediate between the typical incomplete type (in which the young are called nymphs) and the complete type (in which the young are called larvae).

Because thrips have been carried all over the world by man, North America and

88/2

The growth stages of a greenhouse thrips; namely, egg and young nymph, older nymph, prepupa, pupa, and mature insect (imago).

The abdominal musical instrument of a cicada, viewed from below with one side exposed. The large integumental covers (opercula) do not lie snugly against the body, in order to let sound waves pass. The delicate white drumhead (tympanum) bears a thin, sclerotized plate that is connected to the organ of hearing, which is contained in a cavity of the external body wall. Below the drumhead is the columnar muscle that vibrates the sound-producing plate. The latter, here only partly visible from the side, is strengthened by ridges and is protected against damage from without by a clamshell-shaped cover.

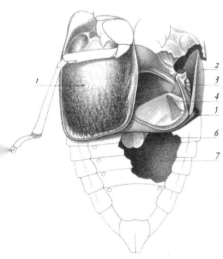

1 *Integumental cover*
2 *Cover of the sound-producing plate*
3 *Sound-producing plate*
4 *Tympanum*
5 *Auditory cavity*
6 *Muscle of the sound-producing plate*
7 *Air cavity*

Europe, as well as other continents, have many species in common. The most important enemies of thrips are predatory insects, among which are little digger wasps *(Spilomena)* that fill their cells with nymphal thrips as food for the brood. Particularly significant are little parasitic chalcid wasps (genus *Thripoctenus*); mites, too, are enemies of thrips. Finally songbirds, especially titmice, decimate thrips that live on bark.

CICADAS, LEAFHOPPERS, WHITEFLIES, APHIDS, SCALE INSECTS, AND OTHERS
ORDER HOMOPTERA

These insects are a large and varied group. About 32,000 species have been described, and they range in size from minute individuals to some more than 2 inches long. They either have two pairs of wings or are wingless. An exception is the male scale insect, which has only one pair of wings. At rest, the wings are held so that they meet over the body and slope outwardly, like the roof of a house.

Though different in many respects, all insects of the order suck on plant tissue. Many excrete a sweet substance called honeydew. The manufacture and excretion of pure wax is another special peculiarity of the order Homoptera.

Many of these insects have an enormous procreative capacity. Their metamorphosis is rather simple. The young hatch without a special egg tooth, and no sooner do they strip off their embryonic integuments than they start to suck the juices of plants. These insects may be subdivided into several groups including: cicadines, comprising cicadas, spittlebugs, planthoppers, treehoppers, and leafhoppers; jumping plantlice; whiteflies; aphids; and scale insects.

SINGING CICADAS

Hour after hour, for days at a time, we can drive through the countryside of the warmer regions without getting beyond earshot of loud-singing insects that are hidden from our eyes in the trees and shrubs. These insects devote their lives to sucking sap and singing, both of which they do at the same time; they are at it from morning to night, constantly following the advancing sun as it shifts from one side of the tree to the other. These insects are members of the Cicadidae, the only cicadine family that produces audible

notes. They are commonly called cicadas; about 1,500 species are known.

People speak of "singing" cicadas, but these insects—especially the large species found in the tropics—produce the uproar of a carnival. Yonder it seems as though an empty tin can were being thumped with devouring zeal; off there it sounds as if a frantically driven saw had struck naked iron; and far away a flute trills shrilly. The way such tones swell in crescendo, shrieking louder and louder until they are roaring, and then suddenly fall, dying away with despairing groans and faint organ sounds, is downright amusing. But in all truth this noise, which a nature lover finds interesting or even agreeable, can drive a sensitive person, or one trying to think, out of his mind.

The cicada's noise-making instrument is the most highly perfected among insects—a mechanism synthesized from an incredible wealth of parts. It plays so dominant a role in the cicada's life that the most vital organs, such as the digestive apparatus, are compressed into very little space in the body.

The males of the singing cicadas do not have "bowed instruments" like crickets and grasshoppers, but have two small drums, each lying in a cavity on the side of the fore part of the abdomen. Females lack such drums and are silent. The shell-shaped drumhead, strengthened with curved braces, is made to vibrate not by means of blows, but rather by a rapid succession of brief tugs from within. These tugs are produced by a powerful muscle that is inserted on the expanded, plate-shaped foot of a small column or tendon that is fused to the lower surface of the membranous drum.

Directly adjacent to these drums, somewhat more toward the underside and further forward on the abdomen, there is on each side a larger cavity, the hind wall of which is a delicate, tightly drawn membrane that usually shimmers in all colors of the rainbow; apparently this is a resonating membrane, although the structure (called a tympanic organ) also has been described as an organ of hearing. These two cavities are not open to the exterior; two gigantic shield- or shell-shaped thoracic sclerites, widening toward the rear, lie over them. The organs can be seen only to the extent one sees the gills of a fish beneath the gill covers, or cannot be seen at all unless one presses the cicada's abdomen upward a little. By means of rhythmical abdominal movements of this kind, which open the orifices of the cavities wider or close them more tightly, these insects modulate the quality and intensity of their tone.

Of similar influence are the smaller covers that partly close off the cavities containing the drum membranes; from species to species their effect varies depending on their size. In some species they are totally absent or are replaced by narrow shelves, which give rise to a different sound effect. As a resonating apparatus for this whole extravagant sound-producing mechanism, there is inside the body an air sac so excessively enlarged that it almost fills the abdomen.

Each species of cicada has more or less distinctively shaped musical instruments and hence produces different tones. Moreover, each possesses a different rhythm. In short, every species makes its own peculiar noise, by which it can be recognized from afar.

What is the function of the cicada's song? The prevalent view is that the music of the males brings individuals together and attracts the silent females to the males. A tympanum inside the sound-producing organ of the male has been described by recent investigators as auditory. It is put out of action by a special muscle when the insect itself is singing. No hearing organ has been identified in females. It is certain, however, that females can hear, for they come considerable distances in the dark to sounding males.

Few studies and experiments pertinent to these matters have been carried out in the outdoors. There are reasons for this. Though these insects are common in warm countries and can be heard close at hand, they are shy and hard to see, partly on account of their barklike coloration and partly because they catch sight of us at a distance and flatten themselves as closely as they can against the opposite side of a twig or treetrunk. And it is next to impossible to catch a cicada, for their long, strong wings carry them rapidly away and out of sight. But if one of them happens to get into the insect net, it immediately announces its misfortune with a continuous damped piping, something like a spinning motor; if the cicada is held between one's fingers, it keeps making the noise until it is released. Especially at such a time, one scarcely can avoid a feeling of great sympathy for the comical originality of this otherwise defenseless creature. [108]

The head of a typical cicada is unusual in that the parietal and occipital areas (regions of the temples and of the back part of the head) are almost entirely lacking. At the two upper angles of the usually three-cornered face, the egg-shaped compound eyes protrude; these are not particularly large, but are distinguished for their great visual capacity. Between them

there gleam, often like tiny rubies, two or three simple eyes, the dorsal ocelli. The two antennae are small and whiplike, as fine as hairs. The large facial plate (clypeus) is bowed out, as if inflated, and is strengthened by cross braces. At its lower end is the strong sucking apparatus.

The sucking apparatus enables cicadas to tap into branches and treetrunks, so that even in the hottest and driest weather they can refresh themselves with the inexhaustible sap. As a cicada sucks, so much sap runs out that the vicinity of the source soon gets damp. Thirsty ants appear and, if necessary, even crowd beneath the cicada, which continues to suck unflinchingly. Larger uninvited guests also gather—wasps, flies, beetles—until the bustle becomes too great and the drinking bout is terminated brusquely by its host. The cicada withdraws its beak and flies away, and all too soon the rest of the assemblage has licked up the last drop from the spring that has now run dry.

HONEYDEW AND CUCKOO SPIT

Many cicadines discharge the residues of digestion from the anus in the form of honeydew, water that usually contains sugar and protein. The quantity excreted often is so great that a small bush or tree occupied by these insects, many of which are tiny, may drip night and day with a sticky fluid. This fluid is consumed by ants and many other insects.

The nymphs of many spittlebugs (Cercopidae) do not squirt their excretions away, but allow them to flow out slowly, wetting both the body and the supporting surface. The fluid of these insects contains an enzyme that can break down a wax that is produced simultaneously by the anal glands. There results a chemical product that is almost unique in the animal world, namely a kind of liquid waxy soap, such as is produced elsewhere only by caterpillars of the wax moth (*Galleria*).

When enough of this soap has accumulated beneath the steadily sucking nymph, the nymph dips the tip of its abdomen into the soap and then out again, meanwhile letting a little air escape and thus forming a bubble of foam. As the process is repeated, another bubble appears about every second. Soon the little insect is completely covered, and all we can see is one of those familiar masses of white foam, so-called "cuckoo spit," that are so conspicuous where they hang on the vegetation.

90/1

Wax excretion is a peculiarity of numerous plant-sucking insects, many species of which thereby modify their outward appearance in a typical manner. This planthopper, from the family of the lantern flies, is wearing wax in the form of an extravagant tail. (→ 19/15)

To breathe inside the blob of foam, the insect raises its hind end to the surface again and again, or sticks the tip of its abdomen into one of the larger bubbles. From here, air is conducted to the spiracles on each side by way of a divided thoracic groove, which is formed by specially modified segmental plates on the underside. Penetration of foam into the spiracles is prevented by special devices that function in conjunction with a nonwettable secretion.

The biological significance of "cuckoo spit" is suspected to be a protective action against enemies and desiccation. As for the former, the degree of protection is limited, for damsel bugs (nabids) suck out the juices of the nymphs through the foam, and digger wasps *(Gorytes)* pull the nymphs out altogether. And as far as a means of defense against drying out is concerned, one may object that at all times the insect is connected directly with the flowing stream of sap in the plant; and further that nymphs of some other species, which suck on subterranean roots where loss of moisture is no problem, also produce this foam. Peculiarly enough, the nymphs of certain genera that range from South Asia as far as Australia build little tubes of lime that stick out from the plants or from the twigs and that serve as cups to contain the foam. Sitting head foremost at the bottom of the tube, the nymph sucks on the plant. [107/9; 109/1-5]

WAX MAKING

Cicadines elaborate wax as a metabolic product. It coats various parts of the body with white powder and often even covers the wings. Or, depending on the species, the wax is shaped into distinct structures by an array of complexly formed molds at the ducts of the wax glands, which frequently open into a special glandular sclerite that resembles a dinner plate. The wax forms flakes, leaflets, disks, rods, ribbons, and simple filamentous or spirally wound strings; these are gathered into clusters, sheaves, or trailing tails. Particularly striking are the wax shapes made by the group called fulgorid planthoppers (Fulgoridae). Their bodies, bizarre in themselves, are made even more so by fountains and trains of wax.

The white or yellowish wax falls off the insect's body easily, and the discarded wax of certain cicadines serves as food for little caterpillars of the moth family Epipyropidae. The wax is thought to afford the cicadine protection against enemies, desiccation, or too much moisture. In any event, the sub-

terranean nymphs of the genus *Oliarius* leave portions of their huge wax trains sticking to the soil as a watertight carpet for the dwelling place. The females of certain species excrete wax from pores on the ovipositors when these are inserted into plants; the wax forms a water-repellent sheath surrounding the puncture. Other females throw a protective blanket of wax from the anus over their eggs. [107/8]

SYMBIONTS

Inside the cicadine body is a fabulous world of microscopic life. Bacteria, yeasts, and ascomycetes (fungi) either live freely throughout the body or are gathered together in special organs (mycetomes). About 40 different forms of such organs are known. There are nodules, clusters, spheres, spindles, sacs, and lobes of all possible varieties. Often, richly branching air tubes (tracheae) from the insect ramify through them and supply them with oxygen. Since these microscopic organisms are so well provided for in the insect's body, they must be of great benefit to the insect. It is suspected that they help the insect digest its food, but their role has not yet been completely clarified.

Up to four different species of these symbionts usually live in a single cicadine. Many of these organisms have two forms—a resting form and a migrant form—and can change from one to the other. At certain times the wandering forms in the female body move into the eggs through a special area of the egg membrane that permits their entry, and either gather in the lower part of the egg or are taken up and enclosed in the yolk. In this process the various species of symbionts are intermingled; not until later, after the egg has been laid and the embryo is developing, does each species migrate into the particular organ prepared for it in the embryonic body. Volumes could be written about the miraculous nature of these symbionts, about their forms, their ways of life, and their interrelationships.

BIZARRE SHAPES

We are far from exhausting all the unusual features that cicadines display. Their body forms often provide a glimpse of the bizarre carried to the point of incomprehensibility. The jutting forehead of certain species of planthoppers, for example, reminds one of structures found on the towers of gothic cathedrals; the inflated forehead of other species looks like the head of a monstrous crocodile.

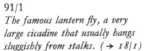

91/1

The famous lantern fly, a very large cicadine that usually hangs sluggishly from stalks. (→ 18/1)

Planthoppers probably number between 5,000 and 10,000 species. Some fulgorid planthoppers have long been called lantern-flies, but they give no light. The mistaken idea that some are luminous goes back to Maria Sibylla Merian, the famous seventeenth-century painter of insects. She received from natives in Sumatra a box of cicadines, and later depicted them in a colored copper-plate etching. One night when the artist opened the lid of the box, some "luminescent" planthoppers flew out. Her etching gives a clue as to what made these insects luminous. It shows a singing cicada with a planthopper's head. This indicates that the box contained not only live cicadines but also fragments of dead ones, and that she reassembled these pieces incorrectly. Now, in the tropics, luminous bacteria settle on dead and decaying substances. Apparently there were luminous bacteria on the pieces of dead insects in the box, and in the narrow confines of this prison some luminous bacteria also got stuck to living specimens and made them shine, too. [18/1; 110/1-4]

Another group of cicadines with grotesque shapes, in addition to the planthoppers, is the treehoppers (Membracidae). In fact, their bodies probably exemplify the apex of eccentricity in the insect empire. Like most other small insects of this order, the treehoppers are sought out by ants for the sake of their sugary excrement. They would be quite similar to their relatives if it were not for a single part of the body, namely the first thoracic segment (prothorax). Depending on the kind of treehopper, this segment looks as though it had been stretched vertically, expanded, lengthened, arched backward and often divided in two, inflated, pressed flat, or wrought like iron and often chiseled or hammered out. These structural extravaganzas are so large compared to the rest of the body that the normal body shape has been wholly lost. The illustrations depict a few of the more than 2,500 described types. Most are tropical, and in South America they reach riotous peaks of profusion. [109/10-22]

In spite of its bizarre shape, a treehopper is well able to run, jump, and fly. Seeing such an edifice flitting right-side up and in equilibrium through the air is enough to fill anyone with amazement and disbelief. An effort has been made to explain these fantasies of form as protective adaptation—more specifically, mimesis—since they appear to imitate acacia thorns, bits of wood, and other objects. But such interpretations often are unlikely, because these insects frequently sit on twigs to which their unusual shape is unsuited.

COLOR AND CAMOUFLAGE

The coloration of the cicadines generally is focused on disguise; green, yellow, brown, and gray are common colors, but some cicadines have bright patterns. In particular, many fulgorid planthoppers have brilliant contrasting colors and, like many butterflies, may even possess eyespots on their big, broad hind wings.

Still more like butterflies and moths are the flatid planthoppers (Flatidae), whose wings are huge in relation to their small body. Thanks to bark-colored fore wings, some nestle invisibly, like flat disks, against the treetrunks; others cling to a stalk like flowers, with their strikingly marked wings raised like a nearly vertical roof. As a result of their broad wings and puny musculature, their flight is more of a fluttering than a whirring, as in other cicadines.

Many of the more than 5,000 species of tiny leafhoppers (Cicadellidae) have brilliant, showy colors with fascinating designs. This is particularly so among members of the subfamily Cicadellinae. With their streamlined shapes and their long, slender, appressed wings, they are extraordinarily elegant spectacles. Certain tropical, heavier-bodied species of such leafhoppers may be seen sitting on leaves, erect and with outspread wings, like fat little elves clad in butterflies' dress.

Even some of the big singing cicadas, the largest of which attain a body length of about 3 inches and a wing span of 7.5 inches, are brightly colored; their wings usually are a dark, translucent green, though they may range in color to satiny black. The wings of most singing cicadas, however, are transparent membranes, glistening more or less with the colors of the rainbow, and the wings of all species are rather regularly creased with crosswise wrinkles. Usually they are adorned with a few dark spots along the veins, more rarely they are cloaked with elegant shaded designs, and at times the front half may bear a feltwork of hairs that glistens like silk.

Many of the 3,000 described species of spittlebugs (Cercopidae), seldom as much as 0.6 inch long, have harder, leathery fore wings and also are reminiscent of beetles because of their short, broad form and frequently variegated coloration—red or yellow, combined with black. [108-109; 110/8, 14-17]

FLIERS AND JUMPERS

Resting cicadines carry their wings in a retracted, rooflike position; many fasten the wings firmly in this attitude by clamping the

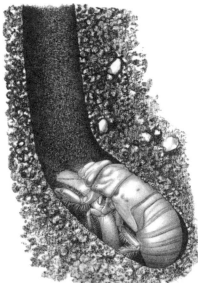

93/1
The last nymphal stage of a cicada, sucking on a root in its tunnel deep in the ground; its proboscis can be seen between the legs.

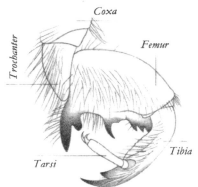

Coxa
Trochanter
Femur
Tibia
Tarsi

The left foreleg, modified as a digging implement.

Schema of a normal insect leg in the same position.

margin of the fore wing into a groove between the thoracic back plates. Some small species have shortened wings or no hind wings at all.

Generally, cicadines are excellent fliers; their rate of wingbeat may be as high as 120 per second. In flight the fore wing and the much smaller hind wing of the same side are united: the down-folded posterior margin of the fore wing fits into the up-turned margin of the hind wing or is gripped by little hooks on the latter.

Cicadines also are fabulous jumpers; mostly they leap with help from the wings, and respond with such alacrity that they evade a threatening danger in the last fraction of a second.

The hind pair of legs do not function as jumping legs in the cicadines, as they do in the grasshoppers (which have exceptionally well-developed femora), for in the cicadines the muscles used in jumping are located within the thorax. The jumping legs are effective because they are particularly long and have a spiny armature that provides the firm support needed for an effective takeoff. Frequently the hind legs bear combs of bristles that are used in distributing over the body the wax produced by the insect.

REPRODUCTION

Theoretically, disregarding nature's checks and balances, a single cicadine female could have about 500 million descendants in a year. When the young insects emerge en masse from the eggs, many species indeed do great damage in fields of corn, rice, beets, sugarcane, and other crops, as well as to fruit trees, roses, and other cultivated plants. The damage is caused by consumption of an excessive amount of sap, by mechanical injuries brought about by the sucking proboscis or by the piercing ovipositor, and by transmission of plant diseases. Certain species cement their longish, oval eggs to twigs, enclosing the eggs in a mass of secretion, and a few others drop the eggs to the ground. But by far the majority bury them in plant tissue, frequently in woody twigs and sometimes several of them in a given region, with the aid of a long, sharp ovipositor or of a short double saw at the tip of the abdomen.

A charming preliminary courtship is displayed by the leafhopper *Cicadula*. On a hanging leaf are a male and a female, one on the front surface, the other on the back. Probably each can perceive only the shadow of the other as the light shines through. Now and again, one moves a bit to one side, and the

one on the opposite surface follows the motion of the other as though magnetized. This game continues back and forth for a time, until finally the two arrange matters in such a way that they run into one another over the edge of the leaf.

METAMORPHOSIS

Cicadines produce from one to several generations a year. The young insects, on hatching from the eggs, begin their development. Usually there are five molts—in the singing cicadas, six. Often one may see all the stages of development assembled on a single food plant. The rudimentary wings and jumping legs grow longer at every molt. Musical instruments are still lacking, but in other respects the nymphs of most species differ significantly from the mature insects neither in appearance nor in their way of living.

There are exceptions. For example, the nymphs of the treehoppers are shaped like cockscombs and often have long dorsal bristles; not until their final molt do they undergo the gigantic modifications of the prothorax and the full extension of the wings that mark them as adults. Many planthopper nymphs stand out from the mature insects because of their especially large wax glands. And particular differences are shown by the subterranean nymphs that suck on roots, above all by the nymphs of the singing cicadas. [99/5]

The forelegs of the cicada nymphs have been modified into extraordinarily strong and effective tools for digging, and the way of life of the nymphs below ground naturally is quite different from that of mature cicadas. With some 30 to 40 incisions, the cicada female sinks her approximately 300 to 400 eggs into erect, dry twigs. In the temperate zone the young hatch in autumn, drop to earth, and bury themselves. They remain quiescent through the winter and begin to suck on roots in the spring. For two to four years, these pale, clumsy nymphs dig their way from root to root below ground.

Great fame has accrued to the "17-year locust" of North America, also known as the periodical cicada, which vegetates underground for 17 years (some closely related species do so for 13 years). Although at the end it lives for only a few weeks as a noise-making and egg-laying cicada, its underground period makes it by far the longest-lived insect in the world.

Before setting out for their transformation into winged insects, the nymphs of the singing cicadas rest for some time, maybe for a week or two, in the ground. In preparation for their resurrection they construct, even in the hardest soil, a vertical shaft about 16 inches long almost to the surface; curiously, many individual 17-year locusts extend the shaft above the ground, in the form of a chimney. The walls of this shaft are hardened as if with mortar. One wonders how the soil removed from this large passageway has been made to disappear without a trace, and where in the earth, dry as dust, so much water for making this mortar might have come from.

The solution of these riddles is the little piece of root evident at the bottom of the shaft. Again and again the nymph has filled up on the sap and then excreted the fluid through its digestive tract, while with its body it compressed into the walls the loose soil it had clawed free. When the forelegs, which function as shovels, get dirty, they are rubbed clean against the rough, bristly facial shield (clypeus).

Now, the nymph rests in its tunnel, climbing up frequently and with its delicate senses taking stock of the weather through the thin layer of soil that has been left as a closure. If the weather meets the requirements the nymph climbs out of the ground, crawls upward some distance on a plant, and bursts its skin. Clinging to the plant, the cicada emerges and expands its wings. Under appropriate meteorological conditions there frequently is a mass emergence.

ENEMIES

In addition to birds, other enemies of cicadines include small mammals, reptiles, spiders, and predatory insects. Large long-horned grasshoppers, for instance, attack and eat the resting cicadas at night in the trees. Specialized cicada-killers include certain digger wasps (sphecids), such as *Sphecius, Stizus, Gorytes,* and *Mimesa.* Numerous tiny parasitic wasps also prey on cicadas and other cicadines. Thus, the larvae of dryinid wasps first cling to cicadines, sucking their juices, and later devour them; also, cicada eggs are stung by chalcidids and proctotrupids. Further, the larvae of certain big-headed flies (Pipunculidae) are parasites that hollow out the cicadine adults. Many of the true bugs likewise suck the cicadines and their nymphs dry, and in fact these natural enemies already have been employed successfully in control operations. Often, too, the cicadines fall victim to various fungal diseases. And in Southeast Asia these insects (and certain others) are even eaten by the natives, or are sometimes used medicin-

ally. The wax of planthoppers is worked into candles.

JUMPING PLANTLICE

The jumping plantlice (Psyllina) are at most about 0.2 inch long. When fully developed, they resemble the cicadines in appearance and mode of life, but differ from them especially in having longer, more movable antennae, which have more subsegments. Nymphs of jumping plantlice, on the other hand, are very different from cicadine nymphs because of their almost sessile way of living and their broad, flat, louselike body with its short, thick, clasping legs. Also, their sucking beak is about as long as the entire body and looks as though it were held in a great loop beneath the head. That the full length of the proboscis, nevertheless, can be inserted into plant tissue is feasible because of special muscles and a clamping device that, working together, give the elastic sheath the tension required for exerting the needed pressure on the points of the stylets.

Mature jumping plantlice, which generally consume much less food, have a proboscis that is not so long relative to the body; still, when at rest, this beak has to be kept bent backward. In the adults the loop is about at the middle of the proboscis and does not lie free, as it does in the nymphs, but is enclosed in a cavity that extends back into the body. We find similar arrangements in various parasitic wasps and gall wasps, but in them it is the ovipositor that is concerned.

The jumping plantlice have a great reproductive capacity, and some of the more than 1,000 described species are harmful, especially to fruit trees; in part they have been spread from continent to continent by man himself. Frequently they suck on buds and young leaves, and in doing so certain species cause galls, tumors, and malformations. Because jumping plantlice transmit virus diseases, a relatively small number of these insects may destroy whole fields of such crops as potatoes. Additionally, plants often are damaged if they are wet too heavily by the sticky, sugary excreta, called the honeydew, of the jumping plantlice.

The female insect deposits its longish eggs on a thin, frequently rather tall pedestal, the foot of which is anchored in plant tissue. The embryo uses a sharp thorn on its head to open the egg membranes and simultaneously begins with peristaltic, wavelike movements to strip off its embryonic integument toward the rear. During this process, the thorn on the cast skin slits the egg open still further length-

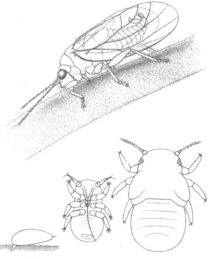

94/1
A jumping plantlouse that feeds on apple leaves. Above is a male; below, the egg, fastened on a stalk, and a young nymph in the second instar (with sucking proboscis extended), as well as an older nymph in the fourth instar (i.e., after the third molt) (greatly enlarged).

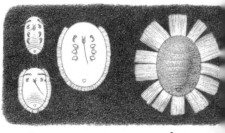

2   3

94/2–5
Whiteflies. (2) Aleurodes young in instars one to three (seen from below, with the sucking proboscis protruding from the mouth); in the second instar middle legs and hind legs are lacking, and forelegs are reduced to clasping appendages; and in the third instar the similarly modified antennae assume this function, whereas only the coxae (segments nearest the body) of the legs are present. (3) Asterochiton nymph in the fourth instar (seen from above). Wax deposits in the form of white or transparent rodlets produce a marginal ridge whose thickness or shape varies with the species. (4–5) A whitefly emerging from the fourth nymphal stage, and another ovipositing.

wise, and the active emerging nymph starts on its hunt for tender sprouts.

After the second molt, the nymphs get their louselike shape and clasping legs, and thenceforth stay in one spot as long as they can, using their long proboscis to suck plant tissue in the entire circumference around them. Certain species excrete from glands along the sides of the body a dense garland of waxen rodlets, which surrounds them like a hedge and gives them a water-repellent attachment to the supporting surface. Many other jumping plantlice coat their entire abdomen with wax and thus prevent the body from being wet by their own excreta.

Not until the fifth and final molt do the nymphs get normal walking legs, the back pair of which is modified to form effective jumping organs. At this time, the mostly transparent, delicate wings attain their full expanse. In flight the fore and hind wings on each side are connected by little marginal hooks. Many species of jumping plantlice, when fully developed, are inclined to go journeying and fly from tree to tree, preferably taking advantage of the wind. In the temperate zone most of these insects have a single annual generation, but some have two. The majority overwinter as eggs, certain species as adults. Like the cicadines, they have mutual relationships with symbiotic organisms that live in their body.

4-5

WHITEFLIES (ALEURODINA)

These little plant-sucking insects, about 0.04 inch to 0.1 inch long, are powdered all over with white wax. About 200 species have been described. They are mainly tropical and subtropical, only a few occurring in the temperate zone.

Whiteflies (Aleurodina) have four almost equally large, delicate, broad wings, with scanty, weak venation. The wings, which at rest are laid back, rooflike, over one another, give the insect a mothlike appearance. The abdomen of a whitefly is narrowed at the base to form a "wasp waist."

Whiteflies are active insects. In the warm, daylight hours one may see them wafted vertically, high in the air, and settling again on the plants, where whole colonies, including individuals in all stages of development, dwell on the undersides of leaves. Whiteflies run gracefully, often with nervous rapidity, on the tips of their feet. They are sensitive to vibrations and jump away at once when the support on which they are resting is shaken. They jump well with their hind legs, the leap usually turning into flight. They fly in a

fluttering manner; the fore and hind wings move rather independently because of their musculature and because they are not linked together.

Each of the two compound eyes of whiteflies is divided into an upper portion, which looks forward and to the side, and a lower portion with coarser facets, whose visual field encompasses the area below that of the upper portion. Some species damage cultivated plants; for example, the "citrus whitefly" damages oranges; the "olive whitefly," olives; and the "greenhouse whitefly," various plants in greenhouses. The harm results mostly from the sticky excretions they spray over the plant's leaves.

Like the cicadines and other members of the order Homoptera, the whiteflies harbor within their bodies various microorganisms. The relationship apparently is of mutual benefit to both parties.

In their development from egg to adult, whiteflies show a special kind of metamorphosis. Their fourth (and final) preadult stage can almost be defined as a pupa; hence the metamorphosis of whiteflies can be regarded as a transition from the incomplete type of metamorphosis (in which there is no pupa) to the complete type (in which there is a pupa).

The whitefly nymph is sessile. With its barely segmented, flattened, oval body pressing against the underside of a leaf, the young insect sucks with its long proboscis, which is like that of aphids; when at rest the proboscis lies beneath the head in a loop that is enclosed in a pouch formed by the integument. The whole body is covered with a secretion of powdered wax, and the sides are fastened to the support by a dense garland of little waxen rods, through which air channels lead to the spiracles, in the abdomen.

During the third and fourth stages, antennae and legs are present only as small stumps. In the fourth instar, the stage after the third molt, curious changes come about. The wax glands themselves no longer are the same and produce some different excrescences than before—for instance, whole crowns of wax, looking as though they are made of fine glass capillaries, or star-shaped structures and lamellae. Most nymphs at this stage have bristles on the back and sides.

It is in this nymph that the transformation to a wholly different adult begins. The body grows obviously fatter and is raised more and more, although it remains attached to the leaf via the wax excreted along the lateral margins. Then there comes into being an odd, box-shaped structure, whose vertical sidewalls

97/1
The biennial life cycle of an oak gall wasp, with a rapidly developing summer generation that produces both sexes, and a slow-growing winter generation that yields only females. After mating with the alate male, the wingless female of the summer generation creeps into the ground and drills her eggs into oak roots. The larvae that develop in the resulting root galls do not emerge until the second winter; then they come forth as much larger females, which differ from their mother in other respects too. They climb up into the tree and insert their unfertilized eggs (virgin birth, parthenogenesis) into the buds on the twigs. Very speedily bud galls arise here; from them males and females of the new generation soon emerge (greatly enlarged). The roman numerals indicate the months of development.

97/2
Mating games of the bristletails. Small silverfishes, the male on the left (enlarged 2×).

97/3
Jumping bristletails; on the inside the female, collecting semen (enl. 2×).

PAGES 98 AND 99

98/1
Springtails. The leap made with the tail, and its phases, in natural size.

98/2
Snow flea, a springtail (enl. 10×).

98/3
Claws, with fingers formed by bristles, for holding a drop of water in order to rinse the body.

98/4
Springtail dermal cells. In bright light, the dark pigment granules gather in the center of the cells; in the dark, the granules migrate to the cell walls, changing the pattern of the markings.

98/5
A springtail in the soil.

98/6
The (smaller) male water springtail that lives on the surface holds fast with its antennal tongs (detailed drawing at right) to the (larger) female's antennae, and is carried about in this way. During the mating act, he drags his partner over a previously deposited drop of semen, which she takes up with her sexual pore.

98/7
Many springtails produce large drops of semen on stalks (detailed drawing

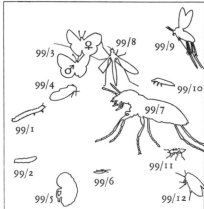

For identification of the insects on page 99

99/1	Fire-colored beetle larva
99/2	Greenhead fly larva
99/3	Common blues
99/4	Wood cockroach
99/5	Cicada nymph
99/6	Springtail
99/7	Purple tiger beetle
99/8	Crane fly
99/9	Fungus gnat
99/10	Firefly larva
99/11	Acrobat ant
99/12	Moth fly

on the right), and the females then run about over them of their own accord.

98/8
A telsontail in moist earth.

98/9–21
Cockroaches are a very ancient stock (half natural size). Photograph.

99/1–24
Small animal life within and upon the North American forest floor. In addition to insects and their young, centipedes and millipedes, a book scorpion, a wolf spider, worms, and ground snakes are also shown.

PAGES 100 AND 101

100/1–10
Various praying mantids or predatory crickets (0.6 nat. size). Photograph.

100/11
The form of the prehensile legs, the number and placement of their spines, and the head with its frequently bizarre horns are the most important features by which to distinguish the numerous mantid species (greatly enlarged).

100/12
From species to species the mantid egg masses are different (enl. 1.3×).

101/1
Oviposition by an Asiatic praying mantis, a species that has become widespread in North America since its introduction there (natural size).

101/2
The Indian praying mantis, the "wandering violin."

101/3
The male of the European praying mantis catching a fly.

101/4
The African "devil's flower" in a posture of defense (left) and in a normal stance (right).

PAGES 102 AND 103

102/1
The few known species of the cold-

loving *Grylloblatta* seem to represent primitive forms of grasshoppers (not quite twice natural size).

102/2
Walkingstick (natural size).

102/3–103/2
Walkingsticks; below, an immature form is emerging from the egg.

PAGES 104 AND 105

104/1
Subterranean mole cricket (enl. 2×).

104/2
On the forehead, some crickets have peculiar lappets of skin, and beneath them the anterior face of the head is flat (enlarged 2×).

104/3
A chirping male house cricket (enlarged 2×).

104/4
One of the wingless saddleback grasshoppers with its powerful saber, which is used for placing eggs in the ground (enlarged 1.3×).

104/5
A loud-voiced katydid (enl. 1.3×).

104/6
A Jerusalem cricket in its excavation (enlarged 1.3×).

105/1–7
Katydids and grasshoppers (natural size).

PAGE 106

106/1–8
Several different kinds of band-winged grasshoppers (somewhat reduced). Photograph.

106/9
A South African migratory locust (natural size); above are immature stages, only the dark-spotted variant of which will develop into the swarming, migratory form; below is an ovipositing female.

106/10
A pygmy grasshopper (enl. 3×).

PAGE 107

107/1–5
Sucking lice. (1) A head louse (enl. 20×); (2) a crab louse (enl. 12×); (3) a dog louse (enl. 15×); (4) an elephant louse (enl. 20×); (5) head louse egg ("nit") glued to a hair with a blob of adhesive material; a section through the egg cover shows its ventilation spaces in detail (greatly enlarged).

107/6
An earwig in a posture of defense.

107/7
An Indonesian species of earwig.

107/8
A detailed photograph of a planthopper (lantern fly family). covered with bits of wax (greatly enl.) Photograph.

107/9
The spittlebug nymph in its blob of "cuckoo spit" (greatly enlarged).

PAGES 108 AND 109

108/1–7
Cicadas (enlarged 1.5×). (1) Death's-head cicada from Taiwan. (2) An African cicada. (3) A North American species of cicada. (4–7) Leafhoppers, including a horned leafhopper with two ear-shaped appendages on the back. Photograph.

109/1–9
Froghoppers, the five small specimens of which are different color forms of the spittlebug. Photograph.

109/10–22
The astounding treehoppers. With the species shown in series (enlarged 4×), only the dorsal plate of the thorax has been colored, in order to reveal its developmental possibilities more clearly. Beside and beneath this series are three species, more highly enlarged.

PAGE 110

110/1–4
Lantern flies (slightly less than twice natural size). Photograph.

110/5–17
Various cicadine types, including the largest of all cicadas (from New Guinea). Photograph.

PAGE 111

111/1–4
A colony of aphids (3) and their enemies. A little aphidid wasp (2) is inserting her egg into the swollen body of an aphid, and another aphid is being sucked dry by the fat larva (4) of the flowerfly (1) (greatly enl.).

(Continued on page 113)

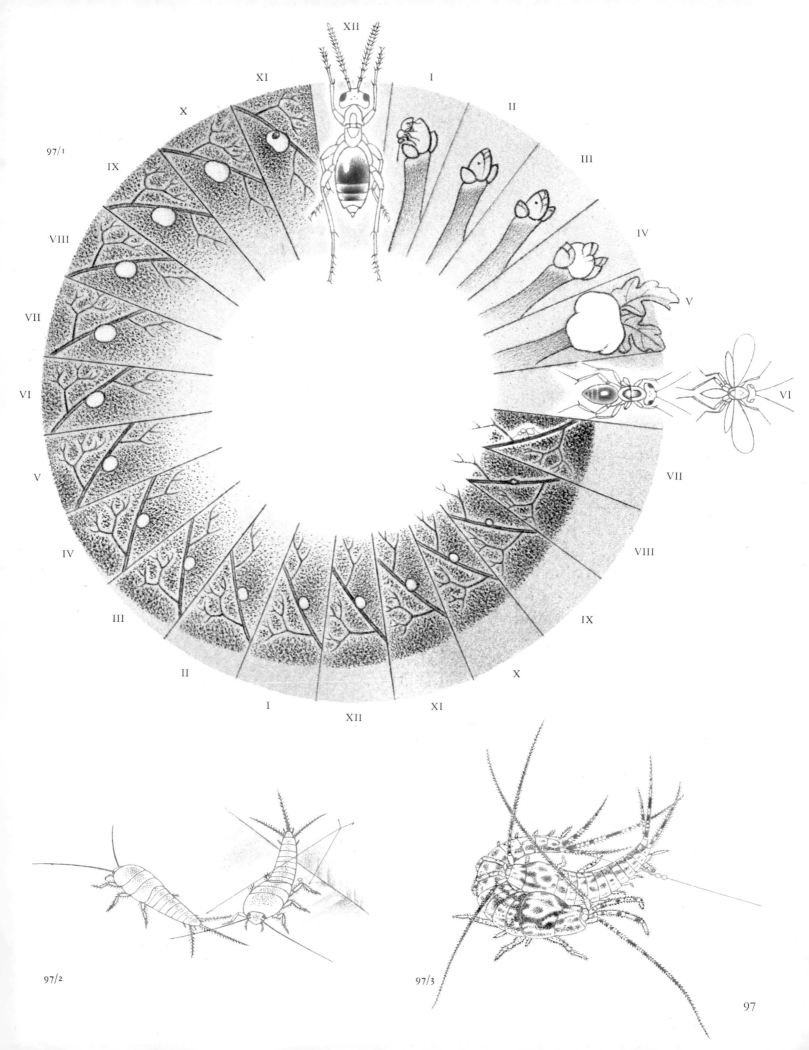

97/2

97/3

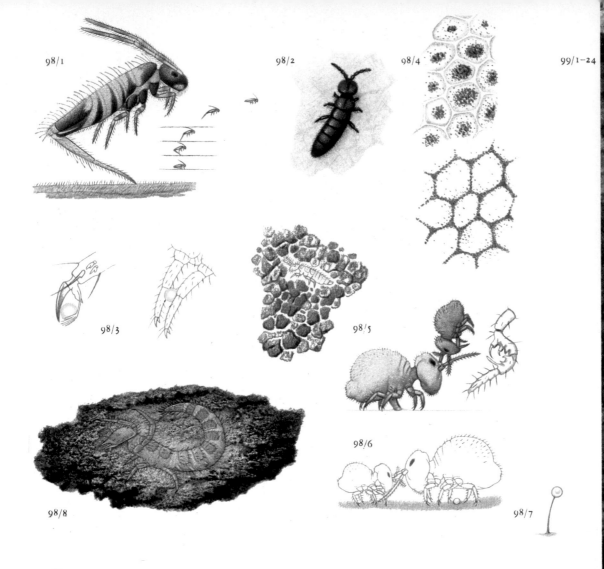

98/1

98/2

98/4

99/1-24

98/3

98/5

98/6

98/7

98/8

98/9-21

9   10   11   12   13   14

15   16   17

18   19   20   21

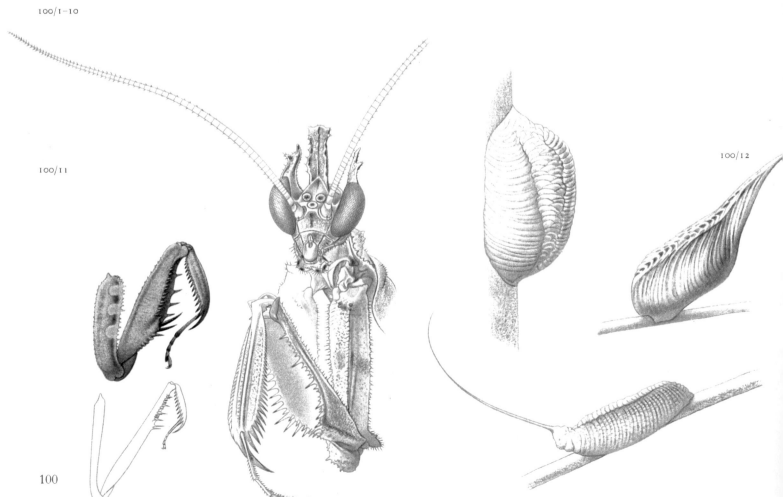

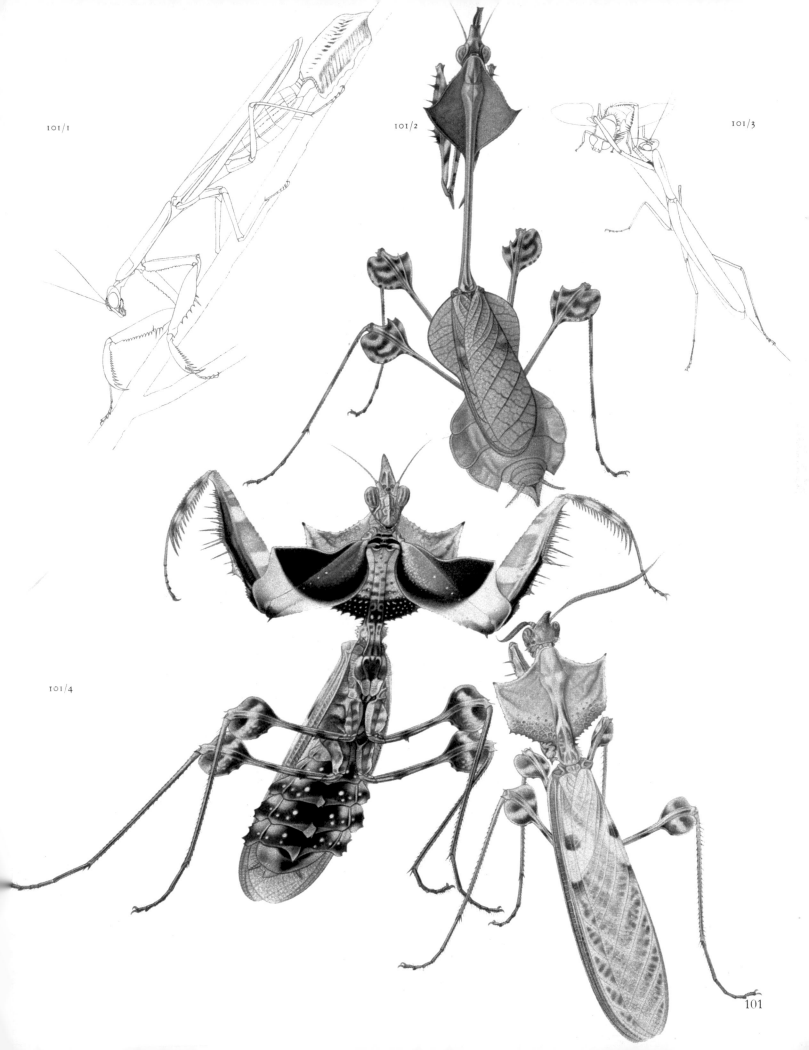

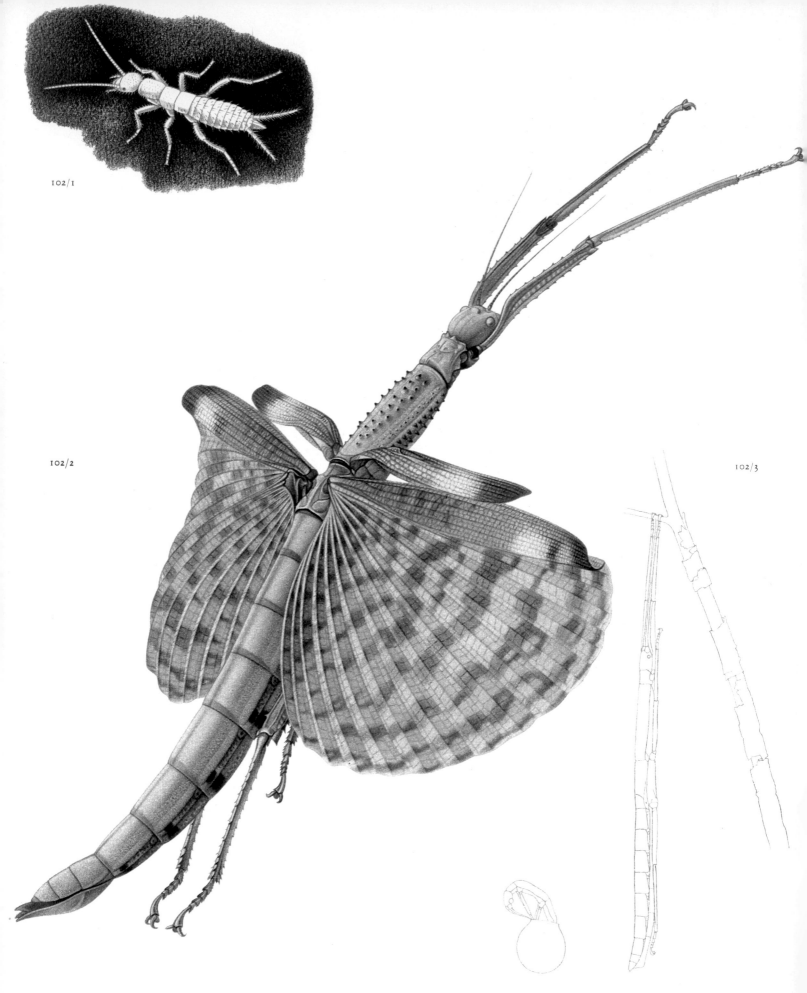

102/1

102/2

102/3

102

104/1

104/2

104/3

104/4

104/5

104

104/6

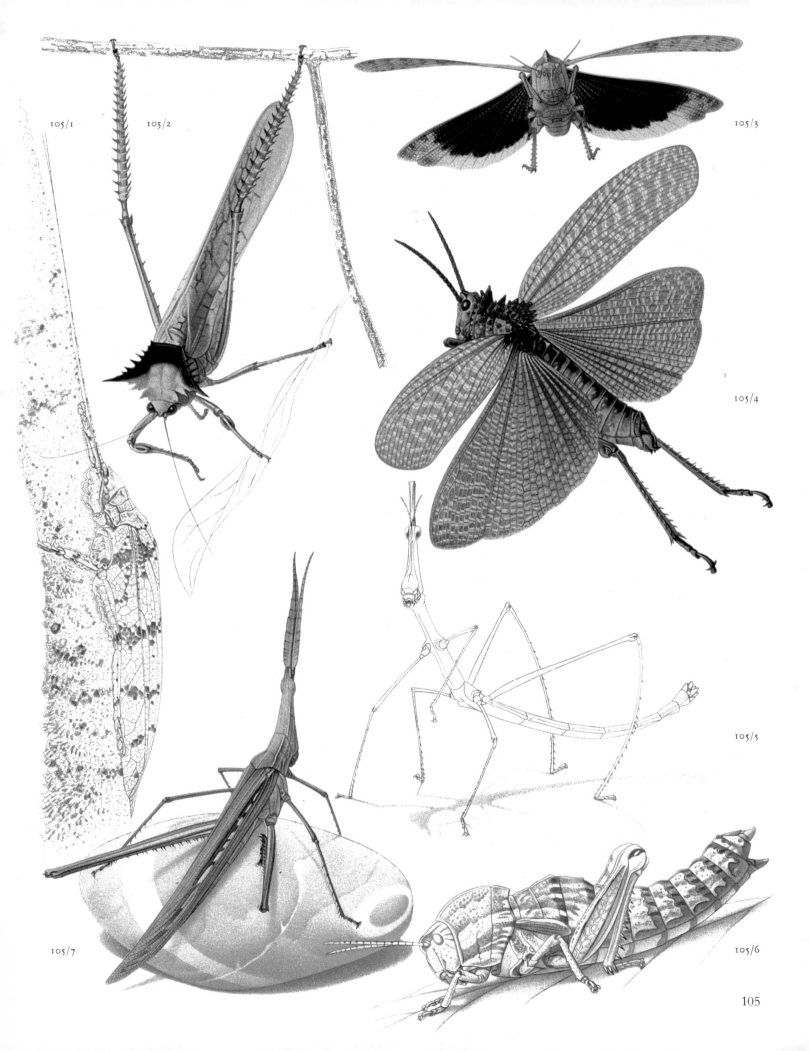

105/1 105/2 105/3 105/4 105/5 105/7 105/6

105

106/1 - 2

106/3 - 5

106/6 - 7

106/8

106/9

106/10

107/1 – 5

1   2   3   4   5

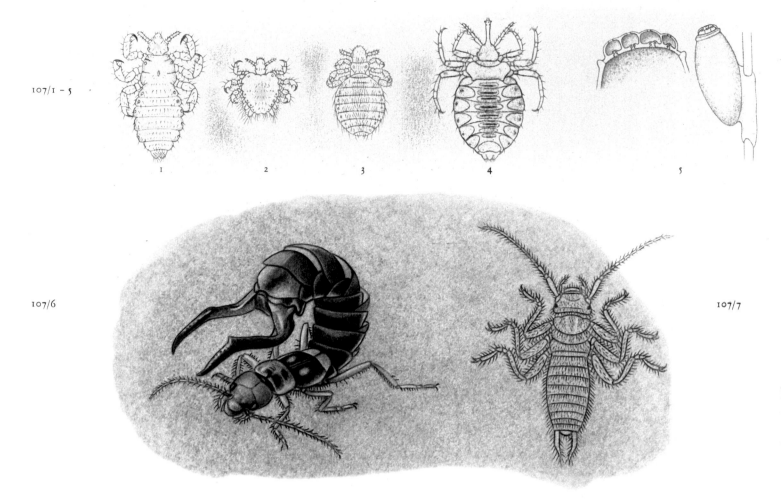

107/6

107/7

107/8

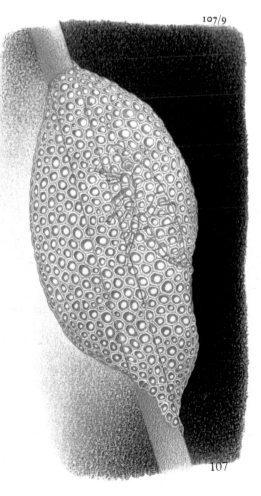

107/9

107

108/1

108/2

108/3

108/4 — 7

108

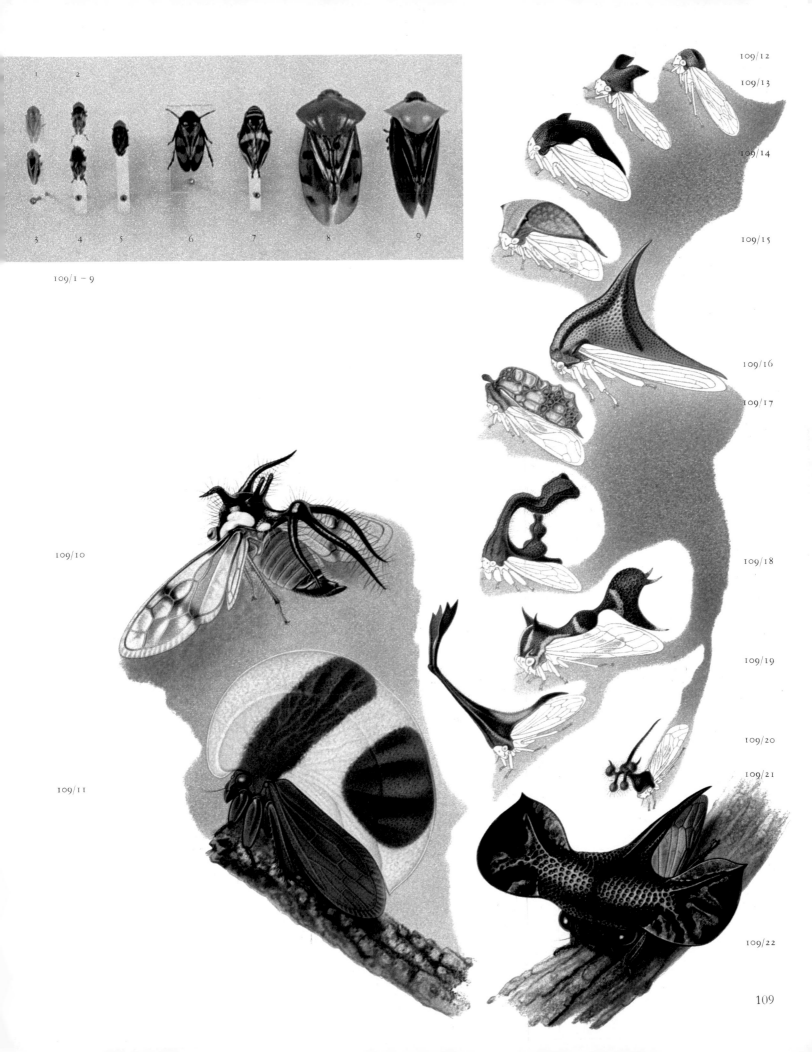

109/1 – 9

109/10

109/11

109/12

109/13

109/14

109/15

109/16

109/17

109/18

109/19

109/20

109/21

109/22

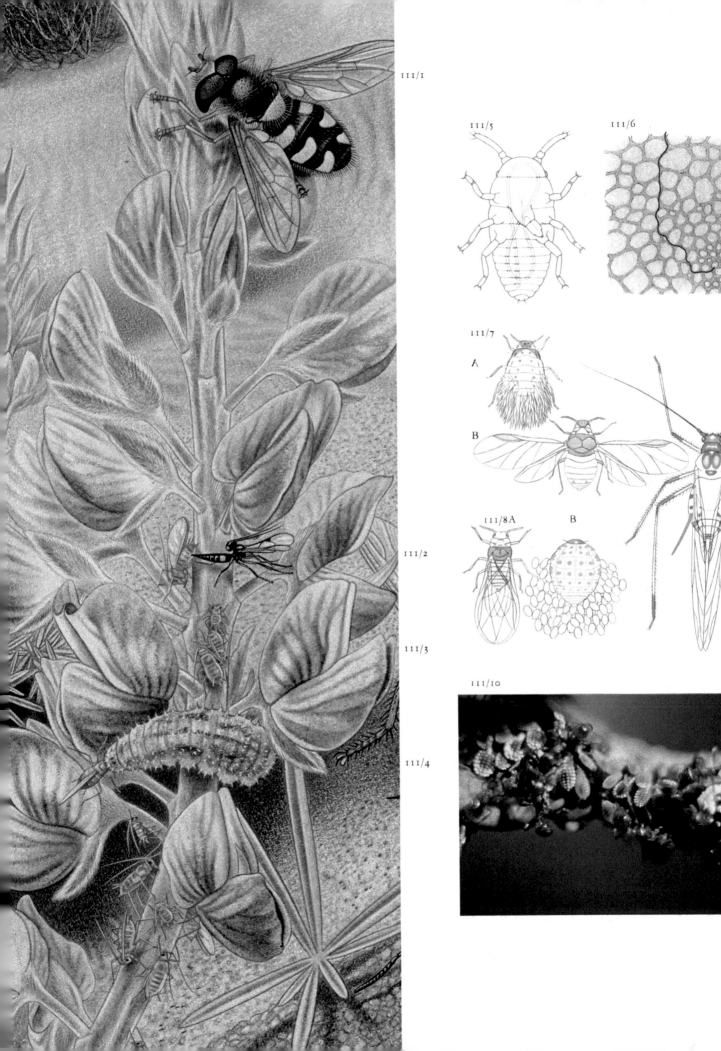

111

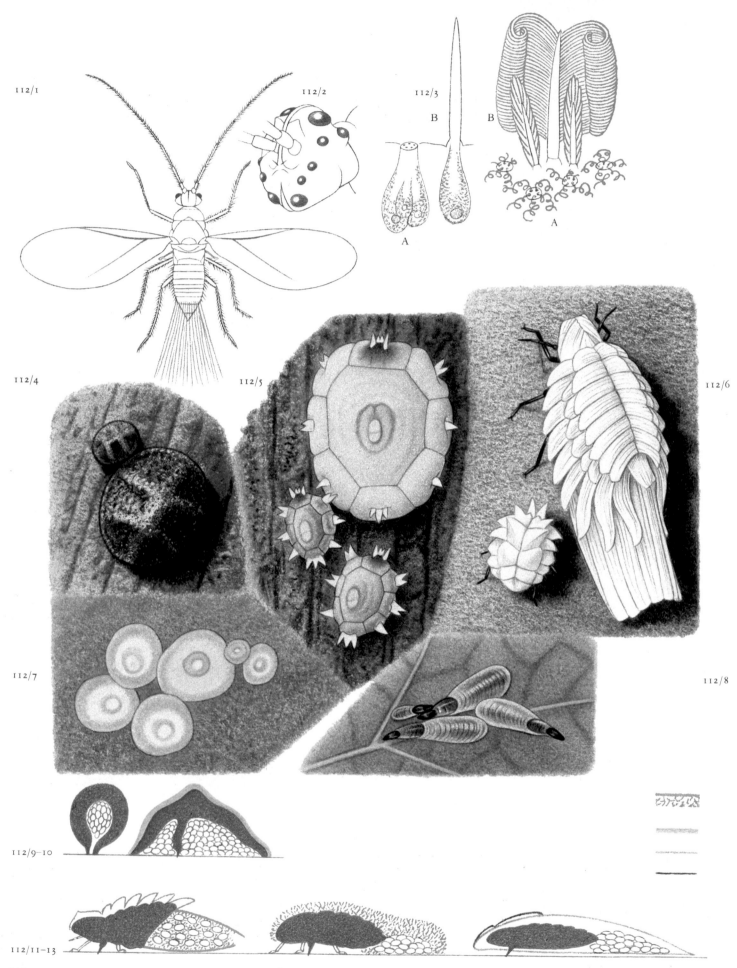

112/1

112/2

112/3
B
B
A
A

112/4

112/5

112/6

112/7

112/8

112/9–10

112/11–13

112

(Continued from page 96)

consist of wax and whose lid is the nymph's own back—that is, its integument.

Eventually an adult whitefly lies in this strange coffin, its head inclined downward, its legs wrinkled and out of shape, and the abdomen somewhat telescoped. When the proper time comes, the whitefly, with one lunge, breaks through the cover along a pre-formed seam and climbs forth, expanding its wings almost at once. The freshly-hatched, still yellowish-green whitefly begins immediately to produce fine waxen threads, glistening like silk, from groups of glands on both sides of the base of the abdomen. These threads are gathered up, as quickly as they are extruded, by special bristles on the hind legs, and are deposited at the base of the fore wings. Taking material from this supply, the dexterous forelegs now start to wax the body.

The forelegs rub the wax over the antennae, the head, and the back of the thorax; the middle legs take wax from the forelegs and the hind legs and brush it over each other as well as over the thorax. The wings are held up vertically and rubbed together, giving the abdomen its coat of wax. Finally, the entire body except the eyes is coated with white wax.

Once this business of grooming is ended, the insects begin sucking on plants and soon follow this with their elegant, long-lasting, and oft-repeated "games of love." Males and females sit side by side in a comical, stiff-legged fashion, but only the male is active. With one antenna the male continually caresses the back surface of his partner's thorax; with the other he drums on her antennae, which are turned towards him.

Notwithstanding such behavior, partheno-genetic reproduction is frequent in whiteflies. Often, as in the case of bees, males emerge from unfertilized eggs and females from fertilized ones. One female may produce up to 400 or more longish eggs, each set on a short stalk. They are deposited on the lower surface of a leaf in close-set garlands of about 40 each. While laying her eggs, the female whitefly keeps her proboscis inserted at one spot in the plant all the time and continues sucking. Only one egg ripens within her every couple of hours; as she lays one egg after the other, she periodically moves her abdomen in a circle. On very hairy plants the eggs may be fastened in irregular groups.

The young hatch with the aid of an egg tooth on the ventral surface of the head, and cast off the embryonic integument at the same time. These nymphs, which excrete wax at once, are indeed oval and flattened already, but they are still quite active until they have taken possession of the site that appeals to

them for sucking on the plant. In molting, the old skin is burst open in front by a voluntary stretching of the body and is peeled back by body movement to the rear end, from which it drops off.

The completion of the life cycle of whiteflies takes varying amounts of time; interpolated rest periods are lacking, and development progresses as temperature permits.

APHIDS (APHIDINA)

Although there are only a few families of aphids, with perhaps about 2,000 species, they are distributed throughout the world and are among the insects most significant to man. He conducts unceasing war against them to defend his plants. These insects, also called plantlice, are rarely more than 0.08 inch to 0.12 inch long, but their powers of increase are almost astronomical. Like other homopterans, they withdraw huge quantities of sap from plants and from this sap obtain the essential materials for growth, especially protein.

The honeydew excreted by the plantlice in this process soon coats everything with a sticky crust, an enormous waste of natural nutrients. As for the plants, their growth is slowed down, many of them wilt, their leaves and sprouts become malformed or develop tumors and galls in forms characteristic for each species of aphid, and they may even receive viral diseases.

Aphids suck on leaves, stalks, woody sprouts, roots, and even on treetrunks; each species is more or less limited to a particular plant. The insect's sucking proboscis, which is laid back beneath the body when not in use, may be so long, especially in the species that live on trees, that it sticks out beyond the end of the abdomen; and in many nymphs, where it extends beneath the integument back into the body, several loops that traverse the entire body (or almost all of it) are required to accommodate the apparatus.

The sucking proboscis is in other respects a marvelous device, a catheter whose tip, extremely sensitive to mechanical resistance and chemical stimuli, penetrates by the most tortuous paths to its goal in the plant tissues, namely to groups of cells that contain definite juices. Frequently it bores straight through individual cells, frequently it winds its way between them like a searching worm, again perhaps it is retracted and then extended anew in a different direction. Over and over it draws in sap, tests it, and thereby determines the route to be followed as the tongue penetrates more deeply. In addition, saliva flows continuously into the puncture and, hardening, stiffens the walls in advance of the probe. The saliva also readies the plant juices for digestion and, by means of certain toxic effects, cripples the plant or stimulates production of galls. [111]

This sucking proboscis, not only in aphids but throughout the Homoptera and Heteroptera, must have evolved from what originally were chewing mouthparts. The proboscis sheath was formed from the labium, the two outer stylets from the mandibles, and the two inner stylets from the maxillae. The outer stylets, in fact, are exclusively tools for piercing, the two juxtaposed inner ones, containing fine canals, form two unimaginably slender pipes. The anterior pipe, with a diameter of 0.001 millimeters (four ten-thousandths of an inch), is the sucking tube proper, and the posterior one, with a diameter of 0.0002 to 0.0003 millimeters (eight to twelve hundred-thousandths of an inch), is the salivary canal.

COLOR AND FORM

The clumsily swollen body of most aphids either is entirely soft-skinned or is somewhat hardened only on the back surface. Such hardened areas stand out because of their dark deposits of pigment and may form designs. In the majority of aphids the general coloring is all varieties of green, but also may be yellow, red, brown, or from bluish to blackish; actually it is merely the color of the body contents—that is, of the blood and fatty substances and also of the symbionts, bright-hued complexes of which often show through the skin. In these insects, as well as in other homopterans, the microscopic organisms that live in the insect body as symbionts evidently are of the utmost importance for metabolic processes.

In colonies of aphids one often sees individuals of different colors, such as green specimens together with red and yellow ones. The color variations may appear irregularly among members of the colony or may be associated with a particular sex or generation.

Not only do aphids display a bewildering complexity of color, but their bodies frequently are covered entirely with white or gray wax. In certain species this wax is excreted only by definite body regions and may be in the form of flakes, ribbons, or other shapes. Certain species, such as the woolly apple aphid *(Eriosoma lanigerum)*, have special plate-shaped groups of wax glands that produce great masses of wax beneath which whole colonies vanish as though covered by dense, snow-white wool. [15/14]

The great majority of aphids have two openings on the upper surface near the rear of the body. Each has a hinged cover operated by muscular contraction. The openings nearly always are elevated in the form of slender tubes that can be aimed at enemies. From them these otherwise defenseless insects expel a sticky, waxlike secretion that clogs up the prehensile mouthparts or other grasping instruments of an assailant.

Except for certain stub-legged nymphs that are reminiscent of whitefly nymphs, the aphids mostly have long, simple legs of the walking type with a cushionlike pulvillus or with spines at the tip of the tibia to give attachment to the supporting surface. Some of the winged forms jump, by suddenly extending their relatively strong forelegs; when flight begins, these are retracted.

WINGS AND FLIGHT

Aphids fly rather slowly and heavily, but with the help of the wind they occasionally make astonishingly extensive migrations. Air currents may carry these delicate organisms to altitudes of 3,000 feet and more. On calm, warm, and humid autumn days one may witness thousands of them floating in and out among one another, all borne in the same direction by the gentle zephyrs, each to resume its own particular course from the place where it next lands. The delicate, elegantly veined fore wings and the much smaller hind wings are united during flight by a few marginal hooks formed of bristles. At rest the wings either are folded flat or are laid rooflike over the back; then, as is normal with all homopterans, their tips extend far beyond the tip of the abdomen.

In almost all species of aphids, both winged and unwinged forms occur, as well as intermediates with rudimentary wings, all of them in both sexes. Aphids in the wingless stages have a rather formless, misshapen appearance, weak compound eyes with perhaps no more than three facets, and no dorsal ocelli (simple eyes). In the winged forms, the three divisions of the body—head, thorax, and abdomen—are distinct, the compound eyes well-developed, and three dorsal ocelli present. Also, the head and the upper surface of the thorax always are armored and darkly pigmented.

Good nutritional conditions, high temperatures, and plenty of light seem to favor winglessness; low temperature, intermittent light, and a gradual reduction in the flow of sap, as may be brought about by increasing aridity, seem to induce the development of wings—that is, the development of migratory

114/1

An aphid colony with one of its enemies, a ladybird beetle larva (enlarged 3×).

sexual forms. In temperate climates the changes from one form to another occur in a rhythm that is determined by heredity.

LIFE CYCLE

In the course of their annual cycle, some aphids go through many forms. The bean aphid *(Aphis fabae),* for example, has eight forms that are unlike in way of life and, partly, in structure. In a year's time, numerous generations of plantlice may succeed one another, for even at moderate mean temperatures the nymphs, which molt four times at most, complete their development in little more than 10 days. The life cycle of aphids is so tangled and so full of exceptions that here we have to confine ourselves to suggesting only the most important possibilities.

Each species, through a series of generations, brings its annual life cycle to completion with definite sexual forms. The whole life cycle is completed either on one and the same plant or in seasonally regulated shifts between various plant species; in the latter case, one speaks of a winter or primary host, and of a summer or secondary host. The aphids live on the primary host, a shrub or tree, through the autumn and until the end of spring; it is here that the winter diapause, or period of suspended development, takes place (usually as an egg). At the end of spring, after the leaves have unfolded fully and their production of nitrogenous compounds has diminished, the aphids emigrate, usually to more herbaceous vegetation, or possibly to roots. In many species all the individuals are involved, but in others only a fraction of them; with the latter, part of the original colony stays on the primary host (perhaps gradually dying off), to which the progeny of the emigrants return in the fall.

Shorter days and lower temperatures are the outward factors that generally cause the aphids to come back in autumn to their first host. The phenomena of emigration and return, however, are by no means fully explained by these outward factors alone. For, in preparation for these journeys very special sexual forms also are developed, namely wingless females (virginoparae) and, in the autumn, winged males. Moreover, the nutritional physiology of these insects is so altered that they shun the previous host plants and accept distinctly different ones. Such changes may be so drastic that the transformed aphids, if prevented from emigrating, will starve to death on the vegetation from which they originated.

Most species that do not shift hosts live on shrubs and trees. Their numbers reach a peak in late spring, then regress markedly during the summer, because of the reduced flow and chemical alteration of the sap that nourishes them. Some species even have a resting stage (latent nymph) in which they spend the unfavorable season without taking food, under the protection of a covering of wax.

The aphid nymph hatches with the aid of a sclerotized saw on its head. The saw cuts through the embryonic integument over head and neck; then the nymph stands upright for a while, swallowing air and bursting the embryonic skin, strips this skin off, and begins to suck on the plant.

All the nymphs that hatch in spring from eggs laid the previous fall are females. No males exist as yet. In many species, especially the tropical ones but also those that live in greenhouses, in cellars, or in houseplants, males do not appear at all. Each female nymph becomes the wingless ancestress of a colony. In certain species she also is the only form that causes plant galls.

When sexually mature, the female parthenogenetically lays eggs or bears living young. The offspring also are females, called virginoparae because they themselves reproduce by parthenogenesis. In the succession of daughter generations that follow, winged specimens may soon appear, or there may be a generation consisting exclusively of wing-bearing virginoparae. The daughters that are able to fly now spread out over the plant, where the same sort of parthenogenetic increase continues, intensified by the improved nutritional conditions there.

Toward the season's end, in late summer or autumn, males at last appear among the offspring, and both males and their winged sisters return to the winter host. Or else the return migration comes before the males appear. Males now mate with the females or with the females' daughters. The offspring of this bisexual generation are then invariably the wingless sexual females that lay the overwintering eggs. In a few families these females are dwarfed and lack any proboscis; after laying a single egg that fills almost the entire body, the female collapses like an empty bag and dies.

That such delicate little insects, mostly devoid of any protection or means of defense, and pursued by a host of enemies, can year after year achieve such eminence in the economy of nature is to be ascribed to just these complex relationships. Coupled with

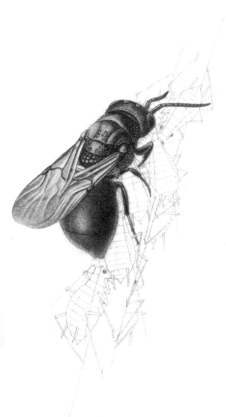

115/1
Not just ants but many other insects, like this cuckoo wasp, refresh themselves with the sugary solution excreted by aphids.
(→ 315/10)

the shifts from plant to plant and from one generation to another is a method of reproduction, predominantly parthenogenetic, with an enormous capacity for multiplication. Here the great adaptability of the insect constitution is shown most impressively. Depending on the time of year and nutritional conditions, advantage is taken now of this plant and now of that, now leaves and sprouts and now of roots. Yet it must not be forgotten that the individual species are amazingly sensitive to environmental changes and require definite microclimates. Thus one species lives only in shady places, another in sunnier ones; one kind only in damp spots and another where it is dry; and any transfer of such species to a different environment would mean their end.

Ants and Aphids

As already mentioned, aphids discharge sugary digestive residues in great quantities. This honeydew constitutes an important source of nourishment for many other insects. Bees, for example, include it in their process of honey manufacture. But preceding all others come the ants.

Ants not only lick up the honeydew discharged, but actually ride herd on the aphid colonies. When the ants drum their antennae on the aphids, the latter produce honeydew more rapidly. Since this intensifies the aphids' sucking of plant juices, the ants indirectly cause an increase in the damage to plants. As a result of their manipulation by ants, many species of aphids have lost the knack of squirting out their excretions, instead discharging them slowly drop by drop; special bristles on the tip of the abdomen prevent the drops from falling immediately, and they are drunk at once by the ants. Some aphid species are not attended by ants, apparently because their honeydew has a disagreeable quality.

Certain species of aphids that suck on roots depend unconditionally on assistance from ants. The latter dig out the necessary cavities up against the roots and keep transferring the aphids from plant to plant below ground. Ants also fetch aphid eggs into their own nest, with the result that the eggs overwinter without freezing. In the spring the ants accompany the newly hatched young aphids to the plants or even carry them there; and, while the nights are still cold, the ants bring the young back into the nest in the evening. Later, the aphids remain outside and are visited at night by the ants. During the day a sentry is left with the aphids; should there be a disturbance she runs back to the ant nest and sounds the alarm. Even mature aphid females occasionally are taken into the ant nest for the winter.

Certain ants build ramparts of earth around aphid colonies living on small plants. Other ants build roofs of rotten wood over aphid herds that live in cracks in bark; extensions of the tunnels formed in this way are connected directly with the ants' nest. Many ants feed more or less exclusively on honeydew. An amusing sight is an ant helping an aphid to pull its long proboscis out of a plant; evidently the aphid finds it troublesome to withdraw the beak only when some danger requires it to run away as quickly as possible. Sometimes aphids are fed by ants. [111/10]

Enemies

Ants to some extent protect aphids against attacks of enemies, but often this protection is not enough. The worst enemies of aphids are the ladybird beetles (Coccinellidae) and their larvae, as well as the larvae of many flower flies (Syrphidae). A ladybird beetle is able to devour about 100 aphids a day, its larva about 50. A recently-hatched flower fly will suck dry about 10 aphids a day, and as many as 300 when full-grown, so that by itself it may liquidate an entire colony. Little red or orange maggots of certain gall midges (Cecidomyiidae), which have a rapid succession of generations, likewise are able to destroy aphids. Other important agents of destruction are the green lacewings (Chrysopidae), which are related to the antlions, and other lacewings and dustywings (Hemerobiidae and Coniopterygidae); both the adults and their larvae eat aphids.

Furthermore, there are little parasitic wasps of the families Chalcididae and Encyrtidae that frequently bury an egg in almost every individual of an aphid colony; certain species of these parasites have been cultured and employed in aphid control. A grotesque spectacle is a shiny little wasp climbing around with vibrating wings over the crowded sucking aphid herd, "stinging" one aphid from a perch on the back of another and in doing so thrusting her abdomen forward between her own legs! The victim seems to notice nothing whatever, but in due course gradually is hollowed out by the wasp larva that hatches and finally, as a dead, empty sack, constitutes the pupal cradle that the newly emerging wasp will forsake by chewing a round exit. Within this skin the wasp larva spins its own cocoon before it pupates, and through a slit in the underside of the host fastens the cocoon to the plant with silk.

There are other, less effective enemies, among them many more or less exclusively predatory insects such as Heteroptera of several families, some of which have such flattened bodies that they can force their way into the galls inhabited by the aphids. There are also digger wasps of the genus *Psen* that, if necessary, drag their victims out of the galls as soon as these begin to open up. The enemy roster includes beetles, earwigs, thrips, and certain butterfly caterpillars (lycaenids). Finally, many songbirds and various diseases help the work of annihilation along, to say nothing of man's refined methods of control. Altogether, it is astonishing that the aphids are able to endure in such great numbers. [111; 182/34]

SCALE INSECTS (COCCINA)

The scale insects, which include more than 4,000 species in a number of families, are distributed throughout most of the world and are among the most destructive pests of plants. They have so much in common with the whiteflies and aphids in respect to body organization, way of life, and relationships to the environment that this description will focus on their distinctive features. The scale insects are mostly tiny, on the order of 0.1 inch or less, but a few range from 0.8 inch to 1.2 inches long. Man has helped spread these pests throughout the world. For example, one of the best known and most destructive of these insects, the San Jose scale *(Aspidiotus perniciosus)*, was brought to California from China and has now spread across the United States.

Like the aphids, but to a lesser extent, certain species of scale insects form galls, and others shift from one kind of plant to another. But scale insects do not have the diversity of generation-types that the aphids do, though the individual developmental stages of scale insects differ much more strongly, as do the two sexes. The females always are wingless, and the highly specialized kinds are so greatly modified, in keeping with their completely sessile way of life, that they scarcely can be recognized as insects. Legs, antennae, and eyes may have disappeared more or less completely; and the broadly oval body, often with a characteristic shield- or bowl-shape, hardly reveals any segmentation. Only the nymphs in the first stage of development are motile and spread over the plant; after these nymphs have settled down, all further developments, such as molting and reproduction, take place more or less in a single spot. For the most part, the body is stuck to the supporting surface by means of wax or gumlike substances; in fact the entire colony of scale insects may be fused into a single secreted mass that covers leaves, twigs, or stems.

These chemical secretions, not all identified completely, are what is extraordinary about scale insects, in particular the amount and the form of these substances. A large role is played by wax that, though it coats some species only as a powder, covers others with a disorderly tangle of rigid threads or irregularly dense masses or may enclose the insects in a tubelike structure. Many species manufacture curls, spirals, plumes, and shafts of the most elegant construction and arrangement, or pegs, knobs, pyramids, bars, and ribbons, in artistic forms that often remind one of the miracle world of small aquatic animals.

Special integumentary molds at the ducts of the wax glands shape these structures, while other neighboring glands simultaneously supply the gum required to make them solid. Most peculiar, too, are long wax capillaries that appear as anal extensions, often attaining grotesque lengths; they serve to conduct away the excreted honeydew, which from time to time appears as a large terminal drop. With species that in their sucking penetrate deeply into bark or other parts of plants, this "dew pipe" constitutes a sewage system leading into the open!

Other gummy secretions are exuded over the whole top (dorsal) surface of the insect's integument. In many species the secretions form armored shields shaped mostly like mussel shells, bowls, or boats; often these incorporate the discarded nymphal skins, and frequently they are made firm by the addition of sticky excretions. Such a covering shield may stand apart from the insect or, woven of secreted threads and penetrated only by the sucking proboscis, may blanket the entire body of a female like a cocoon glued to the supporting surface.

In certain species the female makes an egg pouch at the tip of the abdomen from disks or bars of wax; these are extended farther and farther backward as more eggs are deposited. Females of other species place their eggs behind them, beneath a wax cover. Still others put them underneath the body, so that the dorsal shield comes to arch upward more and more, while the lateral margins of the body and the sucking proboscis remain bound to the plant. This forms a nest, which may take on even a closed, spherical shape, within which eggs and newly-hatched nymphs are protected long after the mother animal above them has died. The females of a few species

117/1
Scale insects are an important factor in agriculture, lead an extremely interesting existence biologically, and secondarily produce, via deposits of wax and other secretions, structures of great aesthetic appeal.
(→ 112/5)

climb down the plant to the ground and lay their eggs there, beneath fallen plant debris or a shallow covering of soil.

According to the species, the number of eggs laid by a female ranges from as few as 12 to as many as 700 to 2,500. Many species are viviparous and do not lay eggs; instead the young nymphs hatch from the egg membranes within the female body, frequently not until after her death. Often there are one or two generations a year, but there may be as many as six. At all events, the reproductive capacity of the scale insects is enormous: theoretically a single female might have as many as 3,000 million descendants a year. Parthenogenetic reproduction is frequent among these insects, although much less so than in aphids. Disastrous outbreaks of scale insects have been controlled successfully by applying their most important enemies, the ladybird beetles.

Male scale insects are much smaller than females, more active, and shorter-lived. They may have wings, wings reduced to vestiges, or no wings at all. In certain species a winged generation alternates with a wingless one. In any case the hind wings are tiny. The head has a strangely comical look, for there is no mouth, and species that lack compound eyes have remarkable arrangements of simple eyes, namely a rather large pair above, another pair directed downward on the underside of the head, and laterally in-between, one or more little ones; or else there may be a double series of simple eyes crossing the whole head capsule. And when compound eyes are present, there is an ocellus (simple eye) on the upper-front margin of each. In the males of a few families, two long wax threads of complex structure are appended to the posterior end of the body. These threads are the product of a group of glands; their significance is no better understood than is that of many other such formations.

The excretions and secretions of scale insects have long been used by man. Shellac, for example, is made from the secretion of the Indian lac insect (*Laccifer lacca*). The Chinese wax scale (*Ericerus pe-la*) secretes a wax used to make candles in Asia. The once important red dyes, kermes and cochineal, come from the scale insects *Kermes ilicis* (of Europe and western Asia) and *Dactylopius coccus* (of Mexico). These dyes have been largely superseded by coal-tar dyes, but the cochineal dye is still used in foods and cosmetics.

The waxen cases of a genus of scale insects that lives on roots in Africa and South America have such a magnificent metallic or golden gloss that they are mined as "earth pearls" and worn as jewelry. In certain countries scale insects are the source of medicines. The honeydew of the tamarisk manna scale (*Trabutina mannipara*), which sucks on tamarisk bushes in the Mediterranean region and the Near East, has long been used as a foodstuff and apparently is the manna referred to in the Bible as having been eaten by the Israelites in the wilderness. The honeydew of aphids and of cicadines often is also called manna, as are some lichens and the sap that flows from certain trees and bushes (European flowering ash, manna oak, manna tamarisk) after an incision made by man or insect. [15/19; 112/1–3]

TRUE BUGS ORDER HETEROPTERA (OR HEMIPTERA)

(Bugs that live on or in the water are described in the section on "Water Insects.")

When bugs are mentioned, some people think of those that drop from the ceiling at night upon a sleeping person. Or they recall the penetrating odor of a green or brown stink bug that they accidentally touched while picking berries. Notwithstanding such unpleasantness, the wealth of form and the aesthetic appeal of the true bugs make them one of the most interesting groups of insects.

Upon the usually flattened backs of bugs, all kinds of distinct shield-shaped plates seem to vie for supremacy. These take the form of triangles, trapezoids, or other polygons, or sometimes strikingly original designs. It is fascinating to follow out, among the different families, the way the plates are grouped and shaped around a single center, namely the shieldlike triangular scutellum, which lies next to the suture between thorax and abdomen. In some bugs the scutellum is expanded to the extent that it covers all or most of the abdomen and the wings.

The diversity of the decorations developed by bugs demands admiration. It appears as though disks of horn, ivory, leather, or metal had been set side by side, often expertly inlaid with what looks like ebony, gold, copper, and verdigris, and frequently sculptured with magnificent chiseled designs. Colors range from a nicely graded gray, brown, or green to glaring yellow and red; from metallic green, blue, and violet to shimmering gold, purple, and highly polished black. And on head and body, on antennae and legs, there appear bizarre extensions and appendages, such as

118/1
A master at concealment is this South American flat bug that lives in assemblages. (→ 51/2)

spines, prongs, flaps, and leaflets; or vesicles, supported by an ingenious network of scaffolding, that may rise above the back.

The bodies of bugs vary as much in shape as in decoration. At one extreme are gracefully slender, rod-shaped insects, with long gnatlike legs; and at the other are shiny, hard, beetle-like hemispheres on short, sturdy props. On the basis of such differences it seems incomprehensible that all these insects are true bugs; and yet all unambiguously display the body form peculiar to their group. [14/6; 57/2; 129–132]

The true bugs are distributed over the world in many families and more than 25,000 species. They are grouped by many entomologists as the suborder Heteroptera of the order Hemiptera, sharing the order with the Homoptera, which includes the cicadas, leafhoppers, aphids, whiteflies, scale insects, and others. Some entomologists, however, give order status to the true bugs as well as to the Homoptera. Most true bugs are small or of moderate size, but some aquatic species are as much as 4.5 inches long. The true bugs have a sucking proboscis similar to that of the cicadas and related insects. But in the true bugs the beak originates at the front of the lower side of the face rather than at the back, as in insects of the order Homoptera; and in the predatory and bloodsucking families of the true bugs, the beak even may extend forward horizontally. Also, the front stylets of the beak often have barbs that make holding onto the prey with the legs superfluous. For example, one occasionally sees a large caterpillar hanging free but spitted on the beak of a much smaller stink bug that is sitting with its head turned aside.

The stylets of the flat bugs (family Aradidae) may be more than six times the length of the body; when not in use, they are coiled up like a watch spring at the front of the head. Flat bugs, of which some 400 species have been described, have a flattened body and reduced or degenerate wings. Found in all regions, they live on trees, beneath bark or fungal mats, or in cracks; with beaks sunk deep into the wood, they suck the juices of fungal mycelia. [130/12; 131/1]

WINGS AND FLIGHT

An especially distinctive characteristic of the true bugs is the structure of their front wings. In most true bugs, only the tips of the front wings, which are laid over one another above the abdomen, are of transparent membrane; the rest is hardened or leathery like the elytra of beetles. But unlike the front wings of many beetles, those of true bugs generally are concerned actively in flight, as they are in other plant-sucking insects. Special devices on the fore wings lock them to the hind wings, and both function together. Yet, in keeping with their rather sluggish nature, not many true bugs are fond of flying, and their rather heavy, audibly buzzing flight usually is pretty much straight ahead.

There are certain exceptions to the structure just described. Some true bugs have partly or wholly reduced wings, and others, such as the lace bugs (Tingidae), have wings that are covered with a honeycomblike network. [131/2]

DISTRIBUTION

As with beetles, there is scarcely a habitable place in the world not utilized by this true bug or that. Many of the largest species have become adapted even to the water. The majority of terrestrial bugs live on plant juices or on fruits and roots, a few of them on wood. In this matter many species are rather nonselective, but others are limited to certain plants or plant families, even to definite parts of plants. In addition many suck on dead animal matter, and other frequently attack living insects. Thus we come without any sharp distinction to the predators and bloodsuckers among the true bugs.

PREDATORS AND BLOODSUCKERS

Species that are predatory, whether exclusively or only occasionally, are found in varying numbers among families whose members are predominantly plantsuckers. These include leaf-footed bugs (Coreidae), chinch bugs (Lygaeidae), red bugs and stainers (Pyrrhocoridae), and plant bugs (Miridae).

Other families consist mainly of insect hunters, with the exception of a few species that ingest the warm blood of man and other mammals. Two such families include the rod-shaped stilt bugs (Berytidae), about 0.1 inch long, of which about 100 species have been described; and the flower bugs (Anthocoridae), at most about 0.2 inch long, with 300 known species distributed for the most part throughout the north temperate zone. Then there are families whose members have forelegs more or less strongly modified for prehension. Among them are the damsel bugs (Nabidae), with about 300 species. These bugs, which frequently have degenerate wings, seize and hold down the prey with their forelegs. Another group is the approximately 100 species of the family Phymatidae (ambush bugs), most of which live in the tropics. They are rather small, but have interesting and even fantastic shapes; their forelegs are unsuited for walking, but have been modified into grasping tongs, similar to the claws of crabs.

Finally, the insect hunters include the huge family Reduviidae (assassin bugs). The nearly 4,000 species, which differ greatly in form, populate the entire earth. Many, wearing bright garb, lurk motionless amid the flowers. The long, hairlike antennae of an assassin bug, bestirred by even the gentlest air currents, detect flying insects far away and prepare the predator to pounce instantaneously upon its victim. Seizing the victim with spiny forelegs, the hunter holds it down and tries to stick the beak into the victim's soft neck. If this is successful, an injection of saliva paralyzes the victim's body at once. In this way the assassin bugs succeed in overpowering big, able-bodied insects, not excepting honeybees.

The reduviid family also includes little, extremely elegant rod-shaped insects, whose forelegs are modified into prehensile claws, like those of praying mantids. Small but broadly built species of another group are given a grotesque appearance by their densely hairy antennae and their legs covered with long spines. Black-and-red species of the genus *Platymeris,* in Africa, measure nearly 2 inches and are covered with sharp, thorny spears that make them difficult to take hold of.

The bite of many reduviids is very painful, even to man; in warm countries certain species even enter homes on occasion at night and suck the blood of people. In North America this may be done by the black "kissing bug" *(Melanolestes picipes).* About 0.6 inch long, this bug prefers to bite the face, especially in the region of the mouth. Particularly feared, however, are the cone-nosed bugs of the genus *Triatoma.* These bugs often live in houses and bore their beaks into persons at night; the bite is painless, but may transmit an exceptionally dangerous trypanosomal infection (Chagas' disease).

The nocturnal reduviid bugs wander about in search of prey and with their extremely sensitive antennal flagellae perceive the slightest vibrations or air movements. A brown species, *Reduvius personatus,* is particularly well-known because it often is seen in houses, where it hunts insects near the lights at night. The nymph of this species covers itself in a curious manner with dust, dirt particles, sand, or soil—materials that are caught fast by its sticky hairs. Of still greater significance

are the hairs of a predatory bug from Java, *Ptilocerus ochraceous,* from which a toxic but apparently sweet secretion is discharged. Ants are attracted, lick these odd hairs, are stupefied, and are sucked dry by the bug. Certain predatory bugs have become exclusively bloodsucking on mammals, in whose burrows they dwell. This brings us to those specialists in bloodsucking, the bedbugs (Cimicidae). [129/3, 10; 130/1-7; 131/3]

The thirty or so species of bedbugs are distributed over the world, many having been spread by man and animals. They suck on reptiles, birds, and mammals, including man, generally not being particularly selective as to their host. Two species of bedbugs that attack man are *Cimex lectularius,* of North America and Europe, and *Cimex hemipterus,* of the tropics. Bedbugs often give away their presence by their disagreeable odor. In rare instances they attack domestic animals, fowl, mice, and rats. *Oeciacus hirundinis* parasitizes swallows and swifts, sometimes sparrows, and occasionally bites people.

All these flattened bugs, which measure about 0.1 to 0.8 inch long, are wingless and lack simple eyes (ocelli). Only at night do they frequent their hosts for sucking blood (at which time many people do not even feel the bite). They spend the day hidden nearby or else in their nests, where the eggs, numbering approximately 6 to 50, are laid. A female bedbug can at one meal ingest almost double its weight in blood, a male about its own weight. After such a meal, these insects can go without food for more than a year. Development from the egg to the mature bug normally lasts about seven weeks, but may be drawn out to more than four months.

Related to the bedbugs are the 18 species of bat bugs (Polyctenidae), which live on bats in the tropics. They probably do not bite humans. Finally, the blind comb bugs, 0.06 inch to 0.08 inch long, of which only a dozen or so tropical species are known, are permanent parasites of mice. They, too, are flattened and wingless, but have backward-directed combs of bristles as well as clasping legs, making them specialized for an uninterrupted existence among their host's hair.

EGGS AND BROOD CARE

The number of eggs produced by the true bugs varies greatly and may amount to as many as 300 or even 500 per female. Many eggs are like jars with covers and often are adorned with threadlike processes or garlands. They are stuck to the supporting surface

120/1
A bedbug in the act of sucking blood; the color of this cosmopolitan creature, which incidentally is not known to transmit disease, runs from brownish yellow to reddish brown or dark brown.

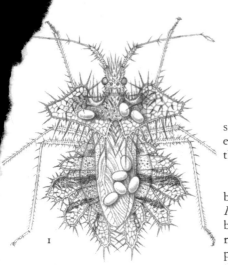

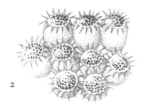

121/1–4
(1) The male of the spiny leaf-footed bug, Phyllomorpha, with eggs that the female has glued to his back. (2) Eggs of a stink bug. (3) Eggs of the burrower bug, Coptosoma, with packets of bacteria (symbionts). (4) An assassin bug's egg, inserted into a plant stem (greatly enlarged).

singly or in batches; in some families they even are sunk into the tissues of plants with the female's pointed or tubular ovipositor.

A few species of true bugs take care of the brood. Females of the leaf-shaped bug (genus *Phyllomorpha*) place their eggs on the concave backs of the males, where the eggs are surrounded by a confused mass of spines and prongs that stick out in all directions. Thus the brood is carried about, well-protected until hatching time. Eggs of the big water bugs, the belostomatids, are similarly carried on the backs of the males.

The females of certain stink bugs stay near their cluster of eggs and cover them with the body when it rains or when danger threatens. In similar circumstances, the gleaming, golden young of *Pachycoris torridus* in Brazil take refuge beneath their mother. And the offspring of the likewise South American *Phloea* hang from the mother's underside. Her irregular, flattened body, which is almost as thin as paper and resembles lichens, is pressed close against the bark at which she sucks. Females of the American predatory bug *Ghilianella* also carry the young; the immature bug clings to its mother by wrapping its long abdomen about her.

Of special interest is the way certain true bugs transmit to their progeny the bacteria and fungi that live as symbionts in the body. The females of the Plataspidae, a family whose members have an unusual humpbacked shape, place their symbionts among the eggs they have laid, in several small packets or clumps surrounded by a membrane; as soon as the young nymphs hatch they suck out the contents. If the symbionts are removed previously by some outside agent, the nymphs grow slowly and are unable to complete their development. In other families the symbionts are smeared over the newly laid eggs and penetrate into them.

But many true bugs don't have any symbionts and apparently do not require them. The diet of these bugs consists for the most part of a diversity of plant and animal juices. The symbionts, which assist in the synthesis of substances essential for growth, are most conspicuous among insects that depend on a limited type of food.

DEVELOPMENT

Metamorphosis in the true bugs is incomplete. The nymphs, some of which hatch with the help of an eggburster, resemble full-grown individuals and have a similar way of life. The wing rudiments, still absent in the beginning, get bigger from molt to molt; they expand to full size and stiffen at the last molt, which usually is the fifth. The most striking increase in body size takes place at the molts and is made possible because the new skin lies more or less in folds beneath the old one. Coloration and design frequently change markedly in the course of the several stages, and hence assemblages of true bugs on their food plant often have a varicolored appearance.

Even in the mature insect the basic color and design may change with age. Thus, during the first four weeks or so after the final molt, many of the handsome stink bugs of the genus *Eurydema* shift in color from white to yellow and red, and also develop a more extended dark pattern. Certain species achieve their final coloration only after they have overwintered. Many of the green true bugs get brown during this time, between autumn and spring, a fact that points to a connection between coloration and the process of feeding on plants. [31/2]

The true bugs mostly have only a single generation a year, sometimes two, and rarely several. In the temperate zone they overwinter either as an egg or as an adult, depending on the genus. Many species migrate in groups into their winter quarters, preferably in the woods or along their margins. On warm days even before the end of winter they sun themselves near their hiding places; at such times flocks of red-and-black-patterned red bugs and chinch bugs, usually glimpsed on the roots of trees and on pathways, are a magnificent sight against the dull-colored landscape. Apparently these are warning colors, which, as is the case with patterns of concealment, are widespread and of great diversity among the true bugs.

DEFENSES

Color is not the only means of protection available to the true bugs. Many have stink glands whose discharge will drive enemies away. These glands, which open on both sides of the thorax in the adults and on the back in the nymphs, secrete an oily substance. It varies somewhat from one species to another in composition and odor. Some big tropical species can spray it a considerable distance. The buggy smell nauseates most people, but is harmless, in contrast to the exhaust gases of our highways. Many true bugs have an agreeable aromatic fragrance, and in some countries are used as condiments.

Another possible means of protection is the ability of various families of true bugs to make chirping noises. Presumably these noises might startle predators such as birds or hunting spiders into dropping bugs they have seized. The stridulatory devices that produce those sounds are mostly small body plates that have sclerotized ridges and grooves like a file. They occur on the underside of the thorax in the assassin bugs, which draw the stubby teeth of the proboscis across them. Certain stink bugs have such instruments at both sides of the midline on the undersurface of the abdomen, and produce sounds by rubbing them with the tibiae of the hind legs, on which there are little warts. Damsel bugs, on the other hand, stroke their hind legs over a row of teeth on the back end of the body. [57/2]

FORM AND FUNCTION

The true bugs usually have well-developed, strongly vaulted, spherical compound eyes. Two simple eyes, or ocelli, may or may not be present. The antennae are very motile, are for the most part slender, and have only a few segments; those of aquatic species are short. Some true bugs are slow-moving and sluggish, but others are agile. Except for the prehensile instruments of the predacious species, the legs are simple walking legs, though frequently grotesquely formed. Certain capsids *(Halticus)* and saldids can jump, although their hind legs are not especially modified for the purpose. Correlated with a marked penchant for keeping the body clean, the true bugs have, either on the forelegs or on the middle legs, cleansing devices in the form of combs, brushes, and tufts.

PESTS

Whereas many species of true bugs are useful to man as predators of aphids and many other pests, others do damage by sucking on cultivated plants and fruits or, more rarely, by transmitting plant diseases. Some of the 3,400 species of stink bugs (Pentatomidae), for example, suck on fruit, berries, and vegetables. One, the harlequin bug *(Murgantia histrionica),* is particularly destructive of cabbage plants in the southern United States. Certain leaf-footed bugs (Coreidae), about 2,000 species of which are distributed over the world, damage vegetables, rice, millet, and cotton. The squash bug *(Anasa tristis)* is well-known in the U.S. for the damage it does to squashes and pumpkins. The Lygaeidae, of which some 1,500 species

are known, do great damage to cotton, but are especially destructive to grains and hay. Among them, the American species *Blissus leucopterus* (the "chinch bug") is particularly notorious; in favorable years its armies migrate in millions from one feeding place to another. The little, often handsomely colored plant bugs (Miridae), a large family of about 5,000 species, have numerous representatives that are pests on all sorts of plants or are vectors of viral diseases. And finally, the genus *Dysdercus,* a member of the smaller family of the red bugs and stainers (Pyrrhocoridae), is a nuisance as the "cotton stainer" that discolors the cotton in the bolls.

Among true bugs, some of the lace bugs (Tingidae), of which there are approximately 700 species, produce galls, particularly in flowers. These tiny insects, true to their name, have a striking lacelike appearance. [14/5, 6; 19/30; 53/1; 129–132]

ENEMIES AND PARTNERS

The true bugs have many enemies, including insectivorous animals, birds, spiders, and countless insects. Some of the insect enemies have been employed successfully by man in the battle against certain bug pests. Many flies (tachinids, sarcophagids, muscids) and parasitic wasps lay their eggs on the true bugs or on their brood, if necessary even under water (some parasitic wasps). All the parasitic larvae that hatch then devour their victims or suck them dry. Also, many twisted-winged parasites (Stylopidae) develop on true bugs, and some of the smallest organisms, the usually microscopic Protozoa, are internal parasites. Great numbers of the bugs perish of fungal infections.

Various true bugs, including a few burrower bugs (Cydridae), red bugs, and plant bugs, have been seen living as guests in ants' nests or else running about with them outside. Most of these guests display a quite startling resemblance to ants. But such relationships are little understood; it is an open question whether the deceptive appearance of these antlike bugs is of advantage to them with respect to the ants or whether it affords some protection against enemies. [19/34]

BEETLES ORDER COLEOPTERA

(Beetles that live in water are described in the section on "Water Insects.")

If a prize were awarded to the insect group manifesting the greatest creativity, the beetles

122/1
Larva of a tiger beetle lurking in ambush in her earthen shaft (enlarged 2 ×)

would probably win it, for they are the most fantastically conceived insects. Certainly the beauty of the moths and butterflies is incomparable and their deftness is decidedly lacking in the beetles. But this very sense of the absence of weight demands a composition limited to the thinnest planes, an image built wholly of colors and of the outline of the wings. The beetles, on the contrary, have the added dimension of depth, as well as the sculptured integumental armor—a branch of art all its own.

The illustrations can only suggest the artistry of the beetle's body. After all, the lustrous brilliance of a beetle's structural colors must appear in a painting as a mere reflection; for what in reality is shimmering light can be expressed on paper only by lusterless, dead pigments. Since the beauty of many beetles surpasses that of precious metals and jewels, it is not surprising that these insects often are used for decorative purposes, especially by primitive peoples. [31/ 1; 133; 180; 182]

Only a few places in the world are without beetles. They even inhabit the water. Almost every organic material is used by them. Their food habits identify some as mold beetles, dung beetles, and carrion beetles, but others are so fussy that only nectar, the sap of trees, and fruits are good enough. Neither beetles nor their larvae have a sucking proboscis like that of the true bugs; instead, they have biting, chewing, or lapping mouthparts.

Especially typical of beetles are their wing covers (elytra). These usually high-arched and hardened front wings generally cover the soft back as well as the larger, membranous hind wings. The latter are folded both lengthwise and crosswise. The elytra of some beetles are reduced in size or absent altogether. In this case the exposed surface of the beetle's back is protected by harder plates.

Although there are many soft species, the armored mail of most beetles is almost as hard as rock; it can withstand a load of as much as several pounds. The strength of these living armored vehicles is extraordinary: some species can carry 800 to 1,700 times their own weight. [133/1]

In addition to these typical characteristics, beetles display an almost inestimable wealth of different body forms, and they vary in size from a few hundredths of an inch (the dimensions of a dust particle) to about 8 inches long. Two main groups, or suborders, of beetles are recognized: the Adephaga, in which the first three abdominal segments are fused; and the Polyphaga, whose abdominal segments regularly are completely independent.

The Adephaga include only a small number of families, mainly the ground beetles (Carabidae), the tiger beetles (Cicindelidae), and a few families of predatory water beetles. Most of these beetles are meat-eating (carnivorous) types, but many also consume vegetable matter, especially fruit.

Among the Polyphaga are some predators, omnivorous species, and parasites, but mostly plant-feeders (phytophagous insects); in addition, some feed on wood (xylophagous species) or on dung (coprophagous species). As is common among other insects, the mouthparts and body structure of beetles are adapted to the method of getting nourishment, and here we find some interesting food specialists.

TRAPPERS AND HUNTERS

The larvae of many tiger beetles live in narrow tubes dug nearly perpendicular to the surface of the ground. Shaped like a short annelid worm with a double-humped back, the larva lurks in ambush near the top of the tube. Supporting itself on three pairs of legs fused to the thorax, and anchored to the wall by two spiny hooks, one on the abdominal hump and the other at the back end, this ugly creature seals the entrance to its burrow with its extended head and ventral neck plate. Usually these parts are brownish, like the ground, but in southern species they may be a brilliant metallic green or blue, a structural color that apparently is not perceived by insects and that can be regarded as a protection against the strong radiation from the sun.

Now, if a small insect happens to tread on this odd door—that is, on the larva's head— the trespasser is seized immediately by the larva's sharp, erect biting jaws (mandibles). The predator also may dart out of the entrance, if need be, or drop back like a trap door. The victim is beheaded, dragged down into the shaft, and devoured. If the insect, such as an ant, is not wounded mortally by the first bite, the beetle larva tosses its head violently, beating the victim against the walls until it is stupefied.

But many of these predators meet their match in a little wasp of the genus *Methoca,* which looks like an ant. The wasp directs its efforts to getting in between the beetle's mandibles. Thereupon she gives it a paralyzing sting in the throat or thorax, and fastens an egg to it. The wasp then closes off the pitfall and hunts for her next victim. From the egg hatches a wasp maggot, which gradually sucks dry the motionless but still living beetle larva.

The tiger-beetle larva's head, with its erect mandibles, flattened plates (sclerites), and convex, hemispherical neck, gives the impression of being upside down. The lower surface, swollen like a balloon, functions as a pestle for polishing the inner surface of the dwelling. Usually the shaft is not more than about 16 inches deep, but in rare instances may be as much as 2 yards. Yet, when the shaft is dug, the soil is not brought out; the larva uses its head to compress the soil against the walls. By constantly turning backward somersaults in the narrow shaft, the larva gradually smooths down the walls. Certain tiger-beetle larvae that live in the forests of Southeast Asia do not build their tubes in the ground but in the pith of branches. Both larvae and adults of other species in warm countries range about at night, hunting in the open. [140/1–13]

Numerous beetles and their larvae feed on snails. A long, slender forebody with a little, highly movable head permits them to eat snails out from within the narrow convolutions of the shells. And high-arched wing covers, extending downward at the sides and thereby covering the spiracles, form an air reservoir over the back—for example, in *Cychrus*. In the midst of the mass of slime ejected by an attacked snail, this air supply can be essential.

The larvae of fireflies (Lampyridae) attack snails with their scythe-shaped mandibles, each pierced by a poison canal. Again and again the larva bites into the head and antennae of the much larger snail, until the latter gradually is paralyzed and killed. Its tissues are first dissolved by the larva's digestive juices and then are consumed. After completing this task, which may take several days, the predator sponges itself off with a clear fluid secretion from a hoselike arrangement protruding from the rear end. This device, the pygopodium, serves also to anchor the larva's body to the snail's shell.

Quite similar are the methods used by drilid larvae, members of a snail-eating beetle family (Drilidae) that is related to the fireflies but that contains only about 100 species. Since the larva molts and later becomes a pupa inside the snail's shell, it often transports the shell into a hiding place, shoving it along or gripping it with the anal fastening device and dragging it. The larva uses its mandibles to force the shell over obstacles. Before the larva molts into the overwintering stage, it cleans out the emptied shell by rolling about within it, and finally stops up the entrance with its shed skin. [99/10; 140/27; 177/1]

DUNG ROLLERS

Many species of the great family of scarab beetles (Scarabaeidae) are dung feeders. A large number prefer the excrement of specific animals, such as sheep, asses, horses, cattle; some want it only fresh, others half-dry, and still others completely desiccated. Among these specialists is the pill roller, or sacred scarab. The ancient Egyptians designated this beetle holy, worshipped it as a symbol of the sun and of the forces of creation, and shaped its image in stone and clay in order to use it for amulets, seals, and jewels. [146/1]

In tropical lands, these broad, black beetles can be seen propelling their balls of dung over the poorly vegetated soil. Although the beetles are only between 0.8 inch and 1.2 inches long, the dung is sometimes as large as an apple. Anyone who has not personally witnessed the diverting spectacle, is probably familiar with pictures of it. The beetle's head, acting as a flat spade with a toothed edge, first cuts off and reduces the dung to small pieces. The widespread front legs, likewise toothed but without feet, seize it like a pair of tongs, or push it along as though with rakes, and function like a bricklayer's trowel in working it over.

Both males and females make balls of dung. Heated by the singeing rays of the sun, these high-spirited beetles work with feverish haste, which is, in fact, dictated by the rapidity with which the material dries out. If the excrement consists of small individual lumps, the beetle takes one after the other, drawing it in with the outreaching forelegs, cutting it to pieces with the shield-shaped headplate, pushing it back between the hind legs, and bit by bit pressing the material beneath the insect into an ever-enlarging ball. The rounded form of the material results from a combination of sense of touch, leg shape, and way of working; the beetle continually turns about in all directions while the curved middle and hind legs embrace the mass like pairs of compasses.

A somewhat different method is used when the material is taken from a larger, coherent mass. After the nature of the pile has been carefully examined, the beetle uses its cephalic spade to open a cleft out of which it rakes material under the body by means of its forelegs. As the beetle continues to rake, the ball of dung grows higher and higher beneath it. When the ball is finished, the beetle, now

125/1

A scarab beetle, rolling its ball of dung backward. The rows of teeth on the head and forelegs are cutting tools; fore tarsi are lacking, inasmuch as they would only be a hindrance in the task of kneading the manure (natural size).

riding on top of it, slides headfirst on his forelegs to the ground. But he keeps hold of the ball with the rest of his legs and, giving a kick, begins to roll it backward with rapid, rhythmic leg movements.

Since pill rollers often work together in a large group they frequently interfere with one another. If a second beetle approaches one that is rolling a ball along, the first stretches out on top of the ball with legs extended toward the oncomer, while the second one comes up and pushes his head and prothoracic shield gently beneath the first. This is an olfactory contact; if the approaching beetle is recognized as being of the same sex, he presently receives a violent shove and goes somersaulting away. But if a pair has met and the owner of the ball is a male, he proceeds to roll it onward, while the female follows. If the ball belongs to a female, she gets off and turns over the job of transporting it to her partner. The mode of progression is not, as one so often sees in illustrations, by means of harmonious cooperative labor, with one beetle pulling and the other pushing. The passive member, however, may occasionally lean the forelegs against the other side of the ball or even sit on it.

Robbery is common. One beetle may drag another forcibly away from the other's ball of dung. Or, as the owner burrows into the ground in order to bury the pill, a second one runs off with it.

Burial is the final objective of all rolling. The ball of dung is enclosed a little below the surface in a hollow about as large as a fist. There, it is devoured peacefully and in concealment by one or two beetles. When the feast is over, the beetle or beetles set out in search of more dung. Matters go along thus for one or two months. The beetles interrupt their activity during the summer and undergo a period of dormancy (diapause) in the cool soil. In autumn, preparations for the progeny are begun; we shall return to them later.

Mouth, Antennae, and Eyes

The mouth of a beetle may face downward or forward. Species of the genus *Stenus* (family Staphylinidae) catch little insects with the lower lip, or labium, which can be thrust forward more than half the length of the body. Weevils (Curculionidae) and brentid beetles (Brenthidae) have the lower part of the face drawn out in a downward and forward direction like a proboscis, often to grotesque lengths. With it, many bore into plants, woody fruits, or seeds, partly to eat

them, but even more to insert eggs into the holes. As might be expected, the females usually have the longer snout.

Weevils of the genus *Curculio* bore into nuts, acorns, and other shelled fruits. In doing so, they circle with almost endless patience, until the nutshell has been penetrated by the slowly turning tip of the thin, curved proboscis, which is about as long as the beetle's body. Next, the channel is extended inward to the milkiest part of the kernel. Finally the beetle places an egg in this spot with its long, slender ovipositor, which stretches out from the tip of the abdomen.

The brentid beetles, thanks to their thin, cylindrical shape, can creep into holes drilled by other wood-boring beetles and lay their eggs in them. Many species drive off the rightful owners or eat them. But the females of many brentids bore their own holes. Using the biting mouthparts at the front of their long, rod-shaped head, they even drill through bark or penetrate deeply into the wood. The larvae then gnaw out shafts of their own and eat the fungi that become established in them. There are about 1,500 species of this family, almost all tropical. Occasionally large groups assemble under bark. A few small species live in ants' nests. [135/1–11]

The antennae of beetles usually are extensively developed and distinctly segmented. They have an extraordinary variety of shapes. In their primary role as odor-perceiving organs, they often are larger and more intricately formed in the males. In many lamellicorn beetles, they are splendid feathery fans. In many long-horned beetles (Cerambycidae), they are enormously lengthened and often fantastically adorned with clusters of hairs. In male timber beetles (Lymexylidae) the palpi also serve as olfactory organs and are feathery or shaped like seashells. Certain tropical representatives of this long-bodied, soft-skinned family, of which only about 500 species are known, have the wing covers (elytra) reduced to short scales. The membranous hind wings, folded lengthwise, merely lie over the back. Often these beetles have such enlarged eyes that they occupy the whole head and meet in the middle of it.

Usually the compound eyes of beetles are on the sides of the head. Their size varies greatly in different species, and they may have as many as 20,000 to 25,000 facets. The eyes also vary in form; frequently they are kidney-shaped or may be indented deeply near the antennal sockets, even to the point of being divided in two. Just a few beetles have dorsal ocelli, or simple eyes, and then only one or two. Certain primitive beetles and beetles that live with ants or in caves lack eyes altogether.

CAVERN DWELLERS

Cave beetles awaken feelings of special veneration in us, and many have been named after legendary figures of the nether world. In the perpetual darkness of their impoverished abodes, they wander as symbols of the tenacity of life. Over millions of years, their eyes, wings, and body pigments have been lost, their groping antennae and legs stretched to absurd lengths, and their abdomen swollen into an almost balloon-shaped air reservoir. Their spiracles and tracheae, which serve for breathing in most insects, are reduced in size, and many cave beetles respire only through the body surface. In these ways many cave beetles are adapted to life in caverns often so full of carbon dioxide that a person can breathe in them only laboriously. Not all beetles that inhabit caves, however, have experienced such drastic modifications.

Almost every cave has its own peculiar, often unique fauna, composed principally of members of the ground beetle family (Carabidae) and the carrion beetle family (Silphidae). These beetles live on other small fellow lodgers or on their decomposing remains. Who knows how many strange, exceedingly rare species may have been extinguished forever by earthquakes or cave-ins. [135/13]

LEGS OF MANY USES

The legs of most beetles are powerful. The mighty goliath beetles *(Goliathus)* of Africa, which hang like monkeys from tree branches by means of their short forelegs, cling so tightly they are nearly undetachable. It is as though they are welded like iron to the trees. If one tries to tear these giant beetles free by force, they can gash the human hand with their claws until it bleeds. Other beetles of many families have climbing and clinging legs whose feet are equipped with broad, hairy padlike pulvilli.

In contrast, some beetles have elegant, slender running legs. These are especially evident in tiger beetles and ground beetles, many of which run from danger with improbable speed. The hind legs of other beetles are developed into leaping organs. This is accomplished by modifications in certain parts of the legs—by thickened femora, as in some leaf beetles (Chrysomelidae), which hop like fleas, or by a long elastic spur at the end of

each of the hind tibiae, as in melandryids (such as *Orchesia*), which can jump 20 inches high. Assisted by the hind legs, the lengthened spine-shaped tip of the abdomen likewise enables the tumbling flower beetles (Mordellidae) to leap into the air when, for instance, they take off in flight.

Forelegs may be modified, too, as in the highly-specialized swimming legs of many water beetles. In many other beetles, the forelegs have become effective digging implements. Ground beetles of the genus *Dyschirius* have such legs. These predators often pursue other, smaller beetles underground. For example, when a rove beetle (family Staphylinidae) digs to escape one of these ground beetles, the pursuer must widen the passage made by the rove beetle. Though the latter usually is the loser, it frequently saves its life by suddenly tunneling upward to the surface and heading for the open, while the pursuer mistakenly digs on for a time in the former direction.

Numerous beetles without specially modified legs dig themselves skillfully and rapidly into loose soil or sand. Certain tiger beetles can do this. So can ground beetles of the genera *Omophron* and *Broscus,* which lurk in ambush for prey at the entrance of their holes in the sand. Beetle legs, which often bear spines and brushes, have an important role in cleaning the body: the forelegs care for the head and its appendages, the hind legs for the wing covers.

The forelegs of certain species seem unnecessarily long, and their function is in doubt. This is true of the South American long-horned beetle *(Macropus longimanus),* the gigantic Asiatic weevils *(Cyrto),* and the Asiatic scarabaeids *(Euchirus).* Since their powerful forelegs often are armed with spines, and in the Asiatic scarabaeids even with mighty prongs, they could be weapons. They usually occur only in the males, and it is a fact that in many beetles, particularly those in which females are scarcer than males, rival males are often seen contesting. One will try to pick the other up and fling him down. Frequently fights occur at the feeding places, also. [134; 181/1; 186/45]

FLIGHT

In general, beetles fly heavily and steer poorly. Often they have to climb to an elevated vantage point for a successful takeoff. Though many sun-loving types, such as the tiger beetles (Cicindelidae) or the metallic wood borers (Buprestidae), fly off swiftly

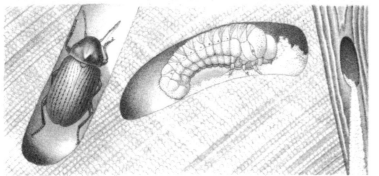

127/1
*A furniture beetle,
the "deathwatch," and its larva,
well-known as the "woodworm"
(enlarged 7×).*

when threatened, most others require fussy preparations before becoming airborne. The body temperature of a resting beetle, which is identical with that of the surroundings, is ordinarily insufficient to permit the beetle to vibrate its wings rapidly enough to support it in flight. So the beetle must first raise its body temperature. It does so by vibrating its wings. This pumps air into its body and expends metabolic energy. The increasing vibrations are accompanied by a buzzing that grows progressively louder and higher in pitch. This buzzing often is heard as a beetle flies by.

Immediately before taking off, beetles of some species—for example, scarabs and long-horned beetles—raise themselves on their forelegs. Right after takeoff, these often heavy insects hang with the body almost straight up and down in the air and assume a more horizontal position only when they have attained full speed. The ineffective, gently vibrating elytra, held diagonally erect, constitute gliding surfaces and stabilizers, while the work of flying is done by the elastic hind wings (alae). These are not simply stretched out flat; their surface is irregularly creased, and their leading edge is stiffened with strong veins.

According to the available data, beetles fly with some 30 to 90 wingbeats per second, depending on species. Many, especially the rose beetles of the scarab family, do not spread the wing covers when flying; the elytra often are fused or stuck together along the midline. The great goliath beetles extend the first two pairs of their powerful legs sideways as substitutes for the elytra. The legs, held out close together on each side, serve for balancing. These monsters fly like bullets and can crash through glass windows.

The orientation of beetles in flight is primarily visual; in flying toward distant objects they are guided by the silhouette of the horizon. Scarab beetles emerging from their places of pupation in the earth (for example, the May beetle *Melolontha*) first fly around in circles a few times and then head at increased speed fairly directly for their goal—a wooded ridge some miles away, for instance. After eating leaves on the trees for some time, they return to the place of their birth and lay their eggs in the ground. Investigations have shown that electric and magnetic influences of the atmosphere and the earth may also be

involved in the orientation of these beetles and, under certain circumstances, may be exclusively responsible. [136/6; 137/1; 180/16A; 183/2]

BEETLE SOUNDS

Apart from the humming and buzzing of their flight, beetles make themselves noticeable acoustically in other ways. Large species, for example, betray their presence in wood by the scratchy noises they make when moving about. The gnawing sounds of wood-eating beetle larvae are audible several yards away from the treetrunks. Likewise to be heard coming from wood is the ticking of deathwatch and drugstore beetles (Anobiidae) and false powder-post beetles (Bostrichidae). At pairing time, males and females tap at regular intervals with the head and prothorax against the floor of their passages, apparently for mutual attraction. Whether they can hear this is doubtful; perhaps their sense of touch enables them to perceive the vibration produced in the wood.

A great many beetle species, including the larvae of passalids and other scarabaeids, have sound-producing instruments (organs of stridulation) with which they chirp, squeak, pipe, grate, scrape, or creak. These always involve the rubbing together of a rough element, usually grooved like a file, and one or a few smooth, rough, or toothed ridges or edges. Amplifiers are supplied by hollow regions in the integumental part that bears one of the sound-producing elements. An amplifier is formed most often by a combination of the back of the abdomen and the underside of the elytra, near their margin. According to the species, sound is produced by longitudinal or crosswise movements of the abdomen. In long-horned beetles, the basal part of the back of the abdomen and the rear margin of the prothoracic back plate bear the stridulatory apparatus and are rubbed together by means of nodding movements of the neck.

Other species have a stridulatory organ on the surface of the throat and another on the adjoining thoracic plate; these are activated by a nodding of the head. Or the apparatus may be situated farther back on two thoracic sclerites that can be rubbed together. Stridulating devices also can occur on the coxae of the middle legs and at the base of the femora of the hind legs (in stag beetles), or on the coxae of the hind legs and the under surface of the abdomen (in scarabaeids); in the latter instance the abdomen is the moving part. In addition, the combination may be

CAPTIONS
FOR PAGES 129 TO 143

129/1–10
*Different heteropteran shapes.
The triangular plate (scutellum) that
is attached to the posterior end of the
more anterior principal dorsal
thoracic sclerite (scutum) is sometimes quite small, but may also be so
exceedingly large as to cover the wings
and the entire abdomen. Of particular
biological interest is a long-haired East
Asian species (3), which discharges
among the hairs a secretion that
attracts ants; the latter are then
seized by the bug and sucked dry. And
the slender ambush bug (10) has
prehensile legs like a praying mantis.
Just as fantastic as they are purpose-
less are the varicolored, leaf-shaped
expansions of the hind legs in certain
South American leaf-footed bugs (6)
(3, 4, and 10 enlarged 4×; all
others enlarged 2.5×).*

PAGES 130 AND 131
130/1–17
*(1–7) Assassin bugs. (8–11) A
series of leaf bugs. (12) A flat bug.
(13 and 14) Two red bug species
(stainers). Below are the slender-
legged stilt bug (15), the red small
milkweed bug (16), and a related
species (17) (enlarged 1.25×).
Photograph.*

130/18–26
*The leaf-footed bugs are a family that
often has distinctive legs and antennae
(enlarged 1.25×). Photograph.*

131/1–2
*Stink bugs. Only the outer half of
the fore wings of true bugs is
membranous. The species (1) in the
illustration is sucking a caterpillar
dry, and at the base of the middle
legs on both sides the slit-shaped
openings of stink glands are visible
(enlarged 4×).*

131/3
*The tropical American bloodsucking
cone-nosed bug, a dreaded vector of
Chagas' disease; and two immature
stages (enlarged 2.5×).*

PAGE 132
132/1–11
*Stink bugs and (below) two
burrower bugs (5 and 11). Many
stink bugs shield their eggs, which are
laid on leaves, beneath them; and next
to their eggs the burrowing bugs set
down packets of intestinal bacteria or
fungi (symbionts) from their own
body. The new generation requires
these organisms for further development
and consumes them immediately on*

hatching (enlarged 1.6×). Photograph.
132/12–15
*Lace bugs are among the most delight-
ful insect forms. For the most part, the
numerous distinct kinds live as groups
on definite species of plants (enlarged
20×).*

PAGE 133
133/1 and 3
*Two snout beetles of extreme
structure, reminiscent of an elephant
and a giraffe. Comparison of the heads
and prothoracic parts reveals clearly
the wide spectrum of forms found
within a single family (1 enlarged
5×; 3 enlarged 8×).*

133/2
*A South American dung beetle,
one of the most beautiful species of
scarabaeoids (enlarged 2.5×).*

PAGE 134
134/1
*On the back of the South American
long-horned harlequin beetle, beneath
the wings, live pseudoscorpions which
subsist on molds that are growing
there, as such fungi do on many other
insects (enlarged 1.75×).*

PAGE 135
135/1–11
*The primitive weevils (Brenthidae)
are best adapted to a life beneath bark
and in holes bored into the wood
(enlarged 1.5×). Photograph.*

135/12
*A tiger beetle from East Asia,
with long slender legs and claws
(enlarged 5×).*

135/13
*A cave-dwelling beetle from
the family of carrion beetles
(enlarged 5×).*

PAGES 136 AND 137
136/1
*The brood pills of Onthophagus are
made entirely of dung; outside is a
hard crust, at the top a lid, and
below this the chamber with an egg
sitting atop a pile of specially
concentrated food. The young
larva eats its way downward, at the
same time filling up the space above
it with its excrement. The pupa
is at first suspended by the rear end in
a cocoon formed of excrement and
saliva, but later stands headfirst on a
peg and has similar supports at the
sides too (on the left) (enlarged 3×).*
136/2
*Structure made by an Onthophagus
pair beneath cow manure on sandy soil.
Via a side passage, roundish lumps of*

*sand are deposited on the surface.
From the balls of dung brought down
into the galleries by the male, the
female shapes the large brood pills and
furnishes each with an egg. Finally, the
galleries and main shaft are refilled
with the material excavated earlier
(reduced).*

136/3–5
*Dung beetle constructions. (3)
Onthophagus; (4) dorbeetle; (5)
bullhead beetle (reduced).*

136/6–7
*A Brazilian lightning bug (a firefly)
(6) and a female glowworm (7), with
their light organs, viewed from below
(enlarged 2×).*

136/8–17 and 137/3–5
*In their body form, the elegant click
beetles are differentiated only slightly,
but there are species with distinctive
antennal shapes (enlarged 1.25×).
Photograph.*

137/1
*Blister beetles are among those
insects protected by having poisonous
body fluids (enlarged 1.6×).*

137/2–2A
*The "typographer" beetle, a bark
beetle, and a piece of bark from a tree
attacked by it (2 enlarged 14×;
2A somewhat reduced). Photographs.*

PAGE 138
138/1–17
*Various beetle families. (1–5) Blister
beetles, with glands that produce the
highly toxic cantharidin, for which
the green "Spanish fly" (2) is
particularly notorious; the meloids (4)
are parasitic on bees. (6–14) The
best-known of the darkling beetles is
the mealworm beetle (13), whose
larvae (mealworms) are used as food
for pet birds. (5) The "tyrant," with
a very few other species, forms a small
but quite distinct Asian family
(Trictenomidae). (15) Fire-colored
beetle. (16 and 17) The rhipiphorids
(wedge-shaped beetles) are principally
parasites of wasps (0.75 natural
size). Photograph.*

138/18–30
*Immature stages of beetles. (19)
The heavily armored ground beetle
larvae hunt insects (18), worms, and
snails above and below ground. (20)
Ladybird beetle larvae live at large on
plants and eat aphids. (21) Carpet
beetle larvae live on dead animal
matter and are pests in houses and,
especially, museums. (25) The
elongate, hard click beetle larvae,
known as wireworms, are notorious
root feeders, and the several species are*

*to be differentiated particularly by
the ingeniously shaped thrusting plate
at the rear end (22–24).
(26) Another supportive organ, in
the form of a protrusible tube, is found
at the rear end of certain rove beetle
larvae. (27) Timber beetle larvae
(Lymexylidae) are wood-feeders.
To move forward the larva first
steadies itself with the hind end,
stretches far out frontward, pulls
the head back, presses the thereby
inflated nape of the neck against the
tunnel wall, and then drags up the
rest of the body. (28) The wood-
eating larva of the poplar borer has
no legs, but crawls along with the aid
of rough pads on the under and upper
parts. (29) Metallic wood borer larva.
(30) Long-horned beetle pupa in
its cradle under the bark.*

PAGE 139
139/1
*A ground beetle overwintering in
rotten wood is chipped out by a
green woodpecker (natural size).*

PAGE 140
140/1–13
*Tiger beetles are light-footed runners
and love sunshine, yet there are also
nocturnal species (1) and others with
long necks and froglike faces that live
in brush (12 and 13). (Enlarged
1.5×). Photograph.*

140/14
*Ground beetles are on the go mainly
at night (enlarged 1.5×).*

140/15–27
*The genus of ground beetles best loved
by collectors is perhaps Carabus, for it
has produced a great many races, many
of which have a truly regal
appearance. Especially fascinating is
the sculpturing of the elytra (wing
covers), composed of ridges and
interlocking links, and differing from
one species to another (natural size).
Photograph.*

PAGE 141
141/1
*A ghostly ground beetle (Mormolyce
phyllodes) of Indonesia, whose greatly
broadened, paper-thin wings and long
neck make it one of the strangest of
beetle forms, has been discovered
beneath the bark of a tree by a slow
loris (natural size).*

PAGES 142 AND 143
142/1–143/3
*The "antlers" of the stag beetles are
elongated mandibles of the males, who
frequently battle over females
(enlarged 2×).*

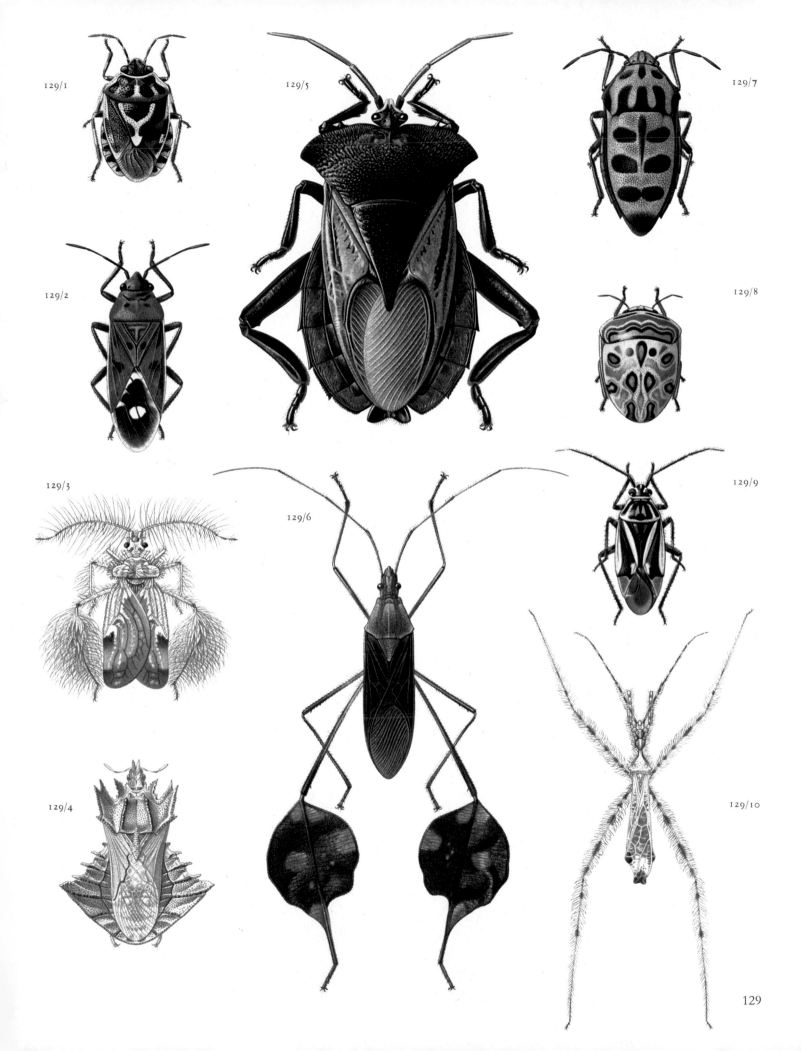

129/1

129/2

129/3

129/4

129/5

129/6

129/7

129/8

129/9

129/10

129

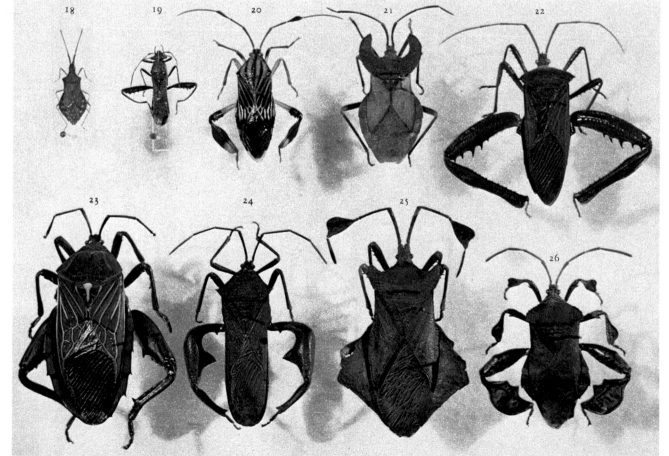

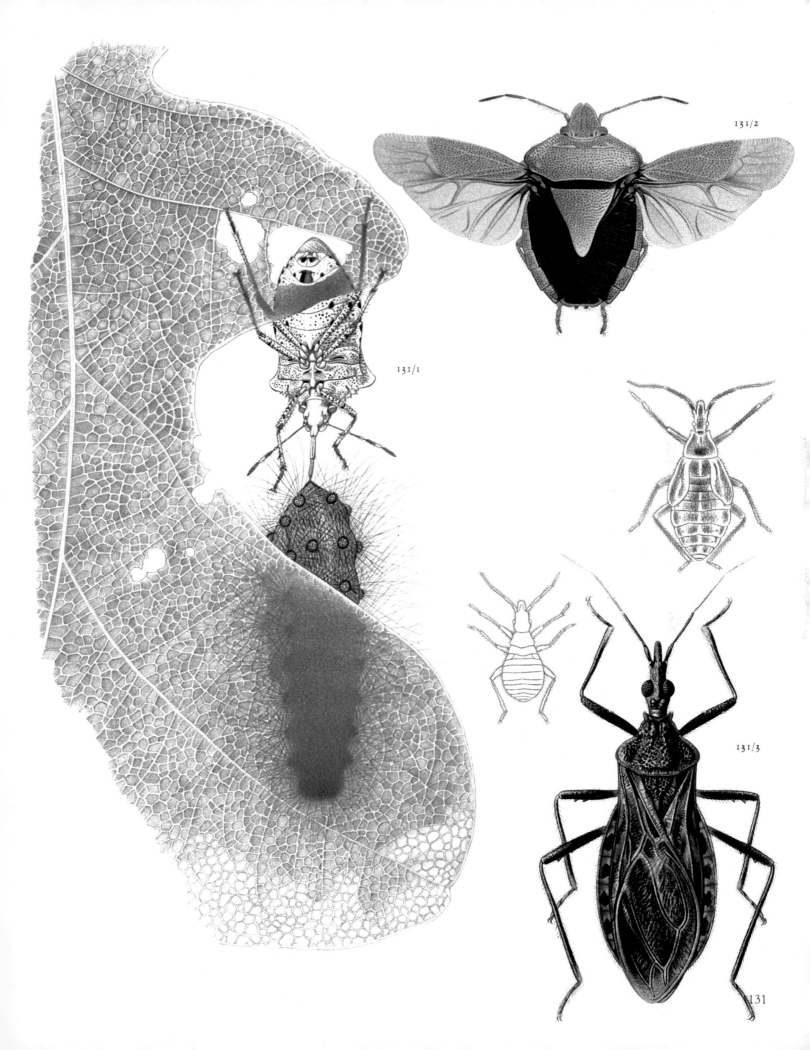

131/1

131/2

131/3

131

132/13

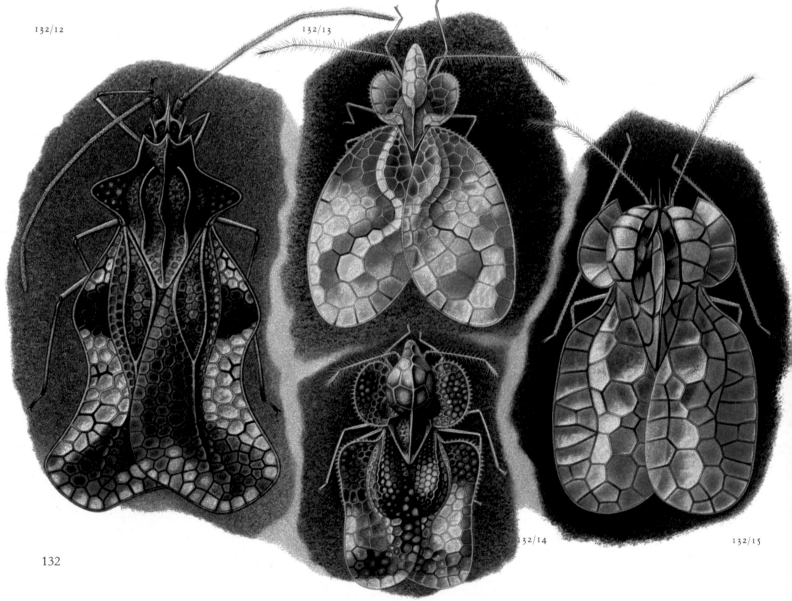

132/14

132/15

133/1

133/2

133/3

133

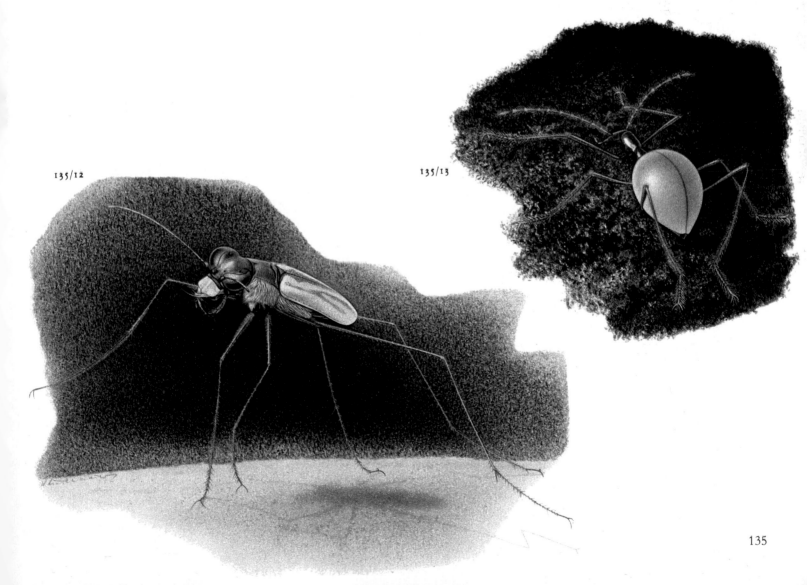

135/12

135/13

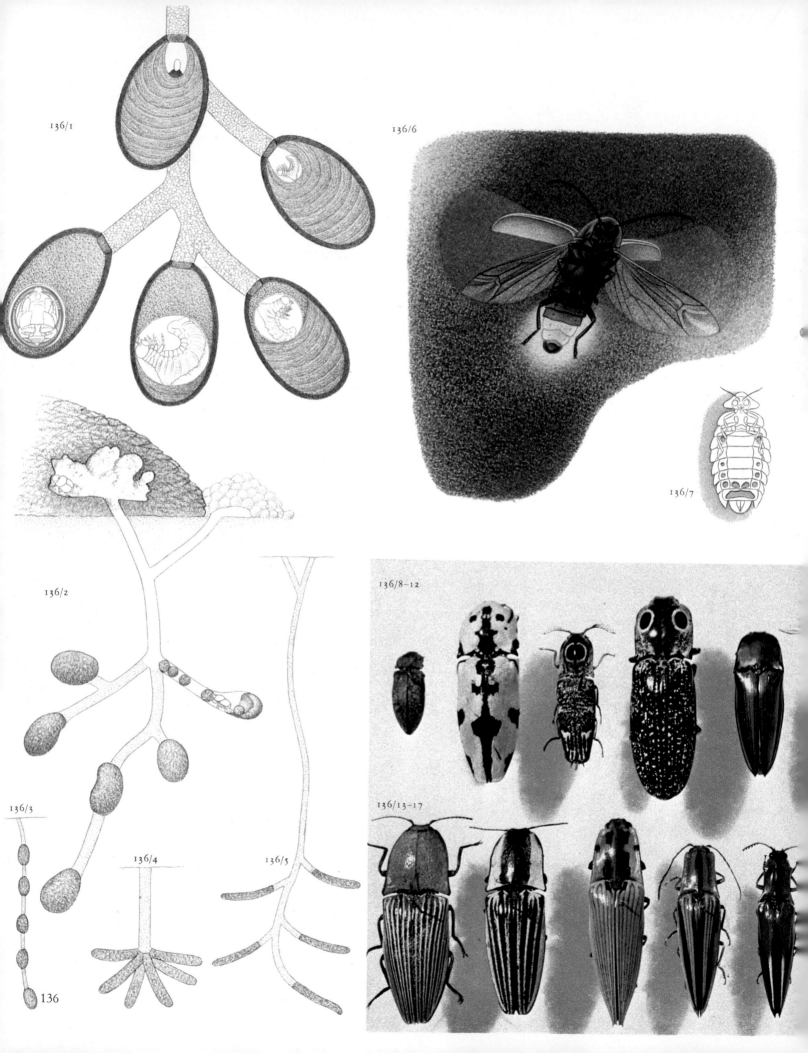

136/1

136/2

136/3

136/4

136/5

136

136/6

136/7

136/8–12

136/13–17

137/1

137/2

137/3   137/2A

137/4 - 5

137

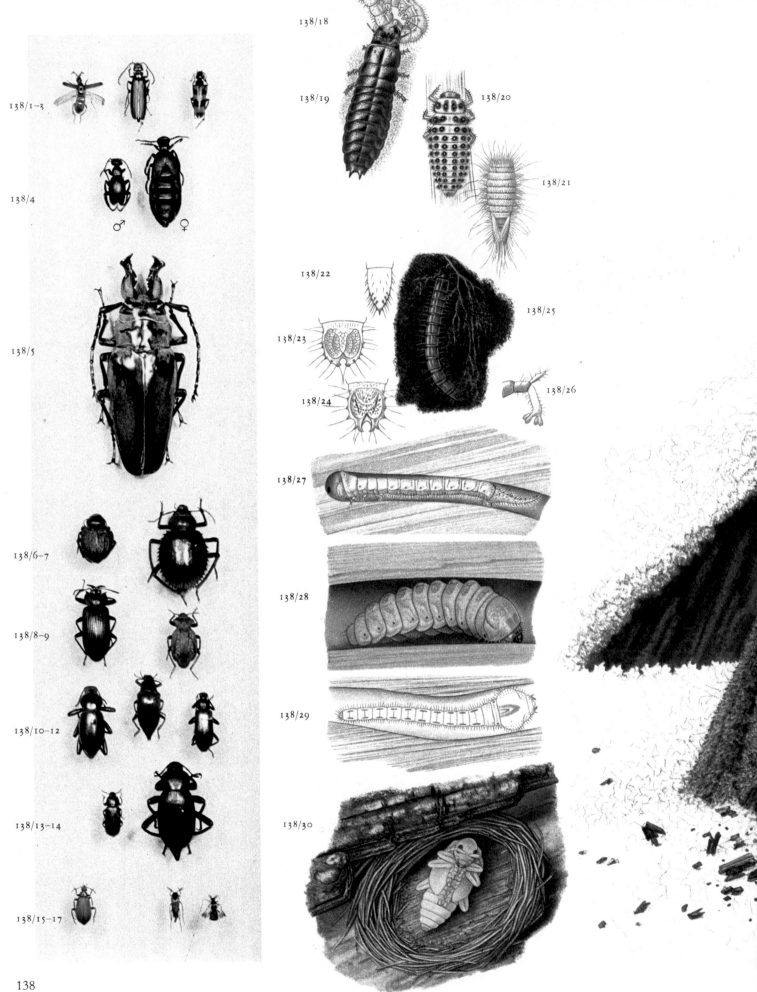

138/1-3

138/4 ♂ ♀

138/5

138/6-7

138/8-9

138/10-12

138/13-14

138/15-17

138/18

138/19

138/20

138/21

138/22

138/23

138/24

138/25

138/26

138/27

138/28

138/29

138/30

138

139/1

140/1 – 6

140/ 7

140/8 – 13

140/14

140/15–21

140/22–27

140

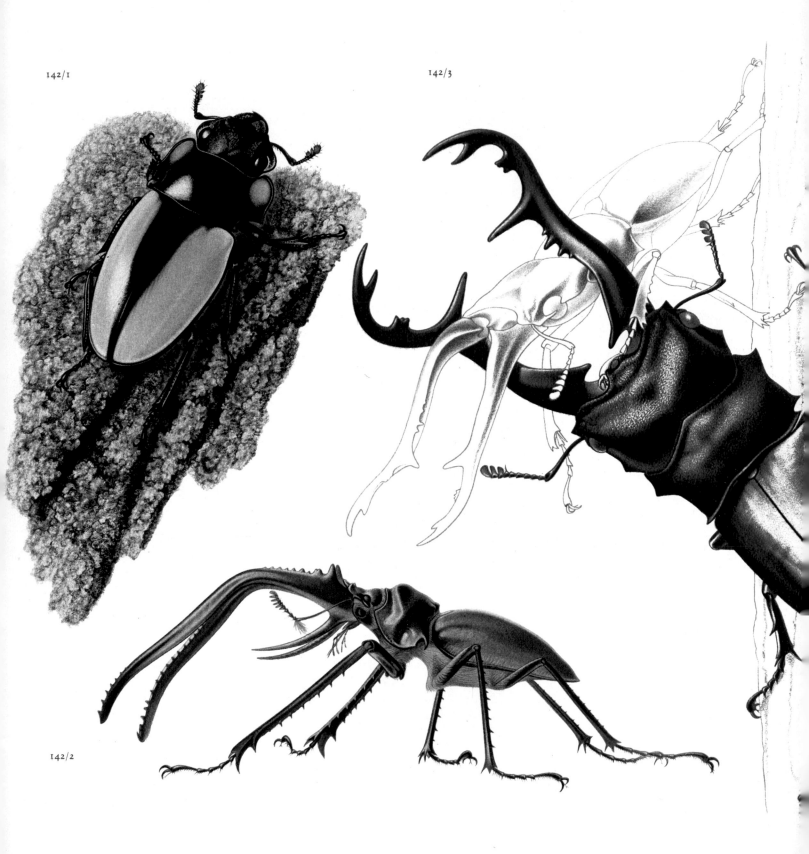

142/1

142/3

142/2

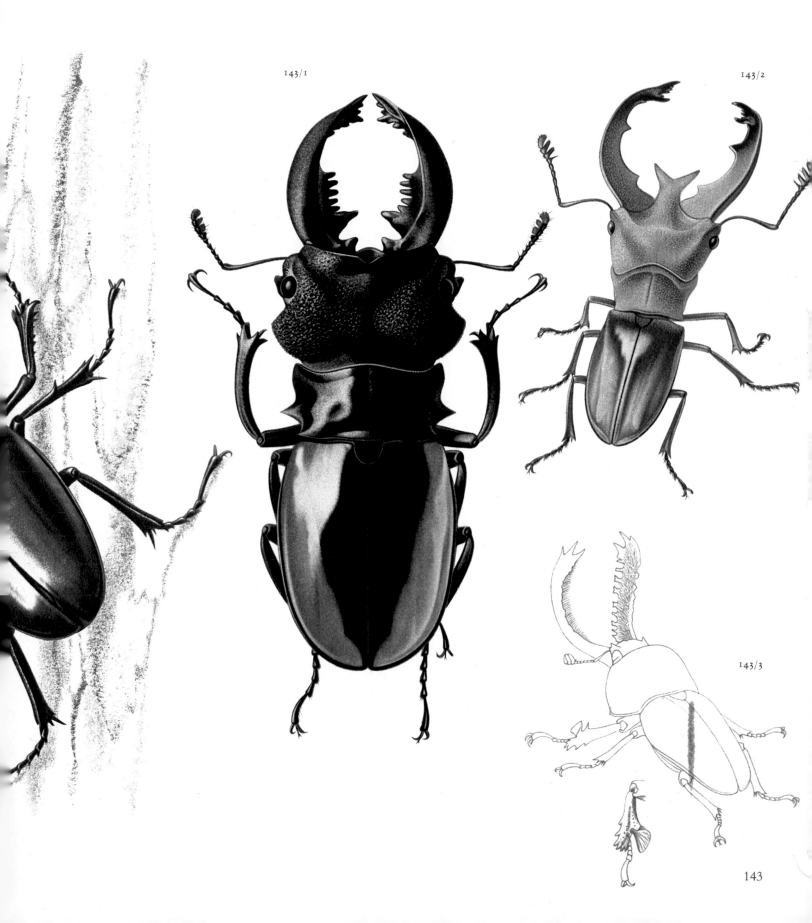

143/1

143/2

143/3

144/1
*The European stag beetle
(enlarged 3×).*

on the sides of the abdomen and on the inner face of the hind femora, or else on the hind tibiae and the elytral margins, in which case, strange to relate, it is the elytra rather than the more versatile legs that are made to vibrate. Certain larvae stridulate with the mouth, namely with the maxillae and the mandibles. And larvae of dorbeetles (*Geotrupes*) have even modified the rear pair of legs extensively as the active element of a sound-producing apparatus.

At this point the question as to the ultimate function of all these instruments becomes particularly insistent. It is hard to discern why *Geotrupes* larvae, buried in a mass of food within deep, closed earthen tunnels, should chirp. On the other hand, one is able to interpret the sounds of passalid larvae as a means of communication, since they live in families together with their parents. Many beetles, usually both sexes, stridulate at mating time, no doubt as a means of mutual attraction and stimulation. Among bark beetles (Scolytidae) only the males chirp. They do so not only at mating time, but also while at work. They are audible for a distance of 6 feet, and if a person is lucky he can hear a whole assemblage "singing" in different tones from inside a treetrunk. Species that play dead when endangered chirp only when undisturbed; in contrast, those that tend to run away are noisiest when threatened. In general, the ability of beetles to stridulate should be regarded primarily as a means of scaring off enemies. [136/6,7]

FIREFLIES

The ability of certain beetles to give light serves both for attraction and for causing alarm. Whereas no sense of hearing has yet been found in beetles, which makes it questionable whether the two sexes actually can hear each other when they stridulate, the strikingly enlarged eyes of the male fireflies (family Lampyridae) undoubtedly are of value in detecting the luminous signals of females. The females of these nocturnal beetles are well known as the larva-like "glowworms," which frequently cannot fly. The female makes the light that shines forth from beneath her abdomen especially visible by climbing up on a plant, by curling up her hind end, or even by turning over on her back. If a light-producing male, which usually flashes more weakly, comes into the vicinity, the female is aroused and shines more brightly.

On warm nights, the greenish lights continually flash on and off as thousands of males fly back and forth over a meadow or among the gigantic silhouettes of trees in a tropical forest. Distinguishable from the stars only by their going and coming against the night sky, they give even the soberest and most matter-of-fact person the impression of a fairy tale brought to life. Unfortunately, when one tries to reproduce this pictorially or with the written word, it sinks almost inevitably to the level of dubious romanticism.

The firefly male and female recognize one another and announce their readiness to mate less from the light as such (the males can be attracted even with a flashlight) than from the duration of intervals between flashes. In other words, communication is by means of light signals. For one of the sexes these are usually short and succeed one another very rapidly, up to 8 flashes per second; with the partner, on the contrary, they are isolated and long drawn out. In addition, the light intensity may either increase or decrease, according to the species. With some fireflies, flashing is much slower; thus, for instance, a male will light up only every 5 to 6 seconds, and the female will answer 2 seconds later.

In the tropics, certain kinds of fireflies gather every night on specific trees; then thousands of males and females run back and forth among one another on the branches, flashing as they go; and more come flying in. The tree is turned into a brightly sparkling pyramid, surrounded by a cold, nebulous gleam. Even heavy rain does not interfere with the activity of these insects, yet their lights are extinguished in moonlight.

One of the most astounding phenomena of the insect empire is displayed by those tropical firefly males that rise at night in thousands from the grass and underbrush, leaving the females, who are not giving light at the time. The males gather in the trees, lights flashing as far as the eye can see. This strange performance reminds one of the males of certain birds of paradise in New Guinea, which assemble in numbers on a single tree and there enact their magnificent courting dances. Yet not all has been told. For the lights of these fireflies all shine forth together, flash after flash, in complete synchrony. As though controlled by a light-producing pulsebeat, the forms of the trees stand out momentarily in the black tropical night, illuminated by the communal effort of countless tiny individual insects.

Fireflies are predominantly tropical insects. Many of the about 2,000 known species are little, unimpressive beetles when seen by day, and the wingless females have the ugliness of larvae. The long, soft body of the male usually is flattened and often bears thin lateral expansions, especially of the prothoracic shield. This forms a roof over his head, but allows light from above to be perceived through transparent, windowlike spots.

Adult fireflies either feed on vegetable matter (obtained principally from flowers) or take no nourishment; the larvae, on the other hand, prey on snails and worms. Any effect the light may have in frightening enemies is disputed and in any event is limited. That frogs are unimpressed by it is evident to anyone who sees the curious spectacle of a frog's stomach shining with the light of the firefly larvae it has recently swallowed.

In addition to fireflies, the larvae or adults of a few other families produce light. Best known are the tropical American click beetles of the genus *Pyrophorus,* often called fire beetles. These useful enemies of sugarcane pests are inconspicuous, brownish insects, usually about 0.8 inch to 1.6 inches long and rarely more than 2.4 inches. Their usually green light appears in two places: on the prothoracic shield in front of its sharply pointed rear corners, and below, at the base of the abdomen. Certain species have a reddish abdominal light and can flash in two colors, like a traffic signal light.

The light of fire beetles is the strongest among fireflies. With one of these beetles in the hand it is possible to read a newspaper at night. As long as the beetle is held, it shines uninterruptedly, but soon stops when it is left at rest, a fact that suggests the function of the light here is as a means of scaring off enemies. Girls frequently fasten these beetles to their hair or clothing in a little lace bag, as a splendiferous ornament; and the beetles even are confined in cages, as living lamps. [34; 181/15,16]

CLICK BEETLES

Fire beetles are members of the family of click beetles (Elateridae), which consists of about 8,000 species and is distributed throughout the world. Its smallest representatives measure less than a tenth of an inch long, the largest more than 3 inches. They are mostly vegetarians. The larvae of certain species live below ground, some for as long as six years, where nearly all feed on plants. Generally known as wireworms because of their hard, slender bodies, they are often among the most harmful of insects.

The click beetles received their name from the loud click they make as they hurl themselves into the air by means of a snapping articulation of the body. Simple though such a mechanism may appear at first glance, it requires an astonishingly complex apparatus whose function remains to be fully explained.

The first segment of the click beetle's thorax is joined to the afterpart of its body by a hingelike joint that enables the insect to bend backward. A spine on the lower side of this prothorax fits into a groove between the basal segments (coxae) of the middle legs. When the insect bends backward the spine pulls out of the groove. In front of the groove is a little barrier or knob. When the insect starts to straighten the body again, the spine meets the barrier, which resists its movement. Activated by extremely forceful tension, the spine suddenly overcomes this resistance and slips into the groove with a snap. This first step, of no effect in itself, immediately releases the essential second step—namely, the reaction produced by the collision of appropriately-shaped bulkheads, ledges, and abutments on various parts of the thorax.

When sitting in the normal belly-down stance, the beetle launches itself by striking the front margin of its prothoracic shield against the surface. But when the beetle leaps from a supine position the shield does not necessarily have to make contact with the ground; the tip of the abdomen may do so, instead. Then the insect usually is hurled aloft vertically, over the tip of the abdomen. In this performance the force of the blow against the support is magnified by the elasticity of the wing covers. Their constitution determines in part the height attained, which may be about 6 inches. The beetle, having shot into the air, may fall back onto the same spot or land as much as a foot away.

Usually click beetles make use of their unique ability only when fleeing danger. In a typical situation the beetle is on a plant when threatened. It immediately drops to the ground and feigns death. Then, suddenly, it snaps itself into the air. This enables it to make a fast getaway or to regain its footing if it landed on its back. At times a beetle on its back will succeed in righting itself only after several jumps, and it is quite possible for a beetle to turn over without jumping at all. [136/8–17; 137/3–5; 312/4]

DEFENSIVE DEVICES

Many beetles besides the click beetles feign death instead of fleeing danger. With legs stiffened in a grotesque attitude characteris-

146/1
South American lightning bugs from the click beetle family. Light signals are emitted by their lamps, which can be turned on and off at will (natural size). Photograph.

tically different for each species, the beetle remains motionless for a few seconds to 15 minutes. A twitching of the legs signals the beetle's return to life. Feigned death is not guile or pretense on the part of the insect, but merely a reflex—an automatic reaction to certain stimuli.

Beetles evade their enemies in many other ways. Their disguises range from the simplest protective coloration to the most refined imitations of lichens, bark, bits of wood or soil, and seed pods. The bodies of a small number of beetles have eyespots, decorative devices that may cause alarm in enemies. Many more beetles wear brightly colored warning costumes. These are found not only in many harmless species—as in mimics that resemble certain wasps or even other, poisonous beetles—but also in species that are equipped with protective glands, a penetrating odor, disagreeable body fluids, or toxic blood.

Among beetles with extremely poisonous blood are the ladybird beetles, also called ladybugs (Coccinellidae). The blood usually is squeezed in drops out of the knee joints (between femur and tibia) when a threatened individual lets itself fall in feigned death.

An especially toxic substance present in the blood and other parts of certain blister beetles (Meloidae)—mainly cantharines, malachiines, and some curculionids—is cantharidin. It acts both as a blood poison and a stomach poison; mere ·contact with the skin causes great burning blisters. A dose of about a two-thousandth of an ounce is fatal to man. Beetles carrying cantharidin are expressly avoided by many reptiles and amphibians, as well as by many predatory insects. Nonetheless, many insectivorous animals, especially birds, eat such beetles without harm. In earlier times cantharidin was employed in medicines as a vesicant, since blistering of the skin was a standard treatment for many ills. It was also used in all kinds of "love potions" (often under the name "Spanish fly"). Without doubt it did much damage. [137/1; 138/1-4]

Other protective juices of beetles and their larvae usually are harmless, though they may cause a burning sensation, especially in the eyes. Such fluids, most of which have a strong smell, can be projected a distance of a foot, or even a yard by some big ground beetles (Carabus); in this case the fluids are digestive juices from the mouth. In other species such secretions are produced by special glands, which may be situated at various locations on the body—in leaf beetles even on the edges of the elytra. Also, the thorax or abdomen of certain beetles has odorous sacs, some of them finger-shaped, that can be forced out by blood pressure. The rove beetles, for example, have a pair of glands at the tip of the abdomen. When threatened, they curl the abdomen upward and eject an odorous secretion. [140/14-27]

A well-known chemical armament is the explosive apparatus of the bombardier beetles (Brachinus and related carabids). These beetles by preference dwell in small groups beneath rocks. Their protective glands, like those of other ground beetles, lie at the rear end. These glands produce both a cohesive fluid and a liquid that evaporates with the utmost rapidity on contact with the air. The resulting gas is emitted in a small cloud that explodes with a slight bang or pop. It carries with it the fluid, which settles afterward as a yellowish precipitate. If the stock of this fluid is exhausted after several shots, the beetle may fire feces from the digestive tract. Certain water beetles (Dytiscus) also do this. [62/1]

Particularly noteworthy is the defense mechanism of the pupae of Melasoma, a genus of leaf beetles (family Chrysomelidae). The larvae of these beetles are equipped with glandular vesicles that produce a strong-smelling secretion toxic to small insects. At the end of its development the larva fastens its skin to a leaf and pupates within the skin. The pupa thereupon begins with writhing movements to work its way out through a slit in the front of the skin, but two great lateral spines, just forward of the pupa's rear end, latch into special folds in the larval skin. The pupa, now mostly free, remains hanging quietly.

But this skin constitutes not only a suspensory device but also an astounding protection. For within the skin the glandular reservoirs of the last larval stage remain intact and still contain protective secretion. When threatened, the pupa exerts pressure on the reservoirs with special movements of its body, with the result that drops of the protective secretion are exuded. After this pressure is released, the drops are sucked back automatically thanks to the elasticity of the vesicles. Thus they remain available for future use.

Beetles need their great array of defense mechanisms, for they have plenty of enemies. Practically all classes of vertebrates share in their destruction, and to these must be added spiders and countless insects, including some of their own kind. Innumerable parasitic wasps and flies carry out their immature stages of growth and their metamorphosis in

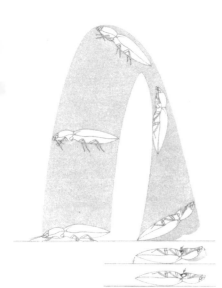

147/1

A jumping click beetle. Simply expressed, the sudden slipping of the thoracic spine, braced against an obstruction, starts the reaction that sets the beetle up on the elastic tips of the wing covers and hurls it aloft.

beetles. Worms, molds, and infectious diseases attack them. To protect his crops, man is forced to combat many species of beetles. And in many countries they are eaten, especially the fat larvae, or grubs, that inhabit live or decaying wood, and the big swimming beetles, enormous numbers of which are cultured as a source of food in Asia.

WAYS OF LIFE

Beetles manage to live almost anywhere. They are guests and lodgers of our houses, living on food, garbage, and filth. Some species eat the remains of insects that have been sucked dry by spiders in their webs, and others feed on excrement and cast skins in the silken nests of wasps, bees (particularly bumblebees), ants, and termites; certain of these attack their host's brood. Such spongers and parasites often let themselves be transported to new nests by clinging to the hairs of the host with their legs or by seizing onto the legs and antennae with their mandibles, a method that is called phoresy.

In common with many other insects, some species depend exclusively upon a definite type of food, such as a single species of plant. Mostly, the larval diet is different from that of the adult. Often, microscopic fungi live in the beetle body and act as symbionts, aiding in digestion, especially among beetles that eat wood; these fungal cells get onto the shell of the beetle egg and are ingested together with the shell by the hatching larva. Beetles that eat plants have feeding patterns characteristic of each species and leave behind them evidence such as skeletonization, arc-shaped cuts, scraped areas, mined-out regions, completely stripped foliage, pockmarked bark, or total destruction.

Certain beetle larvae that live within plant tissue or under bark cause galls, for the most part entirely closed ones. The form of the gall usually is typical for each beetle species, yet a single species may engender different gall forms on different plants. Most of the gall formers are weevils, but a smaller number are bark beetles, long-horned beetles, metallic wood borers, and leaf beetles. A few weevils (*Curculio, Balanobius*) pass through their developmental stages as lodgers in the galls caused by gall wasps and sawflies.

Most adult beetles become able to reproduce only after a period of taking food, a requirement designated as "maturation feeding." Many species, particularly the predatory kinds, continue to eat as long as they live, but others feed only a little (for instance, the stag beetles) or not at all. Commonly beetles have

to drink considerable water, particularly desert-dwelling species; many of these have rigid, high-arched wing covers that evidently constitute a protection against the heat and against a loss of water.

There are day beetles, dusk beetles, and night beetles; many live singly, others in companies that may be brought together accidentally, by the nature of the locale or by their feeding, reproduction, or overwintering habits. Thus, many bark beetles swarm en masse in spring from their hiding places, and the swarming flights of certain scarabs (*Melolontha, Phyllopertha, Amphimallus,* and others) from the places where they were born are only too familiar. Along the seacoast, assemblages of flying beetles sometimes are carried out to sea by strong air currents and then blown back to shore when the wind changes. The majority recuperate and fly back into the interior. [181/2–5]

Actual migrations are rare among beetles and have been seen principally in the ground beetle *Calosoma sycophanta,* swarms of which have descended on city streets, and among the ladybird beetles (Coccinellidae), which in certain years, for example, fly in gigantic swarms from North Europe to England. Features reminiscent of social life are shown by the gregarious games of whirligig beetles (Gyrinidae) on the water surface and especially in the family life of a few genera that practice brood care. [140/16]

EGG CHAMBERS

The round, longish eggs of beetles are shaped like spindles or like tenpins. Those of a few species bear outgrowths. They often are deposited on or in plants on which beetles feed or in chambers in the ground, either singly or in groups. As a rule, eggs hidden away are whitish, and those cemented openly to plants are colored. Often the eggs are protected by a secreted envelope or with bits of plants or dung.

The leaf beetle *Galerucella viburni,* for example, gnaws a series of deep, rounded cavities, one above the other, in a branch, for the reception of about five eggs per cavity on the average. In excavating each egg chamber, the beetle first bites away the bark, then splits the wood up into little fibers that remain attached to the upper circumference of the spot chewed away, and finally hollows out the chamber by eating up the pith. After laying the eggs, the beetle closes the openings. She does this by making a lid of excrement mixed with cement from her colleterial glands and pushing it up beneath the cluster of wood

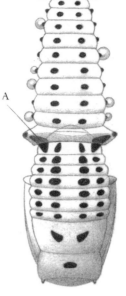

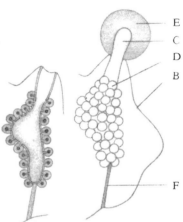

148/1
With two pegs (A) on the sides of its posterior portion, the pupa of the leaf beetle Melasoma hangs in a fold of the last larval skin, from which poisonous drops are secreted on contact (greatly enlarged). Below, a longitudinal section of a secretory gland: B = side of body, C = everted portion of the glandular reservoir, D = secretory cells, E = secretory droplets expelled by blood pressure, and F = retractor muscle.

fibers shredded previously. Thanks to its form and composition the lid not only protects the eggs, but sponges up and stores water that runs down the branch, thereby providing the even humidity the eggs require. Although each egg chamber requires several hours of labor, a single female is able to prepare about 100 of them.

The total number of eggs laid by a female beetle varies according to species from perhaps about 20 to several thousand. The total may be even more than 10,000 for beetles in which the likelihood of a given individual's reaching maturity is slight. This is true for blister beetles (Meloidae), whose young perish in large numbers because many of them must find other insects to transport them to the source of food, and for swimming beetles *(Dytiscus)*, only a few of whose offspring reach maturity.

The provisions for the young made by the female beetle often involve marvelous instinctive acts. A great many larvae must have dying or sickly plant food, and the females themselves produce this by surgical intervention at the time of egg-laying. The long-horned poplar beetle *(Saperda populnea)* gnaws horseshoe-shaped figures superficially into the bark. Their curving course is enriched with transverse furrows, and at the curved end a small hole is dug to the woody tissue. An egg is pushed into this hole and beneath the bark. The bark, at first pressed flat, soon begins to arch spherically outward. After about two days, tumors arise on the damaged tissues of the bark. These gradually lift the bark up slightly in the pre-etched horseshoe shape, thus making room for the egg and the hatching larva. At first the larva feeds on the growing tumors; in fact, unless it devours them, it will be squeezed to death by them. A little later the larva bores its way into the wood, but continues to keep the entrance hole open by repeatedly eating away the bark tumors. The larva is not always the victor in this contest between eating and rate of tumor growth, for often such an insect is suffocated or squeezed to death—for instance, when unfavorable weather slows its development and at the same time accelerates that of the bark tumors. [183/19]

Another beetle of the same family, *Oberea linearis,* inserts its eggs singly between wood and bark of young sprouts and then bites rings above the egg and around the twig down to the level of the wood. The injection of the egg causes an enclosing tumor of the bark; and the tip of the branch beyond the encircling rings eventually is broken off by the wind. Thus the apparently essential and

quite specific diseased conditions of wood and bark are created next to the point of fracture. Later the larva forces its way in deeper, clear to the pith, whence it eats its way first up to the broken surface and then away from it again. [183/20]

A formidable task is performed by the females (exceptionally both males and females in concert) of the American long-horned beetle genus *Oncideres,* known in Brazil by the popular name of "sawyers." By means of one to two weeks of labor, the females, with their mandibles, chew complete rings (rarely on one side only) into branches of the hardest woods, up to 5 inches thick. Thus they perform much as beavers do, although the cut made by the beetles, which are only 0.6 to 1 inch long, has a less pronounced wedge shape, the latter only on the upper side. During their work or afterward, they drill some 3 to 4 eggs with single incisions here and there into the bark of the notched branch. The branch breaks from the force of the wind or falls of its own weight, and the hatching larvae have their dying wood, within which they feed for 8 to 10 months until pupation. Nearly all other female beetles whose young develop in wood seek out material of the proper consistency. But these amazing females create the proper conditions by means of their own preparative acts—of course, with no knowledge of the purpose of what they are doing.

A similar procedure is followed by many weevils that bore into wood and vegetation. These include shoot borers, leaf-vein borers, fruit borers, and bud borers. With a specially-shaped proboscis the weevil makes a hole and lays an egg in it, often pushing the egg in with the snout, and the affected part of the plant dies. Or a fruit borer places its egg in a young fruit and cuts the stalk partly away. Similarly a bud borer causes young flowers to wilt and fall off.

Leaf Rolling

Even more highly specialized are the tooth-nosed snout beetles (Rhynchitinae) and the leaf-rolling weevils (Attelabinae). By cutting into the leaves or the stalk, and occasionally by perforating the whole leaf surface, these little beetles cause the desired parts of the plant to wither and to become pliable and capable of being rolled. There are lengthwise rollers, which roll the leaf with the main ribs in the long axis, and crosswise rollers, which make the main veins perpendicular to the long axis.

149/1
A Galerucella beetle, and its clutch of eggs in the pith of a twig; the cleverly fashioned covers of the chambers (longitudinal section at the right) consist of three parts made of different materials (enlarged 5×)

According to the shape of the rolls, one distinguishes cone rollers and funnel rollers among the lengthwise rollers, as well as cylinder rollers and jar rollers among the crosswise rollers. Depending on the species of beetle, the undersurface of the leaf forms the outside or the inside of the roll. The cone rollers twist one, two, or more leaves together lengthwise—after they have notched the stalk or stalks or the entire shoot farther back. The only known cylinder roller is a single Japanese species, which rolls the leaf up crosswise all the way from the tip to the base. In making their particular style of roll, all other lengthwise rollers and crosswise rollers cut designs through the leaf surface; these figures may be either simple or complex. Normally they leave nothing to be desired in the logic of their design, and arouse much astonishment and admiration because of the calculated geometry and its suitability for the purpose. They even have served as a basis for mathematical computations. Errors in cutting often occur, however, due to various causes. By the tactile sense of their legs and mouthparts these beetles are able to distinguish with certainty not only the uppersides and undersides of leaves, as well as the main and accessory ribs, but also their degree of elasticity, in particular the greater rigidity of the basal and inner parts. The cuts are then directed accordingly. The dependence on innate patterns of behavior is most impressively illustrated when, for example, a beetle has begun its cut too far out on a leaf, so that a portion of the design falls beyond the leaf margin. The beetle cuts onward through the air, symbolically so to speak, until the mouth again reaches the surface of the leaf! [186/38]

With many species, the cut goes completely through the entire surface of the leaf, whose parts then remain connected only by the midrib; the latter, too, is then notched, interrupting the flow of sap. Other beetles do not cut quite all the way across a leaf, or perhaps only a little more than halfway, severing the main rib as they go. Thereupon, the remaining uncut portion often is perforated by a close-set, frequently curving row of holes punched into it, which interrupt the circulation of sap.

The funnel rollers begin the act of rolling at the side of the leaf. With the three legs of one side the beetle bends up the edge of the leaf and rolls it inward, simultaneously walking inward with its other legs. When the roll has attained a certain thickness, the beetle must work the other way around; with legs standing on the leaf's surface, the beetle must now pull the unrolled portion up to the funnel.

Many species creep into their roll and squeeze it together even more tightly from within. A few beetles use cement to make their work firmer. Others fasten the edges by means of punctures made with their snouts; the indentations then fit together like a row of cogs. Often the bottom of the funnel is closed off simply by bending it over, or the tip of the leaf is rolled in. But this effect also is achieved in another marvelous and singular way; the beetle, with legs spread wide, clings with its claws to the lower part of the roll and bends it slowly inward. As a result, there arises a fold that is pressed inward with snout and abdomen; thus the funnel is narrowed or closed off entirely at that point.

The jar rollers make simple incisions that are fairly straight or only slightly curved, but cut notches into all the larger leaf ribs, and sometimes into the whole leaf surface. Then they fold the two halves of the leaf together; they ride on the main rib on the lower side and fold the leaf together lengthwise by pushing with their feet. Then they start to roll up this double layer from the side or from below; from the beginning on, certain species keep putting in stitches with their snout, thus incorporating into the jar and attaching to it parts of the leaf that may protrude laterally. Finally the two ends—that is, the marginal pads that have been formed during the process of rolling—are trampled down with the feet and likewise sewed in.

A female usually rolls one or two leaves a day, perhaps 15 to 30 altogether. In each roll she lays one to six eggs. She either deposits them during the process of wrapping the leaf up or inserts them afterward from outside through holes punched by her proboscis. The larvae feed inside the dying roll and finally pupate in the ground, letting themselves drop from the plant if their dwelling has not already fallen.

The entire task of rolling the leaf up is not always carried through without interruption; occasionally a female goes off to feed. Since one beetle may finish the work on a roll begun by another, changes in individual craftsmanship often occur. Moreover, several females may work peacefully on the same leaf and lay their eggs there, with no attempt at mutual help.

The males have no brood instinct whatever; nevertheless they are present occasionally as onlookers, and then wave their appendages just like the leaf-rolling females, in a wholly superfluous, useless way. If several are there, they endeavor to push one another

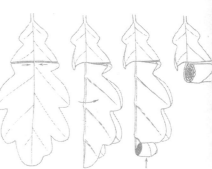

150/1
After making two incisions from each side and flexing the midrib (which also has been nibbled at all along its length in order to render it elastic), the oak leaf-rolling beetle (a snout beetle) lays one half of the leaf over the other and then rolls them up, at the same time tucking in the lobes of the leaf (a cylinder roller). In the course of this procedure as many as seven eggs are gradually laid inside the roll (reduced).

151/1

A birch leaf-rolling beetle (a snout beetle), the leaf viewed from beneath. From the upper surface of the leaf the beetle cuts the geometrically most suitable curves, bends the midrib at a definite place, waits for the onset of wilting, moves to the under surface, and rolls a species-specific form of funnel. Into pockets chewed out in the latter, two eggs are inserted, after which the leaftip is pulled in to close it off (reduced).

off with their hind legs. Other species of weevils, which cannot themselves roll leaves, may also appear and smuggle their eggs, at a favorable moment, into the rolls made by the others.

DUNG COLLECTORS

Dung beetles make provision for their progeny in quite a different way. They dig shafts of various lengths, up to about 6 feet deep, in the type of soil that appeals to them, frequently directly beneath piles of excrement, particularly that of ungulates (hoofed animals). The dorbeetles *(Geotrupes)* if necessary push horse dung off hard roads into ditches. Branching off the main shaft are short galleries or sac-shaped chambers that differ according to the species, or the shaft may have a single such ending; more rarely, several cavities may lie close together at short distances above one another. All of these are brood chambers into which dung (rarely carrion or fermenting vegetable matter) is stuffed for the larvae; often it is molded into a pill. Within, the egg lies in a carefully prepared egg chamber, which often is plastered with a layer of predigested excrement from the mother's stomach as an initial meal for the young larva. From the wealth of methods used, only a few will be singled out for further comment.

The *Onthophagus* female digs her edifice into the sandy soil at the edge of a cake of dung, scraping bits of the soil loose with the forelegs and piling it up in a heap behind her with the help of the other legs. When the pile is about as big as the beetle, she turns around, takes a short run, and butts into it with lowered head; and thus with repeated blows brings it up to the surface and out of the hole. After the beetle has completed her digging, she polishes the walls of the individual brood cavities by the continual turning of her body. She fills the hollow chambers with excrement, bits of which are brought together and pressed together tightly, layer by layer. A space for the egg chamber is left in the upper or anterior end of this plug of dung and closed with a lid of loose fecal material; the egg stands on top of a little mound of dung on the floor. Finally the shaft is partly filled in with sand, which is not invariably fetched in from outside but instead often is obtained, in an astonishingly rational way, from what is being excavated for the next brood chamber.

All this work can be done by a female alone, but often a male helps out. While construction is going on, he stays up above and hauls off the material brought up by his partner. Later, he brings the dung to the female in the shaft. For building a single "plug," a female working alone needs 5 to 6 hours, but one with a male partner can manage in only 3½ to 4 hours. This can increase significantly the number of brood chambers and hence of offspring produced by her, especially at times when the available dung is getting too dry too fast in the sunshine or is being snatched and carted off by other species of beetles.

After about a week, the larva hatches from the egg and gradually devours the soft interior of the plug. But it has barely enough space for twisting, since the space freed by the eaten dung is refilled immediately with the larva's own excrement. The larva molts about every 10 days and is full-grown in a month. But even before this, in its second larval stage, it begins to build a pupal cocoon, a covering formed from its own excrement mixed with sticky saliva. First, the dome-shaped top is molded, allowing the larva beneath to continue feeding, and then the sidewalls grow gradually downward until there is complete closure shortly before the transformation to the pupa.

During this act, the skin last shed is fastened to the ceiling of the cocoon. Anchored to this skin with a bilobed caudal process, the pupa at first hangs free, but soon is braced against the wall on all sides by various special knobs on its body, since the entire capsule contracts to some extent as it dries out. After 10 to 16 days the beetle emerges from the cocoon, waits three days while it completes its coloration, and finally works its way up through the earth to the light of day.

In certain species of dorbeetles, a pair working together digs a shaft up to 2 feet deep beneath horse manure. From the shaft two to eight short lateral passages lead upward obliquely. Each passage is filled with excrement, except for an egg chamber at its end. The beetles drag the excrement with their forelegs as they back down the shaft. As a result, each passage contains a manure sausage some 5 inches long. When the side passages are stuffed full of dung up to the main shaft, the upper entrance is closed with earth. The pair usually digs several such structures. The full-grown larvae overwinter and pupate about the middle of the succeeding year. Four or five weeks later the beetles

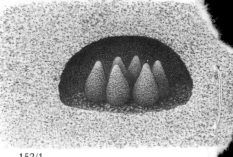

152/1

The scarabaeoid beetle Canthon provides its cavity in the ground with several pear-shaped balls of dung, each with an egg chamber at the tip (reduced).

emerge, but are capable of reproducing only after overwintering another year.

In one species of dorbeetle, *Geotrupes vernalis,* a beetle pair digs a funnel about 2 inches deep beside sheep feces, and at the bottom usually hollows out, in the shape of a star pointing in all directions, horizontal storage chambers about 8 inches long. When the beetles have stuffed these chambers with more than 50 droppings apiece, they fill in the funnel with dirt, burying themselves in the process. They then excavate beneath the funnel a deep shaft with a brood chamber at its end. Then the two beetles fetch down carefully selected material from the storage rooms, and knead therefrom an outwardly smooth mass, some 2 inches long, with a terminal egg chamber. Finally, the space between the mass and the walls of the cavity is filled with sand, and the shaft is stuffed with dung for some distance. One may see these dorbeetles of an evening flying about in search of sheep manure; and in a single night they will dig into the ground a whole heap of it, much more than they can make use of. [136/1–5; 177/31–34]

The pill rollers of the genus *Scarabaeus* have been known for 6,000 to 7,000 years. Yet their breeding customs first were clarified at the beginning of the present century by the unique French teacher and entomologist J.-H. Fabre (1823–1915). For, as already mentioned, the balls that so often are seen being rolled along under the supervision of these beetles usually are intended for their own consumption.

As it now appears, the whole task of arranging for the brood is attended to by the female alone. She rolls the ball, preferably sheep dung, over the surface and, after digging some 4 inches to 12 inches deep in the ground, places it in a smooth-walled spacious hollow at the end of a shaft. Large species make a fist-sized hollow. After about 12 hours of rekneading the dung, she makes it into a thick, erect, pear-shaped structure for the brood; the egg chamber lies in its small upper bulge, and the egg is cemented to the rather sharply pointed roof.

This egg chamber is created by building a parapet around the ball; the wall is extended higher and higher and narrowed down at the top to a tiny opening. Through the latter, the beetle passes an egg; this is followed by a sticky drop, which cements the egg to the inner edge of the opening. The opening is filled with loosely layered particles of dung and possibly also with grains of sand, forming a flue through which air and oxygen can circulate. Finally, the beetle leaves the cavity;

altogether she builds only a few, perhaps five or six.

Within the pear-shaped mass, the hatching larva soon eats its way inward to the center, closing off the egg chamber and the passage behind it with its excrement. The larva continues to eat away the interior of the pear until it changes into a pupa within the vessel, which meanwhile has become as hard as a rock. The pupa, completely incapable of moving, lies on its back, supported by a few callosities. And yet the beetle that emerges in a week is one of the most lively and high-spirited of all.

Deltochilum gibbosum, a tumblebug from the southeastern United States, makes its ball out of feathers or hairs, and the pear-shaped mantle with the egg chamber consists of rotten leaves and earth. The whole affair stands in a rather shallow earthen trough, covered with leaves and straw, at the base of a rock or cliff. Other American tumblebugs, of the *Canthon* species, set up from two to perhaps six brood pears, like funeral jars in a crypt, in especially roomy cavities. The couples work together and often use carrion mixed with mud for their pills.

Phanaeus milon, a dung beetle of tropical America, kneads its sphere together, beneath a decomposing carcass, from damp mud mixed with bits of flesh, skin, hairs, or feathers. The brood cavity is established at a depth of about 8 inches. In it is the ball, enveloped by a mantle of mud about 0.4 to 0.8 inch thick, which grows very hard; on top of this is placed the egg chamber, from which a narrow air tube leads to the surface. After hatching, the larva must bite its way through the layer of hard mud that separates it from the ball of food.

A South American pill roller, *Scaptophilus dasypleurus,* stuffs dung into a long, twisting cavity in the soil, and in the outer layer of this sausage establishes 10 or more egg chambers at fairly equal distances from one another. These are well enough separated so that each larva has sufficient room for feeding without running into its neighbor.

Certain pill-rolling beetles tarry in the brood chambers until the progeny are fully developed, and then all leave together. A pair of the species *Copris lunaris* builds a spacious room, some 6 inches long and as much as 2.5 inches high, underneath cow or horse manure, hauls in dung, and makes it into a large ball of various shapes. After the material has reached a certain stage of fermentation, it is cut to pieces, again by mutual effort, and

153/1

A pair of bullhead beetles caring in common for their brood; this is a very rare phenomenon among insects. Deep down in the galleries the female is molding a food plug for their offspring from the material brought into the shaft by the male (enlarged 1.5×).

the female molds it into 7 to 13 erect brood pears. Male and female remain on watch in the chamber; mostly she stays sitting on a "pear," again and again cleaning fungi off one after another and polishing them with her forelegs. In *Copris hispanicus,* the female of which constructs at most five brood pears, the male leaves her after the chamber has been completed and the material carried in.

A pair of the beetle *Typhoeus typhoeus* digs a shaft as much as 1.5 yards deep, the upper section of which often is forked into two entrances; there are three to eight side passages. The female claws the dirt loose, and the male hauls it up between the fantastic horns of his prothoracic shield. The female also excavates a little egg chamber in the sand at the end of each lateral passage, and fills the whole system of tunnels with sheep dung, firmly stamped down. Thus each egg lies somewhat beyond the end of a sausage of manure, the interior of which consists of fine material surrounded by a layer of coarser substance.

Now, the cooperation of the insect pair in this labor is something truly worthy of admiration. The male fetches sheep droppings, either by holding them with his forelegs while he crawls down backward or by shoving them ahead of him with his horns. He climbs down into the shaft with the first one and fastens it there somewhat above the busy female. After he has brought down two or three more, he uses his horns and forelegs to break up the coarse supply into small pieces; these fall down to the female, who works this shower of manure up into the final form.

CARRION BURIERS

No less admirable is the work of the burying beetles *(Necrophorus)* of the family of the carrion beetles (Silphidae), which number about 2,000 species. The burying beetles are attracted by the odor of dead animals (reptiles, amphibians, mice, moles, birds), which must be neither too large nor too small if they are to be accepted for burial. The beetles carefully inspect the size of the dead animals and the type of ground they lie on. If necessary, the bodies are shoved to a more suitable place. Usually several beetles, both males and females, work together in the beginning; they even may be of different species. Although each member of such an assemblage labors for himself alone, the cooperation of pairs also is frequent.

Soon after the beetles begin digging, the corpse is undermined and sinks into the ground, while a wall of excavated earth rises around it. If there is only a single male at work he soon interrupts his labors and, from a somewhat elevated vantage point, performs a waggle dance in the manner of bees, perhaps for hours at a time. The tip of his abdomen, held up obliquely, is waved uninterruptedly back and forth as it dispenses an odorous substance that attracts females. But if a whole group of beetles has gathered from the beginning, battles soon break out and grow more and more violent; little by little the weaker beetles withdraw until the field is left to the strongest female. Frequently there is one male, too, though usually he also is driven off when the work is finished. Only the males of certain species remain; they help with the feeding of the brood. Often the carrion is buried only superficially, 3 inches or less under the surface. In rare cases it may be sunk as much as 2 feet into the ground.

During the process of interment, which lasts for hours, the female continually forces her way around the corpse in a narrow tunnel, pushing at the corpse and shoving it together from all sides, so that finally it lies in the definitive cavity as an unrecognizable, more or less spherical mass. Here, feathers, hairs, or dirt are cleaned off the morsel, and after a day or two the egg-laying begins. At this time the female digs upward from the cavity a short, fairly vertical passageway, and in its sidewalls establishes one or several (up to 24) little, closed egg chambers, one next to the other. Then she sits down on the ball of carrion and regurgitates over it digestive juices that soften it up. Next she eats out a small crater in it, but closes this over again by pressing its walls together.

The same procedure is repeated several times, at rather long intervals; the crater gets larger and deeper and becomes a basin for the nest. It contains a sort of chyme (partially predigested food) for the emerging larvae, which hatch about five days after the eggs are laid. A few hours before this event, the female often makes chirping sounds, and runs repeatedly into the passageway that shelters the eggs. Soon the new larvae work their way out of the eggshells and the hatching chambers, are led by odor to wander to the ball, and gather upon it in the food cavity.

The mother beetle also climbs onto the ball while the larvae, like young birds, raise the forepart of the body as high as they can. The mother then proceeds to feed the chyme to them. She drums with her forefeet and opens wide her mandibles, and the nearest young one licks up a drop of fluid from her mouth; when the mother turns her head a little to one side, a second larva does the same. The mother takes the chyme from the hollow again and again, giving it to the five or six larvae, one after the other; each is fed for two to four seconds. The old beetle sits on her two hinder pairs of legs and moves the forelegs freely, drumming before each act of feeding and often pushing away overinsistent larvae or grasping one and holding it away from her mouth. The shockingly unconscious rigidity of all these procedures is rendered apparent if the mother is deprived of almost all the young. She then goes through the acts of drumming, feeding, and moving her head from side to side in the same unchanged rhythm and tempo, although perhaps no larva raises itself up.

As soon as the larvae are some five to six hours old they begin to feed independently, but again let themselves be nourished by the mother for two to three hours after their first molt. After the second molt, they eat their way further into the food ball and finally bore through the dried-out walls into the soil. Here they construct a pupation cavity by continually turning about their own long axis. Some species overwinter here as larvae, but others pupate after about two weeks; the pupal stage of the burying beetles also lasts approximately two weeks. [177/21]

FUNGI CULTURE

Among wood-feeding beetles, certain species of pin-hole borers (family Platypodidae), timber beetles (Lymexylidae), and bark beetles (Scolytidae) culture fungi. Almost every species of beetle has its own species of fungus. The individual fungal cells may stick to the beetle's thorax or be caught in the hairs of its head, but mostly they are carried in the digestive tract. When the mother beetle gnaws a passageway in wood, the fungal cells fall or rub off, are regurgitated by her, or are dropped in her feces. The passage walls soon become coated with a thick growth of fungus. This is the primary food of the larvae and often makes available to them nutrients in the wood. The mother beetle carefully tends such fungal cultures and keeps them free of "weeds"; she may even regulate humidity by occasionally blocking the passageway with sawdust. She may also fertilize the culture with excrement.

The fungal lawn dies if not grazed close by the larvae, and it goes to seed if not tended properly by the old beetle. If a fungus-growing beetle is interfered with, she hastily swallows as much of her precious "vegetable"

as possible and uses it again in some new location. (Fungus-growing ants of the genus *Atta* act similarly.) Apparently definite fermentation reactions in the wood are favorable to the fungus or essential to it, for the beetles gnaw the passageway for their brood in diseased wood when they can; most larvae also tunnel into such wood.

FAMILY LIFE OF BARK BEETLES

A majority of bark beetles do not culture fungi; they live in bark or, more likely, place their brood structures between the bark and the underlying wood. After excavating "maternal passageways," the female lays usually 20 to 70 eggs at random, at small intervals, or in close-set rows on each side. Frequently she places them in niches enclosed by the gnawed-off shavings or by a secreted membrane. From these positions the larvae eat out their own tunnels, starting at about right angles to the parental shaft but later running obliquely to it. If space is limited, the larval tunnels cut across one another and get wider and wider as the larvae increase in size. At the end of a tunnel, the larva gnaws out a cavity in which it changes into a pupa.

The larva of one bark beetle, *Hylurgops palliatus,* chews out through the bark near the pupal site, forming an air passage with a little opening to the outside; this is then filled loosely with shavings. The maternal and larval passageways, usually dug simultaneously into the outer surface of the wood (sapwood) and into the inner surface of the adjacent bark, form a pattern of "tattooing" that is a source of worry to the professional forester. It has earned these insects such names as "printing beetles" or "engraving beetles."

The individual species of bark beetles attack one or a few definite kinds of trees, diseased specimens where possible. Each beetle has its own easily recognizable feeding pattern. The tunnels are not invariably cylindrical, but with many species they are irregularly flattened to form what are known as "public squares." In such structures, larvae hatching from eggs laid in groups or piles begin to eat their way forward, side by side, on a broad front.

These larvae exhibit astonishing social instincts. Thus a certain larval group, whose individual composition is shifting continually, carts off accumulating feces, refuse, dead individuals, and invading parasites. By compressing this material and dumping it into "sawdust bins" far to the rear, they clear space for the feeding front rank. If obstacles

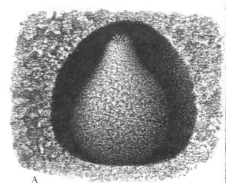

A

154/1A–E
(A) The scarab beetle's ball of dung in its cavity in the ground. (B) The egg chamber, with its ventilation flue, formed of fine passages (laid open for examination). (C–D) Both a younger and an older larva in their

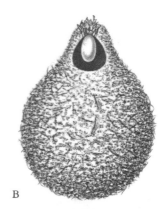

B

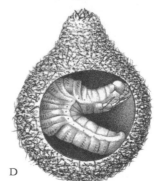

D

155/1
The burying beetle, spotted with black and red, feeds its brood as a bird does its young, in the course of which the larvae rear up instinctively, also like nestling birds (enlarged 2×).

gnawed-out hollow space. When the larva has grown big enough, it crawls downward and braces itself against the walls by means of a dorsal hump and its hind end. (E) The pupa, seen from in front, is lying on dorsal ridges and callosities (natural size).

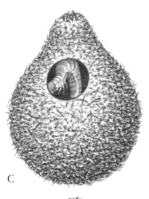

C

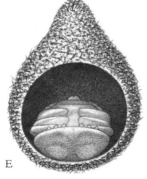

E

break the front rank into separate groups, connecting passages through the "dust bins" are kept open, and a constant interchange of individuals takes place through them. This situation cannot fail to remind the observer of traffic through a city square.

Courting pairs have interesting social customs, too. They hold their nuptials on the treetrunks or inside an entrance to the future dwelling. If another male happens by, the two rivals run together, head against head, chirping excitedly and quivering their antennae, until one gives way. The victor then goes to the female and, still chirping, rubs his frontal brush of hairs against the undersurface of her abdomen. Later, the male draws sentry duty, while the female builds the maternal tunnel, which usually grows in length as eggs are produced and deposited. Sometimes she makes little air holes to the outside, through which she may receive additional "gentlemen" while the first stands watch at the doorway.

Many species live polygamously, one male with several females. The male gnaws out an entrance hole and a chamber, the "mating room." This is an almost unique phenomenon in the insect world, in that elsewhere the male lacks any instinct for seeking out or choosing the proper food plant for the brood. Here he awaits the visits of females, evidently sending out odors that attract them. After copulation, which is repeated later, each female digs a passageway leading out from the wedding chamber. Depending on the number of females that put in an appearance, there may be six to nine maternal tunnels radiating outward like the spikes of a wheel from the mating room. From them the larval passageways lead off to both sides. Among certain fungus-growing wood-feeders, the males of which cannot fly, a single male may have many dozen females.

Males and females may remain for months in their structure, working and watching, until the young beetles are full-grown. Even before egg-laying ends, the female or both male and female often begin to cleanse the maternal passageway of refuse and drillings produced by the first larvae, which already are eating. The beetle's cylindrical body, whose ends are usually blunt but sometimes jagged or shovel-shaped, and which is often covered thickly with hairs like a brush, functions as a dredge and broom. The female uses her legs to scoop up drillings and fill the shovel formed at the end of her body by the tips of the elytra. The male takes this material from her, loads it onto his own shovel, and,

walking backward, dumps it out the entrance, always located obliquely above.

The duration of development averages 1½ to 2 months, but in many species depends strongly on temperature and may last much longer. The young beetles, depending on their species, leave the brood structure either through the maternal passageway or through an exit chewed through the bark. In the latter case, the bark is peppered with little holes.

The bark beetles, which are related to the weevils, are distributed in many species throughout the world. Some, instead of setting up housekeeping in branches or in treetrunks, live in roots, stems, leaves, cacti, nuts and seeds, or even in cellulose-containing materials manufactured by man. The African *Coccotrypes tanganus* establishes its breeding tunnels in palm nuts or in buttons made from them. The female, which can produce well over 4,000 direct offspring in a single nut, remains as a living, protective barrier in the maternal passageway and keeps it clean. Among her progeny are few males. This apparently is no handicap to reproduction since these females lay unfertilized eggs that develop into young, the process known as parthenogenesis. The female mates with one of the few males that develop from the eggs and eats any others that have not left the dwelling. Thereupon she gnaws out a second, larger brood tunnel and lays a new set of eggs, from which both sexes hatch. [137/2, 2A]

All bark beetles are little, most of them only a few hundredths of an inch in length, but some exceptional ones as much as 0.4 inch. Yet a few families, by interrupting the vital layer of tissue between the bark and the wood, can kill a gigantic tree. Many species are dreaded destroyers of forests and cannot always be decimated sufficiently even by their numerous enemies. Among birds, the woodpeckers rate as conspicuous enemies. But much more significant are predatory and parasitic insects, above all various adult beetles or their larvae (clerids, staphylinids, histerids, ostomatids, nitidulids, colydiids), and a great many little parasitic wasps (such as chalcidids, braconids, ichneumonids). Finally, certain harmless "space parasites," namely bark beetles only about 0.04 inch long, lay their eggs in the maternal passageways of certain other species; the larval tunnels of the intruders branch off from here.

OTHER PROVISIONS FOR YOUNG

Also famous for their family life are the passalid beetles (Passalidae), a small family related to the scarabs and the stag beetles, and similarly shaped. Their approximately 300 species, with few exceptions tropical, range from about 0.8 inch to 3.2 inches in length. Parents and larvae live together in rotting wood, the entire family chirping industriously. The young get their food in predigested form from the old ones. Even the male provides food, a phenomenon that occurs hardly anywhere else in the insect empire except among the termites and possibly among burying beetles of the genus *Necrophorus.* [177/24, 25]

The great family of leaf beetles (Chrysomelidae) also makes interesting provisions for the brood and in some cases goes as far as caring for the young. The less specific measures consist of the mother beetle's standing watch or covering the clutch of eggs or the young larvae with her body. Thus the female poplar beetle *Phytodecta rufipes* fastens her eggs to a leaf; the larvae hatch almost at once and stay together while they are feeding. During their first two instars, the stages preceding the first two molts, and sometimes even during the third, the mother sits head down on the twig and bars the way to ants and other insects.

The female of the South American tortoise beetle *Selenis spinifex* fastens her approximately 30 eggs to a stalk made of secreted material. The mother sits on the stalk, which hangs down from the underside of a leaf, until the larvae have hatched. In other species, the young larvae gather during the day under the mother's protecting body shield, and scatter to feed on the plant only at night.

These tortoise beetles, a subfamily (Cassidinae) of the leaf beetles, are only about 0.16 inch to 0.8 inch long and often resemble little turtles. Many tropical species are among the most beautiful of all beetles. The "carapace" (elytra plus prothoracic shield), frequently decorated splendidly with a network in relief, often has spinelike extensions or processes. In certain species it sparkles almost like an electric light, gleaming with a most improbable golden appearance. [186/12–21]

The youthful stages of these beetles are extraordinarily bizarre and interesting, above all because of the singular application made of their own feces, which are extruded from the anus and deposited on the body by means of a long, mobile, proboscis-like integumental tube. This "anal proboscis" is a part of the digestive tract. In a larva some 0.3 inch long it can be extended as much as 0.2 inch. With the feces, the tube expels a sticky fluid that

serves for their attachment. They may be laid down in the form of a seashell covering the whole body or, placed close to one another like sausage links, may assume the appearance of fantastic and relatively huge antlers. Long spiny processes on the body make their attachment possible, and the confusion is rendered complete by the larval custom of loading onto the back, one after the other, the cast skins shed at each molt. A special fork at the rear end, which is bent sharply upward, holds the whole costume in place. Thus there is created finally a chain of five exuviae, each larger than the one before, connected to one another by the posterior fork, which is molted along with them each time.

Often the entire arrangement persists in the pupa, too, as a protective coating. Frequently even the eggs are covered with excrement by the beetles. In certain species every single egg is given a protective shield of secreted material, mostly in the form of a scale adorned with ribs or knobs, so that a clutch of eggs looks like it had a tile roof. There occur also batches of eggs entirely enclosed in packages, fastened to a stalk and roofed over. These are reminiscent of the egg cases of mantids.

Other leaf beetles (clytrines, cryptocephalines, and lamprosomines) enclose each egg in a coat, often of highly artistic appearance. It may be made of bits of wood or vegetable matter stuck together by a secretion, of a paperlike mass of vegetable fibers and saliva, or often of excrement. These little structures, mostly equipped with a small pedestal and looking like tiny pine cones or like seeds, are made in an original way. For this work, many beetles stand on the two front pairs of legs, with the rear end elevated, hold the egg fast with the hind feet as it emerges, press the tip of it into a special pit beneath the rear end of the body, and begin to turn it round and round in this position while feces are attached in definite patterns to its surface. All the egg coverings also serve the larva as a house or case, which is carried along and enlarged to correspond with an increase in body size. In fact, even the pupa is thus enclosed. One structure serves as an egg shelter, a larval shelter, and a pupal shelter, an example of economy in natural housekeeping almost unique in the insect world. The shelters, which are altered from time to time by the larvae, have all imaginable shapes. According to the species, there are cylinders, spheres, hats, capes, and even spiral shells resembling the fossil shells of ammonites. Some shelters are hard enough to withstand a load of as much as 6 pounds. Inside a shelter

156/1
A thorny tortoise beetle, Selenis spinifex, watching over its eggs that are suspended by a secreted stalk (enlarged 2×).

156/2
A clutch of Polychalca eggs on a leaf nibbled at by the beetle; each egg is covered by a scale formed of hardened secretory material (enlarged 2×).

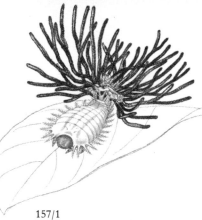

157/1

The Batonota larva; the "antlers," constructed out of sticky excrement—including what has adhered to the cast skins of earlier stages—can be moved both forward and rearward above the back (enlarged 3×).

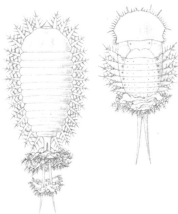

157/2

A Cassida larva with cast skins of earlier stages on the caudal fork; on the right, the pupa (enlarged 3×).

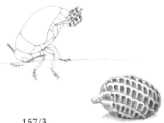

157/3

The biology of case-bearing leaf beetles. During construction of the egg case, as each egg is laid, excrement also is expelled, is held fast with the hind legs, and is shaped into a species-specific container that resembles a seed pod; on it the impressions made by the tarsi are especially prominent (enlarged 4×).

157/4

The egg case, containing a single egg, of another species of case-bearing leaf beetle (enlarged 3×).

the correspondingly-shaped larva is folded up almost like a jackknife, so that the head and the thorax with its legs, which are situated far forward on the body, are visible close beside the rear end in the rather small opening on the lower surface of the shelter. Consequently, these larvae lead a rather immobile existence; most of them eat the bark of plant stems, upon which their houses sit close together. [187/3, 4]

LARVAE

Although beetle larvae have many different forms, they lag far behind caterpillars in wealth of shape and color. This is understandable, considering that the majority of beetle larvae live in darkness. Many are blind, and others have one to six simple eyes on each side of the head. Some are soft and colorless, others clad in armor and pigmented.

Far-reaching differences in body form are recorded. Here, for example, is a fat, white grub, its tender skin wrinkled, living sluggishly and curled-up in its hole in the soil, in rotten wood, or in manure; and over there is a long, black larva of a ground beetle, clad in a coat of mail consisting of hard, smooth segmental plates, skillfully hunting down its living prey. Some beetle larvae are shaped like worms, maggots, woodlice, or brushy caterpillars; then again, those of the ladybird beetles (Coccinellidae) and leaf beetles (Chrysomelidae), which live in the open on plants, bear a greater resemblance to naked caterpillars and often are decorated with bright warning colors.

The larvae of beetles have various kinds of legs, all more primitive than those of mature beetles. Many larvae that live within wood and other substances have no legs at all. Even these may be able to move about by taking a firm bite with the mandibles and pulling the body forward or by crawling along on sharp-edged pads that give a convex contour to the segments and that often work better upside down. Spines and bristles frequently facilitate such movements.

A few larvae have four pairs of spiny knobs on the underside of their abdomen. Others, as already mentioned, have on their rear end an exsertile pygopodium, a fleshy process capable of being thrust out and pulled back. This tube-shaped structure, formed from the integument, is often equipped with a terminal hook or ringlike pad, devices convenient for supporting the hind portion of a larva's long body or for anchoring temporarily the rear end of a climbing species.

The larvae of many ground beetles (Carabidae), in creeping through their tunnels in the soil, make use of two short processes (pseudocerci) that are directed upward; these function either as organs of touch, as supports, or as pushers that gain purchase on the roof of the burrow.

The larvae of pill rollers (*Scarabaeus*) and dorbeetles (*Geotrupes*), lying curled up in their balls of dung, brace the body with their several monstrous humps, which are caused to protrude by means of swollen parts of the gut. The bracing facilitates movement and holds the body away from the wall of the burrow. And larvae of long-horned beetles (Cerambycidae) have paired warty cushions, one each along the upper and under surfaces; by expanding these, a larva can brace its segments against the walls of the feeding tunnels and push itself along.

Certain legless weevil larvae (*Curculio*) move in an unusual way. These larvae grow inside hard-shelled nuts and must leave the nuts and enter the ground before they become pupae. To do this, the larva gnaws a hole large enough to let out the head and thorax, but not the rest of the body, which is much thicker. Gradually the body contents are shifted from inside to the part outside. As a result, the protruding part swells up like a great balloon on the outside surface of the nut. The increasing tension gradually pulls out the thinning abdomen. This is like pushing a sausage slowly through a hole by squeezing its end.

Larval life may last for some weeks only, in which case several generations per year are possible, or may persist for several years. It even may differ from year to year in one and the same species in accordance with variations in temperature and in the quality of food. Long-horned beetle larvae (Cerambycidae) have lived in captivity to an age of 45 years, apparently as a result of the abnormal living conditions; even mature beetles have been kept alive for as long as six years. The longer the larval period, the shorter in general is the lifetime of the adult; thus the larvae of stag beetles (Lucanidae) have a life span of four to six years, but the adult beetles live only for a few weeks.

The young larvae hatch in part with and in part without the help of an eggburster, which may be present on the embryo's skin in the form of spines or teeth on the head, the thorax, the back, or even the labrum (upper lip). Carrion beetles (Silphidae) shed the embryonic integument at hatching, but others retain it until the first molt after emergence. Most beetle larvae have three or four instars (periods between molts), but many have more; for instance, certain tenebrionids have 10 to 16. Before a shedding of the skin, molting fluid produced by glands is poured out between the old skin and the new one lying in folds beneath it. By means of peristaltic movements, the body mass is forced to the front, splitting the skin along the molting sutures on the head and on the back surface of the thorax; from the cleft the new larva wells forth.

Dermestid beetle larvae (Dermestidae) have the extraordinary ability to reduce body size, instead of increasing it, in times of food shortage; when they do so, the cast skin serves as nourishment. In this way temporarily unfavorable conditions may be bridged over. Also, certain larvae may remain in a resting stage for as long as several years. Depending on its species, a beetle may pass the winter in any stage from egg to adult. When it is very hot many beetles estivate in the ground, and under some conditions this period of rest carries over directly into overwintering. Numerous beetles overwinter in groups, often in mixed companies of males and females. Various ground beetles *(Carabus)* do so in rotting stumps, and ladybird beetles under moss. [99/1, 10; 138/19–29; 180/16C; 187/5, 8A; 313/18, 19]

PUPAE

Beetle pupae are mummylike, and the stumps that represent their extremities lie free. Most beetle pupae are soft and whitish, lacking pigment unless they are suspended in the open from plants, as are the pupae of leaf beetles and ladybird beetles. The greatly exaggerated body parts of many genera, such as the antlerlike mandibles, are visibly well-developed though still housed on the ventral surface; often the antennae are greatly contorted. Dorsal ridges, knobs, processes at the hind end, or short tufts of hair or bristles serve as braces or supporting cushions for many pupae, so that close contact with external objects such as damp ground, is avoided. Some pupae are completely rigid, but most can squirm like fish or twist about their long axis. [138/30]

The larvae prepare structures of many kinds such as pupal cradles. They dig cavities in soil, wood, dung, and other materials, often lining them with a water-repellent solidifying secretion. They make cocoons by mixing secreted matter with bits of earth, healthy or rotten wood, vegetable materials, and even their own excrement. Dung beetle larvae use excrement as mortar in plastering the walls of their chambers and in stopping up holes or slits made by aggressors from without.

Cocoons made of secreted or spun material may be glued to plants and hang freely on them or may be hidden between leaves drawn together or in passages mined in the leaves. The fabric of the cocoon made by certain weevils is netlike or wide-meshed; the threads are spun from oral glands or, in rare instances *(Lebia),* from the anus. Certain long-horned beetles pupate under bark within a ring resembling the edge of a bird's nest; it is woven together out of long shavings they have chewed off. Other larvae that live in wood gnaw a short tunnel outward from the pupal cradle and often cushion it with fine shavings. The tunnel runs through the wood or bark almost to the outer surface. When the adult beetle emerges, it can bite its way easily into the open.

A different method is used by the larvae of the pea weevil *Bruchus pisorum,* which belongs to the family of seed beetles (Bruchidae). About 1,000 species, some of them harmful, comprise this family. The larva lives inside a pea and, before pupating, gnaws a hole through which it can emerge as an adult. But it leaves the outer coat of the pea as a cap, simply making a groove around it. Then the fully-developed beetle need only shoulder off this preformed lid.

Certain weevil larvae of the genus *Rhynchaenus,* which mine in leaves, cut out a little flat piece of the leaf surface above and below them in their tunnel; after they have joined the two layers together with spun material, they let themselves fall to the ground in this house and pupate inside it.

The adult beetle usually hatches from the pupa in about 15 minutes. Beforehand, molting fluid is poured out between the pupal skin and the imago (adult) within. Then muscular contractions press the body forward more and more inside the pupa, until the latter bursts along the back—and the still whitish insect can climb out. After the beetle has stretched and smoothed its skin and brought wings, legs, and antennae into their normal positions, a rest period is necessary for hardening of the body and development of coloration. This may last for hours, days, weeks, or even months.

In general, the several instars of beetle larvae are very similar, though insect specialists may see great differences. Thus, the freshly hatched larva of *Hylecoetus dermestoides* (family Lymexylidae), which runs about on bark looking for a suitable spot to bore into, has a pair of eyes that disappear with the first molt. And when it is more fully

158/1
The bonnet-shaped egg case of Lamprosoma, built of shavings of wood and bark, lies with the opening against the surface of a twig; inside sits the emaciated-looking larva, eating bark (the case cut open). In the center is the egg case made by the mother beetle; the larva adds to it as required by the need for space (enlarged 2×).

grown, this larva is equipped with a forked anal process that it uses as a tool in pushing the drillings out of its feeding passage. Changes in form that result in two or more different larvae are known as hypermetamorphosis.

PARASITES

Various parasitic beetle larvae go through dramatic changes in form. The newly hatched larva of the rove beetle *Aleochara curtula* possesses eyes and a mobile yellowish-brown body. In this instar, it bores its way into a fly pupa and eats itself fat. It tarries there, blind, baggy, soft, and white, throughout the second instar. It molts once again into a moving, seeing, and much more heavily armored third stage, is free-living for a while, and finally pupates in the ground. Another form remains more or less shapeless in the fly pupa throughout the third instar, and then emerges as a mature beetle.

Interesting, too, are parasitic larvae of the wedge-shaped beetles of the little family Rhipiphoridae, rare beetles with fan-shaped antennae and often somewhat degenerate elytra. Some species with wingless, larviform females develop as parasites in cockroaches (*Blatta*). Others are parasites in the nest of solitary (nonsocial) bees and wasps. Such a beetle lays its eggs on the ground at the base of a flowering plant. After hatching, the active larva climbs up the plant to a flower, catches hold of a visiting bee or wasp, and rides to its carrier's nest. Here the larva bores into the larva or pupa of its host, molts into a short-legged second stage, and consumes the entire body-content of the victim. Finally it pupates, either within the victim's skin or outside it.

The peak of fantasy in aberrant life cycles is reached by the blister beetles (Meloidae), a family interesting in several respects. Most of the more than 2,000 species, about 0.2 inch to 2 inches long, have a striking appearance because of their warning colors; as mentioned earlier, their bodies contain a toxin, cantharidin. The species known as Spanish flies, blister beetles, or poultice beetles have long, soft wing covers. Most of them feed in groups on leaves and flowers. They belong to the subfamily Lyttinae. The fat oil beetles, black or darkly metallic beetles that crawl clumsily along the ground among the grass, belong to the Meloinae. The wing covers of their females are short and strongly divergent.

In both subfamilies a "false pupa" is interpolated between the next to last and last larval stages. This is a motionless, resting larval stage that has indeed detached the old skin, but remains therein throughout the winter or the rainy season. The females of *Epicauta* and *Mylabris* generally lay their eggs on the ground in the vicinity of the buried pods of grasshoppers; after hatching, the long-legged first-stage larvae make their way into the egg pods, take a meal, and transform into the stub-legged, grublike second stage. In this condition they continue eating the grasshopper eggs and increase in size, molting a few times; finally they dig their way into the soil, molt into a "false pupa," molt once again into a last larval stage capable of some movement, and ultimately change into a true pupa.

The genera *Meloe* and *Sitaris* have similar life histories, but some of the events sound as though they came from fairy tales. In fact, they are so incredible that of a thousand individuals born only a tiny portion ever reach maturity. The females of these beetles lay their eggs in masses on top of the ground or just below the surface, *Meloe* near flowering plants that solitary bees choose to visit, and *Sitaris* in the soil near the entrance holes of the nests of such bees. The yellow, bristly, louselike first-stage larvae of *Meloe*, after having survived the winter without food, climb up the plants and onto the flowers, leap onto visiting bees, and cling to their coat of hairs. In so doing, only a small minority of the larvae have the good fortune of hitting upon the proper bee, namely the nest-building female of certain definite genera.

A lucky rider is flown to the nest and awaits a favorable moment for jumping onto a bee's egg, which is floating on top of a honey solution in a cell that has not yet been closed. If the leap is misjudged, the larva sinks in the solution with no hope of rescue; but if successful, the larva sucks the egg dry and molts upon it into a completely different grub—awkward, bare, and white. The swollen belly of the grub floats like the bottom of a boat on honey, now the grub's source of food. If there is not enough honey, the consumer can bore its way into a neighboring cell.

In contrast, the first-stage larvae of *Sitaris* crawl into the nest entrances of terrestrial bees in the springtime. Since the male bees are the first ones to hatch, almost all the larvae fasten onto male bees, a sex that is of no use to them. Yet a few are lucky enough to be on hand when one of these bees mates and are then able to climb off the male onto the female. What strange instinct ordains this shift? [138/1–4]

159/1
The flattened brown larva of a soft-bodied beetle (family Lycidae) from Indonesia is adorned with glistening tubercles, and is reminiscent of the trilobites of ancient times (natural size).

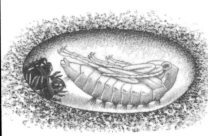

159/2
In its subterranean cavity a ground beetle pupa, supported by dorsal tufts of bristles; at the left, the cast larval skin (enlarged).

Various parasitic beetles have a normal course of metamorphosis. The larvae of a few fungus weevils (Anthribidae), a family closely related to the snout beetles, live within female scale insects (Coccoidea) and eat their eggs. Certain flat cucujid beetles have a much nicer relationship with scale insects. For these beetles and their larvae, which dwell together in families in the hollowed-out stalks of leaves, merely lick up their neighbors' honeydew.

Larvae and adults of a few dermestid beetles (Dermestidae) and darkling beetles (Tenebrionidae) feed on the skin of birds, particularly nestlings and brooding adults. They chew into the skin or flesh and often force their way into an egg as it is hatching. In this manner they cause many deaths among chickens on farms.

Another parasite is the "mouse flea," *Leptinus testaceus,* a blind beetle 0.08 inch long. It lives in the coat of mice and insectivores (such as moles and shrews). A related parasite, the flattish *Platypsyllus castoris,* 0.1 inch long, bears a comb of spines on the back of its head like a flea. All of its stages occur on beavers, and it is known as the "beaver louse." What the "mouse flea" and the "beaver louse" eat among the hairs of their host is not known; perhaps they feed on feces, on scales from the hide, or even on molds. And, speaking of odd parasites, an Australian dung beetle that eats excrement is housed in the rectum of kangaroos.

Finally, there are the twisted-winged insects, whose interesting parasitic ways are described later. An entire literature is concerned with the communal life of beetles with ants and termites. There are bandits and interlopers that live as unwelcome guests (synechthrans) among these social insects and prey on them and their brood. Examples are the rove beetles of the genus *Myrmedonia,* which resemble ants and are warred upon by the inhabitants of the nests. Next comes the great category of the merely tolerated guests (synoecetes). Some are parasites; others live on molds, on dead ants, on excrement and nest material, and occasionally on the brood of termites or ants; and still others seek only protection and warmth. Thus the relatively gigantic larvae of flower beetles *(Cetonia, Potosia)* go undisturbed through their entire development in the rotting building material of wood ants *(Formica),* but when full-grown are attacked by the ants. The leaf beetle *Clytra quadripunctata* encloses its egg in a covering resembling a fir cone

and drops it on or pokes it into an anthill, where the beetle larva lives until it pupates. As already mentioned, the larva remains inside the egg case, enlarges it, and is protected by it.

Many beetles that are guests of ants or termites enjoy similar protection vis-à-vis their hosts thanks to their shape, which prevents them from being laid hold of (for example, the histerids), but more often thanks to a similarity in form and color to their hosts. There are distinct races of rove beetles that vary in appearance according to the particular species of ant with which they live.

A great number of beetles of different families, but particularly rove beetles, are not just tolerated, but are indeed cherished and well-tended guests (symphiles) of ants and termites. The hosts lick up the sweet secretions produced by these beetles from glands most of which are equipped with tufts of hairs. These "cattle" are a pure luxury and command so much attention that masters frequently neglect their own brood. This conduct, if carried too far, can lead to the destruction of an entire ant colony. Actually, signs of physical degeneration may appear in such colonies as a result of the consumption of the beetle secretions.

Rove beetles of the genus *Atemeles* are especially remarkable because their larvae live with a different species of ant than do the adults. These beetles are also unusual in that they lick their food from the mouth of their hosts. Other beetles, such as those of the genus *Lomechusa,* are fed actively by the ants. Wholly helpless and dependent are the blind pselaphids of the genus *Claviger,* which are only a few hundredths of an inch in length. The tips of the antennae of these beetles are swollen into clubs by means of which the ants grasp them and carry them about. In time of danger they often are taken to safety sooner than the ants' own brood. The antennal clubs of the paussids, related to the ground beetles and represented by about 350 tropical and subtropical species, are altogether monstrous; these beetles, too, are valued guests of ants and termites, although they feed on their hosts' brood.

The little beetles *Thorictus* (Thorictidae) have a different procedure. They seize the ants' antennae and let themselves be carried about. Thus they always are close to the source of their food, the ant's mouth.

The larvae of many such guests also are fed and tended by their hosts; but as a somewhat precautionary measure a number of these beetles either carry their eggs around with them until the larvae hatch or even bear

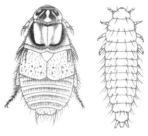

160/1

The "beaver louse"; at the right, its larva. Whether these flattish brown beetles that live in the beaver's coat eat dermal scales and hairs or molds is not known for sure. The two anterior pairs of limbs, having the form of clasping legs, are not visible from above (enlarged 10×).

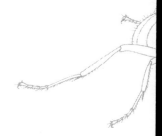

living young. Symbiotic relationships between termites or ants and beetles display an additional peculiar feature in that a highly differentiated antennal language is used by them. In other words, insects from entirely different orders are able to communicate with one another.

Symbiosis, seldom seen among beetles themselves, exists among those that are guests of ants. Thus *Hetaerius ferrugineus,* a hister beetle, rides about in ants' nests on the rove beetle *Lomechusa strumosa,* licking the rove beetle's sweet-tasting tufts of hair. *Dinarda dentata,* a rove beetle, does exactly the same thing, except that it acts not merely to its own advantage, for it also keeps its partner free of mold.

OTHER IMPORTANT FAMILIES

The important beetle families not already discussed in some detail are described below.

TIGER BEETLES

At the head of all classifications of beetles stand the tiger beetles (Cicindelidae), of which about 2,000 species are known. They are distributed over almost the entire earth, but predominantly in the warmer countries. With few exceptions they are of medium size, of slender, fairly uniform shape, and frequently are extremely beautiful. The typical tiger beetle, about 0.6 inch long, likes sunshine and sparsely covered soil. Raised high on its long, thin legs, it runs swiftly and is quick to fly away. It has protruding eyes, lengthy toothed mandibles, and bright, shining metallic colors; on the wing covers the colors are interrupted by bone-colored spotted designs.

In addition to this average form there are a few genera that hunt at night. Among these the African *Mantichora,* with a massive, broad body as much as 2.8 inches long, and powerful, almost antler-shaped mandibles, stands out in contrast to the rest of the family as a ponderous, black giant. A few genera that dwell in the shadows and darkness of the forests have eyes sticking out like telescopes and are almost frog-faced. In fact, the most striking among them, such as *Tricondyla* and *Derocrania,* have knobby, bloated shapes reminiscent of many toads. [99/7; 135/12; 140/1–13]

GROUND BEETLES

The great family of the ground beetles (Carabidae) has a much less uniform appear-

ance. The most typical representative is the famed genus *Carabus.* Beetles of this genus, thanks to manifold differentiation of races brought about predominantly by the glacial area, have provided beetle collectors with one of their favorite subjects of investigation. A few large Chinese species of *Coptolabrus* and closely related genera, with splendidly sculptured tubercles and rows of links on the deep black or shimmering metallic wing covers and with glistening metallic outlines, are true princes among the beetles.

The great majority of the 24,000 species of ground beetles, most of them unable to fly, live as predators on the surface, hidden by day beneath stones, bark, and other objects. Certain of them that inhabit forests have shifted to a life in the trees. Many supplement their meat diet with fruits and parts of plants, and a few have specialized completely on a vegetable diet, among these the destructive grain carabid *Zabrus.*

Yet many are among the most useful insects. At the head of this list is the European pupa-predator and caterpillar-killer *Calosoma sycophanta,* which also has been established successfully in America for the control of certain caterpillars that defoliate forests. During the few weeks of its life in the summertime, such a beetle may slaughter as many as 400 caterpillars, a much greater number than it can eat; and, like its larvae, it pursues them into the loftiest treetops.

The smallest carabids are only about 0.08 inch long, the largest for the most part some 2 inches. The most striking figure in the entire family, the incredible *Mormolyce,* whose outline resembles a musical instrument, is 4 inches long. The beetles of this genus inhabit the Malayan Archipelago, where they live beneath bark and in clefts in wood. They are well-suited to do so, in spite of their length and extraordinary width, because they have a flattened form. [13/2; 14/9; 49/1–12; 62/1; 140/14–27; 141; 177/1–8]

ROVE BEETLES

Also predominantly ground-dwellers are the approximately 20,000 species of rove beetles (Staphylinidae). Most of these are small, many even tiny; the largest are somewhat longer than 1.2 inches. They occur almost everywhere in the world and, with their short wing covers, small but agile legs, and abdomen that can be wagged almost like a tail, are well-known and rather uniformly shaped. Their colors usually are brown to black, yet there are more or less brightly colored species, and in the tropics even some

161/1

A specimen of Lomechusa, an ant beetle from the rove beetle family, is being fed by an ant. On the beetle's back are tufts of golden-yellow hairs, which discharge a fluid that is craved by ants (enlarged 8×).

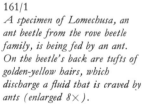

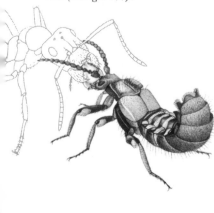

that gleam magnificently with a variety of metallic hues. [177/9–18]

STAG BEETLES

The stag beetles (Lucanidae) are, so to speak, the noblemen among the beetles. With the exception of a few small genera, the males have long mandibles. In the majority these are exaggerated structures, often combined with a massive cranium. The frequently powerful tongs, because of their jagged shapes, are strongly reminiscent of antlers (with which, since they are mouthparts, they have not, of course, the least connection). They may vary greatly in size in one and the same species, and the strongest beetles are the ones with the biggest mandibles. Many tropical beetles have two to four different types of mandibles; the smallest is merely a short, simple biting-jaw, similar to that of the female, but the bigger ones are comparable to the antlers of deer.

On occasion, stag beetles use these weapons in fighting with one another, but do not do so often enough for them to be considered advantageous to or a necessity for the preservation of the species. The stag beetles, usually contending head to head, try to overturn one another by grasping the opponent with the mandibles. During this contest they often punch holes in each other's wing covers with the mandibular branches. Those with longer tongs obviously have an advantage over those with shorter ones, even though the latter may be able to bite harder. But any selection in the struggle for existence in favor of longer "antlers" is not to be discerned. Their size and strength, like those of the beetle, generally depend to too great an extent on the quantity and quality of food consumed by the larva during its many years of eating decaying wood.

Stag beetles lick up sap and fruit juices, and are active principally at dusk and at night. Of the approximately 900 known species, the majority are tropical and large; the giants among them may be about 4 inches long. The much rarer females are smaller. Their coloration ranges mostly from brown—in all the shades of leather—to black; designs either are absent or have the simplest form. A very few species have bright metallic colors. [142–144]

SCARAB BEETLES

One of the most omnipresent families is that of the scarabs (Scarabaeidae). It is dis-

tributed everywhere and has more than 20,000 species. Together with the stag beetles and the passalids, the scarabs are counted among the groups of families of the leaf-horned beetles (Lamellicornia). Their organs of smell are located on movable làmellae, or "leaves," on the clubs (thickened ends) of the antennae. These structures attain their most beautiful development in the May and June beetles (including *Melolontha* and particularly *Polyphylla* and *Phyllophaga*).

The scarabs display a great structural variety, if not in basic body shape at least in its outgrowths and processes. In these respects the great group of rhinoceros beetles and giant beetles (Dynastinae) reaches the summits of formal exaggeration—they are almost surrealistic. The male hercules, elephant, and rhinoceros beetles, whose length of more than 6 inches puts them among the longest and most massive of all insects, have great integumental horns. Those fanciful creations, which may be toothed, forked, or lanceolate, and which frequently are adorned with brushes of hairs, lack practical usefulness and may even be a nuisance. Arising from the head and pronotum, they can be used against other such beetles only to a slight extent by means of nodding movements of the head. Yet they may play some minor part as levers and as implements for thrusting among rivals. They vary greatly in length and development, apparently depending on how well the larval stage, developing in rotten wood or decaying foliage, was nourished. [35/4, 5; 178; 179]

In general the difference between males and the weaponless females is particularly striking among the dynastines. These nocturnal beetles, which frequently fly to electric lights, are quite harmless despite their imposing and almost alarming appearance; they live by drinking sap and the juices of soft fruit. The rhinoceros beetle *Oryctes rhinoceros* of southern Asia is a serious pest, because of the feeding tunnels it makes in cocoa palms and because its grubs prefer to eat the wood in the trunks of these trees.

Similar horns and other such developments on head and prothoracic shield are found among the subfamily of dung beetles (Scarabaeinae), which have been mentioned more than once already. In general these structures are somewhat more modest and of some practical use for digging. Some dung beetles are also massive, heavy creatures, such as the brownish-black *Heliocopris* of the Old World and the South American *Phanaeus*. This last species stands out because of the concentrated strength of its close-knit body and

162/1
An American June beetle, the June bug, having completed development but still in its underground cavity. Below is a click beetle larva (natural size).

because of its frequently splendid, elegantly blended, metallic colors. [133/2; 177/26–34]

When it comes to metallic colors, the shining leaf chafers (Rutelinae) are second to none. Their colors run from broken bronze to highly polished copper, pewter, gold, silver, and resplendent, shimmering sky blue. If one chooses to judge by these physical colors alone, certain American and Australian ruteline beetles are among the most beautiful of all insects. [181/6–12]

The Old World genus *Euchirus,* mostly brown and bronze beetles up to nearly 3 inches in length, contains only a few species. These are distinctive because the males have absurdly lengthened forelegs. [181/1]

Some of the most splendiferous species occur among the flower beetles (Cetoniinae). On their shield-shaped backs they bear colors and designs of the widest range. The structural colors of many species have a molten quality seldom seen elsewhere, with a gentle gleam coming from the depths, an inner flame that defies reproduction. In certain genera the head of the male is adorned with hooks, plates, prongs, forks, or horns, and the forelegs are fantastically toothed. The body surface of many is covered with a delicate feltlike or satiny fuzz. [180/1–15]

The flower beetles include among their members the kings among the beetles, the goliath beetles *(Goliathus)* of Africa. The goliath beetles seem to have borrowed the design on their prothoracic shield from the zebra. These powerful insects hang like gymnasts from the trees, their legs encircling the branches like arms, only now and again hooked fast with their claws. The bellicose males endeavor, with a quickness that is startling in view of their otherwise sluggish behavior, to catch one another on the mighty frontal horn. The object is to hurl the adversary into the air with a violent toss of the head.

The horn is of little use against enemies. A goliath beetle's only defense, other than its hard body armor, is a concealed trap. When danger threatens, the beetle lowers its prothorax, opening wide a sharp-edged joint between the prothoracic shield and the wing covers. This snaps shut powerfully and tightly on any enemy careless enough to come within range. But it is a striking fact that although this snare is employed against anything and everything else, it never is resorted to in contests with their own kind, where unquestionably it could snap off an opponent's leg. [Frontispiece; 180/16]

The goliath beetles live on the sap of trees and on soft fruit; their grubs dwell in rotten wood. Only a few species are known, and some of these are among the greatest rarities. The females are smaller than the males, more modestly colored, and have no cephalic horn.

The scarab family contains many extraordinarily harmful beetles that occur in great hordes. The ruteline beetles are prime examples. They work with destructive thoroughness both as adults, by defoliating plants and especially trees, and as grubs, by consuming the roots. In Europe the May beetle *(Melolontha melolontha)* and in America the imported Japanese beetle *(Popillia japonica)* are the worst. [181/2, 3]

METALLIC WOOD BORERS

These beetles (Buprestidae) have a special right to the name of *Prachtkäfer* (gorgeous beetles), by which they are known in Germany. Like living jewels, though much richer in form and color, they sun themselves on flowers, leaves, wood, and bark, scattering their magnificent hues everywhere. The bodies of some appear to be wrought of steel and fire, glowing from red to white; and where this is veiled by a feltwork or fuzz of hairs, the effect is one of escaping steam. There are, indeed, also some dull, unimpressive species; or the gorgeous colors may be hidden on the undersurface and on the part of the back visible only in flight. Furthermore the colors may be coated over with a deposit of powdery dust, as in one of the largest metallic woodborers, the approximately 2.5-inch-long *Euchroma gigantea* of South America. In collections this beetle shines like smoothly polished copper, but in life it has a lackluster yellowish color. [51/4; 182/1–31]

The mainly tropical buprestids, of which there are perhaps 15,000 known species, are from 0.08 inch to as much as 3.2 inches long; they are vigorous fliers, whose small legs are not particularly suited for walking. Their larvae are as distinctive as the adults; in general they are long, thin, legless maggots whose thoracic region is expanded into a hammerlike shape. The majority of the larvae feed within wood, but they also are found beneath bark (where some form galls) and in the stems of plants. The smallest species are leaf miners. A number of species are pests, in particular many of the elegantly long and slender members of the genus *Agrilus.*

SOFT-BODIED BEETLES

The small- to medium-sized soft-bodied beetles (Malacodermata) include a number of families, among them the fireflies (Lampyr-

163/1
The small shy metallic woodboring beetles are most active during the heat of noontime (enlarged 2×). Photograph.

idae), the timber beetles (Lymexylidae), the soldier beetles (Cantharidae), the checkered beetles (Cleridae), and the net-winged beetles (Lycidae). These beetles have soft wing covers often reduced in size. The soldier beetles, with about 6,000 species, are of wide distribution. Some species gather in large numbers on flowers and regale themselves on nectar and pollen. Often their long, almost clothlike wing covers and brightly colored prothoracic shield remind one of a uniform. The coloration of the checkered beetles, with about 3,000 species, is significantly more intense. A few are notorious as the "bee wolves," because their larvae eat the brood in the nests of bees (including honeybees).

The net-winged beetles likewise number about 3,000 species, most of them tropical; these beetles, with flattened, broad wing covers, crossed by ridges and furrows, frequently resemble moths. Their corrosive body fluids generally make the enemies of insects avoid them, and they are among the insects most typically mimicked. Both helpless insects and those with formidable weapons, including moths, other beetles, bugs, and wasps, wear the same costumes as these beetles, mostly stripes with alternating bands of black and a lighter color ranging from yellow-brown to orange.

The long, flattened larvae of the Malacodermata are active predators. Often they are useful to man because they destroy the young stages of pest insects. [19/32; 136/6, 7; 181/13–26]

LADYBIRD BEETLES

Both larvae and adults of the ladybird beetles (Coccinellidae) are often used in pest control, where they are applied primarily as destroyers of plantlice. These small, rather hemispherical beetles, with flattened undersides and small, agile legs, are held generally in high esteem by man, as is reflected in the many endearing appellations popularly given them in various languages. Nevertheless, it cannot be denied that a few species do damage by eating plants. Nearly 5,000 known species are scattered throughout most of the world, all variations on the same theme. It is astonishing how a single pattern, composed of such simple elements, can be altered again and again to yield countless new variations. [182/32–38]

DARKLING BEETLES

Most of these beetles (Tenebrionidae) are clad fully in black, but in compensation for this sameness have an interesting variety of shapes and sculptured designs. In a few genera these take on quite aberrant forms. Most of the more than 12,000 known species, about 0.6 inch to 2 inches long, live in hot, dry regions—in desert and plains—where they are protected against desiccation by their hard and often highly convex armor. The paucity of metallic colors among tenebrionids is surprising considering the prevalence of these colors in other hard-bodied beetles. Most of the adults and their long, cylindrical larvae feed on dead, dry, or decomposed vegetable matter, decayed wood, or fungi; only a few species take animal food, and some live in ants' nests. Generally familiar as "mealworms" and valued as food for various animals as well as for experimental purposes are the larvae of *Tenebrio molitor*. Like some other members of the family, these are pests that destroy grains and stored products. [32/4; 138/6–14]

DERMESTID BEETLES

Also unwelcome in dwellings are the beetles of the family Dermestidae, though most of their 700 species live in the open. These are all small (rarely as much as 0.4 inch long) and are distributed throughout the world. Their hairy larvae, often adorned with a long caudal brush, inhabit mummified dead bodies or their remains, feeding on hair, feathers, skin, and bones. Many species are found in the nests of animals and insects, and those that have become specialized more and more as our fellow lodgers live on food of animal origin, such as furs or the wool in carpets. [181/27–29]

The larvae of carpet beetles *(Anthrenus)*, at most 0.2 inch long, can quickly render worthless all sorts of zoological collections; they are particularly destructive of insect collections unless these are constantly inspected and treated with disinfectants. Fully-developed carpet beetles, often clothed attractively with bright scales, seek flowers out of doors.

LONG-HORNED BEETLES

Like carpet beetles, many long-horned beetles (Cerambycidae) feed on flowers. With their long, curved antennae, these beetles have a somewhat ramlike appearance. The "horns," shorter in females, may in males of certain species attain a length of five times that of the body. Although they may be slender at their base, they can be extraordinarily strong. The antennae of a few species have a feathery look, achieved by virtue of their enormously long lamellae, or are studded with tufts and brushes of hairs.

This large family, numbering about 17,000 species and distributed over nearly the whole world, has a wealth of coloration and design that places it among the most interesting groups of insects. It has developed almost every possible style of imagery, as well as highly developed disguises and radiant pigments and structural colors. The limits of variation in body form are also extraordinarily broad; the legs in particular occur in a great variety of shapes.

The smallest long-horned beetles measure about 0.2 inch, and the largest 6 to 8 inches. In fact the mightiest of all is named *Titanus giganteus.* This exceptionally rare beetle of the South American virgin forest was long known only from a few specimens that either had drowned and been fished out of rivers or had been recovered from the stomachs of large fish. Thereafter, Indians had some success in hunting out such giant beetles for a European who was living in South America, and from time to time he took them along on his journeys back to Europe. While he was still on the high seas, wealthy French and English collectors would steam out to meet him and to select the biggest specimens. The coveted insects (big indeed, but not particularly beautiful) were purchased at fantastic prices.

The means of defense of long-horned beetles, except for a few that are poisonous because they feed on toxic plants, are limited to the mandibles, which are large in most species and frequently enormous in big species. There are a great many mimetic forms that resemble protected beetles (such as the already-mentioned lycids), bugs, ants, and above all various wasps. Occasionally the resemblance is so complete in even minute details that it goes beyond protective value and casts doubt on the validity of the general theory of mimicry, the more so because the beetles that mimic wasps have also adopted wasplike mannerisms. A few species live in ant nests.

The larvae of long-horned beetles remind one of fat white or yellowish caterpillars. They have either no legs or stunted ones. They feed in wood, predominantly in sick, dead, or rotting wood. They also feed in stems and rarely on roots. Certain species are destructive, the harm they do extending even to milled lumber. The larvae of *Hylotrupes bajulus,* the old-house borer, tunnel in roof beams. [15/21; 19/33; 33/1, 3, 4; 51/1; 134; 183–185]

LEAF BEETLES

These beetles (Chrysomelidae) constitute a great army of serious pests, but an unusually colorful army indeed. One fiery red species of the genus *Fulcidax,* its body divided into strangely sculptured masses, is like a bit of glowing lava. Otherwise, the leaf beetles, except for the interesting tortoise beetles (Cassidinae), mentioned earlier, and a few other small groups, are in general poor in sculpturing; instead they have a gleaming smooth, more or less hemispherical body.

Particularly striking are the thick, powerful, froglike hind legs (toothed in the male sex) of the genus *Sagra* of Asia and Australia. Their ability to jump has earned them the name "kangaroo beetles." These are giants among the family, over 0.8 inch in length, and have magnificent metallic colors. Their larvae feed in wood and stems, and some form galls.

The tiny flea beetles (Halticinae) also are highly developed jumpers, with similarly thickened hind legs. Other oddities are the wedge-shaped leaf beetles (Hispinae), many species of which are covered thoroughly with long spines; their larvae are called leaf miners. For the most part leaf beetles and their larvae feed, often together, on the outer surface of plants. Their most notorious representative may well be the Colorado potato beetle *(Leptinotarsa decemlineata),* which was imported accidentally into Europe from America. No doubt the great effectiveness of a pest of this kind rests on two requirements: the one-sided cultivation of certain plants and the introduction of the pest into new environments in which its natural enemies either are lacking or are unable to accommodate themselves to this stranger.

The family of the Chrysomelidae numbers more than 26,000 species, most of them small. They are distributed throughout the world wherever there is plant cover. [148–149; 156–158; 186/1–21; 187/1–6]

SNOUT BEETLES

With more than 40,000 known species, the snout beetles (Curculionidae) are the largest family in the whole animal kingdom. Among the beetles this is perhaps the most interesting and taxonomically most difficult family; certainly tens of thousands of new species of snout beetles are yet to be discovered. Almost without exception these beetles, many of which are known as weevils, have a hard coat of mail, strong legs, and a prominent snout. In other respects their bodies are more varied in form than in any other family of beetles. Their coloration and design are almost equally as variable. Certain species, such as the incomparable *Entimus* of South America or *Pachyrrhynchus* and *Metapocyrtus* of the Philippines, are adorned with scales that gleam with all the colors of the rainbow. These are among the most beautiful insects. The actual colors are partly determined by a powdery superficial coating that rubs off easily but soon forms anew. Anyone attempting to present a complete account of the marvelous riches of this family would have to set aside several books.

The snout beetles range in size from tiny individuals to giants nearly 3 inches long. All feed on plants. Their larvae, which mine, bore, and dig into all parts of plants—from roots and wood to leaves, fruit, and seeds—are built like maggots. A few that feed in the open on leaves make themselves fast with a sticky, secreted covering. Some snout beetles go through their development in water plants and live in part below the water's surface. [31/1; 133/1, 3; 186/22–48; 187/8–10]

NERVE-WINGED INSECTS
ORDER NEUROPTERA

Delicate wing membranes stretched between a beautifully articulated network of veins, a soft, weak body, and a somewhat secretive way of life endow the nerve-winged insects with an aura of enchantment. The great, clear pinions of an antlion adult that has been flushed from cover glisten like magic as the insect flutters on an irregular, undulant course between light and shadow. Even more delicate are the golden-eyed lacewings, as they flit to and fro in the lamplight of our houses. The most beautiful colors of the rainbow play over their clear, transparent wings, and their eyes gleam iridescently. And yet both antlions and golden-eyed lacewings, as well as most other nerve-winged insects, are insect-eating predators, a thing one hardly would attribute to these slight beings with their tiny heads.

Altogether, there are some 4,300 known species of nerve-winged insects (order Neuroptera). Their four rather similar wings are traversed by a rich network of veins. They have biting mouthparts and small legs. They range in size from about 0.08 inch to 2.7 inches long, with a wing span from 0.02 inch to about 6.6 inches.

LARVAE

Although all nerve-winged insects have biting mouthparts, the mouthparts of the larva serve not only for biting, but also for injecting and sucking. The appressed mandibles and maxillae form a tube, or more rarely the mandible is pierced by a food channel. When the larva bites a victim, it injects a poison that paralyzes the victim and dissolves the body tissue. As the victim's body contents are liquefied, they are sucked up through the mandibles. Many neuropteran larvae have a fastening device, often equipped with little hooks, that can be protruded from the anus in the form of a short tube, peg, or vesicle (pygopodium); using this as an anchor, the larva can keep from being pulled by a stronger insect it has caught.

The neuropteran larva is usually short-legged. Each side of the head bears a group of five to seven eyes. In some larvae, each eye stands on its own pedestal and faces in a different direction. The neuropteran larva passes through only three stages, separated by two molts, the first occurring soon after the larva hatches from the egg.

The young larva escapes from the egg by breaking it with the help of an egg tooth on its facial region or by lifting off a preformed lid in the eggshell. Simultaneously it strips off its embryonic membrane. The freshly hatched larva often is differently formed and more heavily clothed with bristles than it is later, in its second stage.

PUPAE

The hind end of the larva contains spinning glands. When it pupates, the larva spins with its two terminal abdominal segments a round or oval cocoon; this most often consists of an outer loose weft of silk and an inner denser one. It may be glued together with secretion. Frequently bits of vegetable matter, earth, or other substances are included in the outer layer; for instance, the antlion cocoon, which lies in the ground, gets a thick coating of grains of sand. The cocoons of other families may either be fastened openly to plants or bark, or concealed between leaves.

The appendages of the pupa are free, yet seldom are movable. The pupa's mandibles often are longer (as much as three times) and of different form than those of the larva. In the act of emerging, many pupae use the mandibles to bite the cocoon open, force their way partly out of the opening, and then

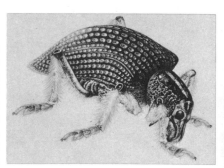

166/1
The linearly arranged grooves of the jeweled snout beetle, a Brazilian curculionid, are inlaid with rosettes of scales that gleam with beautiful colors (see also Figure 31/1).

molt into the mature form. But the pupae of brown lacewings (Hemerobiidae) climb out all the way and hunt for a suitable spot where they transform to the adult. With surprising rapidity, the great wings extend, only to take hours longer to harden. It also takes this long for the insect to achieve its coloration.

ADULTS

Nerve-winged insects seldom are brightly colored. The body usually is an unimpressive green, yellow, gray, or brown to black, often with a faint design of light and dark. In spite of this, many are attractive spectacles, thanks to their two pairs of wings. The most beautiful variants of these are unequaled anywhere in the elegance of their cut and in the aristocratic pattern of their design of spots against a glass-clear background. In their periods of rest, during which many of these insects not only hold fast with their little legs but also bite firmly into the branch or blade of grass supporting them, the wings are laid back over the body like a steep roof.

A great many neuropterans take wing at twilight; their fluttering flight, in which the front and back wings work fairly independently, is of short duration. Certain species (for example, brown lacewings) couple their front and back wings through a special arrangement of bristles. Usually all four wings are about the same size and shape, but the hind wings of threadwinged lacewings (Nemopteridae) have the form of thin blades of grass, and those of the male brown lacewing *Psectra diptera* seem almost degenerate.

Other exceptional phenomena are the presence of scales and wax. The scales on the wing base of the males of a few beaded lacewings (Berothidae) apparently dispense odor that attracts females. The wings and body of coniopterygids, or dustywings, appear to be covered with a white or brown powder. This wax, which comes from abdominal glands, is spread over the whole body by the hind legs. This family is striking also because of its much reduced wing venation and because some of its members are the smallest representatives of the entire order. Their bodies are only 0.08 inch long, and their wing span about 0.2 inch. Except for the cold regions, they occur everywhere, particularly on trees. Eggs are usually laid singly on the leaves or bark. The bristly larvae, clothed with elevated scales, usually are a beautiful rose color with a blue-black design; they are nimble predators of plantlice and other small

insects, and also suck the eggs of insects and spiders.

The compound eyes of the adult nerve-winged insects are large and hemispherical; simple eyes, or ocelli, are found only in the large and slender osmylid flies. The biting mouthparts have somewhat asymmetric mandibles. The antennae are of many kinds, some long and threadlike, others rather short; often the tip ends in a button or club. In the males of dustywings and pleasing lacewings (Dilaridae), the antennae are like a comb, but otherwise sexual differences are not great.

DEFENSES AND ENEMIES

Green lacewings (Chrysopidae) and antlions (Myrmeleontidae) defend themselves with stink glands located in the thorax. Many neuropterous larvae are able to inflict pain by piercing the human skin with their sickle-shaped mandibles, which are equipped with poison glands; the effect is that of a wasp sting. But the adult nerve-winged insects, the great majority of which are fully defenseless, have many enemies. Among them are all insectivorous animals, including spiders and particularly other insects. At any of their stages—egg, larva, pupa, or adult—nerve-winged insects are subject to parasites such as flies, parasitic wasps (ichneumonids, braconids, proctotrupids, chalcidids, and helorids), and even gall wasps (cynipids). Some neuropteran larvae even suck out the juices of their own kind.

IMPORTANT FAMILIES

Nerve-winged insects can be divided into three groups, or suborders: Sialodea, Raphidiodea, and Planipennia. The first includes about 700 species in two families, the dobsonflies (Corydalidae) and the alderflies (Sialidae). Being water insects, these are described in the section of that heading. The second suborder includes one family of about 80 species: the snakeflies (Raphidiidae).

The third suborder, the Planipennia, includes about 3,500 known species, mostly tropical and subtropical. They are broken down into perhaps 18 families. The most important of these families, along with the snakeflies, are described below.

SNAKEFLIES

With their long, necklike prothorax, the snakeflies are as peculiar as they are unmistakable. They occur throughout the world except Australia. The majority are

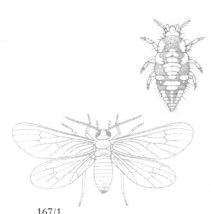

167/1
Dustywings (order Neuroptera), of which only some 60 species are known, are good runners and also go hopping away from danger. At the right, a larva (enlarged 8×).

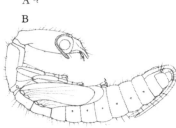

native to the northern hemisphere. In the United States they occur only west of the Rockies. Small to medium-sized, they are useful predators on other insects. The adults, most of them quite black in color, prefer shaded spots, fly both day and night, and subsist mainly on plantlice. [189/1]

The females lay their eggs in masses of some 40 to 50 in cracks in bark or in decayed wood. The female can reach out-of-the-way places with her long oviposition tube, which is capable of snakelike movement. The long, agile larvae that hatch from the eggs live singly. They can run backward just as well as forward, using their sticky hindgut as an anchoring and supporting device. These greedy little larvae spend the entire day on the bark catching all kinds of insects they can overpower with their mandibles. At night or in bad weather they retire into clefts or beneath the bark.

The larva changes into the first pupal stage in a small cavity gnawed superficially into the bark or into rotten wood. Though the appendages are free in this stage, they lie immovable against the body. After about ten days the insect changes into a second, active pupa. After some three more days, the pupa leaves its hiding place and runs nimbly about. Finally it makes itself fast to the bark and molts into the mature insect.

ANTLIONS

At first glance the antlions (Myrmeleontidae) resemble dragonflies, but differ most conspicuously in having antennae with club-like tips. In the smallest species, the usually slender, long wings span about 1.67 inches. The antlion adults are predators, but take little nourishment and live a few weeks at most. They are insects of the summertime, often putting in an appearance around an electric light at night, but also fluttering about in the sunshine. The eggs are laid in loose groups on sandy soil and in the temperate zone hatch into mostly earth-colored, lively, snappish larvae.

Famous among the larvae of antlions are species that build pitfalls in the shape of perfect funnels. Numbers of these funnels often are found side by side in a sandy spot, particularly in the shelter of overhanging cliffs or thickets.

It is hard to comprehend how such a primitive creature, perhaps no more than a quarter of an inch long, constructs a funnel as much as 2 inches deep and 3.3 inches wide; and then, buried at the bottom, waits for an ant or other insect to fall down. The craftsman cannot know he is setting a trap—and the best possible kind at that—nor can he know that something will fall into it, and still less what this may be. Thus the antlion acts not out of prescient wisdom, but according to an inborn urge. The same is true of its perhaps most astounding procedure: As a victim tries to crawl up out of the funnel, the antlion pelts the captive with sand and brings it tumbling down again.

In constructing the funnel, the larva walks backward in a circle, boring its abdomen into the sand. A circular hole results. Continuing similarly, but in an ever-narrowing spiral, it burrows deeper, operating simultaneously as a living excavating machine, for it throws the dirt out regularly with violent tosses of the head. The column of sand that initially stands in the middle grows narrower and narrower at its base, collapses, and finally disappears completely; and the steplike ridges formed by the larva's spirally descending course are smoothed out by the constant flinging out and crumbling of the sand. If the sand is loose, the wall of the funnel is not made as high and steep as it is in somewhat firmer material. When the trap is completed, the bristly larva lies in wait at the bottom, its almost triangular or trapezoidal body hidden in the sand. Only its long, curved, sucking mandibles remain visible.

An antlion often worries a captured insect violently, or beats it against the wall of the funnel until it is stupefied. The stiff bristles on the antlion's body provide the attachment to the ground needed to handle the usually large prey.

Antlion larvae live for about two years. Only a few species construct funnel-shaped traps; the others run freely about hunting on the ground at night, but by day conceal themselves at the bases of plants or in shallow burrows in the soil. There they seize and pull down such insects as walk over them. The larvae turn into pupae that remain still and at rest for from two to several weeks. [188/3]

OWLFLIES

Many similarities to the life of the antlions and especially of their larvae are shown by the owlflies (Ascalaphidae). These are distinguished from the antlions principally by their shorter front thoracic segment (prothorax) and their usually very long, threadlike antennae, conspicuously clubbed at the tip. Because of these features, plus the often broad, triangular wings, usually black and

168/1A–B
Larva (A) and motile pupa (B) of a snakefly.

spotted heavily with yellow or white, and perhaps also because of their very hairy bodies, many species are reminiscent of butterflies and moths. Other species, however, have wings more like those of the antlions.

Most owlflies like sunshine. Excellent fliers, they catch their prey, mainly small beetles and moths, on the wing. Their very active fore wings and their more passive hind wings, which have more the function of parachutes, give their flight its characteristic rapidity and customary combination of whirring and gliding; frequently, too, they ascend vertically.

For short recovery periods, these insects settle with outspread wings on the vegetation, but when at full rest the wings are held back over the body almost like a roof and wrap around the body below, with the abdomen often sticking up above them in a peculiar manner. The ascalaphids usually have a wing span of 1.67 to 2 inches, but the wings of some may measure almost as much as 4.5 inches.

169/1

An antlion adult and its renowned larva (below), the latter with captured prey in its funnel-shaped trap (enlarged 1.5×).

Owlflies have large compound eyes that in many genera look as though they are divided in two by a crosswise furrow. Almost all species glue about 80 to 100 eggs in a thick double row to a blade of grass. The broadly oval, short-legged larvae, which usually live for two years, hunt on the ground, concealed in the grass or at the base of stumps. Many cover themselves with all sorts of matter from the earth. Frequently their bristles are attractively shaped, like goblets or funnels decorated with saw-toothed ridges. The pupal stage lasts three weeks at most. [68; 188/4–6]

SPOONWINGED AND THREADWINGED LACEWINGS

Extraordinary forms confront us in the family of the Nemopteridae. They are puny neuropterans, with slender, bristlelike antennae (which the families to follow also have, for that matter) and with the hind wings modified into improbably long, thin tails, broadened only slightly at the tip. In certain species the tip narrows again at its very end. The larvae of these creatures, which dig themselves into the ground, are as ugly as the adults are attractive. The larva looks like a long-legged antlion on a string, so frightfully long and thin is the neck. [68; 188/1, 2]

GREEN AND BROWN LACEWINGS

Two similar families are the green lacewings (Chrysopidae), also called common lacewings and golden-eyed lacewings, and the brown lacewings (Hemerobiidae). These families extend into the Northland and the Alps. Their larvae, mostly adorned with spotted designs, are the greedy and therefore useful insects called aphidlions. They drink the juices not only of aphids, but also of such other insects as caterpillars or the larvae of sawflies, leaf beetles, or even flower flies. Where possible, the victim is impaled by the mandible from below and lifted high in the air; in this process, the rather long body of the attacker is anchored by a caudal pygopodium, a footlike extension near the rear end. This organ frequently is employed also in locomotion. It is pushed forward beneath the flexed body and glued against the substratum, after which the body is extended frontward.

Many chrysopid larvae cover themselves with the empty skins of their victims or with other objects. With their mandibles, they pile these onto their back where they are caught by hooked bristles.

The cocoon for pupation is concealed between leaves or in some other manner, and within it the larva often lies at rest for months—particularly during the winter—before it molts into the pupa. Many species go through the winter as adults. When green chrysopids do this, they change color temporarily to brown or a reddish shade. Many have only one generation a year, some two, and others as many as six. The adults, like the larvae, are primarily predators on aphids, but some also lick up the aphids' honeydew. Many seldom fly except at night.

Among the hemerobiids are forms whose fore wings are aberrant in their cut and coloration and that are deceptively similar to leaves. Quite logically, then, when these insects are threatened they drop to the ground as though dead. Their eggs, perhaps numbering as many as 500, are placed on the undersides of leaves, mostly singly, or even are put directly beneath the protective scale of scale insects.

Particularly attractive and striking are the eggs of the chrysopids, most of which may be found, like tiny mushrooms, in groups or even in dense clusters, particularly in the neighborhood of aphid colonies. Each whitish or greenish egg sits on a thin stalk, usually 0.20 to 0.24 inch long, which is spun from a thread-producing secretion. While the thread is being exuded during the act of oviposition, the insect needs only to raise its rear end slightly and emit an egg. Then the graceful plantlike structure is complete. With laborious, undulant body movements that may last half an hour, the young larva then hatches. [15/15; 189/2-4]

MANTISFLIES

One of the weirdest families is that of the mantispids (Mantispidae). These nerve-winged insects look like praying mantids, especially because their forelegs are similar grasping organs. This is an impressive case of parallel development in two widely separated types of insect. The mantispids are in general rare; they live hidden in thickets and by preference catch flies.

Their eggs, like those of chrysopids, sit at the end of a thread, though usually a shorter one. The hatching larvae bore into the egg cocoons of wolf spiders, remain in them for weeks, and then molt into a quite different, maggotlike stage capable of only slight movement. Now they gradually suck dry the eggs and the developing young spiders within the spun sac.

Afterward they pupate in a cocoon they have spun themselves, still within that of the spider. And finally this pupa molts into a second, more active pupa, which then breaks through the coverings, climbs out, and at last transforms, in a suitable spot, to the adult. Thus in the life cycle of mantispids two quite different larval forms and two pupal instars succeed one another, an especially pronounced case of hypermetamorphosis. Not all genera of mantispids undergo development in the cocoons of spiders. The South

American *Symphrasis,* for example, does so in the nests of wasps *(Polybia).*

About 25 genera and 350 species of mantispids are known; they are nearly all tropical and subtropical. Their body length varies between 0.12 inch and a little over 1 inch, their wing span from 0.4 inch to 2.2 inches. The coloration usually is from yellow to brown or black; certain species have red and yellow spots. [189/5, 6]

SCORPIONFLIES

Order Mecopera

The scorpionflies form a small but geologically ancient order numbering only seven families and about 300 species; they are related to the caddisflies (Trichoptera). Similar in general to the nerve-winged insects (Neuroptera), the scorpionflies have an interesting and varied body form. Except for members of the genus *Panorpodes* of North America and Japan, the scorpionflies have the lower part of their facial region drawn out into a long beak, at the apex of which are small chewing mouthparts. They have very long legs and caterpillarlike larvae.

Best known are the common scorpionflies (family Panorpidae). On the average 0.6 inch long, these are slender, almost gnatlike insects, the males of which carry the abdomen curved upward in a striking resemblance to the tail of a scorpion. The device is not a weapon, as in a scorpion, but rather a pair of forceps that serves only to grasp the female during the act of mating. During this performance, the male spits out a little blob of sticky saliva that gradually is consumed by his partner. This saliva apparently is important to the maturation of the eggs in the maternal body. In the Australian family Choristidae, the transfer of saliva takes place directly from mouth to mouth.

The common scorpionflies, the majority of which are distributed over the northern hemisphere (most of them in East Asia), like shady places and thickets, fly but little, and fold the wings back horizontally at rest. The four similar wings are mostly marked with dark spots. The eggs, 12 to 20 in number (rarely up to 100) are stuck together and inserted superficially into the soil, where the larvae spend their lives burrowing.

The young are covered with bristles and have at the anal end an exsertile fastening device in the form of four pegs, which permits the whole body to be held freely erect. Such a position is taken, for instance, when the larva is cleaning its legs with its mouth.

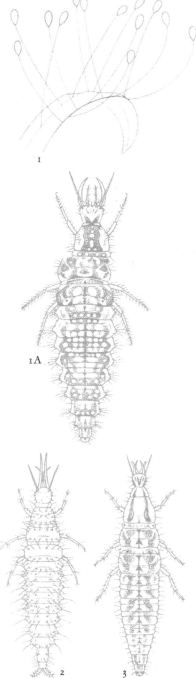

170/1-3
*Immature stages of lacewings.
(1) The eggs of green lacewings, swaying on their slender stalks, are pure white; (1A) a larva (enlarged 4×). (2) Larva of an osmylid; it is able with its spinose rear end, though the latter is mainly a supporting structure, to keep hold of a captured prey, such as small flies (enlarged 3×). (3) Larva of a brown lacewing (Hemerobiidae) (enlarged 4×).*

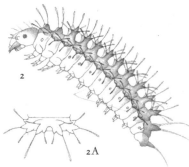

171/1–3
(1) Scorpionfly larva (enl. 3×).

In addition to a half-dozen legs on the thorax, eight wartlike abdominal appendages are present. After five to seven molts, which take place in about a month, the larva is full-grown. It then bores deeper into the earth, hollows out a little chamber, rests therein for up to three weeks, and changes into a motionless pupa with free appendages.

After one to two weeks, the adult emerges. It may live a month or longer. Its food, like that of the larva, consists of small dead or injured insects and other small creatures; the adult also consumes nectar and the honeydew of aphids. [189/7, 8]

HANGINGFLIES

The hangingflies (family Bittacidae) are unusual in being deceptively like large crane flies (Tipulidae), but unlike them have four wings instead of two and fold these rooflike over the back when at rest. They are on the wing at twilight. To some extent, while in flight or while hanging by the forelegs in the grass or brush and swaying freely in the wind, they seize insects flying past or approaching in some other way. Their method of doing this is singular. The terminal segments of the legs, which have only a single long claw, can be snapped shut like a jackknife, and thus serve as grasping tongs. Usually the victim is caught with the hind legs alone and then brought to the mouth. Rather large hangingflies even catch bees and moths, and when flying may snatch a spider from its web.

Hangingflies simply scatter their eggs over the ground, where the larvae hatch. Studded with jagged and bristly processes, but otherwise similar to the larvae of common scorpionflies, these larvae lead a concealed life, the majority as predators. When threatened by danger, they raise themselves up in the form of an S or roll up in a spiral. Pupation takes place in a cavity in the soil, and the adult emerges after about two weeks. There are not many species of bittacids, and they occur only in the warmer regions; they are best known in Africa and North America. [189/9]

(2) Larva of a hangingfly; its body is disguised with bits of dirt that are stuck onto processes of the back. (2A) One segment, viewed from above (enlarged 3×).

SNOW SCORPIONFLIES

The oddest family is that of the snow scorpionflies (Boreidae), the very few species of which live in Europe and North America. These cold-weather gnomes have a blackish or dark bronze-green luster. Their wings, reduced to small scales in the females and to odd, contorted bristly tails in the males, are

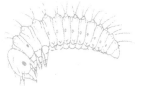

(3) A snow scorpionfly larva; it writhes spirally as it moves forward (enlarged 3×).

hardly more than a tenth of an inch in length. These insects resemble little larval grasshoppers, not only in form, but also in their movements, for they can leap with their long hind legs.

Snow scorpionflies come out between October and March or April, particularly during warm spells in the winter, when crowds of them often may be seen on the snow, thus earning them the nickname of "snowflies" or "snow insects." When on the ground they are scarcely discernible. Frequently they live in concealment among the mosses. Their food is dead or injured insects. When disturbed, a female can expel a sharp-smelling fluid from her ovipositor.

The eggs, about 10 at most, are laid beneath the moss. The larvae, which hatch after perhaps 10 days, resemble grubs more than caterpillars; unlike the larvae of the common scorpionflies and hangingflies, they have neither abdominal legs nor an anal fastening device (pygopodium). They lie sluggishly in passageways in the ground or under moss, which serves them as nourishment, and then pupate below the surface in a vertical tube sparsely lined with silken threads. [189/10]

BUTTERFLIES AND MOTHS
Order Lepidoptera

Among the butterflies and moths are creatures seldom equaled in beauty. Living jewels in the landscape, they flit jerkily over sunny fields, whirl aloft in circles toward the clouds, and sail calmly over forests and chasms as though borne by a sigh. Some may be seen traveling singly from flower to flower, while others congregate in a bright crowd on damp ground. Still others flutter like phantoms through the evening twilight or, as prisoners of light, circle in ever-closer spirals around a lamp. All this coming and going unfolds almost without sound, guided by fragrances and mysterious vision.

Aroused by this world of purely optical experiences, we let the language of images and designs grow within us. And we concentrate our attention on the dual significance of the garb of a butterfly when at rest or when wheeling about.

In flight a butterfly may exhibit the brightest of colors, but when it alights, only the subdued undersides of the wings show, protecting the resting individual. Like as not, the underwings are even more fantastic in their delineation than are the upper surfaces, for they make the entire figure dissolve optically into the background.

Nevertheless, some types maintain a bright-colored appearance in every position, because both upper and lower wing surfaces bear intense, often identical colors. Even the body may be brightly colored. Frequently these are warning costumes, which advertise the inedibility or toxicity of their owners. Or the wearer may merely pretend to have such qualities.

In no other insect order has nature's artistry been expressed so strongly on both adult and immature forms. If all possible optical means have been put to use by adult members of Lepidoptera, the same is no less true of the caterpillars and even to some degree of the pupae. We are astonished by the complete independence of these forms: a caterpillar with harsh warning coloration may become a drab, protectively colored adult, or the color contrast may be reversed. Such thoroughgoing originality in the appearance of the several developmental stages, which goes hand in hand with their particular ways of life, emphasizes the two entirely different worlds of the adults and of the caterpillars and pupae. A better comprehension of these phenomena can be achieved by regarding them separately, and therefore we shall turn our attention first to the mature, winged being. Much about coloration and design, protective and warning costumes, variation, development, migrations, and other information about adult and immature Lepidoptera is presented in the section on "Insects and Their Ways." [62/5, 6]

ADULT BUTTERFLIES AND MOTHS

The systematic arrangement of butterflies and moths into about 100 families is still in part highly controversial; to a great extent it is based on the pattern of veins in the wing, which in general gives reliable indications of the degrees of mutual interrelationship. Primitive or ancestral butterflies and moths have a rich wing venation fairly similar on all wings. But the more highly developed types, which are in the majority, have fewer veins and a different vein pattern on front and back wings. [189/11, 12]

Based on broad natural characteristics more than on systematic classification, these insects may be divided into three great groups: the butterflies (Rhopalocera), the moths (Heterocera), and the micro moths (Microlepidoptera). These general divisions, it is true, do only partial justice to the natural relationships. For, although butterflies are considered children of the sun, certain ones fly at dusk. And many moths, disregarding the night-flying habits moths are known for, take wing only during the day, at times even when the sun is out. In the far north the day-flying butterflies often have to get along with less light than the night-flying moths. As for the "micros," they are neither a uniform grouping nor properly to be separated from the rest of the moths. [210/2–7; 211/5–10]

The uraniid moths of the tropics, which are among the most magnificent spectacles of nature, are day flyers. Their wings, which look as though fashioned of satin or silk bordered with blinding white, shimmer with a deep brown, blue, or gray-black. In the South American and African species this seems interwoven with lustrous golden green or, in some kinds, with purple and fiery hues; but in the Indo-Australian species it alternates with delicate, pastel-green bands that are touched with silver, gray, or blue; with bronze; or with copper. Their beauty is elusive when seen during flight, but commands deep appreciation when these moths sun themselves or drink water at the foot of a dripping, mossy cliff. [223/6; 224/1, 2]

FEEDING HABITS

Most members of the Lepidoptera have a rather strong need for water, especially in warm and dry weather. Some nocturnal species are satisfied with a few dewdrops. Others flutter close to the surface of the water, dipping the proboscis and the anus into it. Still others simply settle on the damp earth. Bright-colored crowds of whites and sulfurs, gossamer wings, swallowtails, and other families gather at times on damp spots, rising in swirling clouds when disturbed. In the tropics, perhaps in a clearing, on a river bank, or on moist cliffs, such events are magnified into overpoweringly grand spectacles, sometimes through the participation of hundreds of gorgeous individuals. A peculiar system of bodily irrigation sometimes is observed in certain papilionids, among others. While they imbibe, they squirt a little stream from the anus every second. [212/1]

One group of small moths with primitive mouthparts, namely the pollen-eating family of the Micropterygidae, possess toothed chewing mandibles. But the rest of the butterflies and moths take more or less fluid food, for their mouth has been modified into a sucking proboscis. This is a tube formed of two appressed half-pipes (the outer parts of the maxillae). When not in use, the tube is rolled up in a spiral. Among many short-lived moths, the proboscis is reduced in size or wholly degenerate, but in general it is well adapted to the structure of the flowers frequented by the particular species. This adaptation seems never to go so far that a lepidopteran has become specialized to feed on a single species of flowering plant.

Certain sphinx moths (Sphingidae) have the longest proboscises, some of them the longest among all insects. The trunk of the huge South American species *Amphimoea walkeri* may exceed 11 inches, more than twice the length of the body and longer than is necessary for the insect to feed. [189/13]

An interesting story concerns the subspecies *Macrosila (Xanthopan) morgani praedicta* from Madagascar, which also has a proboscis about 11 inches long. The English naturalist A. R. Wallace, in his book "Contributions to the Theory of Natural Selection," which appeared in 1870, predicted the existence of a sphingid, at that time unknown, with such an enormously long proboscis. He stated that such a creature must exist for the fertilization of the orchid *Angraecum sesquipedale*. The nectar of this magnificent, ivory-white, star-shaped flower is situated at the bottom of a spur 10 to 14 inches long, and hence could be reached only by an insect with a comparably long proboscis.

Thirty-three years later another scientist actually found in Madagascar the sphingid that is capable of this feat. He named it *praedicta* ("the prophesied one"). Since that time the sphingid and orchid have been cited regularly as the prime example of mutual evolution between flower and insect of a long spur and a long trunk. But today doubt is cast upon this interpretation, for the "prophesied one" has proved to be too rare to be able to fertilize this orchid sufficiently. Besides, the moth usually is not on the wing when the flower is in bloom.

Most butterflies and moths feed on nectar, on the honeydew of aphids, and on overripe fruit. Besides the last, certain families like other fermenting substances, such as dung, carrion, and even human and animal perspiration.

Many families or groups of species prefer certain kinds and especially certain colors of flowers, yet this may vary with the time of blooming, weather, or locality, and also with the mood, age, and physical condition of the individual lepidopteran. So no general rules can be formulated.

Nevertheless, numerous flowers, mostly bright-colored, are specially adapted to moths with long trunks. These flowers wait until nightfall to emit their waves of fragrance strongly, to come erect, or to open. The moths find the flowers, thanks to their odor, at distances as great as 45 yards in still air or 550 yards in a wind.

The sense of smell, located in the antennae, guides the moth to the vicinity. Then, the flight to the goal usually is oriented visually. This is almost exclusively the case with butterflies, although when they are close at hand the sense of smell plays a part in the choice of the flowers with the most honey.

A great many lepidopterans have no sense of taste in the trunk, but often do have such a sense in their legs, especially the front ones. This enables them to detect unimaginably slight concentrations. The ability is of great importance for noctuids and other moths in perceiving weakly odorous sources of nourishment, such as honeydew or the juices of trees or fruit, or in finding damp spots on the ground. In addition, many females use this sense in locating plants appropriate as sites for egg-laying; the females may test the leaves by trilling or drumming on them.

Certain fruit-sucking lepidopterans have a hard or saw-toothed tip on the proboscis. Among them are a group of noctuids comprising about 16 genera. A few species of these living in Asia and Africa take a most peculiar kind of nourishment. For they are found at night around the eyes of resting cattle, often hanging there in a tight circle, poking their trunks under the lids and imbibing the tears. A single individual sucks for about 10 to 15 minutes. The cattle react little, if at all, and their flow of tears is not increased. Nevertheless, the connective tissue in the area may become inflamed, and it is suspected that diseases of cattle may be transmitted by the noctuids, one genus of which (*Calpe*) frequents both fruit and mammals.

Whereas many butterflies loiter from flower to flower more or less all day long, testing first one and then the next, other lepidopterans, especially dusk-flying sphingid moths, have a feeding flight limited to perhaps 15 to 30 minutes. These sphingids rush from flower to flower, visiting as many as 25 in a minute. Hovering with whirring wings above a flower, the sphingid extends its long, curved proboscis into the chalice, and the plant quivers with the vibration of the wings.

Watching sphingids is an absorbing and exciting pastime. Like unreal phantoms, these often powerful creatures flash spasmodically out of the night shadows, and with a gentle, humming sound, visit a flowering, fragrant shrub, only to disappear suddenly into darkness again. The feeding flight usually begins every evening almost at the same time. The time shifts a little in accord with the seasonal position of the sun and, less so, with the cloudiness or brightness of the sky. [190/1]

Within the deeply fissured virgin forest at Rio de Janeiro, a magnificent natural preserve, one of the fascinating hummingbirds visits a flowering tree again and again all day long. One does not tire of watching the skillful techniques of the tiny bird in flight. Now he has dashed off once more with a loud whistle, likely for the last time today, for the sun is about to sink below the nearby horizon of the wooded mountaintop. But at that very moment, four others suddenly appear as black forms against the bright sky, whirring from flower to flower, sinking their beaks into them, and then without warning vanishing like ghosts.

Ten minutes later they come back at one fell swoop as if on command, this time five of them. Oddly, something or other seems not to fit with the so-closely observed hummingbird, and with this thought there comes immediate recognition. These are no birds, but instead sphingids, whose period of flight has begun, just at that minute when the sun vanished behind the treetops.

TERRITORIES

Butterflies and moths have habitual ranges, or beats. Many males try to keep an area to themselves, charging at their own kind and even at other insects that fly into or past it. Such territories are defended particularly staunchly by various nymphalid butterflies and by the magnificent castniids, a day-flying family of moths in tropical America. Most castniid species are huge, have antennae resembling those of butterflies, and possess extraordinarily hard, coarsely-scaled wings with which they develop very high speeds in flight. When such a moth hurls its heavy body onto a flower at nectar-taking time of a morning, it bumps other insects out of the way. Afterward, the male takes his stand on a protruding dry branch and, as he watches for a female, holds despotic sway over as much as an entire clearing in the forest, attacking even the hummingbirds. [191/1]

Many nymphalid males take up positions head downward on a rock, treetrunk, or leaf, to which they return over and over. If such a spot is vacated, it may quickly be occupied by another individual. A scientist in China had an experience in which a male of the genus *Euthalia* settled on a certain leaf shortly after he had captured another one there. A few minutes after the second capture, there sat a third, and in the course of about 20 minutes

he took eight males, one after the other. All these butterflies must have been waiting nearby for a chance to take possession of this one leaf.

Many swallowtail butterflies do not sit still to supervise their territories, but sail about uninterruptedly in flight for hours at a time. A few trees or bushes, a cliff, a body of water, or a footpath may constitute the boundaries of a territory, and the adjacent area may be patrolled by another male of the same species. Skirmishes occur again and again. In a whirling, dashing game, both butterflies disappear into the sky, and shortly afterward each dives back into his own

Here some noctuid moths are sucking at the eye of a domesticated yak (0.3 natural size); beneath is the hard, saw-toothed proboscis tip.

territory, now properly measured off. Maintenance of a territory by means of continuous flight also is seen among the big dragonflies and certain flies (tabanids, syrphids).

Besides water courses, forest paths, or clearings, the tops of trees and ridges with certain configurations of air currents are places where many butterflies of various families assemble, either ignoring one another altogether or causing each other some disturbance. The males in particular engage in sportive flights that often differ markedly from one species to another. Here, the two sexes from the entire environment frequently meet.

It is marvelous how much butterfly life one can see in the course of a day along a little stretch of path in the woods. Not only may the flight periods of the different genera replace one another almost from hour to hour, but the manner of flying of one and the same lepidopteran may change almost beyond recognition. If during the morning a morpho butterfly has been bouncing stormily along the way near the ground, at noontime the same butterfly may perchance be seen cruising about with calm majesty through the crowns of the trees.

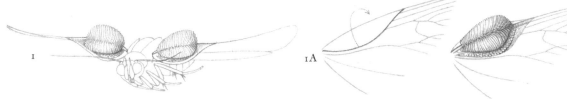

175/1–1A
*Scent organs of male moths, for
arousing the females. Certain
tiger moths have on the upper side
at the base of the fore wing a flap
that can be folded down over the
wing margin, thus exposing a
yellow scent brush (1A).
(1) The moth in natural size,
at which the portion of the brush
on the wing surface cannot be
seen.*

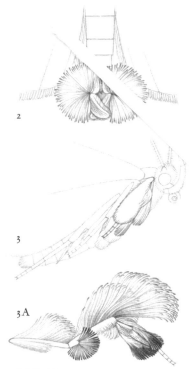

175/2–3A
*(2) Hind end of a geometer with
wings outspread (enlarged).
(3) The forelegs of a noctuid moth,
bearing enormous scent brushes
in the normal, closed posture, and
(3A) with the one on the foreleg
opened (enlarged).*

Or at dusk a covey of males of the great noctuid *Blosyris* may flit hither and yon so wildly at a height of 10 to 12 feet above a 60-foot length of the same path that one imagines he is seeing bats. At that time it is almost impossible to catch these tumultuous fliers, even if one stations himself at the exact place where they regularly make their turn. Even with the quickest, hardest sweeps, the net almost always remains empty, and all one hears is the audible rattling of such a moth dodging the attack with a lightning-fast maneuver. If one then withdraws resignedly a short distance, he may come upon a huge, dark moth patrolling slowly back and forth, whirring along only a yard high over about 30 feet of the selfsame path at a perfectly straight, horizontal level, like a dragonfly. And once in the net this proves to be the identical genus as that of the "bats" storming along a short distance away.

Relatives of these noctuid moths also are widespread in Africa and Asia, and many have two gigantic, specterlike eyes on the fore wings. One of the largest of these species, *da walkeri,* is regarded with dread in Madagascar as "Lulpat," the spirit of a departed person. This superstition is quite understandable in addition to the uncanny appearance of such noctuids, one considers the ghostly quality of their slow, seesawing, whirring flight, conducted at an absolutely constant elevation. Thus evening after evening, "Lulpat" may glide through the dusk along the same path past the where the horrified people get quickly out of the way; and throughout the daytime the moth keeps in quiet, dark hiding places, such as the native houses of the dead. [191/2]

An almost unbelievable loyalty to given localities is shown by many species of metalmarks (Riodinidae), a large family of small butterflies related to the gossamer-winged butterflies (Lycaenidae). With the unprecedented variety of their forms and their often marvelously radiant colors, they are among the most interesting and most beautiful of all. Though they are represented in all parts of the earth, they are in greatest abundance in South America. Year after year, certain species are seen in the virgin forest in only a single place, perhaps only in one and the same bush or even only on a certain branch. Shy, they dash off with a metallic flash, and conceal themselves, with wings flat outspread, under a leaf in the thicket, where they are not to be discovered despite their luminous coloring.

The structural colors of many metalmarks change completely according to the angle at which light strikes them or from which they are viewed—from silver to pure gold, from gold to turquoise-green or to violet and purple. These colors gleam with a radiant intensity unsurpassed throughout the world of nature. As a rare phenomenon, the drop-shaped golden or silver spots on the under-surface of the hind wings of the genus *Helicopis* are elevated convexly, as though hammered out of the surface, which heightens their effect.

Many of the most gorgeous metalmark species come out from the branches in the early morning hours, ascend briefly into the air, and frolic beneath the leaves. The blue males of the genus *Mesosemia* carry out courting dances, hopping from leaf to leaf with the fore wings raised and the hind wings lying flat. [32/4; 192; 209/1–5]

COURTSHIP

Much remains to be learned about the games of butterflies and moths preliminary to mating. These are probably poorly developed among nocturnal species. The males of these species detect their females at unbelievable distances by means of the sense of smell, unless there is a flat calm. Moth breeders take advantage of this ability. They carry females freshly emerged from cocoons to places where they would naturally be flying. While such a person is en route, dozens of males may come swarming about him. If his fingers have touched her beforehand, the males will flutter about the fingers and possibly land on them. Each species has its own set hours for the mating flight, which generally takes place during the first half of the night and again at dawn. [245/1]

The mating games of butterflies are more interesting than those of moths. Many butterflies find one another almost exclusively by sight. Often a butterfly pair, accompanied by additional males, rises a hundred yards skyward in whirling sport and then dives in a mad rush back to earth, with the female in the lead. If she is in no mood for mating, she behaves in a way that causes the male to break off the game.

The introductory steps to mating begin on the ground or on the vegetation. During this phase, the male of the lemon butterfly (*Gonepteryx*) runs excitedly about the female, who sits still with wings outspread. In a delightful game, he is then alternately caught fast between her suddenly uplifted wings and again released. [209/6]

With many satyrid butterflies, the male flies after his partner, settles behind her on the ground, walks forward, and stops direct

177/1–34
*Different families of beetles.
(1–8) Ground beetles. (9–18) Rove
beetles. (19–20) Paussid beetles.
(21–23) Burying beetles and carrion
beetles. (24–25) Bessbugs.
(26–34) Dung beetles
(scarabaeoids), whose notches and
horns are tools for manufacturing
the brood pills (somewhat enlarged).
Photograph.*

PAGES 178 AND 179
*Rhinoceros beetles. The hercules beetle
(Dynastes hercules) (179/2), with
the female beside it, is one of the
largest insects, and its wing covers
look as though they bore a map of
the night sky. Despite the imposing
appearance, these are defenseless
beetles, for the immovable horns on
their head and prothoracic shield are
not weapons; placed next to its
tropical relatives, the European
rhinoceros beetle makes a modest
impression (178/2) (enlarged 1.5×).*

PAGE 180
180/1–16
*Most flower beetles (1–15) and
goliath beetles (16) are of great
beauty, and in spite of their large
size are peaceful vegetarians. In many
species the males have horns on the
head: these are used as pry bars in
their harmless contests of rivalry.
The wing covers are fused along their
inner edges, and hence cannot be
spread apart for flying but can
merely be raised slightly above the
back; instead of them, the legs,
stretched out frontward, function as
stabilizers in the huge goliath beetles
(16A). Below is the (smaller)
female (16B) and the larva (16C)
(1 to 16 enlarged 1.5×; 16A–C
natural size).*

181/1–12
*The huge company of May or June
beetles, together with the dung
beetles and pill rollers, the
rhinoceros beetles, flower beetles, and
goliath beetles, belongs to the great
group of scarabaeoids, and includes
several dreaded pests of plants,
foremost among them the May
beetle (2). The gigantic long-armed
Euchirus (1) are outsiders (natural
size). Photograph.*

181/13–33
*Different families of beetles.
(17–18) Rhipicerids with
fantastically shaped antennae.*

(15–16) *Lightning bugs.
(13–14) Net-winged beetles or
Lycidae are poisonous tropical beetles,
to some extent "mimicked" by other
insects. (26) Timber beetle or
Lymexylidae, whose interesting
larva is shown in Figure 138/27.
(25) These soft-winged flower beetles
(malachiids) and their larvae eat
insects. (23–24) Soldier beetles.
(19–22) Among the checkered beetles,
the checkered ant beetle and the bee
wolves are best known; the former eat
bark beetles, or their entrails; and
the latter grow up as parasites in
bees' nests. (32–33) The wing covers
of many Erotylidae ("pleasing fungus
beetles") are shaped like a tall
pyramid. (30–31) The handsome
fungus beetles (Endomychidae) and
their larvae live on mushrooms and
agarics. Larvae of the larder beetle
(29), the black carpet beetle (28),
and the carpet beetle (27) are
notorious household pests (enlarged
1.3×). Photograph.*

PAGE 182
182/1–31
*The metallic wood-boring beetles.
This enormous family shimmers with
all the structural colors, whose effect
is increased by means of all sorts
of sculpturing. Many of the species,
especially the smaller ones, are decidedly
shy insects with highly acute vision
(somewhat enlarged; 31 much
enlarged). Photographs.*

182/32–38
*The universally liked ladybird beetles
and their larvae destroy plantlice
(enlarged 2×).*

PAGE 183
183/1–27
*The long-horned beetles are a family
with a great number of forms and
species. (4) The house borer is
dreaded as a destroyer of lumber;
below (8–9) are two wasplike
long-horned beetles with their much-
reduced elytra; and (7) one of the
species that imitates the poisonous
Lycidae. There are many beautiful
long-horned beetles. On the other
hand, some have concealing disguises,
among them the carpenter's long-horned
beetle (18) with its long slender
antennae (as is more or less usual in
this family, they are shorter in the
female), and the poplar borer (19)
(natural size).*

PAGES 184 AND 185
184/1–185/3
Long-horned beetles from various parts

*of the globe (184/1, 2 and 185/3
enlarged 1.5×; 184/3 enlarged
3.5×; 185/1, 2 enlarged 2.5×).*

PAGE 186
186/1–21
*Leaf beetles feed on leaves, and are
disliked because they frequently appear
in large numbers. (1) The long-
horned leaf beetle Donacia, whose
larvae are aquatic. (2) Two asparagus
beetles and a case-bearing leaf beetle
(3), which drops as though dead
when endangered. (10) The smallest
ones, called "flea beetles" because of
their talent for jumping. In the lower
half of the figure are tortoise beetles
(12–21), of interest because of their
brood relationships (somewhat
enlarged). Photograph.*

186/22–48
*The snout beetles, with face more or
less stretched out as a sucking trunk
and with integumental armor often
almost as hard as rock, are probably
the most interesting and multisided
family of beetles. At top center, above
one another, are two fungus weevils
(25–26), as representatives of a
different but closely related family, and
beneath them a black and white
Madagascan lichen snout beetle (33),
which lives on lichens of precisely
the same color and shape. Below, on
the left, is one of the leaf rollers (38),
famous for their technique for cutting
patterns, and beside it two American
nut weevils (39). Among the largest
snout beetles are the dreaded palm-tree
pests (45, 47, and 48). (22 to 44
somewhat enlarged; 45 to 48 somewhat reduced). Photographs.*

PAGE 187
187/1–10
*Leaf beetles and snout beetles. Of the
leaf beetles (1–6), the Colorado
potato beetle (4) and its larva (5) are
the best known, and the Javanese
Sagra species (6) with its stocky hind
femora, is one of the largest.
The species in the middle (2)
resembles a glowing coal, and the
tortoise beetle (3) above it shimmers
with delicate colors that vanish
completely after its death. (8) The
boll weevil and its larva (8A).
(9) A Brazilian snout beetle species,
the hind end of which resembles an
animal's face. Finally, at the bottom
an Australian snout beetle (10) is
walking along, and from its looks it
might have come from outer space
(enlarged 3×). Photograph.*

PAGE 188
188/1–6
*Lacewings. (1) A spoonwinged
neuropteran, with its slender
elongated hind wings. (2) The long-
necked larva of another species of this
genus. (3) A giant antlion;
(4–5) owlflies. (6) An owlfly larva
(enlarged 2×).*

PAGE 189
189/1–10
*Lacewings. (1) A snakefly. (2) A
green lacewing. (3) A brown
lacewing. (4) An osmylid lacewing
and two mantisflies (5 and 6), that
resemble a praying mantis because of
their predatory shears. In the right
half of the illustration are
Mecoptera, namely, at the top, three
scorpionflies (7 and 8), the males of
which have a scorpionlike tail; below,
a hangingfly (9) that can snap its legs
back rapidly as prehensile tongs.
(10) Male and female of a snow
scorpionfly (enlarged 1.3×).
Photograph.*

189/11–12
*In those butterflies and moths that are
more highly evolved, the pattern of
the wing ribs (venation) is reduced and
differs more between fore wings and
hind wings, e.g., the cabbage butterfly
(11). The venation is more abundant
and more uniform in primitive
families, e.g., the ghost moth (12);
and here the bases of fore wings and
hind wings are more fully separated.*

189/13
*With certain sphinx moths the
"tongue," transformed into a sucking
proboscis, is three times as long as
the body (natural size).*

PAGE 190
190/1
*The oleander hawk moth on woodbine,
illuminated by searchlight; almost
every year this species migrates northward from the Mediterranean region
(enlarged 2×).*

PAGE 191
191/1
*Patrolling males of the South
American castniid butterflies are
aggressive not only toward other
insects but even toward small birds,
such as this honeycreeper
(enlarged 1.2×).*

191/2
*One of the spooky Patula noctuid
moths, that are distributed widely
through the tropics of the Old World
(natural size). Photograph.*

177/1-8

177/9-13

177/19-20

177/14-18

177/21-23

177/24

177/26-27

177/28-30

177/25

177/31-34

178/1

178/2

178/3

178

179/1

179/2

♀

♂

179

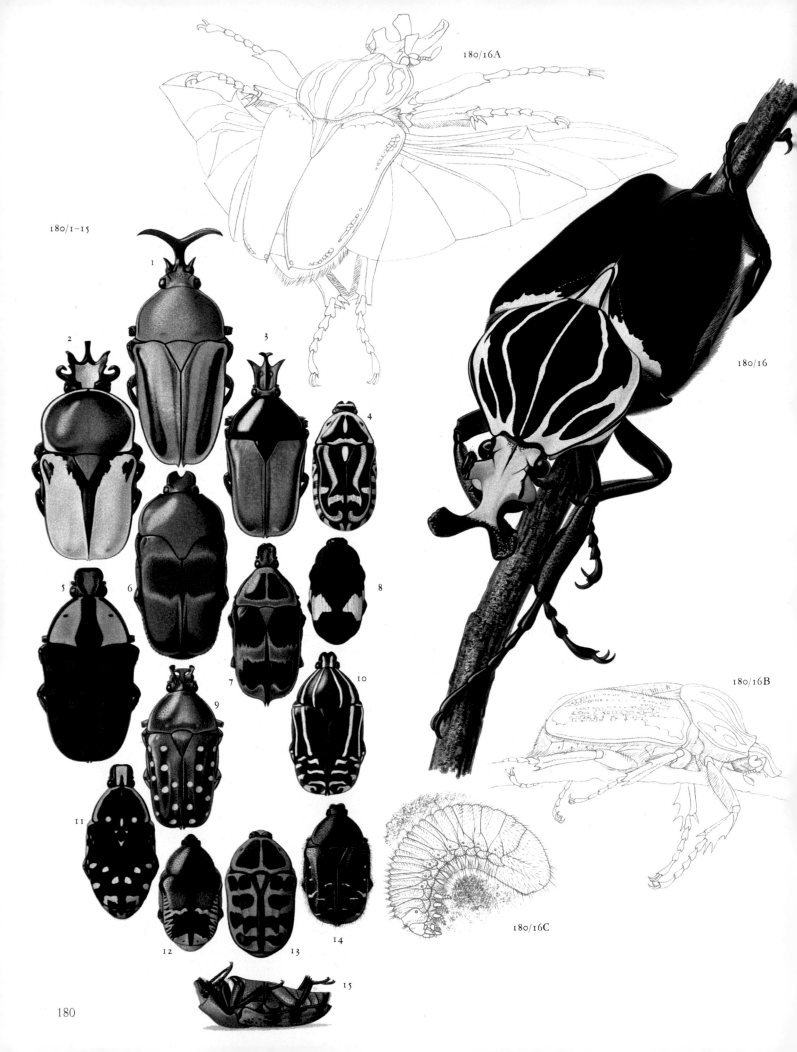

180/16A

180/1-15

1

2

3

4

5 6

7 8

9 10

11

12 13 14

15

180/16

180/16B

180/16C

180

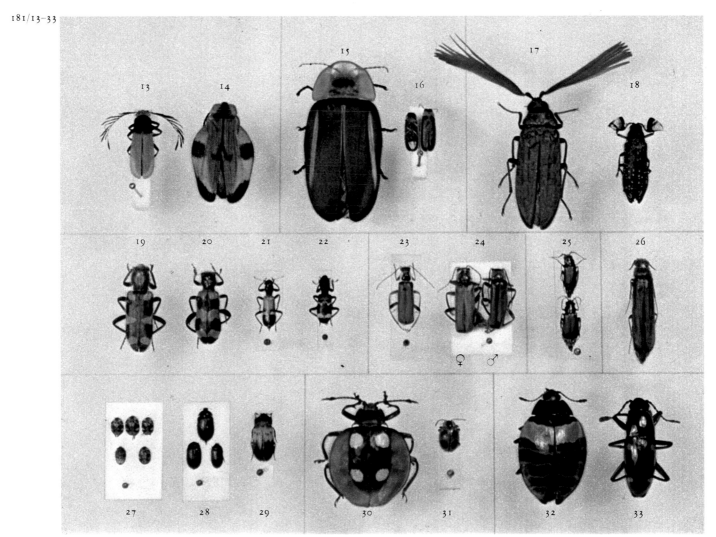

182/1-9

182/31

182/10-13

182/14-17

182/18-21

182/22-25

182/26-30

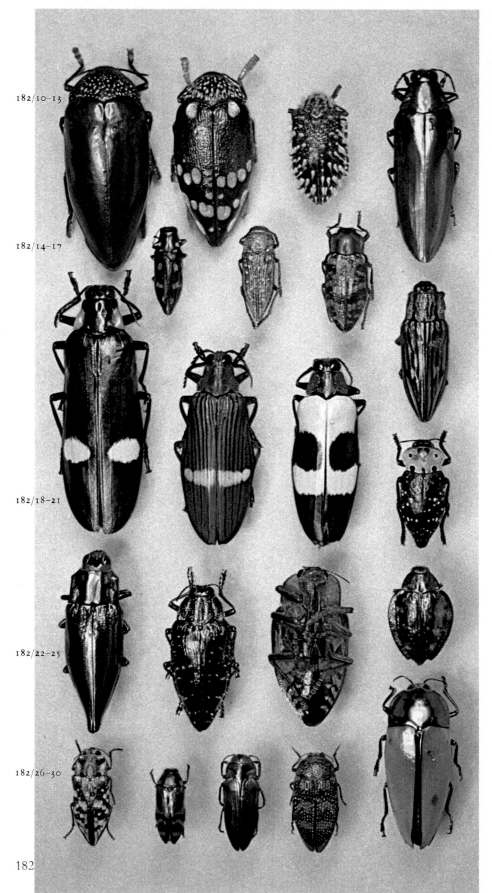

182/32-38

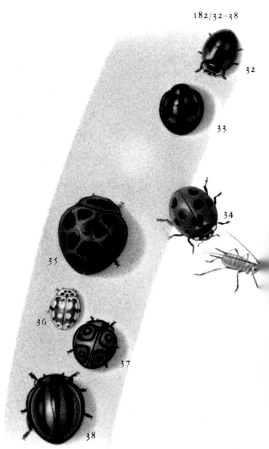

32

33

34

35

36

37

38

182

183/1-3

183/4-10

183/11-15

183/16-20

183/21-27

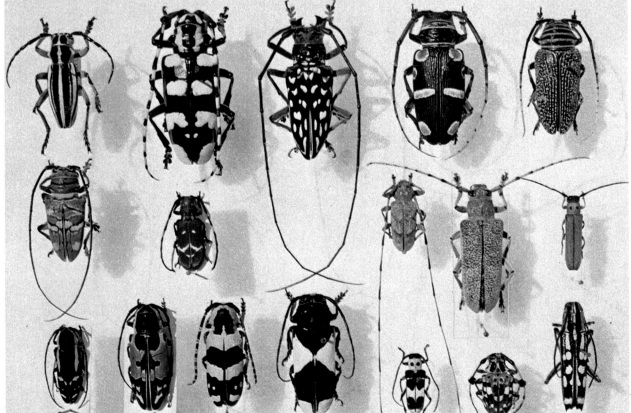

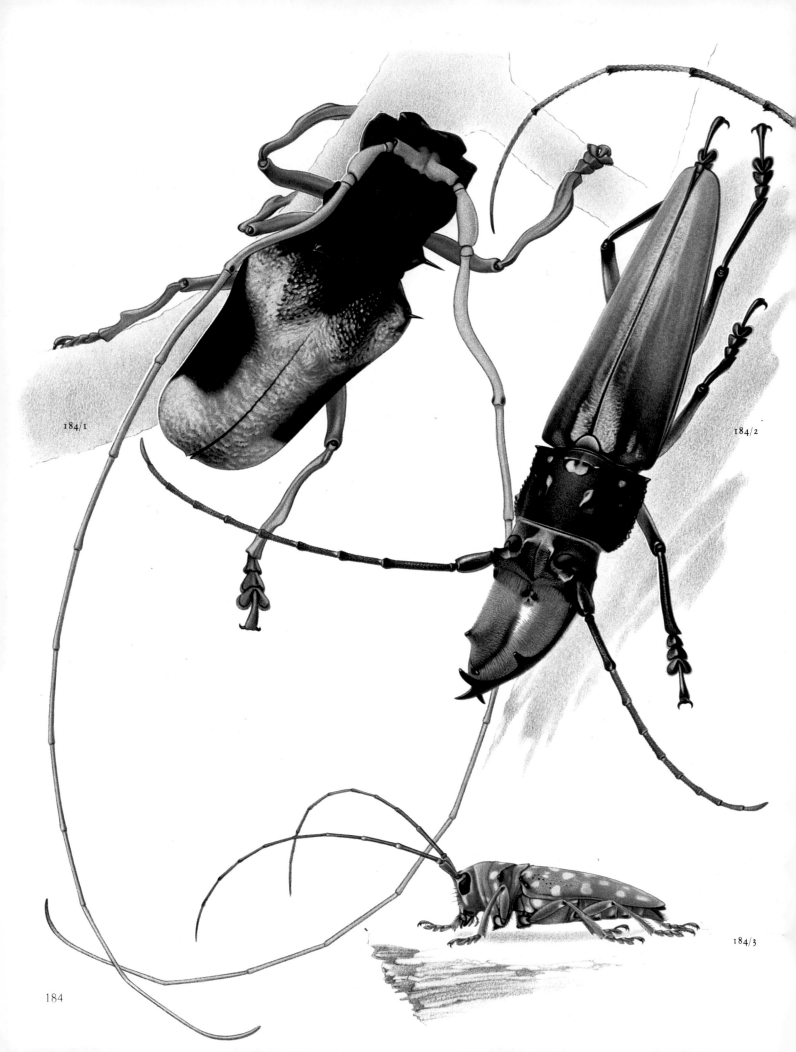

184/1

184/2

184/3

184

185/1

185/2

185/3

185

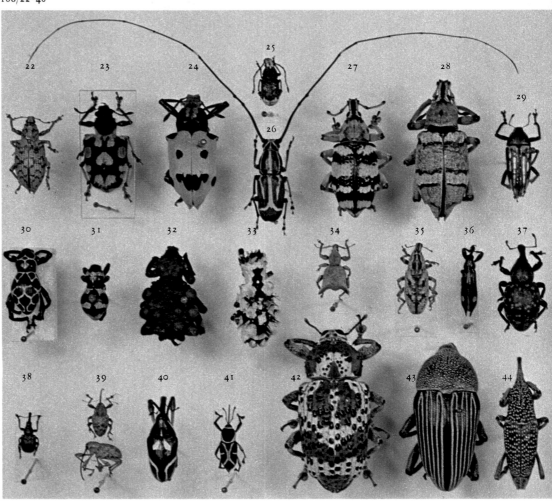

187/1   187/2   187/3

187/4

187/7

187/8

8A

187/5

187/6

187/9

187/10

187

188/1

188/2

188/3

188/4

188/5

188/6

188

189/1–10

189/11

189/12

189/13

189

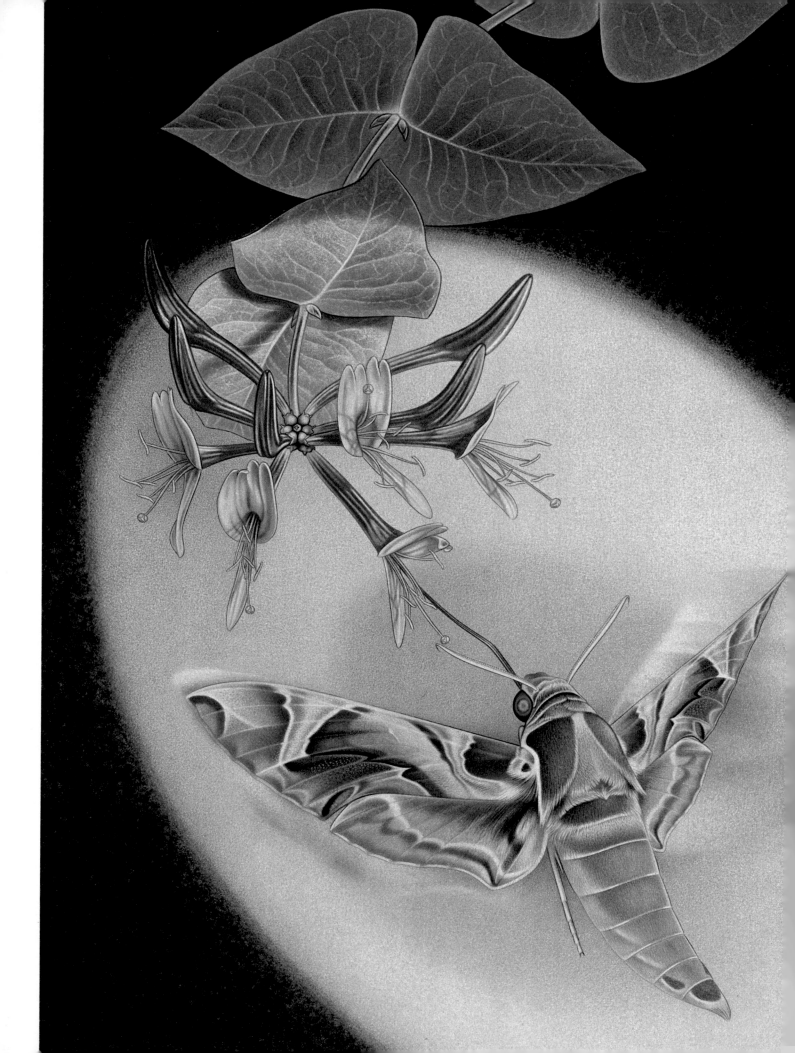

191/2

192/1

192/2

192/3

192/4

192/5

in front of her, head to head. Now he waves his antennae, and opens and closes his wings a few times, and finally squeezes the female's antennae between them. In this way he presses the scent scales on his wings against the female's olfactory nerves, which end in the tips of the antennae, in order to stimulate her to mate. If this succeeds, the male draws his wings back into the normal position, walks around his partner, and begins the act of mating. But it does not come to this every time, for often it all remains a game, though possibly a prolonged one, and the pair separates without having mated. Occasionally the males will even try in this way to lay hold of the antennae of quite different butterflies that don't belong to their family.

While mating is in progress, most moths do not fly. In butterflies, one of the pair usually does, clumsily dragging along the other, who hangs passively. In certain tropical members of the genus *Papilio,* however, both move the wings as they cling breast to breast, the one on the bottom beating them more slowly. This seems like an almost impossible effort at cooperation, but its usefulness is made evident by the ease and speed of their flight.

In general, odorous substances from special glands are responsible for the mutual location and excitation of the two sexes. In the female the glands usually are at the hind end of the abdomen and often can be protruded. Generally the females attract the males, but in some species, especially in primitive families such as certain hepialid moths and micro moths, males attract females with scents. But even in species in which the coming together of the sexes is mediated largely by the optical sense, a great many males—particularly butterflies—have odor-producing organs. The odors serve for recognition and for arousing the mate when she is close at hand. In contrast with the scents produced by the female, they can be perceived, often as being very intense smells, by a person. Thus many butterflies actually have a pleasant aroma—flowerlike, spicy, or fruity, or like chocolate or musk.

These ethereal compounds are given forth by specific scales, usually long and slender, on the wings; either they are scattered at random beneath the rest of the scaly covering or are grouped in particular areas into fields, spots, and stripes; some are intermingled with hairs. Frequently such zones are concealed in folds of the wing bordered thickly with long hairs; this slows the evaporation of the perfume.

Odor-producing scales also may occur on the legs or more rarely on the antennae, grouped in bunches that protrude or that lie in furrows and can be exposed. Milkweed butterflies (Danaidae), for instance, have large protrusible odor-producing hair pencils at both sides of the hind end. Many sphinx moths have odorous organs at the base of the abdomen, and in certain hepialids they lie within pouches on the abdominal sides.

Devices for making sounds also may play a part in the interrelationships of the sexes. Certain moths (predominantly sphinx moths) make chirping sounds by inhaling and exhaling air, and others make crackling and rustling noises by means of elevated rough or toothed veins on the lower surface of the wings; these surfaces may be rubbed together or against the sides of the thorax in flight or frequently may be stroked by or against the legs.

The males of certain noctuids *(Thecophora)* have as a sound amplifier a smooth, vesicular structure in the middle of the hind wings. And a few arctiids have on each side of the thorax a specially constructed vesicle that during flight produces twittering tones so high that not all people can hear them. The moths themselves can hear their sounds by means of so-called tympanal organs, which are on the lower rear surface of the thorax in noctuids, for example, or at the base of the abdomen in geometrids. As noted elsewhere, moths also are able to perceive the ultrasounds emitted by hunting bats. [209/7, 8]

FLIGHT

Most lepidopterans flap their wings continuously while they fly, but many butterflies alternate flapping and gliding, and many moths—typically, the sphinx moths—make the wings whir. Among butterflies, the skippers almost always engage in whirring flight, and male swallowtails of the genus *Papilio,* as well as male pierids, also do so occasionally during the mating maneuvers. Fore and hind wings are coupled by bristles or by the interlocking of their margins (especially in butterflies). The united wings move upward and then forward-downward. In flapping flight, the wings move through an angle of about 150° and beat at a rate of about 5 to 10 per second. In whirring flight, this angle is perhaps only 90°, and the wingbeat 25 to 100 per second. Steering is exclusively by means of the wings. [211/4]

The fastest fliers have more or less pointed wings (although flight performance cannot always be estimated from the form of the wings alone); examples are *Appias,* a pierid butterfly, and the sphinx moths. The ground speed may be as much as 35 miles an hour, or much more with a tailwind. The sphinx moths are among the best insect fliers. They not only fly fast, but also maneuver skillfully and can rise vertically or even go backward.

Among butterflies and moths the type of flight may differ greatly from species to species or, depending on circumstances, even in the same individual at different times. Mimics are particularly interesting in this connection. These defenseless species not only look like certain other species that are protected by their acrid body fluids, but also have assumed their typical, slow wing movements. But if such a mountebank is interfered with, he suddenly reverts to the quite different way of flying characteristic of his own genus, and storms off in a frenzy. Here it becomes particularly evident that mimicry is not a phenomenon of outward similarities alone, but can be comprehended in its full significance and extent only when behavior also is taken into account.

At rest, the wings of most butterflies and a smaller proportion of moths are held together vertically above the back. Only the undersurfaces are visible. The hind wings cover all of the front wings except their tips, whose coloring blends with that of the hind wings. The majority of moths and certain butterflies rest with the wings laid flat or held rooflike above them at various angles; they may be extended laterally to a greater or lesser degree, but mostly are pressed back together in the familiar way or (especially among Microlepidoptera) even are rolled and folded lengthwise around the abdomen. An astounding number of variations is, of course, possible; some alter the accustomed picture of the resting moth to the point where the moth is unrecognizable.

ENVIRONMENTAL INFLUENCES

Lepidoptera occur almost everywhere that insect life is possible; some even develop under water. On the average the minimum temperatures at which they are active are about 46° F to 54° F (8° C to 12° C), but a temperature of only a few degrees above freezing suffices for certain species. Every type of country, every different locality in it, and to a degree even every altitude has its own assemblage of lepidopterous species. The species live where the food plants eaten by their larvae grow. Climate and soil also influence the distribution of individual species.

In the temperate zone the adults of species that overwinter as mature forms—and that frequently fall into lethargy toward the end of summer, but may become more lively once more on fine autumn or even winter days—live to be almost a year old. But in general the life of an adult lepidopteran lasts only a couple of weeks, or only a matter of days in many species that take no food. The daily flight periods often are quite precisely set, a phenomenon that is particularly impressive among forest species, where adaptation to the rapidly changing conditions of illumination is necessary. The customs and ways of flying of lepidopterans during the course of a day also are dictated and modified to a great extent by changes in local temperature or wind.

Very generally, falling barometric pressure and high humidity, warm rain, and, most of all, conditions characteristic of thunderstorms have an enlivening effect on moths, especially on those emerging from the pupa. So where there is a constellation of such factors, there may be a mass occurrence of species that otherwise are seldom seen for years on end.

A different compulsion, just as commonly observed as it is strange and unexplained, is evident in the attraction exerted by sources of artificial light. For example, the illumination of a statue of Christ that stands on the Corcovado cliff near Rio de Janeiro in the midst of a wooded region takes the lives of countless insects, which are unable to escape from the beam for whole nights. Our streetlights have a similar though less decimating effect, partly because they make insect-hunting easier for bats and toads. Flight toward artificial light takes place mostly during certain definite hours that differ according to the species; with many it does not occur until midnight or later. [211/1-3]

Not all moths come to light; in particular the females of many species do not, or they are attracted only after they have laid their eggs. On the other hand, diurnal individuals often appear—probably those whose resting place was in the path of the beam. The impetus toward light can be disastrous in daytime, too, in that lepidopterans may dash themselves into the water surface or, when migrating over mountains, onto snowfields, where masses of them occasionally are found frozen to death.

IMPORTANT FAMILIES

About 100,000 species of lepidopterans are known. The wings of the smallest span

195/1
Zebra swallowtails have more delicate, more highly transparent wings than other related swallowtail butterflies, and can glide elegantly (0.6 natural size). Photograph.

scarcely 0.08 inch, and those of the largest more than a foot. The butterflies lag far behind the others with respect to number of families, genera, and species. They are distinguished most readily by their stiff, threadlike antennae, the clubshaped or button-shaped tips of which usually are thickened (however, similar antennae also occur in certain moths). The most important families are those that follow; the first three have all the legs well-developed, but in the rest the first pair of legs is reduced to mere ornaments of no use for holding onto objects or for walking.

SWALLOWTAILS

In almost every landscape a few of the approximately 600 species of swallowtails (family Papilionidae), thanks to their large size, beauty, and liveliness, appear as the dominant lepidopterans. Straight across fields and gardens, over hill and valley, or even above the hustle and bustle of a city marketplace, numbers of these elegant figures flit and glide; others go sailing about the lonesome peaks or above the lofty crowns of the trees in the virgin forest, or course with rapid wingbeat through the shady underbrush beneath. [19/28]

Swallowtails of the forests, like many other forest butterflies, have dark to black wings adorned with large white or luminous, bright-colored spots and stripes. As they fly, they limit their labor almost entirely to the fore wings, the rear ones fanning gently. Proceeding slowly over the vegetation, they dodge the overly sunny spots and hesitate now and again to sip from a flower. As they sip, their wings beat without interruption, as is characteristic of many swallowtails of the genus *Papilio*. Legs extended and wings whirring, the swallowtail stands on a blossom, its proboscis inserted but quivering nervously. In this position, the strikingly handsome *Papilio (Trogonoptera) brookiana* of East Asia seems like a hummingbird hovering in front of a flower. [210/1]

The grandeur and beauty of the swallowtails is almost too well known to justify further praise. We may feel some regret on hearing the opinion that in the course of evolution the black pigment melanin will gradually become predominant in these butterflies. For example, might not the red of *Papilio rumanzovia semperinus*, which already seems so strangely repressed, be one last outflaring before its extinction—before complete blackening, as seen in other species? For how many centuries or millennia will it hold out? [214/1; 214/2–215/2]

The life cycles of many tropical papilionids are rapid. There may be four, six, or even eight generations a year, even though many species adhere consistently to only one or two. With such a rapid rhythm, changes in form are accelerated. Thus, we find in numerous species both individuals with swallowtails and others without. This is a clear example of older (with swallowtails) and younger evolutionary forms existing alongside one another. Furthermore, the individuals frequently are split up into forms with differently colored costumes. Some of these are mimics that resemble entirely different species, either in their own family or in another (such as Danaidae), which are protected by their toxicity.

Special marginal members of the swallowtail family are three Asian genera: *Lamproptera, Teinopalpus,* and *Bhutanitis.* The small *Lamproptera* species whir over the water like dragonflies. Much of their wing area is as clear as glass, and their large and long tails are folded lengthwise at the base in a remarkable manner. Members of the last two genera, whose wings have several tails, inhabit mountain forests from India to China. *Teinopalpus* butterflies, which like many other papilionids are striking because of the difference between the sexes, are wild stormers of the summits. The two *Bhutanitis* species (*lidderdalei* and *thaidina*), on the other hand, are delicate forms that rock gently in the wind as they glide through the treetops. [35/1; 212/1, 2]

Within the genus *Papilio*, which includes by far the greatest number of species, and which sometimes is divided into several other genera, three groups are distinguished: ordinary swallowtails, kite swallowtails, and pipevine (or Aristolochia) swallowtails. Most numerous and most widely distributed are the ordinary swallowtails. The usually palely transparent and often long-tailed kites also are familiar in the temperate zone. In contrast, the Aristolochia butterflies are limited almost exclusively to South America, with a few ranging from Asia to Australia; beyond this they are represented only by the imposing *Papilio antenor* of Madagascar and a few (such as *Papilio philenor* and *Papilio polydamas*) in North America. The pipevine, or Aristolochia, swallowtails are so named because their caterpillars feed on various toxic pipevine plants of the family Aristolochiaceae. As a result, both the caterpillars and the adult butterflies are poisonous. The adult males have a deep fold, studded with odor-producing scales, along the margin of the hind wing that lies next to the body (also present, though smaller, in most kite swallowtails).

The Aristolochia butterflies include the Indo-Australian bird-winged butterflies, sometimes grouped as the *Ornithoptera* (including *Trogonoptera* and *Troides*). These include not only the largest of butterflies, but also some extraordinarily beautiful ones. The males of a few species, whose wings span about 6.8 inches, are among the most magnificent creatures in nature, whereas their females, whose wings stretch as much as 10 inches, are merely brown with light spots. The sexes are more nearly alike in that series of species that wear a silken or satiny brown or black with a blood-red collar and pleura (sides of thorax). In the male *magellanus* the ground color is a unique opalescent golden yellow. [210/1; 212–215; 30/1]

The majestic bird-winged butterflies again and again arouse the enthusiasm of travelers fortunate enough to see them sail by above the treetops. The species *Ornithoptera priamus*, of the South Sea Islands, has become famous because of its conspicuous geographical variability; according to its particular native land or island, it has evolved into numerous forms, some a fiery orange-red, others green or even blue. [213/2]

APOLLO BUTTERFLIES

Among the few other papilionid genera, which contain smaller but handsome forms, the apollo butterflies (*Parnassius*) stand out because the uniformity of their appearance contrasts sharply with the incalculable variety of other papilionids. The brightly marked wings, in part as transparent as glass, bear black spots and rings, most of them with partly red centers. In truth a very modest palette, but what a maximum of cool, sharp beauty it attains; and what a fascinating effect emanates from the black, red, and white reflecting "eyes" of the apollo butterflies. No other dress could be better suited to that raw world of mountains and glaciers where these jewels flit about somewhat heavily, yet adeptly, along the talus slopes and cliffs, or coast over chasms and gorges.

In the Himalayas, apollo butterflies dwell 19,000 to 20,000 feet above sea level. From their ancestral home in Asia, they have spread across the northern hemisphere to Europe, and a few across the Siberian-Alaskan bridge to North America. The parnassians are preferred objects for geographic studies, inasmuch as the individual species, as a result of their usually more or less isolated occurrence on mountains, have for the most part broken up into numerous races. They are extremely variable in spite of the uniformity of the few

elements in their design. When threatened, these butterflies make crackling sounds. [36/8–13; 216/1, 2]

WHITES AND SULFURS

Butterflies of the family Pieridae, including the whites and the sulfurs, enliven the landscape almost everywhere. They range far into the North, up to the glaciers in the mountains, into the deserts, and onto the plains. A few species are distributed over enormous areas. Thus the imported cabbageworm butterfly (*Pieris rapae*), though introduced into North America only during the last half-century, now occurs over nearly the entire northern hemisphere. The larva of that butterfly has acquired a formidable reputation as a destroyer of cabbages and other crops.

Most of the more than 1,000 known species of pierids inhabit woods, meadows, and plains, but a few are at home in the treetops of forests. Such a one is the Asiatic *Delias*, whose yellow, red, black, and white underside is perhaps unmatched in its magnificence.

The wings of the pierids are usually white, yellow, or orange marked with black. Less frequently their pigments include reds and blues, and sometimes there are delicately shimmering structural colors. The chemical nature of the pigments in all pierids is different from that of other butterflies. In fact the pigments are toxic, just as the body fluids of pierids are. As a result, the family suffers little from the depredations of insect eaters.

In general, the pierids are good fliers, and members of the genus *Appias* are reported to be best among all butterflies. Many species have an intense tendency toward migration; in fact, of about 200 recognized migratory members of Lepidoptera, some 60 are pierids. Enormous swarms frequently fly out over the open sea and come to grief unless they happen to be saved by an island, as has happened in the Bermuda Islands, 600 miles from the mainland of the United States. [18/2, 3; 64/2; 189/11; 209/6; 217/1–6]

GOSSAMER-WINGED BUTTERFLIES

Among the commonest and widest-spread Lepidoptera are the little gossamer-winged butterflies (Lycaenidae), which are of particular interest because of the relationships between their larvae and ants. As the common name of one subdivision known as the "blues" indicates, the upper surface of many of them gleams with all possible blues, from silvery to violet or greenish, but pure

196/1

Parnassius butterflies have relatively hard glassy wings, and being mountain insects are among the Lepidoptera that are most tenacious of life (natural size).

2A

2B

green and fiery golden or coppery structural colors also occur. The intensity of these colors and the very different undersides, often with fine dots or flourishes, the blinding-white wing margins, and the often-present, delicate tails that can be caused voluntarily to quiver in the air current, make the lycaenids exceptionally lovely spectacles.

Much is contributed by the delicate body, the antennae, and the short legs, as well as by the butterfly's graceful motions, especially when, sitting in the sunlight, the insect fans its slightly separated hind wings in the gently rotatory, rubbing movement characteristic of these butterflies alone. In large South American species of the genus *Thecla*, or hairstreaks, both the upper and lower surfaces of the wings are magnificently colored, though in quite a different manner, as also is the case among members of the related family Riodinidae, already mentioned.

The majority of female lycaenids are predominantly dull brown on the upper surfaces or have less extensive and less intense colors than the males. For that matter the males of many species have similarly unimpressive coloring. Frequently there are spotted designs in colors from yellow-brown to red.

Although there are rare solitary species, the gossamer-winged butterflies in general are companionable and frequently gather in great crowds by the water or on certain bushes or flowers. In India, for example, one may see such an assemblage as a compact, glittering carpet of swirling blue floating over the ground.

The hairstreaks love underbrush and woods, where they can slip away beneath the leaves and rest, and many spend their lives and complete their development high in the trees. Amazingly, a number come down at definite times of day to the roads or highways and, with closed wings, take a sunbath in the thick layer of dust; in doing so, they frequently fall over on their sides and remain in this position for some time. A somewhat tilted posture, so adjusted as to receive broadside the full strength of the sunshine, is generally preferred by lycaenids. But when it is too warm they dispose themselves, like all lepidopterans, so that they are exposed to the minimum of radiation from the sun. [32/1; 99/3; 217/7, 8; 220/17–19; 253]

MILKWEED BUTTERFLIES

These butterflies (family Danaidae) are about as sociable as the gossamer-winged butterflies. Though the milkweed butter-

flies have relatively few species, these usually are extraordinarily rich in numbers of individuals. Living principally in the tropics and subtropics, they gather for drinking and sleeping on bushes and trees, often in great crowds. There, above the tips of the branches, the males carry out special courting dances in which no female participates. Nonetheless, some females come along nearby, enticing the males from the swarm and letting themselves be pursued for short distances.

The danaids include the best-known migratory butterflies, such as the monarch *(Danaus plexippus)* of North America. Since monarchs are constantly seen flying over all continents, such as Asia, Africa, and Europe, as well as over the open sea, one might almost suppose that any individuals are capable of crossing the oceans, even taking into account that many are transported by ships.

Most caterpillars of milkweed butterflies eat plants whose sap is more or less toxic, and the resulting toxicity remains as a protection to the butterflies developing from these caterpillars. These butterflies are models for a great number of mimics from other families. A North American brush-footed butterfly, the viceroy *(Limenitis archippus),* provides a particularly impressive example of such a mimic: It looks deceptively like the monarch and completely unlike its own family.

Another model for mimics is the Asiatic genus *Euploea,* which includes many species of tropical forest butterflies whose coloring usually is dark brown, often gleaming with magnificent blue or violet. The males of these butterflies emit a penetrating, often nauseous odor from pencils or star-shaped clusters of hairs, which protrude at right angles from both sides of the tip of the abdomen. The males also issue a fragrance that arouses the females. This fragrance comes from certain patches of scales on the wings. Thanks to their tough, elastic body structures, these and other milkweed butterflies can stand a certain amount of maltreatment and squashing, which may be done, for example, by an inexperienced bird before it recognizes the inedibility of its prey.

A group of milkweed butterflies with remarkably thin bodies relative to their gigantic wings is the Asiatic *Hestia.* Especially weak fliers, they lose control and the ability to steer even in a gentle breeze. These large bone-colored forest butterflies float about like scraps of paper and therefore have received such names as "paper butterflies," "surat" ("letters"), "spirits," and "ghosts." [19/16; 50/4, 5; 64; 218/3, 4]

197/1
The hairstreaks, a large group of the lycaenids, spend most of the time in bushes and trees (natural size).

196/2
The "blues" are low-flying insects that characteristically have a pattern of minute spots on the underside of the wings; as a rule the females have little or no blue (2A). The caterpillars are short and humpbacked (2B) and frequently are on good terms with ants (somewhat enlarged).

HELICONIIDS AND ITHOMIIDS

Best known for mimicry are the almost exclusively tropical American families Heliconiidae and Ithomiidae. These are inedible butterflies with many species and races. Their ranks are joined by almost identically colored companions from various other families, among them both toxic and harmless species, the genuine and the pretenders. The heliconiids and ithomiids, with their long, slender abdomen and lengthy, rounded-off wings, are unique spectacles. Most of them inhabit the woods, cruising slowly back and forth over the underbrush and, whirring and fluttering, often tarrying a while in dancing flight before a flower. One group shines forth conspicuously with splendid compositions of warning colors, some with warm brown, yellow, red, and black tones, others with cool white, lemon yellow, blue, and black. A second group has almost no scales and hence wings that are mostly transparent, often with slight striped designs. These creatures, flitting alertly and unpredictably through the shadows of the forest, are so nearly invisible they hardly need to be poisonous. [19/17–21; 62/2; 218/5–10]

MORPHO BUTTERFLIES

Flying in the same South American forests as the heliconiids and the ithomiids are the *Morpho* butterflies (Morphidae). With small bodies and giant wings, they can be seen in the treetops, flashing in the sunlight like wandering daytime stars. Their glistening brilliance turns the rays of the sun into blue sparks, which on one occasion may float calmly along and on another may turn into wildly leaping flame.

If two male morphos fly too close to one another, there is a sudden flashing gyration. This contrasts with their behavior at a watering place, where they sit peacefully side by side while drinking. The females, not nearly as blue or not blue at all, show themselves less often. In species that fly near the ground in the shadows of the forest, the blue is limited to the wings and is absent entirely in both sexes of the largest species, whose colors are either absent or dull and metallic. Among the giants, *Morpho hecuba,* with a wingspan of about 8 inches, is not only one of the largest butterflies, but also one of the grandest of spectacles. The upper surface of the wings is a picture of majestic calm and completeness, and the underside is decorated lavishly with eyespots. Such spots are more or less pronounced in all morphos. But since the spots

of *Morpho hecuba* do not stand out conspicuously from the brown ground color of the lower surface, the butterflies, despite their size, are excellently concealed when at rest among the leaves.

A few of the approximately 50 species of morphos shimmer whitely, like mother-of-pearl. Among these, *Morpho sulkowskyi* seems to have been given a particularly princely endowment, for in certain light a blinding, bright-blue luster spreads across the surface of its wings. Unfortunately, morpho wings are made by man into all kinds of souvenirs, but a consoling thought is that most of these come from artificially reared specimens. The wild butterflies could hardly be captured in sufficient numbers, and in Brazil they are legally protected. [19/14; 218/1, 2; 219/1, 2]

AMATHUSIIDS

Closely related to the morphos, the family Amathusiidae lives in tropical Asia and on the South Sea Islands, reaching in part as far as Australia. Often similar to the morphos in size, wing-cut, and lower surface, they are not so splendiferous, but nevertheless have many beautiful species. They, too, are forest butterflies, but the majority fly only at dusk and then go deeper in the shadows. The males of most genera have odor-producing organs on the hind wings—either bunches of hairs or cushions of scales. Certain ones have the strongest aroma of all butterflies. The scent is aromatic, resembling that of strong perfume, and on many specimens in collections is still perceptible after years. The most magnificent genera are *Stichophthalmus, Thaumantis, Zeuxidia,* and *Taenaris;* these last butterflies, most of them white and gray, stand out beyond any accustomed frame of reference because of the fantastic eyelike designs on the undersurface of the wings—designs that give the impression of having been artificially exaggerated. [220/12, 13]

OWL BUTTERFLIES

Few butterflies can match the monstrous "eyes" on the undersides of the wings of the genus *Caligo,* already mentioned earlier. This genus is a representative of the purely South American family of the Brassolidae, or owl butterflies. Nearly all of these mostly gigantic butterflies fly only at dusk and near the ground, flitting about through the underbrush with unbelievable skill in spite of their large size. The wings of the males bear scent-producing organs in the form of powdery or feltlike spots or in the form of hair pencils that often are concealed in pouches in the wing membrane and can be expanded. In the males of the genera *Caligo* and *Eryphanis,* on whose giant wing surfaces blue or violet is spread with the lordly gleam of silk, the portion of the hind wing that touches the abdomen has a peculiar polish, as though it had been varnished. At this spot on the abdomen, special glands of unknown function are found. [55/4; 57/4, 5; 220/14]

The brassolids, as well as the morphos and amathusiids, fail to visit flowers, but imbibe the sap of injured trees and bushes or the juice of overripe fruit and other fermenting substances, such as decaying leaves and dung. The same is true of the related wood satyrs, and many species of the family Nymphalidae.

SATYR BUTTERFLIES

Butterflies of the family Satyridae never or rarely have luminous colors, but frequently have attractive eyelike designs resembling little black irises with white pupils, often surrounded with a lighter ring. Particularly enchanting are a few South American genera —for instance, *Euptychia* and *Pierella,* which have a blue-green iridescence; *Callitaera* and *Haetera,* which have transparent wings; or *Argyrophorus,* which gleams like pure silver.

About 2,000 species of satyrs, at most of medium size, are distributed over the entire earth; they are present nearly everywhere and live near the ground. Many settle on the ground, others on vegetation, some on tree-trunks, and still others almost exclusively on cliffs. Most are excellently concealed by their coloration.

Many live only in the forests, but the majority, including many *Erebia* and *Oeneis* species, are mountain butterflies that have a narrowly limited range. These also live in the Far North. Their so-called boreoalpine distribution was dictated primarily by climatic relationships in the Glacial Age. Many satyrs fly even on overcast days or in the evening; *Lethe* and *Melanitis,* primarily Asiatic butterflies, fly almost entirely at dawn and dusk or even at night. Most species are frequent sights in their native habitats. [14/3; 220/15, 16; 221/2–9]

BRUSH-FOOTED BUTTERFLIES

These members of the family Nymphalidae include many of the best-known butterflies as well as the largest number of butterfly species. At home everywhere in the world, their representatives range as high in the mountains and as far northward as insect life

is possible. Of worldwide renown as a migrating butterfly is the thistle butterfly or painted lady, *Pyrameis (Vanessa) cardui,* which has spread to all continents, sometimes traveling in huge assemblages, sometimes in looser formations or singly. A closely related brush-footed butterfly, the red admiral (*Vanessa atalanta),* migrates singly, the mature butterflies traveling northward at the beginning of summer, and the offspring going southward in autumn. [64/3; 220/3]

Other family members include the mourning cloak, *Vanessa (Nymphalis) antiopa;* the peacock butterfly, *Vanessa (Inachis) io,* one of the most beautiful butterflies; the tortoise-shells, including *Vanessa (Aglais* and *Nymphalis) urticae, milberti, californica, polychloros;* and the anglewings, *Polygonia,* in a few species of which a white letter C shines forth, as though punched out of the middle of the lower surface of the hind wing. Other genera of tortoiseshells, such as *Precis,* consist of frequently migrating butterflies of the Old and New Worlds, most numerous in Africa and India. Many of these often magnificently colored species are of interest because of their seasonal dimorphism, in that the dry season generations appear in an often quite different dress than those of the rainy season. [220/4–7]

In view of the multiplicity of the brush-footed family, with its thousands of species, it is not possible to present even an approximation of the whole, and so we shall just touch lightly upon a few additional genera. The thistle-blossom-loving fritillaries (*Argynnis, Speyeria, Boloria, Brenthis),* the most beautiful species of which live in North America, China, and India, glisten with wonderful mother-of-pearl or silver designs on the lower surface of the wings, as do species of the South and Central American genus *Dione.* And the South American genus *Metamorpha* breaks out of the usual framework because of its translucent-green color, so rarely seen in butterflies; it finds an exceptional parallel in the not-closely related *Victorina steneles,* which lives in the same localities, and whose race *pallida* penetrates even as far as North America. Other such cases observed here and there in the insect empire can be a temptation to speak without justification of mimicry. [210/2; 220/2, 7]

A genus as magnificent as it is confusing, because of its almost boundless wealth of male and female forms and geographical races, is *Hypolimnas.* It belongs to the Old World, and yet the species *Hypolimnas misippus,* which has been introduced into America, seems to have become established there. The great, unique *Hypolimnas dexithea* of Mada-

199/1

Members of the genus Limenitis (Nymphalidae), with beautiful patterns and elegant coloring of the lower surface of their wings. are aristocrats among the butterflies (natural size). Photograph.

gascar is one of the most beautiful butterflies in the world, along with certain viceroys, admirals, emperors, and others. [220/9]

In the Old World, two regal, closely related genera, *Charaxes* and *Eriboea,* have designs on their lower wing surfaces that constitute an inexhaustible source of the most beautiful studies possible in the field of natural history. A similar statement can be made about the South American *Callicore, Catagramma,* and *Agrias,* which are strewn with an unbelievable splendor of colors; and quite worthy to stand beside them is *Prepona,* whose overall black color is interrupted by radiant green and blue stripes. These are nervous, shy forest butterflies, which mostly rest head downward high on the treetrunks and which catapult through the air like arrows. Seeing them in their natural haunts is an incomparable experience.

Finally, there are also among the nymphalids many beautiful leaflike forms, whose shapes and pattern, designed for the resting state, actually go so far in their similarity to leaves that they can be said to be unnecessarily exaggerated. This applies to the Asiatic *Kallima* species, and also to the South American *Coenophlebia archidone,* which even surpasses *Kallima,* if that is possible. In *Kallima* a leaf stem is imitated by the apices of the hind wings, lengthened at the ends; in *Coenophlebia,* by a similar construction of the fore wings. [16/1; 32/6; 50/5, 6; 52/4; 54/1; 55/5; 209/7; 220/1–11; 221/1; 223/1–4]

SKIPPERS

An ancient, rather isolated family of relatively homogeneous format are the skippers (Hesperiidae). Whether they should be reckoned among the butterflies or the moths is uncertain. Much about them is similar to butterflies, but certain structural peculiarities tend to set them apart. Anyhow, they are odd creatures, mostly small, with a powerful body and broad head. They also are striking because of their swift, frequently whirring flight, in which they often dart about with somewhat irregular leaps. Usually they gain the ability to fly within a few minutes after emergence from the pupal stage, as befits the impetuous, hasty character of these gnomes. In the Asiatic genus *Tagiades,* pairs have been observed dancing together in flight; they rushed back and forth along the edge of the woods in arcs 20 to 30 yards long.

Most skippers like sunshine and heat, but a few genera are creatures of the twilight and night. All frequent flowers, and some species have a long trunk like sphinx moths. This may be the only means of fertilization for certain flowers with a deep chalice. The relationship of the American skipper *Calpodes ethlius* with the canna plant is a symbiotic one, for the insect fertilizes the plant's flowers, and the plant's leaves provide food for the insect's larvae. A plant that is the source of food for both adults and larvae is a rare occurrence among lepidopterans.

The skippers frequently drink water, and many have a most unusual and typical method of making certain dry foodstuffs edible. For on such foodstuffs they deposit clear drops of water from the rectum, up to 200 drops in a quarter of an hour, and finally suck the solution up again with the proboscis stretched back beneath the abdomen.

When resting, one group of the skippers, mostly those with indented wing margins, holds the wings outspread and even slightly depressed. But most of them clap the wings together above the back like butterflies; yet it is characteristic that during short pauses from flying the front wings often are not closed entirely, and the back ones are held farther open and frequently even are pressed down against the support.

The coloration of skippers frequently is adapted to their resting positions. Those that rest with the wings flat outspread have pallid upper surfaces, and the others often have varicolored ones. Protective colors seldom occur. There seems no need for them since the skippers are extraordinarily skillful fliers and creep into hiding places when they rest. The pattern mostly is very simple, usually being composed of groups of spots, which frequently are transparent.

By far the majority of the 2,500 species are tropical—in fact, predominantly South American, where in a great many localities they surpass all other lepidopterans both in number of species and of individuals. Here they practically besiege flowering bushes. Many have splendid colors, but the few species of the temperate zone are unimpressive. One of these, *Pyrgus centaurea,* has penetrated even into the Arctic, where it has a circumpolar distribution. Best known among the skippers are the golden-brown tawny skippers (Hesperiinae), the males of many genera of which have rows of scent scales in the middle of the fore wing, and the dusky, but brightly-spotted Pyrginae. [221/10–13; 223/5]

The previously described members of the family Castniidae, with few exceptions South American, seem to be related to the same ancient stock as the hesperiids; they, too, occupy an intermediate position between butterflies and moths. Nearly all species of the family are magnificently colored, and some are huge. A few are mimics of the heliconiids and the ithomiids. [191/1]

SYNTOMIDS

The family Syntomidae contains a large number of mimics. Many of these little moths, which love the sun but also fly by night, resemble wasps, especially because of their glass-clear wings that usually are held extended. They often imitate a particular model with an exactitude that extends almost to the last detail. They may, for example, even have a "wasp waist," which is conspicuously abnormal among butterflies and moths. In addition, a few species "copy" the toxic net-winged beetles of the family Lycidae.

Almost all syntomids appear to be inedible to insectivorous creatures; hence some have conspicuous warning costumes, instead of a resemblance to wasps or other insects. Splendid metallic colors are almost the rule; frequently, these are limited to the scales that clothe the body. And where wing scales are lacking, the wing membrane may have a yellowish or even a radiant golden-yellow hue, may shine with the prismatic colors of the rainbow, or may take on an intense milky-blue opalescence by transmitted light.

The beauty of a syntomid unfolds most fully as the moth floats by in its whirring flight or as it sits like a wasp on a flower and spreads its wings when disturbed, making twitching movements like one of these belligerent insects. All the species imbibe nectar or sap from injured plants; more than 2,000 are known, of which more than 1,800 dwell in the South American tropics. [18/7, 10; 19/27, 31; 50/1; 224/18–25]

TIGER AND FOOTMAN MOTHS

These moths (Arctiidae) are so closely related to the syntomids that there is hardly any sharp division between them. Though most of the tiger and footman moths are nocturnal, some of them, particularly the males, fly about during the day. Certain species are large, but not the tropical ones, as is usual among insects. Many have what may be the gaudiest warning costumes of all moths and butterflies, costumes that usually include the abdomen and even may be concentrated there alone. All species are protected by disagreeable sharp-smelling secretions that are expelled as yellow drops from two openings behind the collar. Among pericopines, this fluid, which is forced out with a gurgling noise, foams up and encloses

201/1
In places where the smoky moths live, they appear for the most part in rather large numbers. These sluggish moths, very tenacious of life, seem to have scarcely any enemies, and are also protected by repulsive body fluids and odor (natural size). Photograph.

the insect, which is feigning death. Other arctiids produce twittering, rustling, crackling, or chirping noises.

The tiger and footman moths, of which there are more than 6,000 species, are distributed over the whole world, right up to the foot of the glaciers. Usually sluggish, they have a rather clumsy flight. The females, in particular, which may be filled with several hundred eggs, fly very little, and certain high-Alpine species spend the greater part of their existence beneath rocks. Though many visit flowers, a number of short-lived arctiids have degenerate trunks and take no nourishment at all.

Certain species assemble for resting in caves in the cliffs, and some fly in such enormous crowds they look like a snowstorm. On the Greek island of Rhodes, for example, shining bright clouds of tens of thousands of individuals of *Callimorpha quadripunctaria* may be seen streaming in and out among one another; their luminous red, bright yellow, and bluish-green colors, broken alternately by light and shadow in the bushy gorges, are like an effervescent display of fireworks, a natural spectacle that seems unreal. A moth that migrates in great multitudes is the little, strikingly lovely *Utheisa pulchella,* which is distributed from Africa to the Orient and to Southern Europe. [17/18, 20; 18/13; 30/4; 36/1; 57/3; 62/3; 175/1; 210/4; 224/3–8]

LEAF SKELETONIZER MOTHS

These sluggish and often brightly colored moths of the family Zygaenidae are protected by oily fluids and, in spite of a soft body, have a great tenacity of life. With the extraordinary variety of their wing forms and color patterns, this family of about 900 mostly Old-World species is especially interesting. Many resemble certain butterflies (pierids and danaids) or moths (arctiids, syntomids, geometrids, and others), so that mimetic relationships are to be assumed. And within the group of the Phaudinae, the males of which can protrude an odorous hair pencil from either side of the tip of the abdomen, there are species that look like beetles, bugs, and homopterans.

Because their hind wings have long tails that may be reduced to thin ribbons, the little himantopterines are among the oddest figures within the Lepidoptera and in their body form remind one of nerve-winged insects of the family Nemopteridae. Best-known are the members of the genus *Zygaena.* Since their limited flight activity has favored the development of numerous local races, they are highly regarded as objects of study. With their small wings bearing designs of red, white, or yellow, they are most attractive. [224/9-14]

Now there follows the gigantic host of moths among the silkworm moths, sphinx moths, noctuids, and geometrids. Dazzling costumes are less prevalent among this group. Instead, a wealth of designs and an originality of structures take a leading role. These are expressed particularly in the attitudes assumed at rest. Here, the form and placement of the wings, legs, and often of the abdomen, as well as the frequently tufted or comblike coating of the body with hairs and scales, together with color, line, and shading, conjure up an astounding variety of figures. To a considerable extent the positions adopted in flight present a more nearly homogeneous, anonymous mass.

Mimicry in the sense of similarity to other, protected moths and butterflies is rare. It occurs almost solely among the day-flying geometrids. On the other hand, imitations of surroundings, especially of bark and leaves, are nearly the rule. Warning costumes are rather rare, but startling costumes are common.

Particularly striking are the magnificent *Urania,* already described earlier, and *Alcidis,* of the family Uraniidae; the Indo-Australian genera *Milionia* and *Dysphania,* of the family Geometridae, which are native principally to the South Sea Islands; and the agaristids, which are closely related to the noctuids and live in the tropics and subtropics, most of them in the Old World but a few in America. The majority of all these day-flying moths depart completely from the usual framework of their relationships, not only because of their magnificent, frequently metallic, bright coloration, which is not inferior to that of the arctiids and syntomids and even shows extensive similarity to it, but also more or less through their way of living. They are fond of sunshine, suck on flowers together with butterflies and usually with their wings held in the same way, and for the most part are extremely rapid and accomplished fliers.

The medium-sized agaristids, for example, start the morning by drinking dew or water from the damp ground, then visit flowers, alternately whirring and gliding around blossoming bushes and trees. They reach the peak of their activity in the full heat of noon, when they go shooting about in the treetops, at a time when other insects are seeking the shadows. A few species, it is true, fly only after sundown. In flight many males produce almost whistling, sibilant tones by pressing the rough hind legs against file-shaped scaleless spots on the undersides of the wings. [62/ 4; 224/15-17, 26-29]

OWLET OR NOCTUID MOTHS

With about 25,000 species, these moths form by far the largest family of the Lepidoptera. This family, Noctuidae, is an especially interesting one composed of groups that differ greatly from one another. The wings of the smallest representatives span perhaps 0.2 inch, the biggest almost 12 inches. They are distributed throughout the world wherever there is vegetation—high into the mountains and into the north and south polar regions. Many northern species have attained circumpolar distribution. Many are migratory, and some appear in masses by the millions; in the caterpillar stage they then cause great damage. The "army worms" and "boll worms" are prime examples.

The great majority of noctuids are American; North and South America together have more than double as many species as the Indo-Australian region, three times as many as Africa, and four times as many as the whole Palearctic region from Spain to Japan. As one goes farther north, the species in general become somber and more limited to daytime flight. In warm countries they are more contrastingly colored, and more fly by night as well as by day.

Driven by a need for much food, many suck on flowers, and others on the sap of trees and the juice of fruit. Especially in the tropical species many males are equipped with striking odor-producing organs, in the form of bunches of hairs on the legs, antennae, thorax, abdomen, or wings; most of these can be expanded. [175/3]

Exotic figures with spidery legs, and with extremely long antennae or palpi that often have to be held back over head and thorax if they are not to interfere with freedom of movement, are quite numerous, especially in the hypenine group. Lovely designs in what seems like pure silver, gold, or greenish brass are shown by many *Cucullia,* and above all by the plusiine group, whose grotesque dorsal tufts give a bizarre appearance. The species *Autographa (Plusia) gamma* is one of the best-known migratory Lepidoptera. [32/7]

The underwings *(Catocala)* are unique in having magnificent red, yellow, or rarely blue patterns on their hind wings. These mostly large noctuids are limited to the Northern Hemisphere. When they rest by day on tree-trunks or cliffs, their bright hind wings are covered with fore wings whose colors blend well with the background. In contrast with other night-flying noctuids, they sleep lightly and, when disturbed, flutter wildly off; at the moment of their doing so, the bright colors of the hind wings may so surprise an enemy that he forgets his pursuit. Many large tropical noctuids use similar tactics, but these rest on the ground and have fore wings shaded like leaves rather than like bark or rocks. An example is the group of noctuids of the genus *Ophideres,* distributed throughout the warm regions of the Old and New World. These species, whose hind wings bear a design in orange-yellow and black, damage bananas and oranges by piercing them with their hard proboscis. In addition, there is the African *Miniodes,* whose hind wings are a carmine of almost unequaled intensity.

Another example is the Asiatic *Phyllodes,* whose radiant but elegantly colored hind wings are covered when at rest by fore wings that are among the most beautiful imitations of leaves in the insect empire. In the middle of each there is a perfect picture of a little accumulation of water. These spots are expanded into strange, sultry, gigantic, blinking eyespots in another noctuid group, in which startling colors are absent; by day these Lepidoptera prefer to rest with wings flat outspread in clefts and caves in the cliffs.

The African and Asiatic genera *Patula, Nyctipao,* and *Cyligramma* include great broad-winged species whose dark color frequently is suffused with a splendid glimmer of purple; the males make crackling or rattling noises in flight. The group is represented in the warm parts of America above all by *Blosyris, Erebus,* and *Thysania,* and contains the largest noctuids, among them *Thysania agrippina.* With a maximum wingspan of almost 12 inches (usually at least 9 inches) this species has the longest wings of all butterflies and moths, though others have a greater wing area. The upper surface of the wings of this giant moth is a lusterless bark color, so it is particularly surprising to see the steel-blue radiance of the underside. The flying power of these big species is extraordinary; they shoot about like bats. One species, the somber but lovely *Erebus odora* of South and Central America, frequently migrates northward, often as far as Canada, and even is capable of crossing the ocean. [14/2; 16/10; 17/28, 30; 18/11; 32/4; 36/2–5; 50/3; 51/3, 7, 8; 52/1; 54/2; 56/3, 12; 62/7; 174; 191/2; 210/5; 241–242]

GEOMETRID MOTHS

The geometrids (Geometridae) form one of the largest families, with worldwide distri-

bution. Their numbers press upward in the mountains as well as northward to the limits of possible existence. Some species are circumpolar, a particularly adaptable group being the delicate larentiines. The geometrids have the most universal and most uniform distribution of all families of Lepidoptera, with representatives appearing even in desert regions; their caterpillars are better able than others to feed on nonsucculent plants. Yet most geometrids are fond of the forest, especially on mountain ranges, for which reason the list of known species (most lengthy in America) is far from complete; even more than in the case of the noctuids, new ones constantly are being discovered.

The geometrids are among the commonest Lepidoptera, especially in the cold climatic zones, where certain species may cover the landscape like a blizzard. At an electric light almost anywhere, they make up more than half the moths. There are rather few migrants, although nonmigratory species frequently leave their place of birth in swarms because of special environmental conditions.

Geometrids are often called measuring-worm moths. Both names refer to the caterpillars of the moths. Because they lack abdominal prolegs in the middle of the body, the caterpillars have a characteristic arching manner of progression, as though they are measuring off the distance. The name geometrid also could be applied to the adults, which frequently have a geometric design on their wings. The design often consists of fine, sharply-drawn, intersecting lines or of figures that look as if they had been inscribed with a pair of compasses. These give many geometrids a delicate, decorative appearance.

Most species are small to medium in size and have thin, weak bodies, although some are robust. Protective costumes that resemble bark, lichens, and leaves are predominant, and some species that rest openly on leaves are deceptively similar to a bird dropping. A few groups, such as *Milionia* and *Dysphania,* display bright warning colors, and some of these have mimetic relationships with other families of Lepidoptera. The African genus *Aletis,* which is among the largest geometrids, also belongs to a striking mimicry ring of this sort, which has been described earlier.

Green pigments occur with surprising frequency in geometrids, considering their rare presence in other Lepidoptera. Groups, such as the Hemitheinae, with their apple-green coloration and the brown and white figures on the wing surfaces, are truly beautiful.

The flight of geometrids, in accordance with their slight musculature and gentle wing movements, usually is of limited duration, a rather calm, steady flutter. Most species prefer to fly at dusk and after dark, but many fly by day; nearly all stay alert while at rest and, in contrast with most noctuids, fly off at once if disturbed.

The resting places are chosen in an often astonishing conformity with the moth's own coloring; in treeless localities, such as deserts and plains, these resting places are near the ground. There, straw-colored species sit on stalks, around which they curl their wings. *Zamacra* has an unusual resting attitude, namely with wings rolled lengthwise and sticking up like little rods. But mostly the wings are laid flat and spread out, or less frequently clapped together above the body in the manner of butterflies.

The females of most genera have either no wings or merely stubs; this is true, for instance, of the spring measuring worms (such as *Operophthera* and *Erannis*), which appear during the cold, windy season and whose caterpillars sometimes do great damage, and of species of the heavy-bodied genus *Biston*. These last have achieved a certain degree of fame because blackish variants have become predominant in sooty industrial areas. This phenomenon, often called "industrial melanism," was cited in the section on "Mimicry and Camouflage" as an example of natural selection, since the variants are better concealed than their normal, light-colored sibs. For similar reasons, perhaps, certain species of geometrids and noctuids that live on dunes at the seashore change gradually to lighter-colored, less-distinctly marked forms ("seashore forms"). [35/3]

The geometrids suck on flowers, though much less avidly than noctuids, and imbibe water, particularly dewdrops. Certain tropical species irrigate the digestive tract (as do many papilionids also, for instance) by letting the imbibed water issue at once in drops from the rectum. Thus, one of the American *Panthera* was observed to discharge 50 drops a minute for three hours, which amounts to some 200 times the body weight.

The several families of moths that follow are similar in that the larvae of the majority pupate in silken webs or cocoons. These very hairy moths attract much attention on account of their pronounced sexual dimorphism: the males are smaller and usually darker and have long, comblike, feathery antennae that enable them to detect the scent of the females even at great distance. The proboscis is short or degenerate; correspondingly, little or no food

is taken and life lasts but a short time—on the average about 10 days. [16/16; 18/19; 52/3; 54/3; 62/4; 211/3, 5, 6; 224/26–29; 243/1–13]

TUSSOCK MOTHS

This family (Lymantriidae) is perhaps the most ancient of the Lepidoptera. It includes about 2,000 medium-sized species. In contrast to the often showy larvae, the adults are unimpressively colored and have broad, rounded-off wings that are laid back flat in a rooflike position when at rest. A few genera (for example, *Orgyia*) have wingless females—shapeless, hairy, short-legged cylinders that one would hardly take to be moths. Quite generally the females are very sluggish. Clumsy fliers, they take to the air infrequently, usually late at night. The males of a few genera dash about by day in dancing flight.

Many genera have a characteristic kind of hairy covering. A thick, woolly coat covers the legs (the front pair of which in *Dasychira* species, for instance, is extended grotesquely forward when the insect is at rest), and at the back end of the females a tuft of down serves to blanket the clutch of eggs. In addition, many tussock moths have long and often poisonous hairs on the wings and sometimes on the back; the caterpillars also have these hairs, but in greater number. In certain species, the toxic hairs of the caterpillar may even protect the adult by being incorporated into the pupal web and by being caught in the furry dorsal coat of the emerging adult.

Tussock moths are distributed over the entire world. They are scarcest in America, particularly in South America, which otherwise has almost a superfluity of Lepidoptera. Actually, one might say this family thrives best where others tend to recede; for instance, the largest species, with an 8-inch wingspan, lives in South Australia, where the living conditions generally are unfavorable to butterflies and moths. Matters are quite similar with other geologically ancient families, namely with the psychids, cossids, and many hepialids, which have developed giant forms in generally inhospitable countries.

Tussock moths occur in the icy polar regions and in burning deserts, where their caterpillars inhabit the last pitiful bush. The majority, however, are forest dwellers, among them the destructive gypsy moth (*Lymantria* or *Porthetria dispar*), which was introduced into America during the last century where it became a notorious feeder on deciduous trees. Another forest dweller is the species known in Europe as the "nun" (*Lymantria monacha*), which lives on conifers. It is especially interesting on account of the constant increase during the last few decades of its darker-gray variants. Since this increase began in the less highly developed eastern part of Europe and spread toward the industrial part, the phenomenon cannot be explained by the same "industrial melanism" that has influenced the geometrid genus *Biston*. [210/7; 211/2; 243/14–17]

TENT CATERPILLAR MOTHS

Similar in form and way of life to the tussock moths are the tent caterpillars (Lasiocampidae). A greater number of tent caterpillar species, however, are large—some gigantic—and many have leaflike forms. Some genera hold the resting wings in a rooflike position, and there are females with only vestigial wings.

The 1,000 or so known species are distributed fairly uniformly over the world with the exception of the polar regions. A few are harmful because of the mass occurrence of their larvae; thus some species of the genus *Dendrolimus* damage conifers, and some of the *Malacosoma* destroy fruit trees. During the day the males of certain species engage in wildly leaping flight. [52/5; 210/6; 243/18, 19]

PROMINENT MOTHS

The family of the prominents (Notodontidae) is entirely nocturnal. They were given their family name because of the toothlike projection, formed of scales, on the anal (rear) margin of the fore wing of many species. The sun-loving caterpillars are fantastically grotesque, and the moths, too, are like caricatures, not in body form and wing shape, but because of their peculiar resting attitudes. They are masters of concealment that simulate any solid, sharp-profiled object other than the insect itself, be it a dry, crumpled leaf spotted with silvery dewdrops, the half-wilted petal of a rose-colored flower, or some little nut or fruit.

Most frequently, however, broken bark and splinters of wood or the stumps of branches are involved; often the moths stick out into the air, or lie below like fallen bits of wood, or remain hanging in the underbrush. The broken surfaces may be represented either by designs on the wings or by odd arrangements of hair on the upper surface of the thorax; and bizarre contours are supplied by all sorts of other constructions and by the form of the two scaly toothlike projections of the fore wings, which then are held against one another.

Often, too, there are peculiar fish-tailed formations or bundles of scales at the tip of the abdomen. Many species curl the wings more or less closely about the abdomen, so that it seems to be rolled up in them. On each side of the abdomen there is a glandular apparatus with which special bristles on the hind legs or hair patches on the lower surface of the hind wings are perfumed.

About 2,300 species have been described from all parts of the earth, the majority from tropical America. They are not found in treeless regions, for most of their larvae live on trees, especially on old ones. [16/2, 11, 15; 51/6; 62/5; 211/7; 243/20–24]

GIANT SILKWORM MOTHS

These are the kings among the moths. Outstanding members of the family (Saturniidae) are the magnificent gold and purplish-brown Asiatic Atlas moths *(Attacus)*, whose wings may span as much as 10 inches and have a greater area than the wings of any other insects. Like fluttering silken and brocaded tapestries, these supporting surfaces dwarf the moth's hairy body. The wing surfaces are resplendent with pictorial compositions of unique grandeur, the centers of which consist of transparent, scaleless crescents or triangles. The fore wings have conspicuously extended tips, with impressive coloration, that are reminiscent of the head of a serpent. If the moth is disturbed while resting with outstretched wings, the wings begin to move slowly and majestically in a prolonged, rotary rhythm, and draw one's glance irresistibly to these menacing, protruding tips. [245/2]

In other respects the true wealth of the nocturnal silkworms is represented by the patterns of the central area of the wings, here depicted as gigantic goggle-eyes, there merely blinking sleepily or reduced, like a new moon, to the shape of a sickle. Here lies a tiny transparent spot in the center of the eye, like a piercing glance, and there is a magnificently framed picture window. The ability of these "eyes" to scare off enemies was discussed in the section on "Mimicry and Camouflage." Comparative study of these central structures, with their almost infinitely varied composition, and of the accompanying lines on the wing surface of saturniids, constitutes a fascinating area of natural observation.

The wings occur in all possible pastel colors, often intense, but never gaudy. A costume of concealment is almost the rule. Dry leaves or, less often, green ones are matchlessly simulated. These moths rest by preference at the base of trees and bushes where fallen foliage has collected, usually with the wings laid back or outspread, or less often held like those of butterflies. Most fly by night, but the males of many northern species storm along by day, often in large numbers, leaping wildly in flight. Aided by a great air chamber in the abdomen, they can stay on the wing for hours. The flight of females with egg-filled bodies is heavier, and more as though they were hanging in the air.

Fantastic spectacles in flight are those species whose wings have tails. These reach grotesque lengths in such species as *Actias* in America and Asia, the bizarre South American *Copiopteryx,* the rare African *Eudaemonia,* and what is perhaps the most magnificent lepidopteran of all, *Argema mittrei* of Madagascar, the so-called "comet's tail." It is an unforgettable experience to witness how such a miracle frees itself from its gleaming silvery cocoon. Clinging to the cocoon with its long furry legs, the moth expands its golden-yellow pinions; and, after they have been unfolded fully, it thrusts out like seemingly endless spears the tails of the hind wings, until then recognizable only as pitiful little appendages.

The regal insect now begins to vibrate, and a quivering runs through the wings and their tails all the way to the daintily rolled-up terminal streamers (which are not pressed flat, as they are in museum specimens). Shortly before the takeoff these begin to twitch more and more, and indeed to flicker like flames; when at length the wings have begun to beat violently, so that the yielding tails whip wildly about, the legs release their hold, and the creature drops into the air. Standing upright in the air, with the tails now hanging somewhat more calmly but still twisting like propellers, the insect takes flight—and one feels privileged to have been able to observe such a phenomenon.

The saturniids are an old family. Most of the 1,300 known species, almost all of large or very large size, are tropical, predominantly African and South American; they are fond of open country with trees and bushes. They display a great multiplicity of forms and frequently an extraordinary variation in individual size, which may amount to as much as 50 percent. [15/16; 16/14; 17/19, 31; 53/2; 55/3; 58–59; 63/1; 64/1; 211/1; 244-247]

SPHINX OR HAWK MOTHS

These imposing creatures of the family Sphingidae fly at twilight, their sharply-cut, narrow wings supporting a powerful and elegantly streamlined body. Its usually pointed tip bears an expansible bundle of scales; this is seen in the hummingbird moth *(Macroglossum),* which hovers above flowers in the daytime, and in the glassy-winged bee hawk moths *(Haemorrhagia),* as well as in a few other genera. In contrast to these smaller moths, almost all other members of the family are large, with wingspans up to nearly 8 inches.

Sphinx moths have enormous powers of flight, and many are migratory species that fly for great distances, occasionally approaching ships at sea. But only a very few cross great desert areas, for the sphingids in general have a great need for food and water. Often one sees them dipping into the surface of water in flight, like swallows. Many of the species confined to a given locality do not possess the typical long proboscis, but have one that is more or less rudimentary and nonfunctional.

With their extraordinary flight capacity, it is not surprising that certain species have an almost worldwide distribution and that the formation of new races is rendered difficult or impeded altogether by the repeated influx of individuals even into isolated islands. Nonetheless, some limitation on immigration is seen in the fact that many of the migratory females remain sterile in strange countries and do not reproduce, and that many fertile females produce larvae that are not adapted to the foreign climate.

The sphinx moths, including some 800 species, are distributed over the entire world except the cold regions; much the greater number are tropical. The family takes its name from the sphinxlike defensive attitude of the larvae. The group seems geologically recent since, among other things, it has highly specialized relationships with definite species of the geologically recent flowers.

When at rest, almost all sphinx moths lay the wings back rooflike or else extend them more or less flatly. In this position they have a protective coloration like bark or like dry or green leaves. Bright colors occur frequently on the hind wings and at times on the abdomen. A few species are among the most beautiful of Lepidoptera, particularly the African oleander hawk moths *(Deilephila nerii),* which migrate to Europe annually.

The nocturnal death's-head moths *(Acherontia),* as mentioned earlier, make chirping sounds when disturbed. These well-known migratory moths of the Old World have a skull-like design on the back of the thorax; a similar pattern occurs in a few other species of moths and in certain other insects, but nowhere else is it so striking. [61; 248/1-12]

SLUG CATERPILLAR MOTHS

These moths make up a very old family, the Limacodidae, also known as Eucleidae (Cochlidiidae). The approximately 1,000 species have no relationships with flowers and are represented on all continents, particularly in Australia and in the Asian and African tropics. These moths, some of which are active during daylight, have a somewhat whirring and often undulant flight. They are known for their sluglike caterpillars, a number of which have very toxic stinging hairs.

Certain of these caterpillars look like ugly, shaggy spiders, and many of the adults when at rest, some of them with widespread, bristly legs, also resemble spiders. Others give the effect of small fruits or of green or brown leaves; and although more lively colors or even silvery spots occur, the majority of the cochlidiids are unimpressive. Their designs, which may be regarded as primitive, frequently occur on the legs as well as on the body. In certain species, effects of shading are achieved merely by the incidence of light on areas that are of uniform color, but that have the scales partly flat and glistening and partly ruffled and erect. [56/5; 248/13-15]

BAGWORM MOTHS

Like the slug caterpillar moths, the family of the bagworms (Psychidae) is a primitive group. Because of their nondescript appearance they are infrequently collected and incompletely known, but biologically they are of particular interest. Most of their larvae spin themselves a tubular case, covered in a manner characteristic for each species with all sorts of materials, usually with parts of plants. The larvae carry their cases with them throughout their lifetime. Pupation takes place inside this bag.

In the more primitive species, both males and females forsake the case as flying adults, but females of the more highly specialized kinds remain inside it, and frequently also inside the pupal shell, which then is split partly open. The males mate with the encased females by inserting their abdomen into the shelter from without; the male's abdomen can be stretched lengthwise to an astonishing degree.

Inside the case the female lays 500 to 1,000 eggs, which are covered by the loose down at the tip of her abdomen; she is otherwise bare—a yellow, maggoty creature with a swollen, shapeless body; with no legs, antennae, or eyes; and with vestigial wings or none at all. The tousled males take to wing shortly after becoming adults—some at night, others only at dawn, and still others in the sunlight. The life of both sexes lasts but a little while, often only a few hours.

Colors and designs are weak or lacking altogether in the adult insects. Their delicate wings are either thinly and translucently scaled or completely transparent. The adult consumes no food at all, for its proboscis is vestigial. It is not surprising that bagworms are little noticed, for they not only are inconspicuous in coloration, but are rather small in size, are more or less uniform in shape, occur in narrowly limited localities, and have a very short period of flight.

Considering the complete inability of many females to change their habitat, it is amazing that this family could have spread throughout the world and even to distant islands. That they have done so is largely the result of the way of life of the caterpillars.

After hatching from the eggs, the larvae are very active. Thanks to strong forelegs, they are able to travel quite far, though they do start construction of the shelter very soon.

These caterpillars not only can live on a variety of the constituent parts of plants, even on dead ones, but can withstand starvation without harm for a long time, and in case of need may even subsist on the bits of leaves stuck to their case. It has been observed that a tornado has carried branches many miles with the bags of bagworm moths attached to them, and that such bags have been transported by water, including the waves of the sea. A small branch with lichens growing on it can furnish a caterpillar an abode and provisions for a long journey. Additionally, many bagworms can reproduce parthenogenetically—that is, without males—with the result that a bagworm species can become established in a new locality by means of a single drifting bag containing one developing female. [56/7; 248/16, 17; 250/1-9]

CARPENTERWORM MOTHS

Like the bagworms, the wood-boring carpenterworm moths (Cossidae) are a primitive and omnipresent family, most richly developed in the geographically ancient lands. The majority of their caterpillars feed within wood and, when rivers flood, are distributed throughout an entire continent inside treetrunks. Many carpenterworm moths inhabit plains and deserts. In Australia giant species of the genus *Xyleutes* have a wingspan of as

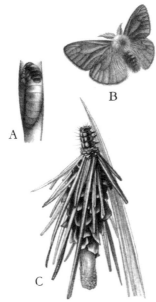

207/1A-C
Bagworm moths. (A) The maggot-shaped female; (B) the male (natural size); (C) the caterpillar in its case, a tube made of spun thread and covered with bits of plants, which are a different selection for each species.

CAPTIONS
FOR PAGES 209 TO 223

209/1–5
(1–5) Riodinid butterflies (see also page 192) (enlarged 1.3×).

209/6–8
(6) Mating play of the sulfur butterfly (genus Gonepteryx), the male above (somewhat enlarged). (7–8) The varicolored Agrias butterflies (7) have scent scales in the form of bushes on the hind wings; and pockets filled with a mat of white scales occur as scent fields in certain swallowtail species (8) (7, 8 enlarged 1.5×).

PAGES 210 AND 211

210/1
Ornithoptera from Indonesia; this species often assembles in crowds at watering places (enlarged 1.5×).

210/2–7 and 211/5–10
Resting moths and butterflies of various families. (210/2) Fritillary butterfly; (3) sphinx moth; (4) tiger moth; (5) noctuid moth; (6) tent caterpillar moth; (7) tussock moth. (211/5–6) Geometer moths; (7) prominent moth; (8) pyralid moth; (9) leaf roller moth; (10) plume moth (enlarged 1.3×).

211/1–3
Moths at a light are proverbial, but the phenomenon is by no means fully understood (enlarged 1.25×).

211/4
The wings of sphinx moths in flight are seen only as shadows (enlarged 1.5×).

PAGES 212 AND 213

The Papilionidae, including the apollo butterflies and the swallowtails, constitute an especially noble group of diurnal Lepidoptera. Marginal members are the water-loving Lamproptera species, with their small, glassy, monstrously tailed wings (212/1), and the weird, multiply-tailed forest butterflies, Armandia (212/2). The swallowtail butterfly pictured together with its egg (far right), caterpillar, and pupal shell is a worthy, temperate-zone representative (212/3) of its stock, the greater part of which is tropical. The species (213/1) found flying on Hibiscus is North American, and is a tropical element of that fauna. Those species that gain protection from their larvae's feeding on poisonous plants are known as Aristolochia butterflies (212/4, 6). A group of blue-green swallowtails (212/5) has

especially regal raiment, and the zebra swallowtails, of which the pictured Celeban species (213/3) is the largest, are strikingly elegant. Finally, there is a pair (213/2) of bird-winged butterflies (Ornithoptera); the upper specimen is the male. Distributed over the island world of the Far East, these butterflies are renowned for their magnificence and gigantic size, and also for their races—blue, green, and golden in the male sex—that differ from island to island (natural size).

PAGES 214 AND 215

214/1
A fluttering Philippine Papilio is sucking water at a moist crag (enlarged 1.3×).

214/2–215/2
Increasing melanism in Papilio species: at the left is an especially light-colored variant of a swallowtail butterfly (214/2) that may have just as strong markings as the second, American species (215/1). The black swallowtail (215/2), likewise an American species, exhibits only remnants of its originally extensive yellow ground color. The evolution of such species is no doubt founded on mutations, and in fact melanic mutants turn up repeatedly, even in light-colored species (somewhat reduced). Photograph.

215/3
A high degree of enlargement of the butterfly wing (here that of a Japanese relative of the swallowtails), impairs the optical continuity of the pattern on the one hand, but on the other reveals the poignant beauty of a background, bespangled with scales, that beckons one on toward impenetrable depths. Photograph.

PAGE 216

216/1
The European Parnassius butterfly (somewhat enlarged).

216/2
A Himalayan Parnassius that lives at an elevation of 16,000 to 19,000 feet (somewhat enlarged).

PAGE 217

217/1–6
White butterflies. (1) Falcate orange-tip; (2) lesser cabbage butterfly; (3) alfalfa butterfly; (4) mountain sulfur; (5) Appias white; (6) harlequin white (genus Delias) (somewhat enlarged).

217/7–8
Blues and hairstreaks, butterflies whose caterpillars frequently live in close association with ants. (8) An African species in premating play. (7) A copper (enlarged 1.3×).

218/1–2 and 219/1
Morpho butterflies in different phases of flight (natural size).

218/3–10
The Danaidae (3–4), the Heliconiidae (5–8), and the Ithomiidae (9–10) are butterflies that are protected by poison, and frequently belong to mimicry rings (half natural size). Photograph.

219/2
One of the largest South American butterflies, a Morpho (both upper and lower surfaces) (somewhat over half natural size). Photograph.

PAGE 220

220/1–11
Brush-footed butterflies (Nymphalidae). (1) A member of the genus Ageronia, that makes a rattling noise. (3) The red admiral, a butterfly that is distributed widely throughout the Holarctic region. (4) Upper and under sides of an angle wing. (6) Spring form and (5) summer form of Araschnia levana. (7) Upper and under sides of a fritillary butterfly. (10) A Prepona male, with its huge odorous hair pencils on the hind wings. (11) A species with astonishingly different sexes, the male at the left (somewhat over half natural size). Photograph.

220/12–19
(12–13) Taenaris, of the Amathusiidae, butterflies with eyespots that are exaggerated especially (or even solely) on the under side. (14) Lower surface of a brassolid, a small family of large species, to which the huge Caligo butterflies also belong. (15–16) Satyrid butterflies. (17–19) Blues (0.75 natural size). Photograph.

PAGE 221

221/1
A rare Javanese brush-footed butterfly (1.25 natural size).

221/2–13
Satyrid butterflies (2–9); below are four skippers (10–13) (0.8 natural size). Photograph.

PAGE 222

222/1–2
(1) Mourning cloak butterfly; (2) peacock butterfly. The former is a

frequently occurring member of the vanessid group, while the latter has become a rarity in the group of the angle wings (enlarged 1.3×).

222/3
A rare European tiger moth (enlarged 1.75×).

PAGE 223

223/1–4
A group of brush-footed butterflies, typical of South America (somewhat enlarged).

223/5
A skipper (enlarged 2×).

223/6
The Madagascan "Croesus" moth (Uraniidae) (enlarged somewhat less than 2×).

209/1

209/2

209/3

209/4

209/5

209/6

209/7

♂

♀

209/8

209

210/1

210/2

210/3

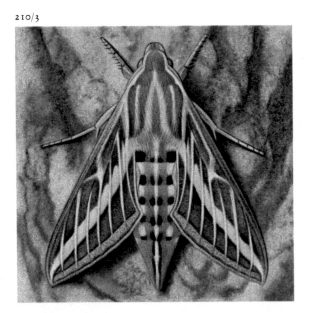

210/4

210/7

210/5

210/6

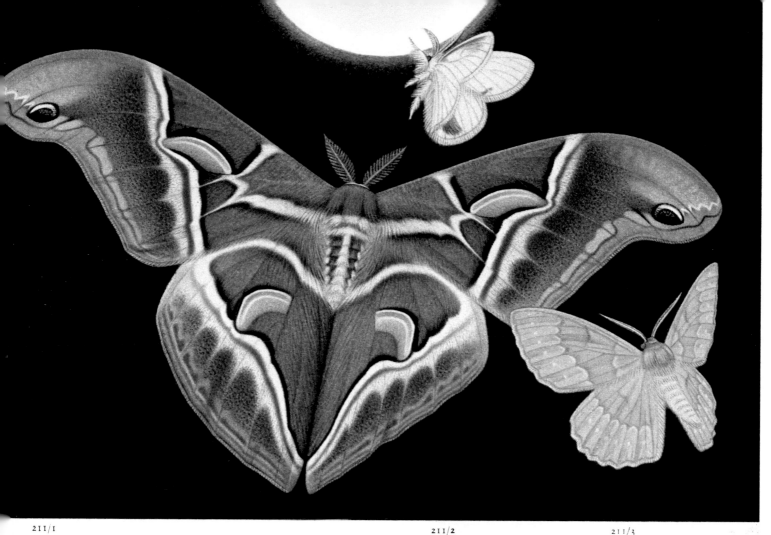

211/1

211/2

211/3

211/4

211/5

211/6

211/7

211/8

211/9

211/10

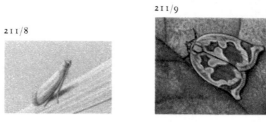

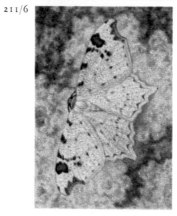

212/1

212/2

212/3

212/4

212/5

212/6

212

213/1

213/3

213/2

♂

♀

213

214/1

214/2

214

215/3

215/1   ♂   215/2   ♀

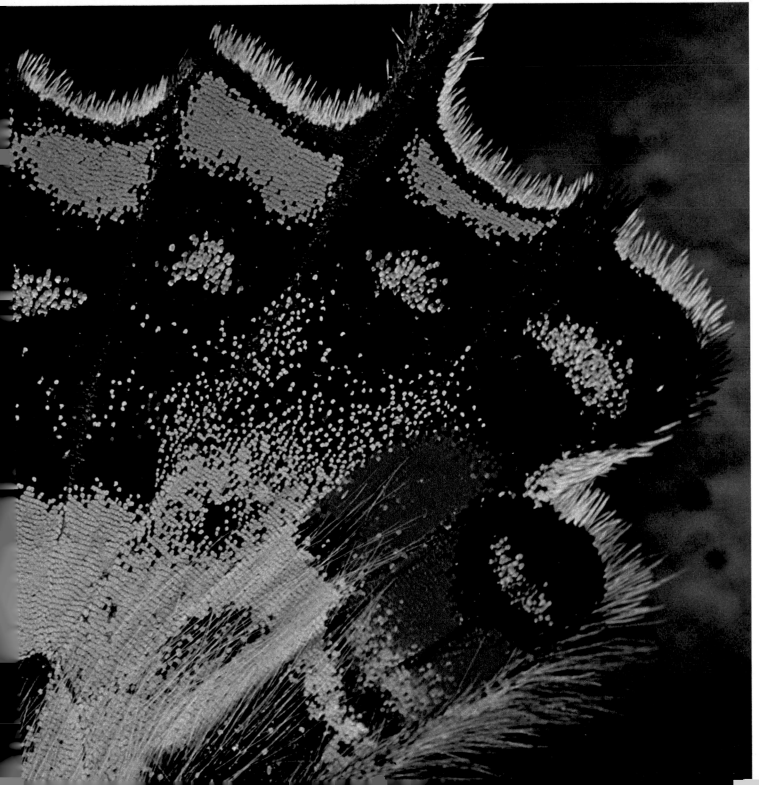

216/1

216/2

216

217/1

217/2

217/5

217/3

217/4

217/6

217/7

217/8

218/1

218/2

218/3-4

218/5-7

218/8-10

219/1

219/2

221/1

221/2-13

221

222/1

222/2

222/3

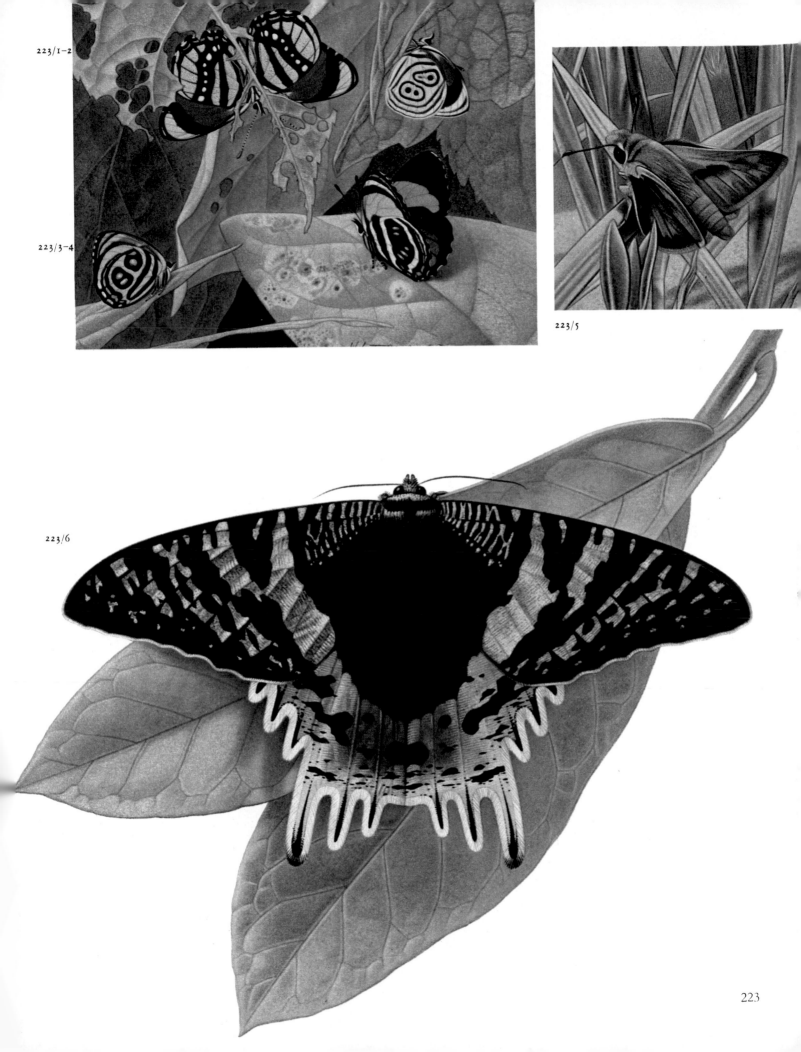

223/1-2

223/3-4

223/5

223/6

223

much as 10 inches and the most massive body of all moths and butterflies. Whereas many of the approximately 800 known species are great rarities, others appear in certain years in enormous swarms almost like locusts, covering the streets, for instance, in South American cities.

The common leopard moth *(Zeuzera pyrina)* is one of the most widely distributed Lepidoptera, being at home in Europe, Asia, North Africa, and North America. The caterpillar of another species, the coffee borer *(Zeuzera coffeae)*, sometimes does damage on plantations. These *Zeuzera,* mostly white but peppered with little glistening blue or blackish spots, are avoided by birds. Their males (like those of related genera) have very characteristic antennae that change abruptly from a broad and densely feathered basal half to a threadlike outer half. Besides, their eyes are so huge they almost meet on the underside of the face. [248/18]

The body of many cossids is very long, and the females have a protrusible oviposition tube with which they insert their exceedingly numerous eggs. The wings are stiff and hard, with a primitive, rich venation, which enables a freshly emerged cossid to let the wings expand vertically upward, rather than letting them hang down, as most Lepidoptera have to do. Moreover, such stable and rather narrow supporting surfaces permit a swift and long-lasting flight, usually at night and often toward electric light.

Throughout the day cossids at rest are particularly well hidden, many of them even somewhat below the soil surface. Although a few strikingly colored species exist, the majority look like bark and bits of wood. Their designs are primitive, consisting of simple spots and speckled, rippling, or wavy patterns. The wings at rest lie close against the body. Certain of these moths, such as the genus *Cossus,* rest on treetrunks with the front part of the body somewhat elevated. In this position they are thoroughgoing imitations of the stubs of broken branches. [16/14; 50/7; 248/18–20]

CLEARWING MOTHS

Similar to the cossids in the type and way of living of their caterpillars are the clearwing moths (Aegeriidae or Sesiidae), likewise an ancient lepidopterous group, though one highly specialized in mimicry. With few exceptions, the approximately 800 known species resemble bees and wasps. The resemblance stems not only from their clear, slender wings, but also from their

often transversely striped body and from their long legs, which in the bee-mimics have a dense, bristly covering of hairs and scales. In addition, they sit and move much as bees and wasps do and even have similar whirring and sometimes buzzing flight.

The family is unusually uniform in structure, and many species are not easily distinguished from one another. They are for the most part pretty, small, delicate insects, for which the name "moth" seems quite unsuitable. Almost all fly in the sunshine, visit flowers, and are especially fond of warm, dry localities. In general the clearwing moths are rather rare. No doubt their shyness contributes also to the infrequency with which they are seen. [50/2; 248/22–29]

HEPIALID MOTHS

This family (Hepialidae) is the very ancestral stem of the Lepidoptera. Its members are almost like dragonflies in that their bodies are extended lengthwise to an extreme degree, the thoracic segments are loosely connected with one another, and the fore and hind wings have a gap between them. This opening is bridged by a membranous fold, the jugum, that originates from the root of the fore wing and is possessed elsewhere by only a single, closely related group, the tiny pollen-feeding Micropterygidae. The huge eyes of many males, which almost come together, also are reminiscent of dragonflies; so are the often tiny, bristlelike antennae. But although they look like dragonflies, their living habits are different. The hepialids are extremely sluggish, mouthless insects that take no food and that, aside from flying perhaps 10 to 30 minutes a day, cannot be induced to take wing. So the astonishing parallels between them and dragonflies, as well as with other very primitive insect groups, such as the nerve-winged insects (Neuroptera), mayflies (Ephemeroptera), and caddisflies (Trichoptera), probably have not arisen from similar ways of living, but indicate true, deeper relationships.

With the caddisflies, the hepialids have in common certain characteristics of the wing venation and of the hairs that are located on the wing membrane; the scales, too, are in part more or less hairlike in form. Reminiscent of the mayflies are the oscillatory or dancing flight maneuvers of many males, the extremely short flight period (mostly at twilight or at night, seldom in the daytime), and the hepialids' very short life. Another similarity is the scattering of innumerable eggs over the ground during a whirring

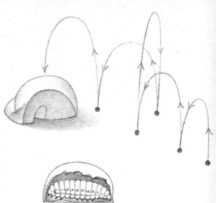

A

flight; some females are estimated to produce about 50,000.

Still another likeness is the way the females are attracted by the males; for example, the hind legs of the Australian genus *Charagia* are modified into great expansible odor-producing clusters, each hair of which is inserted into a little membranous gland and gives off a strongly sweet-smelling fluid at the tip. These males frequently have a uniquely beautiful pale green or opalescent bluish color; and their females display delicate red and green combinations.

Many other hepialids also have green colors and, at rest with the wings laid like a steep roof over the body, are almost invisible on the sprouts of plants. Although the designs of this family consist only of simple patterns of spots, many species have great beauty, such as those adorned with dots of silver. But a large fraction of them are an inconspicuous gray or brown.

One noteworthy species, *Leto stacyi* of New South Wales, is a giant with a 10-inch wing-span, an ancient-looking creature that brings to mind the "lepidopterous dinosaurs" of a vanished epoch when the family was in full bloom. The fore wings of this creature bear somewhat raised eyelike designs, and when at rest it seems to resemble the head of a lizard or snake. Its gigantic caterpillar pupa can travel with astonishing speed, thanks to filelike processes on the abdominal body rings. But most hepialid larvae dwell within (more rarely on) the roots of plants, and many are still wholly unknown.

The tropical virgin forests shelter another genus *(Phassus)* of giants, the largest species of which, from South America, may measure over 8 inches. Numerous hepialid species are great rarities that live on mountains or in swamps, where they are hard to find. Certain ones are attracted by light, and in parts of Australia specimens that fly into the campfire are roasted and eaten at once.

About 250 species are known from the whole world; most live in the mountains and moist valleys, but some have penetrated as far north and south as the Arctic and Antarctic, and up to snowline in mountainous areas. [189/12; 248/21; 249]

MICRO MOTHS

A number of families have been included under the collective concept of the Microlepidoptera, but today the tendency is to consider them as separate groups. It is true that in general these families consist of very small species, yet they are in no way separated from the others (the "Macrolepidoptera"), among which there likewise are many tiny species. Also, among the Microlepidoptera are some ancient, primitive families as well as more highly specialized ones. Ways of life and body forms also vary widely. Thus the microlepidopterous families are not isolated in their phylogeny (with exception of the aforementioned primitive Micropterygidae, of which only some 80 species are known), but are interpolated variously among the families of the Macrolepidoptera. In addition, the systematic position of certain families, as well as how they shall be separated from one another, is still under study by specialists.

If one wished to single out from all Lepidoptera particular species as the most beautiful ones, they might be sought among the micro moths. These magical creations are as enchanting when the wings are outspread for flight as they are in their frequently highly distinctive resting attitudes. Free of misgivings, we squash between our hands, as a loathsome pest, some moth fluttering about the room! Rarely do we think of putting one of these tiny beings in a test tube and taking a look at it under a lens. But what fascinating visions then appear, such as the elegant head, the silklike luster, the satiny sheen, the enchanting linear or speckled patterns, interwoven with bronze, silver, or gold, of the scale-covered wings with their delicate eiderdown-like fringes. These fringes, made of hairlike scales, are broadenings of the supporting surface that are especially characteristic of many families whose wings proper are merely narrow, lanceolate structures. In the plume moth family, adorned with especially long, elegantly spinose legs, the wing margin is indented repeatedly and so deeply that these creatures give the appearance of flying on delicate bird feathers.

Smallest of all Lepidoptera are the dwarf moths (Nepticulidae), whose two fore wings, in most instances marked with transverse silver bands, span only from about 0.1 to at most 0.25 inch. On the other hand, the largest Microlepidoptera are to be found among the broadwinged snout moths (Pyralidae), some genera of which are gayly colored. With over 20,000 species, this is one of the largest families of Lepidoptera. Certain of their caterpillars are dreaded pests of grain, rice, and corn, and even of honeycomb (the wax moths *Galleria* and *Achroea*). Indeed, among the more than 25,000 species of Microlepidoptera that are distributed over the entire world, including arid regions and high mountain ranges, are perhaps the worst insect pests. Most greatly feared are the numerous leaf

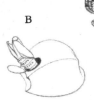

B

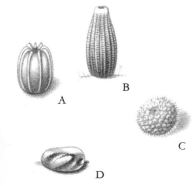

227/1
The gray-brown tortricid moth
Carpocapsa saltitans, with its
caterpillar (A), which lives in a
seed pod: this is the well-known
"jumping bean." In the middle (B)
is the projecting empty pupal shell
(natural size).

227/2A–D
The eggs of various butterflies and
moths differ greatly in form and
sculpturing. (A) Tortoiseshell
butterfly; (B) white butterfly;
(C) purple butterfly; (D) wild
silkworm moth (much enlarged).

rollers (the Tortricidae, many of whose caterpillars live in rolled-up leaves), which are noted for their destruction of fruit, cultivated trees, and entire forests; combatting them requires constant effort. Some other genera have developed into pests of provisions and household wares, like the clothes moths.

The majority of Microlepidoptera are most active at twilight, but others are active in the daytime or at night. Many lead so concealed an existence that collectors try to drive them out of the shrubbery with smoking devices or are able to obtain them only by rearing the caterpillars. Many Microlepidoptera elude pursuit by running swiftly away, or even by jumping, and some let themselves fall as if they were dead. The females of certain species scarcely ever fly, and some are totally incapable of flight.

Bewitching is the effect of the aerial games and dances of the Incurvariidae and Adelidae. Holding outstretched their long antennae, which no doubt serve them for gliding flight, and glistening with purple and gold, they go bouncing up and down between light and shadow amid the green of the vegetation. A few others of the approximately 30 families of Microlepidoptera are the particularly multiform Gelechiidae, with elongated, curved (mostly sickle-shaped) palpi; the Hyponomeutidae, whose "typical" species are recognized by the white fore wings with numerous black dots, and great assemblages of whose caterpillars spin a cover of white silk over entire bushes and strip them bare of leaves; the casebearers (Coleophoridae), with their unobtrusive, uniform coloration, whose leaf-mining caterpillars often are hidden in characteristically constructed bags or cases; the graceful and elegantly marked Lithocolletidae; and the tastefully clad grass miners (Elachistidae)—all these families are distinguished by the curious ways of life of their larvae, to whose incredibly manifold and often extremely peculiar biology we shall presently return.

Well-known, for example, is that Mexican microlepidopteron *Carpocapsa saltitans,* whose caterpillar lives in the seed pods of milkweed plants *(Sebastiana).* If such a seed is lying on the ground in a place unfavorable to the occupant, perhaps where there is too much sun, the caterpillar is able by means of sudden movements within its house to make the latter go leaping away—the "Mexican jumping bean." Before pupating, it makes a circular perforation to form a cap that later can be pushed off easily by the pupa, within which the fully developed moth will then be

contained. Aided by belts of spines on the body segments, the pupa forces itself halfway out, and the insect can now emerge. [16/9; 56/4, 6, 10; 211/8–10; 250/10; 251–252; 364/12]

CATERPILLARS AND COCOONS

Let us now turn the pages of the book of Lepidoptera back to the time of their youth, to the world of caterpillars. This indeed is an almost unbelievably different world, but it contains the same profusion of ways and means for mastering the art of living as does the adult world. The most astounding of those species whose young have become adapted to life in the water will be described in the section on "Water Insects."

HATCHING AND FEEDING

The eggs of butterflies and moths often are adorned with delicate ribs and other sculpturings, but may have only a simple surface, rough or smooth. Depending on the genus, they are shaped like balls, ovals, spindles, bottles, barrels, disks, or plates; most are inconspicuously colored, though this may change markedly in the course of embryonic development.

In general the egg stage lasts one to two weeks, though frequently it is shorter or is much longer, as in those species that overwinter as eggs. The hatching caterpillar eats a round hole in the eggshell, which it then may devour entirely. A very few Microlepidoptera, especially the Asiatic genus *Monopis,* bear living young, more than a dozen of which have been found together in a single maternal body.

The number of eggs differs greatly among different genera. Usually there are about 100, on the average; generally moths have the larger number. Certain kinds, such as the hepialids, produce thousands, which are simply broadcast in flight, so that the young caterpillars have to locate their own food. But as a rule the female chooses the food plant, guided by her sense of smell and taste, and lays her eggs on it.

Whereas many caterpillars can subsist on different kinds of plants, others are so dependent upon a single plant species or group that they will starve to death elsewhere. The caterpillars of related lepidopterous species usually live upon plants that are related to one another; thus the relationship of certain plants of very different appearance was realized because the plants were fed upon by particular species of caterpillars.

Frequently the degree of dependence of such insects goes so far as to encompass definite parts of certain plants. Thus, a leaf-mining caterpillar of certain species of Microlepidoptera will starve to death if its mother has been so oversighted as to insert the egg into the upper side instead of into the lower side of a leaf, since in this special case only the cells of the lower layer of the leaf are consumed. So, as also is customary elsewhere in the insect empire, the degree of this dependence corresponds to that exercised by the mother lepidopteran in her care for the brood.

Most females fasten their eggs to the outer surface of plants—to leaves, buds, flowers, stalks, or bark. Eggs are placed singly, in pairs, or in groups; the latter may amount to whole clutches arranged in piles, in rows, in a layer, or in rings around the twigs. Many moths and Microlepidoptera cover the clutch with sticky cement, mostly mixed with a woolly belt of hairs or scales that hang, often in dense clumps, from the rear end of such females. [254/1–14]

The brood care of the American yucca moth (family Prodoxidae) is a marvelous example of symbiosis between plant and insect. Such a female gathers, with mouth-parts specially constructed for the job, the pollen of a yucca blossom into a rather large ball that hangs below her head. She then forces the ball into the scar on the style of the neighboring flower, as is necessary for its fertilization. Thereupon she inserts one or two eggs into the ovary beneath the style. When the plant's seeds have partially developed, some are eaten by the caterpillar hatching from the egg, but enough are left for the plant's own reproduction, which would be impossible without this assistance from the yucca moth. [252/1]

The females of many species whose caterpillars mine plants bury their eggs in the plant tissues with an oviposition tube. Doubtless almost every plant species—whether an alga, a fungus, a lichen, a moss, or a seed plant—serves as food for the caterpillars of at least one lepidopterous species. Even dead, decaying, or dry substances have their connoisseurs (especially among pyralid moths and clothes moths), and hides, feathers, hair, and other animal material is not excepted, not even after it has been manufactured into textiles, a fact only too well-known by those who have been visited by caterpillars of the webbing clothes moth (*Tineola bisselliella*).

In case of need these insects can even subsist for generations on the excrement left behind by their departed ancestors.

The caterpillars of a few other moths, such as *Tinea cloacella* or *Oenophylla flavum,* live in wine cellars, not only on algae and fungi, but often even in the corks of the wine bottles. The caterpillars of the pyralid moth *Bradypodicola hahneli* eat algae (and perhaps hair, too) exclusively in the fur of sloths. Caterpillars of certain slug caterpillar moths even find their nourishment in the waxy secretions of tropical Homoptera, such as jumping plantlice (Psyllidae), in no wise harming the providers.

Contrariwise, the caterpillars of the genus *Sthenauge* of the pyralid moths live as parasites on saturniid caterpillars; furthermore caterpillars of another pyralid moth (*Pachypodistes goeldii*) are parasites in the arboreal nests of South American ants, just as are caterpillars of the strangely primitive Indo-Australian lycaenid genus *Liphyra* in the nests of the weaver ant *Oecophylla smaragdina.* These caterpillars have an almost hemispherical shape and a smooth, hard skin that protects them against the peril of ant stings and that remains fastened as an armored covering to the outside of the pupa. Most of the adults that finally emerge in the nest reach the open unharmed, since their thick mantle of easily dislodged scales makes both stings and bites comparatively ineffective.

The caterpillars of wax moths (*Galleria* and *Achroea*) live in the nests of bees and to a lesser extent in those of wasps, where they eat not only refuse and honeycomb, but also the brood of their hosts. And finally certain species, partly on account of lack of nourishment and partly without a definite cause, turn into bloodthirsty creatures and eat up both other caterpillars and their own kind, a type of conduct that occasionally may lead to their mutilating themselves. There are also a few insect-eating caterpillars that feed exclusively on aphids and coccids. Thus, for instance, a lycaenid (*Gerydus boisduvali*) in the Sunda Islands lays its eggs in the midst of aphid colonies despite the presence of ants, which seem too busy with the aphids to be concerned about butterflies, eggs, or the caterpillars destroying their "milk cows." The larvae of *Feniseca tarquinius,* in the United States, also feed on aphids.

Numerous are the friendly relationships among caterpillars and ants, and among caterpillars and termites. In particular, many

228/1
The sloth moth develops in the fur of sloths, where the caterpillar subsists on algae (0.5 natural size).

lycaenids live under such symbiosis. For on the upper rear surface of these fat caterpillars, shaped like wood lice, are glands that discharge a sweet secretion. Ants attracted by it lick the caterpillars and protect them, stay with them on the plants, and may carry them into their own nest, where the caterpillars then feed at will upon the ants' own brood. It even happens that the ants bring them fresh leaves from the caterpillars' food plant.

The symbiosis of many lycaenid species has become so restricted that they are unable to develop without their ants and die off if the ants are removed. On the other hand, the friendship that certain Microlepidoptera (*Psecadia* in the family Gelechiidae) have developed with ants is limited to the ants' licking up the sap that flows from the holes made by the caterpillars in their feeding. [253]

The life of a caterpillar is devoted to eating. Some caterpillars eat almost uninterruptedly, others only by day or by night. Most of them remain constantly on the food, but may leave it and go into hiding during their rest periods. Certain noctuid caterpillars, in fact, stay underground more or less all the time, biting off plants and pulling them down into the holes. Little wonder that with such a gluttonous way of life so many caterpillars have become dread pests of cultivated plants.

Often the different species may be identified by their feeding pattern, which may be very different at different larval stages. Most caterpillars gnaw into leaves from the edges. Others (especially young ones) eat out holes or scrape off only the outermost layer from the upper or lower surface of the leaf; or they may skeletonize it, leaving only the ribs.

With few exceptions, such as the bagworm moths (Psychidae), caterpillars quickly die from lack of food. During food shortages, short mass migrations occasionally take place. Strangely enough, almost all migrating individuals proceed in the same direction, and trains have been brought to a standstill by the slipping of their wheels on masses of crushed caterpillars. If unprotected, the caterpillars may soon fall victim to the heat of the sun. Usually a few unfortunates succeed in pupating prematurely, but these at best develop into dwarfed or crippled adults. Species less thoroughly adapted to a specific plant are more likely to come upon other nourishment. This happens in the notorious migrations of the "armyworms" of an American noctuid, *Leucania unipuncta*.

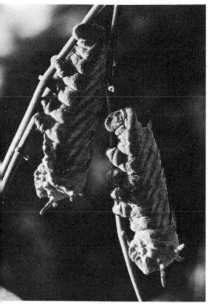

229/1
The caterpillars of the Asiatic atlas moths live on Ailanthus (the "tree of heaven"). Their skin, on which a powdery secretion is deposited, is curiously adorned with pegs; and they have powerful abdominal appendages for walking ("prolegs"). Photograph.

MOLTING

From time to time caterpillars have to molt. The number of molts, which averages four, may differ not only according to species, but also according to whether living conditions are favorable or unfavorable. In preparation for a molt, the caterpillar usually sits motionless for a couple of days, with the old head capsule characteristically displaced forward; afterward, the new one suddenly seems much too big, but does not grow any further until the next molt, as is true similarly for the legs and often for other body appendages, too. These disproportionately large body parts often give freshly molted caterpillars a bizarre appearance.

Certain arctiids (Nolinae) retain the old head capsule for a time on top of the hairy covering of the new one, instead of shedding it together with the old skin and, as usually occurs, eating it up. Since the same thing happens at every molt, the mature arctiid caterpillar finally is adorned with a grotesque crown of three to four heads, the outermost the smallest.

Most astounding is the capacity of many caterpillars for change from molt to molt. At one such event, for instance, fantastic or even gigantic outgrowths, long hairs, or thorny structures may appear without warning; or a caterpillar with such a quixotic shape may emerge from the egg and at the first molt lose forever the entire set of trappings in favor of a second costume. Frequently, too, color changes from one extreme to another. Coloration usually becomes complete shortly after a molt, but in rare exceptions may be delayed for some time. For instance, immediately after its last molt, the caterpillar of a sphinx moth (*Xanthopan*) from Madagascar has the same green dress, striped with white, as before; but two days later it is spotted with bright colors and looks completely different.

LIFE SPAN

The length of life of caterpillars varies greatly. It is longer for those that pass the winter in the caterpillar stage, as occurs regularly two or more times with arctiids in the colder regions or in the mountains. And it is longer for species that live on poorly nutritious foods, particularly for the wood-feeders, such as many clearwing moths, ghost moths, and cossid moths, which usually are caterpillars for two or more years. But in contrast, many butterflies and moths customarily develop two or more generations a year.

Many generations are produced by those caterpillars of Microlepidoptera that mine within green plants, eating their way forward and increasing in size under ideal conditions.

LEAF MINERS

The feeding pathways, or mines, of leaf-mining caterpillars, often visible from afar on leaves as decorative brown or whitish spots or as wormy twisting lines, are hothouses within which development from egg to pupa may be completed within a few days. For the outer surface of the leaf acts as a magnifying glass that raises the temperature within the mine high above that of the environment, and the water-containing leaf cells, bitten into by the caterpillar, produce a constant high humidity.

The danger that the feces may become colonized by harmful molds is met in various ways. Many species deposit them only at certain regions within the mine and place them in rows, allowing them to be aerated from both sides. Others make a little opening through which they eject each fecal pellet, partly with the help of a special comb on the rear end, or else throw it into a special web constructed, no doubt, as a protective measure, on the lower side of the leaf in front of the opening. The simplest procedure is that of species that get rid of their excrement by shifting to a new dwelling place. Certain species move from leaf to leaf without coming for an instant into the open air, since they eat their way down the leaf stalk and onward through the green rind of the branch into the nearest leaf.

Numerous species first bore into leaves and later into flowers, seeds, stalks, or roots; and more still of the "worms" damage fruit and berries, as is well known. Various plant-boring caterpillars—for instance, a few of the minute nepticulids—cause galls, and certain species are lodgers in the galls of other insects. For the rest, many are leaf miners only in their youth; later on, usually quite changed in body form, they lead a free life, often concealed between the leaves.

The leaf blotch miner *Caloptilia stigmatella*, after it leaves the mine, goes to the edge of the leaf, bites off a strip that remains hanging from the end, and rolls this into a capsule-shaped shelter. On the other hand, a corn-damaging pyralid moth, *Ostrinia nubilalis*, first feeds on the outer surface and only later bores into the plant. Certain species cut out a piece of leaf before they pupate and drop with it to the ground.

Leaf mines serve as visiting cards for their inhabitants, which can be identified definitely by the form and color as well as by the location of such feeding passages. In certain cases the affected parts of the leaves are discolored an intense red or violet, occasionally by flower pigments (anthocyanins), the synthesis of which apparently is stimulated by definite changes in the damaged plant tissues. Well-known phenomena, too, are the green spots in browned autumn leaves; such parts often contain the mines of certain Microlepidoptera. Such species, which do not complete development until late in the year, somehow manage to conserve an island of living tissue as food within the dead leaf. [254/17]

CATERPILLAR ANATOMY

The typical caterpillar body is composed of 13 segments, 3 thoracic and 10 abdominal; the last 2 segments appear fused. Each of the 3 thoracic rings bears a pair of true legs, and segments 6 to 9 as well as 13 bear a pair of integumental pegs known as false legs or prolegs. The thoracic legs end in a single claw; the soles of the abdominal legs, in contrast, have rows of hooks ("crochets") on the outer side or, in species that mine and live in feeding passageways, more or less closed wreaths of hooks. Whereas the flannel moths (Megalopygidae) have two additional pairs of abdominal legs (though these are somewhat more weakly developed), the number of legs in a great many genera and even in whole families is reduced. Thus the rear pair of legs of many hook-tip moths (Drepanidae) and prominent moths (Notodontidae) are modified into one or two points.

Also, certain noctuids lack the two front pairs of abdominal legs, and most geometrids even the first three, so that a different technique of walking is demanded. On this account the mostly long and slender geometrid larvae have been known since ancient times as loopers or measuring worms (geometers), for their mode of progression is an alternate extension and pulling after of the body, which is bowed high in the middle after each pull.

Young bagworm caterpillars (Psychidae) have no abdominal legs at first, and walk along with the rear of the body held high like the rove beetles (Staphylinidae). Certain leaf-mining microlepidopterous larvae lack legs more or less altogether. Similar in this respect are the slug caterpillar moths (Limacodidae), so named because of their oval body shape and flat-soled, creeping feet that merely bear suction pads.

In general the capacity of caterpillars for walking differs considerably. For example, arctiids and tortricids go quite fast, and the latter even writhe backward rapidly. On the other hand, many move hardly at all or only enough to take in food.

The visual powers of caterpillars are slight. Most have on each side of the head a row of tiny simple eyes, usually six in number. The micropterygid caterpillars are unique in having little compound eyes.

The powerful mouthparts are of the biting type, rarely (for example, in certain sesiids) modified into tools for boring. Spinning glands open onto the labium (lower lip) via two ducts; in the silkmoths these glands extend throughout the entire body and amount to about one-fourth of its weight.

The respiratory system opens to the outside by means of fine air holes (stigmata), which for the most part are strikingly outlined, one in each side of nearly every segment.

The caterpillar body covering, or integument, which may be delicate or hard depending on the genus and mode of living, forms and bears all possible sorts of excrescences, thorns, bristles, hairs, and scales. Waxy excretions also occur; these have the form of flakes in the caterpillars of certain skipper butterflies, but are fibrous, granular, or powdery in other caterpillars. The gigantic *Attacus* caterpillars often leave a mealy white trail behind them as evidence of these waxy excretions.

Caterpillars that dwell constantly in hiding or in the dark are as a rule of indifferent appearance, usually bare and unimpressive in color. Most leaf miners, for example, are bone-white except for the head and the back surface of the prothorax, which are usually a glistening brown. In contrast, free-living caterpillars frequently have a striking appearance. Many of the elements that make them striking, such as thorny formations of hairs, often have value for the protection of the individual. These hairs may be hard or bristly, or soft as silk, or may even terminate in clubs; they may appear as splendid coiffures in the form of bows, brushes, or pencils; as cushions or down; or as prickly caps on top of warty protuberances. [15/24; 18/8; 30/2; 138/18; 212/3; 250/10; 253; 255]

Defensive Weapons

Caterpillars that defend themselves actively are exceptions; thus cossids and notodontids (*Dicranura, Anurocampa*) occasionally adopt a vigorous biting stance, or squirt at the enemy, from a gland beneath the head, a corrosive secretion that makes his eyes burn. While doing this, *Dicranura* lets two red, evil-smelling glandular threads appear from the caudal fork, and waves them about in spirals. Certain tussock-moth caterpillars have on the upper rear surface two trumpet-shaped glandular warts that can be forced out by blood pressure, but that can serve at most to drive off parasitic insects. [62/6]

A scent gland in the form of a yellowish or reddish forked horn (osmeterium) that can be protruded, like a snail's antennae, from the cervical region is a characteristic mark of a swallowtail caterpillar. The primary function of this horn seems to be that of putting out in gaseous form volatile substances obtained from the food plants, so that any additional action the sharp, penetrating odor may have as a defense probably is to be regarded as secondary. [255/3]

Cossid caterpillars diffuse a constant strong odor of acetic acid, which apparently arises from fermentation of substances in the wood they eat. In spite of it, these caterpillars are eaten by humans in certain countries, as are many other caterpillars. [255/2]

Many wholly harmless caterpillars defend themselves by regurgitating green digestive juice, which is ineffective in itself. Fishlike squirming movements also are used, and under these conditions the hard, pointed caudal horn of many sphingids may become almost a weapon. In certain species of caterpillar, this horn is so long and stringy that it no doubt may be used to whip off attacking flies or parasitic wasps from the back.

Other caterpillars try to flee from danger, perhaps dropping to the ground or letting themselves down on a thread. And many, perhaps most, hairy caterpillars roll themselves up; in many genera, especially in those of lymantriids and lasiocampids, unexpected brightly colored spots or contrasting intersegmental lines then appear. [254/16; 255/7]

But the majority of all caterpillars seek security in concealment. They make use of practically all the methods of hiding available in the insect empire, from the imitation of living or dead parts of plants to the representation of bird droppings, of structures like fungi and molds, and of unrecognizable objects with oddly dissolved contours. Of the last type, many notodontids are masters, resting in apparently distorted attitudes, as though stabbed in the back, so that they just fill the hole they have eaten in a leaf. Stretched out stiff and rigid like twigs or stalks and frequently gnarled with warty excrescences, most geometrids at rest can be distinguished as living objects only by the sense of touch. Many change color from green to brown or vice versa according to the surroundings.

Fantastic attitudes for frightening off enemies are struck by countless caterpillars, even by many that are well masked by their appearance. A well-known stance is the "sphinx attitude"—that is, an elevation and bending inward of the fore part of the body, seen especially in caterpillars of many sphinx moths and giant silkworm moths. In adopting this stance certain caterpillars keep the face continually toward the assailant, moving the jaws threateningly or even clacking them together and making rustling sounds. Here the caterpillar of *Chimabache fagella* (family Gelechiidae) should be mentioned. Particularly at night or when disturbed, it produces chirping, cricketlike noises by rubbing the claws of the last pair of thoracic legs against the smooth upper surface of a leaf.

The startling attitudes of many sphinx-moth and swallowtail caterpillars are supplemented by striking eyelike designs that goggle at one from both sides of the thorax, which in threatening situations is blown up and looks more or less like a head. A few Asiatic pierids, such as *Hebomoia glaucippe*, also have eyelike designs, which have led some local people to fear them as "snakes." Many skipper caterpillars have two spots that also look like eyes in a face; these insects, sheltered in a rolled-up leaf or in a house made of leaves spun together, expose only the head, whose coloration contrasts with that of the rest of the body. The exceptional slenderness of the adjacent part of the thorax gives the head a particularly protruding effect.

The caterpillars of many prominent butterflies (Notodontidae) have the fore and hind parts of the body bent sharply upward and against the back. As a result of this attitude, plus jagged outgrowths, threads, or even long, spidery legs (as in *Stauropus*), strange appearances are achieved. The effect is heightened when certain kinds of caterpillars (such as *Phalera* and *Datana*) sit close together in groups and simultaneously adopt this rigid warning posture. The phenomenon, also known among sawfly larvae, has an almost social quality. [254/15]

Aggregations are especially familiar among caterpillars that are inedible because they feed on toxic plants, or that are armed with poisonous hairs. These caterpillars have harsh colors visible from afar, and the brightly colored masses are like a notice to beware.

Caterpillars studded with toxic hairs are especially well protected, even though some are devoured without harm by such insectiv-

orous creatures as cuckoos or are attacked without hindrance by parasites such as flies and parasitic wasps. With most caterpillars the protective action of thorns, spines, or hairs is only a mechanical one; but with a relatively few species it is also a chemical, urticating one, producing a stinging effect like that of a nettle. Many insects are able to make their covering of hairs or spines stand on end, and some then give twitching movements, driving the tips of the blister-producing organs into an enemy's skin.

The irritant hairs with perhaps the strongest effect on human skin are those of the caterpillars of certain flannel moths. These hairs are scattered among those of the normal wiglike coat. In Brazil the larvae are known as *bizos de fuero* ("fire beasts"), in Paraguay as *iso jagua* ("jaguar worms"). The hollow hairs, which have a poison gland at the base, break off when touched and cause swelling, fever, and pain; in fact, sensitive persons may suffer a paralysis lasting for weeks.

Disagreeable, too, are the slug caterpillars, whose fleshy pegs are studded with spiny urticating hairs that often are a striking red or blue. These blister-producing organs cause pain of long duration, like that of bee stings. *Morpho* caterpillars also have poisonous hairs that produce eruptions on human skin.

The urticating hairs of caterpillars of the brush-footed butterflies (Nymphalidae) are long structures resembling feathers. As the caterpillar sits on the midrib of a leaf, its protective hairs surround the body like a circlet of radiating spikes. In addition, many saturniid caterpillars, especially American ones, often are both extraordinarily brightly colored and have urticating hairs or spines. Thus the elegantly branched spines of the

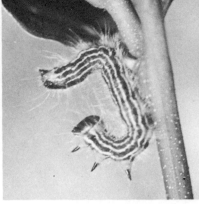

232/1
The singular alarming stance taken by the caterpillar of a prominent moth; this is its sole means of defense. Photograph.

232/2
The caterpillars of the exclusively American genus Automeris are studded with highly irritant, prickly bristles. Photograph.

232/3

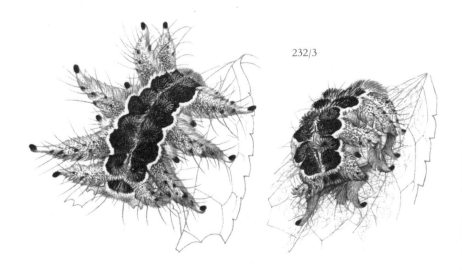

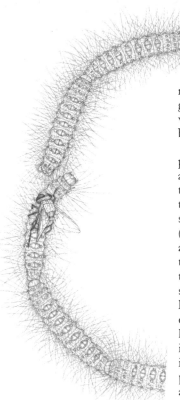

magnificent genus *Automeris* can cause dangerous wounds, for they contain threads whose toxic secretion is stored in vesicles beneath the dorsal integument.

Before pupation, a great many caterpillars pull their hair out in bunches with the mouth and weave it into their web or cocoon, where the blister-producing hairs retain their effectiveness. Inflammatory hairs hanging in the spun webs of processionary caterpillars (thaumetopoeids) are sometimes blown loose and wafted through the air in such masses that to walk through a wood inhabited by these caterpillars is almost impossible. The strikingly colored spots on the backs of these long-haired caterpillars are thickly set with cushions of tiny, easily broken urticating hairs (estimated to number about 630,000 per individual); these are able to cause dangerous inflammations in man and other animals— particularly in the eyes, throat, and stomach— and may retain their effectiveness for as long as ten years. [14/12; 255/4]

COMMUNAL LIVING

The processionary caterpillars, which in Europe reappear again and again in ravaging hordes, are famed for their communal way of living. By day they rest together in their gray-white webs suspended from trees. At night they leave in an uninterrupted column and feed, often making a joint march to another tree, thence to return in the morning to the old nest. Such close-ordered processions often are many yards long and are carried out either in single file or in tight ranks; in the latter case there usually is a single caterpillar at the head, two behind it, three in the next row, and so on, until there are some 15 to 20 marching abreast in the last row. [256/1, 2]

Each individual spins his way along continuously, and the collective strands form a silken path that enables the caterpillars to find their way back to the nest. Yet the continuity of the column is based on tactile stimuli— that is, on bodily contact—in that the head of one caterpillar constantly is touching the tail end of the one walking in front of it. If a gap arises, the ones in front wait until it is closed again. And if by means of artificial interference one maneuvers the whole train into a closed circle, so that the first caterpillar is touching the rear end of the last one, they will keep on marching round and round until they starve to death, which may take as long as a week, unless some piece of good fortune happens to interrupt the diabolical circle.

Pupation also is a communal event, taking place in the nest with one species and on the ground with another. In spite of all this, one cannot speak of these caterpillars as having a social life, for each individual does exactly the same things, and for himself alone.

This is also true of all other sociable caterpillars, such as those of the Australian spinning genera *Epicoma* and *Teara,* the Mexican pierid *Eucheira socialis,* and the American saturniids of the genus *Hylesia.* Like processionary caterpillars, these go forth together at night for feeding and mostly pupate in a communal web. *Morpho* caterpillars, too, live together in webs, but wrangle incessantly. And only too well known are the veils of webbing, often covering entire trees or bushes, of the lasiocampid *Malacosoma americana,* the arctiid *Hyphantria cunea,* and many Microlepidoptera (Tortricidae, Yponomeutidae). [14/10]

Numerous species are sociable only in their youth. On the contrary, Indo-Australian saturniids, such as *Opodiphthera* and *Caligula,* do not assemble until just before pupation, and then weave their cocoons together in piles.

Something akin to a division of labor is seen in caterpillars of the lilac leaf-miner moth (*Gracillaria syringella*). These caterpillars, lacking legs until after the second or third molt, hatch from clutches of eggs laid on the undersides of leaves and eat their way into the plant tissue as a closely-knit group, making a shallow mine. When the leaf has been eaten empty, they all travel together one night to a new one; here, some again bore their way in, while the others work for an hour or two first rolling the leaf up by means of silken threads and then closing off this box at both ends. Only the lower epidermis of the leaf serves as food. Later, as necessity arises, other leaves are treated similarly.

CATERPILLAR CRAFTSMEN

The ability to make silken threads by means of a glandular secretion that hardens at once on exposure to air plays a role in the life of all caterpillars. The silken thread that flows from the mouth may serve as a means of progression; many smaller Lepidoptera haul themselves aloft on it or rise simply by eating it up continuously. Peculiar and at the same time admirable is the technique of certain geometrids, which sit at rest for hours at a time with the body sticking out rigidly into the air. By spinning one or a few threads between the mouth and the nearest point of support, they fasten themselves securely in their perhaps somewhat strained position.

Further, silken pathways or resting surfaces are spun on leaves, giving the legs a firmer hold; some caterpillars do this uninterruptedly throughout their whole life, but most do so only when it is time for molting. The feeding pathways of leaf-mining species frequently are lined entirely with silk, and many species that dwell in the ground or within bark construct webbed tunnels. The spinning of some caterpillars can be extremely troublesome to man. Caterpillars of the Mediterranean flour moth, *Anagasta (Ephestia) kühniella* (Pyralidae), for example, live in flour mills and by their spinning clog the milling machinery.

Among noteworthy protective structures are the nests in which caterpillars of the pierid *Aporia* spend the winter. These nests are formed from leaves whose stalks are spun together so firmly that the leaves cannot fall even after they have wilted. The same "prophetic" instinct is shown similarly by other caterpillars (especially saturniids) in the preparation of cocoons suspended from or among leaves; and it is manifested just as astoundingly by those caterpillars that, contrariwise, bite their support part way through and later fall to the ground with it.

A great many species inhabit typical shelters made of one or more leaves that they gradually consume; some of these containers are left open, and others are closed. The leaves may be pulled together or rolled up with the active assistance of the caterpillar or solely through the increasing tension of the fresh silken thread, which shortens as it dries out. Thus the leaf margins are curled in or pulled together more and more as additional threads are spun between them. A beautiful example is given by the little caterpillar of the tortricid *Ancylis mitterbacheriana,* which stretches short silken bands across the leaf rib in the form of a ladder; like little bundles of muscle, these soon pull the leaf together.

Many caterpillars roll a leaf up only at the edge or roll up only a portion that has been delimited by incisions. The leaf-mining caterpillars of *Lithocolletis* cause infoldings of the epidermis (pleated mines) along the course of the feeding passage by spinning short threads. In northern regions, the *Colias* caterpillar sits on the midrib of a leaf and folds it together overhead at night and during cold weather. It does this by spinning a dense circle of silk strands around itself on the surface of the leaf. When the silk shrinks and the leaf folds up, the two halves of the silken

ring also are brought together and form a closure against wind and cold.

An original sort of house is built by the little caterpillar of the tortricid *Evetria resinella,* which feeds on the bark of pine twigs. From the indigestible excreted portions of the bark, mixed with resin collected from the tree, a rounded shelter ("resin gall") is shaped around a twig, the bark of which serves as the source of the first food. After the caterpillar has overwintered, it adds a second chamber to the dwelling and, now feeding on resin, deposits its excrement in the extra room.

Noctuid caterpillars (*Calymma, Coccidophaga*) that eat fruit-tree scale insects (Coccidae) make transportable houses out of the scales of their victims. Within portable cases and bags, formed of the most varied substances, live the caterpillars and in some cases even the flightless female adults of several families. Those casebearers (Coleophoridae) that mine in the green parts of plants have a simple method: they bite off the bit of leaf that contains their mine, make a case from which only the head and the thorax with its legs protrude, and carry the case with them. They keep on eating their way back into leaves as far as their case permits. The case occasionally is fastened with silk to a leaf.

Other coleophorids have bags of webbing that are oval, irregular, or pistol-shaped. Often parchmentlike, they may be coated with grains of sand or built out of bits of plants, even seed pods. The cases of the almost exclusively South American family Mimallonidae, spun together from various materials such as bits of leaves or even from their own flattened and externally polished excreta, are each suspended freely by a strong thread, which is bitten off when the caterpillar is disturbed or wishes to change location.

Best known are the bags of the bagworms (Psychidae), which usually hang from plants, rocks, and other objects, and look like bundles of conifer needles, straws, or bits of wood. Basically these are silken sheaths spun by the caterpillars; their form is various, and may even be that of a snail-like spiral. Their outer surface is covered densely in a characteristic manner with many kinds of materials, frequently even with snail shells. Indeed it is less the type of objects used than their arrangement that is typical of the individual species. Some bags lack the outer decorations and consist only of woven silk; these hang like balloons from a stalk. All the shelters have at least an opening from which the caterpillar can protrude head and thorax when it feeds or walks about. Additions to the house are made here. At the threat of danger, during

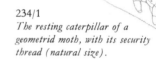

234/1
The resting caterpillar of a geometrid moth, with its security thread (natural size).

234/2
The caterpillar of a leaf roller moth underneath its "silken muscle fibers" (enlarged 2×).

diapause, and before pupation, the shelter is spun fast to a support. [207/1; 250/1-9]

PUPAL SHELTERS

The ability of caterpillars to spin acquires a special significance at the time of pupation. Even in the ground, in passageways in wood or bark, in leaf mines, or in galls, pupae rarely lie within their chambers without any supplement. Instead they are suspended from at least a few threads or are separated from the surrounding walls by a lining of silk. To an even greater extent, caterpillars weave webs typical of the species before pupation; these may be freely visible or hidden away, even in the interior of plants and treetrunks. The webs may be loose, wide-meshed, and of indefinite form, or they may be dense or even extremely hard; further, they may consist of two or more layers, loose outside and firm within.

The pupae of certain arctiid moths lie among a few threads, though more or less concealed among leaves, and the pericopines sway freely among the branches on a single thread, like a spider in its web. The pupal cradle of certain gracillariids looks like a delicate curtain, and that of geometrids of the genus *Urapteryx* is similar, but firmer and more mixed with leaves.

Frequently the web is strengthened with a variety of materials, especially the caterpillar's own hairs. Usually these are used rather inconspicuously, but the stiff, sharp hairs of the lasiocampid *Gonometa* are stuck into the cocoon in such a way that it resembles a hedgehog with the spines on end. In many flannel moths, a special protection is afforded by blister-producing "wig hairs," which are spun into the cocoon in a regular series of curls, like a coiffure.

Many notodontid larvae that pupate on treetrunks gnaw their shelter halfway into the bark or wood and, combining the chewed-off material with webbing and solidified saliva, form an outer vault that becomes almost as hard as stone. For the most part the inner surface of the cocoon also is covered with secretion that often hardens as though it had been polished; frequently this material saturates the webbing and gives it its customary brown color. Yet in many species the silken thread has a beautiful color in itself.

In general much variety and frequently great beauty is displayed in the color, structure, and form of the cocoon. Certain limacodid caterpillars decorate their pupal shelters with delicate designs that make them look like little birds' eggs. The basic form is an

oval one, yet often the cocoons are modified into the shapes of spindles, boats, or pears. They may be closed completely or left open at one or both ends. A structural variant is employed by the nolines (family Arctiidae), which first spin the wall of their boat-shaped cocoon and then add the roof.

The substance of all these shelters may look not only like silk, but also like leather or paper, and the outer surface may be fibrous, almost paper-smooth, or, rarely, ribbed lengthwise. For example, the cocoon of the Madagascan *Argema mittrei* has a metallic, silver-white gloss and is perforated like a sieve or, in some specimens, is even netlike, as is always the case with a few other saturniids, such as *Caligula* or *Cricula*. The cocoons of *Trichostibas* (family Yponomeutidae) of tropical America, only about 0.8 inch long, consist entirely of the most delicate white, waxy, or black network, and festoons of them are worn as adornment about the neck by natives. These beautiful cocoons are particularly surprising in that they open below in an unobstructed tube of the same weave, from which the shed skin of the caterpillar drops at pupation, and in that they are suspended from a many-stranded strong thread often of an improbable length.

One can hardly imagine what it requires, when swaying freely in the air at the end of a thread, to spin a cocoon of definite form and complex structure. The caterpillar begins the task by forming a ring that in the completed wide-meshed cocoon remains clearly visible. In the great Indian silkworm *Antheraea mylitta* the suspension is of a highly original form, being constituted of a long stalk formed of threads and secretion and being as hard as wood; the stalk is wrapped ringwise about the branch above. The bag-like cocoons of other species of this genus, as well as those of *Callosamia,* hang from simple strands of spun silk, although most are also attached firmly by being interwoven with leaves. [14/8; 30/3; 246; 273/1-14; 274/6]

CATERPILLAR SILK

Concerning man's use of caterpillar silk—that is to say, natural silk—a great novel could be written. The source of the famed "Mizteca silk" of the ancient Aztecs was the blinding-white nests, as much as a yard long and spun by 80 to 100 caterpillars, of the Mexican lasiocampid *Eutachyptera psidii,* though the cocoons of saturniids *(Callosamia, Telea, Rothschildia)* no doubt were used frequently also. The cocoons of a few other lasiocampids are usable, too, namely

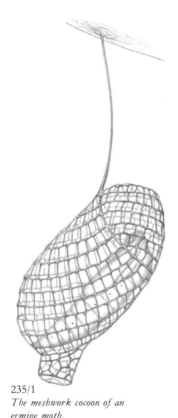

235/1
The meshwork cocoon of an ermine moth.

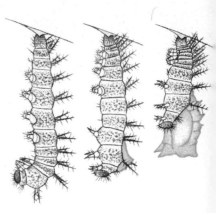

those of *Pachypasa otus* in the central and eastern Mediterranean region, as well as those of certain species of the genus *Borocera* in Madagascar. In fact, the former's silk was valued highly in ancient times, but is less well-known today, and cocoons of the latter still are worked up into silken fabrics by the Madagascans, although doing so presupposes the no-doubt-tedious removal of the countless sharp hairs that have been woven into it by the caterpillars.

Important sources of silk in Africa are caterpillars of the genus *Anaphe,* which belong to the processionary silkworms. Unlike many other communal caterpillars, these do not assemble until just before pupation. They construct three-layered nests up to 20 inches long and a pound in weight. The innermost layer gives the best silk. The threads cannot be reeled off, it is true, because they have been interwoven into a tangle by the spinning of many individuals. Nevertheless the silk is valued because it is better than other kinds for many industrial purposes. From it are manufactured sewing silk and certain textiles, such as satin.

The cocoons of some giant silkworms, or saturniids, have achieved great importance in the manufacture of silk. Whereas American species have been used only for experimental attempts, the few European ones seem hardly suitable, and most African saturniids pupate in the ground without a web, several Asiatic species are employed successfully in silk making. The quality of silk produced by these species varies, however, and the yield is often small because the mass rearing of these species is either impossible or difficult.

The cocoons of the gigantic *Attacus* caterpillars are open at both ends and therefore produce only short lengths of thread, so that the fibers cannot be wound on reels, but have to be combed and spun like wool or cotton; and though the thread is strong, it is somewhat hard and lusterless. Similarly the cocoons of *Philosamia cynthia* consist only of short threads, but are the source of the durable and water-resistant "eria" silk, one of the most important Indian products of this type. This moth was introduced successfully into both America and Europe, but no silk industry has been established from it on either continent. [211/1]

The Indonesian *Cricula* caterpillars give beautiful yellow silk, but are not sufficiently productive, and the amounts of silk obtained from the Indian *Actias selene* are similarly small. From the Chinese *Eriogyna pyretorum,* more silk is gotten, the amount estimated to be about 70,000 pounds a year. This species is of economic significance chiefly for the manufacture of fishing lines from silk taken directly from the silk glands of the caterpillars.

Of much greater importance is the genus *Antheraea,* which is distributed throughout all Asia. From its cocoons the highly valued "tussah" silk is obtained. It was forbidden under pain of death to export eggs, caterpillars, pupae, or adult moths of the original purely Japanese species *Antheraea yamamay,* but in 1860 a French consul managed to send a number of eggs to France; and shortly thereafter a bunch of them, concealed in a walking stick, reached Belgium. As a result, *Antheraea* soon was cultured all over Southern Europe, yet here the silk remained of inferior value, no doubt on account of climatic reasons.

Of comparatively greater significance for the silk industry than all the "wild silks" hitherto mentioned is the true silkworm, or "mulberry worm," *Bombyx mori* (family Bombycidae). It is raised in many places, and different races have been developed by breeding. Its white or yellow cocoon can be reeled off into a single thread ranging in length from many hundred yards up to more than two miles. The resulting silk is still indispensable today in spite of the ever-more-numerous synthetic products. The true silkworm, the economically most important of all insects, was in olden days the foundation of the financial flowering of various Asiatic, Oriental, and Arabian peoples, some of them at times practically wallowing in the luxury of the silk trade. It is not strange that the silkworm had an influence on political developments unmatched by that of hardly any other animal.

Presumably the silkworm's ancestral home was in the Himalayas. It was cultured as early as about 2600 B.C. in China, whose silk monopoly had set capital punishment as the penalty for the export of living material, a penalty that did not prevent the silkworm's gradual spread. In the fourth century, eggs were brought to Buchara, a medieval Islamic center of culture and trade, and, in fact, were transported there in the headdress of a Chinese princess who married into the country. Descendants from this stock reached Rome somewhat later, under the emperor Justinian, and silk thus entered Western commerce. [256/4; 273/15-20]

THE PUPAE

Most butterfly caterpillars do not make cocoons, but form naked pupae that are

236/1
In Asia the silkworm moth has been one of the most important domestic animals since ancient times, and the silk obtained from its cocoons is still unmatched today. (→ 256/4C)

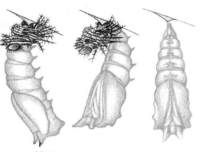

anchored to a little spun cushion by hooklets on the more or less pointed rear end (cremaster). They are fastened to a support, vertically or horizontally, by a strengthened thread encircling the middle of the body (girdled pupae) or else simply are suspended head downward (free-hanging pupae). The latter, frequently decorated magnificently with silver or gold, belong chiefly to the brush-footed butterflies (Nymphalidae). Over and over, they solve a vexatious problem in a simple way.

In this process of pupation, which signifies the final larval molt, the skin is burst in the neck region and gradually pushed backward, while beneath it the still-soft, damply glistening body appears as a rather obscurely delineated pupa that only attains the final form and coloration after an interval of slow hardening. Now, the caterpillar that is transforming into a free-hanging pupa is holding onto its silken cushion with the anal prolegs, so that at the end of the act of pupation, when the shed skin has been pushed almost all the way back, the moment would have to come when the still-delicate, soft-skinned pupa would drop out and squash on the ground. But this disaster is avoided by the caterpillar clamping the crumpled mass of skin firmly between two of its abdominal body rings until its rear end has been reanchored, outside the cast skin, into the silken cushion. [274/1]

Just before they pupate, most caterpillars get somewhat smaller, lose the beauty and freshness of their colors—in which condition certain species grow lethargic and rest for weeks or even months—and undertake instinctive acts that make possible or facilitate the emergence of the future adult. When ready to emerge, the adult makes its way out of the cocoon mostly by means of a fluid that dissolves or softens the spun fabric, frequently assisted by special hooks at the base of the fore wings.

Often, the caterpillar has constructed a closing device that cannot be broken into from without, but that yields under pressure from within. With coleophorids, or casebearers, this is a simple or Y-shaped cleft, placed, oddly enough, at the end of the bag opposite the caterpillar's head, so that the caterpillar inside has to turn around before it pupates, if the moth-to-be is not to die. The cocoon of a flannel moth has a round lid that either is wholly unnoticeable or scarcely visible from outside, but that is easy to raise from within. And particularly noteworthy is the closure of stiff bowed bristles that are pressed forward into a point as though under the tension of a spring, such as are seen in the cocoons of certain giant silkworm moths.

Just before they pupate, many caterpillars that bore in wood, particularly sesiids, direct their feeding passage toward the exterior, leaving intact only a paper-thin layer of bark or else breaking all the way through and closing the opening by spinning a lid. In certain African and Australian bagworms the preparations made by the female caterpillar go so far as to place one of the bits of wood that adorn the bag in such a position that later on it may provide a sitting place for some male that comes to mate with the female, who remains inside the shelter.

Not all butterflies and moths wait until they are mature adults to free themselves from their "prison," but instead may push themselves halfway or almost entirely out shortly beforehand, while still pupae. Such creatures have equipment suitable for the task. Thus the pupae of many Microlepidoptera or of certain notodontids, which are lying in leaf-mines, bore their way out of their firm shelters with the pointed front end of the body, assisted by rotary movements. And the pupa of *Endromis* works its way out of the spun fabric by means of a sawlike comb on the head, helped by rows of spines on the abdomen and by the thorny cremaster at the rear.

Still other pupae that force themselves out in this way not only have wreaths of hooks and spines, but are exceedingly motile besides. Indeed it is the more primitive families of borers, such as castniids, aegeriids, cossids, and hepialids, that do so. It is not just before the emergence of the adult that the pupae of certain aegeriids and hepialids begin to move in this way, but from the beginning they push themselves upward or downward in the vertical tube the caterpillar has spun inside the wood or in the ground, in whichever direction may be required by their humidity needs. Such pupae have a stretched-out shape, and in those of the hepialids the limbs stick out separately besides, whereas in aegeriids and cossids the appendages are not freed from one another until just before emergence. [248/24, 28; 273/2, 3]

Indeed, almost all lepidopterous pupae are of the obtected type, without free appendages, and are able to move at most a few of the abdominal segments, an ability that usually is manifested, however, only when they are disturbed. Exceptional is the reaction to light of the South American butterflies of the genus *Ageronia*. When illuminated they raise themselves into a horizontal stance from the vertical position in which they ordinarily hang in the darkness. [274/2]

Among certain papilionids and pierids, the environment influences pupal coloration. A pupa hanging in the vegetation is green, for example, whereas the same species on a rock is colored gray, a contrast that in extraordinary cases has even found expression on the opposite sides of a single individual. Dry and rainy seasons, as well as summer and winter generations, may also result in different pupae within a single species, and in the tropics may even cause striking differences in form.

Many freely suspended pupae of the butterflies display expansions, outgrowths, combs, horns, spines, or even threads. Frequently their colors and designs are grand devices for concealment. To treat adequately the origin of so great a degree of individual specificity for what is a mere intermediate stage—the pupa—would fill a book. Even within one and the same family the pupa may differ in form, being adapted in various ways to differing situations.

Those pupae that lead a concealed existence are as a rule unspecialized in body parts, cylindrical in shape, and often brown or black. The surface texture may vary from rough to as smooth as china; and a really smooth pupa may be impossible for such organisms as ants to grasp. Rarely the pupa is set thickly with short hairs; somewhat more often it is powdered white or with a yellowish or bluish shade.

In many sphingid pupae, a free-lying proboscis sheath produces a fantastic effect; in species whose trunk is especially long, the sheath may be curved into a high arch or even rolled up into several turns, though in any event it always is much shorter than the tongue of the moth-to-be. Many hesperiids, too, have pupae with a separated proboscis sheath, which also is irregularly bent; in the American species *Calpodes ethlius* it lies extended and well-protected in the tip of a canna leaf rolled into a funnel by the caterpillar. [14/7; 33/2; 212/3; 250/10D; 253/1D; 256/4A; 273/5, 17; 274; 364/12C]

The period of pupal rest may vary greatly in duration, from a minimum of a few days to a maximum of many years. The maximum duration is not customary for any one species, but it is a special device that enables certain individuals to survive during severe environmental conditions. Shortly before emergence, the pupal skin usually becomes soft and fragile, and in the more brightly colored pupae the coloration and design of the future butterfly can be seen clearly. The time of day when emergence occurs is not defined in many species, but in others is set precisely, almost to the hour.

ENEMIES

The enemies of these insects are legion, most dangerous among them the tachina flies (Tachinidae) and innumerable parasitic wasps. But caterpillar diseases, such as break out especially when conditions are too moist, also may have a decimating effect. And to a great extent man has entered the picture, not only by combatting the many pests of cultivated plants, but also through the more intensive use of the land and the accompanying destruction of food plants and other necessary conditions of life for many species.

FLIES, MOSQUITOES, AND GNATS ORDER DIPTERA

(Members of this group that develop in water, including mosquitoes, are treated in the section on "Water Insects.")

Aristotle named these insects Diptera, meaning "two-winged insects," and that is the name of the order today. Instead of the usual rear pair of wings, the flies, which include mosquitoes and gnats, have two little vibratory clubs. These act as organs of equilibrium. Perhaps they also stimulate the movement of the wings, which can start to beat at extreme rates without any preparation; frequently there are as many as 300 wingbeats a second, and a maximum of about 2,000 has been recorded for the tiny biting midges of the genus *Forcipomyia*.

The rapid wingbeat produces the familiar buzzing sound, and in German the fat blowflies (Calliphoridae) are, in fact, called *Brummer* ("buzzers"). The buzzing songs of mosquitoes often would sound almost sweet if they were not so frequently perceived as a threat. Such tones are produced not only by the wing membranes cutting the air, but also by the vibration of the thoracic plates, which move elastically in response to the rapid contraction of the wing muscles. The wing muscles may contribute as much as one-third of the body weight. Members of the order Diptera are not only very speedy fliers, but also are unusually skillful in steering their way.

There are, to be sure, flightless species that have mere stubs of wings or no wings at all. These are the species that live on islands and mountain peaks exposed to strong winds, that

239/1
Flies, with only two wings, can start off like the wind and are highly skilled at steering; their wings beat up to about 200 times per second (the rate for mosquitoes is more than 500 times per second), while their maximum velocity is about 62 miles per hour (the velocity of a few species is several times this value). Flower flies, like the species illustrated here, also like to do aerial acrobatics, such as making occasional somersaults within a hundredth of a second (enlarged 2×).

dwell in caves or within loose soil, or that live as parasites in or on the bodies of other living things. Flight is of no use or is a disadvantage to their way of life.

The eyes of flies, too, have experienced a particularly high degree of evolution. Anyone who has seen the horsefly's powerful hemispheres gleaming with magnificent structural colors, can hardly fail to be impressed. There are flies whose entire head seems to be all eyes. Almost always these compound eyes are larger in the males, often so large they make contact with one another. To the males the sense of sight is of particular importance for finding the females and for detecting rivals. Of course, good vision is crucial for species that hunt other insects; in them the upper-front part of the eyes is composed of different, larger facets than the rest, and this increases their visual capacity. Predators and good fliers, in particular, also have dorsal ocelli, or simple eyes, but not such species as crane flies.

A sense of color has been demonstrated in flies, but so has red blindness. On the other hand, experiments with houseflies, which do not visit flowers, showed a striking preference for red. In the species *Musca domestica,* whose domesticity is of worldwide renown, scientists have observed a herd instinct that may depend strongly on the optical sense. It seems almost as if the individual flies in a room, for example, constantly keep each other in view, for they immediately join a companion that discovers a source of food. In this way houseflies are in general quick to find food that often is invisible.

Food Habits

Diptera frequently find and test their food by probing with the bottom of the forelegs and the tip of the proboscis, the principal bearers of the sense of taste; these organs are subjected to particularly thorough and vigorous cleaning by these insects, which, in general, polish themselves regularly. The mouthparts, which differ greatly in length among different genera, are of the sucking or piercing-sucking types; in the former case they frequently have a spongelike cushion at the end of the proboscis.

Generally the intake of food is facilitated or made possible by a salivary secretion the insect pours over it. Just as the females of many blood-sucking species require blood for ripening their eggs, many nectar-drinking flower flies (family Syrphidae), have to eat pollen for the same reason, and possess a mouth

that is especially constructed for pulverizing it. In certain species that are very short-lived or that are supplied with sufficient reserve foodstuffs, as are gadflies and warble flies, the mouth is vestigial.

In general, the insects of this order seem to have great need of water. Thus the body weight of a housefly falls by about one-third during about ten hours of evaporation in a dry room. The senses concerned with the detection of moisture are almost always situated in the antennae in insects; oddly enough, the feet, which are sensitive to taste, do not seem responsive to water except on contact.

Flies eat almost any liquid or semiliquid organic material, from decomposing substances to nectar and the honeydew of aphids. Among the most astonishing performances in the life of insects is the oral predation of *Harpagomyia* mosquitoes (family Culicidae) on the ant *Cremastogaster.* The mosquito places itself in an ant's way in such a manner that the ant has to run beneath it. At this instant the mosquito begins to drum with forelegs and antennae on the ant's head and thorax. This induces the ant to let a drop of liquid food exude from the mouth, and the waylaying mosquito imbibes it. Mostly the mosquitoes stand with extended legs on treetrunks in the middle of a path followed by the ants and stop those descending from above, where they usually have sucked their fill of the honeydew of scale insects. If an ant tries to force its way past, it is belabored and often turned roughly about until it has paid its tribute.

Odd, too, is the way the bee lice (Braulidae) get their food. These very tiny louselike flies cling to the bodies of honeybees and feed from their mouths. They lay their eggs on the honeycomb, and the hatching larvae bore through it to the honey, which they eat along with bits of dead animal and plant material, feces, and other detritus in the bees' nest.

The milichiid flies of the genus *Desmometopa* keep watch on spiders and predatory insects, including predatory flies such as asilids, and when the hunters have made a kill, the flies come up to lick blood from the wounds of the slaughtered prey. In addition to substances from plants or dead animals, certain Diptera also suck the blood of living insects or of living warm-blooded or cold-blooded vertebrates. Species of the most various families rely exclusively on the sucking of blood; among the many that depend on warm blood are the notorious mosquitoes.

The mosquitoes and many others of the Diptera that develop in water are treated in

241/1

The marking pattern of noctuid moths. The wings are divided into basal, medial, and marginal fields by inner and outer transverse lines, which ordinarily are double and serrated. The medial field contains three spots, namely the kidney-shaped spot (the largest), adjacent to it the ring-shaped spot, and below it, abutting against the inner transverse line, the little peg-shaped blotch. In the marginal field are the toothed undulant lines, which often form a W, and externally, before the fringe is reached, is a marginal line composed of small half-moons. A more or less obvious darkening of the medial field is known as the central shadow. All these designations are of great importance in scientific descriptions and hence characterizing the species. (Greatly enlarged.) Photograph.

241/2

A blue underwing moth pursued by a bat (enlarged 2×).

PAGE 242

242/1–25

Noctuid moths, many of them species with contrasting colors on the hind wings. (24) Male and female of the "black witch" (Erebus odora), a species that in summertime migrates from South America as far north as Canada. (1 to 19 somewhat reduced; 20 to 25 0.6 natural size.) Photographs.

PAGE 243

243/1–13

In the family of geometrid moths refined markings and delicate pastel colors predominate (natural size). Photograph.

243/14–24

Three families of moths. (14–17) Tussock moths, which have wingless females in the genus Orgyia (14–15) and to which belong the gypsy moth (16) and the nun moth (17), which are dreaded pests of trees. (18–19) Tent caterpillar moths; (18) males and females of Dendrolimus pini, a species that now and again appears in great numbers as an enemy of coniferous forests. (20–24) Prominent moths, the largest of their species at the top (0.7 natural size). Photograph.

PAGES 244 AND 245

244/1–245/2

Giant silkworm moths. (244/1–9) Central wing markings of the giant

silkworm moths; the translucent windowlike spots are formed as the result of attenuation of the coat of scales, and hence are bits of bare wing membrane, which here is clearly green in one species. (245/1) A pair of an American species; below, a female emerging from the cocoon. With the odor-dispensing apparatus at the rear end, these females attract their males from distances of several thousand yards. (245/2) The atlas moth, the largest species and, in respect to surface area, the largest of all insects (1 to 9 enlarged; 244/10 and 245/1 somewhat reduced; 245/2 natural size).

PAGES 246 AND 247

Phases during flight from the cocoon by males of the comet-tailed giant silkworm moths. The females' wings have much shorter and broader tails. Species shown: Argema mittrei, Actias isis, Actias leto (somewhat reduced).

PAGES 248 AND 249

248/1–12

The cut of the hawk moth wing reveals the great flight capacity of these insects. The thorax, the fore wings, and often the abdomen also (in species where it remains visible at rest) have concealing coloration, but the hind wings and the abdomen too frequently bear colors that contrast, as is particularly striking in the eyed hawk moths (5) (0.6 natural size). Photograph.

248/13–29

(13–15) Slug-caterpillar moths (Limacodidae). (16–17) Bagworm moths, males; the females are wingless. (18–20) Carpenterworm moths, whose caterpillars bore in trees. (21) Ghost moth. (22–29) Clearwing moths, whose larvae also bore in wood and in plant stems and whose pupae, before emergence of the adult, use rings of spines to help them force their way out of exits prepared in advance in these tunnels by the caterpillars; frequently these moths resemble wasps (somewhat enlarged). Photograph.

PAGE 250

250/1–9

The species-specific dwellings of the bagworm moth caterpillars are remarkably diverse. (9) An Indonesian species, which skeletonizes a leaf by feeding in circles. It then excises such pieces and builds its rosette-shaped home with them (natural size). Photograph.

250/10A–E

The codling moth, notorious among fruit farmers. (A) Caterpillar; (B) egg, on a leaf; (C) caterpillar

letting itself down on a thread in order to pupate; (D) pupa, in its cocoon under bark; (E) adult, beautifully disguised when at rest (somewhat enlarged).

PAGE 251

251/1–48

Various families of Microlepidoptera. (1–8) Pyralidae: (1) Wax moth, which causes damage in bee hives; (3) corn borer; (4) meal moth, unwelcome in the household; (8) Indian meal moth, distributed throughout the world. (9 and 10) Plume moths. (11–24) Leaf roller moths, including notorious pests of trees; (14) codling moth. (25) Glyphipterygid moth. (26–32) Gelechiid moths; (32) Endrosis lacteella, a nuisance to housekeepers. (33–34) Casebearer moths, whose caterpillars construct artful dwellings. (35–36) Adult leaf blotch miners; (36) the Azalea leaf miner. (37) Cosmopterygid moth. (38) Ermine moth. (39) Argyresthia moth. (40–41) Diamondback moths. (42–43) Clothes moths; (43) webbing clothes moth. (44–46) Fairy moths. (47) Shield bearer moth. (48) Nepticulid moth, the smallest of all Lepidoptera (enlarged 1.25×). Photographs.

PAGE 252

252/1–7

Microlepidoptera. (1) Yucca moth inserting a ball of pollen into the stigma of the yucca blossom. (2) Mandibulate moth. (3) Leaf blotch miner. (4) Momphid moth, with iridescent spots formed of bundles of erect scales. (5) Argyresthia moth, gleaming like pure gold, in its peculiar resting position, in which it stands on its head and lays the hind legs against the body. (6) Tortricid moth; the interwoven markings, formed of scales with a metallic gloss, enable the leaf rollers to make a splendid impression. (7) Plume moth. (1 and 5 to 7 enlarged 4×; 2 to 4 enlarged 6×.)

PAGE 253

253/1 A–D

Symbiosis of a blue butterfly with ants. The butterfly has laid an egg on thyme near the nest (beneath a stone) of certain ants. At first the young caterpillar feeds on the flowers (A, beneath the resting butterfly), but later is transported into the nest and fed there by the ants (B). For their part the ants greedily lick the caterpillar's secretions from its

back (C). The larva also eats ant brood and then pupates in the nest (D), protected and watched over by the ants until its development into a butterfly has been concluded (enlarged).

PAGES 254 AND 255

254/1–14

Eggs of butterflies and moths are natural art forms. During embryonic development a number of them change color several times (4–6). (1–3) Three examples of egg clutches (greatly enlarged).

254/15–16

In its defense posture a prominent moth caterpillar (15) distorts its grotesque body, which has antlike forelegs; and the bristle-covered tussock moth caterpillar (16) spreads apart its dark black intersegments (natural size). Photograph.

254/17

Leaves bearing inscriptions made by the caterpillars of a leaf-miner moth; the widenings next to the mines are dying parts of the leaf (reduced).

255/1–11

Various caterpillar forms. (1) Hornworm with the caudal horn that is typical of the family. (2) Carpenterworm, a wood-feeder: a chitinous plate in the neck is characteristic of the more primitive forms. (3) Swallowtail; its differentiated shape and complex markings indicate a more highly specialized family, and the fleshy, extrusible, cervical forked horn (osmeterium) is a distinctive mark. (4) Nymphalid; the longitudinal rows of spines have arisen as modifications of bristle-bearing warts. (5) Geometrid, moving in the manner characteristic of the family; the number of abdominal legs (prolegs) is reduced. (6) Geometrid caterpillar at rest. (7) One of the few long-haired noctuid caterpillars, curled up in response to threatened danger. (8) Indian moon moth (a giant silkworm moth) caterpillar, sitting with the darker underside turned upward and thus producing a less solid impression in light coming from above; this "sphinx" posture is a defensive reaction often seen among hawk moth caterpillars (Sphingidae). (9) Pyralid letting itself down on a spun thread. (10) Underwing moth larva, typical of a caterpillar that snuggles close against the bark, with lateral fringes that soften the contour of its shadow and with prolegs of differing lengths. (11) Brassolid caterpillars whose protruding heads, with their horns, suggest snails (somewhat enlarged).

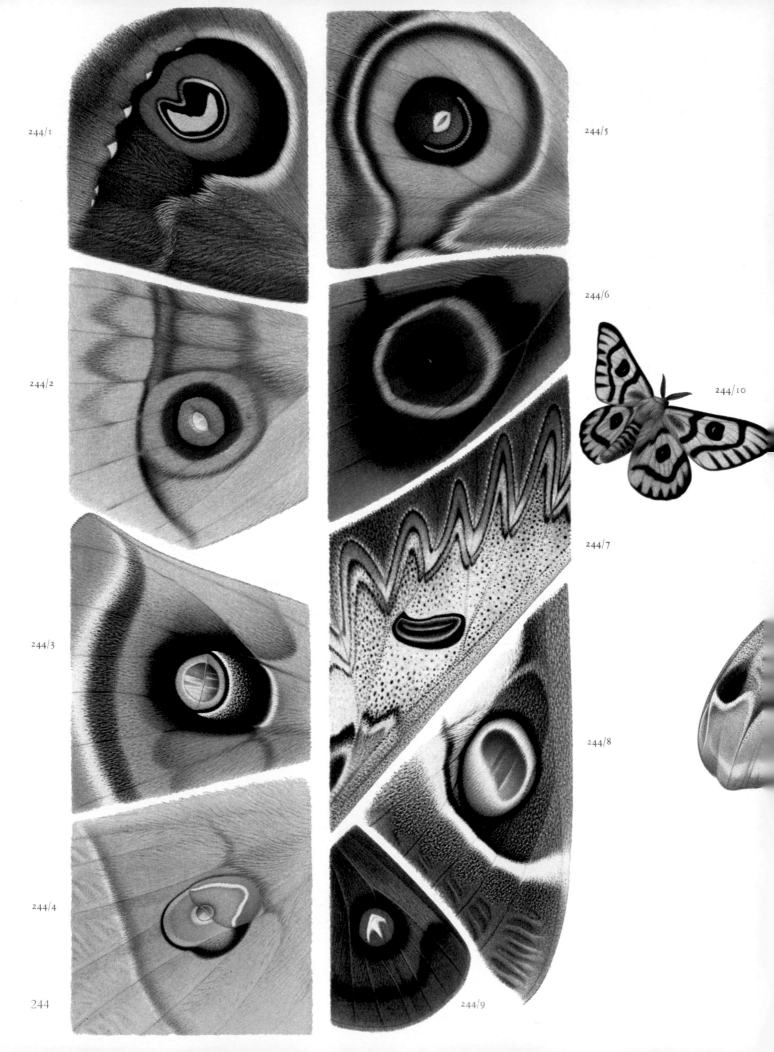

244/1

244/2

244/3

244/4

244

244/5

244/6

244/7

244/8

244/9

244/10

245/1

245/2

247/1   247/2

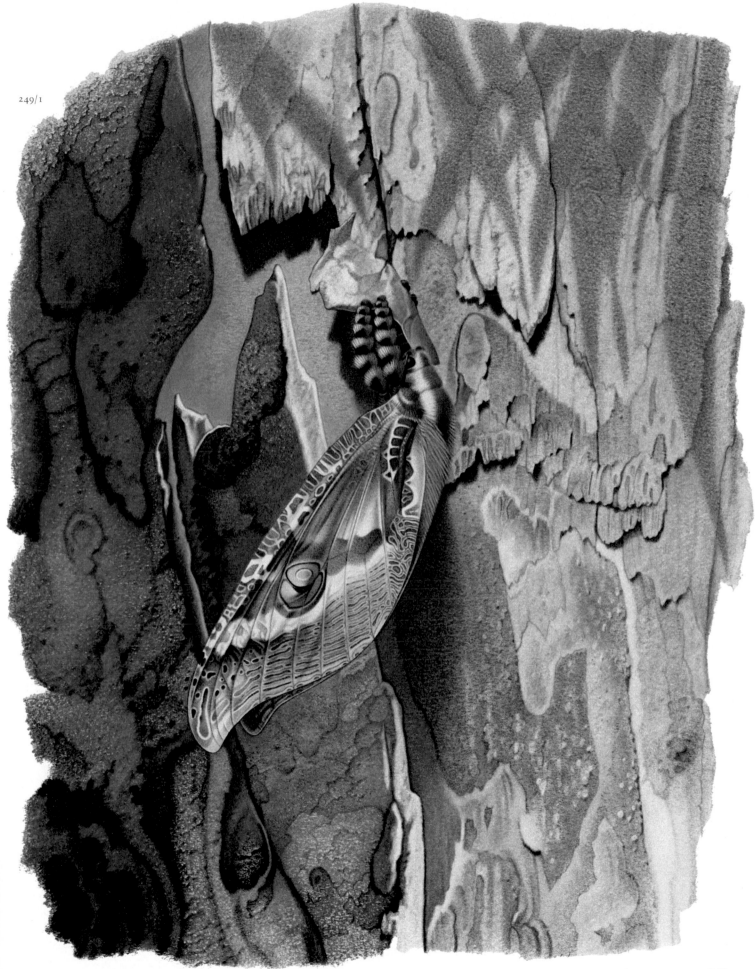

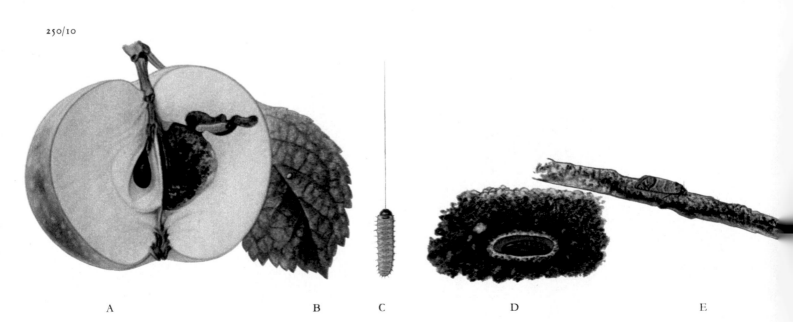

A   B   C   D   E

251

252/1

252/2

252/3

252/4

252/7

252/5

252/6

252

A

B

C

D

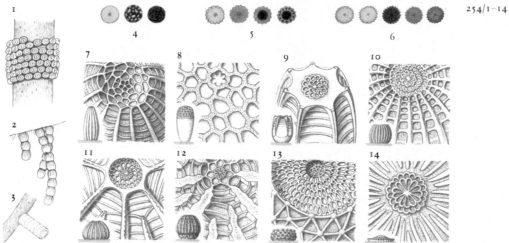

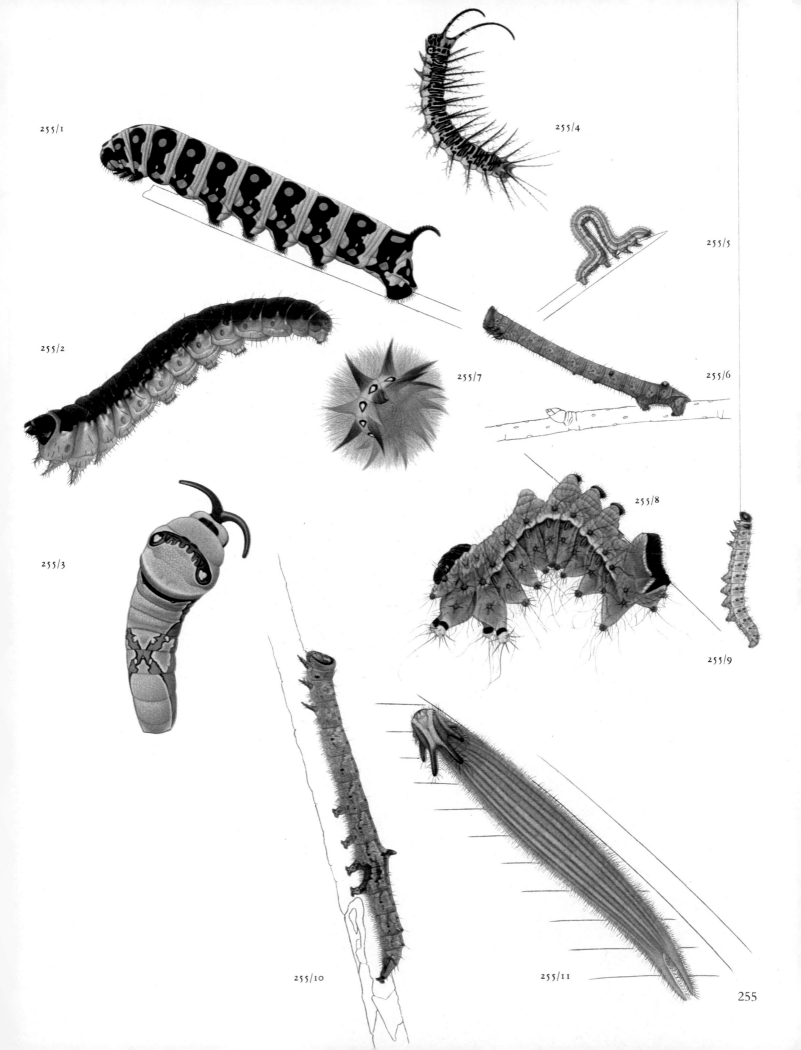

255/1

255/4

255/5

255/2

255/7

255/6

255/3

255/8

255/9

255/10

255/11

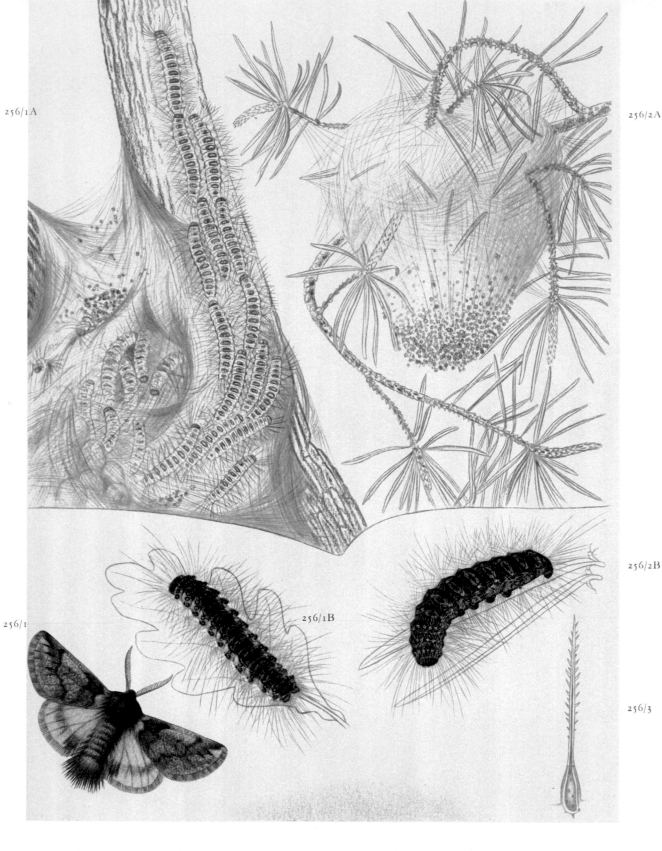

256/1A

256/2A

256/2B

256/1B

256/1

256/3

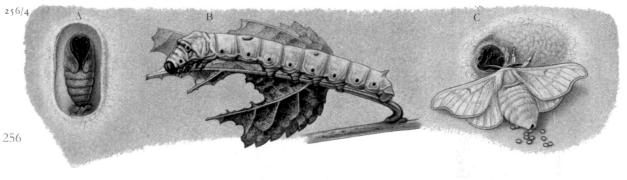

256/4   A   B   C

256

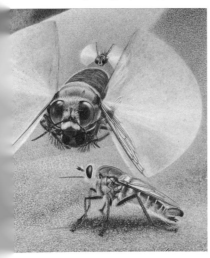

the section on "Water Insects." But two groups are worth mentioning here. One is the group Geosarginae among the soldier flies (Stratiomyidae), whose larvae at all stages live in and eat sap flowing from trees. The other includes those larvae from the families Calliphoridae and Phoridae that get their nourishment from insects that have fallen into the water contained in insectivorous plants (especially the pitcher plants *Nepenthes* and *Sarracenia*). Some of these fly larvae, which evidently are immune to the solvent effect of the digestive fluids of such plants, have gigantic hooks or other devices with which they make fast to the smooth walls of these tubes and jugs. [278/3, 4]

IMPORTANT GROUPS

The flies number about 100,000 species in over 100 families. They have settled the entire globe, insofar as this is possible for insects. The order falls into two parts (suborders): the Orthorrhapha and the Cyclorrhapha. Members of the first group have antennae with more than three segments, larvae with a head or at least a jaw-bearing capsule, and pupae with free appendages (exarate pupae). The more highly specialized Cyclorrhapha have only three antennal segments, headless larvae, and encased (coarctate) pupae.

To the Orthorrhapha belong the delicate and lightly-built Nematocera, a group that includes crane flies, mosquitoes, and fungus gnats. Their slender body is borne by legs that, particularly in the crane flies (family Tipulidae), may be of unlikely length, thinness, and fragility. Frequently these legs are in part expanded by or edged with fringes of hairs. Apparently they function not only as legs but as gliding organs, as do the sometimes enormously extended or long-haired antennae.

The dancing flight of crane flies in the semidarkness of the wood or at dusk is a sight to see, whether it is a female scattering her eggs just above the ground or a company of males getting ready for mating higher up. The wings are a barely perceptible glimmer, and the widespread legs seem no more than detached fragments, just becoming visible now and then as they reflect the light. If the legs and perhaps the body are adorned with white spots and white tips or with glossy metallic scales and hairs, scarcely anything is visible in the deep shadows but these dancing points of light, giving the impression of flickering magic. [276/1–4; 99/8]

How diametrically opposite is the appearance of the snowflies *(Chionea),* though they

are from the same family. These wingless, almost spider-shaped creatures hop about on the snow in winter when the temperature is perhaps no more than 14° F (−10° C). Equally unusual are certain dark-winged fungus gnats *(Neosciara)* that dwell continuously in the darkness of caves. Although they have normally developed wings, they do not fly. They evade pursuit by running or jumping. Similar behavior also may be observed in cellar-dwelling groups of the same family (Fungivoridae) as the fungus gnats. [99/9]

Among the Orthorrhapha there also are a series of other families of flies, most of them grouped together as Brachycera, whose antennal segments are partly fused. Only a few can be mentioned here. Slender ichneumon-like flies (Xylophagidae) suck the sap of trees, and their larvae hunt immature insects and other small creatures in decaying wood. The flower-visiting soldier flies (Stratiomyidae) are mostly gorgeously colored. Broader and flatter in build than other groups, they rest their wings one above the other. They almost always are "armed" with two spines on the rear portion (scutellum) of the upper surface of the thorax. [276/5–7]

Best-known of the sunshine-loving bee flies (Bombyliidae) are the fat, furry *Bombylius* bee flies, which hover above flowers and plunge the long, rigid proboscis into them, and the short-trunked, black-marked bee flies *Anthrax* and *Hemipenthes*. Most bee flies have attractively spotted or shaded wings, and the anthracines in particular also have delicate body designs, most of which are formed by gleaming white or silver recumbent hairs. [49/25, 26; 276/9–14; 285/9]

Finally, there follows a series of bloodsucking families, whose representatives hunt other insects or bite man and other animals. The worst predators on insects are the robber flies (Asilidae) and mydas flies (Mydaidae), mostly rather large species of extended build and with the frons deeply depressed between the eyes. Some tropical species are over 2 inches long and rank among the largest of the Diptera. Hardly any insect is safe from these flying monsters, not even the big, well-armed bees and wasps, to which, oddly enough, certain robber flies show a deceptive resemblance, especially in flight. No doubt this affords them a certain degree of protection against birds, for many birds might well need to shy away from a wasp sting, but not from the poisonous beak of a robber fly, whose paralytic action is designed for the soft neck region of an insect. Like hawks, robber flies dive onto the back of their prey and, with their strong legs, hold such a creature as a

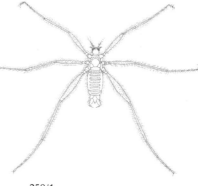

wasp far enough away from their own body for the short time necessary to paralyze the victim. [19/24; 49/27; 276/15–20; 278/1]

Graceful predators by contrast are many species of the long-legged flies (Dolichopodidae), some of which are skillful at running on the surface of the water; the dance flies (Empididae), which "dance" up and down in flight; the stiletto flies (Therevidae), many of which have pointed abdomens; and the shore flies (Ephydridae), small inhabitants of the water's edge. Shore flies of the genus *Ochthera* are equipped like a mantid with predatory shears. Some of the snipe flies (Rhagionidae) have become suckers of the blood of man and other animals. [276/22; 278/8]

Particularly hated by man are the horse-flies and deerflies (Tabanidae). The larger species, up to 1.2 inches long, leave bloody wounds, but molest man less than they do other mammals. Certain species may act as vectors of disease. It is the females that give the family its bad reputation. The males of all 2,500 species frequent flowers and do not bite. [277/1–4]

The second suborder, the Cyclorrhapha, falls into two divisions, the Aschiza and the Schizophora. These differ in the way the adults emerge from the hard puparium in which they are encased as pupae. The Aschiza simply shove a preformed lid off with their sturdy face, but the Schizophora use a special device, called a ptilinum, that is inflated and forced out through an arched cleft in the front of the head. Afterward, the ptilinum is retracted permanently.

In addition to a few families, such as the humpbacked flies (Phoridae), that are of interest because of the varied ways of life of their larvae, the Aschiza include the flower flies (Syrphidae), which are as well-known as they are lovely. These flies, many bearing wasplike designs and some even shaped like wasps, are frequently seen hovering in the air. Some members of the genus *Eristalis* resemble bees; some of the *Volucella*, bumblebees. *Volucella* species go through their development in the nests of bumblebees and wasps.

Whereas almost all of the approximately 4,000 species of flower flies frequent flowers and hence are of great usefulness in fertilizing them, the living habits of their larvae vary greatly. Some live in the ground, in carrion, dung, mud, plants, and fungi; others live in the nests of bees, wasps, and ants, where they feed on excrement or even on the brood; and still others live on plants, principally sucking out the juices of aphids. [111/1, 4; 277/5–13]

The second division, the Schizophora, comprises the many families of the "true flies" (Muscaria) and of the louse flies and bat flies (Pupipara), the adults of which are parasitic. The almost countless species of these are divided among families so similar to one another that the number and position of the bristles frequently constitutes the only distinguishing sign for the specialist. Information about families that are parasitic as larvae or as adults is presented later. Here we mention only a few of the more important of the remaining families.

The little fruit flies (Trypetidae or Tephritidae) are striking because of their particularly beautiful wing designs. Among their larvae, which mine in all possible parts of plants, a few species have achieved ill repute as fruit maggots. These include the cherry maggot (*Rhagoletis cerasi*); the olive fruit fly (*Dacus oleae*); the Mediterranean fruit fly (*Ceratitis capitata*), which has invaded America; and the Queensland fruit fly (*Chaetodacus tryoni*). Wings with gorgeous designs also are borne by members of a few other related families, including most otitid flies (Otitidae), among which the Papuan genus *Phytalmia* has bizarrely formed, antenna-like facial appendages; and some of the almost exclusively tropical stalk-eyed flies (Diopsidae), a group made astoundingly grotesque by their enormously long, stalked eyes, which lack any apparent usefulness. [32/3; 278/7; 277/16–18]

The little tropical celphids are grotesque for another reason. In these extremely rare flies, the upper rear part of the thorax, known as the scutellum, which is usually small in flies, is expanded to such an extent that only the tips of the wings extend beyond it. As a result, these flies look like certain beetles.

Very tiny, but in part responsible for great damage because of their massive reproduction, are the leaf-miner flies (Agromyzidae). Their larvae, with the exception of a few genera (for example, *Leucopis*) that make themselves useful as destroyers of aphids, mine in the most varied parts of plants. Similarly, the larvae of the chloropid flies (Chloropidae) live in stems, especially of the grasses, and many are harmful pests of grain.

The black scavenger flies (Sepsidae), which smell of lemon, make themselves conspicuous by the continuous graceful vibration of the wings; usually the wing tips are marked with a round black spot, by means of which their characteristic frolicsome movements are accentuated. Some ototids, too, vibrate the wings in a striking way.

The little vinegar flies (Drosophilidae) have been elevated to the role of being probably

258/1
A male snowfly (Chionea) (enlarged 2.5×); the female has thinner femora and her pointed rear end bears an ovipositor.

259/1
*Among fly larvae, or "maggots,"
those of the little housefly
are striking because of their
matted tufts of hair, retained even
in the pupal stage, since at this
time the pupae lie encased in the
larval skin, which has hardened
into a small barrel known as a
puparium (enlarged 2×).*

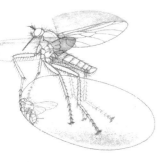

259/2
*Dance flies; the male is flying to
the female with his nuptial gift
(enlarged 1.5×).*

the most significant living forms in the science of genetics. Above all, the species *Drosophila melanogaster* is cultured in countless millions for laboratory experiments that have yielded much information about inheritance. *Drosophila* can be cultured very easily on all kinds of fermenting fruit, have a life cycle of only two weeks to a generation, and are particularly subject to the sudden inheritable variations known as mutations. As a result of such changes, these normally reddish, red-eyed flies occasionally produce individuals that are black, have vestigial wings, and have white or black eyes. [277/19]

There is another reason why these flies are useful in such experiments. Their salivary glands contain chromosomes of about 100 times the normal length; these permit one to visualize the hereditary factors, or genes, as disks lined up one after the other in a series. In fact, the genes for each particular characteristic—for instance, those for white eyes—have been found always to be located in the identical region of the ribbonlike chromosome.

Often occurring together with houseflies in dwellings and, though smaller, so similar as to be confused with them, are the anthomyiid flies (Anthomyiidae). Their larvae have very varied ways of living, but most of them bore into plants. Many are serious pests, particularly the cabbage maggot *(Hylemya brassicae)*, the onion maggot *(Hylemya antiqua)*, and the wheat bulb fly *(Hylemya coarctata)*. The larvae of others, such as the "little housefly" *(Fannia canicularis)*, live on detritus, and a few special genera are insect predators or even parasites. [275/2]

The dipteran type in general is embodied by members of the family Muscidae, above all by *Musca domestica,* the common housefly. At home all over the world, it is properly despised as a carrier of disease germs. Its larvae feed on decaying substances, dung, or meat, and hence get along particularly well where hygienic conditions are poor. [275/1]

The erroneous view that houseflies can bite rests upon confusing them with stableflies (stomoxydines), biting flies that belong to the same family. These are primarily an annoyance to cattle, and their larvae live in dung. The species that is particularly disliked is *Stomoxys calcitrans* which is likely to enter houses toward the end of summer. [277/22]

The tsetse flies (Glossinidae), likewise a group of muscids, are the scourges of the African tropics. Both males and females of these flies, which range up to 0.4 inch in length, bite man and beast. They are dreaded as vectors of sleeping sickness and of nagana

disease of cattle. The females give birth to full-grown larvae, which immediately enter the ground and become pupae after only a few hours. [279/3]

As scavengers of dead flesh, the larvae of the blowflies (Calliphoridae) have eminently useful significance in nature's economy. These flies may be annoying when they gather at open wounds or even dangerous when they lay their eggs in them. Some larvae attack living tissues, causing the condition known as myiasis. But occasionally the larvae are used for medical purposes; young larvae are placed in slow-healing wounds of man and animals, where they devour diseased and dead tissue and exert a disinfecting effect. Some blowflies are metallic in color, among them the handsome green-bottle flies *(Lucilia),* the American species of which now are separated as the genus *Phaenicia.* [275/4; 277/21, 24]

COURTSHIP

The two sexes find one another in various ways. Frequently not only the sense of smell but also that of vision plays a role; often perhaps even a kind of hearing is involved, although a tympanal organ, such as many other insects possess, has not yet been surely demonstrated in members of the Diptera. In any event the flight tones of males and females often are distinct, and the well-known sounds of the dancing swarms of male Nematocera are believed by many observers to attract their females.

The attraction of the partner may be a function of either the male or the female. Thus many male moth flies (Psychodidae) have conspicuously colored markings or scent organs, and females of the biting midge *Palpomyia* bear long scent tubes on the abdomen. A great many of these insects find one another by seeking out definite gathering places, a phenomenon that occasionally becomes striking with horseflies on mountain peaks. Also, among flower flies and horse- and deer-flies, for example, the locality—perhaps an open space in the forest or in the underbrush—is of special significance; here, a single male may hover continuously, awaiting a female, but diving at once upon any rival that appears or even upon other kinds of insects. Such rivalry becomes a ritual of combat among stilt-legged flies (Micropezidae), a tropical family related to the fruit flies. In the presence of a female, two stilt-legged males, rigidly erect, bang together breast to breast. [279/5]

Courting dances of certain dipteran males, as well as mating games, have been observed, and those of the dance flies (Empididae) are among the most astonishing in the insect empire. The male leads a predatory life, especially as a hunter of other flies, and as a wedding gift brings the female a fly he has caught. With the booty held fast between his feet, he flies into a dancing company of females and hovers around one until she drops with him to the ground or until the two make their way to a common resting spot.

The males of certain species wrap the fly they have caught in a fine veil, woven with spinning glands on the forelegs, before they bring the present to a female. In other species this procedure has become an end in itself: the male comes to his prospective partner with an empty web. The male of *Hilara sartor* carries with his middle and hind legs a small, gleaming-white, oval net that floats behind him throughout the course of his dance, which is carried out by flying in quite definite lines and curves. And the American *Empis politea* male holds horizontally between his feet a great egg-shaped balloon, in the fore part of which a little fly frequently is enclosed. But the female pays no attention to the imprisoned prey. No doubt the original purpose of the balloon was to confine this booty, but often it now seems to be a mating ritual. When the male feeds the female before or during mating, this evidently has a stimulatory effect, and is practiced by numerous insects, such as flies, scorpionflies *(Panorpa)*, grasshoppers, blattids, and some soft-bodied beetles (Malachiidae). This is done in part with prey, in part with droplets or little pellets of body secretions, and with mantids frequently even with their own flesh! [259/2]

DEVELOPMENT OF YOUNG

The longish eggs have a variety of shapes and often bear artistic sculpturing, ridges, or other attachments. They are laid singly or in packets or masses, and sometimes are inserted into the ground or into organic materials by means of a female's long, pointed abdomen or oviposition tube. The female of a North American tabanid was observed to protect a newly-laid clutch of eggs for a week by sitting on them. The larvae hatch by secreting a liquid that softens the eggshell, by using a special eggburster on the head, or by pushing off a preformed lid, which may be a round cap at the upper end or a perforated molding along the whole length.

The larvae are adapted to their greatly differing ways of life by their great differences in form, which ranges from the fine-membered, transparent body of many water dwellers to the shapeless, cylindrical fly maggot and the hideous monsters of certain parasites. Most of them are bone-white or dirty gray, and only the relatively few free-living types have the usual sort of coloration or perhaps designs that aid concealment. Included in these few are the caterpillarlike larvae of the crane flies, some of which are bedecked with colored scales, and the flower-fly larvae, which sit among colonies of aphids. Some larval crane flies that live in moss have not only the green color of their surroundings, but also deceptively mosslike excrescences all over the body. Certain sowbug-shaped soldier-fly larvae that live in mud have branched bristles in which bits of dirt get stuck and thus conceal the bearer and keep him moist.

Normally, dipterous larvae lack legs, but some larvae have swellings or rows of spines that facilitate creeping. On the underside, a few crane-fly larvae have warts similar to the prolegs of caterpillars. The larvae of skipper flies (Piophilidae), which grow on cheese among other things, are able to jump; curving the body into a tense circle, the larva catches its mouthhooks in a roughened region near the rear end and then, by letting go, flings itself a considerable distance.

In many families a pair of air holes (spiracles) is found on every body segment. Tabanid larvae have just the terminal pair of spiracles, and in the eristalines (Syrphidae), which live in mud and liquid manure and develop into adults frequently confused with honeybees, this pair of spiracles has been modified into a long, protrusible breathing tube that resembles a tail and works like a snorkel. A similar arrangement occurs in some related species.

The larvae of certain fungus gnats (Fungivoridae), which live in caves and eat algae and fungi, have an open pair of spiracles only on the front part of the body, and the air tubes (tracheae) are confined to the forebody, whereas in other larvae they extend through the body. Hence such cave-inhabiting species have largely gone over to cutaneous respiration, which requires a delicate integument, such as is possible to have only in very moist, dark abodes. These gnat larvae also are interesting because they carpet their paths on the rough cavern walls with salivary threads like "snail tracks," and because they creep about on freely-swinging "ropes" suspended by short threads; these glisten when one enters the cave with a light. [99/9]

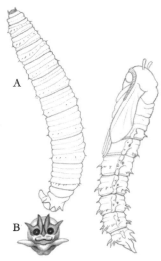

260/1A–B
(A) Crane fly larva, the pupa at the right (enlarged 2×); the larva's rear end (B) differs from one species to another.

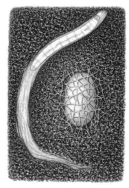

260/2
Fungus gnat larva in its silken tubular home; for pupation a broadmeshed net is spun; below it, the cocoon (enlarged 5×).

260/3
The "rat-tailed maggot" of a flower fly (the "drone fly," a syrphid), with its telescoping breathing tube; it lives in mire and liquid manure (enlarged 2×).

Some fungus-gnat larvae are able to give light. As a result of their performance, the Waitomo cave in New Zealand has become famous; on its ceiling hundreds of thousands of such larvae *(Arachnocampa luminosa)* twinkle like stars in the Milky Way. Another producer of light, the American *Platyura fultoni,* sets up its webs beside shady brooks. It is said to live on little insects that, attracted by the larval light, get stuck in the slimy threads.

Other fungus-gnat larvae are able to spin. Of these, the most skillful is perhaps *Diadocidia ferruginosa,* which pupates within a silken cocoon made from a wide-meshed net of strong, glassy threads. Many species dwell in tubes of silk—or, perhaps more accurately, of slime. The migrations of *Sciara militaris,* commonly called the armyworm, consist of gigantic hordes of individuals, crushed thickly together and on top of one another, that force their way forward within a mutually secreted mass of saliva.

Visual sense organs may appear in the form of so-called eyespots, but eyes are of the greatest rarity among dipterous larvae. Nevertheless, *Corethra* larvae, which lead predatory lives in water, and those of some related species, carry on their head not only larval eyes but the visibly developing compound eyes of the adult-to-be. In the entire second suborder of the Diptera, the typical, true-fly maggots lack a head capsule altogether. At the oral opening there usually is only a mouthhook, which is connected to a movable swallowing apparatus. While the maggots are using this tool for tearing or cutting, they pour out a solvent digestive secretion onto their food and suck in the resulting predigested chyme. Bacteria or yeasts in the gut usually play a further important role in digestion. Species that live on decomposing materials cannot develop without the microorganisms causing the decay; thus these species atrophy on sterilized meat.

For dipterous larvae, practically all organic materials can serve as food, but in the choice of these materials great differences often appear, even within one and the same family. There are both strictly limited food specialists and "omnivores," the latter especially among groups that live in fermenting and decaying substances. Even here, however, there are exceptions. The thyreophorids, for instance, eat only the dried-up remnants of flesh on the bones of the larger animals (including man). Others with similar food habits include many blowflies, humpbacked flies, and vinegar flies. In addition, certain cave-dwelling helomyzids stick to a diet of bat dung, and various *Sarcophaga* blowflies feed on the waxy excrescences of Indian Homoptera.

Countless Diptera develop in dung, liquid manure, waste water, and excrement. These include march flies (Bibionidae), moth flies, flower flies, stiletto flies, humpbacked flies, small dung flies (Sphaeroceridae), lonchaeids, and muscids. The females of the genus *Ceroptera* (Sphaeroceridae) ride on dung-rolling scarab beetles and lay their eggs on the balls of dung when these are buried in the earth by the beetles.

Limitless is the host of plant feeders, some of which develop in living tissue, but most of which live on decomposing matter. In the latter case, mud, damp earth, the upper layers of the soil, or rotting wood are the principal habitats. The seaweed flies (Coelopidae) are specialists of this type. Their larvae live exclusively in seaweed that has drifted onto the shore.

Algae, lichens, and fungi constitute the food of many nematocerous and brachycerous larvae, and the larvae of some crane flies and march flies may be pests of plant roots. Pests also occur among many larvae that bore into flowers, seeds, and fruits. Girdles of little warts frequently assist these larvae to move ahead through their feeding-tunnels. Leaf mines produced by such mining larvae usually are easily recognizable from the feeding traces they have left. For the larvae, lying on their side, move the forebody in such a way that the mouthhook is operated like the sickle of a mowing machine, and this leaves curved grooves behind it. Detritus and excrement produced by the larva are constantly pushed aside, and after the larva has eaten out a somewhat larger space in the leaf, the wastes remain lying there, as does the maggot, and are as conspicuous as dark lines against a mowed meadow.

The larvae of many gall midges (Cecidomyiidae) and certain rust flies (Psilidae) cause galls, and the larvae of the lonchaeids, chloropids, and spear-winged flies (Lonchopteridae) form galls on plants of the grass family. On the other hand, the larvae of a few vinegar flies, chamaemyiids, humpbacked flies, and milichiids are lodgers living mostly on detritus and excrement in the galls of other insects. Feeding within the food tunnels of various insects, such as bark beetles and their larvae, live the larvae of certain lonchaeids and spear-winged flies. And in nests of ants, bees, wasps, and termites there are, partly as harmless lodgers and partly as predators, the larvae of a few families, such as humpbacked

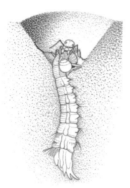

261/1
Snipe fly larva, that builds a funnel-shaped trap like an antlion and that captures insects in it and sucks them dry (natural size).

flies, milichiids, vinegar flies, flower flies, bee flies, soldier flies, and others. Certain of these—the humpbacked flies, for instance—know how to suck away a part of the food proffered by the parent ants as they feed their brood from mouth to mouth. [279/1, 2]

Living in symbiosis as the guests (symphiles) of ants are biting midges of the genus *Forcipomyia* and humpbacked flies of the *Tubicera;* and as the guests of termites, moth flies of the *Termitomastus,* humpbacked flies of the *Echidnophora,* a few muscids, and the termitoxeniids. [359/2]

The fully developed flies of this last family, hitherto found only in Africa, India, and Java, are grotesque in form, are wingless, and have a monstrously deformed, blown-up abdomen. Certain of them give birth to fully formed, mature progeny, which obviously passed through all their development stages within the maternal body; and others deposit a large egg, which hatches into an adult fly. The strangest thing about all this is that during their development the individuals first have male characteristics and later turn into females. In this genus only the female sex is known.

LARVAL PARASITES

The step from symbiosis to parasitism is completed almost as unnoticeably as is the step from predation to parasitism. Thus, not only dead snails, but also sick or hurt ones, are eaten by the larvae of various families of Diptera. The larvae of certain calliphorids, marsh flies (Sciomyzidae), and midges (Chironomidae) feed on or in healthy snails, frequently as specialists limited to this type of nourishment. The polleniines (Calliphoridae) develop within earthworms, the small-headed flies (Acroceridae) in the abdomen of spiders, and certain chamaemyiids within spider eggs. The larvae of many midges live under water on larvae of mayflies (Ephemeridae), on other water insects, or on snails.

The parasitism of Diptera, a stirring and fantastic chapter of insect life, could provide ample material for several authentic horror stories. Not only the gruesome methods of such parasites, but also the monstrosity of their body form can hardly be surpassed. A great many larvae develop within the bodies of other insects. For example, tachina flies develop in caterpillars, beetles, Hemiptera, grasshoppers, and various wasps; milichiids in flies and beetles; certain calliphorids in grasshoppers and crickets; the dixid midges in caterpillars; the big-headed flies (Pipunculidae) in Homoptera; and many

gall midges (Cecidomyiidae), vinegar flies, chamaemyiids, and agromyzids in plantlice.

Certain humpbacked flies develop inside the heads of living ants. Bees and wasps are parasitized by the larvae of many bee flies; the larvae, extraordinarily active in the earliest stage, first have to make their way into the nest of their host. Also parasitic on bees and wasps are the larvae of flower flies and thick-headed flies (Conopidae). Many of the latter are parasitic on grasshoppers. The adult fly dives upon a victim and, forcing apart two segmental plates with a special device (theka), thrusts an egg between them into the grasshopper's body. After hatching, the larva gradually consumes the abdomen of the grasshopper and, after the host's death, pupates therein. [278/2; 285/7]

Many parasitic flies are useful because they decimate insect pests. The bristly tachina flies (Tachinidae) are among the most beneficial living organisms and of eminent significance in the balance of nature. They have been applied successfully by man in combatting scourges of caterpillars. The spectacle of a caterpillar studded with white tachina eggs is well-known, but other insects, such as grasshoppers, beetles, and Hemiptera, also have such eggs deposited on them, either singly or in greater numbers. The maggots that hatch soon thereafter bore their way into the body of the host, unless the latter has chanced to molt shortly beforehand and thus has shed the eggs together with its skin.

Many tachina flies insert the eggs into an adult insect with the help of refined devices, such as an ovipositor curved downward against sawlike ventral combs. Certain little flies *(Rondania)* place themselves some distance ahead of a feeding weevil and extend their enormous oviposition tube forward between their legs into the beetle's open mouth. Many tachina flies, especially those that infect insect larvae that lead a rather well-concealed life, lay their eggs on the ground, in wood, or otherwise near the host in question, and the agile tachinid larvae then locate the latter. Similarly, others fasten little eggs to the food plant occupied by the larva, which eats the eggs together with its food; most of the eggs reach the digestive tract undamaged. [279/4]

Some tachina flies lay large eggs on the food plants, and the larvae hatch at once. They stand up on their rear end in the eggshell as if in a goblet, start to sway the forepart of the body in a circle whenever the plant begins to tremble, and at the same time secrete a drop of adhesive saliva. They thus come in contact with and stick to any larva

262/1
Thick-headed flies, whose larvae develop as parasites in the bodies of bees and wasps, live on nectar (enlarged 4×).

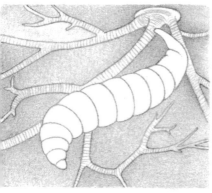

263/1
The larva of a dexid fly, living as a parasite in the body of a beetle and connected at its rear end to a tracheal tube of the latter (enlarged 7×).

263/2
The larva and, at the right, the pupa of a bee fly; the pupa's prongs and horns serve to tear open the pupal skin of the host insect, in whose body these parasites develop (enlarged 3×).

that passes close enough. Certain tachina flies give birth to first-stage larvae instead of eggs.

The number of eggs laid by a female runs from about 200 in species that deposit them directly on the host to many thousand in those whose methods fail to let a high percentage of the larvae reach their goal. As is the general rule among parasites, the tachina maggots first of all consume only the nonvital parts of the host's body, such as fat and blood. If the host goes through a period of inactivity, as when estivating or overwintering, the parasite also rests. An air supply may be provided via the hole made in the host's body upon entering, or through one bored out from within at some other spot. But many young tachina larvae tap an air tube inside the host; and others derive the necessary oxygen from the host's blood. [277/25–27]

When the parasites are full-grown, some leave the host and pupate in or on the ground; others remain within the host's body. If the host is a caterpillar with toxic hairs, its skin, as a covering cloak, is a protection for the pupal parasite. Frequently, a parasitized caterpillar is able to transform into a pupa, from which only the parasite, or a whole flock of them, breaks forth; the host dies as a pupa. In rare instances, the parasite develops only in the fully-developed insect.

Certain sawfly larvae that are parasitized by tachina flies, in contrast with healthy individuals, spin a cocoon that is thinner than normal at the front end, or equip it with a lid, thus giving the deadly enemy within them a means for later escape. Tachina larvae themselves frequently are parasitized, not only by various parasitic wasps, but also by bee flies (*Hemipenthes* and *Anthrax*), which otherwise frequently spend their larval stages in noctuid caterpillars. These hyperparasites first transform into the pupa within the puparium of the tachina fly they have invaded, and the pupa later frees itself with the help of sharp teeth on its head.

PARASITES OF VERTEBRATES

Not only insects and other invertebrates are attacked by parasitic flies, but also vertebrate animals. In birds' nests the maggots of calliphorids as well as nettiophilids suck the blood of nestlings, and heavy infestations of them may have a fatal effect. Similarly, certain tropical flies deposit their eggs on birds they overtake in flight.

A few of the gleaming, metallic *Lucilia* blowflies, probably by their sense of smell, seek out toads or frogs in their hiding places and fasten eggs to the victim's eyes or nose.

The maggots slip into the head and body of the unfortunate host, and gradually skeletonize it. The viviparous flesh flies of the same family (Calliphoridae), particularly the genus *Wohlfahrtia,* squirt their larvae into the ears, nose, or mouth of animals or even of persons asleep outdoors. Serious disease or even death may result. [275/4]

The bot- and warble flies (Oestridae) are parasitic in the skin of ungulates (hoof-bearing animals) and occasionally of humans. The short-stalked eggs may be laid on the hair of cattle, where they may be licked off and thus get into the throat; even more often, the hatching larvae bore through the skin into the body. Once in the body, the larvae wander for months at a time along definite paths between the tissues and through the muscles, feeding as they go. Finally they arrive beneath the hide on the back, where, as a result of proliferation of the tissue, they are encapsulated and form the so-called "warbles."

The full-grown larvae finally bore their way out, or are expelled by twitching of the skin, fall to the earth, and pupate there. The value of the hide for leather is reduced greatly by the ensuing holes; several hundred may perforate a single animal. Although their effects are often apparent, the warble flies and botflies themselves, with their brightly colored hairs, are seldom seen except in specific small areas where they gather for mating. [280/1]

The closely related rodent botflies (Cuterebridae) have a quite similar life; their larvae produce festering sores that are dangerous sources of infection principally in cattle, but also in dogs, in many wild animals such as deer, felines, and rodents, and even in people. Altogether uncanny is the technique of these flies in disposing of their approximately 500 eggs. In flight they fall upon all sorts of other Diptera, even mosquitoes, and forcibly glue a bundle of about 20 eggs to each. If, then, a fly favored with such a burden settles on an animal, the parasitic maggots slip hastily out of the eggshells into the hair. Certain rodent botflies lay their eggs on vegetation, and the larvae attach themselves to an animal brushing past. [281/1]

On mountain peaks, over high treetops, or above steeples, the horse botflies (Gasterophilidae) assemble, and these same customs are shared by other bot- and warble flies (Oestridae). The horse botflies stick their eggs to the head, chest, or forelegs of a horse, ass, pig, or even a rhinoceros, whence they are licked off and get into the animal's digestive tract. According to the species, the hatching larvae attach by means of their

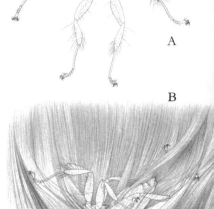

mouthhooks to the throat, stomach, or intestine, where they grow by sucking blood, immune to the animal's digestive juices. They do not let go until ready to pupate; then they are passed out through the colon with the host's excrement.

The oestrids, on the other hand, bear living first-stage larvae, and for the most part squirt them while in flight into the animal's nose or eyes. The parasites wander about in the throat or in the sinuses of nose or head, suck blood, and grow; often present in large numbers and packed close together, they cause inflammation and weakness, and may even bring about the victim's death by suffocation before they finally leave the body and pupate in the soil. Notorious are the various bots of sheep, cattle, horses, deer, and other animals. Occasionally certain oestrids even attack humans, where their goal is especially the eyes. Almost all animals have a strikingly violent fear of the botflies and warble flies, seeming to sense the danger even though these flies do not bite.

LOUSE FLIES AND OTHERS

Less harmful bloodsuckers are the louse flies (Hippoboscidae), bat flies (Streblidae), and bat tick flies (Nycteribiidae). These are grouped together as Pupipara because the larva of each completes its development within the mother's body and is not released until it is ready for pupation or has actually become a pupa.

The members of these families are ugly but interesting, thanks to a remarkably extensive degree of body modification and degeneracy. These flattened, leathery objects have powerful legs and grasping feet. Many females have only rudimentary wings or none at all. Certain winged species shed their wings after finding an appropriate host. The louse-like louse flies are adapted specially to live on birds or mammals, domestic animals in particular. [277/28–30]

The mainly tropical bat flies and bat tick flies almost all parasitize various bats, each kind of fly attacking a different species of bat. Their body, with its almost invisibly small head that can be jerked oddly back and forth, hardly can be recognized as that of a fly. It looks much more like that of a spider, and often moves like one. Especially typical and odd is the unique mobility and flexibility of the terminal leg segments (tarsi), with which the soft hairs of the bat's coat can be swirled apart very rapidly. Within this "plush" the fly frequently moves with great speed by

means of characteristic swimming movements, assisted by the appropriately arranged bristly covering of the entire body.

The females of *Asciodipteron* discard not only the wings but also the legs before they bury themselves superficially in the host animal. Here they remain stuck, like shapeless bags, from the posterior end of which the larvae that are born eventually escape through the perforated hide.

COMPLETION OF DEVELOPMENT

To complete the general account of the development of flies, it should be added that the majority of larvae molt twice and that their life span ranges from a few days to almost a year, depending on the genus. The pupae of the first suborder (Orthorrhapha) are exarate (their appendages are free), and some are very motile. But others are confined within the larval integument, and when they molt to the adult form their shell is split along the back.

In the second, higher suborder (Cyclorrhapha), the transformation of the larva to the pupa takes place within the closed and now contracted larval skin, the barrel-shaped puparium, astoundingly hardened and pigmented from brown to black. Its head end has a fine circular seam forming a lid that can be pushed off.

There are extreme variations within the life cycle of these insects, as shown by certain gall midges (Cecidomyiidae). Their larvae live in colonies on trees and, by means of mutually excreted saliva, change the wood into a broth and suck it up. The midge female lays a very few, extremely large eggs beneath the bark. The larvae that hatch from these eggs live in darkness and mature unusually early. Within the body of each larva, as many as 25 daughter larvae develop parthenogenetically. Eventually these entirely consume the maternal larva's body. Then the daughter larvae become mother larvae, and this process in which the larval stages reproduce (paedogenesis) may go on for generations. Individuals accidentally exposed to light either produce somewhat different, yellower larvae that are led by an inborn migratory urge to go to a new location, or else produce normally pupating progeny that develop into adult flies.

A great proportion of all living organisms feed on midges and flies, both immature and adult. But in spite of their many enemies, these insects have developed no weapons of defense. They evade threats only by means of concealment or by fleeing. Otherwise, they

264/1A–B
A bat fly (A) in wait for a passing bat, with the forelegs held ready to catch hold of it; (B) in the host's fur, with legs held aloft; their tarsi, particularly elastic in construction, twist sinuously and at the same time make swimming motions (enlarged 4×).

are able to maintain their numbers solely by virtue of their enormous reproductive capacity.

FLEAS
ORDER APHANIPTERA (SIPHONAPTERA)

Fleas were once regarded as grasshoppers without wings, and even today systematists disagree about the proper classification of the fleas. Rösel von Rosenhof, a pioneer in research on insects, was the first to recognize with astonishing insight the distant relationship of fleas to flies. He wrote of fleas in his several-volume masterpiece entitled *Insektenbelustigung* ("Entertainment with Insects"), published in 1749. In one place he poked fun at a brochure entitled *A Newly Invented Droll Fleatrap,* which was then in great demand among the fair sex.

The trap consisted of a little ivory tube, pierced with many holes, into the end of which one screwed a stopper that was first to be smeared with warm blood. By means of the stopper one could then extract the fleas that had crept in through the holes and "at will murder them, drown them, stab them to death, behead them, hang them, and consign them to the dark subterranean empire of the moles."

Fleas have achieved a lamentable fame as vectors of the most important bacterial disease caused by insects, the plague. A disease primarily of rodents, plague has its ancestral home in the plains of Africa and Asia. But it has become distributed ever more widely, even into both Americas, and today there are reservoirs from which it might break out into epidemics at any time.

The first epidemic definitely recognized as such was that of the Philistines in biblical times (Samuel). Most frightful was the scourge of all Europe from 1347 to 1350 by the epidemic called the Black Death, which took the lives of 25 million persons, one-fourth of the entire population. Introduced again and again by maritime traffic, the plague reappeared frequently in later times, but after the seventeenth century became gradually rarer in Europe until, for reasons not yet surely known, it all but died out. But toward the end of the nineteenth century, smaller epidemics suddenly struck again in several other parts of the world, the worst in India, where in the course of twenty years some 10 million died. Even today this incurable disease takes thousands of victims annually in tropical countries.

An outbreak of plague in human beings is preceded by an outbreak of the disease in rats or in other rodents. As great numbers of the rodents die, their fleas are compelled to seek new hosts. These fleas—principally the Indian rat flea *(Xenopsylla cheopis)* and the European rat flea *(Ceratophyllus fasciatus)* —bite humans and infect them with plague bacilli. During epidemics, other species of fleas also become carriers from person to person, including the human flea *(Pulex irritans)* and the dog and cat fleas *(Ctenocephalides canis* and *felis)*. In addition, all these and others may be intermediate hosts of various tapeworms, which are transmitted not by flea bites but by the entry of infected fleas or their parts into a person's mouth. Some fleas *(Xenopsylla)* also carry Mexican spotted fever.

A flea bites with its downward-pointing proboscis, which is composed of a long labrum (upper lip) and bristlelike mandibles. Flea bites normally are harmless. Because of the relatively slight toxicity of the saliva, they are not particularly itchy to many people and usually leave behind only a small red dot surrounded by a light ring.

The littlest flea of all, the chigoe flea *(Tunga penetrans),* has a body only a little over 0.04 inch long; its true home is in tropical America, but it has been introduced into Africa and Asia. The females wait on the ground for a chance to attach to some warm-blooded animal. When successful, they bore deep into the skin, continually sucking blood, and swell up to the size of a pea as their eggs ripen. In people chigoes attach themselves mainly to the feet, especially beside the toenails, and may cause dangerously infected wounds. [283/1]

Like the chigoe, certain other fleas remain constantly on their hosts, especially those that parasitize hooved animals, the fledglings of birds, and bats; the way of life of these hosts, without any fixed abode, would make it impossible for a flea to keep getting back onto an animal if it got off. But generally the fleas of mammals and birds, which at times spend considerable periods in their nests or lairs, as well as those of man, stay hidden in the dwelling places and jump onto the host only when they take blood.

The human flea imbibes blood daily if possible, and the digestive process, in which microorganisms in its gut take part, is extremely rapid; during half an hour it excretes perhaps 10 to 20 times. In spite of this the human flea has been observed to live without food for months or even as long as a year.

On the average fleas live to be three to four months old, the females often lasting up to two years. Almost every species has a single definite host, or only a few, but when the source of nourishment dries up or the host is lost in some other way, other animals often are attacked. Thus human fleas may be found on dogs, and dog fleas on people (in many places even as their most common parasite). The fox plays host to the fleas of the prey it has eaten, and to the fleas of the badger if it happens to be using a badger's hole, as frequently occurs.

After their first meal, fleas are capable of reproduction. The eggs are simply dropped, usually four to eight at a time and altogether 100 to 400 during a period of as much as three months. After two days to two weeks, the long, slender, white or yellowish, eyeless and legless larvae, studded with tactile bristles, hatch with the assistance of a frontal tooth. They can move swiftly with jerkily undulant movements. Whereas the adults depend exclusively on the blood of man, mammals, and birds, or in exceptional cases even on that of reptiles, the similarly light-avoiding larvae are not parasites. With their biting mouthparts they eat all kinds of debris and yeasts in the clefts, cracks, or straw of the host's dwelling.

Normally having but one molt, the larva is full-grown after about 10 to 15 days, spins a cocoon made inconspicuous with sand, dust, or bits of dirt, and there transforms into an exarate pupa (one with appendages free from the body). The flea emerges from the pupa after about two weeks, except under conditions of low temperature, when the pupal stage has been observed to last as long as 239 days. Both during their development and adult life the insects are strongly dependent on humidity and temperature. Unfavorable weather is much more destructive than their few enemies (ants, for example, attack the larvae); also, continued exposure to sunlight kills all stages.

The fleas are divided into about 140 genera and some 1,000 species. They are distributed all over the world, together with their hosts inhabiting even the polar regions. In contrast to lice, they have a keel-shaped form, very strongly compressed laterally, and strong, bristly legs with powerful coxae (basal segments); they are excellently equipped to glide through the forest of hairs and feathers on their hosts. The brown, wingless body, some 0.04 to 0.22 inch long and tough as leather, is anchored to the host's body cover by stiff combs of bristles that are directed backward.

Although two dark eyespots are conspicuous on the flea's small head, true eyes are lacking, or at most two ocelli (simple eyes) are present. The very long hind legs enable the flea to make its proverbial evasive leaps; the species that are the best jumpers, among them the human flea, reach a height of about 4 inches and a distance of a foot or more, landing on the hind legs and in a position facing where they come from. The muscular force of fleas is relatively great and since ancient times has induced fun-loving people to harness them as "coach horses" in front of little carriages and to put them on display in a flea circus or in some similar situation, where the propensity of the insects for training as well as the skill of the trainer evokes admiration.

TWISTED-WINGED PARASITES
ORDER STREPSIPTERA

With the exception of a few specialists and collectors, almost no one knows this little secretive family (Stylopidae) of highly adapted parasites. A collector will notice such a parasite when an insect, such as a wasp, seems to have a slightly deformed abdomen; a closer look will reveal a small oval object protruding from beneath a distorted plate on the wasp's back. This is the fore part of the parasite within the wasp's body. Such a wasp differs from other wasps not only in its reduced vitality, but often also through certain abnormalities of body form, coloration, sculpture, and pattern of hairs. Individuals thus altered have time and again misled workers into setting up imaginary new species.

The approximately 250 known species of these twisted-winged insects are distributed over the whole world with the exception of the arctic regions. The largest family is the stylopids, which are parasitic on the most varied species of bees, wasps, and Homoptera (and rarely on the true bugs). The motionless females without exception are stuck fast in the body of the host. This high degree of degeneracy can hardly be equaled anywhere else among the insects. The flattish, scale-shaped, rigidly sclerotized part that extends from the host's body is designated as a cephalothorax; it represents a mouthless, eyeless, and legless fusion of head and thorax. At its end is a transverse cleft (thoracic cleft), the sole body opening, which serves for mating and for discharge of the tiny, first-stage larvae.

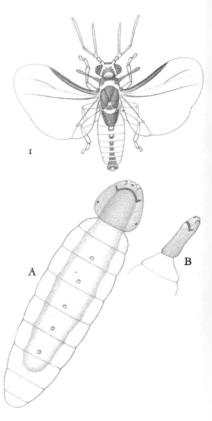

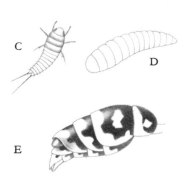

C

D

E

266/1A–B
Twisted-winged parasites.
(1) A male, with his two fore
wings reduced to slender clubs
(enlarged 11×). (A) A female,
seen from below. The head and
thorax are fused and
sclerotized, very flat in the
lateral view (B); the mouth
is in front, the air openings at
the side, and in the body near
the underside is an elongate brood
chamber, from which exits for
the developing larvae are provided
both by the curved slits anteriorly
on the thorax and by the round
openings on the belly (enl. 11×).

267 C–E
(C) A young, very active
larva; (D) a maggot-
shaped larva that has become
sessile within the body of its host
(enlarged 7×); (E) the abdomen
of a wasp that has been attacked
by twisted-winged parasites;
the cephalothorax of a parasite
female is sticking out from
beneath a swollen segment
(enlarged 3×).

The larvae develop in large numbers (about 1,000 to 2,000) in the adjacent, baglike, soft abdomen of the parasite. They are very active, six-legged, and with their two or more long caudal bristles remind one of the bristletails (Thysanura). Moreover, the bristles, when laid forward beneath the body and snapped like the furcula in the springtails (Collembola), give the larvae the capability of jumping.

After hatching, the hundreds or thousands of larval insects first mill about on the body of their mother's host, to which they cling with feet that may be equipped with vesicles instead of claws, and leave at the appointed instant for the source of food. Only a few will succeed in finding it, for they have to bore into the larva of the particular host specified for them, a feat that is quite difficult when the hosts are inside of cells within nests, as is the case with bee and wasp larvae. One possibility is that the larvae of the twisted-winged insect, while still on the maternal host, are carried with her into the home of their host-to-be. Otherwise they leave the maternal host and as occasion offers catch onto others on the ground or on flowers, and in this way may be transported to the right place. Most of the insects to which they attach are the wrong ones, to be sure, but frequently they are the right species, as noted already with regard to the young larvae of the blister beetles (Meloidae).

If the twisted-winged larva has succeeded in penetrating into the soft body of a host larva, the free, active stage of the parasite is now transformed into a simple maggot, which grows as it sucks without interfering decisively with the further development of the host attacked. When the host's growth is completed and the mature bee or wasp emerges from the closed cell—or with the free-living Homoptera frequently in an even earlier stage—the larval parasite, which meanwhile also has matured, bores outward until the fore part of its body breaks through a soft-skinned place, such as between two segmental rings. In this position it molts twice.

The first molt results in transformation to the pupa (exarate, in the male sex) within the last larval skin, and thus to a coarctate pupa similar to that of many flies. The second molt is incomplete in the female parasite, in that the puparial shell is lifted away only on the ventral surface of the body, exposing the thoracic cleft and the brood chamber. This marks the initiation of another life cycle, the duration of which varies greatly in adaptation to the varied developmental times required by the different hosts.

The male individuals, on the contrary, change at the second molt into the mature form, free themselves from the puparium (which remains embedded in the host), and fly off. Their delicate, mainly dark-colored body, at most a few tenths of an inch in length, is borne by two great wings shaped rather like half-moons. These have few longitudinal veins and can be folded like fans. They are the hind pair of wings; the fore wings are reduced to clublike or spoon-shaped outgrowths, approximately equivalent in structure and function to the halteres of flies. On the head with its small mouth, the large, blackberry-like eyes, which protrude somewhat like binoculars, and the antennae, especially expanded as organs of smell, stand out conspicuously. The third antennal segment is lengthened laterally into a process of various shapes that gives the antenna either a forklike or comblike appearance.

The male twisted-winged insects are among the most impetuous of insects and, so to speak, race madly through their life in a few hours. These alert, unresting imps flash through the air in an erratic, buzzing dance, with the forebody held vertical and the abdomen curled upward, too. Flying as fast as lightning, but also, at infrequent intervals, hovering up and down over one spot, these strange gnomes are but rarely seen.

With a body length of as much as 1.2 inches, a few representatives of the family are much larger than other members. These are from the Southeast Asian islands and are parasites on grasshoppers. And some Mediterranean species, which parasitize bristletails (Thysanura), have an aberrant way of life insofar as both the females, though they are quite degenerate, and the last-stage larvae live free in hiding places in the ground.

WASPS, BEES, AND SAWFLIES
ORDER HYMENOPTERA

(Ants and social bees and wasps are described in detail in the section on "Social Insects.")

When the sun's rays have drawn the cool of morning from the last hollows and corners, and are heating up the ravine until it is more and more like an oven, things in the area begin to move. On the hard-trodden ground, in the cracked joints of stone walls, in countless little holes in earthen cliffs, and in the scant grass of talus slopes, the working day of the insects begins. With the body turned broadside to the sun, restless antennae are

drawn through delicate cleaning combs on the forelegs, abdomens are wiped off with leg brushes, wing membranes shimmering with the colors of the rainbow are aired, and a few quick strides are undertaken.

Soon, hundreds of vibrating wings produce a hum ranging from a deep melodious droning to a high-pitched singing tone. Only the bees and wasps can produce this hum in such sharply modulated multiplicity. Bees and wasps, along with ants, sawflies, ichneumons, and chalcids, make up the order Hymenoptera. Seen from afar, many of the Hymenoptera look like flies. But their four wings distinguish them with certainty from those two-winged forms. The much smaller hind wings have a row of tiny hooks that curve around a marginal fold of the fore wings and fasten the two pairs of wings together. Many forms of Hymenoptera, however, go scurrying about without wings, as witness the ants.

A common sight along a path, even early in the morning, are little volcanoes of sandy soil. Shoveled hastily out of tiny holes, these are the piles of refuse unearthed from the shafts of colonies of the mining bees (*Halictus*). Their neighboring big sisters, on the contrary, have strewed to the four winds the soil removed from their holes. One sees these burrowing bees, returning homeward with legs heavily laden with pollen, disappear into the holes and then, wiped clean of their burden, soon fly out again to collect more.

A few steps farther on, one may see fountains of sand spurting from the ground. These are by no means as small as one might estimate from the size of the sand wasps (*Bembix*) that make them. These wasps shovel their nest holes into the depths with the aid of forelegs fringed with stiff bristles, and in doing so fling the material backward beneath them with a highly refined technique.

Paying no attention to all of this, a fat caterpillar bumps its way over the ground, not by its own efforts, but borne along as the victim, stung into paralysis, of the graceful thread-waisted wasp (*Ammophila*), whose little abdomen bobs at the end of an overlong, narrow waist. She stands astride her booty, holding it firmly with mandibles and forelegs, and hastens with it over sticks and stones, through thick and thin, dragging it along more than carrying it.

If we accompany this odd team to its goal, we see the female thread-waisted wasp leave her caterpillar long enough to reopen the nearby entrance to her nest. Previously she had plugged up the opening, apparently as a means of security, making it look just like the rest of the ground; and although it was

invisible she has found it again after a long trek from far away, across territory that could not be seen over, with that phenomenal sense of location that is peculiar to the Hymenoptera. And now the wasp grasps this long-lasting sausage, this caterpillar paralyzed by her preservative sting and destined to be food for her progeny, and, walking backward, slides it into the hole in the earth.

Yonder, where a dry wall beside the path rises especially high and steep, a much smaller spider wasp (Pompilidae) goes through gymnastics with a limp, heavy spider, maneuvering the victim toward her front door, one of the dozens of holes located here and there in the wall. Apparently she gets there eventually, after repeated downhill tumbles and ensuing search for the prey that has slipped from her grasp, even though the struggle may last until long after sunset.

Farther along the wall, on one of the stones that gets plenty of sunshine, a potter wasp (*Eumenes*) builds her beautifully formed nest jugs. Two stand side by side, masterworks not of handiwork, but of footwork and mouthwork. If we observe attentively, then perhaps we will not miss that slowly turning head motion that allows the insect's eyes to follow the curve of such a finished vase, as though its unblemished smoothness should be tested once again, even though it has been palpated and repalpated with the antennae throughout the course of the work.

Suddenly the antennae spread apart, and with an abrupt twitch that makes the whole wasp tremble, the face lifts with wide-open mandibles—but it was only the shadow of the ancestral enemy, the sparkling cuckoo wasp (Chrysididae), whirring past overhead, that momentarily alarmed the potter wasp. Now the wasp packs the just-completed container with little caterpillars, collected after hours of hunting and stung into paralysis, and then she suspends an egg through the narrow opening on a short thread. Finally, the potter

268/1–6
Scenes from the life of Californian wasps and bees. (1) The wool-hanger bee Anthidium is flying to her nest entrance with pollen she has collected and stored up in her ventral brush. (2) With its poison-dispensing proboscis a robber fly is overpowering a sand wasp, in the intention of sucking it dry. (3) A cuckoo wasp is cleaning itself, and is pulling one antenna through

the polishing contrivance on its foreleg. (4) A sphecoid wasp, setting out to hunt for a grasshopper. (5) A resin bee, freeing itself post-developmentally from the cradle its mother has made of resin. (6) A blue mud dauber with her paralyzed prey, a ground cricket, which she is going to put into a previously excavated hollow in the ground as food for her progeny. (→ 111/1–4; → 278/1; → 310/10; → 312)

closes the vessel with round stones brought from a distance but nevertheless fitting precisely, and then both filled jars are sealed completely and formlessly with mortar, mixed from sand and saliva. This final act, perhaps to the regret of one who admires beautifully constructed objects, probably increases the security of the new generation of wasps growing within such vases.

Amid the buzzing along the path, a particularly striking sight is that of green leaf rolls flying past. The observer notes that all come from the same direction and vanish through a cleft in the row of palings that stand oblique to the direction of the wind. These are leaf-cutting bees *(Megachile)*. Beginning at the margin of a leaf, the bee bites out a smooth-edged, oval piece, rolls up the separated piece between its legs, and flies home with it. The bee makes brood cells out of such rolls. Each cell receives as a cover a much smaller leaf disk, cut in the shape of a perfect circle. This is put in place after pollen has been collected industriously, brought in, molded into a ball, and placed in a brood cell, and then an egg added to it.

In another direction, one sees a sphere, gleaming red and blue, rolling down the precipice of the wall. On closer look, one sees a frantic mason wasp *(Odynerus)* struggling between the mandibles of the "ball," which suddenly stretches out and flies off as a cuckoo wasp.

Another sight to see is the digger wasp *(Philanthus)*, known in German as a *Bienenwolf* (bee wolf) because it requires honeybees exclusively as food for its progeny. At a flower it falls upon a honeybee, frequently an old one, stings it to death, throws it on its back, and grasps it with the legs. After first licking up the honey squeezed from the bee's mouth, the digger wasp flies off to its nest with its heavy burden.

Then there are those fat males of the hairy digger bees *(Anthophora)* that in wild and

loudly buzzing flight storm the wall beside the path, snatching any female that happens to emerge nearby.

Interesting as these sights are, they are merely episodes that need to be brought into perspective by examining the characteristic ways of life of these insects. But first it would be well to mention the stinging apparatus of the female and to look briefly at the major groups of the Hymenoptera.

Well-known and rightly feared is the sting of the hymenopterous female. Lying in the tip of the abdomen, it has evolved from the ovipositor tube, a more primitive form of which is present in many Hymenoptera and in other insects too. This sting, bearing tactile organs, is a tube (the sting canal) in which the barbed lancets lie closely appressed, and whose upper end is connected with a large vesicle (poison gland reservoir) that contains the fluid poison. In stinging, the two lancets are moved very rapidly against one another, alternately up and down, and thus saw their way into the skin of the organism attacked. Simultaneously, the poison flows into the bulbous expanded upper portion of the sting canal, and is pumped downward by two integumentary lobes. [284/1]

IMPORTANT GROUPS

The order Hymenoptera can be split up in a number of ways, depending upon the point of view of the entomologist doing the dividing. One way is to divide the order into three suborders: the Terebrantia, the Symphyta, and the Aculeata. The Terebrantia includes the parasitic wasps and the gall wasps; these account for more than half of all the hymenopterous species. The Symphyta comprises the sawflies and the wood wasps, which are distinguished by the complete absence of a "wasp waist." Both of these suborders will be taken up later in the course of examining the relationships of the Hymenoptera. The third suborder, Aculeata, contains many families, the most important of which are described in the paragraphs that immediately follow.

Everywhere in the world, high in the mountains and deep in the ground, there live teeming myriads of ants (Formicidae). About 5,000 species are known, from dwarfs measuring less than 0.04 inch to giants more than 1.2 inches long. They seem quite uniform at first sight, but when studied more intensively disclose a multiplicity of body forms, among which occur bizarre prongs, spines, and hooks. Ants live together in societies, as do certain rather small groups of bees and wasps.

The approximately 3,000 known species of hornets, yellow jackets, and potter wasps (Vespidae), distributed over almost the entire earth up to the margins of the arctic zones, are from 0.12 inch to about 1.6 inches long. These wasps hold the wings folded lengthwise at rest. Among them, several groups can be distinguished according to their way of life, namely the small group of honey-gathering masarines, the solitary wasps, the social wasps, and finally a few species parasitic on these and descended from them. [286/1–21; 320/1–9; 354–357]

Incomparably large in numbers, with perhaps about 20,000 species and about 100 genera, and distributed just as widely as the vespid wasps, perhaps even farther north, is the family of the bumble, carpenter, honey, and stingless bees (Apidae). Most of the species, which measure from barely 0.08 inch to nearly 1.6 inches, are concentrated in the plains areas; very few live in cold zones and in virgin forests. Thus not merely the temperature determines the possibility of an area's being settled by bees, but also the availability of nesting sites, which the ground-inhabiting species lack in solid, damp forests. [306]

Like the vespids, the apids can be divided into different biological groups, namely solitary, social, and parasitic bees; among these—as among wasps, for that matter—there may be some overlapping. At the highest level of community organization lives the genus of the honeybees *(Apis)*; their honey and wax are useful, it is true, but cannot compare to the inestimable value of the entire bee family as pollinators of plants. [320/16–20]

The mutual adaptations and dependence of flowers and bees greatly surpass similar relationships among other insects. A flower-related biology in this sense is almost entirely lacking, for instance, in the very large wasp family of the Sphecidae, from which the bees are thought to have branched off in the distant past. For their brood, the sphecids fetch insects and spiders into their nests, and indeed the individual species have a definite and often very narrow selection of prey.

Another important family is that of the spider wasps (Pompilidae). These spider hunters are extremely agile on foot and have long antennae and legs. The most powerful among them, namely the genus *Pepsis* from the warmer parts and the tropics of America, are up to 3.2 inches long and have up to 6-inch wingspans. They are the largest Hymenoptera of all. Their frightful stinger, together with their remarkable agility, enables them to cope with the mightiest bird spiders, which are almost as large as one's hand.

To strike the nerve cord of these monsters, the paralyzing sting must be delivered from below. Certain *Pepsis* species first try, with a sting in the head region, to put the spider's awesome poison fangs out of commission. Such battles may last for hours and take on an aura of ghastly excitement because of the fantastic leaps and attitudes, particularly those of the huge, bristly spider. But eventually the spider is vanquished. This imposing booty, buried in a shaft excavated in the ground with an egg supplied by the huntress, serves as food for a single one of her offspring.

Both the sphecids and the pompilids include genera that, having given up caring for their own brood, smuggle their eggs into the nests of related kinds. [18/25, 29; 49/19–24; 284/8; 285/1–3; 286/22–35; 287/1–26]

NEST BUILDING

One thing many Hymenoptera have in common is a devouring urge to build nests and collect food. Excluded from this group are the plant wasps and gall wasps, many parasites, and the males of all families. To the males, of course, a nest and food are pure bounty and carry no obligations. Males that help in family duties, as certain beetle males do, are astoundingly rare. But the females work industriously and skillfully.

Aside from the nests made by some species for sleeping or overwintering, all work by the Hymenoptera implies preparation for or care of the brood. Their first concern is mostly with the nest. A separate chamber or cell is built for every individual offspring, except in the nests of ants and a few digger wasps. Books could be filled with descriptions of the systems used by Hymenoptera in nest building, for in their confusing multiplicity they surpass those of all other insects put together, and the materials used arouse astonishment and admiration.

The simplest method of preparing a nest is the one used by those pompilids that seek out spiders in their own holes and, after overpowering them, simply leave them there as food for the future offspring. Also, depressions in the ground, clefts in rocks, and other hiding places may be used as nests without any further intervention, as is done by those *Sphex* wasps that drag into such places grasshoppers they have caught. Not that these wasps have forgotten how to dig, for they do that, too, in case of need, and thereby display a plasticity of instinct that is by no means rare among Hymenoptera. A great many occupy borings and passageways left in wood or in soil by other insects, or use

270/1

Scenes from the life of an aphid wasp of the sand wasp genus Bembix. At the top, the wasp in flight with a captured fly, but pursued by the parasite, a miltogrammatid fly; to the left, one of these wasps is scraping out a nest; beneath it a sand wasp is feeding her larva with flies. At the far left a parasite, the bee fly, has deposited an egg in front of the nest entrance, and the larva that hatches from it will then make its way into the excavation, settle on a wasp larva, and gradually suck it dry. This occurs at the lower right with a larva that already is enclosed in its pupal cocoon; the entryway to the nest has been closed with a plug of coarser material by the mother wasp. On the left side is yet another cocoon, with a circle of tracheal openings around the waist, and below it the pupa of a thick-headed fly (conopid), whose larval development took place inside the body of a sand wasp, in which it also pupated. Parasites too are the hairy "velvet ants"; only the males have wings in this wasp family, which is unrelated to ants. (→ 285)

271/1
A potter wasp (Odynerus), with a captured sawfly larva as food for her progeny, at the nest entrance, which has been built up in the form of a chimney (somewhat enlarged).

plant galls or nests abandoned by other Hymenoptera, clearing out such holes and perhaps also refurbishing them appropriately. Empty snail shells frequently are taken possession of by pompilids and particularly by bees, which mostly select definite species of snails for this use.

Frequently Hymenoptera nest in joints and holes in the walls of huts and houses or, in a pinch, inside dwellings or even in keyholes, telephone receivers, or musical instruments. But in the majority of cases the solitary Hymenoptera themselves dig and bite out the cavities they need. As tools, most use the mandibles and legs, but some also use the tip of the abdomen to push out or tamp down the material; in many genera this part of the body is adapted for that use by having a plate-shaped or pestlelike development (pygidial field) on the upper surface.

Bees usually use the flexed forelegs and the lower part of the face to shove away earth, sand, wood, or pith that they have bitten loose, and may also push it backward into the open with the rest of the body; some bees carry it away bit by bit between the mandibles. And the pollen-gathering bees *(Dasypoda),* colonies of which excavate shafts side by side in the soil up to 2 feet deep, shovel with their forelegs in a very rapid rhythm; walk backward, pushing out the material they have behind them; and brush it to one side with their powerful pollen-collecting hind legs, which have been developed into gigantic brushes; meanwhile the middle legs make slow walking movements. Thus each of the three pairs of legs has a different task and a different tempo, but all of them work together in precise synchrony. [285/2; 310/1]

Sphecids and pompilids have forelegs each equipped with a comb of bristles, and with it they fling sand or earth backward beneath the body. In doing this the forelegs of the sphecids usually work synchronously, and those of the pompilids in alternating rhythm, while all the rest of the legs remain motionless and outspread; yet the insect constantly slips forward as a result of the digging motion of the front pair. The digger wasps *Bembix* occasionally blow remaining sand away from the nest's entrance by whirring the wings. And many ants as well as thread-waisted wasps *(Ammophila)* have on the underside of the head an area bounded by bristles, into which earth can be put and carried away. This is similar to the principle made use of by bees that collect pollen in baskets on their legs.

The debris brought out is not always simply disposed of, but may serve also to construct so-called antechambers, perchance built around the entrance in the form of a ring or funnel or even of a chimneylike tube, as it is indeed with many digger bees *(Anthophora),* pollen-collecting bees *(Eucera, Tetralonia),* honey wasps (masarines), mason wasps *(Odynerus),* and ants. Such a tube, whether it is located on the ground or on a wall of clay, whether it sticks up vertically or is bent over until it lies on the surface, grows simultaneously with the digging out of the shaft for the nest. [290/4]

The lumps of earth bitten off are piled up in layers in the shape of a ring about the excavated hole, the insect using her mandibles to pile the load and wetting the layers with water gathered nearby; usually two buttresses on the outer side provide a stiffer support for the material while it is still wet. Thus the laboring insect comes into view backward, again and again, and kneads a new ball of dirt onto the upper edge. From time to time the female flies off for more water. Now and again she brings up in her mandibles stones that have gotten in the way of the digging and in the course of a short flight drops them elsewhere. The deeper the shaft or the more numerous the chambers excavated, the longer grows the tube.

The tube is polished smooth on the inside and frequently is put together loosely in a latticework. But it is not very solid and soon falls apart. Its function, if any, has not yet been discerned. The excavators seem quite indifferent as to whether they enter their hole in the earth through a chimney or, after this is gone, directly. But sometimes, as occasionally happens by chance, the outermost end of such a tube running along the ground is all that is left, remaining as a ring or a short tunnel. Then, the wasp, peculiarly dependent upon its instincts, is observed to enter the hole into its nest, which now lies open on all sides, only along the path through the gateway.

Certain species of *Odynerus* have been observed to rebuild their tubes at once after they have been destroyed. This would seem to indicate that such antechambers cannot be regarded merely as a means of disposing of the excavated material. In fact, certain wasps do not even use excavated material in building the tubes, but employ mud that they have bitten off elsewhere in the vicinity.

The walls of the cells and passageways in the ground may be merely smoothed down or may be made firmer with saliva. The individual rooms and finally the nest entrance are closed off mostly with lids or plugs made of the loosened material or of other building

CAPTIONS
FOR PAGES 273 TO 285

273/1–14

(1) The delicate silken fabric of a woolly bear. (2) The boat-shaped cocoon of a smoky moth (Zygaena), with semi-extruded pupal shell. (3) The dwelling of a carpenterworm, glued together from gnawed-off bits of wood or bark, with the pupal shell. (4–12) Giant silkworm moths, in some species fastened to the vegetation by a ring and a stalk. (8) The cocoon, opened at the top, of an emperor moth, with its elastic exit. (12) A cocoon with a spring-loaded slit as the means of egress. (13) An emerging silkworm moth, that beforehand has moistened the cocoon at the top with solubilizing saliva. (14) A slug-caterpillar (Limacodidae) cocoon, smooth and hard as a nut (somewhat reduced). Photograph.

273/15–18

(15) Head of the silkworm. (A) Maxillary palpi; (B) labial palpi; (C) labium (lower lip) with the spinning gland; (D) upper jaw; (E) antennae; (F) compound eyes; (G) labrum (upper lip). (16–18) Internal structure of the silkworm (16), pupa (17), and adult (18). (17A) Pupal development of the mouthparts, antennae, legs, and wings.
Red = nervous system,
yellow = circulatory system,
green = digestive system,
brown = sex organs.

273/19

The respiratory system of the adult moth. (A) Air openings (stigmata); (B) a stigma, with its protective bristles (enlarged).

273/20

Spinning glands of the silkworm. (A) Accessory glands; (B) secretory glands; (C) gut.

273/21–22

A butterfly head, with a cross section of the proboscis, which is formed by the union of two half-tubes (22). (21A) Compound eye; (B) antenna; (C) palpi; (D) proboscis; (E) forelegs, reduced (in Nymphalidae) to rudiments. (22A) Muscles; (B) nerve; (C) trachea (air tube).

273/23

The coupling between fore and hind wings, as seen from below at the wing base of most moths. (A) Fore wing; (B) jugum; (C) frenulum, occurring here as a rigid bristle; (D) hind wing.

PAGE 274

274/1

A butterfly caterpillar in pupation (enlarged).

274/2–6

Pupal forms. (2) Ageronia, a brush-footed butterfly (seen from the side). In the daytime these freely suspended pupae, whose heads are adorned with grotesque outgrowths, lean sideways beneath the leaf that protects them from direct sunlight, whereas at night they hang perpendicularly like all freely suspended pupae. These movements are released by light stimulation, and can be induced artificially in swift succession. (3) Ornithoptera (bird-winged butterflies), seen from above; the front portion of the laterally greatly broadened pupa hangs in a noose (a belted pupa), while the rear end stands in a supporting pad, both made of spun silk colored with a black secretion. (4) Giant silkworm moths from a particular African group, extraordinary for their color, spines, tubercles, and artfully modeled cremaster at the posterior end. These pupae, anchored by strong threads, lie amid leaves woven together by spun silk. (5) The pupa of a sphinx moth with an especially long proboscis, taken from its cavity in the earth; it is lying on its back. Eyes, antennae, legs, and wings of the moth-to-be, the last now lying close to the thorax and the ventral abdominal surface, show clearly in relief, while the tracheal orifices are to be seen at the side. (6) Pupa of the emperor moth in the cocoon, which has been cut open. The exit for the future moth is held shut by an ingenious elastic arrangement of bristles (enlarged 2×).

PAGE 275

275/1–4

Flies from the muscid family group. (1) Housefly and eggs (1C). (2) The little housefly. (3) Muscina. (4) A greenbottle fly. (1A) The housefly proboscis and its underside (1B). (1D) The housefly maggot, a highly specialized type of insect larva; it lives on all sorts of decomposing organic substances (enlarged).

PAGES 276 AND 277

276/1–8

Various flies. (1–4) Crane flies. (5–7) Soldier flies, and (8) a large representative of a related tropical family (enlarged 1.25×). Photograph.

276/9–22

(9–14) Bee flies. (15–20) Robber flies, the wing-spreading South American species of which mimics a Eulaema bee. (21) Tangle-veined fly with a long piercing proboscis and particularly elegant wing venation. (22) Snipe fly (enlarged 1.25×). Photograph.

277/1–15

(1–4) Horseflies and deerflies. (5–13) Flower flies. (14–15) Color-winged flies (enl. 1.6×). Photograph.

277/16–30

(16–18) Fruit flies. (19) Vinegar flies (Drosophila). (20) Anthomyid fly. (21) Muscid fly. (22) Stable fly. (23) Phasiid fly. (24) Flesh fly. (25–27) Tachinid flies. (28–30) Louse flies (enl. 1.6×). Photograph.

PAGES 278 AND 279

278/1

A robber fly (Asilidae) has attacked a sand wasp (Bembix) (enl. 2.5×).

278/2

A thick-headed fly is bestriding a sand wasp and, with a special ventrally situated instrument, is pushing two of her dorsal segments apart, in order to thrust an egg into her (enlarged 4×).

278/3

Stealing from an ant's mouth. Harpagomyia mosquitoes from Africa and Asia stand in the way of ants and force them to disgorge a drop of nourishment (enlarged 2.5×).

278/4

The "bee louse," a bee parasite with a worldwide distribution, is scarcely to be recognized as a fly; with its second-stage larva (enlarged 9×).

278/5–8

Exceptional forms among flies. (5) A small-headed fly, a parasite of spiders, with a long suctorial proboscis that is held beneath the body. (6) An aphid fly, the right wing extended; in this species the normally small plate (scutellum) at the posterior end of the thorax is stretched out so as to cover the entire body and gives the fly the look of a beetle. (7) A stalk-eyed fly, whose compound eyes and antennae are set on the sides of the head, which are drawn out into pedestals. (8) A dance fly, with prehensile shears for seizing small insects, especially flies.

279/1–2

Gnat galls on willow in the shape of roses (1) and lentils (2) (reduced). Photograph.

279/3

A tsetse fly; (A) before and (B) after taking blood. (C) Larva;

(D) puparium; (E) the trypanosomes, the cause of sleeping sickness, among the blood corpuscles (greatly enlarged).

279/4

A tachinid fly uses her long ovipositor, that is stretched out forward between the legs, to thrust an egg beneath the mouth of a feeding snout beetle (twice natural size).

279/5

The pappataci moth fly may sometimes transmit pappataci fever, a mild infectious disease. (A) Pupa; (B) egg; (C) larva (greatly enlarged).

PAGES 280 AND 281

280/1–2

The ox warble fly. (1A) Larva and (1B) egg. (2) Eggs of a different species of the genus (greatly enlarged).

281/1

The human bot fly (Dermatobia) and larva (A); (B) a different fly, to which Dermatobia eggs have been affixed; this fly acts as a vector for the phoretic larvae that subsequently hatch (greatly enlarged).

PAGES 282 AND 283

282/1

The rat flea, Xenopsylla cheopis. (A) Egg; (B) larva; (C) pupa.

282/2

Head of the human flea.

282/3

Head of the dog flea.

283/1

A chigoe flea (1) in normal condition; (B) fully fed. (C) Longitudinal section of a chigoe flea stuck in human skin, headed downward, the body full of eggs; (A) the larva (greatly enlarged).

PAGES 284 AND 285

284/1

The stinging apparatus of a honeybee.

284/2–7

Social wasps. (2) Hornet; (3–7) various other species (enlarged 4×).

284/8

An aphid wasp is carrying its parasite, a curled-up cuckoo wasp, out of the nest (enlarged 2×).

285/1–14

Scenes from the life of an aphid wasp of the sand wasp genus Bembix.

285/15

The "bee wolf," a sphecid wasp, holding a honeybee that has been stung into paralysis and that is destined to be food for the brood (enlarged 2×).

(Continued on page 289)

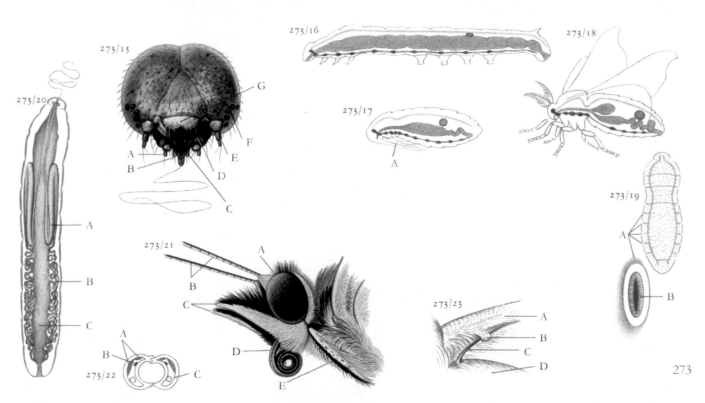

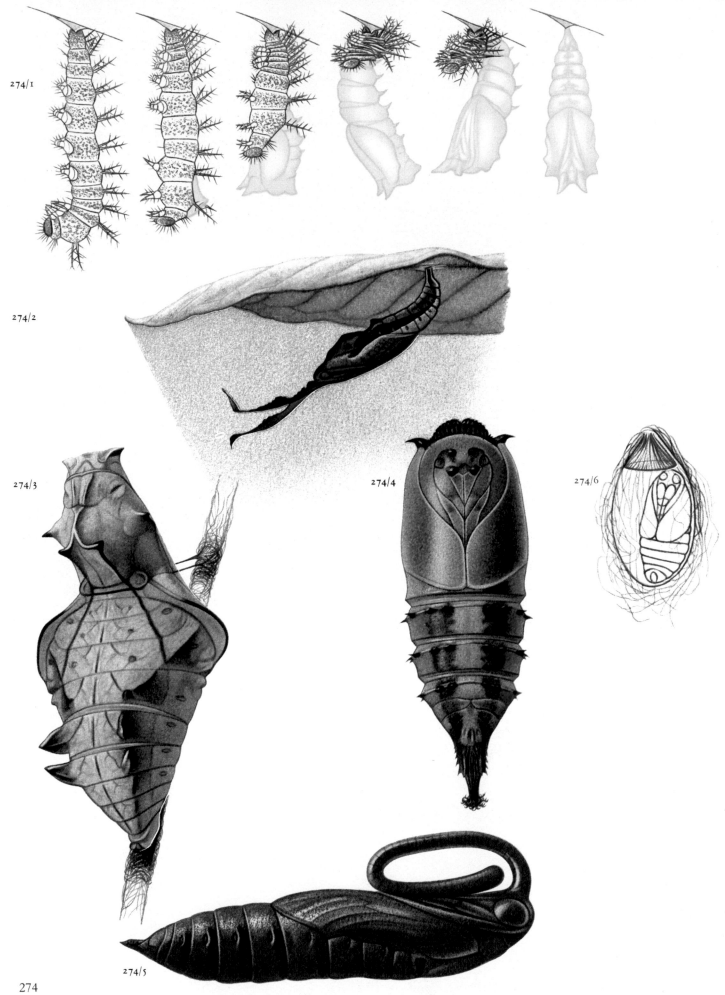

274/1

274/2

274/3

274/4

274/6

274/5

274

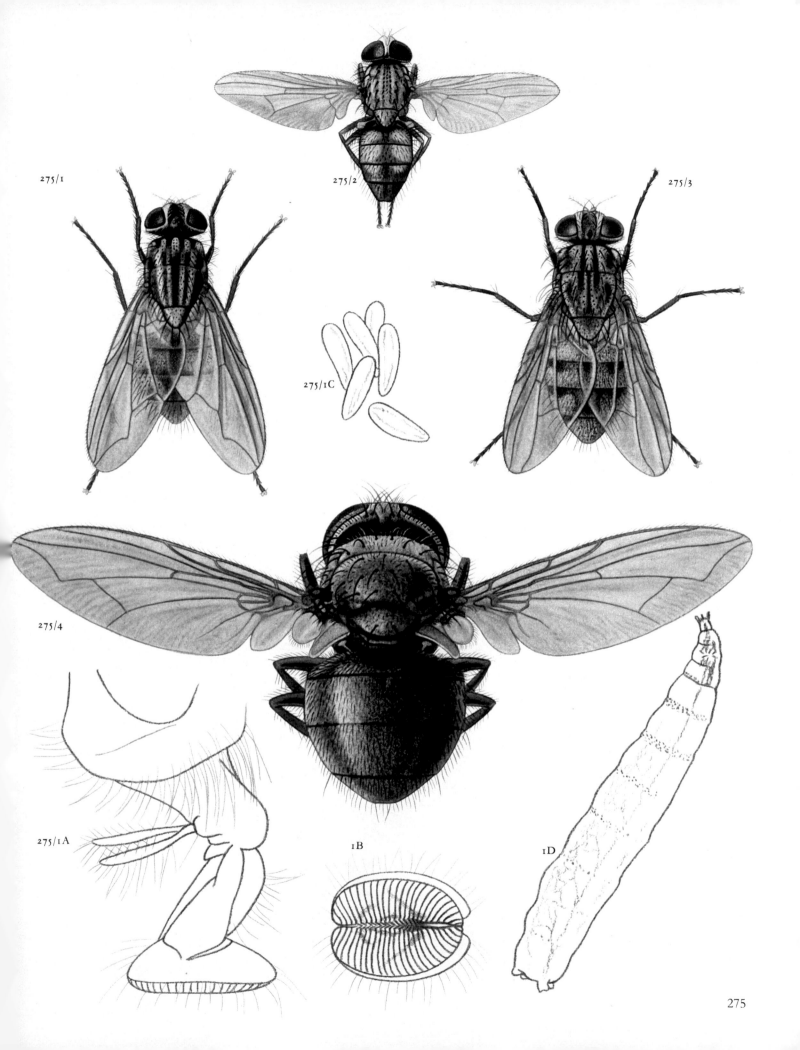

275/1

275/2

275/3

275/1C

275/4

275/1A

1B

1D

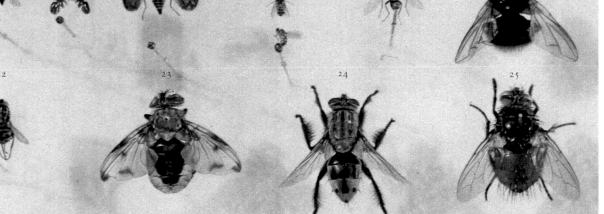

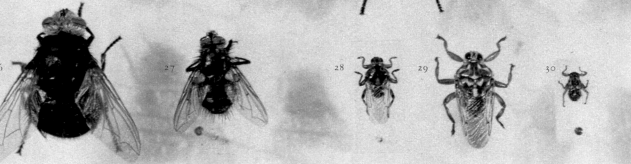

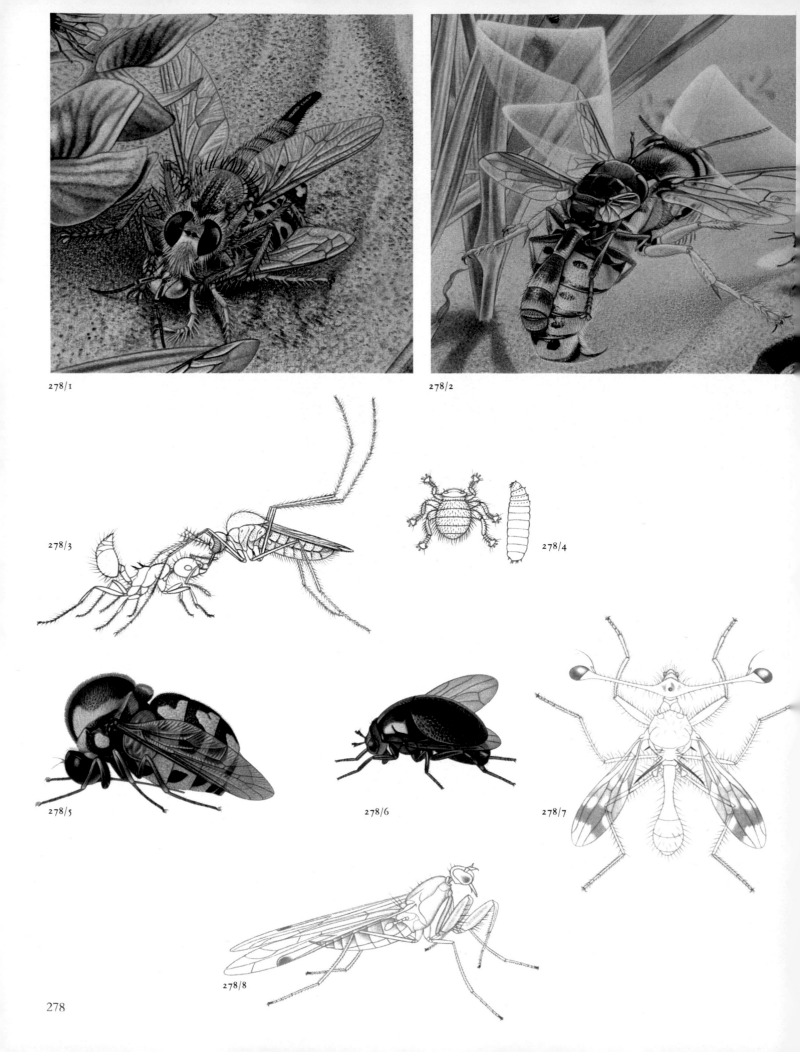

278/1

278/2

278/3

278/4

278/5

278/6

278/7

278/8

278

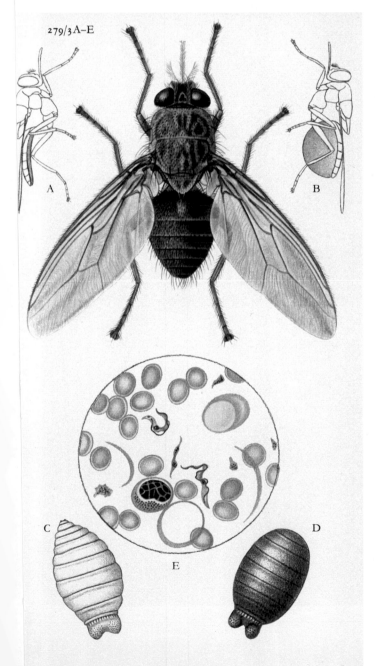

A   B

C   D

E

A   B   C

282/1

282/1 A–C

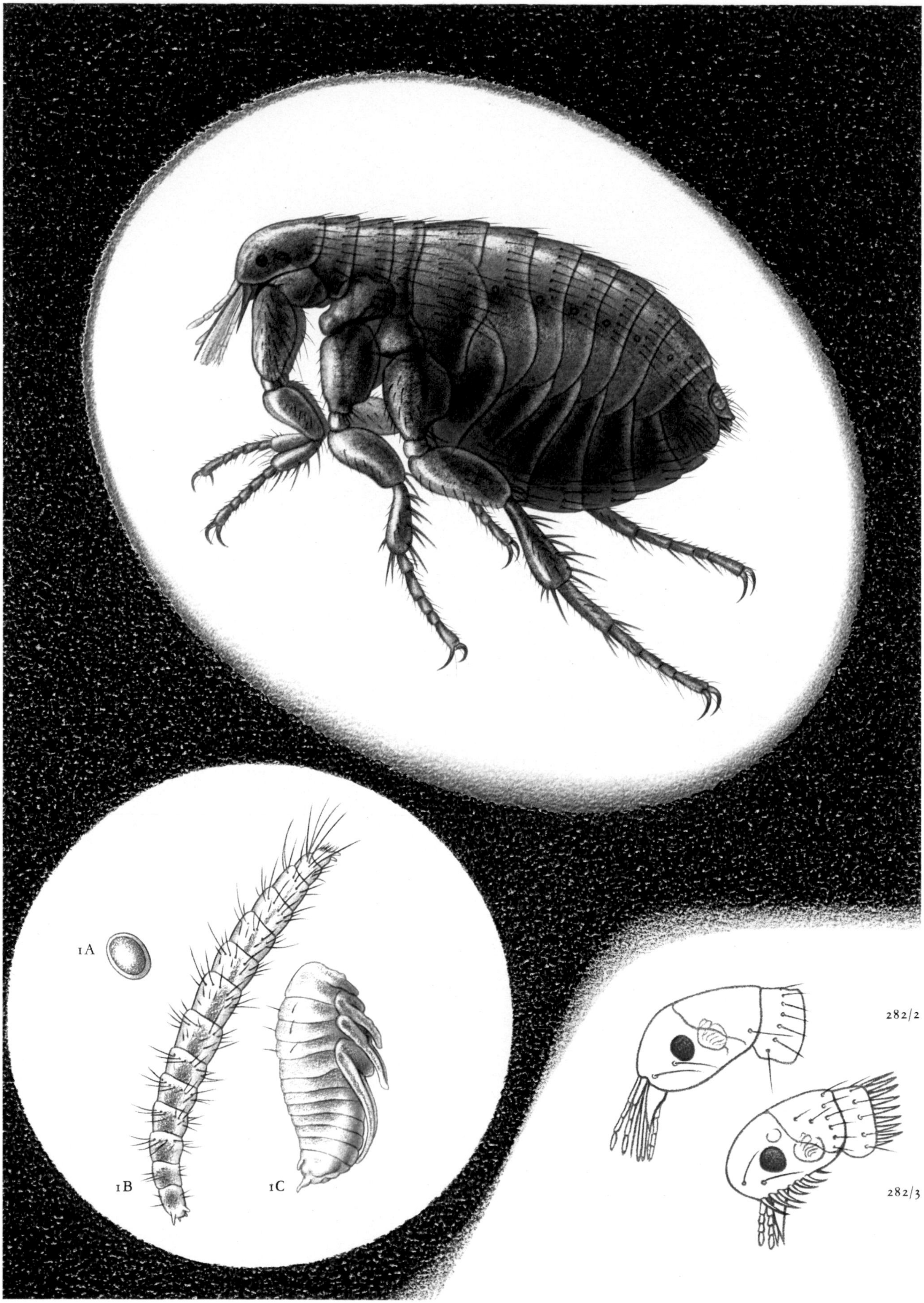

1A

1B

1C

282/2

282/3

282

283/1A

283/1

283/1B

283/1C

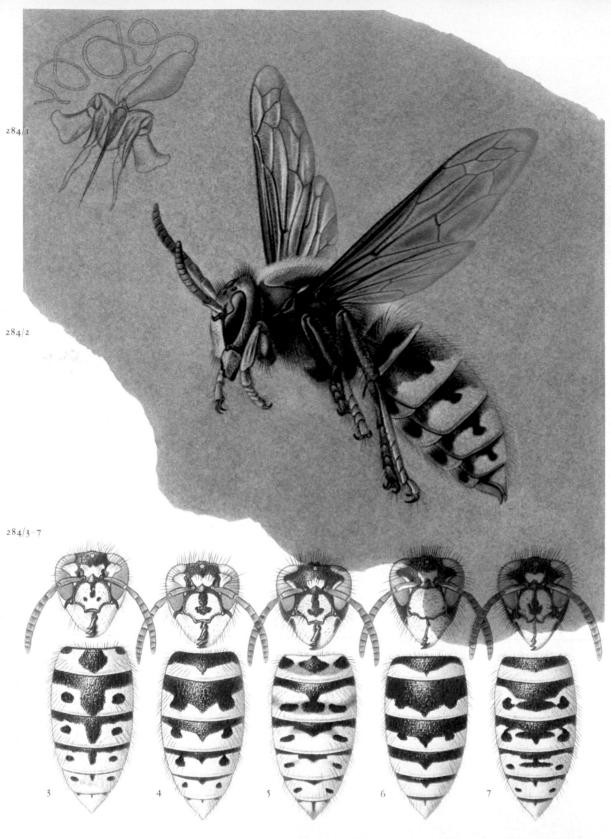

284/1

284/2

284/3-7

3   4   5   6   7

284/8

284

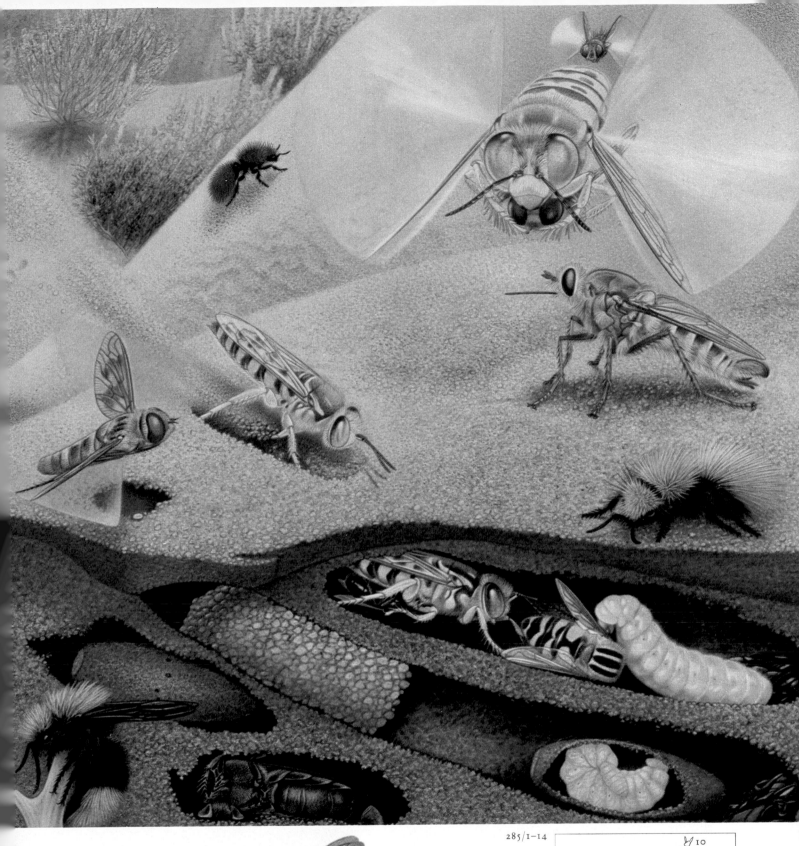

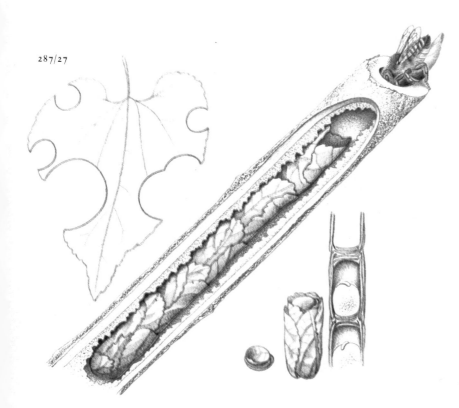

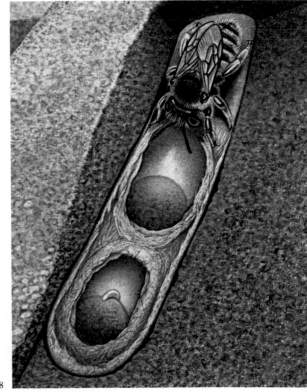

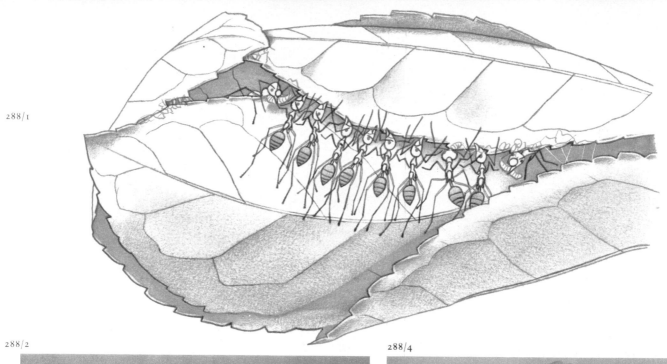

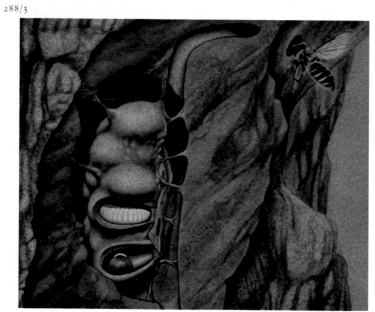

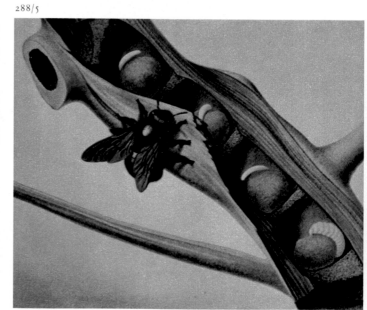

stuff brought in, such as little stones, bits of wood, plant fibers, and straws. Certain pompilids even use bits of earth or bark worked into a felt with spider web. As a finishing touch, *Ammophila* tamps the entrance shut with blows of the head, or even with the help of a pebble held between the mandibles.

Many Hymenoptera establish their cells in wood, pith, hollow stems of plants, galls, holes in rocks, or snail shells. Here, as in the earthen nests already mentioned, the foundation material itself constitutes the cell walls. These cells simply are lined with thin partitions made of various materials mixed with saliva. Numerous species of ants that build in wood merely gnaw out their passageways and chambers, and in doing so the harder layers naturally remain in place as supporting beams and walls. Many ant colonies dwell only in hollow branches, stalks, or aerial roots, in leaf-mines, or in peculiar vesicles in the leaves and stems of certain plants. Well-known is the preference of species of *Cremastogaster* and *Pseudomyrma* for hollow acacia thorns, and of *Azteca* for stems of *Cecropia* trees, which are divided into chambers.

The degree of mutual interdependence, or symbiosis, between such ants and plants is debatable. Nevertheless it is clear, in the first place, that these plants produce from special glands cuplike or egg-shaped bodies containing very nutritious substances that the ants graze on. And in the second place, these ants are invariably biting or stinging species that, in protecting their place of abode, also protect part or all of the tree from the pillaging leaf-cutter ants *(Atta)*. Such a plant also may be immune to grazing by mammals, since masses of biting ants drop from it whenever it is shaken, even most gently.

Other ants incorporate into earthen nests constructed of moist soil the established parts of growing plants in such a way that they function as supports. Protective and warmth-conserving roofs are fashioned from stones, from parts of plants, or from the needles of conifers.

Especially fascinating are the customs of some of the leafcutting bees *(Osmia)* that build in little snail shells. Along the spirals the bees form one or more cells, separating them by partitions of chewed-up vegetable matter; then they usually leave the outer chamber empty and close the opening. This empty outer chamber, also common in nests in hollow stems, probably serves as a measure of defense against parasites. The lid consists of material that differs according to the species of bee. Frequently it is made from a paste of the chewed-up leaves of various plants saturated with saliva, which sets into a hard composition. Sometimes it is mingled with larger grains of sand, with little pebbles, or with splinters from the snail shell. It may be coated with a layer of mortar. More rarely the different materials are kept in altogether separate layers. A few leafcutting bees *(Anthidium)* that build in snail shells use resin instead of plant paste.

Many *Osmia* and *Anthidium* species use only snail shells lying in the open; others choose only hidden ones. Some species drag the shell into a hiding place before or after constructing a nest in it. Taking firm hold of the ground with repeated bites, they grasp the shell with their legs and haul it after them. Some apply plant paste to parts of the slippery shell, enabling their feet to get a firm grip. A few species bury the shell in sandy soil, others protect it with a cover of interwoven pine needles or straws fetched individually in flight, and some disguise it with moss and other things. It is ever a new experience to observe how objectively and with what careful testing such bees work, and how penetratingly thorough is their interest in their productions. [288/2]

The art of building becomes even more intricate. This art, incidentally, by no means serves as a basis for comparing the levels of evolution attained by the various members of the Hymenoptera, since the more highly evolved forms frequently are satisfied with simpler nests than more primitive species. As a further step in constructing the nest, some species line the walls with various materials. Rarely, as is the case with *Anthophora* bees, this is just the nest's basic substance, bitten off and kneaded into a paste with saliva. The primitive yellow-faced bees *(Hylaeus)* and plasterer bees *(Colletes)* use a slime that flows from the mouth and produces threads, which are spun out into a sort of silken carpet. A few wasps *(Odynerus)* form their cylindrical cells with mud, and many bees *(Anthophora, Hemisia, Megachile,* and others) with earth, in certain species mixed with resin or even coated with a thin layer of wax. Numerous *Osmia* species carpet the cells with sections cut from certain petals, gluing them down with saliva and frequently padding them with plant paste beforehand.

Especially widely known are the cells made of interwoven pieces of leaves, or more rarely of thin bark, by many leafcutting bees *(Megachile)*. In individual species the walls of such cells consist of various layers, sometimes being lined with cut pieces of flowers (less often with earth, too) or with pebbles or resin. Frequently resin serves to saturate cell walls made of layers of leaves, as in *Trachusa* and a few *Anthidium* species. Many of the latter genus of leafcutting bees utilize hairs scraped from plants. Load after load of them is brought into the nest in flight, carried under the chin like balls of cotton. The cells are formed from these hairs, and frequently the passageways are carpeted with them, too. [287/27, 28]

A few species of *Sphex* wasps build what look like genuine birds' nests in the joints of stone walls or in clefts in rocks. The nests, oval in shape, measure about 6 by 8 inches, are formed of straws and tufts of grass, and have a hollow of an inch or two deep. They may be cushioned with such material as the silky fibers of cotton grass. Frequently several females build together, as also occurs in numerous other solitary bees as an initial step toward social life. Often, too, very different, rather small digger wasps and bees participate in mixed constructions. Perhaps a stronger species takes possession of a nest entrance after another has already completed a few cells; or perhaps the two are merely living in peaceful coexistence. This sharing may occur naturally in the subsequent re-use of the chambers of an older nest.

The structural pattern of the nest differs according to the species of the builder, but may vary greatly with one and the same species in adaptation to the kinds of cavities available. In the simplest type, the end of a pathway is expanded into a single cell. In the nest of the poppy bee *(Osmia papaveris)* the passageway is so short that the approximately flask-shaped chamber, carpeted with sections cut from poppy flowers, lies close beneath the surface. During construction these bright petals stick up; as a closure their ends are folded in together and finally covered over with soil or sand, after pollen collected from blue cornflowers has been brought in and shaped into a ball, and the more or less banana-shaped egg placed on it. [288/4]

A great many sphecid wasps and spider wasps dig a new shaft for each cell. More frequently, however, and in many very different Hymenoptera, there is a single shaft with several side passages, mostly widened at the ends, or with chambers opening directly from it. In these so-called branched or clustered structures, the cells may lie along one or two sides or may be grouped irregularly on all sides of the shaft. There also are linear structures, where cells are placed one after the other in series like the links of a chain. This last system is the rule among all Hymenoptera

that nest in stems, but also is used in wood, earth, or in clefts in rock, for example.

Most of the heavy-bodied carpenter bees *(Xylocopa)* gnaw linear structures into sticks or dead branches. These are conspicuous, predominantly tropical species. Their wing membranes, buzzing with a deep humming sound and having a magnificent composite radiance of blue, green, gold, or purple, seem to mirror the luminous sky playing on a rippling water surface. A Southeast Asian species, *Xylocopa caerulea,* is covered with blue hairs, a decorative touch almost unique in the insect empire. *Xylocopa* males frequently are completely different in color and hairier than their females. [288/5; 306/2–6; 311/2]

Now, certain digger wasps of the genus *Trypoxylon,* instead of simply taking occupancy of already existing hollow stems or bored holes, as many of their relatives do, construct tubes of mud on vertical surfaces, such as cliffs or treetrunks. The individual cells run the length of the tube, and each offspring emerges through a hole it has bitten out. Among other users of the linear system of construction it is usual that the individuals nearest the end of the tube, and thus the oldest and often the first ones to complete development, cannot make their way into the open until the whole series in front of them has flown out. Similar cell-containing tunnels, made of chips of bark stuck together with resin, are built by a few of the tropical American golden bees *Euglossa,* noted for their magnificent metallic colors. [305/3; 306/18–20]

By way of the bees and wasps that build tunnels above ground, we arrive finally at the stage of so-called "free constructions." These range from simple lumps of earth to combs of paper or wax. Structures that contain only a single cell are naturally roundish or oval, but when the insect makes the small opening into a neck or funnel, they frequently take an attractive juglike or vaselike shape. After the cell is completed and properly supplied, it is walled off. A few potter wasps *(Eumenes)* and certain leafcutting bees *(Anthidium),* which make their nest vessels of mud and resin, respectively, wall them up with little, appropriately chosen pebbles; these insects do the finest kind of work, making clean, smoothly polished joints and inner walls. The working insect is so well adapted to the conditions of its surroundings that the substratum and the nest structures often consist in part of identical material. [312/8]

Frequently the cells occur beside one another in pairs or groups, as do the earthen

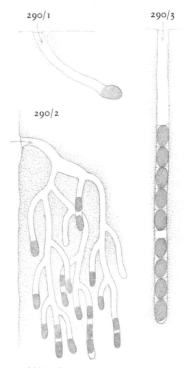

290/1–7
(1) The single cell of a spider wasp's construction. (2) The irregularly branching structure built by a digger wasp (Pemphredon). (3) Linear construction in the ground, in wood, or in stalks is the system followed by many bees, wasps, and digger wasps. (4) The branching linear construction of a digger bee, with a tubular vestibule. (5) The cluster constructed as a nest by a long-horned bee (Eucera). (6) Cells made by a wool-hanger bee in the cavities of a deserted plant gall; the cells are embedded in a mass of scraped-off plant fibers. (7) The heaped-up structure built by a leafcutting bee (Osmia), embedded between stones in chewed-up vegetable matter.

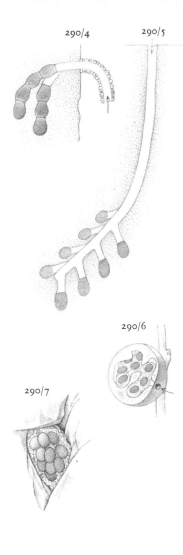

291/1
Resin bees are a group of wool-hanger bees that do not make their cells in existing cavities, but instead build independent vessels out of resin or pebbles (enlarged).

vases of many *Eumenes* or the cylindrical earthen beakers of certain leafcutting bees (*Osmia*). And many species pile a large number of cells together into a great complex, as is the custom of the mortar-making bees in the group of the leafcutting bees (megachilines) and the usually large, graceful digger wasps of the genus *Sceliphron*. These structures, filled with paralyzed spiders, hang from cliffs, houses, and other places, and, because of the way they are plastered over, seem to be nothing but adhering lumps of earth or cement. The mortar-producing bees make unusually firm edifices out of powdered stone and saliva, together with pebbles; one female completes up to a dozen cells, but since several individuals frequently work together at a single location, and since such constructions often are re-used and enlarged by the progeny during the following year, they may grow into complexes covering several square yards. [14/13; 305/1, 4, 5]

The smaller "free constructions," which need not be fastened to a solid surface, frequently are suspended freely from grass stems, twigs, and branches, or are plastered around them. Now, the concept of "free construction," in distinction to the cells formed only by existing cavities or modeled very closely after them, implies the open construction of self-supporting walls, but does not preclude their being located within larger cavities in soil, rocks, or trees, in clefts of cliffs, in masonry joints, and in other hiding places. Thus, certain bees (*Osmia*) plaster their cell complexes of chewed-up leaves freely to rocks or into joints and holes.

Interesting in its application of building material is *Osmia lefeburei*. Like many other *Osmia* species, it works with cement, but overlays the work with apparently superfluous pebbles, setting these in a mortar made of masticated leaves. Also noteworthy craftsmen are some of the primitive yellow-faced bees (*Hylaeus*), striking because of their hairless bodies. Although most of these bees make linear nests in hollow stems, certain species glue together whole piles of cells in masonry joints, using material that apparently flows in large amounts from the mouth.

On the other hand, the one-chambered nests of a few *Sphex* are made of vegetable fibers or the wool of seeds jumbled together. And the many-celled edifice of certain species of the wasp *Zethus*, made of bits of leaves bitten off and stuck together with resin, looks like a ball hanging from a twig. Other wasps of the same genus heap up groups of cells made of vegetable fibers glued together with latex.

Certain species of the social wasps *Stenogaster* suspend their unique structures from a long, thin plant fiber, a straw, or a rootlet. These structures consist either of little bundles of conical cells, numbers of them often hanging above one another, or of a long chain of them, sometimes twisted up so that it reminds one of a braided ribbon. Occasionally, such swaying nests are sheltered by a little umbrella-shaped roof, or even several of these, one above the other. The materials employed are earth, rotten wood or bits of wood, and saliva. [305/8, 9]

What a contrast is the famed "buried comb" of certain mining bees (*Halictus*) and related genera in clayey walls or soils! Here, after excavating and impregnating with strengthening saliva a number of cells that branch off side by side from the main passage, the bees hollow out a narrower room around the entire complex. Since they leave few supporting pillars, the group of cells finally hangs almost entirely free within the ground; it is thus thoroughly aerated, a factor important in preventing or decreasing the destructive formation of molds. Obviously the bees do not know that. And yet they frequently dig out a second shaft to the surface, providing a continuous circulation of air. [288/3]

The nests of ants, though simple in architecture, are fascinating in many respects. The "free constructions" on trees, on trunks, and in all sorts of cavities, even in houses, consist of heaps of cells penetrated by an irregular network of passageways and chambers. They are made out of soil alone or with chewed-up wood added; in the latter case the cardboardlike mass usually is soon pervaded by a specific fungus and thereby becomes satiny. The little ants *Acromyrmex* make bag-shaped nests that consist entirely of interwoven fungal mycelial strands. [353/4]

Peculiarly characteristic are those nests of humus that hang from trees and that soon develop into "ant gardens," so called because the ants (*Azteca, Camponotus,* and *Cremastogaster*) bring in the seeds of epiphytic plants; when the plants grow from the seeds, their roots help to hold the rather loose earthen structure together.

One of the most interesting phenomena is the way certain adult ants use their larvae as spinning implements in the building of silken nests. The adults, which lack the ability to make silk, grasp the larvae in the mandibles and move them back and forth like shuttles on a loom. A drop of secretion exuded from the mouth of these larvae produces a thread when it is pulled away from a point it has touched. The webs made from this silk, frequently intermixed with other materials, are used by certain species of *Technomyrmex, Polyrhacis, Camponotus,* and *Oecophylla*. Sometimes the silk is used only as a carpeting inside cardboard nests or is made into pillars or enclosing shells.

A few of the *Camponotus* and *Oecophylla* species are famed as weaver ants, not indeed on account of their architecture, which consists merely of a pile of leaves pulled together, but because of their methods of working. When fastening two somewhat separated leaves together, these ants line up on the edge of one of them, holding onto it with the legs stretched full length behind them, and, working together, pull up the other leaf with their mandibles. Meanwhile other ants, with the spinning larvae in their mouths, weave the leaves together. If the distance between leaves is too great for an ant to bridge the gap, the ants form ladders; these not only make it possible to pull the leaves closer together, but also serve as a bridge for the weavers.

As if this is not enough, many of the nests serve as homes for the caterpillars of certain moths (pyralids and tineids). Though these caterpillars feed on the ant brood, they are tolerated in the nest because the much denser webs that they make strengthen the walls and help make them impervious. [288/1; 355/7]

At the highest level of building art stand the nests of the social wasps and the honeybees. The six-sided cells of the social wasps fit together in a way that makes a maximum use of the space. The nests may hang free, with perhaps some protection, on branches, on leaves, on cliffs, in houses, or on vegetation. Or they may be hidden in cavities in soil, in trees, in holes in rock, or in the nests of birds and mammals. Certain species of hornets and yellow jackets (*Vespa*) dig holes of their own in the ground or enlarge existing holes. [284/2; 305/10; 307/1]

According to the species and the form of the social organization, as well as spatial relationships, the combs may remain small, with only a few cells, or may become huge, especially if they are reoccupied year after year. The European hornet (*Vespa crabro*), for example, may use the same nest for ten successive years. Edifices of *Polybia socialis* have contained some 60,000 cells, and some structures of *Vespa* species have had perhaps 30,000 cells in 12 to 15 stories. But normally the nests remain smaller.

The generally familiar *Polistes* wasps with rare exceptions build a comb of cells in a single layer. This hangs free and obliquely inclined on a short stalk. Thus, in contrast to the downward-opening cells of most other genera, these cells open in an approximately horizontal direction. [305/11]

Most social wasps build a nest cover that gives protection and helps control temperature, although some species forego this when the nest is well hidden in a confined space, such as in a birdhouse, a hollow treetrunk, or a leaf-roll. The single, frequently gigantic comb of the South American nocturnal *Apoica* wasps, for example, which is suspended flat beneath branches, is covered with a thick, spongy roof of vegetable fibers topped by a varnishlike watertight layer. The outer coat of the nest of the honey-gathering wasps *Nectarina* has a similar porous isolating layer. Such coverings, like the combs, may be either flat or strongly convex downward and may vary from nearly round to long and narrow. In extreme cases they may consist of but two rows of cells.

The building material mostly is a rather fragile mass of paper, a mixture of salivary secretions and gnawed-off wood or bark, more rarely sand or powdered stone. The nests of *Ischnogaster* wasps, in addition, are permeated with wax. The coloration of the nests corresponds to the different kinds of wood employed, which often produce an attractive marbled design. Many of the bright ocher-yellow, cardboardlike structures of the genus *Chartergus,* made of chewed-up vegetable fibers, bark, and pith, are so watertight they can be used as containers for fluids. Certain species of *Polybia* build with mud, in part with an admixture of vegetable materials, and a few *Polistes* with masses of resin.

In general two systems of construction used by social wasps can be distinguished. In the first, used particularly by *Vespa* and *Polistes* wasps, the combs hang one below the other and are fastened to one another by beams or pillars. These are made of material similar to that of the combs but stronger. The size of these nests is increased continually by the addition of new cells all around the comb margins; in case it becomes necessary to enlarge the internal volume, the nest covering (absent in *Polistes* nests) is altered by removing its inner layers and adding new ones on the outside. During the growth in size and weight of such a structure, which together with its contents may weigh several pounds, the wasps constantly widen the weight-bearing pillars, especially in the upper part of the nest. Here these supports finally acquire the shape of broad beams or straps. It is interesting in this regard to consider that wasps scarcely can possess any feeling for the increase in weight of their home, and

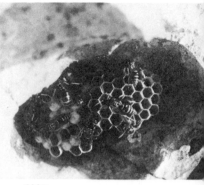

292/1
Paper wasps (Polistes) on their open, papery comb, made out of wood and saliva (reduced). Photograph.

are even less likely to have any realization that, of the many supporting beams, it is the uppermost ones that are of decisive importance. [305/6, 7; 307/4; 320/1]

The second system, best developed in the tropics, uses no pillars. Instead, the combs are fastened together at the margins on all sides by the stable outer covering, and their weight is borne by it alone. Every comb is pierced in the middle or nearer a margin by a passageway that allows traffic to move freely from story to story. Size is increased by additions below. Again and again the floor of the freely suspended nest serves as the ceiling for a new comb.

Every nest, of course, no matter what the type of construction, has at least one entrance and exit, usually in the lower part. This may be drawn out into the shape of a tube or funnel. Frequently a second opening is fashioned at a higher level. This aids in the circulation of air and serves as an emergency exit, as in the nests of certain *Polybia*. Other nests may have many air holes and exits scattered all over them underneath shell-shaped convexities of the coating.

The finest building material, and one produced by the insect's own body, is beeswax. The most complete use of this material is made by the honeybees *(Apis)*. It is exuded from glands at four specific spots on the undersurface and hardens into thin lenses or scales, the front margin of which catches beneath the insect's segmental sclerites. The wax scales are then impaled on particular marginal bristles of the hind legs, drawn back toward the rear, passed forward beneath the body to the mandibles, and here kneaded into a ball ready for use in constructing the honeycomb. [353/1; 355/12]

Honeybees of the species *Apis mellifica* and its races build in hollow trees or, if domesticated, in hives provided by bee-keepers. They construct unenclosed combs, usually a few side by side, that hang vertically and that may contain, on the two faces, about 50,000 horizontal, six-sided cells. For mending the comb or for covering up foreign bodies and rendering them innocuous, the bees use, besides wax, a mass composed of resin and sticky vegetable juices. This is called bee glue, or propolis.

The gigantic Indo-Malayan honeybees, *Apis dorsata,* build free-hanging single combs, up to a yard in length, on branches or cliffs, with a preference for certain huge trees. And the likewise hanging combs of the similarly distributed smallest of the honeybees, *Apis florea,* are a magnificently instructive resume of the life cycle of a bee colony. At the top

there are the approximately 1,000 large honey cells that were the first to be built; then there follow perhaps some 7,000 worker cells, and next below them the larger male (drone) cells, about 300 in number. The comb ends in a point with five huge, plug-shaped queen cells. On the contrary, all the cells are of equal size in the comb of the giant Indo-Malayan honeybees. [307/2]

Quite a different society is formed by the frequently very small, tropical, "stingless honeybees" *(Melipona* and *Trigona)*. Their wax is excreted on the back abdominal surface by males as well as females. It is not employed by itself alone, but is mixed with other materials fetched in the pollen baskets, such as the excrement of plant-eating mammals, bits of bark and sawdust, and frequently clay besides. A large amount of this material, called cerumen, is scattered throughout the nest. [320/12–15]

In a few species, the nests are built so they hang free on trees or on cliffs. Because of their covering layers, they look particularly massive and indeed may weigh as much as 140 pounds. Most other stingless honeybees nest in hollow trees, clefts in rock, and other hiding places. They may be found up to several yards deep in the earth, and certain species live in the nests of termites.

The combs, which are connected to one another by pillars or ribbons, have cells on one side only, like those of wasps and unlike those of honey bees; they differ from the combs of wasps in that the cells usually face upward rather than downward. Combs may also hang vertically or at an angle. The covering layers of the nest are of a loose wax construction that includes air spaces, and in the "free constructions" the inner surface of the mantle, made of a mixture of mud, resin, and other material, constitutes a labyrinth of tangled passageways and cavities.

Many species make nests without coverings, and instead of six-sided cells use oval pots that hang together irregularly like a bunch of grapes or that are bound together with pillars and props of wax. Peculiar to the stingless honeybees is the location of the invariably oval storage jars for honey and pollen, which always are separated spatially from the brood cells; they are usually housed in either the upper or lower part of the nest, and mostly are fastened together in groups.

The entrance to the nest frequently is built out from it in the shape of a tube or funnel made of mud, earth, or resin and wax. As a protection against invaders, certain stingless honeybees set a ring of sticky resin in the mouth of the entrance tube, and ants or other

293/1

Monkshood can be pollinated only by long-tongued bumblebees. Short-tongued species and even honeybees are unable, via the normal route, to reach the nectar, which is up above in the "helmet." But it occurs to many of them to break their way in from outside; they bite or punch holes in the flowers, which are thus not pollinated. Ants too visit flowers, but they help to pollinate only the simplest kinds, if at all (reduced).

trespassers attempting to enter get stuck in it. In other instances, the bees keep out nocturnal visitors by narrowing the entrance or by closing it altogether with a lid equipped with a few holes that permit the circulation of air and enable the sentries to recognize it as an entrance. An especially large *Melipona* nest may contain some 30 combs with about 65,000 cells, which means a population of about 80,000 individuals.

In contrast, those bumblebees *(Bombus)* whose method of building cells together like bunches of grapes is similar to some stingless honeybees construct only small nests. The females (queen and workers) excrete wax from both upper and lower surfaces, and make lumpy, dark-brown brood cells that hang rather irregularly beside and above one another. In them, the larvae grow and, when ready to pupate, spin cocoons that lie close against the walls. They finally emerge from their cells as adult workers. The vacated cells are then used as honey jars. These cells are lighter in color, for they actually consist of the forsaken pupal cocoons from which the bumblebees have scraped off for other applications the wax surrounding the original brood cells.

Bumblebee nests, depending on the species and on environmental conditions, may be located both above and below ground in all possible sorts of hiding places, even in houses. They are frequently embedded in parts of plants or in straw or moss, and in some instances covered with such materials. Especially when it is very damp or cold, many bumblebees add wax coverings that are equipped with air vents. [307/3]

Food for the Brood

Bees and wasps usually begin to gather food for the future brood only after completing the first brood cell. Various digger wasps and spider wasps are exceptions: they first catch prey, hide it by burying it shallowly in the ground, and then dig out a nest. Bees (apids) and a few wasps (nectarines and masarines) provision the cells only with vegetable materials, namely honey and pollen. The activities concerned with collecting them and bringing them in make a particularly engaging bit of natural history. These activities begin with the choice of flowers, a choice that may be quite free or strictly limited.

Bees high in the evolutionary scale—particularly the social bees—almost universally are frequenters of flowers, for their capacity for learning permits rapid adaptation even to flowers of complicated structure. In this connection the inventiveness of single individuals is well recognized; some reach the nectar by biting or stinging a hole in the spur (calcar) of a flower. Even more capable than the honeybees, in all probability, are the bumblebees. They not only have a much longer proboscis, but also their greater strength allows them to force their way into rather tightly closed labiate flowers. But even such adaptable bees display, at least from time to time, a constancy of habit that is useful in the pollination of flowers, in that they fly only from one flower to another of the same or of a closely related species.

Fragrance and color guide the insect to the flowers. Many flowers offer their nectar freely to all comers, but others bar the approach with a variety of highly refined obstacles that only a few selected individuals can surmount. In this way such plants may become wholly dependent on specific insects, as, for example, monkshood *(Aconitum)* on bumblebees. As another example, common red clover *(Trifolium pratense)*, when imported into Australia, grew green and flowered, but it only produced seed after bumblebees also had become established there.

Marvelous are the different mechanisms by which many flowers, like sentient, responsive beings, powder the visitor by touching her lightly or drumming on her, or even glue on or otherwise fasten the anthers to her. With fruitful pollination as the goal, the situation and position of the female stigma is equally precise, whether it is on the same flower or on the next one. Frequently the potential consequence, self-pollination, of the first of these arrangements is avoided by similarly astounding contrivances.

A biology based on flowers, above all as a symbiosis between blossoms and insects, of which the bees are by far the most important, is wonderfully rich and in many features still uninvestigated. Uncounted numbers of plants exist only because of insects, and the insects, in turn, depend for their lives on the plants. Without this worldwide conspiracy, almost all life's bloodflow would come to a standstill!

There exist also some very extreme relationships, such as the "carrion flowers" that smell of decaying flesh and thus attract flies, or the "fetish flowers," namely orchids, that because of their odor and hair patches are mistaken for female insects and visited by the males of certain bees and wasps. Or the variously constructed flower traps, from which insects that have fallen in or have even been flung in by treacherous catapults can

FLORAL BIOLOGY AND
POLLINATION

See pages 308 and 309.

308/1
Nectar presented freely: *A single floret from an umbel flower (enlarged), with exposed drops of nectar freely available to all insects. Visitors get powdered with pollen from the anthers and with it later inoculate the stigmas of other flowers.*

308/2
Temporal separation of sex organs (to prevent self-fertilization): *Male (left) and female stages of the flowering rush (Butomus) (enlarged). In the male phase pollen is produced and the stigmas are immature. Then, during the female stage the anthers have shriveled up and in their stead the ripened stigmas have unfolded.*

308/3
Spatial separation of sex organs: *In the purple loosestrife (Lythrum salicaria), each individual plant has but one of the three different flower forms (enlarged). The flowers with short styles are receptive only to pollen from short filaments, those with styles of medium length only to that from similarly long filaments, and the ones with long styles only to pollen from elongate filaments. The pollinators are bees and Lepidoptera.*

308/4
Entry dimensions adapted to size: *In Gladioli the three floral entrances, marked by means of contrasting color and beard hairs, are suited structurally to bumblebees in particular. The hairy brushes elevate even rather small bumblebees sufficiently to let them rub against the anthers with their back, yet other insects do not reach high enough to do so. When the bumblebees withdraw with pollen sticking to them, they cannot pollinate the small narrow stigma, for only its anterior surface is receptive. Thus fertilization by*

them cannot occur until they force their way into the next mature flower. Other Iris are built to conform to flatter insects, such as flower flies.

308/5

Rings of adhesive: *On the stalk below its blossoms, the catch-fly plant (a pink) produces zones of sticky, pitchlike material that entraps undesired visitors. With their deep, narrow calyces and red tints, the pinks are butterfly flowers.*

308/6
Pollen sac shakers *of the strawberry tree, Arbutus unedo (enlarged). On each anther of plants of the Erica group are two fingerlike bristles. If an insect brushes up against them, the pollen sacs are shaken and let their dust-dry pollen fall from the pores onto the visitor.*

308/7
Pumping action: *The cornflower bears a peripheral rosette of false blossoms while the authentic small flowers are located centrally (below, enlarged). In each individual flower the five anthers are fused together as one tube, not fully closed at the top, in the center of which rises the pistil with its brushy stigma. Every time the sensitive filaments are touched by an insect's proboscis or legs, the filaments immediately shorten elastically, and in doing so draw back the whole anther tube. This causes the stigma of the stationary pistil to push out the pollen that has accumulated in the tube.*

308/8
The "deadfall" system: *Sage (enlarged). The two anthers, here shovel-shaped and fused at the base, are movable on their articulations with the short filaments. When a bee's head touches the shovels, they give way and in doing so lower the lever arm against the insects' back, dusting it with pollen. In flowers of the female stage (below) the style has grown longer and has curved downward, so that the divided stigma is hanging right in front of the entryway and cannot fail to make contact with the pollen brought in by the bee.*
(Continued)

escape only by coming into contact with the plant's reproductive organs, or only after fertilization has taken place. A special group with but few species comprises the carnivorous plants that, by means of their leaves—often flowerlike, equipped with attractants, and modified into trapping devices—entice insects, capture them, and digest them. Best-known are the butterwort (*Pinguiculla*), which catches insects with the help of sticky slime; the sundew (*Drosera*), which operates like coelenterate polyps; the Venus's-flytrap (*Dionaea*); the bladderwort (*Utricularia*), with its trapdoor entryways; and the fluid-filled trapping vessel of the pitcher plant (*Nepenthes*). In the temperate zones about 20 percent of all flowering plants depend on pollination by wind, 80 percent on insects; and in the tropics there are flowers that are adapted to birds. [308–309]

The blossoms achieve the objective of being visited, i.e., the fertilization of the plants, by means of mechanisms ranging from very simple to the highest degree of refinement; these ensure on the one hand that pollen sticks to the insect body, on the other that it is deposited on the stigma of another flower of the same species. Self-fertilization is prevented or impeded by spatial or temporal separation of the pistils and stigmas. The majority of flowers offer nourishment in the form of nectar (carbohydrate) or pollen (protein), and the visitors are lured by odors and colors. Different insects respond to different phenomena, depending on what their sense organs perceive, and thus certain insects choose certain flowers. With flowers whose nectar is readily available, this choice is only a very general one; contrariwise, with those of complex structure, it is a more or less limited one. In the latter case a distinction needs to be made between bee (and wasp) flowers, fly flowers, and butterfly flowers, if only rarely in a mutually exclusive sense. The flowers also offer the flying visitors a landing place, or arrangements for gaining a firm foothold, via appropriately shaped or pubescent petals, long pistils, and lengthy stamens. Frequently butterfly flowers are red, violet, or blue but, in correspondence with the long thin lepidopterous proboscis, are distinguished primarily by a deep, tubular calyx with a narrow entrance. The moth flowers, which do not emit a strong aroma until evening, are generally pallid, often white, and lack any landing surface for the visitors, who drink while hovering before them.

The insects likewise can be grouped: first are the flower visitors with a more or less inefficient approach. To be sure, with their mouthparts that both chew and lap, they get their food from flowers, but remain rather inconsequential with respect to pollination. In this category are many beetles and flies, parasitic wasps and sawflies, many digger wasps and spider wasps, and also social wasps. Second are the well-qualified visitors, equipped with sucking and lapping mouthparts, and usually possessing a hairy covering that serves to store up pollen. Included are especially bees and wasps, Lepidoptera, and flower flies (Syrphidae). Among them are those forms with a long sucking proboscis and highly developed instincts, namely the hawk moths (Sphingidae) among the Lepidoptera, and above all the many bee species, furnished with very special devices for collecting pollen. [190]

Close adaptation between flowers and bees exists not only with respect to nectar and proboscis, but also with respect to pollen and the collecting methods of the female bees. It is true that the primitive *Prosopis* and related Australian bees swallow some pollen with the nectar, to be regurgitated from the crop in the nest, as is also true to a great extent with the carpenter bees (*Xylocopa*). But the rest of the pollen is carried home, stored among abundantly branching body hairs or in special pollen baskets. Bees that gather pollen on their lower surface, like *Osmia, Megachile,* and *Anthidium,* sweep with vibrating movements over the flowers, filling their rather dense ventral brushes with pollen grains. On the other hand, *Systropha,* called spiral-horned bees because the antennae of the males are twisted like a ram's horn, roll around inside funnel-shaped flowers, such as the morning glory, in order to take on a load of pollen with the hairs of the abdomen and legs. Very different, however, are the techniques of those that gather pollen with the legs. The most primitive among them, the ancient *Colletes* and related bees, transport pollen in the loose hairy cover on the hind legs and on the lower surface of the midpart of the body. The same method is used with refinements by the mining bees *Halictus* and related genera, and by burrower bees of the genus *Andrena.* These have more highly developed collecting bristles on the hind legs, predominantly on the femora (third segments), and in part also on the lower surface. The burrower bees frequently have special collecting baskets in the form of great locks of hair at the base of the femora and on the metathorax.

Pollen is stored by other burrowing bees (*Panurgus* and relatives), as well as by the gorgeous pollen-gathering bees (*Dasypoda*),

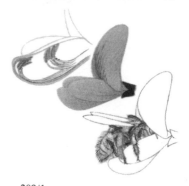

in long fur that forms a dense covering for the hind legs. In gathering pollen, the former roll around on shallow flowers, and the latter struggle about and get the pollen grains in between the long hairs of the monstrous tufts on their legs, perhaps taking on a load equal to more than half their own weight, most of it caught in the trochanters (second segments) or tibiae (fourth segments).

Limited even more exclusively to the collection of pollen on the tibiae are the remaining groups, bees that moisten the pollen with nectar from the mouth. The bees *Meliturga,* which with a loud, buzzing sound often hover in the air like flower flies (Syrphidae), glue the moistened pollen around the hind tibiae in the shape of a broad ring. But the rest, such as the mining bees *Eucera, Tetralonia,* and *Anthophora,* and many related forms, press it into the brushes on the tibiae and the tarsi (parts below the tibiae). The higher bees, such as the bumblebees, have pollen-carrying baskets, namely the bare and somewhat concave surfaces of the hind tibiae, ringed about by bristles inclined inward. The golden bees (*Euglossa*) and the stingless honeybees (*Melipona, Trigona*) frequently have enormous baskets. [310; 330/1]

The collection technique of the honeybees is well worth observing. For these bees are covered almost all over with hairs, even on the eyes. When a honeybee visits a flower, she gets powdered with pollen grains, then cleans herself with the brushes that sit on the inner side of the large first tarsal segment of all the legs. Moistening all the material with honey from her mouth, she constantly passes it back to the particularly receptive brushes on her hind legs. When the bee rubs her hind legs together lengthwise, the pollen is combed out of the brush of one leg by means of the transverse comb on the end of the tibia of the other leg. The pollen piles up here, and, by means of the pressure of a moving, articulated lobe, is transferred to the outside of the leg into the basket, where it is pushed higher and higher as more is added from below. The middle legs cooperate in pressing the mass of pollen together and in rounding it up. If one recalls all the other special pieces of equipment on a bee, such as the sting, wax glands, honey stomach, and mouthparts (with a sucking proboscis, but chewing mandibles), then the impression grows of a creature bristling with tools.

Whereas the social bees fill their cells with honey and pollen, storing them as provisions for both the brood and themselves, the solitary bees usually form in each of their cells a round or elongate ball of a size appropriate to a single offspring, lay an egg on the ball, and close the cell off. The number of such chambers depends among other things on the amount of time at the disposal of the female bee, and this is influenced greatly by the weather. Under the most favorable circumstances there may be about 20 to 30 cells. The pollen-gathering *Dasypoda* display a sure instinct for preventing the formation of mold on the balls of pollen they place deep below ground; they set them on three little legs, so that contact with the earth is reduced to a minimum. [310/1]

The digger wasps (Sphecidae) and spider wasps (Pompilidae), like almost all solitary wasps, supply their brood with animal prey instead of with nectar and pollen. The booty is fetched in from a distance in various ways, according to the species, frequently by means of a tedious, interrupted flight and sometimes by dragging it over the ground. A *Pompilus* wasp has been seen to drag its spider more than 100 yards.

Except for spiders, only insects are brought in; certain wasps take insect species more or less at random, but others confine themselves to a narrow selection. To give a few examples, many digger wasps catch all sorts of flies, as do certain vespid wasps of the genus *Stenogaster,* which even snatch mosquitoes from the webs of spiders; among other digger wasps, certain *Cerceris* species will have nothing but metallic wood-boring beetles (Buprestidae) or weevils (Curculionidae), whereas other *Cerceris* and *Philanthus* species want only Hymenoptera. Still other digger wasps, such as *Stizus,* catch Homoptera, the square-headed wasp (*Crabro*) hunts flies and Lepidoptera, and certain ones take ants from their runways, perhaps about fifty for a single offspring. The vespid wasp *Odynerus spiricornis* ferrets out sawfly larvae in their hiding places between leaves that have been spun together. [271/1; 285/1, 3, 15; 312/1, 2, 9]

All these hunters are equipped with almost unfailing instincts for finding and overpowering their victims; the latter are detected in part with the eyes, but frequently with a very highly refined sense of smell. A few of the smaller pompilids, creeping acrobatically along the threads of a spider web, finally make their way to the concealed spider. Others dig into the earthen tubes of such animals, or open their trapdoors, or even are able from outside to tantalize the inhabitant into jumping out.

Various little digger wasps paralyze their victims by means of crushing bites behind

309/1
The spring-loaded system: *In the broom plant the pistil and the filaments, that are of different lengths, are held under tension in the lower lip of the flower. When the bee (here a large carpenter bee) makes its way in, it depresses the lower lip forcibly. And inasmuch as the two petals that constitute the lip lie close against one another above, but are fused only anteriorly, the increasing downward pressure drives them further and further apart at the top. Initially the five shorter filaments snap upward, striking the anthers against the underside of the bee's body, and then the pistil and the four long filaments also are freed, curling up and beating against the bee's back. The event is as sudden as a smoke-producing explosion, and afterward the pistil is rolled up into a spiral. These flowers have no nectar and dispense nothing but pollen, and they can be opened only by strong bees, like bumblebees, carpenter bees, and honeybees.*

309/2
Adhesive discs: *Certain orchids with numerous little flowers (enlarged), strongly fragrant at night, let their pollen-containing sperm cases, or pollinaria, be torn away from the petals. At the base the pollinaria have an adhesive structure that becomes attached to the moth's proboscis when the latter is thrust down through the narrow opening into the long nectar-containing floral spur. Hence the pollinaria are pulled out when the proboscis is withdrawn, remain glued to it, and after their soft stalk has dried, soon curve forward. When the next flower is visited, they shatter against the adhesive stigma. In lieu of adhesive discs, various other plants have developed a system whereby automatic fastening devices attach the pollinaria to the insect's proboscis or legs.*

296

Fetish flowers: Orchids of the genus Ophrys, by means of their scent and special arrangements of hairs on the strikingly colored lip, have an illusory resemblance to the females of certain species of bees and sphecid wasps, and thus the males make attempts to copulate with these lips. In the process the bee (here, A, a long-horned bee, enlarged) bumps its head against the adhesive pollinaria, tearing them loose as it flies away, and then brushes them against the stigma of the next flower visited. To date, species of andrenids and long-horned bees, members of a sphecid wasp genus (Gorytes), and the scoliid wasp Campsoscolia ciliata have been seen on certain species of Ophrys that are adapted to these insects. The arrangement of hairs on the lip of the flower is very similar to that on the back of the female insects in question, and with some Ophrys they are brushed upward, causing the andrenid males that visit this flower to turn about so that the posterior end rather than the head becomes attached to the pollinaria. In any case, chance pollination by flies and beetles can also occur, and self-pollination is frequent. The weight of the mature pollinaria makes them fall away from the petals, their stalks curl downward thanks to their special construction, and thus they make contact with the stigma (B). As a consequence of self-pollination, different form and color variants of the Ophrys species are created often and in a relatively short time.
(Continued)

the head. Otherwise, the sting is the hunting weapon of the wasps. In contrast, the sting of bees as a rule serves only for defense. Wasps deliver the sting to the softer parts of the body, especially the mouth, throat, or underside. Usually the sting paralyzes the victim. But frequently the prey is killed, particularly by species that continuously supply food to their brood, making preservation superfluous. Some species go further by crushing the back of the head or the neck with their mandibles, as *Sphex* does with grasshoppers, or *Ammophila* and vespids with caterpillars. The usefulness of this act is not surely known, but frequently it signifies a squeezing out of the body juices for the predator's own nourishment. Crushing the legs or even biting them off—occasionally done, for instance, by pompilids with paralyzed spiders—facilitates squeezing past obstacles, such as the narrow tube leading into the nest, but also prevents a later escape in case the victim should regain consciousness.

The method of transportation also differs from species to species. Booty that is not too heavy is carried in flight, usually held close to the body by the middle pair of legs. Peculiar and typical is the method used by little digger wasps of the genus *Oxybelus*. After stinging a fly, they do not remove the sting, but carry the victim home impaled on it and supported to some extent with the hind legs. Here, with their rear part held vertically and the fly poised on the sting, they shovel out the nest entrance. A more pedestrian method is used by the digger wasp *Sphex*. With her mandibles, the wasp seizes one antenna of the big grasshopper it has caught and drags it along, walking backward or astride the victim.

When the female has fully provisioned the brood chamber—with one or more specimens, according to her species—she lays an egg, usually on the victim first brought in and usually on a certain part of its body. Vespids, on the contrary, suspend the egg in the cell on a short thread. A few genera, such as *Bembix,* lay the egg before supplying the cell with food. Certain *Odynerus* and *Rhygium* vespid wasps pile up a stock of paralyzed spiders in a side chamber of the nest before depositing an egg in a new cell. *Odynerus nobilis,* repeatedly interrupting its hunting, takes out of the cell all the beetle larvae collected previously and crushes them up, licking off the juices and probably thereby helping to preserve this food intended for the wasp larvae. The male of the organ-pipe mud-dauber *Trypoxylon rubrocinctum* often stays at the nest, takes the booty from the female as she flies up with it, and carries it inside.

Once the cells have been provisioned and eggs laid, the cells usually are closed and left, never to be seen again by the female. But among the solitary wasps, various species tend the brood, just as the social wasps do. Thus certain *Synagris* species, some males of which have monstrous mandibular horns that may be used in sexual rivalry, feed their larvae with premasticated balls of food. Likewise, many honey wasps (masarines and nectarines) feed nectar to the young from mouth to mouth. And *Odynerus tropicalis* continually brings to its larvae fresh caterpillars, the size of which is adjusted to the age of the young. Similarly, the sand wasps *Bembix* and *Stictia,* most of which shovel the nest entrance shut after each visit, at first usually give their larvae only little flies.

A few thread-waisted wasps, such as the species *Ammophila campestris,* simultaneously take care of a whole series of larvae of different stages, each growing within its own nest. In doing this, the wasps display an astounding memory. For, the underground nests, which are dug and provisioned several days apart, and which are constantly kept closed and hence invisible, are thereafter opened over and over, whether it is for bringing in new caterpillars or merely for inspection. [312/2]

In this procedure three phases per nest may be discerned. First, the wasp digs the nest and closes it, catches a caterpillar and drags it into the nest after reopening it, and lays an egg and closes the nest anew. Second, over a period of days, the wasp opens the nest a few times for inspection and brings in one to three new caterpillars after the young larva has hatched from the egg. Third, the wasp makes additional inspections and brings in from three to seven caterpillars, closing the entrance each time, but with a final, more solid barrier on the last occasion. These phases, carried out instinctively by a wasp, apply to a single nest. When one recalls that a given wasp simultaneously takes care of several nests containing larvae of different ages, then one begins to sense the miracle of the "primitive" insect brain.

One female of the sphecids, pompilids, or solitary vespids has altogether 5 to 12 progeny, of which on the average about half mature. Frequently tachina flies pursue wasps returning homeward in flight or on the ground, with the intention of fastening eggs to the wasps' booty. When they are successful, flies instead of wasps will develop. For that matter, theft of booty is no rarity among digger wasps, and various pompilids will

open a strange nest and steal for their own use the spider stored there. And during times that are unfavorable for catching prey, certain *Eumenes* wasps (Vespidae) simply smuggle their eggs into the still-open cells of others of their kind, instead of first establishing nests of their own and hunting for caterpillars.

SMUGGLERS AND INVADERS

A few pompilids and sphecids *(Stizus)* will enter a strange nest by force, eat the egg already present, and deposit their own in its place. This is not unusual behavior. Numerous species, and even whole genera, in many families have become food parasites of this sort, much as cuckoos are. The ceropalines push their egg into the respiratory opening of a spider captured and stored by the host wasp. They do this in an unguarded moment even while the prey is being transported to the nest or else force their way in later, reclosing the nest carefully after their *fait accompli*. The parasitic larva hatches from the egg after two to three days, before the owner's larva hatches, and hence is able to develop with this advantage and to eat the other, in case it has not already devoured the egg. In the digger wasps the genus *Nysson* similarly parasitizes *Gorytes*. [286/28, 29; 313/ 1–17]

Particularly numerous are the cuckoo bees, which parasitize their relatives. Some are limited to parasitizing a single species, but others have more choice. Often strikingly marked and colored, many have an agreeably aromatic odor. Some are received with friendly tolerance in the hosts' nests, as certain attractive wasplike cuckoo bees *(Nomada)* are by the burrowing bees *(Andrena)*. But otherwise the "cuckoos" must take care not to be detected while smuggling their eggs into strange cells, whether the cells are still open or are closed and must be bored into. [313/3, 4]

If they succeed, then a little later the two hatched larvae, the host's and the parasite's, confront one another within the narrow chamber while eating the brew of honey or the cake of pollen; but soon the parasite has the entire store for itself, for it sucks its legitimate neighbor dry. Not only are the cuckoo larvae older and better developed than the host's larvae, but during their first stage many have sickle-shaped mandibular daggers and can move about more freely. When two or even more parasitic bees lay their eggs in a single host cell, within a short time there likewise is only one surviving

larva, unless the chamber is large and the food plentiful. [315/4]

Among the cuckoo bees, a few species of *Sphecodes,* mostly black and red in color, do not smuggle their eggs, but with naked force invade the nests of mining bees *(Halictus),* when necessary slaughtering everything that opposes them and flinging it out the entrance. A few of these species of mining bees live together in rather large families, and the entire group may be killed off, leaving no survivors. The conqueror takes possession of the edifice, deposits its eggs in the cells, which already are supplied with pollen, and destroys any eggs left by the others. Then, closing up the chambers and the entrance door, she leaves the scene of the crime. [313/1,2]

Social bees, wasps, and ants that have become renegades and gone over to predatory and parasitic ways are described in the section on "Social Insects." Still to be described here are various families as yet unmentioned, in particular those parasites that are not, like those previously considered, in the position of degenerates within their families. Instead, they are, so to speak, dedicated by family custom to this calling.

At the head of the list are the cuckoo wasps (Chrysididae), measuring some 0.08 to 0.9 inch long. Their improbably radiant gamut of structural colors surpasses that of gold or jewels, and their body forms, often appearing to be hammered or engraved into countless facets and, in addition, artistic in cut and harmonious in design, augment still further the gemlike impression.

It would be difficult to contradict a statement that the cuckoo wasps are the most beautiful of all insects. But why should such magnificent dress be worn by smugglers that deposit their eggs in strange nests and presumably should attract as little attention as possible? Or are structural colors, depending as they do upon the refraction of light, perhaps nonexistent to the eyes of insects?

Like many cuckoo bees and other parasites, the cuckoo wasps do not have especially hard armor, but they can roll up into almost unseizable balls, and they gain additional protection by having scent glands that emit an especially penetrating odor; thus, as a rule they can at most be thrown out of the nest. Nevertheless, a few species dig their way only into structures that already have been completed and closed off. For deposition of eggs in the cells, they use a telescopically protrusible ovipositor, which frequently is extraordinarily long; its individual tubular parts are the completely modified terminal abdominal segments. In most genera there are but

309/4
Trapping vessels: *The flowers of the South American orchid genus Coryanthes (here the Venezuelan species albertinae) have what is probably the most fantastic mechanism, far exceeding all that is required for the purpose, in the whole area of floral pollination. Beginning at the top, the lip of these flowers forms a helmet, then elongates downward, and expands into a trough with a beak-shaped rearward extension. In addition, the head of the columella, bearing stigma and pollinaria, reaches so far down toward this beak that only a narrow aperture is left between the two. Above, at the lip basis two short arms are stretched out from the tips of which a clear fluid drips into the basin and fills the latter to overflowing. The flowers are visited by relatively large bees, here a species of Euglossa, which try to reach the nutrient tissue below the helmet but which in the attempt soon slip on the smooth walls and fall into the water. Here their only recourse is to make their way out through the beak, forcing themselves past the head of the columella, and in this process the pollinaria become glued to their back. Later on, in another flower, they brush the pollinaria off in the same manner.*

309/5
A persistent trapping vessel for flies: *During the first hours it is in bloom, the cuckoopint (Arum) has a strong smell of urine and develops a high temperature that may rise as much as 16° C above that of the*

298

surroundings. These factors often attract great numbers of moth flies (upward of 4,000 having been counted on a single flower), which develop in liquid sewage. These insects fall down among the bristles that, together with the smooth walls, later prevent their getting out at the top. Down below, they scrape off on the numerous stigmas of the lower half of the columella the pollen they have brought along, most of it from other flowers. The ring of anthers up above does not ripen until the flies have been trapped in the vessel for some time, have pollinated the stigmas, and have also gotten from them food in the form of drops of nectar. Then the anthers open and pollen falls upon the entire company. The bristles that bar the way out begin to relax, the large covering leaves wilt and separate a little, and the exit is cleared. The cuckoopint is one of the carrion flowers that attract flies and beetles with odors of decomposition and similar smells.

309/6
Insect-eating plants : *The upper portion of the leaves of the Venus's-flytrap forms open traps, in which the midrib acts as a lever. The flap closes quickly as soon as an insect touches one of the six sensitive bristles in the middle of it. Then, depending on the size of the victim, the trap remains closed for from a few days to three weeks, during which time the captured insect is dissolved and digested by the secretions of glands that now become active (at the right, enlarged).*

three of the original eleven segmental sclerites remaining in the actual abdomen.

All wasps and bees are potential hosts of the cuckoo wasps. As is always the case with parasites, some cuckoo wasps are limited to a definite host species, but others have a broader selection. Though the larvae of cuckoo wasps suck dry the prey that has been stored in the nest, the nearly mature host larvae form their principal source of food. If the parasitic egg is inserted into a cell containing an immature host larva, the cuckoo larva that hatches must wait in hunger until the host increases in size. Sometimes two females place an egg in the same cell. Then one of the hatching larvae must be disposed of. In their first stage many kinds of larvae are equipped especially for such contests with strong mandibular tongs and a great degree of mobility, thanks to body bristles and a caudal fork that serves as a supporting organ. [49/28, 30–33; 314; 315]

Although the cuckoo wasps are in general rather rare, they are distributed almost everywhere other Hymenoptera—that is, their hosts—occur; they are most numerous in the plains areas of the warmer regions of the temperate zone. Here, they display the most beautiful golden colors, whereas tropical species gleam predominantly with green and blue. A few groups parasitize insects other than bees and wasps. Thus some species of the genus *Chrysis* develop in the pupae of certain moths, and the cleptines are believed to be parasitic on sawfly larvae.

Another large family of wasp parasites are the velvet ants (Mutillidae), which also are gorgeous, though in quite a different way. Their dress, frequently a mixture of tousled, upstanding bristles and almost satiny hairs, displays attractive designs, most of them in black, red, and white, but also in silver and gold. Whereas the males as a rule have big, dark wings, the usually different-colored and frequently much smaller females are with few exceptions wingless and strikingly similar to ants. Because their heavy armor is almost as hard as rock, they are nearly impossible to take hold of, and in case of need they defend themselves with a remarkably painful sting.

The mutillids chirp with a sound like that of boiling water. They produce this sound by means of vibratory movements of the third abdominal segment, which is rubbed against the margin of the preceding one. The mutillids develop in a way similar to that of the cuckoo wasps. They parasitize not only numerous other wasps and bees, especially bumblebees, but also certain beetle larvae and even tsetse flies (Glossina). The eggs apparently are inserted into the cocoons

of already full-grown host larvae. Both mutillids and cuckoo wasps may at times become so ascendant in certain localities that their hosts are almost eradicated and then require years for recovery during which time, of course, only very small numbers of the parasites are able to develop. [285/12–14; 300/1; 307/3; 316]

Like the mutillids, the scoliids are represented in all parts of the earth, but most richly in the tropics, and are among the most beautiful Hymenoptera. Mostly red or yellow combined with black, they are full of contrast; and their wings frequently are metallic. [313/18, 19]

The larvae of scoliid wasps grow predominantly in the grubs of scarabaeids; the largest, up to more than 2.4 inches in length, develop in the grubs of rhinoceros beetles and giant beetles (Dynastinae). The wasps, armed with a powerful sting and strong digging legs, work their way to these beetle larvae in the ground, in rotting wood, and in deposits of dung or foliage; after stinging them into paralysis, they lay an egg on them on the spot.

Smaller relatives of the scoliids are the tiphiids, likewise parasites of beetle larvae. The wingless females of the genus *Methoca* paralyze the larvae of tiger beetles (Cicindelidae). The tiger-beetle larvae are well-known for their habit of digging burrows in the earth and capturing insects that walk over them. But at the moment a beetle larva seizes the *Methoca* wasp, she stings it in the throat or thorax. [122/1]

The little bethylids, also often wingless in the female sex, have especially interesting ways of living. Many paralyze their victim— usually a caterpillar or a beetle larva—and then drag it into a hiding place, there to lay one or more eggs on it. Others force their way into the cells of wasps after these have been filled with caterpillars or other booty; and still others develop in the nests of ants either on the larvae of the ants or of other insects that dwell there as lodgers and guests. Certain bethylids, frequently several of them participating, stay with the paralyzed caterpillar or beetle larva until the offspring sucking on it are full-grown and have spun their cocoons, or even until the new generation of wasps appears after about a month. For in these cases the booty serves as food not only for the brood but also for the females. At first the females squeeze out juices with their mandibles, but later, when the larvae are somewhat grown, suck at the wounds these have made in boring through the skin of the prey. Frequently, too, the females devour their own eggs or larvae. [317/12]

The dryinids are also small parasitic wasps. The females are wingless and, with the exception of one species, have forelegs modified into grasping tongs. With these they hold down small Homoptera while inserting one or more eggs into their skin. Later a saclike structure grows at the infected spot. It is formed of the shed skins, pushed into one another, of the larva sucking beneath. The homopteran does not die until the larva is almost full-grown, and then finally is consumed entirely. In Australia, dryinids are useful because they destroy Homoptera that damage sugarcane. [317/5–11]

PARASITIC WASPS AND GALL WASPS

These groups include families whose members are almost all parasitic. It should be mentioned here that, in the strict sense of the word, parasite means an organism that does no serious harm to its host. Since most "parasites" of the Hymenoptera destroy the host, they are not true parasites. Instead they are more accurately called parasitic predators or parasitoids.

One of the few true parasites among the Hymenoptera is the tiny parasitic wasp *Rielia manticida*. This wasp lands on a praying mantid, presses its way beneath the wings against the body, and, soon shedding its own wings, sucks on the mantid as an external parasite. If the host is a female and produces an egg packet, the wasp climbs over and deposits its own eggs in it. If the host is a male, the wasp soon dies. Although the adult *Rielia* wasp is a true parasite, its larvae are not, for they develop in the mantid eggs and destroy them.

Although it is important to know the distinction between parasites and parasitoids, in actual practice even entomologists tend to use the word parasite for both. To simplify matters, this book will do likewise.

The parasitic wasps are among the most important forces in the balance of nature's economy. Moreover, many parasitic wasps are hyperparasites—they infest the eggs or larvae of other parasites. Since many of these parasites benefit man by destroying harmful insects, the hyperparasites that prey on them hence are pests from the standpoint of human interests. Parasitic wasps are scourges of the eggs, larvae, and pupae of all insects; some even attack adult insects, as aphidiids do with aphids, and braconids do with certain beetles. Besides insects, these wasps afflict spiders and their eggs, mites, ticks, centipedes,

and millipedes. For this parasite, a certain species is host; for that one, others are. The picture is frequently a confusing mosaic of hosts, parasites, and hyperparasites. [111/2]

One tiny chalcid species (*Trichogramma evanescens*) has been shown to have some 150 hosts in seven orders, and to complicate matters wasps of this same genus are known to have as many as thirty consecutive generations in a year. On the other hand, from a single caterpillar host there may develop ten different parasites, and it is difficult to know which is a parasite of the caterpillar and which is a parasite of another parasite. One may believe he has identified the cocoon of a definite wasp, as it lies inside the emptied host pupa, because the wasp hatched therefrom. But if the cocoon were opened, one might find in it still another cocoon, which actually belonged to the wasp in question.

The typical parasitic wasps, particularly those of the family Ichneumonidae, develop primarily in caterpillars. Graceful and long, the ichneumons run with agility and glide through the vegetation. Some are active at night. Their long, threadlike antennae, quivering nervously all the time, can detect a larva concealed deep in wood or beneath the water's surface. Thus a female of the family Agriotypidae dives below the water's surface and remains there for perhaps ten minutes as she places an egg in a caddisfly larva. The larva that develops from this egg is especially interesting because it produces an air-containing ribbon 0.4 to 2.4 inches long and usually rolled up in a spiral. It is spun before pupation in such a way that it sticks out of the case of the host larva, which is then consumed. This ribbon serves to supply oxygen to the wasp, which is almost fully developed, but still must rest for four to five months over the winter in its own pupal cocoon within the caddisfly house. [318/1–12]

A few ichneumons and braconids also parasitize water insects, pursuing them on or even under the water. And the chalcid *Prestwichia aquatica*, less than 0.04 inch long, stings the eggs of various insects under water, inoculating them with its own eggs. From 12 to more than 30 of these wasps may develop from a single water-beetle egg, and there are several generations a year. The males are wingless, and the females may have normal, shortened, or rudimentary wings. Both sexes swim with leg movements, and remain dry within a surrounding mantle of air.

Equally small and also at home in the water are a few proctotrupids. The young of the genus *Polynema*, for example, develop

300/1
Among "velvet ants" only the males have wings. This is a family of parasitic wasps, most of them with lovely tricolored markings of black, red, and white (enl. 3×).

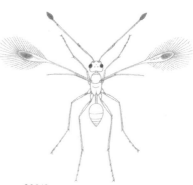

300/2
One of the tiny "fairyflies" (mymarid wasps), whose wings are suitable both for flying and for swimming underwater (enlarged 20×).

300/3
The case of a caddisfly pupa, that instead of its proper inhabitant contains (in the pupal state) the latter's parasite, an ichneumonid wasp (enlarged 2×).

particularly in the eggs of dragonflies and of aquatic bugs. Males and females are able to fly with their delicate wings, modified into fringed oars, both in the air and under water, where they can remain all day long. The first-stage larvae of such water-inhabiting proctotrupids are extremely odd forms, rather more like snails.

Only about 0.008 to 0.032 inch long, the mymarids, or fairyflies, are the smallest of all insects. They parasitize aphids as well as the eggs of Lepidoptera and of water insects. Their oar-shaped wings are long and fringed; the species that inhabit water use them together with the legs for swimming.

Some parasitic wasps insert their eggs inside the host, which frequently has been stung into paralysis or even killed beforehand. Often the eggs are placed in definite parts—for example, in the brain, mouth, or gut. But other wasps merely glue or otherwise attach the eggs to the skin. The tryphonines, for example, attach their eggs by means of a stalk equipped with anchors; after hatching, the larvae often remain within the securely anchored eggshell, holding themselves fast within it by means of their specially developed posterior end. Other larvae may bore their way into the host's body.

The larvae either consume the host from within or cling to the host's body and suck on it as ectoparasites. Not every insect attacked by an endoparasite is doomed, for within the body a battle, initially undecided, may begin, in which the parasite egg is encapsulated, and it counters by producing solubilizing substances. At first the parasitic larvae consume only blood and fatty tissue—that is, the less vital parts. As a result, the host continues to live until the development of the parasites is almost completed. Some parasitized insect larvae live until they have transformed into pupae, but usually die soon thereafter. From the host there then emerge, either singly or *en masse,* either the parasitic larvae, which at once spin and pupate, or the already mature wasps of the new generation.

Parasitic wasps specialized as egg parasites may be so large that a single egg does not suffice to nourish the wasp larva, but that whole clutches are necessary; or the parasitic larva may have to wait for the host larva to hatch and grow bigger. On the other hand, as many as 70 individuals of the tiny Trichogramminae (Chalcidae) may appear from a single lepidopterous egg.

As a matter of course the life cycle of the parasite has to be synchronized with that of its host in respect to the duration of the intervals between molts, periods of diapause, and sequence of generations; such synchronization may cause difficulties when biological pest control is attempted by rearing and releasing such parasites for the destruction of pest insects, especially when the parasites are introduced into other countries or continents.

But even under natural conditions, many parasites do not have an easy time. Consider certain hyperparasites of the genus *Eucharis* of the family Chalcidae, a family conspicuous for its enormous variety of frequently bizarre forms and often, too, for its splendidly metallic colors. Since these *Eucharis* wasps do not lay their eggs on the host, but insert them into buds or leaves, the larvae hatching from the eggs must seek out an appropriate host, namely an ant larva that is ready to pupate. To this end, the active first-stage larvae, called planidia, wait on the plant or, if it is not frequented by ants, let themselves drop to the ground, attach themselves to a passing ant, and hitch a ride to the ant's nest. There both the visiting larvae and the adults that develop from them not only are tolerated by the host ants, but frequently are licked and fed, although they are parasites of the ant larvae and pupae. The heavy odds against an individual *Eucharis* larva reaching its objective are offset by the enormous number of eggs, up to 15,000 per female, that are deposited. [317/1–4]

Even more complex are the ways of the chalcids of the genus *Perilampus*. The newly-hatched larva seeks out a caterpillar and bores into it. But this does not end the job, for it is not the caterpillar that is the host, but a parasite living within it, usually a tachina fly or a parasitic ichneumon wasp. Only if the caterpillar in question is thus parasitized can the hyperparasite reach its goal; otherwise it dies. Still, many such parasites are able to wait for a long time within the caterpillar's body or even in the pupa for such an invasion. If the invasion occurs, the hyperparasite waits until the deposited egg has hatched into a larva, bores into it, and waits therein for it to reach the stage of pupation—that is, until a cocoon is spun if it is the larva of a parasitic wasp, or until its skin hardens into a puparium if it is a fly larva. [317/3]

Now, the *Perilampus* larva again bores its way out of the host's body, finds itself in the narrow space between this and the wall of the cocoon or puparium, molts and changes into a maggotlike form, and then begins as an ectoparasite to suck its victim dry, although it is within the latter's pupal house. And all

301/1

The egg of an ichneumonid, held fast by a claw-shaped hook beneath the host's integument (much enlarged). Whenever the victim molts, the egg is drawn in through the old skin, and thus remains affixed to the same spot (much enlarged).

301/2

An ichneumonid larva in the first, second, and third stadia; the caudal appendage is used for moving about (natural size).

this takes place within the still-living caterpillar.

Generally, in accordance with the species and size of the parasitic wasps, a single egg may develop into one, a few, dozens, hundreds, or even thousands of young, the last occurring among certain braconids and chalcids. The production of more than one progeny from a single egg, known as polyembryony, results from unusual cell divisions within the egg. Similar phenomena may take place in man and other mammals, the birth of identical twins being an example.

Virgin birth (parthenogenesis) also is no rarity among parasitic wasps and gall wasps. Unfertilized eggs produce usually only males, but more rarely both sexes or only females. In many instances the ways and means of such sex determination are mysterious. In chalcids, for example, males may result from eggs laid in rather small hosts, and females from those in larger ones. Or the female larvae of one species may develop as parasites in scale insects, whereas the males appear as parasites of other chalcid larvae, which in turn are parasites of different scale insects or in some instances may even be hyperparasites of females of their own species.

Many gall wasps (cynipids) are well known for heterogony, or the production of differing generations; normal bisexual generations alternate with generations of females that reproduce only parthenogenetically. Odd relationships also occur in the chalcids of the genus *Melittobia*. These live as parasites or hyperparasites in the nests of bees and wasps. As befits their life in darkness, they frequently have degenerate eyes, wings, and colors. Usually there are few males. So an unfertilized female lays only a small number of eggs and waits until she has copulated with one of the males that develop from them before she deposits her extensive store.

A small percentage of the chalcids and the cynipids have become *parasites of plants*. Among the chalcids, the larvae of certain agaonines, torymines, and eurytomines also parasitize insects during their early life. Both groups consist for the most part of species that parasitize the larvae of gall wasps and other gall-causing insects. A few develop in galls of other insects, living as lodgers on plant tissues, but more live on seeds, a few of them as pests of grain, fruit, and other domestic plants, frequently producing galls themselves.

The fig wasps (agaonines), only about 0.04 inch long, live in remarkable symbiosis with fig plants. The female fig wasp inserts her eggs into the urn-shaped flowers inside the fig of the wild fig tree *(Caprificus)*. The flowers are degenerate and sterile in the lower portion, but have normal parts above. Following the insertion, the flowers become modified into galls and furnish the hatching wasp larvae with their food. When a male fig wasp reaches adulthood, this short-legged, almost eyeless, wingless creature begins searching for a mate. Climbing from one flower chalice to another, he soon detects a gall housing a matured female, gnaws an opening in the wall, and, stretching his abdomen through it, mates with her from the outside.

The fertilized female emerges from the narrow exit of the urn and gets powdered with pollen as she brushes past the anthers located in the upper part of the flower. She then flies to flowers in other figs and, finding a suitable one, lays her eggs. In this way the flowers are pollinated.

The wild fig tree, which plays host to these wasps, does not produce edible fruit. The figs we eat come from cultivated trees developed from the wild tree. One of these trees, the Smyrna fig, produces ripened fruit only when pollinated with pollen from the wild fig, and this pollination is successfully accomplished only by the fig wasp. The female wasp visits the flowers of the cultivated tree in her search for a place to lay her eggs. But because of her short ovipositor, she cannot insert her eggs in these flowers; she can achieve this goal only in the flowers of the wild tree. When the Smyrna fig tree was introduced to countries such as the United States, efforts to grow the fruit failed until wild fig trees and fig wasps were also brought in.

GALLS

A highly interesting science, known as cecidiology, is devoted to the study of plant galls. This is a complex and confusing subject as a result of the enormous variation in such phenomena as the responses of the plants, the relationships to them of the gall-producing organisms, the frequently curious reproductive processes of these insects, and the often extensive living communities of gall-producers—parasites, hyperparasites, and lodgers in one and the same gall.

Seventy-five different insect species have been obtained from galls of the gall wasp *Biorhiza pallida* alone. These gall wasps emerge in winter, solely as large, wingless females, from little, one-chambered root galls, often lumped together in groups, on oaks. The insects are seen sitting on a tree-

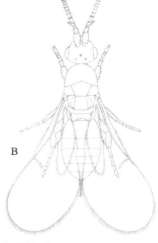

302/1A–C

The fig wasp. (A) Single female flower, taken from the inner portion of a vase-shaped inflorescence of the wild fig; the female wasp (B) thrusts an egg down through the pistils. Flowers thus taken possession of turn into galls, and on such a gall (C) is crouched the smaller, wingless male (whose forelegs and hind legs are monstrously thickened, whose eyes are small, and whose fore tarsi have but two subsegments). Through a hole bitten into the gall, he is mating with a newly born female (enlarged 20×).

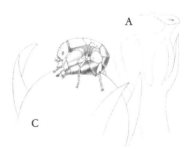

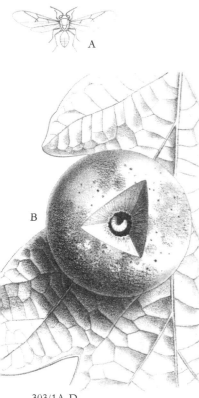

303/1A-D

An oak gall wasp. The female of the summer generation (A) implants her eggs in the ribs of oak leaves, and at each place stabbed there arises a spherical gall within which a larva is growing (B, cut open). The generation developing therefrom consists solely of females, which emerge in winter and lay their eggs in buds (C), which turn into bud galls (D). In summer these yield the new, once again bisexual, generation (enlarged 2×).

trunk even when the weather is freezing and they perhaps are covered with a coating of ice; finally they crawl upward and sink their unfertilized eggs into buds on the branches. After the larvae hatch they begin to form large, round, multi-chambered galls. The larvae that mature in these galls develop into the generation of adult males and females that emerge in the summer. Only a portion of the females are able to fly; after mating they creep deep into the ground and deposit their eggs on the roots.

Among the various producers of galls, such as gall gnats, sawflies, and beetles, as well as threadworms and fungi, the cynipids cause especially complete and strikingly developed galls, tumorous structures that frequently are astoundingly fantastic and often beautifully colored. Galls occupy all possible parts, even woody ones, of plants, and are particularly numerous on oaks and rose bushes. Their position and appearance are characteristic for each species of gall wasp. They are formed by the plants in response to the excretion of hormones by the wasp larvae inside them. Infrequent parallels to plant galls are found in the living animal body. For example, the host containing a larva of certain ancyrtines (Chalcidae) forms within itself tracheae that branch off from the respiratory system and lead to the parasite.

Plant galls are filled with loose tissues, the center of which, usually enclosed by a skin or hardened layer, consists principally of cells containing oils and proteins. These constitute the food of the larva which lives here, in one or more chambers. If it should die, all further growth of the plant gall would end, too. The larva, which after each molt regularly devours its cast skin, pupates without a cocoon. When mature, the insect emerges from the gall. [14/11; 97/1; 319/3–5]

OVIPOSITORS

The ovipositor of the parasitic wasps and gall wasps is a particularly marvelous instrument. And the structure of the body, above all that of the abdomen, seems to have been adapted to it, in correspondence with the demands of egg-laying, which differ according to the species. For example, the evaniids, or ensign wasps, sometimes called famine wasps on account of their grotesquely small abdomen, which is attached to the thorax by a short stalk, have an almost invisibly short ovipositor; this is sufficient, however, for the insertion of eggs into the egg capsules of cockroaches. In the pelecinid wasps, on the other hand, the abdomen itself has been

modified into an almost unbelievably long and slender ovipositor tube, which can be pushed deep into the earth to pierce beetle larvae. [318/10, 12]

Similar extensions of the abdomen are necessary in wasps that do not retract their overlong ovipositor into the body, but carry it openly. For to place it beneath them in position for a vertical thrust, the insect must raise its rear end a corresponding distance in the opposite direction. Frequently such action is assisted by extensible membranes between the segmental sclerites in the outer part of the abdomen, which must curve over if it is to guide the ovipositor along beneath the body. Further, lengthening of the legs, in particular of the hind legs, enables the insect to take a high stance, and the coxae of the legs may also help direct the slender, elastic instrument that could easily be bent out of line. [318/7, 8, 15]

This kind of construction, typical of parasitic wasps, is embodied strikingly by the large ichneumons *Ephialtes, Rhyssa,* and *Megarhyssa,* and by the more delicately and bizarrely built gasteruptionids and stephanids. The ichneumons plunge their eggs deeply through even very hard wood into the insect larvae living there, first having ascertained, from without, their presence and precise position by means of unimaginably acute antennal senses. Others pass the ovipositor through the openings leading to the nests of Hymenoptera, or into the feeding passages of beetle larvae; certain braconids are well equipped for such work, having an ovipositor tube that may be about seven times as long as the body. [15/18]

Overly long ovipositors may be concealed partly within the body and partly in an external sclerotized sheath. Frequently nature follows strange ways of construction. *Leucospis* wasps, for example, parasitize solitary bees, and their ovipositor, unusually long for members of the family Chalcidae, is bent forward and runs along the back. *Inostemma* wasps, of the family Proctotrupidae, have an unusual handlelike receptacle that begins at the top of the base of the abdomen and bends forward frequently to a position above the head. The long ovipositor of these wasps, which parasitize the larvae of gall gnats, lies within the body, running forward into this extension and then backward in it again into the abdomen. Another example is the ovipositor of the big gall wasps *Ibalia,* parasites on siricid larvae that live deep in wood. Almost three times as long as the wasp's flattened, compressed abdomen, the ovipositor runs in loops through it. [318/13, 14, 16]

305/1–5

*Plaster nests of wasps and bees.
(1) Thread-waisted wasp
(Sceliphron), with cocoons (or their
remains) made by the larvae before
they pupated. (2) Mud dauber wasp
with remnants of the spiders dragged
in as larval food. (3) Potter wasp.
(4) Spider wasp. (5) Potter bee
(Osmia) (reduced).*

305/6–11

*Structures made by wasps.
(6–9) Stenogaster species from
Sumatra. (10) The initial stage of a
wasp nest. (11) Paper wasp
(natural size). Photograph.*

PAGES 306 AND 307

306/1–6

*Carpenter bees. Blue hairs, such as
are sported here by an Asiatic
species (4), are a great rarity in the
animal kingdom. (1) Little carpenter
bee (Ceratina) (enlarged 1.5×).
Photograph.*

306/7–28

*Yellow-faced and plasterer bees: (7)
Yellow-faced bee. (8) Plasterer bee.
Brush-legged bees: (9) Ramshorn bee
(Systropha). (10) Halictid bee.
(11) Panurgus bee. (12) Sand bee
(Andrena). (13) Long-horned bee
(Eucera). (14–17) Digger bees.
(18–20) Euglossa bees.
Social bees: (21) Bumblebee.
(22) Stingless bee (Trigona).
(23) Honeybee (Apis).
Brush-belly bees: (24–26) Potter
bees (Osmia). (27–28) Wool-hanger
bees (Anthidium) (enlarged 1.5×).
Photograph.*

307/1

*In very constricted, protected places
hornets forego building any nest
covering (reduced). Photograph.*

307/2

*The freely suspended comb of the
Indian dwarf honeybees (Apis
florea), with the queen and workers
(0.5 natural size).*

307/3

The stone bumblebee's nest.

307/4

*The paper nest of an (American)
bald-faced hornet, cut open for
viewing (reduced).*

PAGES 308 AND 309

*Floral biology and pollination. See
description on pages 294 to 299.*

PAGES 310 AND 311

310/1

*Dasypoda, an andrenid bee, with its
enormous leg brushes loaded with
pollen (nat. size); at the left the nest
built in sandy soil, with eggs and
larvae on pollen balls equipped with legs.*

310/2–9

The gathering methods of bees.

310/2

*The ventral brush of a leafcutting bee,
Osmia; at the right, full of pollen.*

310/3

*The ramshorn bees (Systropha), at a
low level evolutionarily speaking, have
no special brushes for collecting
pollen; the latter is merely loaded into
the hairy covering of the abdomen and
hind legs.*

310/4

*Bees of the genus Meliturga moisten
the pollen and knead a ring of it
around the hind femora.*

310/5

*In andrenid bees, both femora and
tibiae, as well as the coxae, have
special hairs for pollen.*

310/6

*Bees of the genus Dasypoda gather
pollen with the lower parts of the legs
and the "ankles" (tibiae and tarsi),
inasmuch as here the huge pollen
brushes extend distally even as far as
the first tarsal subsegment.*

310/7

*For taking up pollen or material for
building (resin), South American
golden bees (Euglossa) have powerful,
swollen hind femora, onto which the
concave comb of bristles on the middle
leg fits as an instrument for removing
such substances.*

310/8

*On the plate-shaped hind tibiae of
the tropical stingless bees (Trigona),
there is room for large amounts of
pollen or resin, and they are held fast
by stiff bristles.*

310/9

*Hind leg of the honeybee. (A) With
a full pollen basket; (B) the basket
with a ball of pollen that begins at
the lower end; (C) the inner side of
the collecting apparatus; (D) the
route taken by the pollen, from the
tarsus through the gap between it and
the tibia to the outside of the latter
and upward into the pollen basket
(brown = first tarsal segment,
red = auricle, blue = pecten, with
which the pollen is combed out of the
tarsal bristles of the opposite leg).*

310/10

*A wool-hanger bee flying to her nest,
her ventral brush laden with pollen.
In back is the funnel of an antlion
(greatly enlarged).*

311/1–3

*Various bees. (1) Stone bumblebee,
Bombus lapidarius. (2) Large
carpenter bee. (3) Steppe bumblebee,
Bombus fragrans (greatly enlarged).*

PAGES 312 AND 313

312/1–2

*Hunters with their prey, which has
been paralyzed by stinging and which
is destined for the progeny.
(1) Oxybelus, a sphecid wasp that
transports her victim impaled on the
poisonous stinger, digging into the nest
entrance. (2) Ammophila, a
sphecine caterpillar hunter, with a
noctuid moth larva, holding the latter
with mandibles and forelegs (enlarged).*

312/3–9

*Insect life in California. In front is a
thread-waisted wasp (7), stalking a
wingless grasshopper (5); at the right
is a blue mud dauber (9) with a
ground cricket. Above (8) is a newborn
wool-hanger bee (Anthidium),
freeing itself from its cradle of resin,
and in the center (6) is another species of
the same family building a nest cell.
Nearby is a click beetle (4), and
above on the left (3) a sand wasp
(Bembix) diving on a victim.*

313/1–15

*Hymenopterous hosts and parasites
together. There are many such "pairs"
among the bees, wasps, digger wasps,
and spider wasps, and for the most
part they have evolved from related
stocks. Nearly all these parasites act
like cuckoos, but there are also
murderers like Sphecodes or the
cuckoo bumblebee Psithyrus that kill
their hosts (enlarged 1.5×).*

313/16–17

*A digger bee, followed by its
"cuckoo" (17) (enlarged 3×).*

313/18

*A scoliid wasp digging into the
earth, in order to lay her egg on a May
beetle grub (enlarged 2×).*

313/19

*A scoliid wasp paralyzes a rhinoceros
beetle grub in its chamber by stinging
the ventral nerve cord (somewhat enl.).*

PAGES 314 AND 315

314/1

A cuckoo wasp (greatly enlarged).

315/1–12

*Cuckoo wasps have a fantastic wealth
of structural colors and sculpturing.*

*For the species shown in the center (7)
the female is red, but the male is
green; at the right (10) a cuckoo
wasp is partaking of aphid honeydew,
and below another one has curled
up into an armorplated ball while it is
being harshly ejected by the host wasp
Eumenes (12). A line drawing
shows a cuckoo wasp larva (4)
sucking on an Osmia larva that is
feeding on its ball of pollen, and at the
right is the beaker-shaped, parchmentlike cocoon of a cuckoo wasp
larva (11) (enlarged 7×).*

PAGES 316 AND 317

316/1–5

*The "velvet ants" are cuckoo wasps
with wingless females (enlarged 5×).*

317/1–4

*The chalcidoid wasps, most of them
tiny, are also parasites; they are a
large group, of great importance for
the balance of nature. Their often
magnificent structural colors have
brought them the name "hummingbird
wasps," though some are grotesque
dwarfs (greatly enlarged).*

317/5–11

*Dryinid wasps are parasites on
leafhoppers. With one of their
prehensile legs, which differ from
species to species, they seize an
immature leafhopper, hold its jumping
legs down with the other, and glue an
egg to the victim's body (greatly enl.).*

317/12

*A bethylid wasp, a parasite of beetles:
male and female (greatly enlarged).*

PAGE 318

318/1–16

*Parasitic wasps (ichneumons,
chalcids, and others) make a great
group among the Hymenoptera.
There are different families with
almost innumerable species, many of
which can be distinguished only by
specialists. (13) An especially large
chalcid wasp, and a specimen of its red
race (14); the ovipositor sheaf is
carried arched up above the back, but
the ovipositor is lowered during the
act of stinging. (16) A gall wasp
(ibaliid) that lives as a parasite.*

318/17–33

*Sawflies, horntails, and wood wasps,
easily recognized by the unconstricted
waist. The horntails and wood wasps
are shown below (30–32), the
females with a boring ovipositor.
Among these wasps too is a family of
parasites (33) (greatly enlarged).
Photograph.*

(Continued on page 321)

305/I–II

305

307/1

307/2

307/3

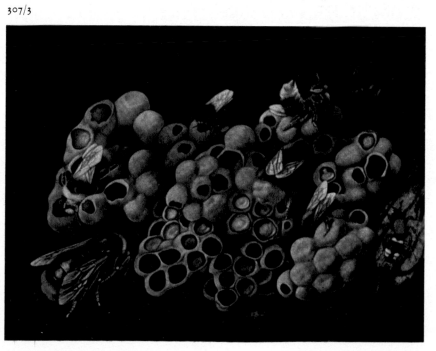

307/4

308/6

308/7

308/8

308/1

308/4

308/2

308/3

308/5

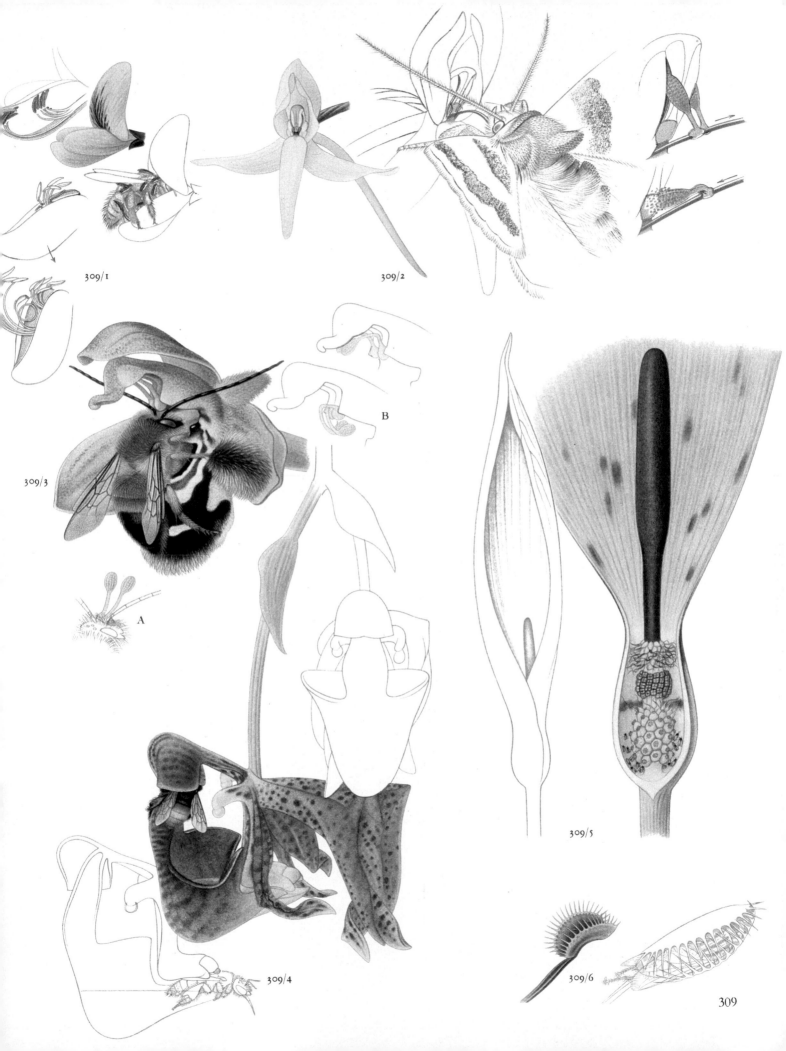

309/1

309/2

309/3

A

B

309/4

309/5

309/6

309

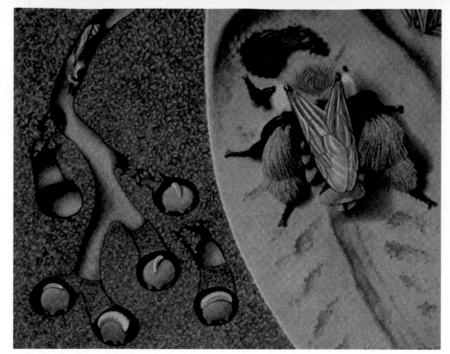

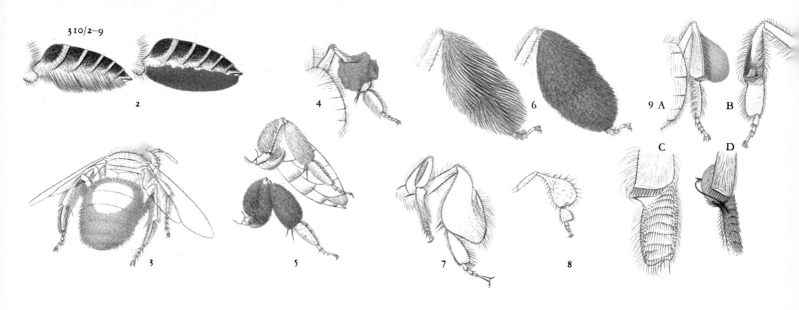

2

4

6

9 A   B

3

5

7   8

C   D

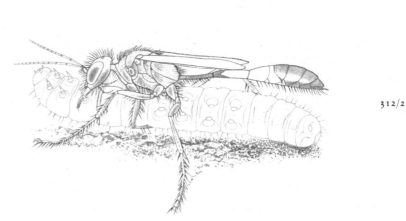

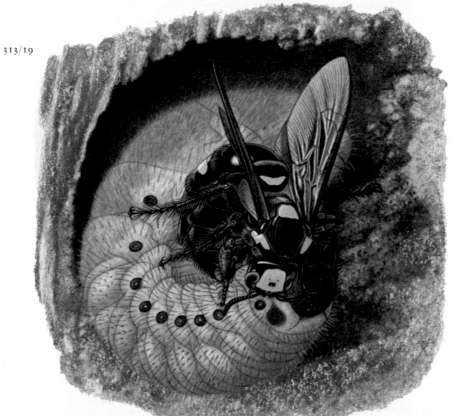

314/1

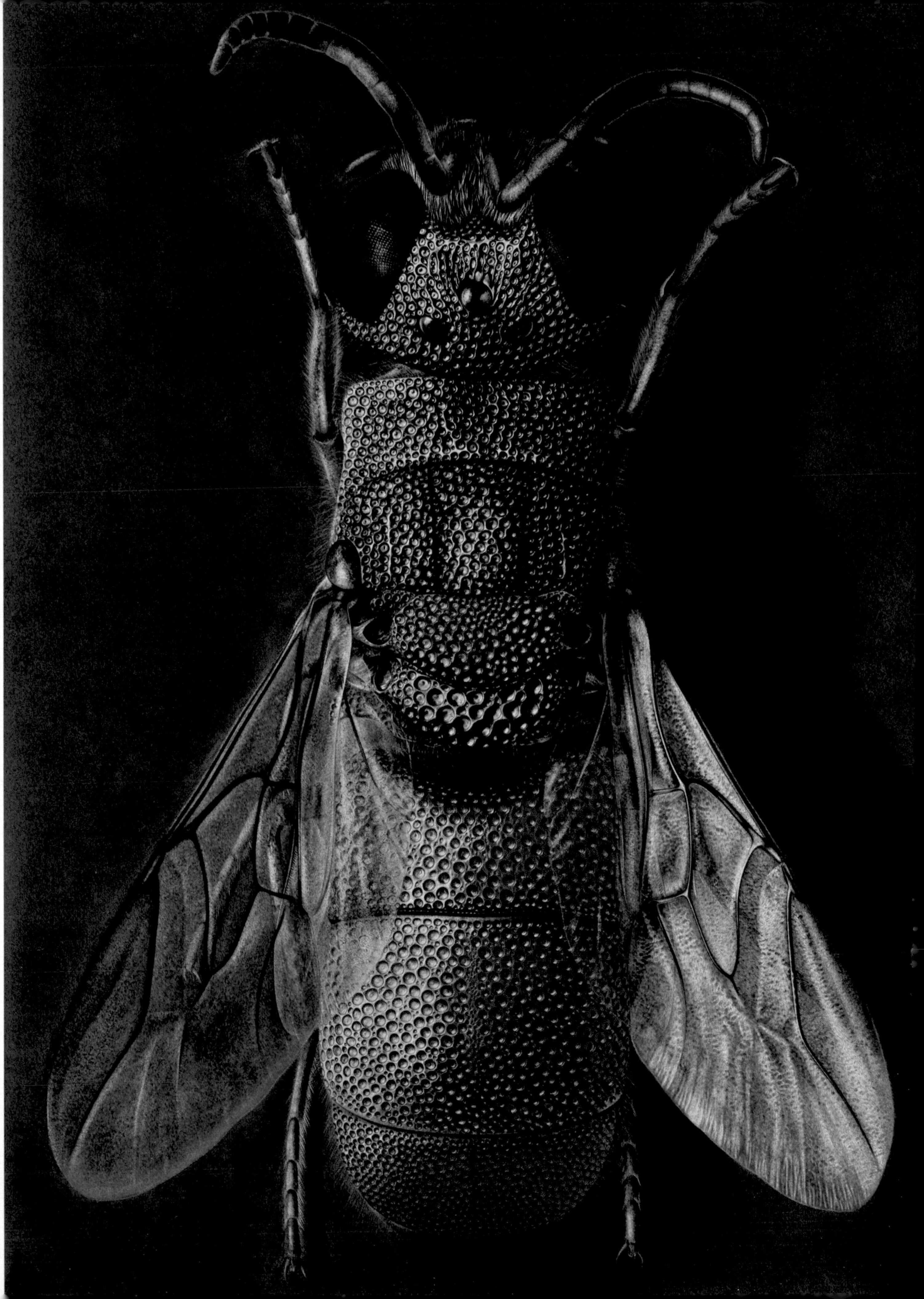

1

6

9

2

7 ♀

♂

3

8

10

4

11

5

12

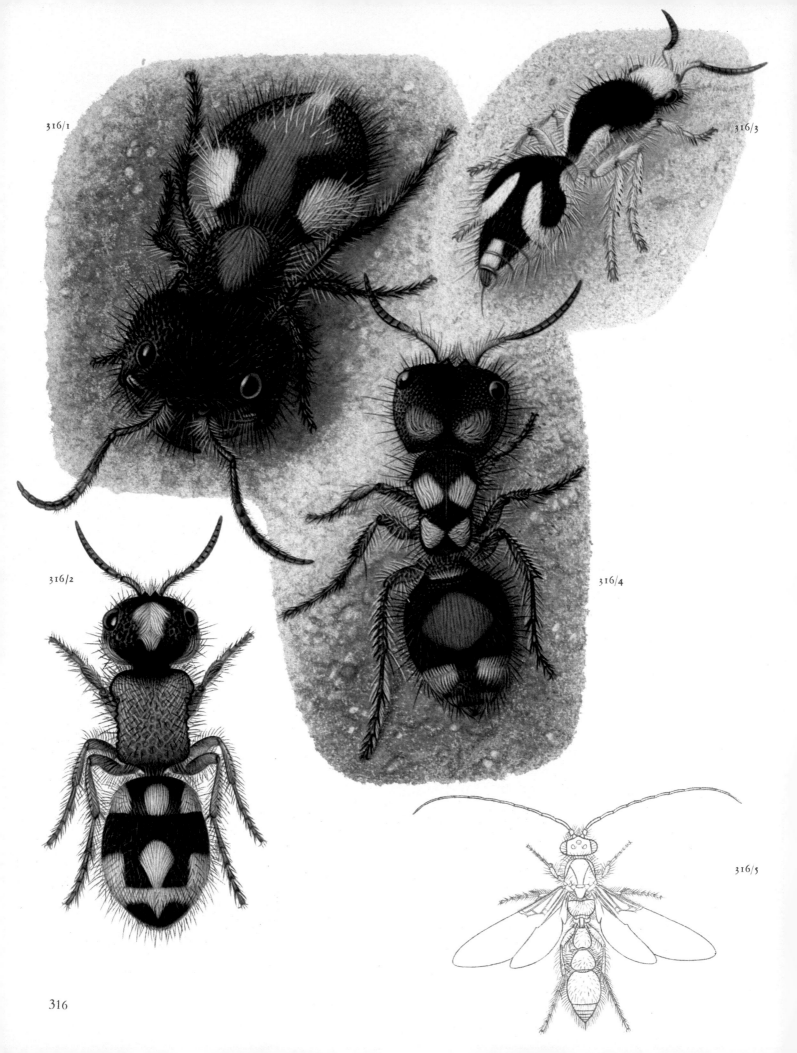

316/1

316/2

316/3

316/4

316/5

316

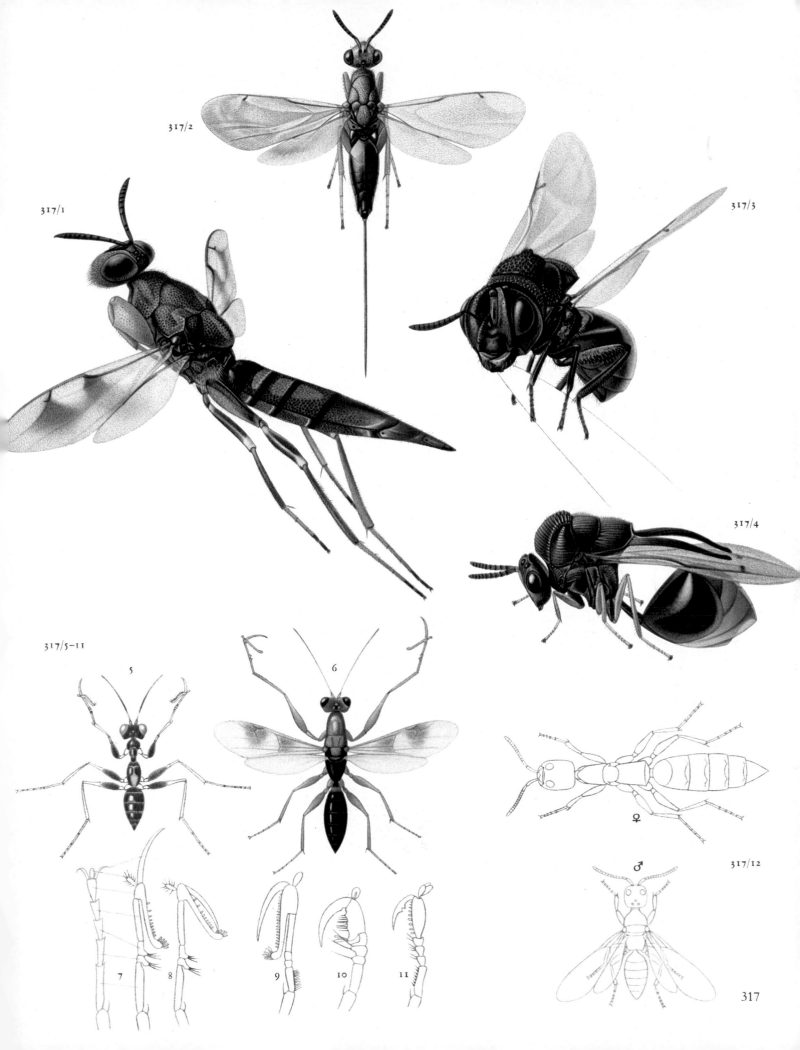

317/2

317/1

317/3

317/4

317/5-11

5

6

7   8   9   10   11

♀

♂   317/12

317

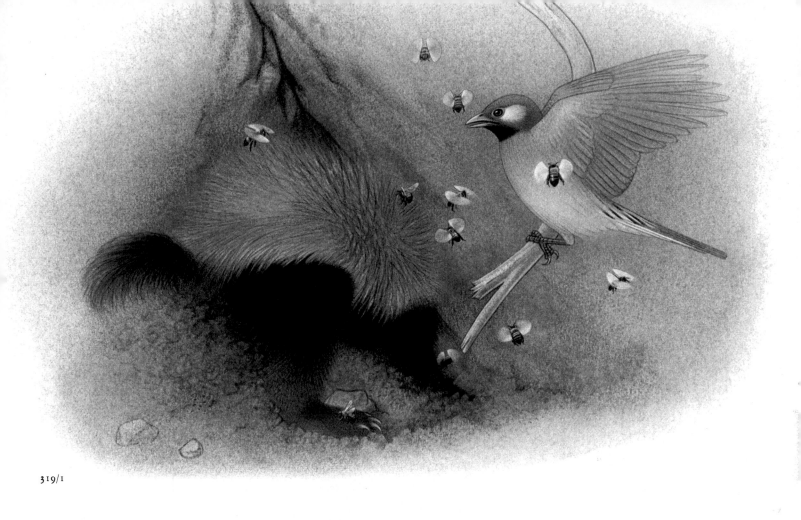

319/1

319/4

319/2

319/3

319/5

319/6

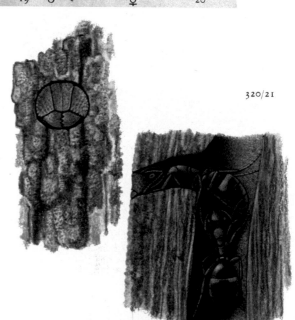

In many species of parasitic wasps and gall wasps, the ovipositor is connected with poison glands. These are weaker than those of other wasps and bees, but nevertheless can temporarily paralyze or even kill a victim. Primarily the ovipositor serves for egg-laying, but it is also used frequently for puncturing a victim, the wasp then licking up the body juices that well from the puncture; occasionally even the males, which invariably are unarmed, also partake. Infrequently the females sting in defense, as is customary with bees and wasps. Many parasitic wasps that sting free-living insects bend the abdomen forward beneath them in the process; those of the aphidiid genus *Trioxys* in addition take hold of the aphid that is to be parasitized with a pair of tongs formed from two handle-shaped processes on the lower body surface, as the upper member, opposed by the thrusting ovipositor below. Its two serrated, gutter-shaped stylets, that fit together to form the ovipositor tube, penetrate even into solid tissue, by pushing downward and sawing away with an alternating rhythm. In the parasitic wasps the sheath often is separated from the borer itself during the piercing, yet its tip, set against the substrate, may also serve as a guide. Finally, the very elongate eggs are forced through this tube by means of a liquid; they do not always have to be so small as its extraordinary slenderness would seem to require. For they have a long, tubular stalk into which their entire content can be displaced under the pressure of the narrow passage; the content returns into the actual body of the egg only after the egg has passed out of the ovipositor. The eggs of many tryphonines (Ichneumonidae), however, are too firm and too big for this method and, held fast only by the stalk, slide out along the tube; there they frequently remain hanging like a bunch of grapes and are glued onto the victims, mostly the larvae of sawflies. [111/2]

LARVAE AND PUPAE

The larvae of all the Hymenoptera considered up to now, with the exception of the especially active and frequently exotic first-stage larvae of many parasites (parasitic wasps, gall wasps, and certain parasitic bees), are maggot-shaped, narrowing in front and at the rear. But in contrast with many similarly shaped fly maggots, they have a well-developed head and mouthparts, especially the mandibles. The usually soft-skinned body—white, yellow, or sometimes brown, greenish, or reddish—is either bare or is dotted with short hairs, bristles, or spines; frequently, these, together with humps, pads, and supporting caudal processes, enable certain slight movements to be made.

Such movements may be essential, as when the parasitic larva leaves its host prior to pupation. This is done in a particularly original manner by certain dryinids with the help of their spinning ability. Lying supine, with bristles anchored in threads, they spin continuously over the substratum, and worm their way forward. Many ant larvae have hooks, branched or otherwise, and sometimes sticky processes, by which they can be held; these help the worker ants transport them.

On the average, hymenopterous larvae molt five times, scarcely changing their form in the course of growth, if we overlook the possible disappearance of the caudal outgrowths of certain species. When fully developed, the larva shrinks somewhat, after emptying out the gut contents accumulated during larval life, and begins either a frequently long period of diapause—lasting through the winter, the dry season, or even for several years—or molts at once into the mostly white pupa. In numerous species the pupa, like the larva, is equipped with attachments or processes. No doubt these serve to keep the delicate entity from too intimate contact with the substratum.

COCOONS

Although many species spend their resting and pupal stages lying free within a cell or other cavity, the majority rest in a cocoon spun beforehand. In the nests of certain bees and digger wasps a mutual separation of the several individuals, such as otherwise is provided from the beginning by the mother's construction of cells, does not even occur until the grown larvae begin their active spinning. The spinning secretion that exudes from the mouth is not invariably drawn out into slender threads, but can flow in rather broad ribbons or be rolled onto the cell walls by the body, thus yielding delicate, parchmentlike cocoons. In general these are cylinders, rounded off fore and aft, but frequently they range from oval to almost round; they may be whitish, yellow, brown, or rarely blackish or green. In the cuckoo wasps they resemble goblets. [315/11]

A few genera that are at the point of abandoning the spinning of a cocoon now make only a rudimentary one. The little digger wasps *Pemphredon* and relatives make a cocoon

321

that covers just the head, like a hood, and the black-and-white-spotted bees *Melecta,* on the contrary, spin one that covers only their rear half. Certain species build ventilating systems into the cocoon wall, such as the conical points that are permeable to air at the head end of the cocoons of crabronines (Sphecidae) and a few solitary bees, or the series of holes, each widening inwardly like a funnel and here bespun with loose cushioning material, that are arranged in a beltline in the cocoons of *Bembix* (Sphecidae). [285/6]

In many parasitic wasps the cocoons, which are made outside the host, are spun fast to the substratum or more rarely fastened to it with columns of thread at both poles, or else are supported freely by threads. Thus there dangle on long threads the delicate pupal cradles of the genus *Meteorus* and the attractively designed cocoons of *Charops.* The almost spindle-shaped cocoons of certain braconids have strong, lengthwise ribs, and those of dryinids are clad in bitten-off pieces of leaves. The cocoons of parasitic wasps are found grouped in conspicuous, feltlike masses on the empty hide of the devoured caterpillars; best known are those of *Apanteles,* on the caterpillars of pierids and silkworms. Sometimes these are referred to erroneously as "caterpillar eggs."

The Hymenoptera emerge mature and fully colored from the pupal skin. With wings unfolded, they free themselves from the cell or the cocoon by cutting open a lid or gnawing a hole, though with ants the workers often have to lend assistance. Many species emerge from the pupa as early as autumn, but only open their cocoon after a long winter's rest.

SAWFLIES AND WOOD WASPS

The most primitive Hymenoptera, designated as Symphyta, differ from the others in having no wasp waist. The body continues through thorax and abdomen without any intervening constriction. Their larvae are also different. This suborder includes the families of the sawflies (Tenthredinidae), stem sawflies (Cephidae), horntail wasps (Siricidae), and parasitic wood wasps (Orussidae). The approximately 7,000 species, ranging from 0.2 inch to 2 inches long, are by far most prevalent in the north temperate zone. They are distinguished by their rich, strong wing venation; the other extreme, namely an almost complete absence of wing veins, is shown by the chalcids. [318/17–33]

Typical of the sawflies (Tenthredinidae and Cephidae) is the ovipositor, the two stylets of which are developed into broad saw blades that can be swung downward out of their sheath. Together with the trough that guides them, these constitute a canal through which the eggs glide. The eggs are pushed into deep pockets or shallow slits (often in rows) cut by the blades into plant tissue. They are placed beneath the leaf epidermis or inserted into stalks, stems, twigs, shoots, buds, or flowers. *Hoplocampa* species, for example, insert their eggs in flowers, and the hatching larvae develop in and damage the fruit. A few sawflies produce galls, which seem to arise not from larval activities but from material secreted when the eggs are laid.

The horntail wasps, which inject their eggs deep into wood, have a slender boring device instead of the saw blades. The parasitic horntail wasps, whose limited number of species attack insect larvae living in wood, have a very long ovipositor that, when retracted, makes several turns within the body. [318/30–32]

The life of sawfly larvae is significantly more interesting than that of most other Hymenoptera, because the majority of sawfly larvae are free-living feeders on plants and hence usually are equipped with thoracic legs and abdominal prolegs. The numerous prolegs, which lack the circles of crochets, or hooks, found at the tips of the prolegs of butterfly and moth caterpillars, work as suction cups. The body is cylindrically round, but is flattened in mining species and in many that feed on the surface of leaves rather than on their edges; rarely it even is shaped like that of isopods (sow bugs). The skin may be bare, dotted with short hairs or little warts and spines, or coated with a thin layer of powdered wax or with flaky excretions. *Caliroa* species not only have the form of nocturnal snails, but also are coated with a thick, black slime that comes from glands between the forelegs.

Sawfly larvae usually have protective costumes, in which green predominates, but bright warning colors also occur. In defense, depending on species, stench glands may come into action, or fluid may be squeezed in drops or even squirted from the sides of the body. Particularly interesting as a reaction to danger are the startling postures of certain species that live in companies. In unison, as though on command, all the larvae throw their abdomens upward in an S and go through lively twitching movements. Most sawfly larvae roll up when threatened. [319/6]

Their capacity for spinning also frequently serves for protection, whether it is by the production of common webs or by the use

322/1
The cocoon, suspended by a thread, contains an ichneumonid pupa (enlarged 2×).

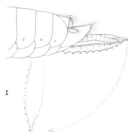

1

323/1–3
The biology of sawflies.
(1) Posterior end of a female
with her ovipositor, which can be
swung downward; plants are cut
open with the saw and the eggs
thrust in (greatly enlarged).

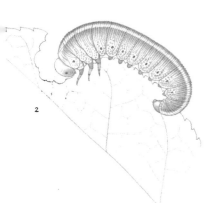

2

3

(2) Sawfly larva, which differs
from caterpillars of moths and
butterflies especially in the greater
number of abdominal legs
(prolegs), in its more sharply
set-off head, and in the involuted
way it carries the rear end
(natural size). (3) Young
sawfly larva hauling itself aloft
with the aid of encircling threads
spun beforehand (enlarged 4×).

of silken threads to pull leaves together or roll them up into tubes and houses that can be carried along. Although many larvae spin silk all along their way, they do not let themselves down on a thread as caterpillars do, but simply drop. In climbing up again or moving ahead in any direction, certain species employ a method that is as astonishing as it is original: they spin over the body a belt fastened on both sides to the substrate; hanging on it, for the most part supine, they can propel the body forward with wormlike movements while constantly spinning additional threads.

Among sawfly larvae there are many pests, some dreaded because of mass outbreaks, especially on conifers and grains. Among those attacking wheat and other grains are the slender stem sawflies (Cephidae), which also may do damage by boring into stems and twigs; the members of one genus, *Calameuta,* live in reeds below the water surface. Cephid larvae, like those of pamphilines (Tenthredinidae) and horntail wasps (Siricidae), lack abdominal legs. The pamphilines, which live in webs or houses of leaves, have instead a hook on the upper side of the posterior end and a slender process ("cercus") on each side, as organs of support.

A strong, spinelike structure at the posterior end of horntail larvae has the same function; moreover, their thoracic legs, too, are only weakly developed. These wood-eating forms, colored white like many other larvae that live in parts of plants, take several years to develop. This slowness is due to their poorly nutritious food, the digestion of which is aided by molds transferred to the egg by the mother and living as symbionts in the larva's gut.

Horntail larvae, in spite of being hidden deep in hard wood, frequently are parasitized by wasps of the genera *Rhyssa* and *Megarhyssa,* which are equipped with an efficient boring ovipositor. When the parasites complete their development, the adults must free themselves from the wood by eating out a passageway, and hence may even appear in houses, coming out of beams and furniture made of new lumber.

Most sawfly larvae pupate in the ground, some in cocoons, others in earthen chambers with walls frequently hardened and made watertight with secretion. Still others pupate beneath bark or in stalks, twigs, buds, fruit, or rotten wood. But many spin free-lying cocoons. The cocoons of the cimbicines, for example, may be very tightly woven or latticelike. Members of the genus *Arge* make splendid net bags within which the actual cocoon lies. The individuals of certain species gather together before they spin, and then make common heaps of cocoons; species of *Dielocerus* arrange their cocoons regularly in a honeycomb pattern and cover them with a great spun cloak made earlier by communal effort. [318/25, 26]

Before they pupate, most sawfly larvae lie at rest in the cocoon for a long time, frequently for several years. Adults emerging from the free-lying cocoons cut out a round lid and swing it open. Frequently they are rather sluggish Hymenoptera, among which parthenogenesis is no rarity. In the Australian sawfly *Perga lewisi,* brood care has been seen; the female continuously sits straddle-legged not only over her clutch of eggs, but also for additional weeks over the growing larvae.

ENEMIES

As enemies of the Hymenoptera, vertebrates generally are of less importance than predatory and parasitic insects, especially other Hymenoptera. The most significant predators are robber flies (Asilidae), assassin bugs (Reduviidae), a few digger wasps, and other wasps. Crab spiders, which lie in wait in flowers, are also high on the predator list. Among vertebrates a few concentrate to a greater or lesser degree on eating Hymenoptera, their brood, or their combs. These include badgers, honey buzzards *(Pernis),* tropical bee-eater birds (meropids), and certain other birds, not least swallows. Consummate specialists are the numerous eaters of ants (and termites), such as anteaters, armadillos, aardvarks, spiny anteaters, and others.

RELATIONSHIPS AMONG INDIVIDUALS

In many species of insects there are definite relationships among individuals, but only in the Hymenoptera and the termites has this led to organized societies. First, let us consider the relationship between the sexes.

Considering the highly developed visual sense of the Hymenoptera, the flying forms of which, at least, display very large compound eyes and three well-developed simple eyes (ocelli), it is no wonder that the females usually are first detected by the males by means of sight. Thereafter, at short distances, the sense of smell comes into action for the decisive test. Thus many males of the carpenter bees *(Xylocopa),* sitting at the tip of a branch or hovering with a loud buzz over one spot, occupy a given post until they can dive upon an approaching female. Usually these males choose their point of vantage in such a way that the sun is at their backs and that an oncoming, brightly marked female stands out against the background.

But in other circumstances scents may play a primary role, as has been observed in various other bees, especially bumblebees, as well as in cuckoo wasps (Chrysidae). For, except for taking food, these males seem to be occupied during their entire lifetime in constantly repeating their flight around certain definite circuits, in the course of which they pass the same signposts again and again. A day's journey of about 37 miles has been determined for a bumblebee flying in this way.

Many cuckoo wasps arrive at regular intervals at the bases of certain telegraph poles, whir upward to the tops of the poles, and fly off. Such signposts also may include individual leaves, twigs, recesses in the roots of trees, rocks, or circumscribed areas of the ground. All are marked with specific scented materials usually laid down by numerous males in a network covering the area in which the species flies. They not only afford an odorous train for the patrolling males, but also induce the females to fly into the pathways.

Contests of rivalry can be observed particularly in those places where the males, which almost always have developed somewhat sooner than the females, fly about in front of the nests waiting for the females to emerge.

Various Hymenoptera flock together or form colonies for resting or dwelling. These initial steps toward a social way of life are taken also by other insects. Since many solitary and parasitic bees, as well as digger wasps, use their bite to take a firm hold of a grass stem or twig for resting, frequently with the body extending rigidly out from the support, the often thickly crowded sleeping companies formed by such insects may take on a bizarre aspect.

Overwintering may also be a communal activity, perhaps even taking place in a nest dug especially for the purpose. Thus mining bees *(Halictus)* pass the winter in tunnels dug in the ground, and small carpenter bees *(Ceratina)* have been found in groups of up to 30 individuals crammed into a hollowed-out stem.

Certainly the herd instinct often is responsible for the origin of nesting colonies, but many times individuals are brought together simply because they are attracted by the same suitable place. And yet, many of these insects are not content with mere neighborliness, but certain solitary bees, for example, dig a common entrance to their still separated nests. Likewise, a few solitary bees work together on one and the same structure, and occasionally this is done, too, by digger wasps of the genera *Eumenes, Zethus,* and *Ischnogaster.* In such cases, however, every female takes care of her own cells.

A striking phenomenon in big colonies is the aggressiveness of the single individuals, a trait apparently awakened by their herding together. Normally these solitary species merely fly about an intruder at some distance, no doubt familiarizing themselves with his appearance, just about as they do in becoming oriented to the environment and to the entrance of the nest. But now they may attack him directly *en masse.* It is well known that among the social Hymenoptera, too, large swarms are more aggressive than small ones!

Other stages leading toward a social way of life are visible in the continued feeding of the brood, as in certain bees *(Allodape)* and in a few digger wasps and vespids *(Synagris, Odynerus, Zethus, Ceramius).* Some species feed the brood premasticated food in the form of balls of paste. Although the fully developed progeny of these Hymenoptera forsake the nest entirely, a few bees of the genus *Halictus* are exceptions. One such is the species *Halictus malachurus,* whose females build several cells at a time before each oviposition. The first brood, as a result of sparingly-doled-out food, develops into small females that stay in the nest helping their mother care for the brood. Division of labor even occurs, such as sentry duty at the nest entrance, which is carried out by certain individuals, frequently including the mother herself.

The young females have a limited reproductive capacity. They lay unfertilized eggs that hatch into more small females. Later in the year, usually not until the third generation and thanks apparently to the joint exertions in caring for the brood, there appear normally large individuals of both sexes. Then matings take place, partly within their own group and partly outside it. All die except the fertilized females, which remain alive through the winter and start another brood the following year.

With this preamble we are face to face with the organization of life among the social Hymenoptera, and propose to discuss it together with the similar institutions of a different insect order, namely the termites (Isoptera).

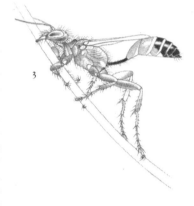

324/1–3
The sleeping arrangements, frequently communal, of wasps and bees. (1) Honey wasp (masarine), whose somewhat concave ventral side leaves room for antennae, legs, and wings (enlarged 4×). (2) Digger bee (enlarged 2×). (3) Sand wasp (enlarged 2×).

Social Insects

SOCIAL BEES, SOCIAL WASPS, AND ANTS — Order Hymenoptera

Although ants (like termites) live solely in organized societies, bees and wasps may have either a solitary or a social way of life. Sometimes the boundary between the two is hazy. Various simple forms of family life are shown by a few mining bees of the genus *Halictus,* as described earlier, and by a few vespid wasps.

Vespid wasps of the genus *Stenogaster* include both solitary species and species whose members live in united families. Among the latter, the females reared by the mother remain in the nest for a short time giving help. After their departure, they are replaced by younger sisters. Frequently such offspring, instead of establishing their own nests at a distance, attach them directly to the maternal structure, forming a home that contains a loose federation of families.

The Workers

In other social bees and wasps, the female progeny do not leave the home, but continue to live there. They participate, as workers, in the care of the brood, in building activities, in the preservation of hygienic conditions in the dwelling, and in sentry duty. Domestic tasks include cleaning out of empty cells, removal or walling off of foreign bodies, and temperature regulation and renewal of air by fanning the wings in the vicinity of the nest entrance and air vents. This last is done in concert and mostly silently, except by bumblebees. Early in the morning a single bumblebee, dubbed a "trumpeter," takes a position immediately beneath the roof of the nest and ventilates it, with a loud buzzing.

Another chore of the workers is to receive food and building material fetched home by their foraging sisters. The food is eaten by the workers and fed to the larvae right away or is first stored in special provision cells. The building material is used at once.

An especially important job is the care of the brood and, for honeybees and ants, care of the nest mother or queen. Without proper attention the eggs may die. The larvae, which live in groups within the structure, have to be shifted again and again from chamber to chamber, according to the temperature and the humidity. Even newly matured insects may need to have the cells opened for them when they emerge, or may have to be freed from the pupal skin, as happens with ants.

Aside from these chores, nursing is confined to distributing food adapted to the age of the brood. In general, wasps and ants proffer food prepared from captured insects, spiders, or even fresh meat; the wasps provide it in the form of little balls saturated with saliva, the ants usually as droplets of predigested juice. Bees, on the contrary, feed the brood only with pollen and honey. Just as young songbirds, apparently by means of their strikingly bright-colored and widely opened gullets, keep alive and augment the urge of the old birds to continue feeding them, the larvae of wasps and many ants (but not of bees) again and again offer a drop of secretion on their extended mouthparts. This is greedily licked off by the older insects and thus indirectly stimulates them to feed the larvae. Such exchange of food, called trophallaxis, may also induce a swarm to rear as many offspring as possible. Moreover, many ant larvae do not produce this delicacy from the mouth, but instead exude it from peglike processes or even from the entire body surface.

In the vespids of the genus *Belonogaster* the assisting daughters are just like the mother. Since their urge toward nest construction and search for food awakens only with sexual maturation, they are occupied during their first week solely with cleaning operations and with distribution of food in the nest. Then they begin to lay eggs, gather food, and enlarge the nest as needed. Nevertheless, the family still needs the original mother, for if she were lost the daughters would finally devour their own brood, and the entire society would gradually die off. But otherwise the family gets bigger and bigger, and males, too, are developed. For four to five days the males are fed in the nest with stored-up honey by their sisters or else, pilfering on the sly, lead a parasitic life, as is also the case with various species of the wasps *Polistes.* [292/1]

If the members of the community become so numerous that for technical reasons the structure no longer can be enlarged sufficiently, some of the wasps depart and found a new home. But they do this in a most indelicate manner. They not only bite off material from the old home for use in the new one, but even pillage it of the larvae, feeding them to the new brood, with the result that the old nest soon is destroyed. *Polistes* wasps are of a rather predatory nature anyway, and occasionally they plunder one another's nests.

In other wasps, such as *Ropalidia* and some species of *Polistes,* the worker caste begins to show some of the differences that among the rest of the social bees and wasps make it a clearly distinct form. The offspring of the nest mother are smaller females and have reduced fertility or lack it entirely. This results from a restricted supply of food. Except in honeybees and ants, the later offspring, as the family grows in size and the amount of feeding becomes larger, develop into bigger and bigger individuals. With wasps such as *Polistes* and occasionally even with bumblebees *(Bombus),* the later-emerging females scarcely can be distinguished from the mother any longer, but with the other wasps and hornets *(Vespa)* they always are clearly smaller than the queen.

The tasks of the workers in the nest frequently are determined by their age—that is, by the degree of maturity of definite internal organs—and thus the life cycle of the individual unfolds in a predetermined sequence. Such a sequence of duties has been best studied in honeybees and, with some exceptions, follows the schedule described here.

Life Cycle of the Honeybee

For the first two to three days of their life, honeybees take care of cleaning tasks and the regulation of warmth. By means of community cooperation, they maintain a continuous brood temperature of about 95° F to 97° F (35° C to 36° C). Ventilation and cooling are accomplished by means of whirring the wings, in case of need even by fetching water and pouring it over the combs. On the other hand, heating results from vibratory activity of the flight muscles, from which the wings have been uncoupled, and thus from burning the carbohydrate that has been derived from the honey.

From the third to the sixth day of their adult life the bees use pollen and honey to feed the medium-sized to full-grown larvae, which are four to six days old. Both of these foods are stored, carefully separated, in different groups of cells in the combs. From the seventh day onward, for about a week, two large glands develop in the bee's head. These are vitally important to the colony in that they secrete an extremely growth-promoting, predominantly protein-containing fluid, the royal jelly. This flows from the worker's mouth and is fed to the young larvae and the queen. Unlike them, she is given royal jelly continuously, for to ripen about 100 eggs every hour of the day and night her body must have an enormous metabolic turnover. The "royal court," whose members feed and lick their queen, consists of individuals of various ages.

The queen does nothing but deposit an egg at the bottom of each cell prepared for it. Every day she lays over 2,000 eggs, with a total weight more than her own. At any one time the bees in a colony have perhaps 10,000 larvae to feed, and each of these may receive several thousand feeding visits during the six days it takes to mature.

In a strong hive with 50,000 to 80,000 individuals, the 2,000 to 3,000 males (drones) that develop are also fed with royal jelly. But gradually the males come to be regarded as useless parasites, are starved to death or killed by stinging, and are thrown out.

During the twelfth to eighteenth days of a bee's existence the wax glands begin to function; in addition to construction tasks the workers have much to occupy them during this second period of their life. Above all there is the reception of the honey and pollen brought home by the other bees, the feeding of the larvae with it or the storing of it, and finally the assumption of sentry duty at the hive entrance. In defense of the nest, the bee is ready to sting an intruder, whether it is a larger animal, another insect, or even a bee from another society. [319/1]

Particularly when times are bad, bees turn into honey thieves. If they succeed in overpowering the guard at the gate, they fetch their companions and raid the nest. Among the stingless honeybees (meliponines) there is even one species whose societies specialize in organized predatory invasions of other

327/1
The slaughter of the drones in honeybees. Once the males (drones) have become superfluous, they are killed by the workers and tossed out of the hive.

nests. There they pillage the honey stores and also steal wax for use as building material.

The third phase of a bee's life, beginning at an age of about three weeks, is one of active service in the field. The worker prepares herself by undertaking several preliminary orientation flights in which she impresses upon herself the location of the nest and its immediate surroundings. Now she begins her food collections, and when she finds sources of food learns how to pass on information about them to her comrades. After perhaps ten days of this, the bee's life is at an end; the average age is 30 to 35 days, with a probable maximum of 55 days.

One might be tempted to regard the division of labor within the bee society as merely an automatic consequence of various glandular functions. But experiments have shown that such conduct can be repressed or can be forced ahead of schedule if conditions so demand. In other words, the requirements of the social organization are the moving force of all behavior. Thus, if a hive happens to lose its normal building workers, old bees whose wax glands have regressed will experience a redevelopment of these glands and will begin to produce wax again.

Or suppose a hive is divided into two nests, one with only young bees and the other with only older ones. In the first of these the catastrophe of starvation seems about to take place. And yet many of these young bees go flying out betimes to gather food, although this is not their job, and they do this in spite of their active royal-jelly glands, which then degenerate prematurely. On the other hand, in the older bees' nest, these glands continue to function in a number of bees longer than normally, simply because, for lack of young nurse bees, this has become a vital necessity.

ANT WORKERS

In an ant society, though brood care and division of labor are more highly organized, the type of work seems to be less definitely regulated than it is with bees, and its individual facets are only slightly dependent on the age of the individuals, or not at all. So the society is much more adaptable. In place of females that merely are reduced in size and more or less sterile, there are workers with distinctly different body structures specially suited to the tasks at hand.

The workers of a given ant species may be more or less uniform in size and shape (monomorphic), may be variable (polymorphic), or may appear as two distinct types (dimorphic). These last, known usually as "workers" and "soldiers," may represent the extremes of an originally continuous chain of variations, the intervening links of which no longer exist. In genera with a single type of worker, only one variant, usually a smaller one, has remained; with ants low in the evolutionary scale such monomorphism may be a primary manifestation.

Where a species has different types of workers, the large ones are designated as "soldiers," yet by no means are they always the defenders or the warriors of the society. Big heads and mandibles of extraordinary shape may be based upon other biological prerequisites; for instance, they may be necessary for mincing up seeds or animal prey. In some species the nest entrance is closed off by the head of a "porter" stationed there; in certain genera the porter's head is so constructed that the door is not only barricaded but is concealed besides. [320/21]

Various worker forms, ranging from about 0.08 to 0.6 inch in length, are found among the leafcutting ants *(Atta)*. As in other ant societies, the different tasks appear to be parceled out to the types best fitted for them. The dwarfs take care of the mushroom garden, the middle-sized individuals gather leaves and work them over in the nest, and the big workers guard and defend the nest.

In general, the different tasks in the nests of ants all can be carried out by any worker, and usually a single worker executes a particular job only for a limited length of time. Nevertheless, the small individuals seem to devote themselves preferentially to the actual care of the brood. Both the eggs and the larvae are licked over and over and put in piles, arranged according to their age, and the pupal cocoons (often mistakenly called "ant eggs") are also separated and heaped up in different chambers. Ants mostly feed their larvae, as they do their queen, their fellows, and their guests, from mouth to mouth with drops of nutritive juice from a "crop" or "social stomach" that, like the honey stomach of bees, lies in the fore part of the abdomen. But more primitive species, such as many ponerines, proffer chopped-up insects; and a few genera offer balls of minced tissue as food, in some cases from a special oral pocket.

FORMS OF SOCIAL LIFE

After this consideration of the worker caste and its duties, we return to the forms taken by family and civic life. In the tropics the life span of families of vespid wasps and bumblebees *(Bombus)* does not depend on the season, but in the temperate zone they die out toward the end of the year. Here, only the new, fertilized queens live through the winter and found new societies in the spring. But, thanks to their higher degree of organization, the societies of honeybees and ants are able to persist continuously even in the north; ant colonies have been observed to last for over eighty years.

Many wasps and bumblebees have simpler and more similar forms of social life, and an example will describe their normal course. A bumblebee queen, after overwintering, finds a site that appeals to her and prepares it for nesting. After plastering a spot on the ground with wax, she mixes a lump of pollen and honey, builds a circular wall of wax on top of it, lays some 7 to 16 eggs inside, and closes the cell with a wax roof. From the same material she builds a storage vessel for pollen and honey to one side, placing it where she can reach it without leaving the waxen cell. Sitting on the cell, she keeps the eggs inside warm, and they soon hatch into larvae. These are fed from time to time by the mother, who bites a hole through the lid of wax and then closes it afterward. The larvae also eat the mass of pollen and honey on top of which they were born in the cell, which the mother enlarges as they grow bigger, until finally they spin cocoons that hang together; in these they pupate.

The queen then attaches more waxen egg chambers here and there to the old cell, using in part material from it, so that the lighter-colored cocoons now lie bare. After the first bumblebee workers emerge, these cocoons are used as storage vessels. The workers help the mother, and the more numerous they become the less she works herself, until she perhaps has become nothing but a producer of eggs. Thus the bumblebee queen in two ways embodies the transition from the solitary to the social bees. First, she gathers food like the solitary bees and closes off the cell after laying eggs, but on the other hand constantly feeds the young through openings. Second, in the beginning she carries out all the tasks, but later merely lays eggs like a queen bee.

In midsummer, when the family has become numerous and food is plentiful, new queens are reared. Bigger and bigger workers develop, and some lay unfertilized eggs. If there are excess eggs, the bumblebees frequently feed on them. The unfertilized eggs always develop into males, as is everywhere the case among social Hymenoptera. Thus males may be descended from workers. But more often they are produced by the queen,

who is able voluntarily to prevent access of semen to the egg she is laying. This semen, which suffices for the entire duration of her life, was received from the male with whom she mated in the preceding year.

The emerging males, fed by their sisters, remain in the nest for a few days until their hairy covering, at first a whitish-gray, has gained its full color. Then they fly off, visit flowers, and mate.

In the tropics bumblebee societies may last for years; then, instead of a single queen, a whole group of them is active in the nest. In the far north, there frequently is another variant. During the very short period of the year when flight is possible, the mother's offspring may not develop into workers but instead directly into males and new queens, as is customary in the solitary bees. [311/1, 3; 320/10, 11]

The family life of many vespid wasps corresponds in great measure with that of the bumblebees, apart from the wholly different manner of constructing the nest and feeding the young. In both groups, the mature insects imbibe nectar and sweet or fermenting plant substances, as well as honeydew. But the vespids, with the apparent exception of the nectarines, feed their brood with a paste of chewed-up insects.

In the spring two or several vespid queens occasionally found a nest in common. In *Polistes* wasps, this urge for sociability may even extend to where a female will leave her own nest and her still-young brood in the lurch and will attempt to join a distinct family. Whether she succeeds is another matter. For the majority of species drive away intruders, even those of the same line of descent; the cause of this is nothing else than that very possessiveness toward the brood that to some degree has been lost by the worker caste in correlation with their degenerate sexuality, a loss that has made possible the selfless cooperation of the individuals in a society. Through this loss a certain loosening of the rigidly established instinct for the care of the brood also entered and brought with it space for other, new tasks.

The most highly developed social organizations among the wasps are those of certain species of *Polybia* in South America. They are said to surpass in this respect even the social organizations of honeybees, which are very similar. With one and the same *Polybia* species the establishment of new colonies can take place in very different manners according to the circumstances. It can take place by swarming, as in honeybees— that is, through the departure in flight of a

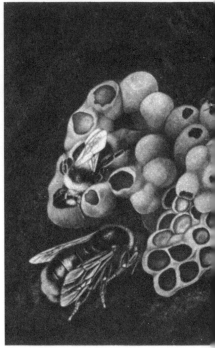

328/1

The stone bumblebee's nest, with the queen (in the middle), male (at the far left on the comb), and workers, one of them in a posture of defense (above). The comb (exposed) consists of honey jars and cocoons, many of them already abandoned, spun by the larvae for pupation. Also in the nest are parasites: at the left a cuckoo bumblebee (Psithyrus), and at the right a so-called velvet ant, which is actually a wasp, whose larvae feed by sucking dry those of the stone bumblebee (natural size). (→ 307/3)

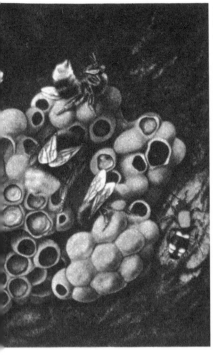

portion of the hive together with one or several queens—or else, as in other wasps, simply by individual fertilized females. These *Polybia* wasps, moreover, have the strange peculiarity of flying soundlessly, and are particularly prone to attack intruders within a circumference of about two yards of their nest. The bleeding puncture made by their sting is very painful and makes the affected part of the body whiten at once, yet causes only a slight swelling. [320/3]

The frequently large societies of the "stingless" honeybees (*Melipona, Trigona*), which do have a sting, though an ineffective one, seem more primitive than the societies of *Polybia*. For these honeybees close off their brood cells, as do the solitary bees, after providing them with honey paste and an egg. Further feeding, with consequent relations between larvae and workers, does not occur at all. But again, the queen of the nest is more highly specialized than the queens of bumblebees and wasps. With shortened wings, small aggregations of pollen on the legs, a little head, and weak mouthparts as well as a reduced brain, she is greatly dependent on the assistance of the workers. [320/12–15]

With a single queen, stingless honeybees form societies that endure for several years. The queen tolerates the presence of other, virgin queens. Where they are lacking, the colony dies after the death of the queen, for another queen cannot be reared, from such larvae as are present, through special feeding by the workers, as can be done by honeybees (*Apis*) and by the more highly organized among the wasps. On the other hand, the queen by herself is unable to establish a colony. This has to be accomplished through the formation of a swarm led by a young female. In fact, among meliponines such young females usually are immature initially; later, the great swelling of their abdomen makes flying out impossible.

SWARMING

After the sexual forms—males and females (queens)—have been reared, swarming occurs. Since in many species, including the honeybees, these forms are larger than the workers, sometimes far larger, they have to be reared in special large cells. One might imagine that honeybees would construct their cells of a size proportional to their own body mass. But where do honeybee workers get the proper measure for their fatter brothers, the future males (or drones), which they have never seen before in their lives? What

signal suddenly causes these bees to build larger cells in the comb, and impels the queen to deposit eggs that are unfertilized and that therefore produce males?

Truly they have great power over the life of their folk, these workers. Ultimately, too, they determine the number of the young queens. These are reared with special food in the few big, pendant, peg-shaped queen cells, which strangely enough bear on their surface the six-cornered pattern of the comb. Inside the cells the young larvae hang head-downward. When they are ready for pupation, their cradles are closed over with waxen covers. The worker caste is then gripped by that feverish, pervasive agitation, the swarming mood. This leads to the departure, as if on order, of about half the population, after each of the individuals has filled up on honey from the plentiful stores in the nest.

In the course of only a few minutes, they fly off from the exit, perhaps some 30,000 of them, together with the old queen. Not being an especially good flier, she soon settles somewhere on a branch, and the whole billowing swarm of bees gathers around her like a bunch of grapes. From this place, usually a few hours later, they make off to a new nesting place that has been explored meanwhile by scouts. Or perhaps the swarm is packaged up by a beekeeper and given a home in his apiary. It is precisely this situation that has enabled man to culture bees, a practice known to the Egyptians over 5,000 years ago.

Among the ancestral stock that stays behind when the swarm leaves, there emerges after about a week the first of the young queens. Excitedly singing "tu-tu" she opens the remaining queen cells and stings to death her rivals who lie within them and respond with hollow sounds to her call, for in the bees' society such a rival cannot be tolerated. But frequently the swarming mood among the colony has not yet subsided, and this murdering of her sisters is prevented by the workers, for a second swarm is about to break forth, perhaps still others are to follow, and each of these supplementary swarms, smaller than the first, requires a queen. Often two or several queens fly along, but only one of them is left alive. The South African honeybees do not absolutely have to have a queen, for with them the workers are capable of producing female progeny. [353/1]

Since a queen, who lives to be four to five years old, is not able all by herself to found a new bee colony, the swarm constitutes the only possibility of increasing the number of bee populations and thereby preserving the species. Lack of food or any kind of disturbance or menace can also provoke bees into swarming; such migratory swarms then represent merely a change of dwelling place and not a fractionation of the population.

The honeybee *Apis mellifica*, originally from the Old World, has been spread by man over the entire earth. Until recently its races were not products of intentional breeding, but were primal geographic forms. Today, at all events, crosses can be produced by artificial insemination of queens. Of the remaining three *Apis* species (*dorsata, florea,* and *indica*), all of which live in South Asia, only the last has been domesticated. [320/16–20]

A quite different kind of swarming is seen among ants. Excited workers appear before the nest entrance and get more and more numerous. Finally there appear the winged, sexually mature individuals, which usually are reared in large numbers only some years after the society is founded. First come the males, and then the females. They rise into the air, perhaps like clouds of smoke, later to cover the earth with a layer of ants.

This is no swarming in the sense of the bees, for these are mating flights. In many genera the males and females, which as a rule are equipped with huge wings, are almost equal in size, but in other genera they are very different. One may even see a tiny male riding about on his partner's abdomen as if on a dirigible. Verging on the incredible are the differences in size between sexually mature forms and workers, especially in legionary ants (dorylines). Here, a male may measure 1.2 inches, and the smallest worker a mere 0.08 inch; or a worker 0.12 to 0.16 inch long may have a queen more than 2 inches long.

The males are of no use in a hymenopterous colony. After mating, they die. The fertilized females then found their purely female societies, as queens with a final cohort of many myriads of workers.

There are ant societies with over a million individuals, and one population may hold sway over an area of hundreds, even thousands, of square yards. Certain *Formica* ants pile on top of their nests heaps of earth more than a yard high and perhaps four yards in diameter. Such digging by ants is of great benefit to man in loosening and aerating the soil.

On the average the workers live to be about three years old. Thus they have much more time than bees, for instance, to gather

impressions and gain experience, and their adaptability is decidedly greater than one might credit insects with. The queens may live for as long as three decades, not as rulers, it is true, but merely as producers of eggs, for among ants even more exclusively than among bees it is the colony that does the deciding.

In the simplest case, a fertilized female founds a colony by enclosing herself in a hole she has dug or in some other hiding place, after shedding her wings, which is facilitated by a preformed line of rupture. Here the ant remains closed off from the world at large until the emergence of her first workers, which may take a year. She ingests nothing but moisture, living on her bodily reserves, a good part of which come from the breaking down of the thoracic flight musculature. This source of nourishment also enables the queen to rear her first larvae on glandular secretions in spite of the long period without food. The queen may eat some of the eggs she lays, but they, of course, are products of her own body.

When the larvae are fully grown, the mother helps them in the spinning of their cocoons by providing them with bits of dirt, which they incorporate in the structures. Later, she helps the workers emerge from the cocoons. At this point her instincts for the care of the brood usually disappear, since subsequent brood care is taken over by the workers; only in the smaller societies of certain ponerines and *Leptothorax* does the queen continue to help. Societies of a few of the primitive ponerines may be no larger than ten individuals. In founding them the queen does not enclose herself, but goes on the hunt, fetching food for her brood in the manner of the solitary wasps.

Frequently several females work together in establishing the nest, but when the first brood of workers appears, the mothers battle one another until only a single one survives. But several or even many of them are tolerated when spatially more extensive societies are concerned. The young queens then settle down in outbuildings after their mating flight. This procedure is also followed by species in which the queens have lost their capacity for digging or for some other reason are unable to found a society by themselves. By remaining within the existing society, they have ant helpers at their immediate disposal.

A young queen of the genus *Carebara* solves this problem by taking along with her on her mating flight a number of tiny workers from

330/1
The largest honeybee species, the Asiatic Apis dorsata, with full pollen baskets (enl. 2.5 ×).

the nest; these cling fast to her en route. Or a female of *Formica sanguinea,* a species that is particularly many-sided in its methods of establishing colonies and its ways of life, first joins forces for founding a common nest with a female from the company of one of her slave species; then, as soon as the latter's first workers appear, she kills her.

When females that are not self-sufficient but are dependent on worker ants establish branch settlements of a flourishing colony, there frequently are schisms and estrangement between the original population and its offshoots. On the other hand, the adoption of young queens is by no means limited to populations of their own species, but strangers of the same genus are accepted, resulting in mixed communities. These occur frequently, especially in the genus *Formica,* and also in *Lasius* and others. They are only temporary, however, if the queen of the original population dies, and often enough she is beheaded or murdered by the adopted stranger or the latter's workers. In this case, a pure stock of the adopted species gradually arises.

Communities that have lasted a long time frequently consist of several mixtures and a confusing diversity of interrelationships. For instance, a female of a third species may establish her nest in a *Formica* colony that already consists of two species; and, in addition, the workers may sally forth to capture slaves, bring home pupae of still another species, and let the ants that hatch from them likewise become servants of the state. Such mutual associations of different species stretch through countless possibilities, including mere neighborly activity, the mutual benefits of symbiosis, hospitality, and larceny. They range in one direction to slavery (in which only the ruling ants produce males and new colonies, while the helping ants are allowed to produce only workers), and in the other direction to parasitism (in which species that have become incapable of feeding themselves or are no more than wretched cripples have to be supported by the others).

Slavery

The custom of capturing slaves seems to have developed from the dependence of those queens that are able to establish a nest only with the help of workers. The pupae of foreign societies are stolen, and a permanent supply of the enslaved working population that emerges from them is assured to the society by forays repeated annually. But occasionally the slaveholders eradicate all the potential sources of slaves in the area and have to return gradually to self-sufficiency. Slave hunts may be extended over such great distances that the soldiers establish guarded camps at intervals of a day's march from home.

The dependence on slaves varies from one society to another. The saberlike mandibles of the Amazon ants *(Polyergus)* make them fine fighters, but also make them so incapable as workers at home that they are fully dependent on their slaves, which usually far outnumber them. On the other hand, many *Formica* communities are not unconditionally dependent on slaves, and keep only a modest number of them; in fact, the larger the community and the greater its own resources, the fewer slaves it maintains. The species of *Formica* that steal slaves, although they are less capable soldiers than *Polyergus,* thus remain good workers. But the Amazon ants must depend on their slaves even to feed them, for their daggerlike jaws, tailored for piercing the head of adversaries, do not permit them to chew their food. In addition, these implements are no good for caring for the brood or for construction, and apparently this formal specialization is accompanied by a degeneration of the corresponding instincts.

Thus the true masters in the *Polyergus* community are the slaves, which happen to be *Formica* species. These would by no means exchange their life of slavery for one in the maternal nest, for among the warrior-folk they are better protected, quite apart from the fact that ants (and not only these ones) feel at home in the place where they were born. And more than ample food is at hand, for during the summer the daily slave-hunting expeditions yield an abundance of captured larvae and pupae that can be eaten.

The predatory attacks of Amazon ants on *Formica* communities are carried out with refined tactics adapted to prevailing conditions, and are uncannily abrupt. After the return of scouts sent out to ascertain the route to be followed for attack and the proper initial dispositions of the forces, the soldiers assemble before their nest, excitedly drumming each other's heads with their antennae. As if responding to an order, part of the population, numbering from many hundred to perhaps 2,000 warriors, sets out in a close column, marching directly at full speed and perhaps straight through heavy grass to the gathering place near the selected nest.

When the attackers have consolidated here, they carry out an assault so suddenly and with such concentrated force that the *Formica* community is caught by surprise and in a few minutes is sacked. Nevertheless, in the first confusion of battle, many *Formica* ants succeed in fleeing to a place of safety, carrying part of the brood in their mandibles. A *Polyergus* colony has been observed to undertake 44 expeditions in 33 days, collecting a booty estimated at 40,000 slave pupae.

In addition to various species of *Formica* and *Polyergus,* the myrmicine genera *Strongylognathus* and *Harpagoxenus* take slaves. *Strongylognathus* ants have saberlike mandibles, but unlike the Amazons are capable of feeding themselves. And they have different tactics or battle methods. Thus certain *Strongylognathus* communities maintain throughout the duration of their attack a constant liaison between their own nest and the *Tetramorium* nest they have assaulted; their aim is to intimidate the inhabitants of the latter, namely to render them more or less defenseless by pinching them suddenly from behind with the mandibles. But if battle is joined, nonetheless, fights break out between the robbers' slaves, participating in this expedition, and the similar workers of the besieged community, from which it is possible that slaves themselves have descended, having been captured in an earlier raid. Consolingly, however, such an occasion may end in reconciliation, with attacker and attacked giving up the battle and joining forces.

The methods of slaveholders vary. Colonies of *Harpagoxenus sublaevis* drive *Leptothorax* societies out of their own nest, set themselves up in it, and obtain the indispensable helping ants from the *Leptothorax* pupae left behind. For these slaveholders, which even try to make workers out of already-hatched queens by biting their wings off, are unable to rear their own brood.

Neighbors, Guests, and Thieves

Composite nests also are shared by very different groups of ants and even by ants and termites. Frequently societies of this sort are brought together by such things as the presence of favorable dwelling places—for instance, hollow branches or the houses made by termites. Each of the species, more or less forced by circumstances into a neighborly existence, has its own dwelling, but with a common entrance to the nest. This may result in various forms of symbiosis. A defenseless species may live with a species capable of defending itself and may bear a deceptive resemblance to it. The combined defenses of two or more populations living in a given habitat may enhance the safety of each.

In the outer parts of the ant gardens of a *Camponotus* colony, for example, a population of *Cremastogaster* may establish itself. Under moderate menace only the latter takes the appropriate measures of defense, but when seriously threatening attacks occur, the fundamental owners appear from the depths of their spherical nest.

A few genera of tiny ants live as obligatory lodgers; they build their little cities and dwellings in the middle of the nests of much larger species, being tolerated as friends of the latter and fed by them on solicitation. Certain *Leptothorax* species are ant guests of this sort. They often ride on the backs of their host ants, licking them. Other such guests include a few *Formicoxenus* and *Symmyrmica* ants, the males of which, as a rare exception, are wingless.

Except in human society, hospitality probably is nowhere manifested in so varied and interesting ways as among ants (and, to a much lesser extent, among termites). In addition to welcomed and uninvited ants, guests include certain mites and isopods (sow bugs). One may estimate at several thousand species the number of living forms that, by craft or by friendly means, overcome the natural standoffishness of ants and profit directly from them in one way or another.

There are a great many thieving ant species whose workers settle among other ants as bad, antagonistic neighbors or even as lodgers, frequently in numbers nearing the hundreds of thousands. They are dwarfs only about 0.04 to 0.08 inch long, almost too small to be taken hold of, and some also have a bad smell. Masses of them will attack their much larger hosts, if these put themselves in the way, and by stinging them, especially in the antennae and the mouth, make them incapable of fighting. These tiny devils eat the hosts' brood and get into the hosts' chambers by making fine passageways that course like a network throughout the structures of the host ants; the hosts cannot possibly pursue them through these little tubes.

Solenopsis and many other genera are thief ants of this sort, and they dwell also among termites. Since the smallest workers are best adapted to this way of life, these species have developed from originally larger forms, as is still shown by the sexual individuals, above all by the queens, which frequently are veritable giants in comparison with their tiny workers. Thus, the workers of *Carebara,* which live with termites, seem like little lice hanging to the legs of their queen.

Less harmful thieves are those highwaymen that settle in the vicinity of another nest with the intention of plundering the ants that are bringing foodstuffs home. Both robbery and quarrels over boundaries can lead to open war or perhaps to feuds lasting for years between different stocks.

Contests of a more ritual nature also occur among ants. *Camponotus* ants, for example, run headlong against one another, with the abdomen audibly beating the ground. But ants in general engage at once in mortal combat. The principal weapons are the mandibles and, among the more primitive ants (ponerines, myrmicines), the toxic sting. In lieu of stinging, *Formica* curls the abdomen forward between the legs and sprays out its poison, formic acid. Certain species disseminate repugnant odors (for example, many *Lasius*), and dolichoderines plaster the enemy's antennae with a sticky, ill-smelling secretion from the rear end. And finally, the soldiers of many species are able to blockade the nest entrance with their head. [353/2]

ANT HARVESTERS, FARMERS, AND HUNTERS

The food of ants consists of plant juices, nectar, and honeydew, as well as insects (ants not excepted), worms, and other small animals. Insect-eating ants can be highly useful to man. A large community of wood ants of the genus *Formica,* for example, destroys about 100,000 insects daily.

In specializing on certain types of food, some ants have developed unusual organizations and ways of life. Ants that feed on honeydew, a sweet excretion of aphids, are a good example. These ants in their own nest raise aphids, feeding them leaves or roots and even building special chambers—stalls, so to speak—for such "milk cows." The ants comprehend to an astounding degree the essentials of aphid care, a capacity that has probably developed in great part from the instincts for the care of their own brood.

Instead of letting "domestic animals" furnish a continual supply of the desired juice,

certain ants (such as *Myrmecocystus, Prenolepis, Leptomyrmex, Melophorus,* a few *Camponotus* and *Plagiolepis*) of warm, dry countries store it in the bodies of their own workers. A number of such workers are fed by their sisters until their expandable abdomen inflates into a gigantic, amber-colored, shimmering sphere, upon which the normally contiguous segmental sclerites are widely separated from one another. These "walking honey jars" can creep forward only slowly and with difficulty, and usually remain hanging calmly in groups on the ceiling of a cavity in the nest; particularly when food is scarce they dole out their store from the mouth drop by drop to their entreating sibs. [354/16]

Man gathers and eats the bodies of such honey ants, or at least their contents, rating them as a delicacy that surpasses the honey of bees. Incidentally, the honeydew of aphids is not the sole constituent, for these ants frequently also gather nectar and exudations from plant galls, in America particularly those from oaks.

Quite different specialists are the harvest ants, especially *Messor, Pheidole, Holcomyrmex,* and *Pogonomyrmex,* the last of which stings energetically. These collect plant seeds, preferentially those of grains and grasses, and accumulate them in their nests. The seeds, later to be broken up and eaten, are laid out in the sun to dry; if they nevertheless sprout, the sprouts are often bitten off. Certain species throw such unwanted seeds out of the nest, and surrounding the nest entrance there soon grows a dense fringe of grass, a phenomenon that has led to the erroneous designation of these ants as "farmer ants." The harvest ants are not only eaters of seeds, but also hunters of insects; in addition, a hard-stinging American species (*Solenopsis geminata*) eats fruit and cultures aphids.

In contrast, the well-known leafcutting ants *(Atta)* of tropical and subtropical America are one-sided specialists that grow "vegetables." Their vegetables are the protein-containing bodies that grow on the mycelia of certain fungi. And the majority of these fungal species will flourish only in the gardens of certain leafcutting ants. The culture medium in which the fungi grow is prepared by these ants and consists of a fermenting mass of chewed-up leaves carefully manured by the ants' own excrement.

The amount of plants that an *Atta* community will cut up in a very short time and carry into the fungal chambers is so great that the result is frequently as destructive as a catastrophe of nature. The nest workings, which may be many yards below ground

333/1
Harvester ants gather seeds in provision for the dry season.

333/2
Leafcutting ants require green leaves on which to grow their fungal food (enlarged 3×).

I

2

and spread over a wide area, may perhaps have a volume of several hundred cubic yards. [354/7-9]

No matter how familiar the illustration showing the ants transporting sections of leaves, direct contact with the processions out of doors is always an overpoweringly impressive experience, especially when almost every "banner" borne is of a different color. Rocking and reeling, the ants hustle nervously along their routes, stumbling past their fellows coming the other way, who draw aside for them, and, falling suddenly into the aperture of a nest entrance, are swallowed up by the earth, one after the other, or even two at a time, over and over again.

On her flight into new country, a young queen, as founder of a colony-to-be, brings with her not only the instinct for tending a fungus garden but, in a special pouch of her head in back of the mouth, a tiny wad of fungal mycelia from the maternal home. In the new little brood chamber the ant puts this down, deposits five or six eggs on it, and manures the fungus by pushing little bits of it beneath her anus and then returning them to the pile. The wad grows, and yet the young queen takes none of it; instead she eats some of her own eggs and also feeds her first hatching larvae exclusively on these.

The tiny workers that after a few weeks have developed from these larvae are the first to consume the "vegetables" that have grown on the fungus plant, which now is about 0.8 inch in diameter. The mother and brood still partake only of eggs. The workers also manure the precious fungus, open the brood chamber perhaps some ten days later, and gather and chew up pieces of leaves. This now permits the vitally important vegetable to develop adequately.

Certain attines are not leaf cutters, but culture their fungus on insect feces, especially that of caterpillars, or on all sorts of decaying plant tissues.

In great contrast to these vegetarians are two groups of warlike carnivores. First, there are the primitive Australian ponerines of the genus *Myrmecia*, known as bulldog ants and notorious for their stings and furious attacks. Like certain other ponerines *(Odontomachus, Harpegnathos)*, they are able to leap upon their adversary by snapping themselves backward from the ground with their powerful mandibles. Otherwise, ability to jump has been seen among Hymenoptera only in a few chalcids, and here is done with the legs. In their organized predatory raids, the bulldog ants hunt mostly termites. [354/6]

The second group of carnivores are the driver, or migratory, ants (dorylines). They also prey on termites, as well as on other ants. In tropical America the driver ants are represented especially by the genus *Eciton*, and in Africa by *Anomma*. Their sexual individuals are gigantic, the males resembling wasps more than ants, the females wingless from the beginning. The workers, remarkably unequal in size, have saber-shaped mandibles. In large-headed individuals these are awesome and in certain *Eciton* species take on grotesque dimensions. [355/8-11]

The driver ants travel in well-organized formations that differ according to the species of ant. Some columns may be more than 100 yards long and several yards wide. At times, the workers with the most formidable mandibles march on each side of a column. Biting, stinging, murdering, and pillaging, these armies move over the countryside, some traveling more through open territory, others through woods and thickets. Whatever is unable to flee from them is torn to pieces and carried forward in little bits. The ground, vegetation and trees, holes, caves, nests, even houses are in a short time completely cleared of every living thing, and even larger animals and people take flight. Clamoring antbirds accompany these horrifying processions and eat their fill of the insects fleeing before them.

Many driver ants migrate below ground, and others under the protection of leaves and fallen debris. In case of need they may even build uninterrupted tunnels above ground over open stretches. The driver ants build no nest, but in a sheltered place crowd together in a heap, leaving cavities that constitute the brood chambers. These satisfy all requirements for the care of the brood.

In the nomadic life of these ants, resting intervals approximately twenty days long alternate with slightly shorter migratory periods, a rule that is determined by the rhythm of egg-ripening in the queen, for she hardly could take part in the march with her abdomen swollen with ripe eggs. In a circle of as much as a mile around the resting places, everything edible is soon eradicated, yet the signal for a new migration apparently does not stem from a shortage of food, but rather from the 25,000 or so larvae produced from the previous egg-laying period. In fact, this signal seems to emanate from their secretions, which are licked up by the attending workers and stimulate them. Because of their social effects, these secretions are called "social hormones."

Certain other insects go along as undisturbed guests on the expeditions of migratory ants. Rove beetles (Staphylinidae) frequently accompany the ants. That they are allowed to do so may seem odd, for they rarely resemble the hosts in appearance. But with the exception of the males, the ants have no compound eyes, and at most have ocelli; the majority are blind and gauge their environment exclusively by the senses of smell, taste, and touch. Evidently these guests meet the specifications covered by these senses deceptively well. Along with such adaptation, the guests have developed to an astonishing degree the ability to respond satisfactorily to antennal "fingering," the so-called "antennal language," despite the difference in the structure of the host's and guest's antennae.

When the migratory ants raid termite houses, frequently some of the accompanying guests get into the termite chambers, perhaps lose touch with the ants when these withdraw, and are left behind, usually to starve to death or to be killed. But certain of these guests are able to make themselves acceptable to the new hosts and live henceforth as guests of the termites.

COMMUNICATION

The ability of insects to live together in communities rests on the means of communication among them. Such communication is based first of all on the odors of the species and nest, which are perceived through the antennal sense organs. Sentries at a nest entrance admit no individuals contaminated with the odor of a strange nest, and populations refuse to accept them. But if strangers somehow succeed in taking on the community odor, they are adopted without further ado. Some ants regularly use this "fifth column" system to gain entrance to a nest, and certain others are rendered inconspicuous naturally by the possession of a deceptive body odor.

Mother and children (or workers) recognize one another by smell, even after long separation, at least up to a certain age; after that, recognition may fade, for older workers often change. Odors serve not only for recognition, but also for marking pathways. By their odors, for example, honeybees become direction signs for their companions returning homeward. In front of the hive entrance, bees stand and do a waggle dance, during which fragrance is emitted from an exsertile, membranous organ between the last two segments. The odor is disseminated to the winds by means of continual fanning movements of the wings. In the same way bees that have discovered a source of food call in their fellows. Or the fragrance of the flowers, clinging to a bee that returns home successful, can induce her nest-fellows likewise to scour the vicinity in search of such blossoms.

The simple urge for imitation may play an especially large role in ant communities; it seems that there the older workers, leading the way in all actions, set an example for the younger ones. When a large prize is being transported by several individuals, for instance, there is a constant participation of new individuals that, attracted by what is going on, hasten up and crowd into the work. Thus there is a constant succession of more or less compulsory relief of those already on duty, and the object passes through many "hands" before it is finally fetched home. Such community transport takes much longer than that engaged in by individual ants, principally because the differing temperaments and intentions of the participants are likely to be a mutual hindrance.

Quite similarly, any moods or conditions of excitement may be disseminated, via imitation, throughout the population, yet ants also have at their disposal concrete means of expressing themselves. As one instance, there is the capability of many species of producing high-pitched chirping notes by rubbing two abdominal segments together. And, of course, there is the "antennal language," which is rooted in the sense of touch. Definite signs and signals are given by antennal movements, which include stroking, tapping, and drumming; with these may be included similar motions of the forelegs, as well as blows with the head.

Added precision frequently is given the communications not only by the varying intensity of the movements, but also by the production or transmission of odorous materials. Within the community, the most frequent signs of this sort no doubt are connected with the mutual solicitation of food. This situation also may render more comprehensible the astounding initiation and acquisition of such signs by many ant guests that belong to different insect orders.

BEE LANGUAGE

The honeybees (*Apis mellifica*), and quite similarly a few advanced wasps, have developed an incredibly highly differentiated sign language. For if a honeybee has found a source of food in the immediate vicinity of the nest, say up to 50 or even 100 yards distant, once home she executes a small circle on a comb, first to the left and then to the right, and so on. This is done in the midst of her sisters, both busy and idle, and they, carried away by the display of so much zeal in their immediate vicinity, are infected by her spirit and join the leader in her circular dance. Thereafter the bees fly out and round about the hive until, by means of the particular flower odor on the leader of the dance, they have located the source of honey or pollen she has announced so ingratiatingly by her dancing.

But this is only part of the story. For if the flowers are farther away, then the discoverer, still dancing alternately to the left and to the right, changes from a single circle to a broad figure eight, the longer middle portion of which is a straight line. Every time the dancing bee runs over this stretch, she waggles her abdomen, surrounded and followed by her sisters, who are not just looking on but are taking the message in. For the more slowly the dancer runs, the more her waggling movements over the middle part of the course are accentuated, and the farther is the distance to the source of food. Not just an approximate distance but the precise one is communicated and comprehended, measured by the bees not in units of length but in terms of the required expenditure of flight energy, which has to be greater in a head wind, for example.

Yet the most incredible feature of the dance is that it communicates the exact compass direction. As is well-known, the sun serves as a compass for bees, even when hidden behind clouds, as long as a clear patch of blue sky is visible. If the dance takes place on the "flight board" in front of the hive entrance, then the mid-stretch of the dance points straight as an arrow to the food source. But this direct indication of direction is impossible in a dance within the nest on the comb, which hangs vertically. Here the straight part of the path is run through from below to above when the location to be indicated is in a compass direction exactly toward the sun, and from above to below when it is away from the sun. But if the source of food, as viewed from the hive, lies to the right or left of the sun, the bee dances the straight stretch upward at the same angle to the right or left of the vertical by which the direction of the discovery site departs from that of the sun. Hence, vertical direction on the comb is equivalent for the bees to the position of the sun, which signifies a translation of the direction learned through orientation in sunlight into perception of the force of gravity.

Astonishingly, the dancing bee also indicates the precise compass direction when the place she has found cannot be reached in a straight line of flight, but only by means of side excursions, such as flight around a mountain. But since the bees reading her message are oriented by the dance as to the distance, they now produce the required amount of exertion in flight and, after flying around the obstacles but always holding to the proper compass direction, they arrive at the goal.

The dance expresses, in addition to distance and direction, the productivity of the source of food, which is communicated by the degree of liveliness. After a rich discovery the dance is a correspondingly excited one, and even an arousing one.

The dance is also used by swarming bees in searching for a new home. Each bee returning from the search dances on the hanging mass of the swarm. She communicates not only the location of the place she has found but also how good it is. The discoverers of the best situation prove to be the most infectious dancers, and induce more and more of their comrades to fly out and inspect the place. These return, dance with equal elan, and soon the other scouts, which are behaving less convincingly, are ignored and either give up or simply join in with the rest. Thus finally all are doing the same dance, the decision is made, the swarm breaks forth, and, led by the many dancers, they fly off to the new home. In this way, the swarm is likely to select the best hollow tree even though it may be miles away. [355/12]

WINTER SWARMING

Bees swarm densely not only when seeking a new home, but also when passing the winter in the hive. A single inactive bee, like all resting insects, has inappreciable body warmth of its own and is therefore at the mercy of the environmental temperature. When the temperature drops to about 46° F (8° C), the bee is incapable of moving and soon dies. Nevertheless, together in the hive, bees are able to survive a rigorous winter. They cluster in a thick spherical mass around the empty inner combs, and individual bees inside the cluster produce heat by vibrating their wing muscles. In this way they are able to maintain a temperature in the center of the swarm of 68° F to 86° F (20° C to 30° C) even when it is as cold as –4° F to –22° F (–20° C to –30° C) outside. The temperature of the outer layer of the swarm is about 45° F to 46° F (7° C to 8° C). When raising a winter

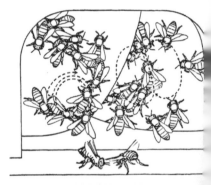

336/1

Honeybee dances. On the comb at the left is a round dance, on the right hand one a tail-wagging dance, in which the leader is vibrating her abdomen. Below, with the odor-producing organ in front of the hind end uncovered, two wagging bees are dispensing scent (clarification in drawing at the top).
(→ 355/12)

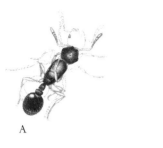

A

B

337/1

A parasitic ant is perfuming itself with the body odor of its hosts (A), another ant species; later, without being molested, it will throttle their queen (B) (enlarged).

brood, the bees raise the cluster temperature to 95° F (35° C).

Ants spend the cold season of the year in deeper chambers or in special winter nests. A few house ants—such as the notorious yellow pharaoh's ants *(Monomorium pharaonis)*, which have been spread all over the world and which establish their colonies everywhere, even in the handle of a table knife— live in comfort in the heated houses of humans and avoid the problem of overwintering altogether. [354/5]

SOCIAL PARASITES

Among certain bumblebees, wasps, and ants, individual social species have become parasites. They differ from their hosts in that they have lost their worker caste and, in part, their own instincts for brood care. Whereas a few *Polistes* and *Vespa*, which resemble their wasp hosts almost to the last hair, live quite peaceably in the latters' nests and lay their eggs in the comb, the female parasites of bumblebees and ants are compelled to gain possession of foreign workers for rearing their own brood. With some exceptions, this can be accomplished only by disposing of the host's queen. This is done usually with naked force, but among certain ants with treacherous guile.

A parasitic bumblebee *(Psithyrus)* forces her way into the nest of her host *(Bombus)*, intimidates the workers with her bites, slaughters the queen, and destroys eggs and larvae. In some cases, *Psithyrus* will spare the life of the bumblebee queen, which then no longer pays any attention to her own progeny. In either event the bumblebee colony perishes. [307/3, left]

In rare instances a genuine bumblebee *(Bombus)* adopts the despotic methods of a *Psithyrus,* kills a relative, and with the latter's workers founds her own community. But *Psithyrus* founds no new community, merely rearing a few new males and females.

In ants, social parasitism may transpire in a significantly more peculiar manner. Parasitic queens frequently have arisen from former slaveholders, whose own workers, instincts for brood care, and even ability to feed themselves independently became superfluous and gradually were lost altogether. Some of these ants are pitifully reduced creatures, unable to rear their offspring, yet they are endowed with the refined cunning needed to compel others to carry out these tasks. The female of a *Bothriomyrmex,* for instance, climbs onto the back of the much larger queen of a

Tapinoma community, bites her head off, and now usurps her place in the society, to which she gained access thanks to her similar body odor. Other parasitic females are not in so simple a position; first they must patiently make friends in the outlying quarters with the workers, and attempt to accustom these to themselves, until their own body odor has become imbued sufficiently with the family smell.

Still another procedure is used by the female of *Epimyrmex stumperi;* she takes a firm seat, from which she cannot be dislodged, on the back of a worker of the selected *Leptothorax* colony, and for a long time brushes the worker as well as herself with her bristly forelegs. Thus the crafty *Epimyrmex* perfumes herself with the *Leptothorax* odor. And then finally, being unrecognized in the darkness of the passageways and chambers of the nest, she comes upon the queen, rolls her over, and bites a firm hold in the throat of her victim, who is much larger but does not defend herself. There the *Epimyrmex* hangs for days, until the queen dies or is completely exhausted.

Workers are in the vicinity, no doubt, but none offers help against the perfumed strangler; no one knows of the drama that is being played out silently in the middle of the community. Finally their own queen, perhaps still alive though paralyzed, is not heeded any further and must slowly starve to death, while the monster sets out after another queen, if there is one, but leaves her unmolested if she is young and has not been fertilized. What a horrible triumph of bare natural instincts.

How friendly, in contrast, seems the relationship of *Teleutomyrmex schneideri* with their host ants *Tetramorium caespitum.* For here these little invaders are tolerated, and hence, as a rare exception in ant communities, the queens of two different species dwell in peace side by side. Not literally side by side, it is true, for the parasites, themselves pitiably incapable figures, ride upon the host queen and are tended by her royal court. [356]

TERMITES ORDER ISOPTERA

Termite populations run into the millions. They forge the complexion of a landscape like no other organism except man. Their secretive activities result in almost uncanny accomplishments; these grow out of their remarkable social organization.

Termites are often called "white ants," a description that is only partly true. The majority are white, the lack of color being an adaptation to a life in the dark. But they are not even closely related to ants. Primitive creatures, their nearest relatives are the cockroaches (Blattaria). [359/1]

To be sure, there are striking parallels between termites and ants, such as the method of nest building, the use of fungal culture, and the relationships with guests and soldier castes. Moreover, there are parallels between termites and honeybees, in that termite workers feed both the young brood and the royal pair from modified salivary glands with an almost miraculous fluid, or "royal jelly."

But in speaking of a "royal pair," we already have come upon the first of the great differences between ant and termite communities. For whereas Hymenoptera form strictly female organizations, from which males, as a necessary evil, are supposed to disappear as quickly as possible after performing their function, the termites have not only a nest mother, but a permanent parental pair and even workers and soldiers of both sexes.

As a second fundamental difference from Hymenoptera, termites hatch from the eggs as freely active nymphs that resemble the parents. They do not go through a pupal stage. As a result, the working potential of a termite colony is greater, for instead of time and strength being spent in the rearing of helpless, maggotlike larvae, the young can immediately give assistance.

FOUNDING A COLONY

The way a termite community is founded also differs from the same activity in other social insects. The fully developed male and female termites swarm, frequently in great hordes, rising like dark clouds through shafts or apertures in the nest opened by the workers and guarded by the soldiers. But they are not on a nuptial flight, as is the case with swarming bees, wasps, and ants, for all of the termites are still sexually unripe. Yet, in spite of this, thanks to the activity of scent glands at the rear end of the female, they come together in pairs, land on the ground, break off their four long wings at a previously formed suture, and start for the nuptial chamber. Either they find a suitable place or dig one, perhaps in mutual effort.

Here the pair tarries for a while as an "engaged couple," mating some time later, perhaps after weeks, when the gonads have matured. There is not just a single mating, which is sufficient for the whole life of ants and other Hymenoptera, but repeated matings throughout their marriage, which may last for twenty years.

For weeks the first few eggs are licked by the parents, and then the nymphs that hatch are fed with oral secretions. Frequently these workers grow faster than normally, but remain somewhat smaller than the succeeding ones, which require about three to six months and several molts to reach their full size. The first soldiers are reared later, and usually new sexual individuals are produced only after some years.

The dwelling chambers are enlarged gradually, as needed, at first giving no inkling of the future huge structure that will house a population of millions. But even after things have gone that far, the parents' apartment—in other words, that of the king and queen—usually is still near the original spot. Thus in species that build skyscrapers it is usually in the middle of the base, and in correspondingly excavated structures it is far below ground.

THE ROYAL APARTMENT

Looking into the royal apartment may afford one of our most impressive experiences of nature. Here, scenes and characters seem to present themselves as in a fairy tale. Beneath the low-arched ceiling of the chamber, a broad, thickly-crowded ring of termite workers is jammed around an odd ridge, and outside the ring stand soldiers with gigantic heads and powerful mandibular tongs. In the midst of the milling throng of workers there rests one particular dark-colored termite, the king, and at one end of the long hill we now recognize the head and the thorax, with its legs, of a yet larger termite, the rear end of which seems to be imbedded in the mountain.

That would be our actual impression if we did not know, in fact, that the hill is nothing but the enormously swollen abdomen of the termite queen. Continually the hill quivers as though gripped by internal spasms, and at its posterior end there appears one egg after another, as many as 10,000 of them in a day, perhaps over 10 million in 10 years! Walled in and unable to move from the spot, this fabulous being, 4 inches long, is fed and licked uninterruptedly by the surrounding workers. They also continually remove eggs into the nearby nursery and feed the king and the soldiers.

Only certain termites display this "classic" picture, the grandest of them all. One such group is the genus *Termes,* in which one king may be together with two or more queens. In species that build less populous communities, the queens have a much less distended abdomen and remain active.

being excreted from the workers' anus. For termite populations are socialists through and through. Their food frequently is excreted in a semidigested condition from mouth or rectum and is taken in again by

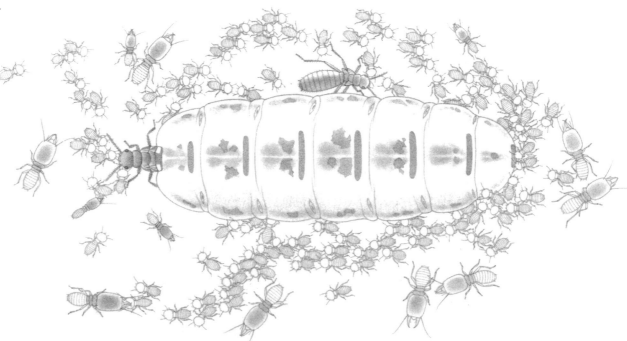

SOCIAL STRUCTURE

In contrast to the different types of ant societies, the nature of termite societies is rather uniform and, having been developed in very ancient times, seems to abide unchanged. The majority of the population are workers, which vary in size among most species. The same is true of the soldiers. The several termite species may be distinguished more certainly by the characteristics of the soldiers than by those of the sexual individuals and workers, which are very similar. The soldiers' heads not only are larger and more heavily sclerotized than those of the workers, but are also more strikingly shaped. According to the species, they are armed either with a frontal horn that is directed forward and gives out or even sprays ahead a sticky, glandular secretion, or with strong, sword-shaped mandibles. In certain species these mandibles, oddly and irregularly contorted, have become slings of a sort. The termite runs the mandible beneath an adversary and hurls him away with a violent toss of the head.

Termite soldiers are not able independently to feed themselves. Like the sexual individuals, they are fed by the workers with salivary secretions, but also eat feces

other individuals, thus passing through several bodies before it has been completely utilized.

At the same time, secretions are thought to be exchanged; they are suspected to contain "socially active substances," similar to hormones, that help determine the relative numbers of the various castes in the community. The queen's "hormones," namely the secretions continually exuded from the entire surface of her abdomen, are licked up by the workers and thus reach the population as a whole. They are regarded as somehow impeding the production of further sexual individuals. For, if the matriarch dies by accident or grows weak with age, cutting off the supply of hormone, a substitute queen is reared from an older nymph by feeding it with "royal jelly." Similarly, if the king dies, a replacement for him is reared.

These substitute parents, in contrast with all other potentially reproductive males and females in the population, become sexually ripe prematurely and often even acquire eyes in the process. But they never get wings, as do those that swarm. Yet they are complete substitutes so far as the society is concerned. Many species rear such secondary sexual individuals in spite of the presence of the king and queen.

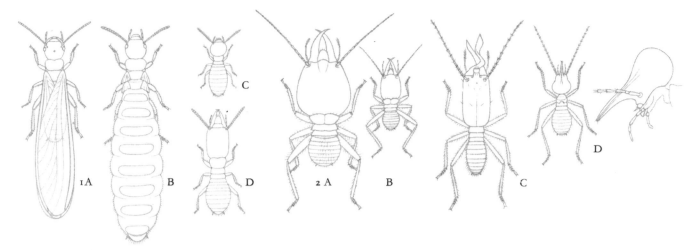

The worker-soldier population may be of different composition in the various species. Thus there are societies with only a few soldiers or none at all, and in others nymphal soldiers constitute the worker caste; or there is no full development of soldiers and workers, but only nymphal forms.

FOOD HABITS

In general, three groups of termites may be distinguished by what they eat: the humus eaters, the omnivores, and the wood eaters. The humus eaters, predominantly forest dwellers, live on decomposed organic materials. The omnivores, from which scarcely anything is safe, have a diet ranging from artists' materials and building supplies to grass and trees. The exclusively African and Asiatic fungus growers belong to this group.

The fungus growers accumulate their excrement in special nest chambers and mix it together with vegetable fibers to form spongy structures about the size of a fist. The fibers are obtained from fallen trees or perhaps from wooden dwellings; frequently chewed-up parts of plants are included. The masses of mixture are stored below ground along pathways over which covering tunnels are quickly built. They are soon thoroughly overgrown with fungal mycelia, whose protein-containing ambrosia bodies are harvested by the termites, but fed only to nymphs and sexually mature individuals. Frequently the young nymphs live right in the fungus gardens. Above the gardens are mostly store rooms filled with wood fibers.

Certain other species of termites collect only arboreal lichens or grasses. Thus various South African and Asiatic harvesting termites and the Australian *Eutermes* cut grass into pieces and carry them into the nest.

Termites that feed exclusively on wood are especially dreaded by people whose homes are made of wood. These termites would be unable to digest their cellulose nourishment without the help of certain flagellates (Protozoa) that live in the gut, most of them, in fact, in a vesicular appendix of it. Frequently bacteria and fungi also are concerned. The wood is ground up in the proventriculus (gizzard) of these termites and is then taken in by the flagellates and given off by them after having been broken down into grape sugar (dextrose). But the termites also digest a great many of the rapidly multiplying protozoans and bacteria, thereby obtaining protein, which ultimately will no doubt be regarded as the most important food of these wood eaters. The newly hatched nymphs suck at the anus of workers and soldiers, thus infecting themselves with the indispensable inhabitants of the gut.

The wood-eating Australian termites *Mastotermes darwiniensis* mine in tree stumps and do not have a closed nest structure. These are very primitive termites. The female sexual individuals have only short rudiments instead of long wings, and in this way resemble many cockroaches. The cockroaches of one group are also wood-feeders and live together in parental families, a situation that is outstanding evidence of a common origin of cockroaches and termites. As further evidence, the *Mastotermes* termites do not lay their eggs singly, but glue them together with a sticky paste in rows of 16 to 24, just as similar egg packages are formed by cockroaches.

TERMITE HOUSES

Termites are especially famed as builders. But some (*Kalotermes, Reticulitermes,* and others) do not live up to this reputation. They simply excavate passageways and chambers in wood and earth, or plaster covered vaults and tunnels along treetrunks and branches or over the ground and rocks.

Except for the swarming of the sexual individuals, only a few termites venture forth beneath the open sky; among those that do are the grass collectors, such as the South African *Hodotermes*, which are different also in being dark brown or black and in having eyes. Such termites, which, according to the species, gather pieces of grass and leaves, lichens, or seeds, as the harvester ants do,

340/1–2

Termite forms and castes.
(1) Reticulitermes. (A) Male,
still bearing the four superimposed
wings; (B) female (the queen)
after fertilization, without wings
and with her abdomen bloated
with the ovaries; this has forced
the segmental plates apart;
(C) worker; (D) soldier
(enlarged 2.5×). (2) Various
species of soldier, equipped
primarily for combat with ants,
the chief enemy of termite
communities. (A–B) Two different
forms from a Termes colony
(enlarged 2.5×); (C) so-called
"goat termite" with their
spiraling left jawpiece or
mandibular tong which, when used
as a vaulting pole, makes the
insect fly some distance through
the air (enlarged 5×);
(D) nasuti; these soldiers,
incapable of biting, have a pointed
extension of the frons that squirts
out a sticky toxic fluid
(enlarged 5×); at the right is
such a head seen from the side.

usually move about at night in snakelike columns as much as 200 yards long.

Typically, termites build concentric structures. Frequently these are fully closed off from the outside. Labyrinths of passageways and chambers surround the royal cell. The circulation of air through these is aided by shafts, figures, and pores. Passages leading downward allow water to run off or give access to moisture from the ground.

The actual nest complex in a termite hill may be a hanging structure whose upper portion is fused continuously with the thick mantle; or it may be a standing structure surrounded by a cavity and supported by pillars. An extensive network of roadways through tunnels below ground or along the surface leads to the nest structures. [358]

As building materials, termites use soil, sand, plant substances, and their own feces, suitably dampened with rapidly hardening secretions from the mouth or rectum, or in certain species also from the frontal gland of the soldiers. Termites that nest in trees employ a semidigested mass of wood (alone or mixed with soil) that acts as a sort of cardboard as tough as leather. Some nests that hang on trees are lumpy or spherical and are connected with the ground by tunnel-like runways molded of masses of earth. The structure built by certain *Eutermes* termites is a similar but unattached sphere lying on the ground.

Many species have their entire colony below ground, frequently beneath a hill built of the excavated debris and perhaps criss-crossed with air channels; the hills of other termites enclose the chambers above the ground. The forms of such structures often are fantastic. There are little mushroom-shaped ones and larger ones resembling columns, organ pipes, pyramids, steeples, and miniature mountain ranges. A termite hill may be more than 12 feet wide at the base and may tower some 20 feet into the air. On a scale of relative size, a manmade pyramid would have to be about 2.5 miles high.

Especially striking structures, frequently forming almost ghostly cities, are erected by the "compass termites" (*Hodotermes meridionalis*) of the Australian plains. These edifices are slender, almost wall-like blocks of about 11 feet in height. The two narrow sides, tapering toward the top, face precisely north and south; thus the fairly rectangular broad sides face east and west. This orientation no doubt is based on the temperature

sense of the termites. For one or the other of the two walls is always in shadow, causing a temperature gradient in the nest and thus enabling the termites to select a temperature of their choice. [358/6]

But the cleverest structure is the small subterranean house of the African *Apicotermes,* where a regular system of galleries and connecting passages, supported by pillars, is enclosed in a mantle of highly refined construction from the point of view of ventilation technique.

How is it possible for myriads of laboring individuals, without any structural plan or supervision, to erect an edifice of definite form—for example, one shaped like a mushroom? No one can know. [358/5]

New structures are built particularly after rains, if the materials are moist. The termites' method of building is much more rapid than that of bees, wasps, and ants, since termites begin simultaneously on a broad base, instead of constantly enlarging the structure outward. How swiftly termites work is shown by partial destruction of a nesting hill, a feat that demands good tools or even dynamite, for the hills are so flintlike that natives make ovens and smelting furnaces out of them. When one has succeeded in making a breach, one sees the workers vanishing into the depths with nymphs and eggs, forewarned by a hissing sound produced in the narrow passageways by the soldiers, who with violent nodding movements beat their heads against the walls. The soldiers then burst forth in hordes and, with their antennae twitching in agitation, blockade the aperture. And in spite of the dazzling sunshine hundreds of workers appear among the soldiers and begin to plaster up the hole with lumps of earth. After perhaps an hour, the job is done.

Although the workers are blind, they do not seem handicapped by it, for the countless antennae of the group measure and probe the shapes of the walls. Termites also use these organs to feel and smell their companions and to communicate with one another.

Among termites, as among ants, two or more societies of different species may live together in a common dwelling, in various degrees of neighborliness or sociability. There are fewer warlike disagreements between them than between ants, even though cannibalism is normal among termites. Frequently colonies of smaller, different populations occupy the thick mantle of termite hills. And just like thief ants, certain termites dwell as tiny thieves in the homes of larger

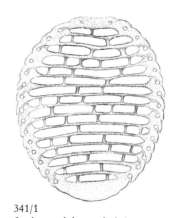

341/1

In the rounded nest of Apicotermes, instead of rooms there are broad galleries supported by numerous little pillars. Within the wall are circularly horizontal air channels (visible in section as round openings); these vent to the outside through small tunnels. From them curved passageways (of which but a little can be seen in the section), resembling spiral staircases, unite the several stories. These fist-sized blackish-brown nests, fashioned of quartz, sand, their own excrement, and saliva, are among the most ingenious structures made by the animal kingdom.

species, although they make inroads not on the brood but on the food stores.

As remarked earlier, termites and ants sometimes live together, and even certain bees (*Trigona, Hemisia, Acanthopus*) set up their societies unmolested in the arboreal nests of termites. The same is done by a few parrots; and in Africa the great Nile lizard (*Varanus niloticus*) lays its eggs in a hole it has clawed out of a termite hill, where the constant temperature and humidity are favorable for brooding.

Termite guests include members of the most varied insect orders, as well as mites and spiders. Many insect guests that are greatly desired and well-tended by the termites have strongly swollen, often grossly misshapen abdomens (physogastry), as in the wingless flies *Termitoxenia,* which live in the fungus gardens, and in numerous beetles of the family Staphylinidae, among which there is a viviparous species from Brazil (*Corotoca melantho*) that deposits first-stage larvae instead of eggs.

Broader Relationships

Practically all insect-eating organisms are active as enemies of the sexual individuals, which swarm in huge numbers, and during such swarming even man traps termites as food. But the pursuit of termites within their structures requires specialists. Among vertebrates these include the armadillos, anteaters, and a few others usually adept at digging. Among birds the woodpeckers take precedence. But none of these is as destructive as bulldog ants, migratory ants, and a few others. These decimate the termites, emptying an entire house at a time and then frequently taking possession of it, or even eradicating the termites from whole localities. In general termites cannot cope with these enemies. But the so-called "nasute" forms are exceptions. The sticky excretions from their "nose" gum up beyond repair the antennae and mouth of the attacking ants and thus are much more effective than implements for biting.

Humans that inhabit the warm countries must be on guard against the termite hordes, for these insects devour almost anything and everything, even (possibly with the help of their solvent saliva) metal and ivory. Coming from the ground, they penetrate into the wooden parts of the houses, hollowing everything out yet leaving the outer layers deceptively untouched, and in the same way get into furniture and utensils of all sorts. In addition to nonliving materials, they attack trees and other plants. As proof of their destructiveness, man has been forced to establish institutions for testing termite-proof materials, of which there are incredibly few.

A problem everywhere in the tropics, termites also threaten to become one in the temperate zone. Notorious pests there are *Kalotermes minor* and *Reticulitermes* in North America, and *Kalotermes flavicollis* in Europe.

Although considered destructive by man, the armies of termites have inestimable value in the natural economy of the tropics. Their dissolution of dead materials, above all fallen timber, and their loosening up of the soil enable new generations of plants to grow. On the other hand, in certain districts the secretions given off by termites during the activities of building can harden the ground to such an extent that it becomes unsuitable for cultivation.

Classification

About 2,000 tropical and subtropical species of termites are known. They range from about 0.08 to 0.9 inch long (large queens up to 4 inches). Of the three to five families of termites, the kalotermitids and the mastotermitids seem the more primitive; the latter are represented only by the single Australian species *Mastotermes darwiniensis,* which has been designated the most primitive of all.

Rich in species and more advanced in their organization are the termitids and rhinotermitids. Only among them is there, strictly speaking, a true worker caste, namely fully developed workers and soldiers no longer capable of transformation. Those of the other groups are merely nymphs of different stages. Such nymphs can be developed into workers, soldiers, or sexual individuals by special feeding applied at a definite period of their development.

At first glance, insect societies may seem strangely similar, or at least comparable, in some ways to human societies. But it is well to keep in mind the infinite distance that separates the two. Our social existence is based on the family as a unit, has been developed by human intellect, and depends upon the free will of the participants. Insect societies, on the other hand, recognize no unit other than the population as a whole, are governed by instinct, and have compulsory memberships. There is really no need to make comparisons; the life of social insects is marvelous enough in itself.

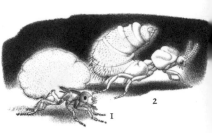

342/1–2
Highly specialized guests of termites. (1) Termite fly, native to Africa and India, whose body is bloated with growing ovaries; such flies are hermaphrodites that are able to fertilize themselves as well as each other. (2) Rove beetle (Staphylinidae); the abdominal swelling (physogastry) of these South American species is due to the dermal glands that discharge a secretion for which the termites are avid. (→ 359/2, 3)

Water Insects

Insects live in the clear, cool springs at the foot of glaciers and in the warm, yellow courses of tropical streams. They live in the wet moss of dripping cliffs, on the leaf surfaces of bromeliads high in the trees of tropical forests, in the exuding sap of trees, and in the digestive juices of insectivorous plants. Insects are at home in rushing brooks, in still water, in azure lakes, and in the morass of swamps. From the mountains to the oceans they inhabit all waters, forming in each kind the type of living community peculiar to it.

Insects live and develop in hot springs throughout the world; larvae of certain flies and beetles exist in water whose temperature remains at 135° F (55° C) even when air temperatures drop well below freezing. And the larvae of the fly *Psilopa petrolei* live in the California oil swamps, breathing by means of a tube that reaches above the surface and taking in food through a double-layered digestive tube whose inner wall holds back the petroleum but not the digestible matter.

In their adaptation to life in the water, insects exhibit a multitude of clever refinements. In some groups, although the fully developed insects are much alike, the youthful stages differ completely in body form in accordance with their different environments and ways of life. But in other groups, exceedingly diverse ecological conditions are mastered by a single larval type, whereas the adults look very different from one another.

Almost all the more important orders of insects are represented in the wet element. Only a few species spend their lives uninterruptedly in water. Some live out of water only as pupae. But most pass through all their developmental stages in water and take to the air as adults. To the latter type belong those four orders—mayflies, dragonflies, stoneflies, and caddisflies—that may be regarded as the "most genuine" aquatic insects, since all of their members without exception are bound to the water. Among the other orders only a very few species or groups generally are water insects.

Various scientists believe that land insects such as cockroaches, praying mantids, walkingstick insects, grasshoppers, and crickets are the descendants of originally aquatic species. In actual fact, swimming cockroaches, grasshoppers, and crickets have been discovered; and walkingstick insects, whose bodies have certain features adapted to life in the water, have been found clinging to submerged stones. What is more, the stoneflies, which belong to the most typically aquatic insects, seem to be distantly related to the grasshoppers.

The first prerequisite for living in water is breathing. Water insects have two types of respiratory systems: closed and open. In a closed system, oxygen from the water is taken up through the body surface or through special extensions of it, such as the gills. But in an open respiratory system, air passes from the atmosphere or from the air passages of water plants through openings such as spiracles directly into the air tubes. During its various stages, which frequently are subject to different conditions, a water insect may at times use a closed respiratory system and at others an open one.

Breathing through the skin without special adaptations represents the simplest closed system. Beneath the skin, in this system, there usually are little integumentary sacs, called blood gills, the circulating blood in which takes up oxygen; often these are employed only when breathing conditions have become especially unfavorable. Simple integumentary breathing is possessed particularly by insect larvae that live in highly oxygenated water. These larvae frequently promote the circulation of oxygen with rhythmical body movements that increase the circulation of water, as well as by intestinal breathing, in which the rectum pumps water in and out.

But by far the majority of water insects with a closed respiratory system breathe through tracheal gills. These are extensions of the integument that are richly supplied with air tubes; frequently they have a beautiful shape, like leaves or clusters, or they may be highly branched or in the form of bristles or threads. The tracheal gills are not always freely visible, but in many larvae are located in a depression with a movable cover at the end of the abdomen or within the hind gut. Often gills are still lacking when the larva hatches from the egg, and first appear in later stages.

There are wide variations in the open respiratory system, whereby air enters the tracheae, or air tubes, directly through little spiracles. As is normal in all insects, these spiracles are arranged along the sides of the body, two pairs on the thorax and seven pairs on the abdomen. Yet in water insects not all spiracles are open, and the method of taking air in at the water surface depends on the position of the functional spiracles. In many insects only the last pair is operational, and these insects breathe through the tip of the abdomen, which in many larvae is drawn out into a more or less lengthy respiratory tube. In the process, the used air first is expelled, and then the tracheae are pumped full, after which a part of the air flows out again through other spiracles and is caught on hair patches or in various depressions of the body surface, very often beneath the wings.

Frequently there are also air chambers inside the body, such as thoracic sacs, tracheal vesicles, and parts of the gut. The air thus stored outside the tracheal system serves as a reserve, used especially when the insect is obliged to stay under the water for a long time or even to pass the winter beneath the ice.

The air also has an important function as a hydrostatic device that helps regulate body density, and therefore buoyancy. Water insects that live predominantly on the bottom carry little or almost no air in their respiratory system and are heavier than the water. But most become lighter than water by virtue of their air store; if they are not to be carried to the surface, they must hold themselves down by clinging to submerged objects or must work their way down by expending energy.

By voluntarily displacing its mass of air, an insect can alter the position of its body in the water, as is important when a certain part of the body must be elevated to the surface for taking in air. Many insects, by regulating the pressure of their air store, are able to rise or fall slowly, or to float at a desired level. The ideal situation where the body weight is exactly equal to that of the displaced water has astonishingly seldom been realized by

insects. It is also surprising that only a very few forms live in the open sea.

A special role is played by the water surface. Its uppermost layer is a fine, elastic skin, that enables many water insects to suspend themselves from it, to brace themselves against it from below, or to walk upon it. As suspensory and bracing devices, bristles, hairs and hair circlets, spines, and integumentary pegs are used, and in mature insects the feet are particularly useful. Various insects are able to walk on the water surface—that is, on the surface film—because their legs and frequently their entire underside are rendered unwettable by a dense feltwork of hairs.

The springtails that live on the water surface differ in two respects from terrestrial springtails. First, their leaping organ is expanded like a beaver's tail. Second, from their venter they are able to push out into the water a peg that, unlike the rest of the body, is wettable and holds these excessively light creatures to the surface, lest they be too severely buffeted by the wind. [90/6]

Complete or partial unwettability is of vital importance to many water insects, since they would find it impossible to breathe and would drown if they got wet. But they remain dry thanks to a thick coat of hairs or scales or to fatty materials exuded from glands. In some caterpillars that live under water and in parasitic wasps that attack various water insects, special structures of the body surface prevent them from getting wet. The unwettable parts of insects are coated when under water with a thin film of air, and therefore gleam like silver. Certain water insects spend the winter or pass through the pupal stage inside an air bubble, and some rise in one as in a balloon to the surface after they have emerged from the pupa.

The little larvae of the dixid midges lie bent in the shape of a U at the boundary where water and land meet; although only the head is below water level, the rest of the body, because of its constitution, is encircled by the surface film. Hence this insect lives under water even though its body is on land. Only at one spot is the aqueous skin interrupted— at the single unwettable part of the larva where the respiratory organ is situated.

The hairs, as already noted, are important not only as organs of touch and of other senses, but also as clinging and bracing devices and as a covering that permits air storage and keeps the insect dry. And they find still further applications in water insects. Many breathing apertures are ringed with hairs that hinder the entry either of water or of dirt particles. Various cleaning devices or brushes on the mouth, legs, or hind end of water insects are built of hairs, as are the sievelike snares or prehensile devices for catching food. Hairs also serve as fans that swirl food into the mouth or even move the whole body slowly along. Hairs frequently support larvae and pupae so well they do not come into direct contact with the substratum; and in rapidly flowing streams fringes of hairs fasten to the substratum those flattened larvae that are continually in danger of being swept away by the current.

The movable organs of the body, the gills and legs of many larvae, are broadened by means of hairs, thereby promoting circulation of water. Fringes of hairs also can serve as devices that assist the insect in maintaining a constant depth by reducing the speed of sinking. Finally they increase the propulsive surface of legs, swimmerets, or, in certain larvae, the rear end.

Actually, only a minority of water insects are swimmers. They propel themselves by paddling movements of the legs, by writhing and beating movements of the body, occasionally by expulsion of water from the rectum, and rarely by rowing motions of the wings. The capacity for swimming is most highly developed in certain beetles and bugs whose legs have been modified into oars.

The most frequent means of progression in water, however, is crawling, which by no means always requires the participation of the legs. Thus, the body may be shoved forward with the help of projecting warts or segments stiffened perhaps with swallowed air. Or the body may be dragged along after the mouthparts, which repeatedly take a more advanced hold on the substratum. Or, the hind end, endowed with various specializations such as hooks, or the extruded hind gut, can be used as a continuously advancing point of support, in which action sticky secretions occasionally may play a part. Certain larvae are nearly sessile, some of them in motionless tubes, others attached with silk or fastened with hooks to objects under water, or possibly clinging to rocks by means of suckers.

The water insects include the oldest known insects. Traces of them have been found from a time about 150 million years ago. The original ancestors of all insects lived in water. But as far as the known water insects are concerned, it can be deduced from anatomical characteristics of the respiratory organs that in earlier geologic eras these insects lived through long periods as land insects and

must have reentered the water only much later.

MAYFLIES ORDER EPHEMEROPTERA

The light of the sun sinking on the horizon is broken up by the gray-green webwork of the willows along the shore. The last rays wander over the ripples of the slowly flowing stream, here quivering in the rings made by a leaping fish, there vanishing quickly in transient whirlpools. Occasional insects appear at the surface, slip from their skin, rise from the water on shimmering wings; and others follow, more and more of them. Like summoned spirits, hundreds, thousands, millions, arise from the water.

Over the wavelets there is a twitching, a hissing and a rustling, a moving mosaic of bodies, wings, and empty skins. A cloud, like whirling snowflakes, rises and grows denser and denser, now ascending like a mighty column of smoke toward the heavens, then wafted abroad by the gentle evening zephyrs. In this unforgettable drama of nature, the principal players are the mayflies (order Ephemeroptera), those images of the transitory that long ago were celebrated in song by the ancient Greeks.

For one, two, three, or even four years these insects exist as nymphs, striving to meet their vital requirements in the water and perhaps shedding their skin as many as twenty times, all in seeming preparation for a dance of only a few hours—the nuptial flight that marks their adulthood. In adults, the mouth and digestive tract become exclusively an aerostatic apparatus for regulating the center of gravity of the body in the air. Driven by rapid wing movement, with the body held almost vertically, at one instant they shoot nearly ten yards upward. Then, turning horizontally and beginning to hover, they sink slowly, borne up as though with parachutes by the outspread wings and caudal filaments, only to rise once again. Up and down they go, in form and movement a picture of perfect grace. Their eyes, which seem to gleam, are among the most beautiful and most capable in the insect world.

Almost always only the males dance thus. But one female after another flies into the swarm. There, she is seized by the long forelegs of a male, which at other times are stretched out in flight like antennae. Female and male drift downward together, mating in flight, and the female lets her eggs drop into the water either one after the other or in a single big package. Soon thereafter she dies,

345/1

Mayflies: Ephemera male (enlarged 3×) and the head of a Baetis species with its yellow glowing "turbaned" eyes (greatly enlarged).

and the male returns to his companions. The eggs, numbering from 100 to 3,000, sink into the water, catching here or there by means of the threads that spread in tufts from both poles of each egg.

The course of events is not identical in all species. In *Palingenia* the female remains at the water surface and the male flies down to her. Or the package of eggs is not cast off at once, but sticks for a while to the abdomen or to the caudal filaments of the female. A few species from more rapidly flowing streams go beneath the surface, cloaked in a fine mantle of air, and glue their eggs to rocks; the *Baetis* mayfly even submerges in foaming waterfalls. And a very few are viviparous. *Cloeon dipterum,* for example, hangs hidden in the thickets along the bank for ten days to two weeks, during which the eggs in the abdomen develop into tiny nymphs that only then are borne to the water.

Corresponding to their dissimilar living conditions the nymphs of mayflies differ greatly in form. Very flattened types develop in rapidly flowing water; their body and legs are broad and compressed, the separate parts pieced together like the plates of a knight's armor. By means of their almost knife-sharp contours and the frequent trailing fringes of bristles, these insects are enabled practically to weld themselves to the rocks to which they cling. The violent current finds no surfaces to seize upon, and instead of washing the body away presses it more forcefully against the substratum. A few species make themselves fast with gills that act as suction devices, and others use the labium (lower lip) as a suction plate. In the quieter streams nymphs of a more cylindrical build sit on the bottom or on plants. Hairy species creep through the mud, sometimes at depths as great as 30 feet. Others excavate passageways along the shore with forelegs modified into digging implements. A species in Indonesia bores into wood and has been known to damage wooden water conduits. Many nymphs swim along in open water in spurts, assisted by their caudal fans, formed of three elegant bristles broadened with fringes of hairs, and by two series of gills of various leaflike shapes; the gills, moreover, are in constant waving motion as respiratory organs. In an escape from danger, the first swift movements may be speeded greatly by the expulsion of water from the rectum.

A very few mayfly nymphs lead predatory lives, but most are vegetarians. They scrape algae from stones or leaves with their mouth, or whisk it off with their forelegs, which bear hairs especially adapted to the job. The *Oligoneura* mayfly sifts plankton through such hairs, and *Isonychia* catches plankton in a basket beneath the mouth, a basket open against the current and formed from rows of hairs on the forelegs. [359/5–13]

Toward the end of its development the mayfly nymph accumulates air beneath its outer skin and rises to the top of the water. Floating on the surface or clinging to some object, it swells by swallowing air; suddenly the skin bursts and in an instant there seems to be a mature mayfly fluttering along the water. But it only seems so, for the too-short caudal filaments, the too-heavy, luster-less wings, and the eyes betray their immaturity. On a plant at the water's edge, or on the water surface, or maybe even in free flight, the true final molt soon occurs.

The pre-adult form, inserted between life in the water and life in the air, is unique in the world of insects. It is only after the final molt that the mayfly attains the degree of completion essential for life in the new, quite different medium, the air. This achievement, however, entails very great sensitivity to even the least amount of water. The most extreme form of an air-bound life is exhibited by a South American species that falls over and dies if it touches the ground; instead of legs this mayfly has only little useless stumps, except for the male's forelegs, which are essential for seizing the female.

Mayflies belong to the most ancient of insects and are distributed over the whole world; about 1,400 species are known. North as far as Alaska and south as far as New Zealand and Patagonia, they fly above fresh water, especially in the forenoon and evening, but also at night, when they frequently are attracted to electric lights. They dance in small groups, large groups, and in swarms, and in many lakes and rivers for unknown reasons there occurs a nearly simultaneous mass emergence of millions. In such numbers they can force ships to heave to, can darken light buoys, and can extinguish campfires, and on the next day cover the shore and roads in deep layers. They have been spread as fertilizer on the fields.

In the economy of nature mayflies are of crucial importance, for countless fish live almost exclusively on them and their nymphs. And they supply the basis of life for many birds, as well as for many other water insects. Year after year life manifests itself in uninterrupted abundance in these delicate, frail creatures. What an impressive demonstration of its strength! [359/4]

DRAGONFLIES
AND DAMSELFLIES

Order Odonata

347/1
*Damselflies of the group
Zygoptera are the Odonata most
frequently seen; and there are
numerous species, most of them
sky-blue (somewhat enlarged).*

The heat of summer lies over the pond. Water birds doze in the half-shadow of the scarcely moving reeds. The gentle buzzing of innumerable insects seems woven softly into the midday silence, like an audible veil. An odor as of the primeval world, of wet plants and heated mud, saturates the air. This is the kingdom and the time of the dragonflies and their smaller, more fragile relatives, the damselflies.

As curious testimonials to their resurrection after a long underwater existence, their empty nymphal shells hang everywhere on the plants, grotesque in form and position, as though the life that now goes gliding away, ghostly and silent, decked in kaleidoscopic color and borne on shimmering wings, had not entirely left them. Like flashing needles the small species crisscross the luxuriant tangle of swamp vegetation. Larger ones whir glitteringly through the reeds and rushes. And huge dragonflies dart mutely, like an artistic mosaic of festive colors, over water and countryside.

On the shore is a fisherman. In spite of his careful tread, the carpet of moss squishes and the water quivers beyond the heavy belt of grass. For a few moments, a big dragonfly hangs motionless above the man's head, and its rattling wingbeat draws his attention. The fisherman's actions seem odd, for on one occasion he hangs a dragonfly on his hook, and another time only a dragonfly's wing, and instead of fishing in the water he lets the line dangle in the air. We have guessed the riddle: he is a naturalist who is experimenting with dragonflies.

The study of behavior, of animal psychology, has been extended even to insects, and besides the social insects dragonflies and damselflies seem especially suitable for such attention. In some dragonflies, not only does an individual or pair take possession of a territory, but also the sexes cooperate to an astounding degree in the process of egg-laying. Big dragonflies, such as *Aeschna,* take charge of a hunting preserve with definite boundaries, and seldom tolerate trespassing by another dragonfly, least of all one of the same species. Individual domains abut, but frequently it is possible for an interloper to force his way between two occupied zones. Then three smaller preserves are formed. But apparently such subdivisions are permitted only up to a certain degree of saturation of this imaginary mosaic of hunting areas. [361]

This staking out of territory is also common in the damselflies *Calopteryx,* which flutter up and down, almost like butterflies, along streams and brooks of the Old World. Their satiny dark blue, violet, or purple wings gleam in intense reflections through the dark green shadows and the scattered rays of sunlight in the midst of the bushes along the shore. A male will defend an area of about 15 square yards all day long against penetration by his companions. Frequently the males come together in small companies for sleeping, then next morning take over new hunting preserves, entry to which is granted only to females. By use of the casting rod, it has been shown that the females recognize males of their own kind by the distinctive color of the wings, which differs from species to species.

If both sexes are in the right mood, the male begins a dancing flight, turning hither and yon with quicker wingbeats and coming nearer and nearer to his prospective mate, who waits quietly. Perhaps on one occasion he drops quickly onto the water surface with the tip of the abdomen uplifted; the abdominal underside is a luminous light color or red. Finally he drifts down over the female's wings, which are held together above the back, and runs quiveringly forward to her head, bending the tip of his abdomen forward beneath him and filling the sperm reservoir that is situated there. He then seizes the female's neck with his terminal claspers, and stretches out again. While the two are resting thus connected, the female, who is behind, bends her abdomen forward beneath her partner's sperm reservoir. The "mating wheel" is now complete, and it is without parallel in the insect world. [362/1]

Many of the larger dragonflies mate during flight; the union of two bodies in the form of a "wheel," made possible by the shift of the sperm reservoir far toward the front, permits continued directed flight with the full cooperation of both partners. This flying machine is unique in the entire animal kingdom.

After mating, the female *Calopteryx* begins at once, and as though under the supervision of the male, to insert her eggs into the stems of plants just beneath the water surface. She is stimulated by the presence of her mate, no doubt in the same way as before copulation by the latter's dominating, colorful appearance. Beyond this, however, the male occasionally dips his abdomen suggestively into the water in front of his mate.

Many damselflies do not disjoin completely after they have mated. One sees them hanging in a chain or in tandem, the male in the lead, for he has not loosed the grip of his claspers on the female's neck. In such a way pairs of the genus *Sympetrum* seesaw up and down, while the female brushes the water with her abdomen on each excursion and lets eggs drop into it. Aroused by this spectacle, other males often fly up and join solo in the seesaw flight, or may even attach themselves to the pair as a third member. In the American genus *Tramea,* the "tandem" hovers over water; the female is released, drops to the water surface and deposits eggs, rises vertically, and once again is seized behind the head with astounding assurance and carried off in flight by her partner, who meanwhile has been hovering nearby.

In the majority of species, which deposit their eggs under water, the male accompanies his attached partner, who descends backward. While she is inserting the eggs one after the other into a long plant stem, the two vanish gradually beneath the water surface, cloaked in a delicate, silvery mantle of air.

Among broad-winged damselflies (Agrionidae) the male stands still and vertical on the female, attached to her neck only by the claspers at the hind end of his body, frequently letting his wings quiver or buzzing them excitedly, and stimulating his companion to oviposit. Often whole groups of such pairs assemble, and a series of them lined up on a stem at the water's surface resembles a beautiful ballet of breathtaking delicacy.

Another enchanting scene is presented by an *Agrion* pair on a floating water-lily leaf. The female sticks her posterior end into the water through a hole previously eaten in the leaf by beetles, and bending it forward inserts the eggs one after the other into the leaf from below. Meanwhile she is slowly rotated like an hour hand by her mate, who is standing on her neck and either whirring perpendicularly or creeping along on the surface of the leaf. When the first circle of eggs is finished, the female sinks her abdomen deeper, and the procedure begins anew, with an increased radius. For the third circle, the entire abdomen disappears into the water. The final result is eggs inlaid in circles into the underside of the leaf, like a handsome piece of embroidery. [361/3, 4]

The dragonflies and damselflies are one of the oldest groups in the animal kingdom; they are incomparably older than man. Their typical form, completed in primeval time, seems inalterable. We are acquainted, of course, with some aberrant ancient types, yet we see no deep-seated changes since the Jurassic. Dragonflies and damselflies have in part highly primitive and in part highly specialized characteristics, including numerous peculiarities found only in this group of insects. [8]

The dragonflies and damselflies comprise the order Odonata, which we divide into three suborders. The suborder Anisozygoptera is an especially old group, a remnant of which survives only in a single living Japanese species. The suborder Zygoptera includes long, slender insects whose very similar fore and hind wings are held erect during rest and whose eyes are widely separated. These are the damselflies. The third group, Anisoptera, contains the dragonflies. Their wings always are held outspread after maturation, and the hind wings usually are wider than the fore wings. [360/1–16]

The dragonfly-damselfly flying machine may well be the best on our planet. The center of gravity lies between and below the bases of the wings, which, in contrast with those of nearly all other insects, are connected directly with the very strong flight muscles. Consequently dragonflies and damselflies are masters of every type of flight, even when the position of the body makes flight almost impossible. They can fly backward, move vertically like helicopters or even like rockets, or stop and turn in the midst of the most rapid progression, as if they had been rammed into. So violent are these maneuvers that it is surprising the wing membrane is not torn to shreds. Yet it withstands these strains, for it is not smoothly stretched out, but is ribbed with a bountiful system of veins that make it elastic.

The speed of a big dragonfly may reach about 60 miles an hour; and flight is noiseless, since the wings beat too slowly to produce a hum. In small species there are some 50 to 90 beats per second, but only about 15 in certain damselflies. The latter have an alternating wing movement, in that the hind wings are elevated while the fore wings are depressed. But other dragonflies and damselflies move both pairs of wings together, only alternating while hovering, at which times the wing margins brush against one another and cause the rustling that differs so slightly and yet so insistently from the sound of reeds rubbing together in the wind.

Many species spend their entire lives, including procreation, in flight, with the exception of nightly pauses or those compelled by bad weather. For the most part the insects spend these intervals in trees, suspended by the legs. These limbs, unsuitable for walking, are raptorial (adapted for seizing prey) appendages situated far forward and armed with spines; their potential is increased by the uniquely movable first thoracic segment. With them the prey is ensnared during flight as in a basket and is at once conveyed to the mouth, which is equipped with sharp, toothed, knifelike mandibles.

All dragonflies and damselflies are voracious predators, and many are cannibalistic. Some species catch mosquitoes almost exclusively, but larger ones prefer butterflies and moths, as well as smaller members of their own group. These predators have been seen chasing moths in the dusk in the company of swallows and bats. Some dragonflies, like their enemies, the kingfishers, even plunge into water in their effort to catch prey.

The little damselflies snatch aphids from leaves as they fly past, and some of the large darners *(Aeschna)* occasionally may be seen fluttering along treetrunks or cliffs, probing every cleft for resting moths or other insects. Once a resting underwing moth *(Catocala nupta)* was seen to be roused in this way by a darner, but due apparently to its size and strength was able to escape, which few prey succeed in doing. It is astonishing that the darner discovered this completely camouflaged lepidopteran, inasmuch as experiments have shown that large dragonflies ordinarily respond to objects in motion.

The magnificent iridescent eyes of dragonflies and damselflies probably are the best in the whole world of insects. According to the species, one eye is composed of about 10,000 to 30,000 facets. As a further aid to vision, the head is exceptionally movable, as may be observed in dragonflies that lie in wait for their prey at the tips of branches or on the stems of reeds. They can twist the head sideways 180°, backward 70°, and forward and downward 40°. This gives an enormous visual field for the eyes, which already have a large visual field, since they cover almost the entire face. Moreover, a highly refined system of joints in the neck compensates for all involuntary movements of the body—for instance, those caused by the wind shaking the perch—so that any object that has been fixated visually is held precisely in focus. The actual field of observation of these insects lies above them and in front of them, so they always attack their prey from below.

Since their eyes are capable of seeing at night, dragonflies and damselflies may hunt until late evening and in almost complete darkness. In Java there lives an exclusively nocturnal species. South American damselflies of the family Pseudostigmatidae sail almost invisibly through dark parts of the forest in spite of their size. These are ghostly creatures, venerated by the natives more or less as the souls of the departed. In the deep shadows of a luxuriant vegetation, where the smell of mold holds sway, one sees transparent, iridescent wings shimmering like a quivering veil. The four wingtips rise and fall as deep blue-violet, opalescently-ringed spots, or again seem to dissolve into an undulant reflection. Occasionally, perhaps, one can imagine he sees a long, slender body floating horizontally behind them, like a magic wand. And involuntarily one doubts that all this belongs to a single being.

Species with such long abdomens develop in the water reservoirs of the bromeliads that grow as epiphytes on the trees of the virgin forest. In the clear water that collects at the base of the leaves, the nymphs grow up, subsisting on other water insects that live there. The long abdomen permits the female to insert her eggs deeply enough into the narrow base of a leaf of these plants. [360/8–10]

In this act of oviposition, dragonflies and damselflies exhibit peculiar specializations. Many go beneath the water surface, some alone and others accompanied by the male, and work there for up to an hour, thanks to the layer of air surrounding the body. In mountain streams species fly into the white spray of the raging water and lay their eggs on foam-covered moss. Many dragonflies and damselflies bore their eggs into living or dead plants, or even into wood, with the help of a cutting device at the tip of the abdomen. For each species there is a typical arrangement or grouping of the eggs, and some species make attractive incised designs. [361/5, 6]

Others bury their eggs in sand, mud, or moss in shallow water or along the shore. In doing this, the huge dragonflies *Cordulegaster* hover erect on the tip of the abdomen and force themselves downward rhythmically once a second, by means of special wing movements, each time boring an egg into the ground. Another species hovers in a horizontal position, and with corresponding wing strokes hammers its eggs into the earth with a sharp ridge, directed downward, on the tip of the abdomen. [360/1]

A great many dragonflies and damselflies tap their eggs into the water with an up-and-down movement while they are flying, or place them in this way onto floating foam, wood, or the damp bank. A few species dart through the surface film, hissing like speedboats, and in this way brush the eggs off.

An *Aeschna juncea* female frequently creeps into a dark hole in the bank and lays her eggs, while the males patrol outside.

The females that insert their eggs into plants produce several hundred, of rather large, elongate form. On the other hand, those that oviposit freely produce thousands of smaller and rounder eggs, most of which are laid in series or in large batches. These eggs are enclosed in a gelatinous layer that swells strongly in water and that frequently takes the form of strings that twine about water plants.

At first ensheathed in a membrane like little mummies in their wrappings, the hatching nymphs squirm forth from the eggs. If the eggs were deposited on shore or in overhanging twigs, the nymphs work their way into the water with fishlike undulations. But most nymphs hatch in the water, free themselves at once from their first skin, and then, as much more finely articulated nymphs, take up their predatory, aqueous life. This lasts in rare instances only a few weeks, but mostly from one to three years, or even for four, with perhaps 10 to 15 molts.

Rather inactive beings, they are well camouflaged by their color, which changes according to that of the bottom. They live there on submerged plants, or in mud or sand, frequently deeply buried. They eat everything they can, including little fishes and slightly smaller nymphs of their own kind. Lurking motionless or creeping slowly, these uncanny creatures suddenly shoot out their raptorial tongs, previously folded almost invisibly beneath the head, and grasp the prey.

The respiratory organs of the nymph are in its expanded rectum, which contains up to 24,000 gill leaflets arranged in six double rows. A strong intestinal musculature pumps water in and out. But atmospheric air also can be taken in, as happens when the oxygen content of the water falls too low. Thus such nymphs change without difficulty from aquatic to aerial respiration; this also is the case with those neotropical species that live on damp pillows of moss, on rocks at the edge of gushing waterfalls, or on dripping crags.

In addition to getting rid of the remains of digestion and taking in oxygen, the rectum of many nymphs has a third important function as an organ of locomotion. It can expel with great force the water taken in. This provides rapid movement.

Damselfly nymphs frequently also have at the posterior end three handsome gill leaf-

lets; these, however, have only a very limited respiratory function and serve for the most part as oars. In the species that lead a buried life the tip of the abdomen frequently is lengthened into a breathing tube that extends out of the mud into free water or even beyond into the air.

Not all dragonfly and damselfly nymphs live exclusively under water. An Australian species digs passages in the banks to just above the water's surface, where it hunts at night. In Hawaii, some species come ashore when food is scarce, and one even lives solely on land beneath plants. Many nymphs can withstand for more than two months the drying up of a puddle; they dry out in the mud and reawaken when it is moistened anew.

When the time has come, the adult dragonfly or damselfly is formed inside the nymph. The nymph, as a type fully coordinated and shaped for a creeping, underwater existence, produces the basis for a completely and incomparably different being. From the one comes the other, without transition.

The nymph spends its last days at the water surface. In front on the thorax, above the level of the water, spiracles have opened, allowing air to enter. The former intestinal respiration no longer functions. A thin layer of air already has freed the nymphal skin from that of the adult, which lies beneath. This double creature in its nymphal shell climbs yet higher and finds something to cling to. It is strange that in this grasping reflex the nymph seems to live on in the empty skin, even after the adult has freed itself at the front end and, exhausted by this effort, remains for some time bent back and hanging downward. It then frees itself entirely, its wings and body expanding as blood is pumped through them, and again rests, hanging while it hardens a little, until it finally soars into the air. [360/6, 7]

Still soft and completely helpless, the new dragonflies or damselflies frequently fall prey to their enemies, especially to birds. They are easily visible because of their still light-colored, almost white skin; the final coloration first appears with sexual maturity, which, according to the genus, may require at least several hours, but more likely days or even weeks. The length of life also varies greatly, from two to three weeks in some to three to six months in others, and as long as ten months in the overwintering *Sympecma* species.

Dragonflies and damselflies by no means always stay near water, but frequently hunt

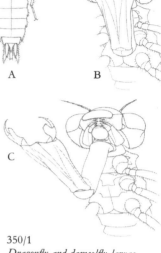

350/1
Dragonfly and damselfly larvae. (A) Aeschna; on the back the four wingpads, and at the hind end various appendages that can be clapped together to form a pointed closure for the anal opening (natural size). (B) Head and thorax of the same larva, seen from below; the lower lip (labium) has been modified into a prehensile trap, armed with hooks (C).

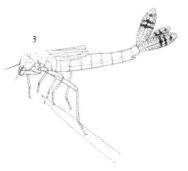

350/2-3
(2) With its tongs an Aeschna larva is capturing a water beetle larva (Acilius). (3) The larva of the damselfly Agrion; below the head is the hinged labial trap, and at the rear end are three platelike oars that are also respiratory. From the form, venation, and markings of these the different species can be distinguished (enlarged 2×).

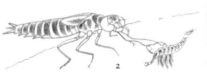

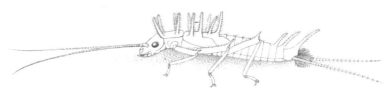

The nymph of a South American stonefly; particles of mud stick to its projecting processes and conceal the insect (enlarged 3×).

far away in woods, over fields, and even in the middle of cities. These insects are distributed over the whole world, as far north as the Arctic Ocean, but the majority of the 4,500 species live in the tropics. A few develop in salt water lakes and in brackish pools, others in hot springs.

Apparently overcrowding and special weather conditions can trigger mass migrations of certain species, in Europe mostly of *Libellula quadrimaculata,* in Australia of *Hemicordulia tau.* Such hordes, with which isolated individuals of other species may join, frequently number tens of thousands, flying calmly and regularly in a single direction. In the South American pampas, dragonfly migrations are feared as harbingers of tornados. Along the seacoast, migratory companies are formed rather frequently, and occasionally whole swarms will land on a ship in the open sea. Mass migrations of other insects, particularly butterflies and moths, are known, too, but their causes are still riddles, as is so much in nature.

STONEFLIES ORDER PLECOPTERA

Though they are distributed in some 2,000 species throughout the world, the stoneflies (order Plecoptera), which lead somewhat concealed lives, are familiar to few persons besides fishermen. Dependent more exclusively than many other insects on water rich in oxygen, their nymphs with few exceptions inhabit only brooks, rivers, or clear lakes; they are absent from waters polluted by civilized man. Stoneflies, sometimes called perlids, choose cold, flowing water, and ascend mountain streams to the foot of glaciers; many are looked on as relics of the Ice Age.

Stoneflies are rather elongate insects with parallel sides, slightly reminiscent of the distantly related grasshoppers. With the exception of a few tropical species, they lack striking colors; from a large head, long antennae protrude. Their wings are folded back against the abdomen and extend beyond it. The second pair of wings is folded fanlike beneath the first pair. In spite of having large wings with strong veins, the stoneflies are poor fliers; the two pairs of wings beat slowly and asynchronously, producing a characteristic fluttering flight.

Shortly before the female lays her eggs, she brings them together in sticky clumps beneath the abdomen, or in the form of strings on its upper surface; then she flies low over the water until the eggs are washed off by the waves, finally to adhere to submerged stones.

In adaptation to swift-flowing waters, the nymphs mostly are flattened and resemble the nymphs of mayflies. But since oxygen uptake occurs predominantly through the skin and perhaps also through the rectum, gills frequently are lacking or are present only as rudimentary clusters at the base of the legs and, occasionally, at the front and back ends.

Stonefly nymphs usually sit on or under stones and pressed tightly to them; they are skillful at crawling about and swim with undulating movements, assisted by their hairy legs. Some are voracious predators with saw-toothed, dagger-shaped mouthparts; others are vegetarians. For their development they require one, two, or even as much as four years, with up to 33 molts. At the last molt the nymph changes outwardly but little, yet it has longer wingpads, is much more sluggish, and no longer takes any food.

For their transformation into adults, the nymphs usually crawl from the water onto stones or branches, frequently in large groups. Certain species fasten themselves to the steep, smooth, foam-flecked cliffs and rocks of raging mountain torrents by means of a sticky crop, extruded from the mouth.

Eventually the stoneflies emerge from the nymphal skin and are fully developed within a few minutes.

A few species are found on snow as early as winter's end, but most appear in spring and summer. Some live only a short time, others up to half a year. They do not feed, but consume fat stored up during the nymphal period. Stoneflies of a few genera perform mating dances, during which they beat the abdomen against stones so hard one can hear it.

WATER BUGS ORDER HETEROPTERA

When sunlight bewitches the brook, casting the reflection of sky, thickets, and trees in cool colors onto the surface, and making the water below luminous with its warm light, here and there it traces on the bottom silhouettes composed of symmetrical spots. At one instant they are still or flowing slowly along, then suddenly they dart jerkily away in ghostly, disembodied designs over the golden yellow of the bottom, the copper of sunken leaves and the shining green of the water plants.

Soon we recognize the cause as insects flitting over the surface. These are the water

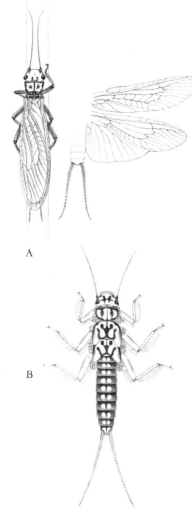

A

B

(A) Stonefly (Plecoptera) and (B) its nymph (natural size).

CAPTIONS
FOR PAGES 353 TO 366

353/1
The first young queen bee to emerge from one of the big queen cells kills any sister queens that come out subsequently (enlarged).

353/2
A red wood ant, defending her nest with formic acid (enlarged).

353/3
The ant garden, a part of the nest in which fungi are cultured (natural size). Photograph.

353/4
The pasteboard nest of a house ant built of chewed-up wood; inside it contains passageways and chambers (reduced). Photograph.

353/5
A hitherto unknown ant nest, made of pasteboard (nat. size). Photograph.

PAGES 354 AND 355

354/1–15
Ant forms. (5) Pharaoh ant; (6) bulldog ant from Australia; (7–9) leafcutting ants; (7) worker, (8) soldier, (9) queen. (13–15) Carpenter ants; (13) wingless queen, (14) male, (15) winged queen (1–6 enlarged 1.5×; 7–15 enlarged 1.2×). Photographs.

354/16
Honey ants in California; in the central chamber (that contains the cocoons) is the queen; below are the "living honey jars" (enlarged 2×).

355/1–11
Ant forms. (7) Weaver ant; (8–11) army ants; (8) queen (1–7 enlarged 1.4×; 8–11 enlarged 1.7×). Photographs.

355/12
Honeybee dances (somewhat enlarged). See description on page 336.

PAGES 356 AND 357

356/1
Three females of a parasitic ant, tolerated in friendship and taken care of, are riding on a queen ant who is accompanied by a worker. The front two are not yet fully mature, and one of them still has wings (greatly enlarged).

357/1
Friendship between ants and the Indian ant woodpecker. The bird digs its nesting cavity into the ant nest, and is tolerated by them (natural size).

PAGE 358

358/1
Only a few termite genera rear fungi.

In fungal gardens deserted by the termites, those fungi they cultivated may develop the fruiting bodies.

358/2
Diagram of a termite nest. In the hill are large air shafts and numerous fungus chambers interconnected by passageways. Down below in the center is the queen's cell. Subterranean passages lead away to the food supplies (dead wood), and where the latter come to the surface they are roofed over like tunnels.

358/3
Section through an African Bellicositermes hill. The thick covering layer, pierced by a network of passageways, encloses a central cavity beneath which are the fungus chambers and the queen's cell.

358/4
An Apicotermes nest.

358/5
The mushroom-shaped structure built by Eutermes, about 20 inches high.

358/6
A "termite city," made by the Australian compass termites, 10 to 13 feet high. Its wide sides are precisely in the east-west direction.

358/7
A tower constructed by Eutermes, 23 feet high and thus 2,500 times as high as the body length of the insect.

PAGE 359

359/1
North American termites; workers and soldiers (enlarged).

359/2–3
Termite guests. (2) Termite fly. (3) Rove beetle (greatly enlarged).

359/4
A North American mayfly, about to be eaten by frogs (reduced).

359/5–13
Immature stages of mayflies. (5) Caenis eggs: in water their polar spiral structures dissolve into long threads that catch on plants. (6) One of the digging larval forms in its U-shaped tunnel, in the bank below the water line; its thin gill leaflets are curled over the back in the shape of an S. (7) Typical free-resting and free-swimming larva. (8) Larva typical of those that creep through mud; in them the second, very large pair of gills covers those that follow. (9) Larva that is adapted to torrential currents; it presses its flattened body against the underside of rocks. (10–13) Different forms of gill leaflets (greatly enlarged).

PAGES 360 AND 361

360/1–7
Dragonflies of the group Anisoptera, with empty nymphal skins (exuviae) (somewhat reduced). Photograph.

360/8–16
Damselflies are Odonata that belong to the group Zygoptera (0.75 natural size). Photograph.

361/1–2
An imperial dragonfly (1) has dived upon another species in order to drive it from his own "beat" (1.6 nat. size).

361/3–6
Reproduction in dragonflies and damselflies. (3) Agrion pair during oviposition on a water-lily leaf (natural size). (4) Slits, each of them containing one egg, in the underside of the leaf (somewhat reduced). (5–6) Rows of eggs of species of Lestes in plant stems (laid open artificially); (5) two elongated eggs per insertion; (6) four.

PAGES 362 AND 363

362/1–2
(1) The mating wheel formed by damselflies. (2) Whirligig beetle (natural size); at the back, a pike.

362/3
A water strider, an aquatic bug of the family Gerridae (enlarged), and its characteristic shadow. Additionally a pond snail, fingernail clam, fairy shrimp, and a bullhead are shown (North America).

362/4
A backswimmer, an aquatic bug of the family Notonectidae (enl. 2×).

362/5
A caddisfly larva in its case (enl. 2×).

363/1–11
Aquatic bugs. (1) Water strider. (4, 5) Backswimmers. (6, 7) Giant water bugs (Belostomatidae), the largest of all Hemiptera. (9) Ranatra, a water scorpion. (10, 11) Other water scorpions (genus Nepa) (nat. size). Photograph.

363/12–15
Dobsonflies and alderflies (nat. size). Photograph.

PAGES 364 AND 365

364/1–11
(1–7) Caddisflies and (8–11) the cases built by the larvae (enlarged 1.3×). Photograph.

364/12
(A) Aquatic moth (Nymphula:

Pyralidae), running along the surface with whirring wings; (B) the caterpillar with its dwelling; (C) the pupa in its cocoon (the enclosing housing has been opened); (D) moth at the moment of emergence (enlarged 1.5×).

364/13
(A) The yellow fever mosquito, Aedes aegypti; (B) egg; (C) larva; and (D) pupa.

365/1A–E
(1A, B) Malaria mosquito, Anopheles; (1C) eggs; (1D) larva; (1E) the fever curve (°C) of malaria, which is caused by the microbes injected during the mosquito bite. Depending on the species of the disease organism, attacks of fever occur every 48 or 72 hours, when the (round) blood corpuscles burst in consequence of the proliferation of the microbes, which then go on to attack new corpuscles.

365/2A–C
(2A) Ordinary biting mosquito, Culex, recognizable from its characteristic resting position; (2B) eggs; (2C) larva that (in contrast with Anopheles) hangs down from the water surface (greatly enlarged).

PAGE 366

366/1A–C
(A) Buffalo gnat, or black fly; (B) larva: (C) pupae in their dwellings (greatly enlarged).

366/2–4
Fly larvae under water (greatly enl.).

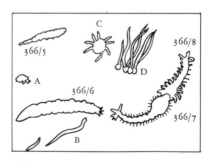

366/5–8
(5) Larval horsefly. (6) Crane fly larva. (7 and 8) Phantom midge larva pulling a mosquito larva down beneath the water surface (from a North American brook). Also shown are (A) water flea, (B) threadworms, (C) water mite, and (D) oligochaete worms.

366/9
A predaceous diving beetle, Dytiscus, with an air bubble at the rear end.

353/1

353/3

353/2

353/4

353/5

353

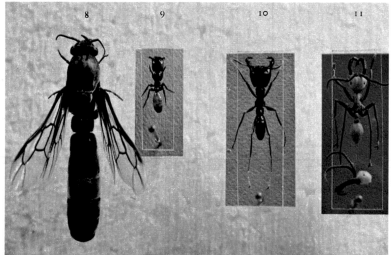

356/1 ▶

357/1 ▶▶

355/12

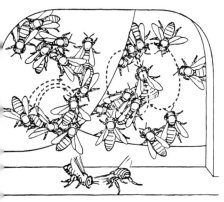

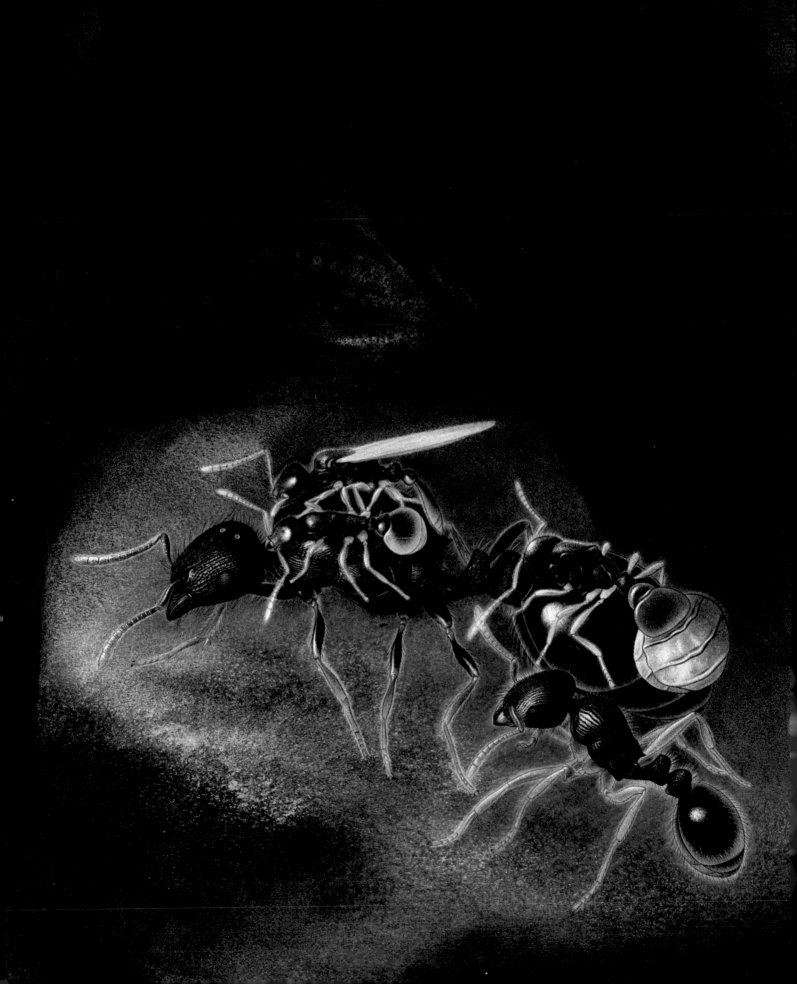

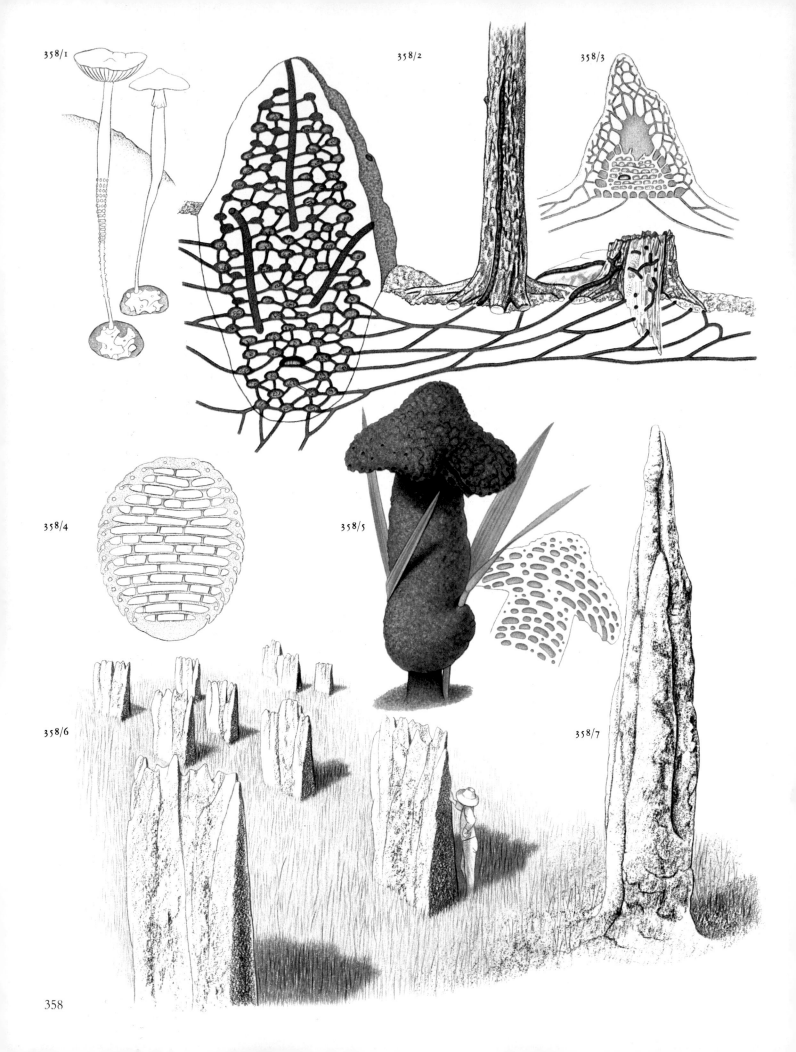

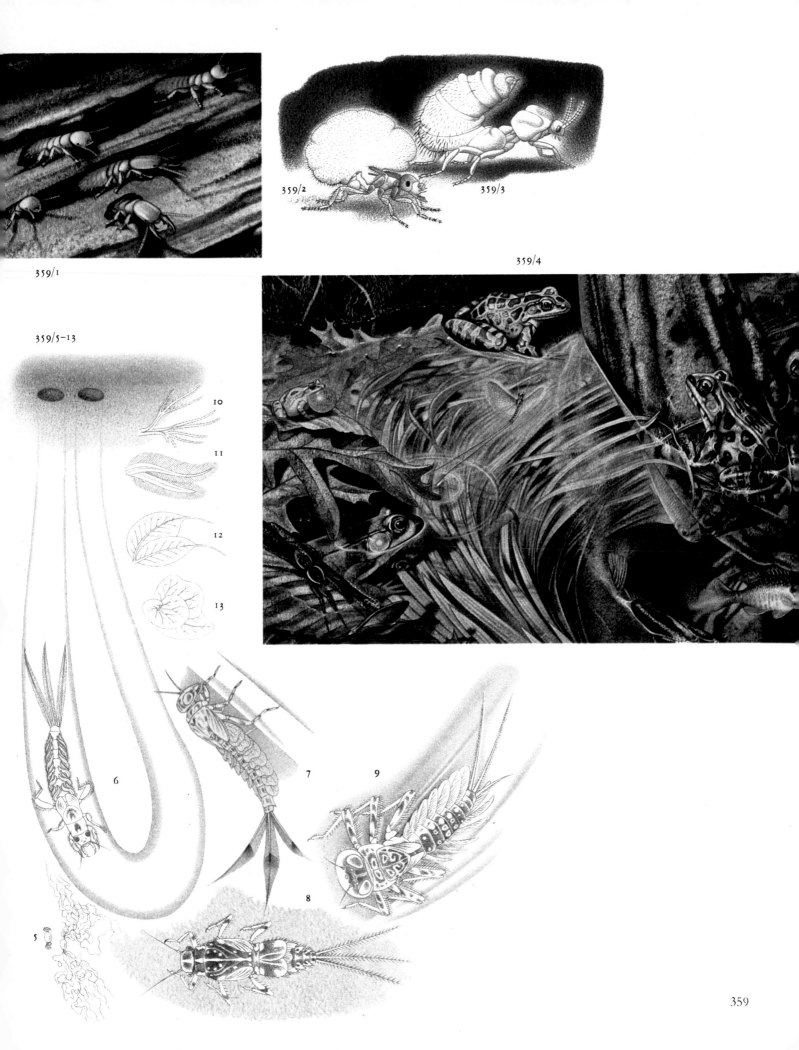

359/1

359/2   359/3

359/4

359/5-13

10

11

12

13

6

7

9

8

5

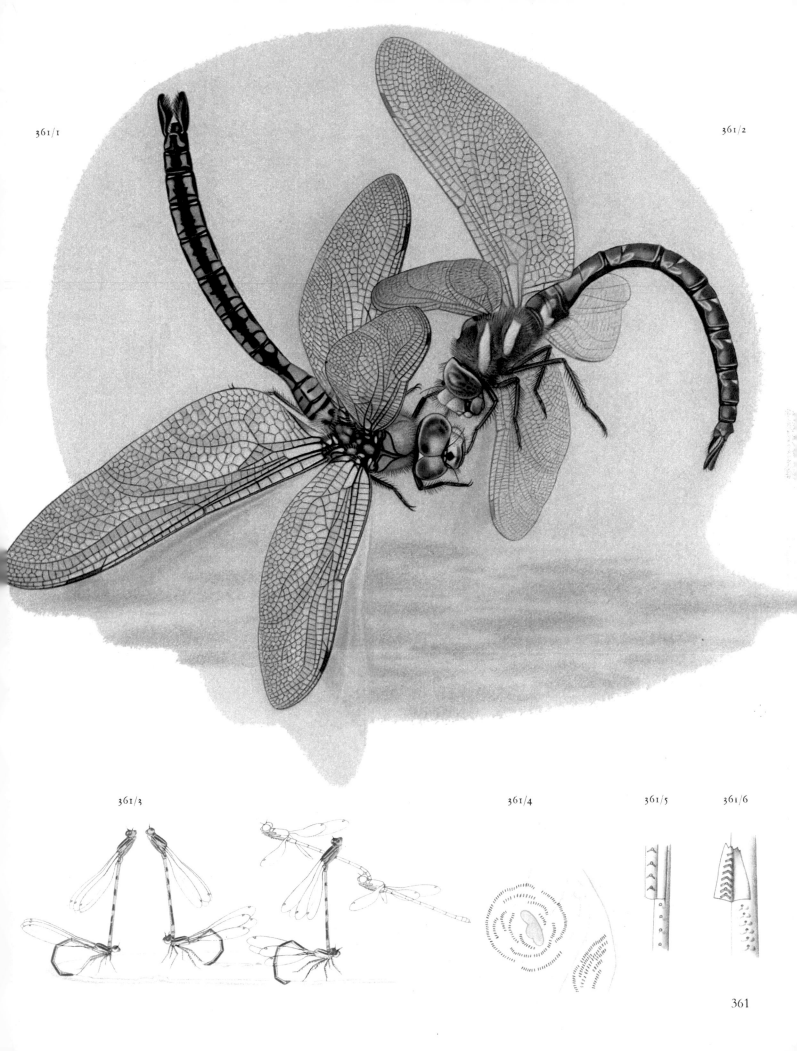

361/1   361/2

361/3   361/4   361/5   361/6

361

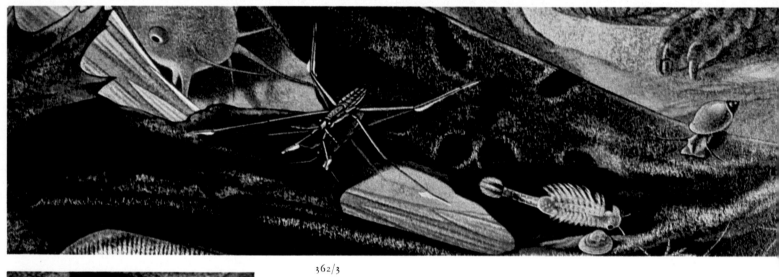

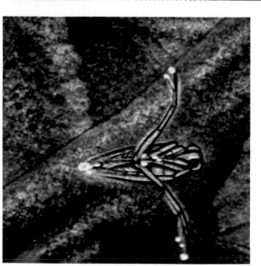

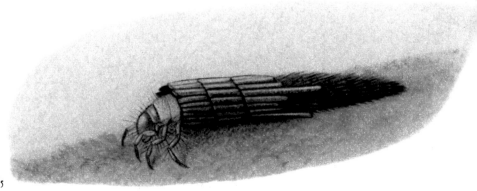

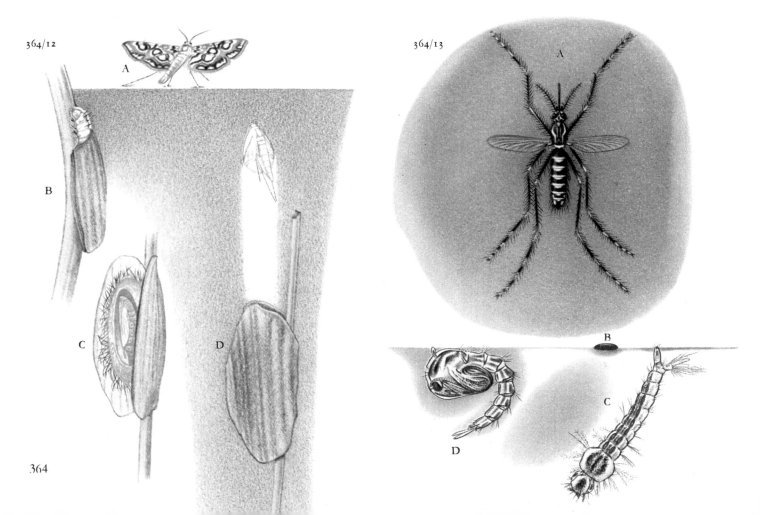

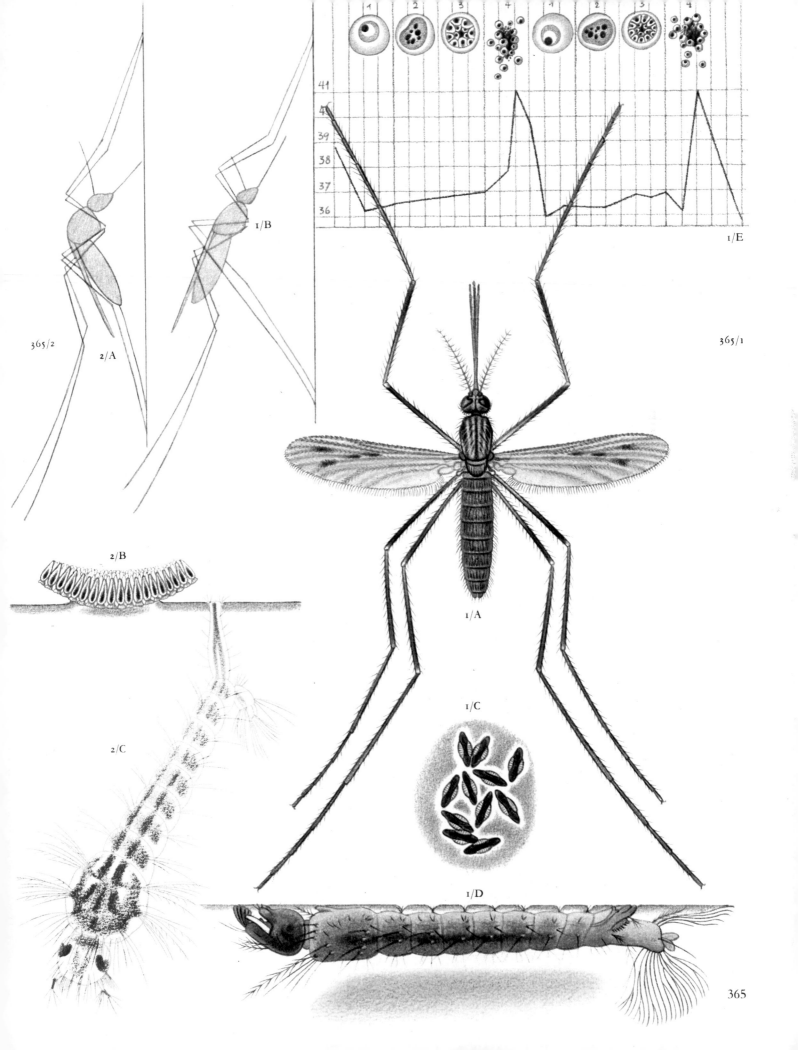

1/B

365/2

2/A

1/E

365/1

1/A

1/C

2/B

2/C

1/D

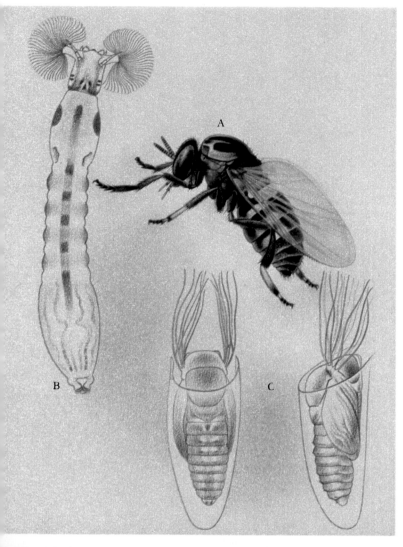

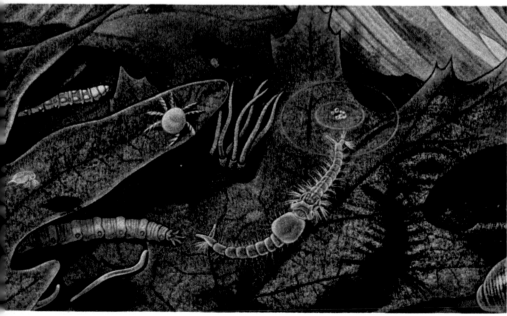

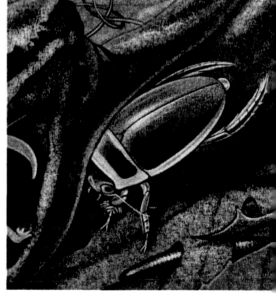

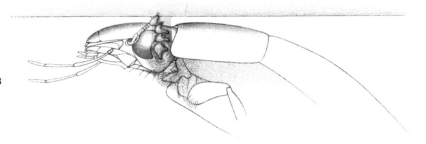

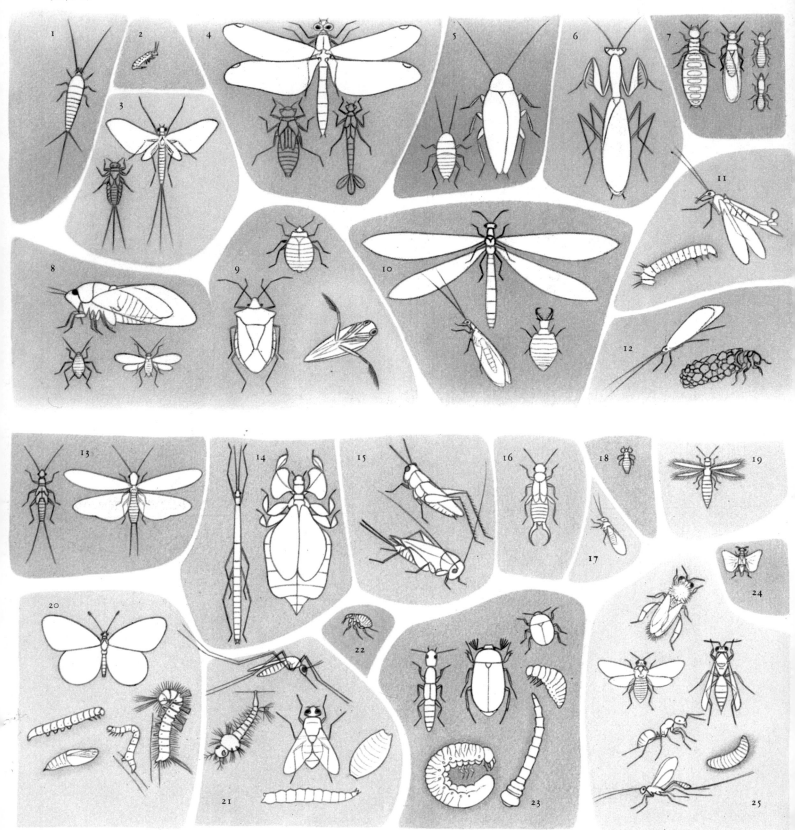

striders, bugs of the family Gerridae. Their legs, kept dry by a dense feltwork of oily hairs, indent the uppermost layer of the water a little; these impressions cast the striking silhouettes, which are much larger than the insects and seem hardly to belong to them.

The body of the water striders is always dry, too, thanks to an oily, silvery coating of hairs, for if it got wet these insects would drown. There is indeed one North American species that dives to the bottom and catches its food there, but otherwise the water surface exclusively is the environment of the water striders. Upon it they rest with their long, slender legs extended crosswise like the outriggers of a boat; upon it they dart forward for perhaps as much as a yard with a single stroke of the middle legs, or perhaps proceed in jumps as high as 4 inches.

Their claws are not at the tips of the legs, as in other insects, but are located in a depression a little above and to the side. In this way rupture of the surface film is avoided. The hind legs serve as rudders, and the forelegs are borne bent over the head, above the water. With their forelegs the water striders seize their food, which they suck dry. This consists of little insects that have fallen into the water; their struggles on the water surface are perceived at a great distance by sensory hairs on the water striders' legs.

Among the water striders, as among many other bugs, a species may have winged individuals and others that either are wingless or display various degrees of wing reduction. Why this is so has not yet been satisfactorily explained. Water striders spend the winter under moss or leaves on the bank or further inland, and are in the water again early in spring, when little open channels first appear in the ice. They lay their eggs on plants or on wood just below the surface, and the hatching nymphs first sink to the bottom and only later swim to the top. At first the nymph is normal in form, but then for a while seems to have lost its abdomen, which becomes only a very small and compressed protuberance at the end of the large thorax. But the abdomen is extended again after the third molt.

Water striders are sociable insects, and at times hundreds may assemble in the shade of a bush. There are species that live at sea, certain ones often hundreds of miles from land, laying their eggs on floating objects such as pieces of seaweed, feathers, or snail shells. [362/3; 363/1]

In shallow water close to shore, among all sorts of stranded plant parts, lives another odd family, the water measurers (Hydrometridae). Walking along slowly and as though uplifted on stilts, these needle-thin creatures, with eyes that seem to be attached to their neck, may be seen seeking their prey on the water surface. Their eggs are sculptured works of art. [363/2]

A family whose members prefer running water and are active at low temperatures is the veliids. These bugs walk on the water with alternating movements of their legs, which are shorter and more strongly flexed than those of the water striders. Frequently they anchor themselves with two legs to the bank and wait for small insects carried along by the stream. The species of the more tropical genus *Rhagovelia* even walk across raging rapids with the help of large swimming fans near the tip of the middle leg. These feathery circlets, which are kept folded up in a crease of the leg, can be spread at need and act like oars pulled just beneath the water surface. All the veliids dive often, cloaked in a layer of air, and frequently run about hanging from the underside of the surface film. [363/3]

In contrast to the surface dwellers are the genuine aquatic bugs. The best-known representatives surely are the backswimmers (Notonectidae). With the keel-shaped back down, the flat venter up, and the hind legs widely spread, like oars, these insects rest and swim close beneath the water's surface. On various parts of their body and also beneath the wings, a layer of air is held; the greatest store of air lies on the ventral surface in two channels formed of four dense rows of hairs that are unwettable on their inner faces. This is the cause of the upside-down position of these bugs.

Being less dense than water, the backswimmers are carried to the surface unless they drive themselves downward with rowing movements of the hind legs, which are especially adapted by means of hair fringes as swimming organs, or unless they hold themselves down by means of the four front legs while the oars, directed forward, hang free in the water. The backswimmers seem to be suspended from the water surface by means of their four front legs and hind end, but actually they are being pushed upward against it, so that at the five points of contact the water surface bulges outward slightly. But, if the backswimmers come up with the back on top, they break through the surface film and are forced out of the water, as occurs when they crawl onto some object and fly away.

The backswimmers are excellent fliers. They swarm, occasionally in large numbers, especially in autumn when they seek other bodies of water, where they will overwinter. In certain species it is the egg rather than the adult that overwinters, and egg diapause may last eight to nine months.

The backswimmers are voracious predators. They capture aquatic insects swimming in the upper levels and other insects that have fallen in, sucking them dry with the strong, piercing proboscis. With their bite they can even kill small fish, tadpoles, and other aquatic animals. Their bite is painful to people and cattle, which is why they have also been given the name "waterbees." Certain species, like a few other aquatic bugs, are able to produce clearly audible sounds; they do this by rubbing the forelegs over ridges on the proboscis.

The female inserts her eggs into water plants with her sharp ovipositor, or cements them to the plants with a viscous fluid. The nymphs, which hatch after three to six weeks, resemble their elders fully except for their lack of wings. They mature, after five molts, in five to six weeks.

One group of backswimmers (Anisopinae) has a few peculiarities. For one thing, these insects as a rule are in equilibrium with water; they come to the surface only to get air, and at other times float through the water like the plankton they gather in a basket formed from the legs. For another, these bugs have red blood, which makes the ventral surface frequently look red. [362/4; 363/4]

A family at first glance much like the backswimmers is that of the water boatmen (Corixidae). But these do not swim on their back and do not live on the surface. They spend more time on the bottom, gathering their predominantly vegetable food with their forelegs and sucking at it with their weak proboscis.

The water boatmen fly frequently, especially at night, when they are attracted to electric lights. Their takeoff is swifter than that of most water insects. Much lighter than water, these bugs shoot away from the bottom as soon as the grasp of their abnormally long middle legs is released. They hurtle through the surface film into the air, where their very rapid course may pass over directly into flight.

Their method of taking in air when in water is very different from that of the backswimmers, for the water boatmen have no special ventral channels. They hold the greater part of the air mass beneath the wings, and a thin layer of air by means of hairs on the ventral surface; the two air supplies are connected between thorax and abdomen. And the water boatmen do not come to the surface hind end first, like the backswimmers, but stretch head and thorax out into the air and also frequently leap out of the water like fish.

These bugs also chirp by means of the proboscis and forelegs, particularly at mating time, and hence have received the designation "water cicadas." The eggs are glued usually to plants, but by certain North American species even to living crayfish.

With about 300 species, of which many have a delicate transverse pattern of wavy lines, the water boatmen are the largest family of the water bugs. They have worldwide distribution, occurring in all possible bodies of water up to 16,000 feet above sea level, and even in brackish estuaries. Occasionally they appear in great swarms. Their eggs are used as food by the poorer people of Mexico and Egypt. [363/5]

Broadly oval, like beetles, are the creeping water bugs (Naucoridae). They are conspicuous because their forelegs have been transformed into prehensile hooks with long, dagger-sharp points. With these the living prey is seized, then pierced with the poison-bearing proboscis and the juices sucked out. The bites of these bugs are very painful and sharper than those of bees and wasps.

The creeping water bugs swim very well thanks to their hair-fringed hind legs and also fly very well, even though only very rarely. Air for breathing is taken in at the water surface with the posterior end and stored as a layer on the underside as well as beneath the wings. These bugs swim with the back uppermost, as well as in the reverse position, and frequently walk belly upward beneath the water surface. The eggs are inserted into plants or merely stuck to their surface. [363/8]

Similar in structure and way of life to the creeping water bugs are the giant water bugs (Belostomatidae), known particularly in America as "electric light bugs," because they frequently fly to electric lights, and as fish-devouring "fish-killers." This predominantly tropical and subtropical family contains about 200 species. Some are more than 4 inches long and hence among the largest of all insects.

These insects have become especially well-known not only because of their size, but because care of the young, though of a rather involuntary sort, has been observed in a few species. For, after the male has fought against it for hours and has made innumerable vain efforts to escape, eventually he is overpowered by the larger female and forced

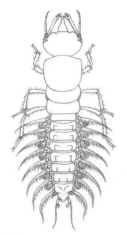

371/1
*Larva of a dobsonfly
(Megaloptera); the gill
appendages on the sides of
the abdomen are usually carried in
a laid-back position (natural size).*

to hold still while she at her leisure plasters his whole back with eggs. To no avail the male rolls and scratches afterward, for his weighty gift is glued on too firmly. The first-stage nymphs hatch after only ten days, freeing the father of his burden. But usually he is fallen upon anew, and the female polishes the empty eggshells from his back, making room for a new clutch.

In flight the giant water bugs breathe through big thoracic spiracles. In the water these become nonfunctional, and the insects inhale by suspending themselves from the surface and taking in air through a short respiratory tube protruded from the posterior end into the air like a periscope. Air is stored both on the ventral surface and in the thorax. With their poisonous proboscis the giant water bugs kill insects, frogs, tadpoles, salamanders, and fish, and their bite is very painful to man. In certain South American and Asiatic countries these great bugs are eaten by the natives, and some are used also in the manufacture of medicines. [363/6, 7]

The oddest forms among the water bugs are the water scorpions of the family Nepidae. These distantly resemble real scorpions because they have two grasping legs far forward on the body and a long respiratory tube at the rear. They may be seen crawling about on floating plants or on the bottom in very shallow water, or resting half buried in mud, while the tip of their breathing tube sticks up through the surface. The tube is composed of two trough-shaped staves.

Like almost all water bugs, the water scorpions are predatory, stalking their prey slowly or lying in wait for it, seizing it like lightning with their raptorial tongs, and killing it with their toxic beak. Their bite is painful to man, and they are not called "toe biters" for nothing.

The two subfamilies of water scorpions, Nepinae and Ranatrinae, are similar in structure and way of life, but are different in appearance. Members of the Nepinae have an oval shape, and those of Ranatrinae have a long, thin, sticklike form. The grasping legs of the latter group are much like those of praying mantids in function and attitude.

The Nepinae seem hardly ever to fly despite their large wings, which, retaining a store of air beneath them, cover the curiously gaudy, red back; but they are able to swim slowly, even though their legs do not seem particularly well-suited for doing so. The Ranatrinae, on the other hand, fly frequently and have been seen even in migratory swarms.

Water scorpions pass the winter on the bank under stones and cast-up remnants of plants, or in the water beneath the ice, where they can live for a long time almost without oxygen. They insert their eggs at the water surface into rotting plants, moss, or algal carpets. The eggs of Nepinae have on the upper side a wreath of short threads that serve as respiratory tubes. The eggs of the Ranatrinae, which are laid in rows, have only two of these tubes, but they are much longer. [363/9–11]

ALDERFLIES, DOBSONFLIES, AND SPONGILLAFLIES

ORDER NEUROPTERA

A small minority of nerve-winged insects (order Neuroptera) live in the water, but only during their larval stage. These include the alderflies, dobsonflies, and spongillaflies.

In the spring the shores of many bodies of water are swarming with small brown thick-headed gnomes. On their four large prominently veined wings they fly ponderously and shakily over short stretches between the vegetation or across the water from one twig, post, or stone to another. Over the ground they run in pairs, with wings laid back against the body and the antennae extended forward, the larger female leading the male.

These are the alderflies of the family Sialidae. During their adult life of but a few days, they mate and lay their eggs. They take little or no food, possibly nibbling a bit at flowers. The female glues her approximately 1,000 eggs in several groups on plants, wood, or stones, close together and at an angle with the vertical. The hatching larvae burst the eggshells with a special tool situated on the head, drop into the water, and swim off, rowing with the legs and undulating the body.

The larvae are predators that dismember their prey with their sharp jaws. In their later stages they usually creep about in mud on the bottom. They breathe through long gill chambers on the sides, seem to be independent of vegetation, and penetrate to depths of up to about 65 feet. Molting nine times, they live as larvae some two years, and then go ashore, frequently very far inland, where they pupate. The pupae, which lie on their side in a cavity in the ground, are able to crawl if they are disturbed. The adults are fully developed in one to two weeks. [363/15]

Closely related are the dobsonflies of the family Corydalidae, of America, Africa, and Asia. Their extraordinary size (usually more than an inch long) and quixotically shaped head render them especially striking insects. Huge, crossed mandibles jut out like sabers

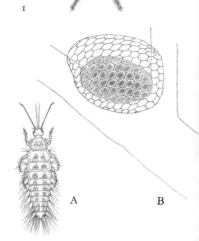

from the head of the male, but dangerous as they look these are hardly of any use in biting; rather, they probably serve as claspers in the act of mating.

The dobsonflies live predominantly near swift-flowing water, and with their very large, frequently spotted wings, fly at dusk, often to electric lights. Eating little or no food, the males live but a few days, the females perhaps one to two weeks. The female fastens as many as 3,000 eggs to leaves, frequently three to five yards above the water. The larvae creep about as voracious predators for two to three years, and are able to swim backward as well as forward. In North America they are known as "crawlers" or "hellgramites" and are often used as fish bait. [363/12–14]

A close relationship to the water also is shown by the spongillaflies (Sisyridae). They are distributed over the whole world except for the Arctic and Antarctic regions. Near the water, on branches or other objects, sit these little, dull-colored insects, whose wings are hairy on the margins and on the veins.

The females fasten their eggs to plants above the water. After hatching, the larvae drop into the water and swim away with kicking movements, buoyed up by an air bubble in the gut. Eventually they develop a series of abdominal gills that look like the opposed legs of a millipede.

The larvae hunt out freshwater sponges, no doubt homing on the gentle currents that emanate from them, and suck on them with two long, slender, independently movable oral tubes. By moving over the sponges in a special manner, the larvae avoid being gashed by the spines sticking out in every direction. The two long antennae, serving as crutches, are moved forward alternately step by step and, with the help of the propelling legs, lift the soft body over the sharp points of the sponge. Another peculiarity of these larvae is that they vomit the indigestible parts of their food.

Pupation takes place out of the water in a cocoon spun on plants from threads that flow from the rectum. The cocoon of the American genus *Climacia* is a magnificent net woven with hexagonal meshes.

CADDISFLIES ORDER TRICHOPTERA

Wading in a brook, we may have seen tiny houses, artistically put together from pebbles or all sorts of rubbish, on the bottom of the stream. We may also have seen the protruding, caterpillarlike fore part and six tiny legs of

the little artisans that pulled their houses along after them.

These are the larvae of caddisflies (order Trichoptera), and their skill at construction arouses our admiration. The whitish larvae, like hermit crabs, have to hide their soft bodies inside a house. They make it by spinning a tube, open at both ends, from a silken thread that flows from the mouth and that is manipulated with the help of specially adapted forelegs. Most species disguise the outside of these cases, into which they are anchored with two hooks on the posterior end, with all kinds of materials found in the water. For instance, they use minerals such as grains of sand and pebbles, all possible parts of plants, bits of wood, or animal matter such as snail shells and the shells of little bivalves. By means of sticky silk these things are mounted on the tube lengthwise, crosswise, or spirally. [362/5]

The cases themselves may be cylindrical, flattened, four-cornered, or triangular in cross section. They may widen conically from back to front, in correlation with the growth of the larva, which builds on at the front end and requires a more capacious dwelling as it increases in girth. Or they may have a regular cylindrical form when the posterior part of the house keeps wearing away or is removed. Furthermore, the house may be straight, curved, or twined like a snail shell; and at the rear it is narrowed down into one or more apertures for the circulation of water.

In many instances the individual species may be recognized from the style of construction and the material employed. Often enough, however, these matters give difficulty even to the experienced scientist, since many species use different material or vary the style of construction according to the environment, and both things may happen simultaneously. The particular virtue of these dwellings resides in their adaptation to environment and way of life. From the wealth of innumerable variations we shall emphasize a few examples, turning our attention first to those of still or placid waters.

The beautiful, regularly cylindrical case of a species of the family Phryganeidae is a spirally twisted ribbon of bitten-off plant stems of equal length, apparently measured by the larva against the fore part of its body. This form of case combines lightness with the potentiality of slipping unhindered through narrow passages and a tangle of plants. It thus affords the larva, which is predatory on other water animals, the requisite motility.

372/1A–B
(1) Spongillafly (Neuroptera) and (A) its larva, which lives on freshwater sponges and sucks on them with its oral bristles. (B) Cocoon of a related species, with its netlike covering (enlarged 4×).

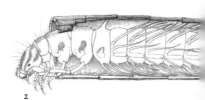

372/2–3
The biology of caddisflies. (2) A Phryganea larva with its many gill threads, in a case that has been laid open (enlarged 1.5×). (3) The Triaenodes larva, in its case built of bits of stems, swims undulantly in calm water, using its long hind legs that have been modified to serve as oars (enlarged 1.5×).

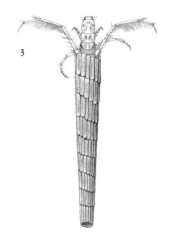

373/1
*Kitagamia cases, from Japan,
are made fast by a strong silken
strap.*

373/2
*The cases of the larvae of
Limnophilinae, which live in calm
water, may be made of very
different materials by one and
the same species (natural size).*

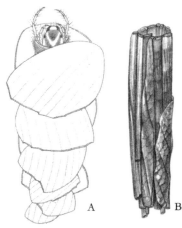

373/3
*In summer Glyphotaelius larvae
live in the upper layers and in winter
at the bottom of permanent bodies
of water; to do so first they have
a floating, flattish case (A) made
of excised bits of leaves,
and second, another (B) made of
heavier material (natural size).*

The European *Crunoecia irrorata* also lives in a specially regular structure. After the larva has been content for more than half its life with a simple case made of sand, it then constructs one out of many small, transversely placed parts of plants, arranged in four rows that meet at right angles. Each individual bit of plant is gnawed out circularly on the inside in such a way that the cavity of the case makes a smooth tube. Very intriguing also are the structures put together out of snail shells, especially where larger and larger snails are used toward the front end, corresponding to the growing size and strength of the caddis larva.

Certain phytophagous species, which in their youth live on the bottom, rise in the course of the year, together with the growing vegetation, and finally live for a while on the surface. These larvae then cut large pieces from green leaves and affix them crosswise to the upper and lower sides of the house, thus giving it a flattened form and buoying it up by the air contained in the leaves. When these wilt, they are replaced again and again with new ones. In the autumn the larvae once again go to the bottom, and their case now is given a wholly different appearance through the lengthwise attachment of tiny dead bits of plants.

Oxyethira has a case made of transparent silk; like a spider this caddis larva pulls a thread along behind it at all times. It also stretches about its abode a crisscrossed network of threads, and does acrobatics on it like a rope dancer, or perhaps lets itself down to the bottom supported by a thread.

A few species simply cut off a length of reed, line it with silk, and so have their finished case. An American species gets along similarly, boring its way into a little bit of wood or twig, hollowing this out, and then carpeting it with silk.

Let us now visit turbulent waters—rushing brooks and rivers, or the shores of large lakes pummeled by wind-whipped waves. Here the animals have the task of not being swept away, and frequently utilize the current in obtaining food. They are forced not only to orient their body against the flow, but also to move about as little as possible, and the ways and means of their battle for existence are fascinating.

Many species build flattened cases that offer fewer surfaces for the water to attack and that are especially well adapted to hugging the substratum; frequently these have leaf-like expanded margins, made of sand or little pebbles fastened with silk or with sticky material, that surround them and lie close against the bottom. The apertures for water circulation that are essential for respiration are constructed by a few species in the form of two or three big, pyramidal, stone chimneys. Other larvae weight their stone houses additionally with larger fragments, frequently with a large flat stone on each side, the firm attachment of which seems almost impossible for such a small creature.

Outriggers, which function as brakes, in the form of pieced-in, long bits of wood or stems, are found in the cases of other species, and frequently the entire structure is interwoven with rough staves, crisscrossed and sticking out in all directions. Houses with cylindrical or smooth constructions are curved like horns, and hence are less easily rolled over by the current; others are anchored by a strong rope woven of silken threads.

The cases of certain species stand out like pointed teeth from the stones to which they are held by suction. The head of such a larva fits exactly into the case's opening, which lies close against the substratum, and is withdrawn slightly so that a little space of lowered pressure is produced and effectuates the strong, sucking attachment. All these caddis larvae feed on algae.

Certain species that lack cases gnaw long grooves into the surface layer of rocks, which consists of soft lime and algae, and at the same time spin a tunnel-like covering for their feeding grooves, including in it particles of lime. These tunnels are migratory, since they are constantly being broken away in back and added to in front.

One group that lives in swiftly flowing water and builds no cases subsists principally on small aquatic life and water insects. A few larvae of this group move about freely in the water with the help of their swimming legs, or creep assuredly with the aid of a thread. When not moving, they anchor themselves with their two posterior hooks.

Many lead an existence almost like that of spiders, catching their prey in nets. Special brushes on the forelegs and in some species on the posterior end serve to sweep together the plankton that is caught, as well as to clean the net. The nets mostly are irregular webs on the bottom or on plants, thickened medially into a funnel that narrows below or at one side into a silken tube that leads finally into a hiding place. When prey has strayed into the net, the larva seizes it.

But there are much cleverer plankton nets that have been used by these insects for

millions of years, nets of a type that man has made for only slightly more than half a century. These are spun tubes, broadened in front into the shape of a funnel and stretched between plants or stones with the opening facing the current. The net of the species *Neureclipsis bimaculata* is curved like a trumpet. The owner sits at the bottom of the funnel or in an attached side tube.

Masterpieces are provided by the species of the genus *Hydropsyche;* between stones or plants they build a chamber whose entrance widens on the upstream side, and the rear portion of which is closed off by latticework made of two-ply spun threads that are bound together with sticky material at the intersections. The artisan sits in front of this net, hidden either in its case, which is fastened to the bottom, or in a dwelling tube, and has nothing to do but to collect whatever is left behind by the water that streams through, and to clean the filter now and then. Several of these structures frequently are found lined up in a series, constituting a system of traps built by an insect.

The larvae of caddisflies live for the most part in rather shallow water, yet they have been found in depths of over 20 feet, even as deep as 130 feet. They respire either through the entire skin, or, more often, through gills, which run along the body as two or more rows of threads or tufts; at times these are only on the lower surface. In their houses these larvae circulate the water by an almost constant oscillation of their bodies. Effectiveness is promoted by lateral lines, such as rows of hairs on both sides, that increase the moving surface. The body floats freely within the house, supported fore and aft by humps on the back.

During their growth the larvae molt from five to seven times and ultimately pupate, frequently gathered together in large groups. Thus, by including a pupal stage, their metamorphosis is a complete one, in contrast with such insects as dragonflies and mayflies.

Case-bearing larvae fasten the cases to the substratum, perhaps also weighing them down with rather large pebbles, and close them off except for small openings for circulation at both ends. The spun closures are variously constructed covers that differ according to the species. Some have only a single, rather large, round or slit-shaped aperture, and others have several little ones, up to about 30.

Species of the genus *Heliopsyche,* which live in little snail-shell-shaped cases in the thin layer of water on dripping cliffs, fasten down only the closure before they pupate. Before emerging as a mature insect, the pupa bites off the cover, and the house is carried to calmer water. Many larvae in strongly flowing water spin an additional leathery cocoon inside their case and pupate there; in highly oxygenated water respiration is possible in spite of a completely closed cocoon.

Some larvae that are free-swimming or that live in webs build themselves a spherical house of sand for pupation, others spin an enclosure between leaves, and many merely bury themselves in the bottom or hide in holes or in clefts in rocks. Thus may the beetle galleries in the branch of a tree, which for years thereafter may have served many a small bee or a wasp as a dwelling place, in later years eventually become useful under water to quite different insects. But certain caddisfly larvae themselves bore deep holes into wood and may damage old bridges or vessels that are laid up for long periods. Even ancient scientists such as Aristotle and Pliny designated these larvae as "destroyers of wood."

The pupae, which already resemble the mature insect slightly, have free antennae, legs, and wings, and frequently free jaws, too. Like the larvae, the pupae maintain a circulation of water in their house by means of constant movements. The appropriate openings in the sieve are kept clear at all times with the aid of specially adapted cleaning instruments on the front and rear ends of the body. These take the form of brushes, pegs, or shears, and are present only in this pupal stage, which lasts scarcely more than two weeks. At emergence time, the oral shears serve also to cut open the front closing membrane of the house. As additional organs peculiar to it, the pupa has on its back special hooks that enable it to make the forward and backward movements essential for cleaning.

When the time of emergence has come, the pupa frees itself from the cocoon or hiding place, and crawls upward on a plant or on any other object. Many pupae can swim upward with strong strokes of the middle legs, which are equipped with swimming hairs, and others are borne by air to the surface. There they support themselves by means of the hairs of the lateral lines or else by grasping something with their jaws, until the mature insect emerges and flies off or walks ashore on the surface film.

In contrast with their larvae, the mature caddisflies ultimately display few differences among themselves. Rather monotonous in shape and drab in coloration, they resemble

374/1
The small rare Ithytrichia larvae, like their cases made of opaque secreted matter, are compressed laterally; these larvae have pear-shaped gills on back and belly and live in running water (enlarged 9×).

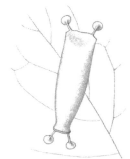

374/2
The Oxyethira case, which consists only of spun secretory material and which is fastened down by four plate-shaped feet, is made especially for the pupal stage (enlarged 2×).

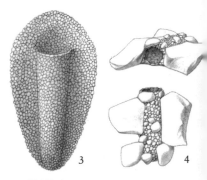

374/3-4
(3) The larval cases of Molanna, which are made of sand, and are from the surf zones of the larger lakes, are expanded in a shield-shape and hence are not carried away by the waves (viewed from beneath). (4) Goera cases, with their stony outriggers (enl. 1.5×).

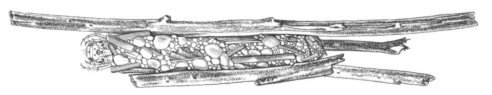

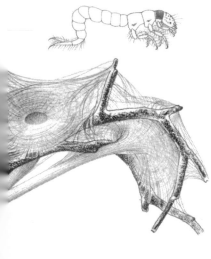

in form and attitude little moths, to which they are distantly related. Their wings, however, are covered with recumbent hairs rather than with scales. With few exceptions hidden throughout the day, the caddisflies appear in clumsy, reeling flight toward evening, when they are attracted to electric lights.

The caddisfly mouth is best suited for lapping, and many of the adults take no food whatever. The nuptial dances of caddisflies are enchanting; frequently they circle with whirring wings above the water surface, paddling vigorously with the middle legs, the female in advance and the male following. Or other species dance in a vertical posture in the air, with the very long antennae diverging. The flight period may last three or four weeks, or for some species only a few days. [364/1–11]

The eggs—some 20 to 800, according to the species—are thrown in a gelatinous, swelling mass into the water, scraped off in flight by the surface film, glued to twigs or to other vegetation along the bank, or deposited deep beneath the water. Eggs fastened outside the water are protected by a gelatinous mass from drying out, and the first-stage larvae that hatch can afford to wait there to be washed into the water by rain or dew.

The life cycle of caddisflies mostly is an annual one, but frequently there are two generations a year. In a few species, the egg is the overwintering stage, but in most the larva overwinters on the bottom.

Caddisflies develop in almost all fresh waters of the world. The larvae of various species also live in damp moss on trees and cliffs, in salt and brackish water, in the icy water of grottoes, and in the water collectors of bromeliad plants growing on the trees of tropical forests. They even are able to develop in the fluid of a tropical insectivorous pitcher plant *(Nepenthes),* apparently protected by their thick skin from the fluid's dissolving action.

Occasionally mass swarms are observed, and then even in cities the house fronts along whole streets facing a river may be covered with these brown insects. Caddisflies are very ancient insects, known as early as the Lower Jurassic period and very richly represented in the Tertiary. Over 150 species have been preserved in amber, but none of these exists today.

Present-day caddisflies are divided into two suborders with more than 20 families and over 3,000 species. Their great importance in the pattern of nature is as one of the most important sources of food for fish.

AQUATIC MOTHS

ORDER LEPIDOPTERA

That there are water moths probably is not generally known. In fact, only a vanishing minority, with representation from a few families, have become adapted to the water. The degree of adaptation varies widely, with all kinds of intermediate forms between land and water insects. Thus some caterpillars of the family Arctiidae feed on plants extending over the water and, in doing so, occasionally crawl partly or wholly beneath the surface, and others of the same family dwell under water, swimming and crawling along with air carried in their hairy coat and constantly renewed at the surface.

Caterpillars of different families, such as noctuids, cossids, and pyralids, burrow in plants below water level, often clear down to the roots, without coming in contact with the water itself except perhaps when migrating from one plant to another. For doing this, moreover, certain caterpillars bite off a piece of the plant and use it as a float. Another species builds itself a little boat out of a short, hollow stem, closing the two openings with silk.

More highly specialized water insects are found among the micro moths of the family Pyralidae. These sometimes appear on summer evenings over bogs, ponds, and little lakes, in swarms like undulant white veils. Or the individuals, like snowflakes, may chase after one another over the water surface in graceful nuptial dances.

Their larvae build themselves houses of varied form, typical for each species. These houses in the water are made from leaves spun together, or simply from a piece of hollow plant stem; mostly they are filled with air, but by some species with water. Some float and some are dragged along as if by caddisfly larvae. Many larvae, especially those that live in flowing water, spin nets on stones or plants and live in them, inhaling air bubbles that get stuck in the nets and likewise eating algae that are caught there.

For pupation, astonishingly appropriate pupal cradles frequently are constructed. *Cataclysta* simply uses the caterpillar's case, namely a piece of hollow stem, and attaches it with spun silk at the water surface at right angles to a plant; or else makes a floating, oval, air-filled chamber out of the tiny leaves of rushes, carpeting the inside with silk. On the chamber's bottom the caterpillar lies enclosed in a silken tube.

Similar houses of certain American and Chinese species do not contain air, but oxygen-rich water flows through them without being able to wet the pupa resting within. The cocoon of *Hydrocampa,* covered with two large pieces of leaf and fastened below the surface to the skin of a plant, is a silken web inside which the pupa stands upright. The web is filled with air that has escaped from holes bitten into the plant stem by the caterpillar; in other genera, on the contrary, the caterpillars themselves extrude air into the case from the supply stored within the body.

It is amazing how the moths emerging from such cocoons under water manage to remain dry while getting to the surface; for them to get wet would mean certain death. Before they emerge, air is concentrated beneath the pupal skin. At the moment when the moth breaks out of the shell, the air is stowed away under the wings, as though in a diving bell, and lifts the insect to the surface. The pathway remains visible for a while as a vertically suspended white column of wax particles in the water, which have been brushed off the wings during the swift ascent. This waxen coating is the waterproofing that keeps the insect fully dry until it reaches the surface, crawls ashore, and unfolds its delicate wings.

Many caterpillars that live their whole lives under water breathe through the skin or through gills that cover the body in tufts. They promote the circulation of water through their webs with oscillatory movements of their bodies. Whereas most water moths dip only the abdomen into the water when depositing eggs on plants, a few species with an unwettable garment of scales go completely beneath the surface; for example, the female of *Acentropus niveus,* which lives only in water, swims with the help of legs fringed with hairs and with wings reduced to little oar-shaped stumps. The males have normally developed wings and go whirring over the water in search of some female that comes briefly to the surface. Strangely enough, in many regions there also are females of this species with complete wings. Thus the species has developed two different female forms, one adapted to air and the other to water. [364/12]

MOSQUITOES, GNATS, AND AQUATIC FLIES

ORDER DIPTERA

Rare is the person who has not had the experience of drifting contentedly off to sleep only to be awakened by the insistent buzz of a mosquito. Mosquitoes have earned a worldwide reputation as torturers of man

and animals, and as disease carriers they have helped shape the world's history. They have made regions of the earth uninhabitable and have extinguished thriving cultures. Malaria-carrying mosquitoes helped free ancient Rome from the besieging hordes and likewise brought her people into great danger. Mosquito-transmitted yellow fever forced the French to give up construction of the Panama Canal after the loss of 20,000 lives.

Of the thousands of different species of mosquitoes (family Culicidae), only a few are vectors of the dreaded tropical diseases, such as elephantiasis, yellow fever, and malaria, the last of which at times penetrates far into the North. The disease-causing mosquitoes are among the best-investigated animals in the world, for in combatting them a gigantic amount of scientific work has been done and is being done in many countries. Nevertheless, much remains to be learned, since the subject is a complicated one.

Among the malaria mosquitoes, for example, some species bite only animals, and others also include man, but these and other characteristics may change from locality to locality. The activity of mosquitoes is affected by climate, light, and temperature. Thus they have two generations a year in the North, but up to ten in the South; and a northern European female produces 100 to 350 eggs, an Italian female perhaps 1,300.

The females of the most important European malaria mosquito, *Anopheles maculipennis,* live and overwinter, so far as has been observed, mostly in the stalls of cattle, where at night they suck the blood of the animals, preferably from their eyelids. Almost all female mosquitoes require blood meals, since it is only thereafter that their eggs can ripen; the males are not bloodsuckers, or only in exceptional cases. In many localities, the *Anopheles* females go into dwellings, too, infecting people with malaria; to transmit malaria, a female must have previously imbibed blood containing the malaria parasite in a quite specific stage, from a person with the disease. For another tropical disease, yellow fever, the mosquito *Aedes aegypti* is chiefly responsible, yet in the South American virgin forest the disease also has been transmitted from apes to man by species of the genus *Haemagogus.* [364/13; 365/1]

The proboscis of mosquitoes is a tube formed from the labium (lower lip). It does not itself penetrate, but serves as a sheath enclosing a combination of six stilettos. These are sharp as knives, some of them saw-

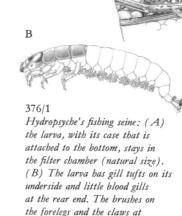

A

B

376/1
Hydropsyche's fishing seine: (A) the larva, with its case that is attached to the bottom, stays in the filter chamber (natural size). (B) The larva has gill tufts on its underside and little blood gills at the rear end. The brushes on the forelegs and the claws at the back end serve to cleanse the sieve window (enlarged 2×).

376/2
A tube spun in the shape of a horn, attached both fore and aft and with the opening facing the current, catches the food of the Neureclipsis larva, which stays back in the hind end (natural size).

376/3
The helical cases of Heliopsyche, built of sand and gravel, are so like snails that at one time they were referred to this group of animals (enlarged 3×).

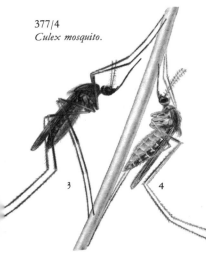

toothed and others with tips as smooth as daggers. When these pierce the skin, the mosquito's saliva flows at once into the puncture, and the victim's blood is sucked in as a continuous stream by the pumping action of the digestive tube. [20/5G]

There are multitudes of harmless bloodsuckers, such as many of the mosquitoes of the genus *Culex,* which are known only too well in human habitations. From these, the biting (female) malaria mosquitoes *Anopheles* are readily distinguished by their angular resting position, where the body is not parallel with the substrate but is elevated obliquely toward the rear, by the frequently spotted design on their wings, and by their palpi, which are as long as the proboscis and much longer than those of *Culex.*

Many mosquitoes are specialized for taking blood only from certain animals. Some, for instance, suck only on amphibians or reptiles, as is the case with tropical species of the group Sabelini, which are adorned with magnificently colored hairs or scales. Others attack small mammals, birds, or even other insects. A few *Aedes* mosquitoes inhabit the nest holes of crabs and imbibe their blood; the mosquito larvae develop in the water at the bottom of the holes. The notorious yellow fever mosquito wants almost no blood other than that of man, and even seems to prefer certain human races. But the fundamental and general food of mosquitoes is almost any vegetable fluids from flowers, fruit, leaves, or bark.

The eggs of mosquitoes are handsome boat-shaped structures equipped with air chambers or belts, which are incorporated as a very fine filigree into the surface. The eggs are laid mostly on water, floating singly, in star-shaped groups, or stuck together like little rafts. Usually any collection of water suffices, and it may even be dried out temporarily at the time of egg-laying.

The hatched larvae are found in wagon tracks and hoof marks along the road, in all possible cavities in wood, in the axils of leaves, in discarded tin cans, and in flower vases and fonts. A few species even live in the digestive juice of carnivorous plants, feeding on the remains of digested insects or predatory upon other water insects that likewise are adapted to this extraordinary milieu. And yet others are at home in pools of salt or brackish water and in holes in the rock.

In the far North the eggs laid in the summertime in dried-out puddles remain at rest for eight to ten months, frozen solid in the winter. Also preserved in ice for the winter, in

the tubular traps of the insectivorous *Sarracenia* plants in North America, are the larvae of the mosquito *Wyeomyia smithi.*

The larvae of mosquitoes are just as striking as they are characteristic. The majority, including those of *Culex,* hang stiffly in groups beneath the water surface, with the head extended; again and again undulant wagging movements come over the whole assemblage. The sides of the short, thick forebody and of the cylindrical, clearly segmented abdomen bear tufts of long bristles that stand stiffly away from the body; and the rear end is divided into a cone-shaped propulsive organ bearing swimming fans, and a somewhat longer respiratory tube with a tiny, star-shaped wreath at its tip. By means of this wreath the body is suspended from the surface film of the water.

In contrast, the larvae of the fever mosquitoes *Anopheles* float horizontally, fastened to the film along the back by means of special bristles and warts and by means of the respiratory shell, into which open the two principal air tubes of the body. This shell replaces the respiratory tube.

The food of mosquito larvae consists of little particles in the water, especially of algae, but also of animal substances, that are swept in by means of a current engendered by two large, hairy fans, beating in opposition, on the outer mouthparts. Before the accumulation is swallowed, it is sorted over with other oral parts, and balls of what is deemed unsuitable thereafter sink to the bottom. The water thus filtered by a single larva in a day may amount to 2 quarts or more.

On the fourth molt the mosquito larva transforms to the pupa; frequently the massive numbers of pupae cover entire ponds with a black layer. These creatures, slightly less motile than the larvae, have a thick, lumpy forebody, an abdomen curved halfway beneath it, and leaflike caudal fins. The pupae also hang from the surface film, fastened to it in the fore part of the back region by two short, continuous respiratory tubes that, because of their basal articulation, accommodate any movements of the water and thus prevent changes in the position of the body. Although the pupae are lighter than water, since expired air is stored as a large bubble between the apposed wings, legs, and antennae, they dive headlong downward when threatened, with forcefully delivered, undirected strokes of the tail.

Before emerging, the new, fully developed mosquito within the pupa blows air beneath the pupal skin from the respiratory openings; the skin swells, raising the pupa somewhat above the water surface, and then bursts. The insect swallows air, climbs forth from the floating empty skin, and flies off.

The male of a mosquito in New Zealand runs hither and yon over the water surface looking for an emerging female, frequently even sticking his head underneath. He mates with the female before she has had time to emerge properly, even helping her tear away the pupal shell.

Many mosquito larvae have an aberrant way of life. Some species, for instance, are predatory feeders; their mouth has jaws as sharp as knives instead of the pliable sweeping organs. Larvae of the genus *Mansonia,* one of the groups that transmit elephantiasis, live on the bottom of bodies of water; they breathe by boring the tip of their respiratory tube into the lower shoots of water plants.

Mosquitoes are distributed in about 2,000 species over almost the entire world, with by far the greatest number of species (not of individuals) in the damp tropics. Remarkably, Iceland has no mosquitoes, and although three species are known in the Hawaiian Islands, none is malarious. Besides amphibians and fish, the most important destroyers of the mosquito brood are other water insects, especially the larvae of aquatic beetles. Mosquito males live some two to three weeks, the females three to four months, and under favorable conditions development from the egg to the adult may be completed in less than two weeks. The tropical genus *Psorophora* even does it within five days; the egg hatches on the first day, and a molt occurs on each day following.

The tiny flies known as gnats also suck blood. Of these, the biting midges, or punkies (Ceratapogonidae), in spite of a body length of only 0.04 to 0.08 inch, sting more painfully than mosquitoes. Some are vectors of disease. Many species attack only amphibians, reptiles, or insects; one of them sucks mammalian blood from the abdomen of a mosquito that has ingested it. Others visit flowers, and certain tropical species are useful as pollinators of cocoa and rubber trees.

The larvae of many gnats, especially the bloodsucking ones, develop in water. Shaped like worms or wires, they move with undulations, seeking prey on the bottom or in the mud; their body length of about 0.8 inch is larger than the gnat that arises from them. The females deposit eggs in gelatinous masses, at times in long strings.

In certain years, many places in the world are besieged by the tiny, dark, humpbacked

black flies (Simuliidae). Called buffalo gnats in America, black flies in the Canadian woods, and Columbian gnats in Europe, they fall upon animals and people in swarms of millions. They penetrate beneath clothing and into the nose, ears, and eyes; their bites, containing a poison that affects the nerve centers, leave red, bleeding spots. Black flies kill buffalo, cattle, reindeer, deer, and horses, by the thousands; human beings have died also, for 20 to 30 bites may cause a fever of as much as 104° F.

These gnats develop only in flowing, and especially in cold, water, where their wedge-shaped larvae cling to plants and rocks in part by a suction plate and in part by spun threads at the rear of the body. A few larvae walk along the threads of a web they have spun, by putting out a drop of sticky material from the mouth, by flexing the body and attaching the rear end to the drop, and then by stretching out forward again and setting the next attachment point on the thread. Black-fly larvae have two large fans of bristles spread out in front of the head that act as a sieve. Algae or other particles carried in by the current stick to these bristles, are swept off from time to time with special oral bristles, and are swallowed.

The pupae, by means of threads and numerous hooks, are caught fast in a basket of sticky webbing; this basket, with the opening facing the current, is hung on plants or rocks and comes to a point at the rear. Out of this house there project upward from the pupal head two bundles of long, thin, silvery threads, through the entire surface of which oxygen is taken up from the water. Toward the end of development, the pupa stores air beneath the skin, and this air carries the emerging gnat to the surface. [366/1]

Certain moth flies and sand flies (Psychodidae) also bite painfully and in the tropics and subtropics transmit various diseases. These tiny insects hold their broad, hairy wings in a mothlike position. Many of their larvae live in the zone between land and water, where they feed on rotting plants. In the water they take air through open spiracles at the rear end. Certain larvae live in flowing water, holding onto objects with their stiff hairs, and a few tropical species that inhabit waterfalls are fastened to the rocks with a series of suction cups. (99/12; 279/5]

The bites of the much larger horse flies and deer flies (Tabanidae) are pure torture. Although in Africa and India these insects transmit certain diseases of cattle, elsewhere they cause annoyance only by means of their itching bites, which may cause appreciable

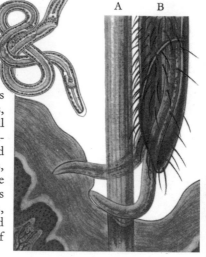

378/1A–E
A mosquito of the tropical genus Mansonia transmitting elephantiasis.
(A) The stinging proboscis in human skin; (B) proboscis sheath, from which are emerging two of the disease-causing organisms (threadworms), in order to move into the body. (C) The threadworm. (D) The larva of a Mansonia mosquito getting air from an aquatic plant. (E) The pupa too is connected by means of two little stigmatal horns to the air tubes of a plant.

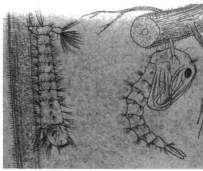

losses of blood. Only relatively few of the larvae live in water; these are predators, either on the bottom, in lower layers of mud at the surface, or frequently on the banks. They are spindle-shaped maggots that inhale through a protrusible but short breathing tube formed from the last segment. [366/5]

Among the most interesting water insects are the larvae of the family Corethridae, whose members are closely related to the mosquitoes. Respiration takes place through the skin of these freshwater predators, for the tracheal system has been reduced to two paired, curved air vesicles that act exclusively as a hydrostatic apparatus.

Living in little puddles as well as in big lakes, and of all insect larvae probably the best adapted to a pelagic way of life, they float at any desired depth in the water, wholly independent of atmospheric air or of any point of support, as completely planktonic organisms. They swim with the help of a large fan of hairs, directed downward at the posterior end, and eat all possible living aquatic things; these are seized with the two antennae, which are lengthened with stiff, curved tufts of bristles, and then cut up with the razor-sharp mandibles. [366/7]

The *Corethra* species, which live in large numbers as deep as 120 to 160 feet in big lakes, bury themselves by day in the bottom mud, perhaps more than 70,000 larvae per square yard, and then ascend at night. Astonishingly, a pressure change from 4 atmospheres to 1 atmosphere within the space of perhaps a single hour is thus no problem to these organisms, which look as though they were made of the most delicate glass. Thousands of their pupae float vertically in the water and apparently rise or sink automatically to the level with which they are in equilibrium. When the gnats emerge from the pupae and their swarms fill the air, frequently with a high-pitched buzzing but often without sound, the empty pupal cases are washed ashore by the waves and look like a broad band of white foam.

A few peculiarities are displayed also by the water-dwelling larvae of soldier flies (Stratiomyidae). Those of the genus *Stratiomys,* which are long, legless maggots drawn out posteriorly, hang from the water surface as though glued to a single point by means of the slender rear end, but with the body constantly undulating or writhing. At the posterior tip of the abdomen, where the two spiracles open, there is a beautiful outspread wreath of hairs; the wreath lies on the water surface. At a sign of danger it is clapped together in the shape of a bell, containing

a large bubble of air; with this the larva glides to the bottom. [366/4]

In spite of their tininess, the mouthparts are astonishingly diverse and complex; they not only shave the algal layer from leaves, but also sweep in free-floating food. Moreover, they are able to move the whole body forward slowly by means of their constantly moving rows of "cilia." The integument of these larvae is very thick because of the large amount of incorporated lime; and it gets much thicker still before pupation. Ultimately this protective coat of mail conceals a much smaller cocoon containing the resting pupa.

In gorges as far north as the glaciers, live the flattened larvae of the net-winged midges (Blepharoceridae) during eleven months of the year. Amid the strongest currents they are fastened almost immovably to rocks by means of six big suction cups along the middle of the underside; these are among the most perfect retaining devices in the animal kingdom. By pulling in a fleshy cone beneath the cup, a space with reduced pressure is formed, producing the suction; the cups also give off a sticky material. Grazing on the algal layer, these larvae move both forward and sideways by alternately releasing the suction in the individual cups. [366/2, 3]

Among the strongest currents, the pupa is glued to rocks slightly below the surface by means of special plates. During the instant of emergence, the gnat clings with its long hind legs to the pupal skin while the forelegs rest on the water surface; then it flies off. In torrents this maneuver frequently fails, and hence adults are rather rare. Their wings have few or almost no veins, but are crossed by a network of folds; and the eyes are divided into an upper zone with very large facets and a lower zone with little ones, a division that enables the insect to see when it is light and when it is dark. The majority of females suck the blood of insects, especially of other gnats, but the males frequent flowers.

The water insects that most universally have mastered the most various environments are the larvae of the shore flies (Ephydridae). These are thick-skinned creatures of simple, maggotlike form, lengthened posteriorly into a forked respiratory tube. They crawl by means of eight pairs of spiny warts, or swim with violent twitching movements of the body. They live in salt lakes and salt bogs, in salt pits, in hot springs, and even in oil swamps, where almost no other living thing is able to exist.

One and the same species seems to live just as well in warm as in cool water, or in

379/1
The petroleum fly Psilopa (enlarged 2×).

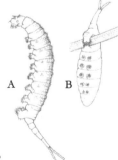

379/2
The larva and pupa of a salt lake fly (Ephydra). To pupate, these larvae (A), whose hind end terminates in a forked breathing tube, suspend themselves from a stalk; then the skin contracts and becomes a hard armored coat, which does not, however, impede the respiration of the fly developing within (B).

fresh, brackish, or sea water; and it lives in pools on the seashore no matter whether these have dried up today, are filled with rain water next week, or later are inundated again with sea water. These pools, which are evaporating and being refilled constantly, finally attain a much higher salt content than the sea itself, and may reach temperatures approaching 104° F (40° C). As is well known, other water animals die when changed suddenly from fresh to salt water and vice versa. When large numbers of these flies all deposit their eggs on the water at one time, they frequently develop swarms that move along the shores of salt lakes as compact, black belts visible miles away. Peculiar salt-water flies are the little Pacific *Pontomyia* (Ephydridae). Using their middle and hind legs and their oar-shaped wings, the males run along the surface, forelegs held aloft and bent toward the rear. The females, larval in shape, have only the two posterior pairs of legs, both greatly reduced, and they live under water in mud tubes they have built.

Some of the larvae of another family have the ability to live both in fresh and salt water. This family is the midges (Chironomidae), which resemble mosquitoes. A few, as a very great rarity among insects, live exclusively in the ocean. Where there is surf they live in the canals within sponges, and are found at depths of over 90 feet. The mature female gnat of one species herself has only a maggot-like form, almost without legs, antennae, and wings; she does not leave the canal within which she developed, but mates by stretching her rear end out of the water. Some of these gnats walk on the water with the hairy soles of their feet, or fill the air with dense swarms.

Of all water insects, the midges are the family that probably is richest in number of species. Their larvae show the greatest diversity of ways of living, and yet almost all have an identical wormlike form. They live on land in plants and rotten wood, in hot springs, in icy lakes at elevations above 15,000 feet in the Himalayas, in subterranean caves, in waste water, in wells, and in the ocean.

The best-known midge larvae no doubt are those red worms of the *Chironomus* group, which cover the bottom of lakes like a carpet. Their mass surpasses the combined masses of all other living organisms in these bodies of water. Like few other insects, they have red blood. Protruding vertically from their tubes buried in the mud, they wave back and forth, catching particles sinking from above. The pupae likewise remain in the tubes, but rise to the surface when transforming

to the adult, and do so in such masses that the emergence of these insects from the water makes an audible rustling. In buzzing clouds that fluctuate in shape from steeples to mushrooms, the midges fill the landscape for miles around, slipping into the eyes, ears, and nose of persons and animals. Meanwhile the empty pupal shells on the shores are heaped together into broad ribbons by the waves. Midges and their larvae, like mayflies, are an important source of food for water insects, fish, birds, and other animals.

Many larvae build dwelling tubes from webbing or gelatinous masses. These tubes differ from species to species. Tubes that lie in or are stuck into mud mostly are curved, so that both open ends protrude into the water. Frequently tubes are fastened to plants, some by threads that let them wave freely back and forth in flowing water. Many species include sand or algae in their spun structures, and carry these houses around with them like caddisfly larvae; others build on rocks masses of adjacent tubes of webbing, which become more and more heavily petrified by depositions of lime.

Before pupation, the various houses are enlarged at the front, forming a chamber, and are closed over with a spun lid. A few species bore passageways lined with webbing into colonies of sponges or moss animalcules (Bryozoa), and others eat grooves into the upper sides of green leaves and close these over, like tunnels, with spun material. Many mine all the way into plants, and such mines sometimes are filled with air; more often, water is circulated through them by continual oscillatory movements of the larvae. A North American species spins a net in its passageway about every ten minutes, and then eats the net together with the plankton caught in it.

WATER BEETLES

ORDER COLEOPTERA

Beetles show many gradations from land insects that like moist conditions to the most highly perfected water insects. In the boundary zones between land and water, in wet sand that at times is inundated, in mud or moss of pools, brooks, lakes, and seas, underneath stones washed by the water, or on plants sticking out of the water, there is abundant beetle life. By far the majority of the species that have settled in such places nonetheless have no particularly close relationships to the wet element. Yet some show in at least one developmental stage the be-

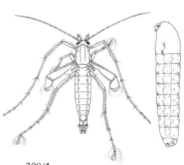

380/1
The male of a salt water fly running along the surface; at the right, the female.

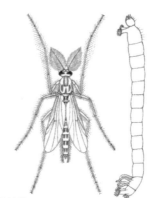

380/2
Male and larva of a chironomid midge (enlarged 2×).

ginning of an adaptation to water. Certain larvae, for example, though much like land-dwelling larvae, nevertheless respire through gills located on the rear end and live in a chamber that can be closed by a lid and from which the body can be protruded.

Among beetles the first adaptive stages toward a life in water show in the form of an unwettable feltwork of hairs on the legs, which enables them to walk on the water surface, or a hair-covering on the body, in which a layer of air is taken along when the insect lays its eggs under water. The pupa of certain heloids is bedded down in an air bubble under a stone in the water, and this air bears the emerging beetle to the surface. A few weevils (Curculionidae) that crawl on floating leaves and on underwater plants near the surface have larvae that mine in stems below water level and that breathe air from the plants.

The larvae of the long-horned leaf beetles (donaciines) of the family Chrysomelidae inhale air through two big posterior spines hooked into plant roots, while the used air escapes through special spiracles. Perhaps never moving more than an inch or so away, these larvae mostly hang motionless throughout their two-year life, sucking sap from a hole they have bitten out and keeping it watertight by forcing in their head and first thoracic segment. When ready to pupate, the larva builds a house by enclosing its body and its support in a waxlike secretion and then expanding the enclosure to the proper shape by inflating itself with air. In addition, the larva curls up into a humpbacked position with the support of a cushion of air it has collected beneath its body. Afterward, the larva collapses again, becoming much smaller, and ultimately paints over the whole inside of the house with a layer of varnish made of water-repellent saliva and of sap from the gut; thereafter it pupates. [367/1]

In one genus of these long-horned leaf beetles, namely *Haemonia,* even the adult beetles spend their whole life deep under water without coming to the surface. Their slight oxygen requirement is satisfied by a thin layer of air held beneath the hairs of the body.

The little beetles of the family Helmidae are equally perfected for a life in water. They likewise remain in the water during all stages, scarcely ever coming to the surface at all. They take up little bubbles of oxygen from algae and rocks with the mouth and conduct them by way of body grooves to the spiracles as well as to the lower body surface.

Generally, the term "water beetles" refers to the families of the whirligig beetles (Gyrinidae), the predaceous diving beetles (Dytiscidae), and the water scavenger beetles (Hydrophilidae). Their highly polished, broad, and frequently flattened body, kept greased constantly by means of countless glands, seems as though molded into one single, streamlined figure. The individual portions of it are indicated merely by finely engraved lines. The legs are flattened, with sharp edges, and the hind legs in particular are modified into oars, most of them further expanded by means of borders of hairs. The mature beetles and the larvae live under water, but the pupae live on land, in the soil, under moss, or on plants.

A fascinating spectacle is offered by a group of whirligig beetles dancing on the water. Their blue-black streamlined bodies, almost penetratingly brilliant, dart back and forth among one another in turbulent circles and spirals, seemingly making the water surface boil. Although they swim only in curved paths on the surface they swim in straight lines under water. Because the air they carry makes them much lighter than the water, they bob to the surface unless they keep themselves down by swimming or by clinging to something. [362/2; 367/2]

Their well-lubricated and always dry body has neither sharp edges nor projections that might rupture the water surface when they go tearing along. The form and cooperative action of their four swimming legs are impressive miracles. Their eyes, too, are fantastic: one pair is above the water level, and one below it. The beetles look upward into the light and air, and simultaneously down through the water into the interwoven shadows of the bottom.

The whirligig beetles represent a very ancient group, belong to the most highly specialized of water insects, and are geniuses at almost everything. They swim and dive, sit on rocks on the shore in the sunshine, and in the evening and at night fly around for great distances in the vicinity. And in spite of the unimpressive appearance of the legs, the beetles progress quite well on dry land, even hopping when necessary, and the species that prefer swiftly running water swim quite fast against even a strong current.

On land and on the water surface the whirligig beetles breathe through spiracles like land insects, but under water they carry on their rear a bubble of air that is renewed from time to time. These beetles overwinter both under ice in a big air bubble on plants, and on land under stones. They collect dead

381/1
A whirligig beetle and its larva (greatly enlarged).

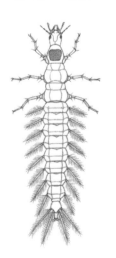

or living animal food on the water surface, seizing it with long forelegs.

The eggs are attached to plants under water, and the elongate larvae, which breathe through rows of narrow, lanceolate gills along the sides of the body, crawl on the bottom, but also swim very well with undulant movements. They catch living prey, which they kill with their poisonous mandibular tongs. Pupation takes place in a cocoon on the bank or above the water on plants.

Likewise carnivorous are the predatory diving beetles (Dytiscidae), some 4,000 species of which are distributed over the world, principally in the northern hemisphere. These beetles, some very large and most of them with yellow margins, are distant relatives of the very abundant family of ground beetles (Carabidae), which live on land. The big species and their larvae even attack amphibians and fish, and it has happened that ponds for the culture of fish have had to be given up because of this.

The yellow-margined *Dytiscus* beetles are rather rarely seen, except possibly when getting air at the water surface or on the streets at night, to which they are attracted by electric lights during their frequent nocturnal flights from one body of water to another. Often, too, they drop onto the glass panes of greenhouses, the shining surfaces of which seem like water.

The air these beetles need under water, for respiration and the regulation of specific gravity, is held in the space between the back and the wings; this space is made watertight in a complicated manner through the participation of wings, wing covers, thorax, and abdomen (with its felt-covered tip). The spiracles open into it. Certain of the smaller beetles of this family, which have a small air space of this type, also carry air as a permanent bubble on the rear end or beneath the coxae of the hind legs.

Without their air reservoir, the predaceous diving beetles could not come to the surface readily and would soon drown. A yellow-margined *Dytiscus,* like many other water insects, is able to subject its store of air to changes in pressure, and hence to rise or sink at will, or to float at a desired depth. The beetle is often seen suspended from the water surface at three points, namely the posterior end and the two hind legs, which are spread far apart and directed frontward and upward. This posture, with the posterior end sticking upward, is essential for taking air at the surface. It is made possible by displacing the air into the hinder part of the air chamber.

Dytiscus beetles live for two to five years, overwintering under the ice. In the spring the female, with the aid of a special cutting instrument, bores her approximately 200 eggs into plants close beneath the water surface. During mating, which often may last all day long, the male clings to his partner's back principally by means of the front legs, which are modified into suction disks; these suction cups also give off a sticky material.

The larvae of beetles in the genus *Dytiscus* hang downward from the water surface, connected at their posterior end with the atmosphere, their body curved like a question mark and their legs sometimes supported lightly by a plant. Those of the genus *Cybister,* in contrast, sit stretched out on plants, with the posterior end likewise at the water surface. And the larvae of smaller water beetles of the genus *Acilius* float in the water in a more horizontal stance; when breathing they adopt this position at the surface or else are suspended at an angle.

Both by day and by night all these larvae are enormously voracious predators. Propelled forward by undulant body movements made more efficient by fringes of hairs on the legs and on the posterior end, they hurl themselves upon their living prey and plunge into its body the two widely opened, long, dagger-shaped mandibles. Through these oral daggers a toxic, solvent fluid from the gut is poured into the victim's body, which, with the exception of the integument, is liquefied within a few minutes and then is pumped into the body of the larvae. Thus digestion occurs first outside of the larval body.

Dytiscus larvae are full-grown after some five to six weeks, molting thrice within this time, and the big ones devour perhaps 30 victims a day. When ready to pupate, the larvae go ashore, progressing by hooking the jaws into the ground and dragging the body along; then they bury themselves in the soft earth, where they prepare a smooth-walled cavity. A short time thereafter the pupa is suspended in it freely, supported against the wall only at the front and rear ends, the rear being drawn out into a short, pointed tip. After some two weeks, the beetle emerges, lets itself harden on the bank, and enters the water.

Besides these highly perfected predaceous diving beetles, many smaller, less specialized species belong to the family Dytiscidae. In fact, the family members exhibit quite different stages of adaptation to an aqueous life. Some larvae simply crawl about on the bottom, rarely take air at the water surface, and when they do so have to hold fast to the

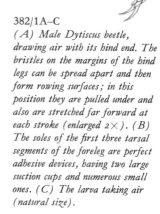

382/1A–C
(A) Male Dytiscus beetle, drawing air with its hind end. The bristles on the margins of the hind legs can be spread apart and then form rowing surfaces; in this position they are pulled under and also are stretched far forward at each stroke (enlarged 2×). (B) The soles of the first three tarsal segments of the foreleg are perfect adhesive devices, having two large suction cups and numerous small ones. (C) The larva taking air (natural size).

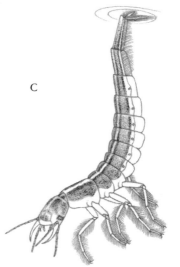

bottom. Other forms can swim more or less capably, thanks to swimming hairs on the legs, but spend most of the time clinging to plants. And the most highly evolved larvae, such as *Dytiscus,* not only can swim elegantly, but also can float at a chosen depth, assisted by the outspread legs with their fringe of hairs. As outsiders, there exist a group of burrowing larvae with digging legs and toothed, chewing mouthparts. These larvae insert themselves in mud along the bank and let the posterior end stick out above the water.

In the mature beetles, too, the capacity for swimming is variably developed; it is most highly perfected in *Cybister* and *Dytiscus,* the hind legs of which are formed into efficient oars, which can be rotated about their own axis and which work in unison. During the backward (effective) stroke, their surface is expanded by fringes of hairs that stand erect; these collapse during the forward movement. The middle pair of legs serves for steering. [366/9; 367/3–5]

Similar in way of life and body forms to the predaceous diving beetles are the water scavenger beetles of the family Hydrophilidae. The approximately 2,000 species are distributed over the whole world, but prefer warm countries and rather shallow water with rich vegetation. Their most prominent representatives are the big, pitch-black water scavenger beetles *(Hydrous).* With few exceptions all these water beetles are plant eaters, only the larvae being in part predatory.

These beetles swim much less well than dytiscids. In contrast with the latter, their hind legs alternate in their swimming strokes, rather than row together. Moreover, many small species live on land, developing in plants, fungi, decaying matter, and dung; certain larvae can live both on dry land and in the water. But the real water beetles are so bound to the wet element that only in the pupal stage are they in the ground or above the water.

A small number of water scavenger beetles carry their store of air under the wings, as do the predaceous diving beetles, but most store it on the under surface of the entire body. A little air is held by various areas of dense, fine hairs, but the bulk of it is contained between the projecting lateral margins of the wing covers and a deep longitudinal keel on the thorax, which is extended posteriorly as a spine.

Oddly enough, the beetles come to the surface head first rather than hind end first when replenishing their air supply, and the method they use is highly unusual. An air bubble on the neck grows in size, bursts, and makes a rent in the surface film. Simultaneously, the beetle applies to this funnel an air conduit that is unique in the animal kingdom.

One half of the tube (imagining it in longitudinal section) is formed by the four successive segments of the antennal club, which are hollowed out and furthermore are fringed with marginal hairs. The other half of the tube is a pathway, fenced in by erect bristles, that begins at the level of the eyes, curves downward to the underside of the head, and there opens into the feltwork of hairs that retain the air on the underside of the body. The antennae are bent and laid against the head in such a way that the two unwettable halves just described constitute the pipe that connects the atmospheric air and the layer of air on the underside of the beetle's body.

With twitching movements, the beetle begins to pump in air, which arrives at the prothoracic spiracles after following the descending course just described. It then is expelled through the spiracles of the metathorax and the abdomen, is retained beneath the wing covers, and from here distributed to the underside of the body. [367/6–8]

Another unusual aspect of the life of hydrophilids is the little, closed, silken boats the females spin to hold their eggs. These boats float on the water and are equipped at one end with a little, upright mast that ensures a supply of air if the water should rise but the cocoon be caught in the vegetation and held below the surface. The beetle builds this vessel out of silken threads unreeled from her posterior end over two motile spinning staffs.

The insect starts by gathering a large store of air beneath the body. Supporting herself on plants, she then weaves a flat web on the underside of a thin, floating algal layer or on a floating leaf. Below this web the beetle then places a large bubble of air swept from her lower surface with the legs; this bubble, together with the whole rear end of the beetle, is now enclosed with spun silk. Then there follows a pause of about an hour, during which the beetle deposits inside the cocoon some 50 to 100 eggs, each one of which receives its own silken wrapping.

Now she withdraws gradually from the cocoon, which rises higher and higher in the water as she forces air into it and closes it completely. Finally the mast is molded onto it, with the help of the spinning staffs, from a sticky mass that comes from the spinning glands. The time required for the entire construction amounts to about four hours. The inside, between parchmentlike walls, is interwoven with the most delicate, loose

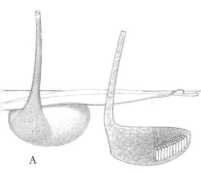

A

383/1A–B
(A) Egg cocoon (at the right, cut open) of the water scavenger beetle (family Hydrophilidae): the larvae that have hatched inside leave this "ark" through its dark-colored, more thinly woven portion at the bottom of the webwork. (B) Full-grown larva (natural size).

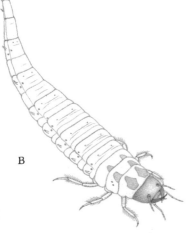

B

webbing. The eggs are nicely lined up on the bottom, and the air is above them under the roof.

The little boat rocks on the water, light as a feather, and moves about easily without tipping over; in between the algae and even covered over with them it is almost invisible. The mast looks like one of the erect straws in the vegetation. In a year a female is able to make two to five such egg cocoons.

The hatching larvae tarry a few days in the nursery, eating the fine silken webbing that is inside. Frequently they climb onto the roof or up the mast and sun themselves, vanishing again into the boat during the night or at a sign of danger.

Smaller beetles of the genus *Hydrophilus* build their cocoon out of a bit of leaf that is rolled up, carpeted with silk, equipped with a mast, and filled with air. Others prepare a plate-shaped float in the middle of which is a bowl-like, roofed-over depression that holds the eggs. Certain species fasten the cocoon to plants somewhat below the water level, and instead of the mast there is a ribbon of material leading to the surface and glued to the vegetation.

The larvae of the water scavenger beetles are ugly maggots that crawl on plants or on the bottom, frequently with the help of undulant movements of the body. With their hairy legs they can swim a little, too. They obtain air by holding up to the surface, with the two spiracles opened, their little posterior respiratory shell, which is closed in its underwater portion. Slow-moving, lurking predators, they seize every living thing that is not too big, preferably snails.

Like the larvae of the predaceous diving beetles *Dytiscus,* they ingest food that already has been digested, before entering the mouth, by means of a fluid that liquefies the tissues. This fluid does not flow, as it does in *Dytiscus,* through mandibular canals into the interior of the victim, but merely is poured out over the prey from the mouth. In contrast with the sucking *Dytiscus* larva, this does not take place under water, since too much of the dissolved food would be washed away. The larvae of the water scavenger beetles climb up on a plant to the surface and stretch the head with the prey up vertically, far out of the water. They adopt a characteristic position in which the rear end is bent upward, too, in the act of respiration. When the larvae have grown enough to attack larger snails, they eat their meal on the bottom, for then the soupy food is contained by the victim's shell.

Hydrous larvae live about two months,

molting three times, and after a diapause of two to three weeks transform in a cavity in the ground to a pupa that lies supported fore and aft by spines. After two to three weeks the beetles emerge, in the autumn, and, frequently flying some distance, seek new bodies of water in which they overwinter beneath the ice. The pupa of certain rather small water beetles floats among the carpets of algae, in a sphere spun of algal filaments.

Many differences among species also are seen in the mode of life of the larvae and mature beetles. Thus certain genera do not spin any boats for the eggs, but carry the eggs about beneath the abdomen, stowed away in a silken packet suspended from the legs by means of strong filaments. Many larvae stay almost always at the surface, sometimes crawling about beneath the film with the air-filled lower side uppermost. And a few live in hollow plant stems, where they eat the owners of such passages, namely other beetle larvae.

Perhaps best adapted to a life in the water are beetles of the genus *Berosus.* These unusually agile mature beetles live in brackish pools and carry a thick cushion of air beneath the body. Their larvae, equipped with long, bristly gills, crawl about on the muddy bottom and never come to the surface.

Interesting for their extraordinary adaptability are the little black beetles of the genus *Ochthebius,* which may be seen in the sunshine flying from one body of water to another. Indeed these beetles are found both in fresh water and in pools of sea water or brackish water, mostly hanging beneath the surface, but also digging in numbers in the bottoms of the pools.

In conclusion, two other unusual larval types may be presented. First there are the larvae of the little water-penny beetles (Psephenidae), a family known only from America and Asia. Their back has been flattened to form an exceedingly thin, broadly oval shell, consisting of platelike segments articulated together. These larvae live in rushing water, pressed flat against rocks and held to the substrate by means of a surrounding fringe of fine hairs. Fully concealed under the shell are the head and the rest of the body, which along the sides bears rows of gill tufts.

The second peculiar form is shown by a few larvae of the firefly family Lampyridae, namely of the genus *Luciola,* known in India, Indonesia, and Japan. These larvae, which live under water, creep about in brooks or in standing water, as in ricefields. At night they shine with a beautiful blue light, and are perhaps the only luminous freshwater animals.

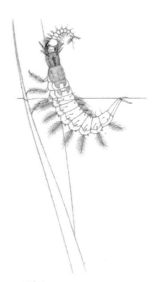

384/1
The larva of a rather small water beetle (Hydrophilidae) with prey, a mosquito larva (natural size).

384/2
The Psephenus larva, the water penny, from below (enlarged 5×).

INDEX OF ILLUSTRATIONS

This index lists all the insects shown in the book in numerical order, and gives their areas of distribution.
The following abbreviations are used for continents:

AF = Africa   AS = Asia
AU = Australia   EU = Europe
NA = North America   SA = South America

murinus, EU. 136/9 *Alaus speciosus*, Cent. AS. 136/10 *Lycoreus* sp., Madagascar. 136/11 *Alaus oculatus*, NA. 136/12 *Campsosternus auratus*, SA. 136/13 *Chalcolepidius* sp., Brazil; 136/14 *C. zonatus*, SA. 136/15 *Semiotus imperialis*, SA; 136/16 *S. distinctus*, SA; 136/17 *S. sanguinicollis*, Peru. 137/1 *Lytta* sp., West NA. 137/2 *Ips typographa*, EU. 137/3 *Oxynopterus* sp., Philippines. 137/4 *Selatosomus aeneus*, EU. 137/5 *Elater sanguineus*, EU. 138/1 *Cerocoma schreberi*, South EU. 138/2 *Lytta vesicatoria*, EU. 138/3 *Mylabris (Zonabris) variabilis*, South EU. 138/4 *Meloe violaceus*, EU. 138/5 *Autocrates aeneus*, South AS. 138/6 *Pimelia boyeri*, North AF. 138/7 *Prionotheca coronata*, Egypt. 138/8 *Tauroceras aries*, SA. 138/9 *Entomoderes dentipes*, NA. 138/10 *Elaeodes dentipes*, NA. 138/11 *Blapida spixi*, SA. 138/12 *Strongylium violaceum*, SA. 138/13 *Tenebrio molitor*, cosmopolite. 138/14 *Blaps gigas*, South EU. 138/15 *Pyrochroa serraticornis*, EU. 138/16 *Metoecus paradoxus*, EU. 138/17 *Rhipiphorus subdipterus*, South EU. 138/18 Noctuidae. 138/19 *Carabus*. 138/20 Coccinellidae. 138/21 *Anthrenus*. 138/22 *Dolopius marginatus*. 138/23 *Limonius aeneoniger*. 138/24 *Corymbites castaneus*. 138/25 Elateridae. 138/26 *Quedius*. 138/27 *Hylecoetus dermestoides*, EU. 138/28 *Saperda carcharias*, EU. 138/29 *Buprestis*. 138/30 *Harpium inquisitor*, EU. 139/1 *Carabus hispanus*, South EU. 140/1 *Tetracha euphratica* and 140/2 *Cicindela flexuosa*, Mediterranean; 140/3 *C. campestris*, EU; 140/4 *C. tricolor*, West AS; 140/5 *C. galatea*, Cent. AS; 140/6 *C. regalis*, AF; 140/7 *C. formosa*, NA. 140/8 *Pseudoxycheila bipustulata*, SA. 140/9 *Cicindela purpurea splendida*, NA; 140/10 *C. sexguttata*, NA; 140/11 *C. chinensis*, East AS, Japan. 140/12 *Tricondyla punctipennis*, Philippines. 140/13 *Collyris lissodera*, Indonesia. 140/14 *Carabus violaceus*, EU. 140/15 *Calosoma aurocincta*, Mexico; 140/16 *C. sycophanta*, EU. 140/17 *Ceroglossus chilensis gloriosa*, Chile. 140/18 *Carabus clathratus*, EU; 140/19 *C. rutilans*, South EU; 140/20 *C. olympiae*, North Italy; 140/21 *C. vietinghoffi*, NA. 140/22 *Carabus (Procrustes) sommeri amasicus*, Turkey; 140/23 *C. (Coptolabrus) ignimetallus*, China; 140/24 *C. augustus*, East AS; 140/25 *C. lafossei*, East AS; 140/26 *C. lafossei coelestis*, China; 140/27 *C. (Damaster) viridipennis*, Japan. 141 *Mormolyce phyllodes*, Southeast AS. 142/1 *Odontolabis lacordairei* ♀, Sumatra. 142/2 *Chiasognathus granti*, SA. 142/3 *Cladognathus giraffa*, Southeast AS. 143/1 *Odontolabis wollastoni*, Sumatra. 143/2 *Cyclommatus lunifer*, Sumatra. 143/3 *Neolamprima adolphinae*, New Guinea. 144 *Lucanus cervus*, EU.

PAGES 145–175

146/1 *Pyrophorus noctilucus*, SA. 147/1 Elateridae. 148/1 *Melasoma 20-punctata*, EU. 149/1 *Galerucella viburni*, EU. 150/1 *Attelabus nitens*, EU. 151/1 *Deporaus betulae*, EU. 152/1 *Canthon muticus*, SA. 153/1 *Typhoeus (Ceratotyphus) typhoeus*, South EU. 154/1 *Scarabaeus*, Mediterranean. 155/1 *Necrophorus vespillo*, EU. 156/1 *Selenis spinifex*, SA. 156/2 *Polychalca laticollis*, SA. 157/1 *Batonota spinosa*, SA. 157/2 *Cassida vittata*, EU. 157/3 *Megalostomis gazella*, SA. 157/4 *Metalactus nigrofasciatus*, SA. 158/1 *Lamprosoma seraphinum*, SA. 159/1 *Dulticola* sp., Indonesia. 159/2 *Carabus granulatus*, Palearctic. 160/1 *Platypsyllus castoris*, EU. 161/1 *Lomechusa strumosa; Formica sanguinea* (Ant), EU. 162/1 *Polyphylla decemlineata*; Lycaenidae-Larva (above) and Elateridae-Larva (below), NA. 163/1 *Anthaxia hungarica*, South EU. 166/1 *Entimus imperialis*, SA. 167/1 *Coniopteryx tineiformis; Semidalis aleyrodiformis* (right), EU. 168/1 Rhaphididae. 169/1 *Hesperoleon papaga; Myrmeleon* (below), NA. 170/1 *Chrysopa vittata*, EU. 170/2 *Osmylus fulvicephalus*, EU. 170/3 *Wesmaelius quadrifasciatus*, EU. 171/1 *Panorpa*. 171/2 *Bittacus italicus*, EU. 171/3 *Boreus hyemalis*, EU. 174/1 *Lobocraspis griseifusca*, AS. 175/1 *Euplocia membliaria*, Indonesia. 175/2 *Chloroclystis rectangulata*, EU. 175/3 *Zanclognatha tarsiplumalis*, EU.

PAGES 176–182

177/1 *Steniridia andrewsi barksdalei*, NA. 177/2 *Scarites buparius*, South EU. 177/3 *Abax ater*, EU. 177/4 *Chlaenius velutinus*, EU. 177/5 *Lebia crux minor*, EU. 177/6 *Eudema brevicolle*, AF. 177/7 *Agra plaumanni*, Brazil. 177/8 *Eccoptoptera lagenula*, AF. 177/9 *Phaedrus litoralis*, EU; 177/10 *P. sanguinicollis*, EU. 177/11 *Staphylinus oleus*, EU; 177/12 *S. caesareus*, EU. 177/13 *Emus hirtus*, EU. 177/14 *Glenus regalis*, SA. 177/15 *Eulissus chalybaeus*, SA. 177/16 Staphylinae sp., New Guinea. 177/17 *Leptochirus scoriaceus*, SA. 177/18 *Thinopinus pictus*, West NA. 177/19 *Paussus bova*, Madagascar. 177/20 *Platyrhopalopsis picteti*, East AS. 177/21 *Necrophorus germanicus*, EU. 177/22 *Oeceoptoma thoracica*, EU. 177/23 *Silpha nigrita*, EU. 177/24 *Proculus goryi*, Cent. America. 177/25 *Popilius disjunctus*, NA. 177/26 *Heliocopris gigas*, AF. 177/27 *Phanaeus ensifer*, SA. 177/28 *Catharsius molossus*, Southeast AS. 177/29 *Phanaeus mimas*, SA; 177/30 *P. festivus*, SA. 177/31 *Onthophagus vacca*, EU; 177/32 *O. rangifer*, AF; 177/33 *O. negus*, AF. 177/34 *Geotrupes mutator*, EU. 178/1 *Golofa pizarro*, Peru. 178/2 *Oryctes nasicornis*, EU. 178/3 *Xylotrupes dichotomus*, Philippines. 179/1 *Megaceras chorinaeus*, SA. 179/2 *Dynastes hercules*, Cent. America. 180/1 *Eudicella grolli*, East AF. 180/2 *Ranzania bertolonii*, East AF. 180/3 *Neptunides polychromus*, East AF. 180/4 *Eupoecilia australasiae*, AU. 180/5 *Amaurodes passerinii*, East AF. 180/6 *Ischiopsopha jamesi*, New Guinea. 180/7 *Heterorrhina dohrni*, Nias. 180/8 *Glycyphana tricolor*, Ceylon. 180/9 *Stephanorrhina guttata*, Cent. AF. 180/10 *Rhabdotis chalcea*, AF. 180/11 *Eurochea histrionica*, Madagascar. 180/12 *Euphorea biguttata*, Mexico. 180/13 *Pachnoda cordata*, West AF. 180/14 *Cetonia aurata*, Palearctic. 180/15 *Argyripa lansbergi*, SA. 180/16 *Goliathus goliathus*, Cent. AF. 181/1 *Euchirus parryi*, South AS. 181/2 *Melolontha melolontha*, EU. 181/3 *Polyphylla decemlineata*, NA. 181/4 *Polyphylla fullo*, EU, West AS. 181/5 *Lepidiota stigma*, Southeast AS. 181/6 *Chrysophora chrysochlora*, SA. 181/7 *Anoplognathus frenchi*, AU. 181/8 *Hopeia coerulea*, EU. 181/9 *Phyllopertha horticola*, Palearctic. 181/10 *Antichira festiva*, SA. 181/11 *Rutela histrio*, SA. 181/12 *Anoplognathus olivieri*, AU. 181/13 Lycidae sp., New Guinea. 181/14 *Lycus elegans*, AF. 181/15 *Cratomorphus giganteus*, SA. 181/16 *Luciola italica* (at left, from below), South EU. 181/17 *Callirrhipis philiberti*, Seychelles. 181/18 *Rhipidocera pulverulenta*, AU. 181/19 *Trichodes favarius*, EU; 181/20 *T. apiarius*, EU. 181/21 *Targostenus univittatus*, cosmopolite. 181/22 *Thanasimus formicarius*, EU. 181/23 *Cantharis discoidea*; 181/24 *C. pellucida*, EU. 181/25 *Malachius bipunctulatus*, EU. 181/26 *Hylecoetus dermestoides*, EU. 181/27 *Anthrenus scrophulariae*, Holarctic. 181/28 *Attagenus pellio*, Holarctic. 181/29 *Dermestes lardarius*, Holarctic. 181/30 *Eumorphus marginatus*, Indonesia. 181/31 *Endomychus coccineus*, EU. 181/32 *Erotylus loratus*, SA. 181/33 *Coptongis sheppardi*, Moluccas. 182/1 *Buprestis octoguttata*, EU. 182/2–4 *Anthaxia hungarica* (2 ♂, 3–4 ♀ upper and lower side), South EU. 182/5 *Anthaxia candens*, South EU. 182/6 *Chrysobothris affinis*, EU. 182/7 *Amorphosoma penicillatus*, SA. 182/8 *Corcebus bastanus*, East AS. 182/9 *Agrilus biguttatus*, EU. 182/10 *Sternocera marseuli*, South AS; 182/11 *S. rothschildi*, East AF. 182/12 *Julodis cirrhosa*, South AF. 182/13 *Chrysochroa chinensis*, East AS. 182/14 *Metataenia clothilda*, AF. 182/15 *Psiloptera plagiata*, SA. 182/16 *Chalcopoecila ornata*, Southeast AS. 182/17 *Chalcophora japanica*, East AS, Japan. 182/18 *Megaloxantha bicolor*, Southeast AS. 182/19 *Catoxantha purpurea*, AU. 182/20 *Chrysochroa buqueti*, Southeast AS. 182/21 *Capnodis carbonaria*, Southeast EU, West EU. 182/22 *Cyphogastra javanica*, Indonesia. 182/23 *Polybothris sumptuosa*; 182/24 *P. quadricollis*; 182/25 *P. orbicularis*, Madagascar. 182/26 *Achardella americana*, SA. 182/27 *Conognatha compta*, SA. 182/28 *Belinota sumptuosa*, Indonesia. 182/29 *Stigmodera roei*, AU. 182/30 *Calodema kirbyi*, AU. 182/31 *Julodis manipularis*, North AF. 182/32 *Adalia bipunctata*, EU. 182/33 *Oreus australasiae*, AU. 182/34 *Coccinella 9-notata*, NA. 182/35 *Solanophila insignis*, East AS. 182/36 *Vibidia marshali*, AF. 182/37 *Solanophila tetracycla*, AF. 182/38 *S. v-pallidum*, SA. 183/1 *Polyoza lacordairei*, SA. 183/2 *Cerambyx cerdo*, EU. 183/3 *Batus barbicornis*, SA. 183/4 *Hylotrupes bajulus*, EU, AF. 183/5 *Callichroma suturale*, SA. 183/6 *Megacyllene robiniae*, NA. 183/7 *Amphidesmus apicalis*, West AF. 183/8 *Necydalis major*, EU. 183/9 *Callisphyris macropus*, SA. 183/10 *Cosmosoma ammiralis*, SA. 183/11 *Dorcadion crassipes*, West AS. 183/12 *Cyriocrates horsfieldi*, China. 183/13 *Stellognatha cornutus*, Madagascar. 183/14 *Zographus oculator*, South AF. 183/15 *Sternotomis regalis*; 183/16 *S. pulchra*, West AF. 183/17 *Callimation venustum*, Madagascar. 183/18 *Acanthocinus aedilis*, EU. 183/19 *Saperda carcharias*, EU. 183/20 *Oberea oculata*, EU. 183/21 *Tragocephala nobilis*; 183/22 *T. guerini*, West AF; 183/23 *T. knenckeli*, Madagascar. 183/24 *Phosphorus gabonator*, West AF. 183/25 *Paraglenea fortunei*, China. 183/26 *Anisocerus* sp., Peru. 183/27 *Sphenura elegans*, Indonesia. 184/1 *Petrognatha gigas*, West AF. 184/2 *Callipogon barbatus*, Cent. America. 184/3 *Sternotomis variabilis*, AF. 185/1 *Rosalia alpina*, EU. 185/2 *Plagionothus bayi*, NA. 185/3 *Batocera wallacei*, New Guinea. 186/1 *Donacia bicolor*, EU. 186/2 *Crioceris asparagi*, EU, NA. 186/3 *Cryptocephalus aureolus*, EU; 186/4 *C. primarius*, EU. 186/5 *Doryphora arcuata*, Peru. 186/6 *Chrysomela menthastris*, EU. 186/7–8 *Chrysochloa gloriosa* (variants), EU. 186/9 *Paropsis intacta*, AU. 186/10 *Chalcoides aurata*, EU. 186/11 *Hispa testacea*, South EU. 186/12 *Tauroma casta*, Cent. America. 186/13 *Pseudomesomphalia punicea*, Mexico; 186/14 *P. chalybaea*, SA; 186/15 *P. imperialis*, SA. 186/16 *Selenis venosa*, SA. 186/17 *Acromis sparsa*, SA. 186/18 *Omoplata bonifilii*, Peru. 186/19 *Aspidomorpha fenestrata*, New Guinea. 186/20 *Syngambria bisinuata*, SA. 186/21 *Cassida nobilis*, EU. 186/22 *Ischnomias nobilis*, SA. 186/23 *Cyphus myrmosarius*, SA; 186/24 *C. schönherri*, SA. 186/25 *Anthribus albinus*, EU. 186/26 *Xenocerus rufus*, Aru-Islands. 186/27 *Eupholus linnei*, New Guinea; 186/28 *E. schönherri*, New Guinea. 186/29 *Lordops decorus*, SA. 186/30 *Pachyrrhynchus reticulatus*, Philippines; 186/31 *P. gemmaus*, Philippines. 186/32 *Brachycerus manifestus*, AF. 186/33 *Lithinus nigrocristatus*, Madagascar. 186/34 *Apirocales cornutus*, NA. 186/35 *Cleonus piper*, EU. 186/36 *Belus plagiatus*, AU. 186/37 *Liparus germanus*, EU. 186/38 *Rhynchites bacchus*, South EU. 186/39 *Balaninus nasius*, NA. 186/40 *Alcides richteri*, New Guinea. 186/41 *Eugnoristus monachus*, Madagascar. 186/42 *Ceratosomus roddani*, SA. 186/43 *Rhinastus sternicornis*, SA. 186/44 *Sphenocorynus meleagris*, Borneo. 186/45 *Cyrtotrachelus buqueti*, Southeast AS. 186/46 *Rhina barbirostris*, SA. 186/47 *Rhynchophorus pascha*, Indonesia. 186/48 *Protocerius purpuratus*, Indonesia. 187/1 *Asphaera octoguttata*. 187/2 *Fulcidax (Chlamys) cuprea*, SA. 187/3 *Coptocycla arcuata*, SA. 187/4–5 *Leptinotarsa decemlineata*, NA, EU. 187/6 *Sagra buqueti*, Indonesia. 187/7 *Platyomus niveus*, SA. 187/8 *Anthonomus grandis*, NA. 187/9 *Platyomus boisduvali*, SA. 187/10 *Mecopus* sp., AU. 188/1 *Halter halteratus*, West AS. 188/2 *Necrophilus* sp. 188/3 *Palpares solidus*, West AS. 188/4 *Puer* sp., North AF. 188/5 *Ascalaphus macaronius*, EU, West AS. 188/6 *Ascalaphus* sp. 189/1 *Raphidia notata*, EU. 189/2 *Chrysopa vulgaris*, EU. 189/3 *Drepanepteryx phalaenoides*, EU. 189/4 *Osmylus chrysops*, EU. 189/5 *Mantispa pagana (styriaca)*, EU. 189/6 *Paramantispa decorata*, SA. 189/7 *Panorpa germanica*, EU; 189/8 *P. communis*, EU. 189/9 *Bittacus italicus*, EU. 189/10 *Boreus hyemalis*, EU. 189/11 *Pieris rapae*, EU; 189/12 *Hepialus humuli*, EU. 189/13 *Cocytinus lucifer*, SA. 190/1 *Daphnis nerii*, Mediterranean. 191/1 *Castnia licus licorides*, Peru. 191/2 *Patula macrops*, AF, AS. 192/1 *Ancyluris ocollo*, Columbia. 192/2 *Symmachia rubina*, Cent. America. 192/3 *Helicopis eudymion*, Guyana. 192/4 *Ancyluris pulchra*, Peru. 192/5 *Mesosemia mevania*, Ecuador.

PAGES 193-207

195/1 *Papilio (Iphiclides) podalirius*, West Palearctic. 196/1 *Parnassius apollo*, West Palearctic. 196/2 *Lycaena (Plebejus) acmon* (above ♂, below ♀), NA. 197/1 *Strymon melinus*, NA. 199/1 *Limenitis rivularis*, EU. 201/1 *Zygaena*, EU. 207/1 *Pachythelia unicolor*, EU.

PAGES 208–224

209/1 *Helicopis acis*, Brazil. 209/2 *Mesene phareus rubella*, Brazil. 209/3 *Mesosemia croesus*, Brazil. 209/4 *Ancyluris aulestes pandama*, Peru. 209/5 *Zeonia faunus*, Peru. 209/6 *Gonepteryx cleopatra*, Southwest Palearctic. 209/7 *Agrias lugens*, SA. 209/8 *Papilio childrenae oedippus*, Columbia. 210/1 *Papilio (Ornithoptera) brookiana*, Southeast AS. 210/2 *Argynnis (Speyeria) aphrodite*, NA. 210/3 *Celerio lineata*, NA. 210/4 *Callarethia virgo*, NA. 210/5 *Autographa (Plusia) mortuorum*, NA. 210/6 *Malacosoma americana*, NA. 210/7 *Dasychira pudibunda*, EU. 211/1 *Philosamia cynthia*, EU, NA, East AS. 211/2 *Porthesia similis*, EU, NA. 211/3 *Hipparchus papilionaria*, EU. 211/4 *Protoparce pellenia*, NA. 211/5 *Mesoleuca gratulata*, NA. 211/6 *Semiothisa enotata*, NA. 211/7 *Phalera bucephala*, EU. 211/8 *Rhodophaea rosella*, EU. 211/9 *Cacoeia crataegana*, EU. 211/10 *Pterophorus monodactylus*, EU. 212/1 *Lamproptera meges decius*, Celebes. 212/2 *Armandia (Bhutanitis) lidderdalei*, Himalayas. 212/3 *Papilio machaon*, Holarctic. 212/4 *P. antenor*, Madagascar. 212/5 *P. ulysses telegonus*, Moluccas. 212/6 *P. latreillei*, South AS. 213/1 *P. cresphontes*, NA. 213/2 *P. (Ornithoptera) priamus croesus*, Halmahera. 213/3 *P. androcles*, Celebes. 214/1 *P. rumanzovia semperinus*, Philippines. 214/2 *P. machaon*, Holarctic. 215/1 *P. zelicaon*, NA. 215/2 *P. polyxenes*, NA. 215/3 *Luehdorfia puziloi japonica*, Japan. 216/1 *Parnassius apollo*, West Palearctic. 216/2 *P. charltonius*, Himalayas. 217/1 *Anthocaris genutia*, NA. 217/2 *Pieris rapae*, Holarctic. 217/3 *Colias eurytheme*, NA; 217/4 *C. phicomone*, EU. 217/5 *Appias zarinda*, Celebes. 217/6 *Delias harpalyce*, AU. 217/7 *Chrysophanus (Lycaena) phlaeas*, Palearctic. 217/8 *Jolaus prometheus*, AF. 218/1 *Morpho papirius*, Peru; 218/2 *M. cypris*, Columbia. 218/3 *Euploea hansemanni dürrsteini*, New Guinea. 218/4 *Hestia idea*, Moluccas. 218/5 *Heliconius egerides*, Brazil; 218/6 *H. phyllis anacreon*, Bolivia; 218/7 *H. bicolorata*, Peru; 218/8 *H. charitonius*, Florida, SA. 218/9 *Dircenna euchytma*, SA. 218/10 *Ithomia agnosia*, SA. 219/1 *Morpho anaxibia*, Brazil; 219/2 *M. hecuba obidonus*, Brazil. 220/1 *Ageronia arinome*, SA. 220/2 *Victorina steneles*, Florida, SA. 220/3 *Pyrameis (Vanessa) atalanta*, Holarctic. 220/4 *Polygonia faunus*, NA. 220/5–6 *Araschnia levana*, EU. 220/7 *Argynnis lathonia*, Palearctic. 220/8 *Charaxes smaragdalis*, Cent. AF. 220/9 *Hypolimnas dexithea*, Madagascar. 220/10 *Prepona omphale*, SA. 220/11 *Chlorippe zunilda*, SA. 220/12 *Taenaris dimona sorronga* (lower side), New Guinea; 220/13 *T. bioculatus charon*, New Guinea. 220/14 *Eryphanis zolvizora* (lower side), SA. 220/15 *Neorina lowi*, Indonesia. 220/16 *Polymastus whitelyi*, SA. 220/17 *Chrysophanus (Heodes) virgaureae*, EU. 220/18 *Lycaena bellargus*, EU; 220/19 *L. meleager*, EU. 221/1 *Eriboea dehaani*, Indonesia. 221/2 *Callitaera pireta*, SA. 221/3 *Pierella nereis*, SA; 221/4 *P. dracontis*, SA. 221/5 *Antirrhaea philaretes avernus*, SA. 221/6 *Satyrus actaea cordula*, EU. 221/7 *Enodia portlandia* (lower side), NA. 221/8 *Satyrus parisatis*, West AS; 221/9 *S. bischoffi*, Turkey. 221/10 *Hesperia carthami*, EU. 221/11 *Abantis zambesiasca*, AS. 221/12 *Zemadia geneta*, SA. 221/13 *Yanguna staudingeri*, SA. 222/1 *Vanessa (Nymphalis) antiopa*, EU, NA. 222/2 *Vanessa (Inachis) io*, Palearctic. 222/3 *Arctia hebe*, Southwest Palearctic. 223/1 *Catagramma cajetani*, Peru. 223/2 *Callicore clymena*, Peru. 223/3 *Catagramma peristera*, Peru; 223/4 *C. aegina salamis*, Peru. 223/5 *Ochlodes agricola*, West NA. 223/6 *Chrysiridia (Urania) croesus*, Madagascar. 224/1 *Alcidis aurora*, New Guinea; 224/2 *A. metaurus*, AU. 224/3 *Utetheisa pulchella*, EU, AS, AF, AU. 224/4 *Estigmone acraea*, NA. 224/5 *Eucharia casta*, EU. 224/6 *Orodemnias cervini*, Switzerland. 224/7 *Eucyane bicolor*, SA. 224/8 *Pericallia matronula*, EU. 224/9 *Campylotes histrionicus*, South AS. 224/10 *Erasmia pulchella*, South and East AS. 224/11 *Zygaena transalpina*, EU; 224/12 *Z. transalpina maritima*, South EU; 224/13 *Z. ephialtes*, EU; 224/14 *Z. occitanica vandalita*, Spain. 224/15 *Euthesanotia unio*, NA. 224/16 *Eusemia bisma*, Indonesia. 224/17 *Agarista agricola*, AU. 224/18 *Trichura cerberus*, SA. 224/19 *Dinia aeagrus*, SA. 224/20 *Synthomis phegea*, EU. 224/21 *Euchromia sperchia*, Madagascar; 224/22 *E. orientalis*, Ceram. 224/23 *Histiaea prosperina*, Amazonas. 224/24 *Macrocneme* sp., Columbia. 224/25 *Isanthrene porphyria*, SA. 224/26 *Dysphanis militaris isolata*, Southeast AS; 224/27 *D. subreplecta*, Indonesia. 224/28 *Automolodes tricolor*, New Guinea. 224/29 *Milionea paradisea*, New Guinea.

PAGES 225–239

225/1 *Leto stacyi*, AU. 227/1 *Carpocapsa saltitans*, Mexico. 227/2 A *Vanessa*, B *Pieris*, C *Limenitis*, D *Saturniidae*. 228/1 *Bradypodicola hahneli*, SA. 229/1 *Attacus edwardsii*, South AS. 232/1 *Datana ministra*, NA. 232/2 *Automeris flexuosa*, Brazil. 232/3 *Phobetron hipparchia*, SA. 233/1 *Thaumetopoea pithyocampa*, West Palearctic. 234/1 *Urapteryx sambucaria*, EU. 234/2 *Ancylis mitterbacheriana*, EU. 235/1 *Urodus parvula*, Florida. 236/1 *Bombyx mori*. 237/1 *Vanessa (Inachis) io*, Palearctic. 239/1 *Syrphidae*, NA.

PAGES 240–256

241/1 *Anaplectoides prasina*, EU. 241/2 *Catocala fraxini*, Palearctic. 242/1 *Acronicta occidentalis*, NA; 242/2 *A. alni*, EU. 242/3 *Bathyra sagata*, SA. 242/4 *Triphaena fimbria*, EU. 242/5 *Polia arctica*, NA. 242/6 *Calotaenia celsia*, Palearctic. 242/7 *Cucullia argentea*, EU. 242/8 *Lamprosticta viridana*, EU. 242/9 *Criposia aprilina*, West Palearctic. 242/10 *Trachea atriplicis*, EU. 242/11 *Dicycla oo*, EU. 242/12 *Autographa (Plusia) pulchrina*, EU; 242/13 *A. festucae*, EU. 242/14 *Plusia balluca*, NA. 242/15 *Cymatophoropsis hieroglyphica*, SA. 242/16 *Catocala concumbens*, NA; 242/17 *C. sponsa*, EU; 242/18 *C. patala*, Japan; 242/19 *C. actaea*, Japan. 242/20 *Ophideres fullonica*, Indonesia. 242/21 *Phyllodes meyricki*, New Guinea. 242/22 *Nyctipao albicinctus*, AS. 242/23 *Miniophyllodes catalai*, Madagascar. 242/24 *Erebus odora*, NA, SA. 242/25 *Ischyja maculia*, Southeast AS. 243/1 *Selenia lunaria*, EU. 243/2 *Casipeta divisata*, NA. 243/3 *Fidonia plumistaria*, Area of the Mediterranean Sea. 243/4 *Annemoria unitaria*, NA. 243/5 *Elphos hymenaria*, Southeast AS. 243/6 *Biston strataria*, EU. 243/7 *Problepsis plenorbis*, Southeast AS. 243/8 *Geometridae sp.*, Sumatra. 243/9 *Agathia codina australis*, Indonesia. 243/10 *Hipparchus papilionaria*, EU. 243/11 *Lygris prunata*, EU. 243/12 *Calocalpe undulata*, Holarctic. 243/13 *Cidaria (Eulype) hastata gothicata*, NA. 243/14 *Orgya (Hemerocampa) leucostigma*, NA; 243/15 *O. dubia*, South EU. 243/16 *Lymantria (Porthetria) dispar*, Holarctic; 243/17 *L. monacha*, EU, West AS. 243/18 *Dendrolimus pini*, Palearctic. 243/19 *Gastropacha quercifolia*, EU. 243/20 *Anurocampa mingens*, SA. 243/21 *Lirimiris lignitecta*, SA. 243/22 *Procolax apulana*, SA. 243/23 *Phalera bucephala*, EU. 243/24 *Pheosia tremula*, EU. 244/1 *Salassa nola*, South AS. 244/2 *Nudaurelia gschwandneri*, AF. 244/3 *Telea polyphemus*, NA. 244/4 *Antheraea roylei*, South AS. 244/5 *Antherina suraka*, Madagascar. 244/6 *Lobobunaea phaedusa*, AF. 244/7 *Rhinaka zuleica*, South AS. 244/8 *Epiphora bauhiniae*, AF. 244/9 *Aglia tau* (Melanismus), Palearctic. 244/10 *Pseudobazis eglanterina*, West NA. 245/1 *Hyalophora (Samia) gloweri*, West NA. 245/2 *Attacus caesar*, Philippines. 246/1 *Argema mittrei*, Madagascar. 247/1 *Actias maenas*, South AS; 247/2 *A. maenas latona*, Celebes. 248/1 *Protoparce occhus*, SA. 248/2 *Megacorma obliqua*, Indonesia. 248/3 *Amplypterus gannascens*, SA. 248/4 *Prosperpinus juanitus*, NA. 248/5 *Smerinthus planus*, East AS. 248/6 *Theretra alecto*, AS. 248/7 *Celerio euphorbiae*, West Palearctic. 248/8 *Oryba kadeni*, SA. 248/9 *Euchloron magaera lacordairei*, Madagascar. 248/10 *Xylophanes titana*, SA. 248/11 *Macroglossum stellatarum*, Palearctic. 248/12 *Hemaris thysbe*, NA. 248/13 *Euclea delphinii*, NA. 248/14 *Parasa pastoralis*, Indonesia. 248/15 *Cochlidion limacodes*, West Palearctic. 248/16 *Psyche viciella*, EU. 248/17 *Solenobia triquetrella*, EU. 248/18 *Zeuzera pyrina*, cosmopolite. 248/19 *Cossus cossus*, West Palearctic. 248/20 *Hypopta caestrum*, North EU. 248/21 *Hepialus fusconebulosus*, EU. 248/22 *Chamaesphecia seitzi*, North AF. 248/23–24 *Synanthedon formicaeformis*, EU; 248/25 *S. scoliaeformis*, EU; 248/26 *S. vespiformis*, EU. 248/27–28 *Paranthrene tabaniformis rhingiaeformis*, EU. 248/29 *Sanninoides exitiosa*, NA. 249 *Leto stacyi*, AU. 250/1 *Pachytelia unicolor*, EU. 250/2 *Psyche viciella*, EU. 250/3 *Phalacropteryx graslinella*, EU. 250/4 *Solenobia clathrella*, EU. 250/5 *Rebelia danubiella*, EU. 250/6 *Clania sp.*, Sumatra. 250/7 *Oiketicus kirbyi*, SA; 250/8 *O. geyeri*, SA. 250/9 *Eumeta* sp., Sumatra. 250/10 *Carpocapsa pomonella*, West Palearctic, NA. 251/1 *Galleria mellonella*, cosmopolite. 251/2 *Crambus myellus*, EU. 251/3 *Pyrausta (Ostrinia) nubilalis*, EU, NA. 251/4 *Pyralis farinalis*, cosmopolite. 251/5 *Nephopteryx semirubella*, EU. 251/6 *Pyrausta purpuralis*, EU; 251/7 *P. funebris*, EU. 251/8 *Plodia interpunctella*, cosmopolite. 251/9 *Alucita pentadactyla*, EU. 251/10 *Orneodes hübneri*, EU. 251/11 *Euxanthis zoegana*, West Palearctic. 251/12 *Phalonia aleella*, EU. 251/13 *Phiaris arcuella*, Palearctic. 251/14 *Carpocapsa pomonella*, West Palearctic, NA. 251/15 *Pamene regiana*, EU. 251/16 *Pandemis corylana*, EU. 251/17 *Evetria (Rhyacionia) buoliana*, Holarctic. 251/18 *Cacoecia aeriferana*, EU; 251/19 *C. piceana*, EU. 251/20 *Argyroploce betulaetana*, EU. 251/21 *Tortrix viridana*, West Palearctic. 251/22 *Notocelia uddmanniana*, West Palearctic. 251/23 *Evetria edella*, EU. 251/24 *Laspeyresis compositella*, West Palearctic. 251/25 *Glyphipteryx thrasonella*, West Palearctic. 251/26 ♂, 27 ♀ *Chimabacche fagella*, EU. 251/28 *Psecadia pusiella*, West Palearctic, 251/29 *Depressaria arenella*, West Palearctic. 251/30 *Gelechia rosalbella*, EU. 251/31 *Alabonia staintoniella*, EU. 251/32 *Endrosis lacteella*, West Palearctic. 251/33 *Coleophora pyrrhulipennis*, West Palearctic. 251/34 *C. onosmella*, EU. 251/35 *Lithocolletes strigulatella*, Cent. EU. 251/36 *Gracilaria azaleella*, East AS. 251/37 *Stathmopoda pedella*, EU. 251/38 *Hyponomeuta cognatella*, EU. 251/39 *Argyresthia conjugella*, Holarctic. 251/40 *Plutella maculipennis*, cosmopolite. 251/41 *Theristis mucronella*, West Palearctic. 251/42 *Tinea granella*, Palearctic. 251/43 *Tineola bisselliella*, West Palearctic. 251/44 *Adela viridella*, EU; 251/45 *A. degeerella*, EU. 251/46 *Nemotois auricellus*, EU. 251/47 *Antispida treitschkeella*, EU. 251/48 *Nepticula malella*, EU. 252/1 *Tegeticula yuccasella*, NA. 252/2 *Micropteryx allionella*, Cent. EU. 252/3 *Lithocolletis roboris*, EU. 252/4 *Stagmatophora heydeniella*, EU. 252/5 *Argyresthia goedartella*, EU. 252/6 *Ancylis lundana*, EU. 252/7 *Pselnophorus brachydactylus*, EU. 253/1 *Lycaena arion* and Ants *Myrmica rubra*, EU. 254/1 *Malacosoma neustria*, Palearctic. 254/2 *Araschnia levana*, EU. 254/3 *Hemistola chrysoprasaria*, EU. 254/4 *Acronicta euphorbiae*, EU. 254/5 *Erebia ligea*, EU. 254/6 *Trachea atriplicis*, EU. 254/7 *Leucochloe daplidice*, Palearctic. 254/8 *Erannis defoliaria*. 254/9 *Vanessa (Inachis) io*. 254/10 *Satyrus semele*, West Palearctic. 254/11 *Thanaos tages*, EU. 254/12 *Ipimorpha subtusa*, EU. 254/13 *Lycaena idas*, EU. 254/14 *Craniophora ligustri*, EU. 254/15 *Stauropus fagi*, Palearctic. 254/16 *Dasychira pudibunda*, EU. 254/17 *Lyonetia clerkella*, EU. 255/1 *Celerio nicaea*, Area of the Mediterranean Sea. 255/2 *Cossus cossus*. 255/3 *Papilio scamander*, SA. 255/4 *Eueidis dianassa*, SA. 255/5 *Bupalus piniarius*, Palearctic. 255/6 *Urapteryx sambucaria*, EU. 255/7 *Acronicta aceris*, Palearctic. 255/8 *Actias selene*, South AS. 255/9 *Loxostege similalis*, NA. 255/10 *Catocala coccinata*, NA. 255/11 *Opsiphanes tamarindi*, SA. 256/1 *Thaumetopoea processionea*, EU; 256/2 *T. pithyocampa*, EU, West AS. 256/4 *Bombyx mori*.

PAGES 257–271

257/1 Sand wasp: *Bembix* sp.,; miltogrammatid: Miltogrammatinae sp.; flower fly: *Rhaphiomidas trochilus* (Aphioceridae), West NA. 258/1 *Chionea lutescens*, EU. 259/1 *Fannia canicularis*, cosmopolite. 259/2 *Empis* sp. 260/1 *Pachyrrhina maculata*, EU. 260/2 *Diadocidia ferruginosa*, EU. 260/3 *Eristalomyia* sp. 261/1 *Vermileo degeeri*, South EU. 262/1 *Conops* sp., West NA. 263/1 *Prosena siberita*, EU. 263/2 *Hemipenthes morio*, EU. 264/1 *Penicillidia dufouri*, EU. 266/1 *Elenchinus delphacophilus*, EU. 266/1 A–D *Stylops melittae*, E *Xenos vesparum* on *Polistes*, EU. 268/1 *Anthidium* sp. 268/2 *Asilidae* sp. 268/3 *Chrysis* sp. 268/4 *Sphex ichneumon*. 268/5 *Anthidium* sp. 268/6 *Chlorion* sp. and Nemobiinae sp. (ground cricket), West. NA. 271/1 *Odynerus spiricornis*, EU.

PAGES 272–288

273/1 *Rhyparia purpurata*. 273/2 *Zygaena*. 273/3 *Cossus cossus*. 273/4 *Attacus*. 273/5 *Rothschildia*, SA. 273/6 *Antheraea myltitta*, AS; 273/7 *A. roylei*, AS. 273/8 *Saturnia (Eudia) pavonia*, West Palearctic. 273/9 *Rothschildia*, SA. 273/10 *Copaxa lavenderae*, SA. 273/11 *Dictioploca simla*, South AS. 273/12 *Rhodinia fugax*, Japan. 273/13, 15–20 *Bombyx mori*. 273/14 *Monema flavescens*, Japan. 273/21 *Nymphalidae*. 274/1 *Vanessa (Inachis) io*. 274/2 *Ageronia amphinome*, SA. 274/3 *Papilio (Ornithoptera) aeacus*, Formosa. 274/4 *Pseudantheraea discrepans*, AF. 274/5 Sphingidae, SA. 274/6 *Saturnia pavonia*. 275/1 *Musca domestica*, cosmopolite. 275/2 *Fannia canicularis*, cosmopolite. 275/3 *Muscina stabulans*, EU. 275/4 *Lucilia caesar*, EU. 276/1 *Pachyrrhina analis*, EU. 276/2 *Tipula gigantea*, EU; 276/3 *T. heros*, EU. 276/4 *Ctenophora ornata*, EU. 276/5 *Stratiomyia chamaeleon*, EU. 276/6 *Chloromyia formosa*, EU. 276/7 *Chrysochroma bipunctata*, EU. 276/8 *Raphiorhynchus pictus*, SA 276/9 *Bombylius discolor*, West Palearctic. 276/10 *B. analis*, Area of the Mediterranean Sea; 276/11 *B. boghariensis*, North AF. 276/12 *Hemipenthes morio*, West Palearctic, NA. 276/13 *Exoprosopa jacchus*, Palearctic. 276/14 *Thyridanthrax perspicillaris*, South EU, AS. 276/15 *Laphria ephippium*, EU; 276/16 *L. aurea*, Area of the Mediterranean sea. 276/17 *Mallophora fascipennis*, *Eulaema*-Imitation (see 17/23), SA. 276/18 *Andrenosoma atra*, West Palearctic. 276/19 Asilidae sp., Sumatra. 276/20 *Asilus crabroniformis*, Palearctic. 276/21 *Nemestrinus albofasciatus*, North AF. 276/22 *Rhagio scolopaceus*, EU. 277/1 *Tabanus bovinus*, EU. 277/2 *Straba regularis*, EU. 277/3 *Styporhamphis barbara*, Area of the Mediterranean Sea. 277/4 *Chrysops caecutiens*, EU. 277/5 *Baccha elongata*, EU. 227/6 *Eristalis nemorum*, EU. 277/7 *Volucella bombylans*, EU; 277/8 *V. pellucens*, EU. 277/9 *Phalcromyia* sp., SA. 277/10 *Tubifera trivittata*, EU. 277/11 *Merodon clavipes*, South EU. 277/12 *Milesia semiluctifera*, South EU; 277/13 *M. crabroniformis*, South EU. 277/14 *Acalyptrata* sp., Sumatra. 277/15 *Otites lamed*, South EU. 277/16 *Rhagocarpus permundus*, EU. 277/17 *Aciura coryli*, EU. 277/18 Trypetidae (Tephritidae) sp., NA. 277/19 *Drosophila* sp., EU. 277/20 *Anthomyia pluvialis*, EU. 277/21 *Mesembrina mystacea*, EU. 277/22 *Stomoxys calcitrans*, cosmopolite. 277/23 *Ectophasia rostrata*, South EU. 277/24 *Robineanella* sp., South EU. 277/25 *Peletieria ferina*, EU. 277/26 *Echionomyia grossa*, EU. 277/27 *Nemeraea strema*, EU. 277/28 *Hippobosca equina*, Palearctic; 277/29 *H. camelina*, North AF, AS. 277/30 *Lipoptena cervi*, Palearctic. 278/1 Asilidae on Bembix, West NA. 278/2 *Conops* sp. on Bembix, West NA. 278/3 *Harpagomyia* sp. and Ant *Cremastogaster*. 278/4 *Braula coeca*, cosmopolite. 278/5 *Vyrtus gibbus*, South EU. 278/6 *Celyphus* sp., Sumatra. 278/7 Diopsidae sp., Sumatra. 278/8 *Hemerodromia* sp., EU. 279/1 *Rhabdophaga rosaria*, EU. 279/2 *Hartigiola (Hormomyia) annulipes*, EU. 279/3 *Glossina palpalis*, AF. 279/4 *Rondania dimidiata* and beetle *Brachyderes incanus*, EU. 279/5 *Phlebetomus papatasii*, Area of the Mediterranean Sea, East AS, NA. 280/1 *Hypoderma bovis*, EU. 281/1 *Dermatobia cyaniventris*, SA, Cent. America. 282/1 *Xenopsylla cheopis*, AF, South AS. 282/2 *Pulex irritans*, cosmopolite. 282/3 *Ctenocephalides canis*, cosmopolite. 283/1 *Tunga penetrans*, AF, South AS, SA, Cent. America. 284/2 *Vespa crabro*, Holarctic; 284/3 *V. germanica*, West Palearctic; 284/4 *V. vulgaris*, Holarctic; 284/5 *V. rufa*, Holarctic; 284/6 *V. sylvestris*, Palearctic; 284/7 *V. saxonica*, Palearctic. 284/8 *Pemphredon* sp. with *Omalus* sp., West NA. 285/5–7 *Bembix* sp., West NA. 285/8 Syrphidae sp., West NA. 285/9 *Exoprosopa* sp., West NA. 285/10 Miltogrammatinae sp., West NA. 285/11 *Rhaphiomidas trochilus* (Aphioceridae), West NA. 285/12, 14 *Dasymutilla sackenii*, NA; 285/13 *D. coccineohirta*, NA. 285/15 *Philanthus triangulum*, West Palearctic. 286/1 *Eumenes bolli oregonensis*, NA; 286/2 *E. unguiculus*, Area of the Mediterranean Sea; 286/3 *E. maxillosus*, AF; 286/4 *E. flavopictus*, Southeast AS. 286/5 *Ischnogasteroides leptogaster*, Northwest AF, Palestine. 286/6 *Katamenes niger*, Arabia. 286/7 *Odynerus grandis*, West AS, Palestine; 286/8 *O. interruptus*, Southeast EU; 286/9 *O. macedonicus*, Southeast EU; 286/10 *O. niloticus*, Arabia; 286/11 *O. meyeri pseudolateralis*, North AF; 286/12 *O. bifasciatus*, EU. 286/13 *Pterocheilus mirandus*, NA; 286/14 *P. pedicellatus*, NA; 286/15 *P. diversicolor*, NA. 286/16 *Alastor antigae*, Southwest EU. 286/17 *Synagris carinata*, AF; 286/18 *S. cornuta*, AF. 286/19 *Celonites abbreviatus*, EU. 286/20 *Masaris vespiformis*, Palestine. 286/21 *Ceramius beaumonti*, North AF. 286/22 *Pepsis staudingeri*, SA; 286/23 *P. smaragdina*, SA. 286/24 *Hemipepsis barbara*, North AF; 286/25 *H.* sp., Sumatra. 286/26 *Pepsis* sp., Venezuela. 286/27 *Hemipepsis* sp., Thailand. 286/28 *Pompilus plumbeus* and its parasite, 286/29 *Ceropales maculatus*, EU. 286/30 *Pompilus orbitalis*, South EU. 286/31 *Episyron albonotatus*, South EU. 286/32 *Batozonellus lacerticida*, EU, North AF. 286/33 *Paraferreola syraensis*, South EU. 286/34 *Cryptochilus octomaculatus*, Area of the Mediterranean Sea. 286/35 *Pseudopompilus humboldti*, Area of the Mediterranean Sea. 287/1 *Chlorion lobatum*, Southeast AS. 287/2 *Sphex macula*, Southeast AF; 287/3 *S. latreillei*, SA. 287/4 *Ammophila extrematata*, NA. 287/5 *Philanthus triangulum*, West Palearctic. 287/6 *Aphilanthops laticincta*, NA. 287/7 *Eucerceris arenaria*, NA. 287/8 *Stizus vespoides*, North AF. 287/9 *Steniolia duplicata*, NA. 287/10 *Stictia signata*, SA. 287/11 *Sphecius speciosus*, NA. 287/12 *Gorytes spilosternus*, NA; 287/13 *G. concinnus*, South EU. 287/14 *Cerceris rufipes*, South EU; 287/15 *C. frontata*, NA. 287/16 *Palarus rufipes*, North AF. 287/17 *Tachytes spatulatus*, North AF. 287/18 *Liris haemorrhoidalis*, North AF. 287/19 *Tachysphex ashmeady*, NA. 287/20 *Trypoxylon figulus*, EU. 287/21 *Pemphredon lugens*, EU. 287/22 *Diodontus minutus*, EU. 287/23 *Crabro zonatus*, EU; 287/24 *C. clypeata*, EU, North AF; 287/25 *C. schmiedeknechti*, South EU. 287/26 *Oxybelus maculipes*, South EU. 287/27 *Megachile versicolor*, EU. 287/28 *Anthidium* sp., West NA. 288/1 *Oecophylla smaragdina*, Southeast AS. 288/2 *Osmia bicolor*, EU. 288/3 *Halictus quadricinctus*, EU. 288/4 *Osmia papaveris*, EU. 288/5 *Xylocopa violaceus*, EU.

PAGES 289–303

290/1 Pompilidae. 290/2 *Pemphredon*. 290/4 *Anthophora*. 290/5 *Eucera*. 290/6 *Anthidium*. 290/7 *Osmia*. 291/1 *Anthidium strigatum*, EU. 292/1 *Polistes* sp., EU. 293/1 *Bombus lapponicus hypsophilus* and honey bee *Apis mellifica*, EU. 296/1 *Xylocopa violacea*, EU. 297/1 *Eucera longicornis*, EU. 298/1 *Eumorpha pulchra*, SA. 300/1 *Dasymutilla coccineohirta*, NA. 300/2 *Mymar regalis*, EU. 300/3 *Agriotypus armatus*, EU. 301/1 Tryphoninae. 301/2 *Exochilum circumflexum*, EU. 302/1 *Blastophaga psenes*, South Holarctic. 303/1 *Dryophanta quercus-folii*, EU.

PAGES 304–320

305/1 *Sceliphron destillatorius*, EU. 305/2 *Deuteragenia variegatum*, EU. 305/3 *Trypoxylon politum*, NA. 305/4 *Eumenes dubius*, South EU. 305/5 *Osmia fuciformis*, EU. 305/6 *Stenogaster micans*; 305/7 *S.* sp., Sumatra; 305/8 *S. depressigaster*, Indonesia; 305/9 *S.* sp., Sumatra. 305/10 *Vespa media*, Holarctic. 305/11 *Polistes bimaculatus*, EU. 306/1 *Ceratina chalcites*, South EU. 306/2 *Xylocopa violaceus*, EU; 306/3 *X. aestuans*, North AF; 306/4 *X. caerulea*, Southeast AS. 306/5 *Neoxylocopa* sp., Brazil. 306/6 *Xylocopa latipes*, Southeast AS. 306/7 *Prosopis variegata*, EU. 306/8 *Colletes hylaeiformis*, EU. 306/9 *Systropha curricornis*, EU. 306/10 *Halictus* sp., North AF. 306/11 *Panurgus banksianus*, EU. 306/12 *Andrena agilissima*, South EU. 306/13 *Eucera grandis*, North AF. 306/14 *Anthophora nubica*, North AF; 306/15 *A. zonata*, Southeast AS. 306/16 *Hemisia mariae*, SA; 306/17 *H. mocsaryi*, SA. 306/18 *Eumorpha* sp., Bolivia. 306/19 *Euglossa brullei*, SA. 306/20 *Eumorpha mariana*, SA. 306/21 *Bombus affinis*, NA. 306/22 *Melipona fasciata*, Surinam. 306/23 *Apis mellifica cypria*, Cyprus. 306/24 *Osmia balearica*, South EU, North AF. 306/25 ♀ and 26 ♂ *Megachile sericans*, EU. 306/27 ♀ and 28 ♂ *Anthidium manicata*, EU, North AF. 307/1 *Vespa crabro*, Holarctic. 307/2 *Apis florea*, South AS. 307/3 *Bombus lapidarius*, lower left *Psithyrus rupestris*, at the right *Mutilla europaea*, Eu. 307/4 *Vespa maculata*, NA. 308/4 *Bombus terrestris*, *Lycaena*, EU. 308/8 *Apis mellifica*. 309/1 *Xylocopa violacea*. 309/2 *Plusia chrysitis*. 309/3 *Eucera longicornis*. EU. 309/4 *Eumorpha pulchra*, SA. 310/1 *Dasypoda argentata*, South EU. 310/2 *Osmia adunca*, EU. 310/3 *Systropha*. 310/4 *Meliturga*, South EU. 310/5 *Andrena*. 310/6 *Dasypoda*. 310/7 *Euglossa*, SA. 310/8 *Trigona*. 310/9 *Apis mellifica*. 310/10 *Anthidium* sp., West NA. 311/1 *Bombus lapidarius*. 311/2 *Xylocopa violacea*. 311/3 *Bombus fragans*, EU. 312/1 *Oxybelus*. 312/2 *Ammophila* with Noctuidae caterpillar. 312/3 *Bembix*. 312/4 *Elater*. 312/5 *Tettigonidae*. 312/6 *Anthidium*. 312/7 *Sphex ichneumon*. 212/8 *Anthidium*. 312/9 *Chlorion* with cricket (Nemobiinae), West NA. 313/1 *Halictus sexcinctus*, EU. 313/2 *Sphecodes albilabris*, EU. 313/3 *Andrena thoracica*, EU. 313/4 *Nomada goodeniana*, EU. 313/5 *Anthophora quadrifasciata*, EU. 313/6 *Crocisa histrionicus*, EU. 313/7 *Eulaema fasciata*, SA. 313/8 *Megachile ericetorum*, EU. 313/9 *Coelioxys aurolimbata*, EU. 313/10 *Chalicodoma muraria*. 313/11 *Dioxys cincta*, EU. 313/12 *Stelis nasuta*, EU. 313/13 *Anthidium interruptum*, EU. 313/14 *Stelis freygessneri*, EU. 313/15 *Exaereta frontalis*, SA. 313/16 *Anthophora* sp., West NA. 313/17 *Melecta* sp., West NA. 313/18 *Elis* sp., West NA. 313/19 *Scolia procer*, Southeast AS. 314/1 *Chrysis scutellaris*, EU. 315/1 *Cleptes dubuyssoni*, SA; 315/2 *C. ignitus*, Area of the Mediterranean Sea. 315/3 *Hedychridium vachali*, Southwest EU. 315/4 *Chrysis*-Larva. 315/5 *Chrysis ignifrons*, South EU; 315/6 *C. hemipyrrha*, *Celebes*. 315/7 *Euchroeus purpuratus*, EU. 315/8 *Chrysis excavata*, SA; 315/9 *C. fascialis daphne*, Japan. 315/10 *Omalus purpuratus*, NA. 315/11 *Omalus*. 315/12 *Stilbum viride* and *Eumenes* wasp, Madagascar. 316/1 *Atillum bellatrix*, SA. 316/2 *Mutilla barbara*, South EU, North AF. 316/3 *Dasymutilla* sp., Brazil. 316/4 *Hoplocrates subtilis*, SA. 316/5 *Apterogyna savigny*, Arabia. 317/1 *Lycisca* sp., 317/2 *Diplolepsis rosae*, EU. 317/3 *Perilampus auratus*, South EU. 317/4 *Isomerata* sp., Brazil. 317/5 *Platygona buyssoni* ♀, EU. 317/6 *Lestrodryinus formicarius* ♀, EU. 317/7–8 *Platygonatopus buyssoni*. 317/9 *Chelogynus angusticollis*. 317/10 *Anteon marginatus*. 317/11 *Xenanteon reticulatus*, EU. 317/12 *Scleroderma domestica*, EU. 318/1 *Ichneumon xanthorius*, West *Palearctic*. 318/2 *Amblyteles quadripunctorius*, EU. 318/3 *Trogus lutorius* in *Papilio alexanor*-pupa, West Palaearctic. 318/4 *Catadelphus arrogator*, West Palearctic. 318/5 *Caenocryptus* sp., South EU. 318/6 *Enicospilus* sp., EU. 318/7 *Arotes amoenus*, NA. 318/8 *Glyptomorpha desertor*, Area of the Mediterranean Sea. 318/9 *Vipio impostor*, South EU. 318/10 *Evania punctata*, EU. 318/11 *Gasteruption pedemontanum*, EU. 318/12 *Pelecinus polyturator*, SA. 318/13–14 *Leucospis gigas*, EU, North AF. 318/15 *Stephanus coronator*, Indonesia, AU. 318/16 *Ibalia leucospoides*, EU. 318/17 *Tenthredella maculata*, EU. 318/18 *Tenthredo scrophulariae*, West Palearctic; 318/19 *Z. bifasciata*, EU. 318/20 *Tenthredopsis austriaca*, EU. 318/21 *Rhogogaster viridis*, Palearctic. 318/22 *Arge pleuritica*, East EU, West AS. 318/23 *Abia (Zaraea) aurulenta*, Cent. EU; 318/24 *A. nitens*, EU. 318/25 *Pseudoclavellaria amerinae* with cocoon, West Palearctic. 318/26 *Trichiosoma tibiale* with cocoon, Palearctic. 318/27 *Cimbex lutea*, EU. 318/28 *Melanopus fabricii*, West Palearctic. 318/29 *Eumatabolus troglodyta*, EU. 318/30 *Xiphydria prolongata*, EU. 318/31 *Paururus juvencus*, Palearctic. 318/32 *Sirex gigas*, EU, North AS. 318/33 *Oryssus abietinus*, West Palearctic. 319/1–2 *Apis unicolor*, AF. 319/3 *Rhodites rosae*, EU. 319/4 *Neuroterus*, EU. 319/5 *Dryophanta quecusfolii*, EU. 319/6 Tenthredinidae. 320/1 *Vespa maculata*, NA; 320/2 *V. mandarina*, Japan. 320/3 *Polybia jurinei*, SA. 320/4 *Vespa tropica*, AS. 320/5 *Polistes hunteri*, NA; *P. gallicus*, Palearctic. 320/7 *Apoica* sp., SA; 320/8 *Synoeca* sp., SA. 320/9 *Metapolybia* sp., AF. 320/10 *Bombus argillaceus*, South EU; 320/11 *B. dahlbomi*, SA. 320/12 *Melipona mandacaia*, SA. 320/13 *Trigona apialis*, South AS. 320/14 *Trigona* sp., Paraguay; 320/15 *T. fulvopilosella*, Southeast AS. 320/16 *Apis mellifica*, EU. 320/17 *Apis unicolor*, AF; 320/18 *A. indica peroni*, Indonesia. 320/19 *A. dorsata*, South AS, Indonesia; 320/20 *A. florea*, South AS. 320/21 *Colobopsis truncatus*, EU.

PAGES 321–351

322/1 *Charops obtusus*, Sumatra. 323/1 *Dolerus*. 323/2 *Cimbex*. 323/3 *Acantholyda*. 324/1 *Celonites abbreviatus*, EU. 324/2 *Anthophora plagiata*, EU. 324/3 *Sphex albisectus*, EU. 326/1 *Apis mellifica*. 328/1 *Bombus lapidarius*, EU. 330/1 *Apis dorsata*, AS. 333/1 *Messor*, South EU. 333/2 *Atta*, SA. 336/1 *Apis mellifica*. 337/1 *Epimyrma* on *Leptothorax*, EU. 339/1 *Macrotermes natalensis*, AF. 340/1 *Reticulitermes*, Holarctic. 340/2 *Termes lilljeborgi*, AF. 340/2 C *Capritermes latignathus*. 340/2 D *Eutermes diurnus*, Indonesia. 341/1 *Apicoterma occultus*, AF. 342/1 *Termitoxenia bugnioni*, South AS. 342/2 *Thyreoxenus autuorii*, SA. 345/1 *Ephemera danica*, EU (above), and *Baetis binoculatus*, EU (below). 347/1 *Ccenagrion* sp., West NA. 350/1 A–C *Aeschna*. 350/2 *Aeschna* larva with *Acilius*. 350/3 *Agrion*. 351/1 *Griopteryx*, SA. 351/2 *Perla maxima*, EU.

PAGES 352–368

353/1 *Apis mellifica*. 353/2 *Formica rufa*, Holarctic. 353/3 Formicidae. 353/4 *Lasius fuliginosus*, EU, AS. 353/5 *Polyrhachis emmae*, East AS. 354/1 *Ponera coarctata*, EU, North AF. 354/2 *Odontomachus chelifer*, SA. 354/3 *Dinoponera australis* bucki, SA. 354/4 *Diacamma rugosum*, Indonesia. 354/5 *Monomorium pharaonis*, cosmopolite. 354/6 *Myrmecia gulosa*, AU. 354/7–9 *Atta cephalotes*, SA. 354/10 *Zacryptocerus clypeatus*, SA. 354/11 *Deromyrma swammerdami*, AF. 354/12–15 *Camponotus ligniperda*, EU. 354/16 *Myrmecocystus* sp., West NA. 355/1 *Camponotus sericeiventris* rex, Mexico. 355/2 *Polyrhachis ypsilon*, Indonesia. 355/3–4 Camponotinae sp., Philippines. 355/5 *Camponotus gigas*, South AS. 355/6 *Cataglyphis setipes*, West AS. 355/7 *Oecophylla smaragdina*, Southeast AS. 355/8–9 *Dorylus fulvus*, AF. 355/10 *Anomma nigricans*, AF. 355/11 *Eciton burchelli*, SA. 355/12 *Apis mellifica*. 356/1 *Teleutomyrmex schneideri* on *Tetramorium caespitum*, EU. 357/1 *Cremastogaster dohrni*, South AS. 358/3 *Macrotermes natalensis*. 358/4 *Apicoterma occultus*, AF. 358/5 *Eutermes fungifaber*, AF. 358/6 *Hodotermes meridionalis*, AU. 358/7 *Eutermes pyriformis*, AU. 359/1 *Reticulitermes flavipes*, NA. 359/2 *Termitoxenia bugnioni*, South AS. 359/3 *Thyreoxenus autuorii*, SA. 359/4 Ephemeridae, NA. 359/5 *Caenis*. 359/6 *Polymitarcys*. 359/7 *Siphlurus*. 359/8 *Caenis*. 359/9 *Ecdyonurus*. 360/1 *Cordulegaster annulatus*, EU, North AF. 360/2 *Crocothemis erythraea*, South EU, AF, AS. 360/3 *Orthetrum brunneum*, Palearctic. 360/4 *Libellula pulchella*, NA; 360/5 *L. luctuosa*, NA. 360/6 *Aeschna grandis*. 360/7 *Libellula fulva*. 360/8 *Microstigma rotundatum*. 360/9 *Mecistogaster lucretia*,

INDEX

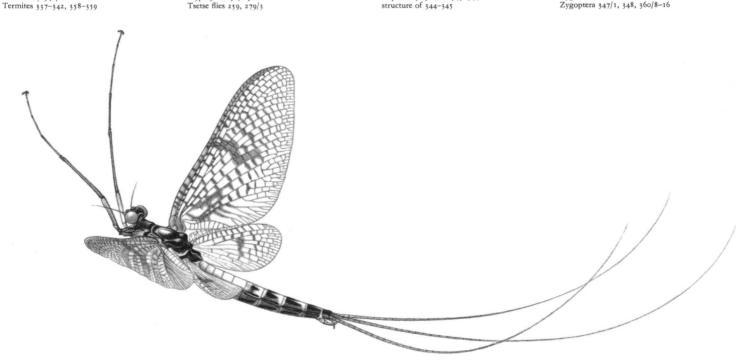